D1535516

DIASPORA

DIASPORA

Jews amidst Greeks
and Romans

ERICH S. GRUEN

HARVARD UNIVERSITY PRESS
Cambridge, Massachusetts
London, England
2002

Library of Congress Cataloging-in-Publication Data

Gruen, Erich S.
Diaspora : Jews amidst Greeks and Romans /
Erich S. Gruen.
p. cm.
Includes bibliographical references (p.) and index.
ISBN 0-674-00750-6 (alk. paper)
1. Jews—History—586 B.C.–70 A.D.
2. Judaism—History—Post-exilic period, 586 B.C.–210 A.D.
3. Jewish diaspora.
4. Jewish literature—History and criticism.
I. Title.

DS121.65 .G78 2002
933—dc21   2001052767

Designed by Gwen Nefsky Frankfeldt

TO JOAN

my wife, best friend, and lifelong companion

PREFACE

THE JEWS of classical antiquity dwelled predominantly in the diaspora. Palestine may have been the cradle of their culture, but most Jews lived elsewhere—in Syria, Egypt, and Mesopotamia, in Asia Minor, the Aegean, and Greece, even in Rome and Italy, The Jewish experience was largely a diaspora experience.

The image of dispersal looms large in the popular perception. The destruction of the Temple in 70 CE would seem to mark a watershed: loss of the homeland engendered the scattering of Jews around the Mediterranean, a scrambling to recreate abroad the culture that had been crushed in Palestine. That perception is fundamentally erroneous. A fact of compelling significance complicates the picture: the dispersal of Jews had begun long before the Temple fell and the native land came under Roman control. The fact is well known to specialists in the field. But it has rarely reached the notice of other scholars, even those of classical antiquity, let alone a wider public.

Such was the genesis of this project. It focuses on that remarkable span of time, stretching from Alexander the Great to the emperor Nero, nearly four hundred years, in which Jews dwelled in the diaspora—*before* any threat to the Temple materialized. They evidently preferred it there.

My objective is to bring this fascinating feature of Jewish history to the forefront, to emphasize its importance to my colleagues in the classical world, to pique the interest of scholars in other areas of Jewish studies, and perhaps to reach a wider readership. The book presents a preponderantly positive picture. It questions the drastic alternatives often posited: that diaspora Jews either assimilated to classical culture by diluting their own traditions, or separated themselves from the larger world to maintain the purity of their faith and heritage. This study holds that, for most Jews, retention of a Jewish identity and accommodation to the circumstances of diaspora were joint goals—and often successfully achieved. Many readers will find this conclusion too sunny or upbeat, even counterintuitive and implausible. But if it can stimulate a spirited discussion, it will have served its purpose.

I have enjoyed considerable help in the completion of this labor. A fellowship from the University of California Humanities Research Institute at Irvine enabled me to spend a very fruitful term, the fall of 1997, with a lively, multidisciplinary research group exploring the topic of "Jewish Identity in the Diaspora." This resulted in the composition and profitable discussion of a key chapter. The bulk of the book was subsequently drafted in the friendly confines of my neighbor to the south, the Stanford Humanities Center. Two generous grants enabled me to spend the academic year 1999–2000 there, one from the Center itself and one from the President's Fellowship in the Humanities awarded by the University of California. The center too supplied an intellectually engaging, interdisciplinary group of scholars and graduate students from whom I took much profit.

Chapters 7 and 8 appear elsewhere in different versions. Chapter 7, in a previous incarnation, formed part of two edited collections: I. Malkin, *Ancient Perceptions of Greek Ethnicity* (Center for Hellenic Studies, 2001), and J. J. Collins and G. E. Sterling, *Hellenism in the Land of Israel* (University of Notre Dame Press, 2001). Chapter 8 appears in a new edited volume: H. Wettstein, *Diasporas and Exiles: Varieties of Jewish Identity* (University of California Press, 2002).

Individual portions of the manuscript were read by colleagues and friends whose criticisms and suggestions have resulted in many improvements—though far fewer than they might have liked. I note with gratitude the acute advice I have received from Daniel Boyarin, Robert Cousland, Robert Doran, Claude Eilers, Shaya Gafni, Martin Goodman, Benjamin Isaac, Lee Levine, George Nickelsburg, Maren Niehoff, Miriam Pucci Ben Zeev, and Tessa Rajak. I gained considerable benefit from the forceful disagreements delivered on one chapter by Daniel Schwartz. He deserves credit for a number of salutary changes—which will not, however, win him over to the conclusion. Maren Niehoff's new book, *Philo on Jewish Identity and Culture* (Tübingen, 2001), arrived too late to appear in the notes. But I have taken much profit from our mutual exchanges during the period in which we were both engaged in our respective compositions. Finally, I owe a heavy debt to John Barclay, whose recent book on the diaspora has helped to change the shape of the field, and whose generous comments on my chapters were a source of reassurance even in my flights of fancy.

As always, many of the ideas expressed here gained initial airing in graduate seminars and were sharpened in the course of seminar discussions.

Numerous participants in those classes have contributed (even unknowingly) to the advantage of the book. I give no exhaustive list here. But I note in particular the insights gained from Ory Amitay, Chava Boyarin, Bridget Buxton, Jo Crawley, Sandra Gambetti, Bradley Ritter, and Chris Seeman.

I am grateful to Peg Fulton of Harvard University Press, a longtime friend, for encouraging this project through its various vicissitudes, and to Mary Ellen Geer for editing the manuscript. Most important, I received invaluable service from Chris Seeman, who shouldered the formidable tasks of checking the notes, reading proofs, compiling the bibliography, and composing most of the index.

Berkeley, California
September 2001

CONTENTS

DIASPORA

Introduction

DIASPORA DOMINATES the history and imagination of the Jewish people. Jews have brooded about it for two and a half millennia. For many, it constitutes the defining characteristic of Jewish experience. The notion of removal from the homeland is firmly entrenched in the mythology of the Jewish people. In the Book of Genesis, Adam and Eve barely came to self-consciousness before they were sent packing out of Eden. Cain, after his foul fratricide, fell under an irredeemable curse, condemned to perpetual wandering over the earth. Abraham, patriarch of the nation, migrated from Ur of the Chaldees to Canaan, to Egypt, and back to Canaan. Joseph could fulfill his destiny only in an alien land. The return of the children of Israel from enslavement and oppression in Egypt required much meandering in the wilderness. And recovery of the Promised Land proved tenuous and temporary. Exile lay ahead still again, and more than once. The symbolism haunted Jewish consciousness. The figure of the "Wandering Jew" serves as emblem of the people's fate, a repeated theme in art and literature through the ages.

In fact, of course, Jews have no monopoly on diaspora. Other diasporas existed in antiquity. Warfare among Greek states regularly involved exiles, deportation, and dislocation. The destruction of cities sent whole populations into exile. And Roman conquests could expel people from their lands, place them on the slave marts abroad, or even prompt massive population transfers. In the modern era, other displaced nations parallel or eclipse the fate of the Jews. The Armenians spring first to mind, but one can cite also the diaspora of Poles in France, Turks in Germany, Gypsies in Central Europe, and Palestinians in various parts of the Arab world, among many others. Yet "diaspora" remains quintessentially associated with Jews. They have occupied the role of the outcast par excellence. They lost their homeland in the "Babylonian Captivity" of the sixth century BCE, thus beginning a dispersal that continued over centuries in lands all

over the Mediterranean and the Near East, and then suffered the catastrophic demolition of the Temple in 70 CE. The image of Jewish scattering,
of resettlement in alien places, of insecurity, powerlessness, marginality,
and repeated readjustments, holds sway.

For the Jews of antiquity, the loss of the Temple represented an enduring
trauma. The date of its destruction, which by a quirk of fate or fabrication
is identical to that on which Jerusalem succumbed to Babylon, is still commemorated annually in Israel. Of course, prior catastrophes had marked
Jewish history. But the fall of Jerusalem to Rome represented a wholly different order of magnitude. It must have been clear to most, and soon to all,
that recovery of the Temple could no longer even be contemplated for
the indefinite, perhaps the infinite, future. In the general view, the resound-
ing reverberations of that event determined the diasporic consciousness of
Jews throughout the centuries to follow. The eradication of the center,
which had given meaning and definition to the nation's identity, obliged
them to alter their sights, accommodate to a displaced existence, and re-
think their own heritage in the context of strange surroundings.

Focus on the consequences of the Temple's destruction, however, overlooks a fact of immense significance: the Jewish diaspora had a long history
prior to Rome's crushing of Jerusalem. The Babylonian Captivity was just
the beginning. Jews entered (reentered?) Egypt already in the sixth century,
as the Elephantine papyri reveal. But the scattering gathered real momen-
tum in the years and decades that followed Alexander the Great's conquests. Greeks and Macedonians came to conquer and stayed to settle in
the lands of the Near East. New communities sprang up; old ones were re-
populated or expanded. The collapse of the Persian empire brought a wave
of migration and relocation, and Jews participated in that development in
substantial numbers. Nor did they confine themselves to the East. On the
information of I Maccabees, composed in the late second century BCE,
Jews had found their way not only to Egypt, Syria, Mesopotamia, and the
Iranian plateau, but to the cities and principalities of Asia Minor, to the
islands of the Aegean, to Greece itself, to Crete, Cyprus, and Cyrene.[1]
Gentiles too took notice. Strabo, writing at the end of the first century BCE,
remarked that there was hardly a place in the world that did not possess
members of this tribe and feel their weight.[2] A generation later Philo reinforced that impression, with specifics. In his formulation, Jerusalem had
sent out colonists over the years who had now established themselves in
communities far and near: in Egypt, Phoenicia, and Syria, throughout Asia
Minor, in all parts of mainland Greece from Macedon to the Peloponnese,
in the islands of Euboea, Cyprus, and Crete—not to mention the lands be-

yond the Euphrates where Jews are ubiquitous.[3] And even these impressive statements do not tell the whole story. We know, for instance, of Jewish communities in Italy, including large settlements in Rome and Ostia. Precise figures are well beyond our grasp. Only a few isolated notices exist, with reference to particular places and occasions.[4] There is no mention of overall totals. But a confident conclusion can be voiced. By the time that the Roman commander Titus leveled the Temple, Jews abroad far outnumbered those dwelling in Palestine—and had done so for many generations.

What induced so massive a migration? Some of it, to be sure, was forced and unwelcome. Prisoners of war followed Ptolemy I to Egypt after his victories in Palestine in the late fourth century BCE.[5] Others unquestionably suffered in the cross-fire between Ptolemaic and Seleucid armies in the third century and were carried off as slaves to Syria or Egypt, depending upon the victor.[6] That fate certainly befell Jews who had the misfortune of being on the losing side in conflicts between the Hasmoneans and the Seleucids or Ptolemies in the second century.[7] Internal battles in Palestine, of course, produced political refugees.[8] The coming of Rome did not immediately improve matters. Pompey's conquests in Judaea in 63 BCE, plus the battles on Palestinian soil in the course of contests over the next three decades, brought a large number of Jews as captives and slaves to Rome itself.[9]

Compulsory dislocation, however, cannot have accounted for more than a fraction of the diaspora. In the case of the initial deportations by Ptolemy I, an alternative version reports that the Jews moved to Egypt voluntarily.[10] Whatever the truth of the matter, even according to the grimmer version Ptolemy employed many of the Jews as soldiers in his army, and the rest were liberated by his son.[11] Neither tale is verifiable, but the upshot is that Jews remained in Egypt of their own volition. Capture in the course of the Syrian wars or the Hasmonean battles often resulted in ransoming and restoration, and never involved large-scale or long-term exile.[12] Antiochus III, we are told, moved two thousand Jewish families from Mesopotamia and Babylonia to garrisons in Lydia and Phrygia. But they went as supporters of the regime and with many inducements, not under constraint. And it is noteworthy that such numbers were in the lands of the Tigris and Euphrates to begin with.[13] Many suffered enslavement or removal to Rome as a consequence of Pompey's intervention. Yet Jews had already been in Rome in appreciable numbers for some time before that—hardly under force.[14] Evidence for later deportations to Rome is slim. And, in any case, most of those enslaved in Rome were manumitted thereafter but continued to live in the city.[15]

The vast bulk of Jews who dwelled abroad in the Second Temple period did so voluntarily. Even where initial deportation came under duress, the relocated families remained in their new residences for generations— long after the issue of forced dislocation had become obsolete. No single objective impelled them; there were multiple motives. Overpopulation in Palestine may have been a factor for some, indebtedness for others.[16] But hardship need not have been the spur for most. The new and expanded communities that sprang up in the wake of Alexander's conquests served as magnets for migration. And Jews made their way to locations in both the eastern and western Mediterranean. Large numbers found employment as mercenaries, military colonists, or enlisted men in the regular forces.[17] Others seized opportunities in business, commerce, or agriculture.[18] All lands were open to them.[19]

Four centuries elapsed between Alexander and Titus. How did Jews conceive of their lot in a Greco-Roman world where they dwelled in large but dispersed numbers for decades upon decades? Two potent and recurrent images, with quite distinct messages, dominate the discourse on this subject. The haunting refrain of Psalm 137 still lingers:

> By the rivers of Babylon
> we sat and wept
> at the memory of Zion . . .
> How could we sing a song of Yahweh
> on alien soil?
> If I forget you, Jerusalem,
> may my right hand wither!
> May my tongue remain stuck to my palate
> if I do not keep you in mind,
> if I do not count Jerusalem
> the greatest of my joys.[20]

These verses allude to the Babylonian Exile that followed the fall of the First Temple. And the melancholy reverie signals the lament of the exile crushed by enforced removal, incapable or unwilling to make peace with an alien environment, and pining away for Palestine as the authentic soul of his being.

By contrast, the prophet Jeremiah, addressing the exiles in Babylon and reporting the word of God, delivers a very different manifesto for the diaspora:

> Build houses, settle down; plant gardens and eat what they produce . . .
> Work for the good of the city to which I have exiled you, since on its welfare yours depends.[21]

The prophet counsels adjustment and accommodation, a recipe for successful diaspora existence—an identification of Jewish interests with those of the community at large.

The two approaches suitably symbolize the discordant strategies that have long characterized and continue to characterize discussions of diaspora life: either resistance to assimilation and longing for Jerusalem, or conformity to and embrace of the alien environment. For victims of the Babylonian conquest (or for those who subsequently reconceived it), the alternatives may have been stark. But a comparable dilemma did not face the Jews who dwelled in Greco-Roman communities in the Second Temple period. Jerusalem (for most of that time) stood under Jewish rule, welcoming to pilgrims, visitors, or repatriates. The Jews abroad had chosen their residence voluntarily and (in many cases) had been there for generations. They had no cause to ache for Jerusalem. Nor, by contrast, were they obliged to adopt a new guise and sacrifice their identity to blend in with their surroundings.

Individuals, to be sure, made individual choices. No formula or pattern dictated decisions. Assimilated Jews certainly existed. One can point, for instance, to the (otherwise unknown) Jew in Oropos, a city bordering Boeotia and Attica in central Greece, who dedicated a stele to the divinities Amphiarios and Hygieia in whose shrine he had been vouchsafed a propitious dream.[22] Or, much more prominently, the notorious Ti. Julius Alexander rose to the prestigious posts of procurator of Judaea and even governor of Egypt in Roman service—having abandoned the customs of his people.[23] On the other side, some Jewish voices insisted on a rigid apartheid, asserting a sharp divide between ancestral traditions that identified the nation and the practices of the Gentiles. The High Priest Eleazer in the *Letter of Aristeas* spoke of impregnable fences and iron walls that separated Jew and non-Jew in accordance with the laws of Moses.[24] And the verses of the Third Sibylline Oracle, also a Jewish composition, trumpeted the righteousness and virtue of faithful Jews who shun the misguided beliefs, absence of morality, and reprehensible behavior of their Gentile contemporaries.[25]

But the radical alternatives were by no means the only options available. Nor is it likely that many Jews resorted either to isolationist purity or to outright apostasy. The Jewish communities in Alexandria offer an informative and revealing instance. Jews could and did live anywhere in the city, but the majority chose to make their residence in two particular districts that became known as the Jewish quarters.[26] In other words, Jews had access to all parts of Alexandria, mingling freely and (in some cases) living

among the Gentiles, but most preferred the company of their co-religionists. Greek and Latin authors refer with some frequency to Jews dwelling in
their midst. They were not ghettoized. But, at the same time, their identity
was undisguised and their peculiar customs conspicuous. Pagans noticed
their tendency to keep to themselves.[27] But they *did* notice them. Numerous comments from a wide range of writers point to Jewish adherence to
monotheism, observance of the Sabbath, dietary restrictions, and the practice of circumcision.[28] Attachment to distinctive traditions continued to
mark diaspora existence. And Jews did not have to hide them away in sub-
terranean regions.

We can therefore abandon simplistic dichotomies. Diaspora Jews did
not huddle in enclaves, isolated and oppressed, clinging to a heritage under
threat. Nor did they assimilate to the broader cultural and political world,
compromising their past, ignoring the homeland, and reckoning the Book
(in Greek) as surrogate for the Temple. The stark alternatives obscure understanding. A complex set of circumstances, diverse and dependent on local conditions, produced a mixed, ambiguous, and varied picture.

Maintenance of a Jewish identity and accommodation to the circumstances of diaspora were joint objectives. According to most analyses, the
combination created strains and tensions: Jews struggled to reconcile competing tendencies, felt pressure to justify deviations or compromises, found
it necessary to devise apologetics either to Gentiles or to themselves, forever grappling with dissonance in their daily lives. That conceptualization,
however, may be off the mark. Jewish experience in the diaspora need not
have been so labored. It is striking and significant that Jews in the Second
Temple period omitted to contrive a theory or philosophy of diaspora. Although the issue seems gripping in retrospect, it does not appear to have
been compelling at the time. That fact should give pause—and prompt a
fresh look.

This book concludes with the coming of the Great Revolt against Rome
in 66 CE and the consequent destruction of the Temple. That watershed left
a profound and enduring impact on both the center and the diaspora. Relations between Jews and the world of Greece and Rome took an irrevers-
ible turn. For that very reason it will be beneficial to set our sights exclusively on the Second Temple era, without encumbering the analysis by
dragging in an embittered future as yet unknown to contemporaries. Diaspora Jews themselves took little part in the conflagration of 66 to 70,
which confined itself largely to Palestine and its environs. The fact bears
notice. The revolt did not betoken smoldering discontent among Jews who
had made their homes abroad. To be sure, outbreak of the insurrection

brought reprisal outside the homeland. Inhabitants of cities in the vicinity of Judaea made haste to exhibit loyalty to Roman power by turning upon Jews who dwelled in their midst and whose retaliation escalated the violence. Large numbers fell in towns and villages of Galilee, Syria, Phoenicia, and across the Jordan.[29] The riots soon spread to Alexandria, and eventually to Antioch.[30] But pragmatic and cynical considerations prevailed. Alexandrians, Antiochenes, and others were eager to distinguish themselves sharply from the Jews in their cities, in order to avoid the potential wrath of Rome.[31] The grim episodes left irreparable scars. When Jews again engaged in open rebellion against Rome two generations later, the contest took place primarily in the diaspora—in Egypt, Cyrenaica, Cyprus, and across the Euphrates.[32] But it will be prudent not to read that fierce dissension and embitterment back into the centuries that preceded the loss of the Temple. Very different circumstances held in that era for the life of diaspora Jews. It merits close examination in its own terms.

The inquiry of this book proceeds along two broad fronts. First, it endeavors to elicit, as far as evidence allows, the realities of diaspora experience, the situations in which Jews found themselves, the positions they occupied, the rights and privileges they possessed, the obstacles they encountered, the institutions they developed, and the strategies they employed in order to commingle a local patriotism with traditional allegiances. Second, and at least equally important, the study seeks to identify traces of diaspora as a concept that imposed itself (however subconsciously) upon Jews prior to the destruction of the Temple, the implications it had for the Jews' sense of themselves, and the consequences for the shaping of a Jewish identity (or identities) when the vast majority of Jews dwelled outside the homeland. This is the more difficult and controversial part of the project. The conspicuous absence of a philosophy of diaspora is itself an item of real consequence. It means that Jewish attitudes concerning diaspora need to be extracted from texts composed for other purposes, in a variety of genres, but offering hints and glimpses of the Jews' perceived (even when unexpressed) relations with Greco-Roman culture and the circumstances of Gentile authority. This book does not aspire to exhaustive coverage—or anything near. In dealing with a period of four centuries and a geographic spread that extends from Italy and North Africa to the Black Sea and the Fertile Crescent, severe selectivity is imperative. With regard to realia, the work concentrates primary attention upon periods and locations where evidence is adequate to draw plausible (and some novel) conclusions—namely the Jews of Rome, Alexandria, and Asia Minor, with briefer excursions into other areas of the ancient world. On literary and intellectual conceptualization, only a sampling of texts is attempted, although this traverses a range of genres and authors. Special focus falls upon constructs that convey humor, wit, even a dash of mischievousness, for they give insight into a diaspora mentality that is rarely noticed or acknowledged.

The book falls into two parts along these lines—first on the realia, second on the constructs—with a final chapter on the balance maintained by Jews between identification with a homeland and engagement with diaspora communities.

Part I opens with the experience of Jews in Rome, the political center of the ancient world. Jews moved to the city of Rome in substantial numbers during the first and second centuries BCE, some as slaves and war captives, others as visitors, immigrants, and settlers, rising to as many as 20,000 to 40,000. Chapter 1 examines the available evidence for governmental actions, especially the periodic expulsions of Jews from Rome in the late Republic and early Principate, and the perceptions of Jews as articulated by Romans who encountered them in the streets, had some awareness of their strange ways, took note of their tight-knit communities, and drew their own conclusions. It attempts to put the expulsions into a broader context of Roman policy and to reassess the idea of "persecution" of Jews in a city that conducted such sweeps very rarely and with only fleeting consequences. Effects on the continuity of Jewish communities in Rome seem negligible. This makes it all the more imperative to understand the normal place of Jews within Roman society and the meaning of the diverse, ambiguous, and intriguing comments they provoked from Roman observers.

Alexandria was the queen city of the Hellenistic East—and a major magnet for migrating Jews. It also supplied the site for one of the most celebrated and painful episodes of Jewish history in antiquity: the catastrophic pogrom of 38 CE. Jews fell victim to devastating assaults, confiscation of property, destruction of synagogues, and personal violence. That deeply disturbing event is too often taken as only the most dramatic example of what Jews could anticipate in any diaspora community where they led a vulnerable and marginalized existence and where small provocations could trigger explosive consequences. The second chapter takes on this subject of high controversy and offers still more controversial suggestions, seeking to set the pogrom within a wider spectrum of the Jewish experience in Alexandria from the founding of the city to the time of the Great Revolt. On that larger canvas, the brief episode in 38 looks very different indeed. Jews held an active and rewarding place in the life of Ptolemaic Alexandria. And the prevailing, nearly unquestioned, notion that they were thrust on the defensive by the coming of Rome, exposed to the envy and brutality of their enemies, requires serious scrutiny. The evidence points in quite another direction. A new analysis may stimulate salutary rethinking.

A dossier of documents preserved by Josephus opens a critical vista upon Jews in the Roman province of Asia. They consist largely of Roman responses to Jewish appeals for assistance or protection of rights endangered by the actions of Greek cities in Asia Minor. The testimony, not surprisingly, has served as chief witness for the argument that Jews perched on a precarious precipice in the region—subject to the persecution of Hellenic officials and regularly rescued by Roman intervention. Chapter 3 revisits and revises that conclusion. Most of the documents, in fact, belong to a concentrated period of time, when this region, like so many others, was thrust into the maelstrom of Rome's civil war and the realignments that came in its aftermath. Circumstances were exceptional rather than representative. The chapter ties this testimony to international events that helped to determine the specifics of the situation in Asia. And the documents indeed disclose the existence of flourishing Jewish institutions in various Asian communities that put into question the idea of dependence on external defense against the oppression of local officials.

Chapter 4 takes a much broader look at the variety of ways in which Jews organized themselves for both religious and civic purposes in communities all around the Mediterranean. It surveys the quite remarkable range of testimony, whether literary, epigraphic, papyrological, or archaeological, for the existence of Jewish synagogues in the Second Temple period. Synagogues supported a plethora of activities that declared the distinctiveness of the Jewish people within the structure of a larger Greco-Roman society. They possessed official personnel and wholesale administrative structures. They served as schools of instruction, houses of worship, record offices, financial depositories, political assemblies, and judicial tribunals. The survey serves as a means to address a number of key questions: the degree to which the synagogue imitated or compensated for the Temple, its relation to pagan conventions or models, and the nature of its association with the surrounding society. Diaspora life, however, by no means confined itself to the synagogue. Individual Jews could and did participate in the wider affairs of the places in which they dwelled; they had access to the gymnasia, to the higher learning, and to the athletic competitions of Greek society, to some share in the civic privileges of Hellenic cities, and, on occasion, even to the ranks of the officialdom that governed those cities. A picture emerges that is quite distinct from conventional assumption.

Part II turns to literary manifestations of Jewish responses to diaspora

life. The allusions are less than explicit, requiring interpretation and imagination. Texts are numerous, and only a selection can be accommodated.
Chapter 5 discusses several appealing works either written in the diaspora
or employing diaspora settings for the creation of historical fiction. Their
authors (generally anonymous) set the narratives within an ostensibly historical frame, with familiar figures and events of the past, only to revise,
adorn, or freely fabricate tales to attract and amuse readers. This chapter
treats the stories of Esther, Tobit, Judith, and Susanna, as well as the fancies indulged in by the author of II Maccabees. Emphasis falls on an ingredient too rarely noticed in these and other Jewish texts: their humor. The
fiddling with pseudo-history gave scope for imaginative play. And even serious historiography (as in II Maccabees) could be enlivened by novel
touches that slipped into comedy. What all this signifies invites speculation.
The idea that such a resort to humor indicates repression of an unwelcome
reality does not easily capture the tone of the texts. It may, in fact, betoken
a more buoyant and self-confident attitude that better characterizes the
mood of diaspora Jews.

Chapter 6 explores a different mode of literary expression. Jewish writers indulged themselves regularly in the recasting of biblical stories. Reverence for canonical texts did not prevent additions, subtractions, enhancement, or wholesale inversion. And here too humor pops up with frequency.
The chapter scrutinizes three diverse and fascinating examples: the Testament of Abraham, the Testament of Job, and the fanciful rewriting of
the Abraham, Joseph, and Moses legends by the whimsical Egyptian Jew
Artapanus. The comedic aspects of these tales, largely ignored or under-
played by moderns, provide critical clues to the Jewish response to diaspora. Not that the subject is directly addressed—hints and suggestions
need to be brought to the surface. The chapter endeavors to follow leads
that reflect on relations between Jews and Gentiles and give access to a diaspora mentality that welcomed mirth and amusement.

Yet another vein is mined in Chapter 7: the images of Greeks and Greek
culture as constructed by a variety of Jewish authors, through both direct reference and indirect allusion. The discussion ranges over historical,
philosophical, apocalyptic, and novelistic texts. No neat and tidy picture
emerges. Jewish intellectuals had a complex and ambiguous relationship
with the Hellenic world, both critical and admiring, scornful and laudatory. Conflicting signals occur in the same writers and the same works. But
important echoes arise from the dissonance. Jews condemned those aspects
of Greek culture that permitted them to highlight their distinctive advantages, and embraced others that they could label as derivative from their

own traditions. The Jewish elite immersed itself in that culture and refashioned it to suit their ends—a means of enunciating the tribe's moral and intellectual superiority. There is little sign here of a nervous and insecure minority.

A concluding chapter addresses the larger question of diaspora and homeland on a more theoretical level. It questions the dichotomy itself and ponders the validity of privileging homeland over diaspora or, for that matter, vice versa. Were diaspora Jews compelled to make such a choice? Their writings do not suggest that they had turned their backs on the center, having elected to sever themselves from Jerusalem, or that they grieved over an unfulfilled existence, deprived of their roots. Nor do they express apology or embarrassment. Respect and awe paid to the Holy Land could coincide with commitment to local community and allegiance to Gentile governance. Jews in Greco-Roman cities felt no obligation to rationalize their life-style or explain their decision to dwell at a distance from their nation's origins. Nowhere did they define themselves as part of a diaspora. And it is no accident that they never constructed a theory of diaspora.

JEWISH LIFE IN
THE DIASPORA

The Jews in Rome

THE POPULATION of Rome exploded during the second and first centuries BCE. Some came involuntarily, as slaves or war captives. Others arrived as visitors, immigrants, and settlers. As the center of an expanding empire, the city held great attraction; it drew peoples from all over the Mediterranean. Jews were among them. When they first came and in what numbers requires guesswork. Evidence on the beginnings is altogether absent. Figures of any kind emerge only in the Augustan era—and even then they are of dubious value. We can be sure only that Jewish communities in Rome continued to grow in the late Republic and early Principate, with modern estimates of the Jewish population ranging from 20,000 to 60,000 (the reality, in all likelihood, being closer to the lower number).[1] The process remains obscure. But the appeal of the imperial city is obvious. It would naturally serve as a principal pivot for the diaspora.

Ancient writers paid little heed to the Jews of Rome. The latter rarely attracted attention and even more rarely attracted comment. The few nuggets of information float in an otherwise vast void. That frustrating circumstance enforces caution in any conclusions. What survives, however, piques our curiosity—and can also stimulate fruitful hypotheses.

The first mention of Jews in Rome comes out of the blue. A strange, disputed, and possibly garbled notice appears in the text of Valerius Maximus, an idiosyncratic collector of anecdotes designed to convey moral lessons or make philosophical points, in the reign of the emperor Tiberius. Embedded in that collection is a peculiar report that has Jews actually expelled from Rome in the year 139 BCE.[2] Hence they must have been there to be ousted. No context or background is provided. And without Valerius' testimony, few would have imagined the existence of a Jewish community in Rome as early as the mid-second century.

Standard opinion in Philo's day, almost two centuries later, had it that

the large majority of Jews who dwelled in Trastevere derived from prisoners of war, enslaved and subsequently manumitted.[3] That may, as is cus-
tomarily supposed, refer to Pompey's campaign in Judaea, the capture of
Jerusalem that occurred in 63 BCE, and the transfer of Jewish prisoners to
Rome.[4] Yet Jews were hardly strangers to the city before that time. Cicero's
reference to crowds of Jews around his tribunal in 59 BCE, presuming full
familiarity with this group on the part of his audience, implies that they
had been ensconced in Rome for some time before.[5] How long before remains a matter for speculation. Had they really come a century earlier, a
troublesome lot who made themselves sufficiently obnoxious to be driven
out of the city by 139? And, if so, why had they come and in what numbers? These are vexed questions, perhaps ultimately unanswerable. And
yet the problem, of high importance, lures on the investigator.

What exactly does Valerius Maximus say about the matter? There is no
easy answer even to that. Roadblocks arise right from the beginning. We
do not, in fact, have Valerius' text, only two epitomes of it by two separate Byzantine excerptors—and they provide two somewhat different versions. The first, by Julius Paris, probably dating from around 400 CE, states
that the Roman praetor peregrinus, Cn. Cornelius Hispalus (an error for
Hispanus), in the consulship of Popilius and Calpurnius (i.e., 139 BCE), ordered the Chaldeans to leave the city, indeed the country, within ten days;
he further compelled the Jews who had attempted to infect the Romans
with their cult of Jupiter Sabazius to return to their own homes.[6] The second version, composed or preserved by Nepotianus perhaps a century
later, offers a variant: Cornelius Hispalus expelled the Chaldeans from
Rome and ordered them to leave Italy within ten days, lest they peddle
their alien wisdom. He also banished the Jews from the city for attempting
to transfer their sacred rites to the Romans, and he threw out the private
altars they had established in public places.[7] Either way, the circumstances
seem serious and disturbing. Were Jews really there in sufficient numbers
to alarm the authorities? And what were they trying to transmit?

The connection with Jupiter Sabazius can be dealt with swiftly enough.
It appears only in Paris' epitome, and even that has textual problems of its
own.[8] The cult of Sabazius, an eastern form of Dionysos, has nothing in
common with Jewish practice and could hardly be confused with it.[9] More
likely, Valerius, his source, or a later copyist conflated the two, perhaps
blundering because of the superficial similarity of Sabazius and Sabaoth.[10]
The error would be still more likely if, as is quite possible, the adherents of
Sabazius were also booted out of Rome.[11]

But that is the least of the problems. The idea of Jews making a substantial nuisance of themselves in Rome by the mid-second century is not easy to swallow.[12] One might solve the problem by rejecting the testimony of Valerius Maximus' epitomators altogether.[13] That, however, is a bit extreme. What in the world would have possessed Valerius Maximus to enter this fictitious item into the record? Did he invent the episode as a precursor to the real expulsion of Jews in 19 CE, of which he was a contemporary?[14] Not very likely. On that theory Valerius must have gone to considerable trouble to produce a circumstantial account of events in 139. Another explanation has won some favor: that an embassy from Judaea's new ruler, Simon Maccabee, arrived in Rome about this time to renew friendly relations, and members of the delegation may have used the occasion to engage in some missionary activity (or inspired other Jews to do so), thus irritating the Roman authorities, who threw them out.[15] But the envoys of Simon Maccabee almost certainly came in 142, not 139, and would hardly have lingered in Rome to proselytize for three years. Besides, those envoys received very hospitable treatment by Roman officials.[16] Furthermore, what about the demolition of altars supposedly put up by Jews in public places? Jews do not go about erecting private altars in the midst of a Gentile city. The suggestion that these altars were really synagogues has little credibility.[17] Valerius must have expressed himself very badly, on that hypothesis. Did Romans who sympathized with the Jews erect these altars in standard pagan fashion?[18] That would seem an excessive display of admiration.

Where does this leave us? The notice in Valerius Maximus cannot be dismissed or explained away. That some Jews were in Rome by the middle of the second century should cause no great surprise. The Romans had fought a major war against Antiochus III, monarch of the Seleucid realm, in the years 191 to 188. The great king was defeated and humbled. Prisoners of war followed the Romans home. And the conclusion of any conflict provided a bonus for slave traders, who could find eager purchasers in Rome and Italy. There is no mention of Jews in this connection, but we do know that Jews had benefited substantially from the favors of Antiochus III. More to the point, this king had transported two thousand Jews from Mesopotamia and Babylonia to key sites in Phrygia, where they would undertake garrison duty and protect the interests of the Seleucid realm in Asia Minor.[19] That Jews fought in the cause of Antiochus is logical, even inevitable. And some surely found themselves in Rome and Italy as captives, slaves, and eventually freedmen.[20]

But there need not have been many. Nor does Valerius' account require many. Few scholars have paid attention to the fact that the expulsion order included others besides Jews. The Chaldeans too were ordered out of the city, astrologers who, as Valerius states, misled foolish and giddy minds with their mendacious interpretations of the stars and took profit from them.[21] This was no campaign against the Jews as such.[22] And it did little or nothing to discourage Jews from dwelling in the city. They were there in notable numbers by the age of Cicero. Nor did astrologers vanish from the Roman scene.

How then does one explain the decree of expulsion? The answer lies not in Jewish proselytizing nor in Chaldean chicanery, but in Roman public relations. A close parallel occurred about twenty years earlier. In the year 161 BCE another Roman praetor, M. Pomponius, proposed a resolution which was adopted by the senate, authorizing him to ban philosophers and rhetors from the city.[23] On the face of it, execution of that order would entail a serious impoverishment of education for Roman youth. But the decree had little practical effect—and probably intended little practical effect. Eminent Greek philosophers were in Rome a few years later in 155 as diplomatic representatives of Athens, and stayed to deliver lectures to enthralled audiences.[24] In 154 came a new expulsion order: two Epicurean philosophers were singled out for deportation on the grounds that they introduced unnatural pleasures to the young.[25] That clearly was a caricature of Epicureanism rather than a serious effort to root out unsavory philosophers. We know that learned men from Hellas continued to find a place in Rome and to mold the minds of the younger generation.

Why then go to the trouble of periodic expulsion decrees? Posturing rather than pragmatism took precedence. The second century witnessed a rash of sumptuary laws sponsored by Roman legislators, regulating everything from expenditures on smoked meats and green vegetables to the species of fish and fowl that could be served at the table. The measures were plainly unenforced and unenforceable. Hence, their repetition. Five of them at least were passed in the second century, sometimes in close conjunction with the expulsion of designated groups.[26] One came in 143, the *lex Didia,* extending the restrictions on luxury to all of Italy.[27] That entered the books within a very few years of the order directed against astrologers and Jews. Still another bill imposing sumptuary limitations of some kind, the *lex Licinia,* followed in the next decade or two, and yet another, the *lex Aemilia,* was promulgated in 115. The satirist Lucilius took pleasure in recommending evasion or simply lampooning such meaningless measures.[28]

In fact, of course, these laws did carry meaning. And so did the order to deport Chaldeans and Jews, passed in their midst. But the significance rests in the image projected by the regime. The second century marked a time when Rome came into frequent and regular contacts with the worlds of Greece and the Near East, contacts which enriched but could also embarrass the imperial power. Periodic expressions of superiority and control seemed necessary to maintain the proper image. Thus sumptuary legislation declared resistance to debilitating luxury associated with the infiltration of eastern habits. And occasional removal (or, at least, proclaimed removal) of foreign groups with alien practices could cleanse the conscience without risking serious disruption. Rome's *principes* paraded their protection of the nation's values against too much contamination from abroad. Symbolic significance rather than any systematic expulsion held primacy.

Thus the episode as described by Valerius Maximus or his excerptors can stand. In 139, as often before and after, Roman authorities found the need to reiterate the undiluted character of their ancestral traditions and to make an example of foreign groups whose strange ways were unacceptable to proper Romans. The Jews' peculiar practices were undisguised and conspicuous, hence readily identifiable and easily censured when convenient for the government. But they were not the sole, perhaps not the main, target. Chaldean astrologers came in for comparable condemnation, and so, apparently, did the worshippers of Sabazius. The latter, in fact, may have been the perpetrators of private altars set in public places, wrongly ascribed, in the confused text, to Jews. The government, in short, was making a statement, not purging itself of alien ethnic groups. And the statement, characteristically, included dubious charges to justify the action: astrologers sold their fallacious wares to unsuspecting and unwitting victims, and Jews sought to transfer their sacred rites to Romans. This does not constitute serious evidence for proselytism—let alone for genuine Roman hostility to Jews. The Jewish community that existed in Rome by the mid-second century clearly endured, indeed grew in size and significance, in the decades that followed.

Not that Roman contemporaries or later historians writing on this period paid much attention to the Jews. They appear nowhere in the testimony for two generations. Jews, one might surmise, were too inconsequential to capture notice. Or they minded their own business, perhaps blended inconspicuously into the social landscape, and thus provided no interesting material for writers engaged in reconstructing and interpreting the travails of the later Roman Republic.

The Jews of Rome resurface briefly and surprisingly—but most tellingly—in the record for the year 59 BCE. The evidence comes in an oration of

Cicero, the principal defense speech for L. Valerius Flaccus, ex-governor of the Roman province of Asia. Flaccus came under indictment for a range of alleged felonies committed against Asian provincials during his tenure in the province. Among them was a relevant and intriguing item: Flaccus passed an edict forbidding the export of gold from Asia, a reinforcement of earlier senatorial decrees against the export of gold and silver, the most recent one in 63.[29] Flaccus' action hit the Jews of Asia particularly hard. They had long adhered to the practice, as did Jews elsewhere in the Mediterranean, of contributing their annual half-shekel payment to the Temple in Jerusalem for maintenance of the sacrifices. The funds, it appears, were collected city by city in Asia and converted to gold equivalents for shipment to Jerusalem. Flaccus had seized them publicly in Apamea, Laodicea, Adramyttium, Pergamum, and doubtless other cities of the province.[30] Of course, the Jews of Asia set up a howl. But, more interestingly, the Jews of Rome made their presence felt as well. They came out in force to the vicinity of the Aurelian Steps where the case was being tried, a favorite place, it seems, for vociferous demonstrations. Not for the first time, if one believes Cicero. The *multitudo* of Jews had occasionally expressed itself with fervid fierceness in Roman *contiones,* i.e., informal gatherings for expressions of opinion and discussion of public issues prior to the promulgation of decrees and laws.[31] On this occasion, as is clear, Jewish passions were aroused by the prospect of suppressing this entrenched means of demonstrating devotion to the Temple. As Cicero himself knew (and this was evidently no secret to other Romans), Jews from Italy and every province of the Roman empire sent annual contributions to Jerusalem.[32]

What is to be made of this? Much ink has been spilled over the attitude of Cicero toward Jews. Does he represent a virulent form of anti-semitism, an example of Roman hostility to that religion and its practitioners? He certainly has some harsh things to say. After all, Roman troops under Pompey had only recently, in 63, marched into Jerusalem, took sides in an internal dispute, and crushed the opposing party by capturing the Temple Mount and slaughtering its defenders.[33] Cicero could thus rail with impunity. He branded the Jewish faith as "barbaric superstition," deplored its practices as deliberately divorced from the splendor of the empire, the seriousness of the Roman name, and the ancestral institutions, and boasted that its defeat at Roman hands proved its unworthiness in the eyes of the divine.[34] None of this, as is now generally recognized, amounts to anti-semitism. Cicero's rhetorical outbursts did not restrict themselves to the Jews, even in this speech—let alone elsewhere in his vituperative repertoire. The needs of the moment dictated the level of vitriol. Cicero also lambasted the Asian Greeks who had come to testify against Flaccus, contrasting them unfavorably with the sober and respectable Greeks of the mainland, like Athenians, Spartans, and Achaeans. Those in Asia barely qualified as rational beings. Nothing said by Lydians, Phrygians, or Mysians could be believed—especially if they were speaking under oath.[35] If Cicero's verbal explosions exhibited prejudice against Jews, they disclosed even more profound prejudice against the Hellenic inhabitants of Asia Minor. Plainly prejudice is not the issue here, only the strategy of the advocate.[36]

Was the measure itself, however, the ban on export of gold and silver, directed explicitly against Jews? Nothing suggests it, and plausibility stands against it. Cicero says only that Flaccus' edict forbade shipment of gold from Asia and that this followed frequent senatorial pronouncements, including one in the orator's own consulship of 63.[37] The Roman senate surely did not make repeated efforts to curb Jewish collection of contributions to the Temple. Cicero's own testimony about annual deliveries to Jerusalem from all provinces of the empire belies the notion.[38] Flaccus, to be sure, blocked consignments of gold from the cities of his province, including those destined for Jerusalem. But that hardly means that he specifically targeted Jews. Other motives drove Roman public policy on this score. Flaccus simply implemented previous decrees of the senate in Rome, the latest of which had come in 63.

Why then? Surmises are possible. Perhaps monies had begun flowing abroad in the wake of Pompey's victories in the East, thus to take advantage of opportunities in that newly pacified area, leaving shortages or potential shortages in Italy.[39] Or else the economic troubles produced by recent wars, culminating in serious debts that helped to provoke the Catilinarian insurrection in 63, prompted action by the senate.[40] Or, on another hypothesis, the panic created by Catiline's movement led to a shortfall of coinage as persons of wealth sent monies abroad for safekeeping.[41] Comparable circumstances, relating to financial crises or opportunities, may have lain behind earlier (undated) senatorial decrees. But hostility or resentment toward Jews played no discernible role.

The evidence of Cicero has greater value on a different subject: the significance and cohesion of the Jewish presence in the city of Rome. His remarks, hostile and distorted though they may be, afford valuable insight into a subject consistently ignored by pagan writers. When Flaccus came to trial in 59, the charge of confiscating Jewish gold may not have loomed large in the overall indictment. But it certainly stirred the Jews of Rome into activity, with vehement protests registered around the tribunal. This, of course, supplies clear testimony for communication between Jewish communities across the Mediterranean. Roman Jews took up the cause of their fellows in Asia. Cicero, however, reports something at least equally interesting: demonstrations by Jews at Roman public gatherings had taken place before, a not unfamiliar feature of the political landscape.[42] Jews stick together, he said; they come out as a crowd, and they carry considerable weight in the *contiones*.[43] The audience presumably was acquainted with the phenomenon. Cicero gives no hint that these demonstrations were illicit or illegitimate—only unwelcome (to him). Jews could freely voice their views and press their case on the public stage. The notion, widely embraced by scholars, that Jews were egged on and mobilized by Roman politicians and that they formed a cadre for the *"populares"* is pure construct, nowhere buttressed by testimony.[44] The Jews of Rome had solidarity when they needed it. And they could lobby for their causes with impunity. The episode discloses both an integration of Jews within Roman society and a strong sense of their own identity.

Who were these Jews? Ex-slaves, prisoners of war liberated by their masters, and permitted to participate on Roman sufferance? Hardly. The captives brought to Rome as a consequence of Pompey's victory in Judaea had only been in the city for two years, barely enough time for a few manumissions, and certainly not enough to constitute a cohesive community. Were they the descendants of freed slaves who had come in the wake of the Antiochene war of the early second century? Perhaps. But, if so, three or four generations had intervened. The stigma of the freedman would long since have evaporated. And one should not rule out the possibility, even the probability, that many Jews migrated to Rome and Italy for purposes of commerce, to join families, to seek employment, or to enjoy the advantages of attachment to the center of power in the Mediterranean. Cicero had no kind words for the Jews who rallied in public against his client. He would not have missed an opportunity to stigmatize them as *libertini*—if he could. The absence of any such slurs is telling. The Jews in Rome of the late Republic were predominantly free persons, whether citizens or *peregrini*.[45]

We have been bedeviled for too long by a notorious notice in Philo. The philosopher, as mentioned above, declared that the majority of Jews who dwelled across the Tiber were Roman freedmen, originally taken to Italy as enslaved war captives, later manumitted by their owners.[46] That presumably alludes to the victims of Pompey's campaign in Judaea in 63, to those who fought unsuccessfully against Gabinius, the Roman governor of Syria in 57, and to the captives of Cassius, who took over the province in 53.[47]

No known prisoners arrived from that land between the time of Cicero and that of Philo. In what numbers Jewish captives came to Rome in the 60s and 50s, we cannot tell.[48] In any event, a century had elapsed, nearly three generations, before Philo penned his lines. And he refers only to the Jews of Trastevere. We know from archaeological and epigraphic evidence that Jewish communities established themselves elsewhere in Rome as well—although the chronology eludes us.[49] They certainly did not comprise only captives, chattel, and refugees. And even those who fell into that dismal category may have escaped it within a generation or two.[50]

Roman practice, as is well known, was strikingly liberal in the ready manumission of slaves. Freedmen enjoyed civic status, the privilege of citizenship, albeit with some legal restrictions and social liabilities. And sons of freedmen had largely shaken off the taint of their origins, even gained eligibility for office in the political order.[51] This broad-minded attitude surprised the ancients and continues to intrigue moderns. Romans raised no insurmountable barriers to the transition from slavery to citizenship.[52] Among other things, this created the rather anomalous, even paradoxical, situation in which free-born immigrants, the *peregrini,* actually exercised fewer civic privileges than did manumitted slaves who, in some form, entered the citizen body. Romans evidently regarded the exposure to the social and cultural scene that came with service to an aristocratic family as providing credentials for citizenship upon emancipation.

Whatever the motives of this generous convention, Jews were certainly among its beneficiaries. The existence of an established Jewish community or communities in Rome by the early first century BCE is clear, and the origins probably go back a good deal earlier. In all likelihood, the communities combined descendants of freed slaves with immigrants, descendants of citizens with non-citizens. Although few, if any, could aspire to political prominence, their collective presence on the public scene was acknowledged and uncircumscribed. Jews could exhibit their views and exercise pressure when interests of the clan were at stake. Nothing suggests any desire to pull up stakes and head for the homeland. But the Jews in Rome maintained ties both to Jerusalem, as demonstrated by adherence to the annual contribution to the Temple (a symbolic as well as a tangible act), and to fellow-Jews elsewhere, exhibited by protests on behalf of their compatriots in Asia Minor. Roman Jews kept a very clear perception of their own identity.

The authorities in Rome had no cause to harass Jews—nor indeed to "tolerate" them. The practitioners of that faith were simply part of the social/

cultural landscape of the city. A crackdown against foreigners had come in
the year 65. The assembly of the people, on motion of a tribune of the
plebs, passed formal legislation to expel all *peregrini* from Rome.[53] What
prompted the measure is obscure. Political agitation of some sort may have
lain behind it, perhaps demonstrations on behalf of the franchise for those
Italians dwelling beyond the Po, an issue of prominence at the time.[54] But
if, in fact, any significant numbers of aliens were driven out of Rome, that
action seems to have left the Jews unaffected. They were still there in 59 to
push their claims at the trial of Flaccus. In the following year of 58, the senate did order the destruction of idols and altars to Egyptian gods that had
been constructed on the Capitoline Hill without official permission.[55] The
motive for this action eludes us. But it entailed no governmental sweep
against foreign sects.[56] The Jews came away unscathed.

A more serious move by the officialdom in Rome during these years surfaced in efforts to control the *collegia*. These voluntary associations, corporate groups organized either as trade guilds or as religious and social
clubs, had a long history in the city.[57] In the late Roman Republic, freedmen and slaves consituted a substantial proportion of the membership in
the *collegia*. A potential for disruption lay there, especially in the tense political scene of the 60s and 50s. The senate at least became sufficiently
alarmed to sponsor a decree in 64 to abolish those *collegia* that it regarded
as formed against the interests of the state.[58] Which and how many of the
collegia were suppressed at this time is a matter of considerable debate, but
it has little relevance for our purposes.[59] The *senatus consultum* was un-
done in 58 when the popular tribune P. Clodius sponsored a measure that
canceled previous legislation, renewed the legitimacy of the old *collegia*,
and authorized the creation of new ones.[60] But other measures followed
in subsequent years, both senatorial decrees and *leges,* that curtailed the
collegia, exempting only those few that were of service to the community,
such as guilds of craftsmen and artisans.[61]

Did Jews fall under these strictures? They are nowhere mentioned in this
connection; nor indeed is the term *collegium* ever applied to them in the extant evidence. The Jews of Rome in general did not reckon themselves as a
corporate entity organized as a religious club. They employed none of the
terms normally adopted by the officials of such organizations. And the notion that individual synagogues received government sanction as *collegia*
falls well short of persuasive proof. The character of the Jewish communities set them apart from the usual criteria that applied to *collegia*. They did
not form a voluntary association, their membership was determined by

birth and ethnic identity, their bonds crossed the lines of individual syna-gogues, their communal interests and connections extended to Jews well outside the boundaries of the city, and the regulations governing particular communities were less important than the overarching laws of the Torah.[62]

None of this, in principle, would preclude Roman authorities from clas-sifying, even licensing, Jewish groups as *collegia*. Did they do so? The critical evidence concerns a purported piece of legislation by Julius Caesar, promulgated during his dictatorship, probably in 47 or 46 BCE. Suetonius provides a terse and tantalizing description: Caesar dissolved all the *collegia*, apart from those established of old.[63] That Caesar sponsored and implemented such an act need not be doubted. A subsequent measure by Augustus alludes indirectly to it.[64] Just which *collegia* qualified as old and established can be debated but need not be here. They presumably in-cluded the ancient priestly colleges, some harmless religious, social, and cultural clubs, and the associations of craftsmen, artisans, and other pro-fessionals.[65]

Were Jewish groups included among the *collegia antiqua*? Suetonius supplies no answers. But a highly problematic and much disputed passage in Josephus steps into the breach. The Jewish historian includes in his col-lection of documents detailing Roman affirmation of Jewish privileges in the East a letter from a magistrate probably written in the mid-40s and probably to the island of Paros. He reasserts Roman policy that frowns upon local decrees limiting the practice of Jewish rites and customs. And he cites explicit precedent for this position: "Gaius Caesar, our commander-in-chief, in his decree prohibiting the assemblage of associations within the city, exempted the Jews alone from the ban on collecting money or having common meals."[66] That can hardly be a reference to anything but the same Caesarian measure summarized by Suetonius, even if the terminology in Greek is less than a precise rendition.[67] How likely is it that Caesar inserted a special exemption for Jews in a sweeping administrative measure de-signed to control *collegia* that had disrupted or might disrupt public or-der?[68] Would he single out Jews alone as immune from the provisions of the law? To be sure, they might not otherwise qualify as *collegia antiquitus constituta*. But many other associations, harmless and useful to society, had emerged in recent decades without claims on great antiquity. They surely did not all come under the ban—and it is very hard to imagine a lengthy appendix listing every *collegium* still reckoned as legitimate. Caesar might indeed have been grateful for Jewish cooperation in his civil war in the East. But that would bear little or no relevance for the reconstitution of *collegia* at home. To include an exemption clause for Jews alone could only have invited a flood of applications (or widespread resentment) from other groups.

Where then does this leave us? One could cut the knot by tossing out the Josephan document—or, at least, this portion of it—as forged, fabricated, or doctored.[69] But there is no need for such radical surgery. The Roman magistrate does not purport to quote Caesar's measure verbatim. (He is unlikely to have had a copy of it with him in Asia.) He calls upon it simply as a buttress for his instructions to the officials of Greek islands to leave Jews practicing their rituals in peace. After all, Caesar let them do it. If the Caesarian law omitted specific mention of the Jews (as is most probable), the magistrate could interpret that, for his purposes, as giving them free rein. One might even suppose a particular application by Jewish representatives after passage of the measure, seeking and receiving reassurance that their gatherings would be unaffected. But the idea of an exemption written into the law, with explicit reference to Jews alone, cannot be sustained. The Roman magistrate in Asia took some liberties—or perhaps Josephus did.

The ground is now cleared. Testimony on Jewish communities as *collegia* evaporates. Jews did not conceive of themselves as forming social clubs or even religious societies in the Roman sense. And there is no good reason to believe that the Romans set them in those categories.[70] Legalistic questions have plagued us too long. Inquiry as to whether Judaism was a *religio licita,* whether Jews received official sanction, whether they were arrayed amidst the *collegia,* threatened by the ban, and required exemption, or even whether their practices needed governmental "tolerance," may miss the point.[71] Their presence in the city of Rome during the late Republic created no ostensible problem for the stability or integrity of Roman society. Many of them were Roman citizens themselves. Their associations had become part of a colorful urban scene, distinctive and recognizable, but hardly threatening and rarely noticed. Roman writers, like the Roman government, passed over them almost altogether. The political turbulence of the era, it seems, left the Jews untouched.

What evidence we possess—not much, to be sure—indicates a thriving, active, and engaged community in the age of Augustus. The *princeps* himself paid them heed, so it appears. A crisis occurred in Palestine in 4 BCE upon the death of King Herod, the controversial but powerful ruler who had held the land in thrall for a generation. Riot and rebellion burst out in Judaea, prompting the intervention of a Roman procurator, who roiled matters further, issuing in greater violence, more widespread uprisings, and forceful repression by Roman legions from Syria. The question of succession to Herod—or indeed the continuance of Herodian rule—stirred fierce passions.[72] Herod's will had designated his son Archelaus as successor, but the claim was challenged by another son, Antipas, while other Jews clamored for removal of the Herodian dynasty altogether, even at the expense of direct Roman rule. Parties representing each claim gathered in Rome, seeking the sanction of Augustus. The *princeps* duly assembled his *consilium* to sit in solemn judgment in this complex controversy.[73] An initial decision was postponed so that Augustus could ponder the conflicting testimony.[74] In the interim, violence broke out in Judaea, heightening the intensity of the issue confronting the emperor in Rome. A delegation of fifty Jewish leaders arrived, requesting "autonomy" for their nation.[75] That term, flexible and malleable at all times in antiquity, had a special connotation here. For the Jewish envoys and those whom they represented, it was entirely compatible with the status of a Roman province and the oversight of a Roman governor. "Autonomy" meant, in a word, independence from Herodian rule.[76]

Augustus reassembled his council to hear the dispute. And the Jewish envoys swiftly found that they were not alone. No fewer than eight thousand Roman Jews, according to Josephus, materialized to express their support and exhibit their solidarity.[77] The numbers may very well be an exaggeration, but the crowd was conspicuous and the exertion of pressure was uninhibited. The Jews of Rome stood shoulder to shoulder with the delegates from Jerusalem.[78] That Augustus eventually found for Archelaus and authorized his accession to the throne did not constitute dismissal of Jewish concerns (Archelaus' supporters, after all, were Jews as well). It was a matter of imperial policy: Roman interests in the East seemed best assured by continuance of the Herodian dynasty. But the demonstration by Roman Jews, bold and unhindered, remains the most striking feature of this episode. They showed no hesitation in arriving in force to express their connection with the aims of compatriots from the homeland. They clearly feared no reprisals—and they got none.

It was not the first time, nor the last. At the funeral of Julius Caesar in 44 BCE large crowds of foreigners had gathered to express their grief, and the Jews were most prominent among them. They showed up at his funeral pyre for several nights in succession.[79] That notice comes from Suetonius, who had no axe to grind on behalf of Jews. And another occasion brought out Jewish throngs later in the reign of Augustus. A young Jew from Sidon traded upon his remarkable resemblance to Alexander, son of Herod, who had been executed on his father's orders in 7 BCE; he claimed to be that son, allegedly spared by his would-be executioners. He persuaded Jews in

Crete and then in Melos, who hailed him and supplied him with cash. The pseudo-Alexander then made so bold as to arrive in Rome in order to press his claims upon the Judaean throne. The advent astonishingly brought out crowds of Jews in the city, not just through curiosity but to cheer him on. To no avail. The plot soon collapsed; the imposter was unmasked and sent to labor amidst the oarsmen in Roman galleys.[80] But the outcome matters little. The most striking feature of this event is the behavior of Roman Jews. Large throngs sprang up to show their enthusiasm for a supposed scion of the Herodian house. For Josephus, not averse to hyperbole, they constituted the "entire Jewish population of the city"![81] Few will credit that exclamation. Josephus himself had affirmed that only a few years earlier vast numbers of Jews had turned up to back those who sought to shake off the hegemony of the Herods. The incident, if anything, discloses divided opinions among Jews in Rome, mirroring divisions in the homeland. This is not surprising. A significant fact remains: Jews in the city had free rein to display their sentiments and demonstrate their political passions. In that regard the coming of Augustus, so momentous a milestone in Roman history, represented a comfortable continuity for Jews dwelling in the capital.

The Jewish philosopher Philo, writing in the reign of Claudius, has nothing but praise for Augustus. For some, that may arouse suspicion rather than supply confirmation. Philo, it can reasonably be surmised, dwelled on Augustus' solicitude for Jews in order to paint a contrast with Caligula and offer a model for Claudius. To be sure. Yet there is no reason to question the basic presentation of Augustus' relation to the Jews of Rome. What is striking about Philo's account is the emphasis on the *princeps*' passivity. He does not claim (with one exception) that Augustus enacted measures for Roman Jews, intervened to protect them, or promoted their prosperity. What he does say, in effect, is that the *princeps* let the Jews go on precisely as they had in the past: he altered none of their traditional practices; he had no problem with their meetings in synagogues or sending their tithes to Jerusalem; he did not expel them from Rome or deprive them of citizenship. Philo thus concentrates upon what Augustus did *not* do.[82] If he could cite explicit legislation or official action, he would hardly have missed the chance to do so.[83] The one positive act of Augustus with regard to Roman Jews is noteworthy and interesting. When monthly distributions of grain took place for the needy, Jews among others were eligible. But if the allocations took place on the Sabbath, the observant among them would lose out. Augustus rectified the anomaly by affirming that, in that event, officials in charge of the distributions would reserve a portion of the grain due to the Jews for the next day.[84] This, of course, was far from a center-piece of Augustan policy. Jewish representatives must have called the problem to the attention of those who supervised the allocations. And once the issue surfaced, Augustus had no difficulty in remedying the problem. It implies no special concern on the *princeps'* part for the welfare of Jews in Rome.[85] They did not, on the whole, require it.

The testimony has an added dimension as well. The Jews eligible for grain distributions must have enjoyed Roman citizenship.[86] We cannot begin to estimate the numbers, but they were sufficient to prompt action by the *princeps*. This furnishes further insight into the successful integration of Jews into the social and economic life of the city. In general, the Jewish community in Rome appears to have survived quite satisfactorily without special protection or privilege from the crown.[87] Rome did not have a "Jewish problem."

Circumstances changed in the reign of Tiberius. Or did they? A notorious episode occurred in 19 CE, much discussed, analyzed, and brawled over. The emperor turned on the Jews and expelled them from Rome, perhaps from Italy—the first such deed in a century and a half. Had the Jews suddenly made themselves offensive or reprehensible? Were they victimized by a hostile ruler prepared to undo generations of laissez-faire? Did they become embroiled in a larger social and economic upheaval from which they suffered governmental backlash? Or does any such explanation suffice for so drastic a turnabout? The event itself cannot be dismissed or discounted. Several sources converge, both Jewish and pagan, to record it, each in a somewhat different way but all pointing to the same episode. What to make of it?

The evidence needs to be set forth, at least in summary and outline. Josephus has the fullest account, over-full in fact, for he supplies introductory narratives that either include folkloric elements or seem unmatched to the governmental acts that followed. He gives two independent tales. The first has the priests of Isis who ministered to the goddess' temple in Rome engage in a devious scheme to deceive and debauch a Roman noblewoman who was also a devotee of Isis. She was led innocently into a trap, expecting to have intercourse with the god Anubis in the temple, and succumbed instead to a lustful young man who had found no other way to seduce her. When the plot was disclosed and word came to Tiberius, he reacted swiftly and fiercely. The emperor ordered the crucifixion of the priests and a freedwoman who arranged the tryst, the razing of Isis' temple, and the ignominious dumping of her statue in the Tiber. The young man was hustled off into exile.[88] At the same time, according to Josephus, a parallel tale unfolded, involving the Jews of Rome. An unscrupulous character, a fugitive from justice in Judaea, showed up in the city and enlisted three other dubious characters in a scheme to wheedle money out of the aristocratic lady Fulvia, who had become a convert to Judaism. The wicked plotters induced Fulvia to supply purple and gold for the Temple in Jerusalem—only to pocket the goods themselves. This scam too was reported to Tiberius, who proceeded to crack down on the Jewish offenders, but not on them alone. The emperor ordered the entire Jewish community to evacuate Rome. Four thousand of the Jews were rounded up by the consuls, who enlisted them in the army and forthwith sent them off to Sardinia, a hell-hole for military service. Others who refused to enroll lest they break Jewish law suffered unspecified penalties.[89]

The pagan sources are briefer and more pointed. Tacitus reports that in the year 19 the senate debated the matter of banishing Egyptian and Jewish rites. The resultant decree directed that four thousand persons of freedman origin, imbued with that superstition and of appropriate age, should be shipped off to Sardinia to crush the brigands there, and that all the rest be obliged to leave Italy by a certain day—unless they had abandoned their profane practices.[90] A comparable but by no means identical version appears in Suetonius' biography of Tiberius. He has the emperor suppress foreign cults, especially the Egyptian and Jewish rites, even compelling their devotees to consign their religious garb and all that went with it to the flames. He sent Jewish youth to provinces of dreadful climate, on the pretext of military service, and expelled the rest of that sect or those of similar persuasion from the city—with a threat of permanent slavery for those who did not cooperate.[91] The notice in Dio Cassius, writing in the early third century, is briefer still. In the fragment preserved for us, Dio asserts that, as numerous Jews collected in Rome and persuaded many of the indigenous population to adopt their customs, Tiberius banished most of them.[92] Only one contemporary voice makes allusion, or apparent allusion, to these events. The philosopher Seneca speaks of the days of his youth in the early years of Tiberius, when certain foreign rites were being stirred up and abstinence from animal food was reckoned among the proofs of adhering to their beliefs. Under advice from his father, Seneca gave up his vegetarian ways.[93]

How is one to interpret—let alone reconcile—these texts? Did Tiberius turn long-standing Roman policy on its head and suddenly find Judaism to be a loathsome or menacing sect? One answer might be that Jewish proselytizing had finally snapped the patience of Roman officials. They would tolerate Jews so long as they confined their peculiar practices to themselves; but they were fed up with missionary activity that infiltrated the upper strata of Roman society. That thesis has had—and still has—its advocates.[94] But the basis for it is thin and brittle. Only Dio Cassius serves it up as a motive.[95] And his text arrives at second or third hand: we have it via the seventh-century Christian author John of Antioch, an isolated excerpt not in the manuscript traditions of Dio. Moreover, the fragment bears little relation to anything else in the testimony. That does not in itself suffice to discard the comment.[96] But the absence of context creates some nervousness, and the excogitation of motive may be Dio's own, based on the experience of the third century rather than on any testimony from the beginning of the first.[97] The others say nothing about proselytizing, and it won't do to try to wring it out of their texts.[98]

We need not pause over the explanation offered by Josephus. The idea that Tiberius would penalize every Jew in Rome for the misbehavior of four Jewish rascals cannot be taken seriously. Among other things, it would be wildly out of character for that emperor, who frequently mitigated punishments, to indulge in overkill of such proportions. Josephus plainly had no plausible reason to provide. The paired tales of Paulina, the deceived Isis worshipper, and Fulvia, the deceived proselyte, represent an artificial coupling. They reek of folk-tale, romance, and fiction.[99]

Were the Jews ousted as a turbulent and unruly people? Did their participation in disturbances during the early years of Tiberius provoke expulsion from Rome? That thesis has drawn some support in recent years.[100] One can certainly find ancient references to the Jews as disorderly, troublesome types. Cicero, as we have seen, branded them as such at the trial of Flaccus. Suetonius reported that they "flocked" around the funeral bier of Caesar, and Horace, like Cicero, described them as a "mob."[101] But no action was taken against the Jews at Flaccus' trial or at Caesar's funeral. And Horace's allusion to a *turba* is a jocular one.[102] The stray comments do not account for an expulsion in 19 CE. No reference to Jews as a troublesome lot appears in the testimony on that event. To be sure, the early years of Tiberius were unhappy ones for the less affluent in Rome. Grain shortages and natural disasters hit the poorer folk hard, and generated some upheaval.[103] But the same can be said of many other periods of Roman history that did not issue in the banishment of the unruly en masse. And the proposition fails to explain why Jews (nowhere mentioned among the perpetrators of unrest at the time) were singled out for punishment.

A different line of reasoning, more direct and distressing, also needs consideration: that Tiberius' action represents imperial policy against Judaism as a religion. Governmental action, on this view, simply aimed to stamp out alien rites as practiced by Jews, a cult reckoned as offensive to the establishment in Rome.[104] The texts might indeed give some support to this theory. Tacitus speaks of the senatorial discussion as focused on the driving out of Egyptian and Jewish rites, and offers indulgence to those who would renounce their profane practices.[105] Suetonius has the emperor repress foreign rituals and banish Jews or those holding similar beliefs.[106] Dio makes reference to Jews converting others to their customs.[107] And Seneca's contemporary remark about dietary restrictions as evidence for adherence to alien ways and superstitions appears to fit this pattern.[108] Yet the conclusion that Tiberius was bent upon the suppression of a distasteful and repugnant religion falls well short of conviction. Not only do the sources refrain from ascribing such motives to the emperor. The thesis also sidesteps the explicit statement of Philo that Tiberius, after the death of Sejanus, intervened, with directives to governors abroad, to protect Jews from hostilities in the provinces and reassert the inviolability of their customs.[109] Philo's comments, of course, are partisan and apologetic, designed to maximize imperial favor to the Jews by contrast with Caligula's wickedness. But his statement cannot be erased from the record as if it were pure invention.[110] And it demonstrates that Tiberius had no determined policy to stifle Jews as a sect and Judaism as a religion. More significantly, even if one interprets all the collected evidence as making reference to Jewish rites and practices as the primary targets of repression, this speaks only to the public posture of the authorities, not to authentic motivation. If the government were determined to rid Rome of alien rituals and their practitioners, they could have done so long ago. Why wait until 19 CE? And why not do the job more thoroughly? Jews were still in Rome in the later years of Tiberius, objects of Sejanus' slander.[111] And they were there in substantial numbers at the beginning of Claudius' reign a few years later.[112] A satisfactory explanation for the episode in 19 CE is still wanting.

One point, often neglected, needs emphasis. Jews were not the only sect named in the edict or edicts of that year. Tacitus reports the senatorial debate as treating Egyptian and Jewish rites alike. Suetonius even has the target as foreign sects generally, while singling out Egyptians and Jews. Seneca speaks only broadly of alien rituals, and the potential problems with his vegetarianism may not relate to Jews alone. Josephus' paired stories about Isis worshippers and Jews makes it clear that both fell under the punitive edicts of the regime. In short, as in the case of governmental action in 139 BCE, the Roman establishment needed to present a proper face to the public. Emperor and senate reaffirmed their commitment to antique principles and the religion of their ancestors. They would make an example of alien groups. Never mind that the eviction was far from thorough. The point had been made.

But why in 19 CE? Yes, there was a grain shortage and a public outcry.[113] But that does not explain why religious groups should be targeted. Another episode in 19 CE, entirely neglected in this context by modern scholarship, but of high drama for Rome and its inhabitants, may supply the needed clue. Tiberius' nephew and adopted son Germanicus, Rome's prime hope for the future, at least in the public imagination, perished in the East in that year—amidst mysterious and controversial circumstances. Suspicion fastened upon Cn. Piso, governor of Syria, who had quarreled with Germanicus and engaged in a heated competition concerning rival authority over the armies and provinces of the Roman East.[114] Whatever Piso's responsibility may have been, rumors swiftly flew about regarding magic spells, strange signs, and objects that may have hastened Germanicus' demise. Report had it that in Germanicus' house in Syria, where he lay gravely ill, menacing items were found beneath the floor and behind the walls: disinterred remains of human bodies, incantations, curses, the name of Germanicus inscribed on lead tablets, decayed organic matter, ashes, and other evil charms, by which souls were believed to be dedicated to the spirits of Hell.[115] Plainly the arts of black magic had played a role in promoting the last illness of the heir-apparent—or so it was widely believed. Word of the prince's deteriorating condition got to Rome, amplified and exaggerated, as was common with rumors. And when the news of his death arrived, grief, rage, and mourning pervaded the city, calling a halt to public business and paralyzing all official activities in Rome.[116]

The gods were evidently angry. One can readily imagine the exertion of popular pressure to find some means of appeasing divine wrath. It may be no coincidence that Tacitus records the expulsion of Egyptians and Jews in a chapter immediately following his treatment of public reaction to the death of Germanicus.[117] The historian, it is true, draws no direct connection. And the chronology is murky. Tacitus changes subjects in *Annales*, 2.85, when he reports the banishments, prefacing the chapter with *eodem anno*, i.e., 19 CE. The events might have happened any time during the year. The death of Germanicus, as we know from independent testimony, occurred on October 10 in that year.[118] But the rumors of grave illness, with the alarming details about magic spells and the black arts, would likely have arrived well before. Nothing forbids the conjecture that action against alien religions took place in the wake of those revelations. Tiberius, as is well known, had some suspicions to dispel. Many surmised

that the emperor secretly hoped for (and possibly planned) the death of
Germanicus.[119] A public show of commitment to the ancestral divinities,
punctuated by expelling practitioners of alien rites, would be most appropriate, even necessary, at a time of anxiety over the effects of sorcery and
popular outcry at the fate of Germanicus. Proof of the connection is wanting. But suitable circumstances existed, and the confluence of religion and
politics makes for a tempting association.

A closely comparable situation just three years earlier lends support
to the reconstruction. Libo Drusus, a kinsman of Augustus through the
princeps' first wife Scribonia, was accused of treasonable ambitions, led on
by Chaldeans, fortune-tellers, and dream-interpreters. His accusers conveniently turned up some mysterious texts, allegedly in Libo's handwriting,
with hostile or obscure markings that contained the names of senators and
members of the imperial house. It bears special notice that after Libo committed suicide in advance of his trial, the senate directed that astrologers
and magicians be expelled from Italy.[120]

If this conjecture has validity, the expulsion in 19 had more to do with
religious concerns than with xenophobia. The edict that banished Egyptians and Jews could serve its purpose without a sweeping search to dig up
every member of those ethnic groups in Rome. The continuing residence of
Jews in significant numbers in the city thereby finds explanation.

How then to account for four thousand young Jews of military age sent
to the unhealthy isle of Sardinia?[121] Tacitus refers to them as men *libertini*
gentis. Many scholars have worried over the question of whether he means
persons of freedman descent or simply freedmen *tout court,* with subtle
and legalistic arguments brought to bear.[122] They may all miss the historian's purpose. Tacitus has little but scorn for these foreigners kicked out of
Rome as practitioners of despised rites and adherents of superstitious sects.
To brand them further with the status of ex-slaves or the descendants of ex-
slaves may be mere slander, not a reference to the actual origins of Roman
Jews—let alone to the formal wording of the edict. Tacitus adds for good
measure the scornful aside that if they should perish in Sardinia it would be
a cheap loss.[123] But why Sardinia? The need to repress brigandage would
hardly have surfaced conveniently in 19 CE. It was doubtless a recurring or
continuing problem. Perhaps appeasement of the gods may have a part
here as well. The dispatch of conscripts to a dangerous and disease-prone
island could have the effect of supplying victims without engaging in executions. That might supply a plausible solution in a tricky business where
the public posture was paramount.

Jews, it seems plain, were not driven out in droves. But the taint associated with usage as scapegoats could embolden others to exploit the situation. Tiberius' ambitious and manipulative praetorian prefect Sejanus found occasion to take advantage. Although generally labeled as a virulent anti-semite, Sejanus may simply have seized an opportunity to advance his own authority. The testimony is confined to a few sentences in Philo, much overblown in modern discussions.[124] A cryptic comment comes at the beginning of the *In Flaccum*. Philo introduces the treatise by stating that Flaccus (in Alexandria) took up where Sejanus left off in his assault against the Jews—only he did not have the authority or resources to damage the nation as a whole.[125] The case is fleshed out, though only slightly and obscurely, in the *Legatio ad Gaium*. There the philosopher speaks of stirrings in Italy when Sejanus conceived his attack. But the emperor came to his senses after the fall of Sejanus, and recognized that the charges leveled against Jews in Rome were false slanders, creations of Sejanus who wished to eradicate that people.[126] Tiberius then wrote to all provincial governors instructing them to reassure Jews in the cities under their charge that only the few guilty ones would be punished, and to make no changes in the policy of permitting Jews to follow their own practices.[127]

How should we best interpret these phrases? It seems clear enough that Philo is not here offering a different version of the expulsion in 19 CE. He had reason to pass over in silence an episode that set Tiberius in a bad light.[128] Sejanus, though already praetorian prefect by that time, had not yet ingratiated himself with Tiberius to the extent of manipulating affairs to his whim. Tacitus, who records the episode in 19, would have missed no chance to refer to Sejanus' wicked designs. The praetorian prefect did not wield his baleful influence until after 26 CE.[129] And the Philonian passages suggest strongly that Sejanus' maneuvers against the Jews came in the last years before his death in 31. The prefect, it appears, spread slurs against the Jews of Rome. Why? The notion of inveterate anti-semitism seems hard to swallow. And Philo's explanation, that Sejanus, already plotting Tiberius' overthrow, knew that Jews would be the emperor's staunchest shield, is patently preposterous.[130] A campaign of calumnies, however, could serve to reinforce Sejanus' show of loyalty to the emperor. Jewish communities in Rome must have gradually resurfaced after lying low in the wake of the measures of 19 CE. It might seem advantageous for the minister to reproduce charges to which Tiberius himself had subscribed a number of years earlier. But Sejanus miscalculated. And after his fall in 31, Tiberius could conveniently make his prefect the scapegoat for policies that he himself could now renounce.[131] The Jews of Rome were once again the beneficiaries of imperial favor. The episode of 19 had only fleeting impact.

The imperial government thus seems generally indifferent, if not tolerant, and certainly no relentless persecutor of Jews. Our sources record very few occasions of victimization, even in the company of others (as Jews usually were). One can hardly imagine a continuous cowering in fear. Even the reckless and maniacal Gaius Caligula, whose antics threatened sacrilege in the Temple of Jerusalem, left the Jews of Rome alone. Scapegoating, however, could recur. Special circumstances might prompt the need for a public polishing of the imperial image.

Such circumstances, it seems, arose in the reign of the emperor Claudius. That individual could hardly be categorized as a Jew-baiter. In fact, Claudius' somewhat tumultuous ascent to the throne, after the sudden assassination of Caligula in 41 CE, came, so Josephus would have it, with the vital assistance of the Jewish ruler Agrippa, grandson of Herod, a boyhood friend of the new *princeps*. Whatever the validity of that tale, Claudius shortly thereafter bestowed upon Agrippa additional holdings in Palestine, beefing up his kingdom to the size of that once ruled by Herod.[132] And Claudius responded to the tempestuous situation in Alexandria that embroiled Jews, Greeks, and Egyptians in a firm but even-handed fashion. He delivered a stern lecture to Jews, as he did to other Alexandrians—but he also insisted that Jews be allowed to keep to their traditional ways unmolested.[133] The emperor could hardly be reckoned a fervid advocate of the Jews. But he began his reign by reaffirming their sovereignty in Judaea and their ancestral traditions in Alexandria.

Rome, however, was a different matter. Claudius had achieved supreme power in questionable circumstances; he was an untested ruler whose marginalization by the imperial family must have provoked grave doubts about competence and authority. He needed to erase them. The third-century historian Dio Cassius reports a noteworthy act taken at the outset of the reign. Claudius, recognizing that Jewish numbers in Rome had increased to such an extent that they could not be removed from the city without turbulence, chose instead to ban the gatherings in which they practiced their traditional ways.[134]

What is one to make of this? The date seems firmly fixed in 41 CE, the first year of Claudius' principate. Dio sets it in that year, amidst other events that belong there, and there is no sound reason to question his chronology.[135] But the meaning of the event remains puzzling and problematic.

Was Claudius' first impulse to expel Jews from the city, thinking better of it only when he realized that the difficulties involved in removing so large a number of people would cause more trouble than they were worth? So says Dio. But it must be recognized and emphasized that this reasoning is Dio's or that of his source. It can hardly derive from a document. No such explanation would emanate from the regime—it would only suggest weakness. Surmise alone, no hard data, lies behind it. One interesting item does indeed emerge: the Jews in Rome had multiplied yet again.[136] That gives the lie to any broad roundup in 19 CE or in the years of Sejanus' ascendancy. If Jews had gone underground for a short time, they were back in force now. But the notion that Claudius refrained from expelling them because they might stir up too much of a ruckus is pure conjecture. Dio may well have had Tiberius' order to expel Jews in 19 CE, which he had also recorded, in mind.[137] But it does not follow that Claudius did. The record in Dio shows only that he expelled no Jews in 41. The idea of expulsion may never have come up.

What Claudius did do was ban convocations. Did he also clamp down on the practice of Judaism generally? The text of Dio delivers frustrating ambiguity: τῷ δὲ δὴ πατρίῳ βίῳ χρωμένους ἐκέλευσε μὴ συναθροίζεσθαι. This could be construed as forbidding Jews from gathering to practice their religion.[138] Or, by contrast, it might mean that Jews could practice their religion, but could no longer assemble to do so.[139] The latter has both logic and context in its favor. Roman decrees regularly confirmed support (usually verbal rather than practical) of other people's rights to adhere to traditional ways. Parallel phrases recur frequently in the documents transmitted by Josephus regarding pronouncements by Roman officials on behalf of Jews.[140] More to the point, we have a precisely contemporary document, recorded on papyrus and independent of Josephus, in which Claudius makes a closely comparable pronouncement, directing that Alexandrian Jews be allowed to practice their conventional customs: ἐῶσιν αὐτοὺς τοῖς ἔθεσιν χρῆσθαι.[141] It is hardly likely that in the very same year, the emperor would deliver two public declarations, affirming this privilege for Jews in Alexandria and repressing it in Rome. And one needs to attend to the context. Scholars who focus on the predicament of the Jews commonly ignore the textual setting in which Dio places his report. The immediately subsequent sentence asserts that Claudius dissolved the clubs that had been reinstated by Gaius. And he proceeds to record the new *princeps*' actions in abolishing taverns where the common people gathered to drink and engage in unacceptable behavior.[142] The historian plainly points to a series of imperial edicts whereby the emperor cracked down on undesirable assemblages, thus to exhibit a public posture decidedly distinct from that of his predecessor.[143] The Jews, once again, fell under a broader imperial policy designed to advance the image of the ruler. They were not alone. A long list of groups, for all we know, may have been restricted by imperial decree, of which Dio gives only a sample. The action, in any case, directed itself against objectionable convocations, not against Judaism.

But there is more. A highly controversial and endlessly discussed passage in Suetonius continues to bedevil scholarship. The imperial biographer of the Hadrianic era asserted that Claudius expelled Jews, persistently tumultuous at the instigation of Chrestus, from Rome.[144] Wherein to set this tantalizing tidbit? Suetonius, as usual, supplies no chronology. The jumble of anecdotes and semi-digested information does not flow in historical sequence. The episode could have come at any time in Claudius' reign. Some have amalgamated the testimony with that of Dio: both refer to the same event, and Dio simply used the occasion to correct or refute Suetonius by insisting that Claudius did not, in fact, banish Jews from the city. Or else Claudius intended to expel Jews but changed his mind and just banned assemblies instead.[145] But amalgamation is strained and implausible. The two texts intersect nowhere. If Dio's negative evidence implies a positive expulsion notice, he is thinking of an action by Tiberius, not an error by Suetonius.[146] Moreover, the date of the episode in Suetonius seems to be different from that given by Dio. At least Orosius thought so. He read Suetonius and cites him but adds a date: the ninth year of Claudius' reign; i.e., 49 CE.[147] Where he got this information remains forever elusive. But it is unlikely that he invented it out of whole cloth.[148] Support comes from an altogether independent direction. The Acts of the Apostles reports that Paul arrived in Corinth from Athens, where he encountered a Jew named Aquila who had just come from Italy with his wife Priscilla because Claudius had ordered all Jews to leave Rome.[149] The dating of this event evades absolute precision. We know that Paul, not long thereafter, came before the tribunal of Gallio, the Roman governor of Achaea. And Gallio's proconsulship can be dated to 50/51 or 51/52.[150] This is close enough. It is hard to escape the conclusion that Acts and Suetonius refer to the same event. Orosius evidently had good reason to place it in 49.

But why the expulsion? Suetonius' phrase, *Iudaeos . . . assidue tumultuantis,* does not supply the answer. The good secretary of Hadrian wrote his words after Rome had experienced two major Jewish rebellions against Roman authority abroad. He could well have equated Jewish behavior with repeated upheavals.[151] None of that had happened, however, by the time of Claudius—and no such activity is otherwise recorded as ever having occurred in Rome.[152] Some episode in 49 may have triggered—or provided a pretext for—government intervention. But the adverb *assidue* lacks any supporting testimony. Suetonius injected his own interpretative phraseology. He surely did not get it from an edict in the archives. Many have found a clue in the mysterious and enticing *impulsore Chresto*. Oceans of ink have already been spilled over the possible involvement of Christians in this affair, and it would be unhelpful and unwelcome to add further to that speculation.[153] Chrestus can hardly be Jesus Christ, since the text clearly implies his presence in Rome at the time. To postulate a blunder or confusion on Suetonius' part—failure to see that followers of Christ rather than Christ himself were creating havoc in the Jewish community—only increases the speculative quality of any reconstruction.[154] Little likelihood exists that Chrestus (if there was indeed such a person) will ever be identified. The name is widely attested; it was a common designation in Rome not only for freedmen but also for free foreigners from the East, even second-generation Romans or beyond. The record indeed shows many Chresti who held office in Rome.[155] The ubiquity of the name makes the association with Christianity an uphill battle, best given up.[156] As it happens, no Chrestus is a known Jew. But authorities could always finger a troublemaker if they sought a pretext to take action against a group, whether or not the miscreant could be discovered among its members. An *impulsor* could come from anywhere.

Pretexts, however, are not motives. Reasons for the expulsion decree still need to be sought. And no solution will satisfy all. But a promising procedure suggests itself: to look beyond the Jews themselves. The few official actions taken against them in the past always involved other groups as well; Jews were never the sole targets. That may well be the case here also.

Claudius' public concern about religion provides the context. We need not postulate deep-felt religiosity. The image of the regime was what mattered. Religion, politics, and publicity were intertwined. Claudius presented himself as a guardian of ancient Roman rituals. It was a valuable posture whereby to contrast himself and his policies with the madcap antics of Caligula, who had regularly mocked and parodied the obeisance of men to the gods. Claudius had already signaled his devotion to antique piety in the year 44 CE, when he ascended the steps of the Capitoline on his knees to celebrate his triumph in Britain, a strikingly conspicuous homage to Jupiter Capitolinus.[157] In the year 47 CE he presented a motion to the senate to reconstitute the college of *haruspices,* that ancient guild of Etruscan diviners who had so often in the past prescribed religious rites to pull the state out of dire circumstances. Claudius made a point of affirming the necessity of reviving this most ancient Italian institution lest it sink into obsolescence.[158] In the same year Claudius celebrated the Secular Games, a commemoration of Rome's centennial and a major religious ceremony, even juggling the calendar somewhat to bring the date into line with his own purposes.[159] He provided an equally dramatic occasion in 49 when he formally extended the *pomerium,* the sacred boundary of the city, signifying a corresponding expanse of the borders of the Roman empire. This too required the revival of an archaic ritual, only very rarely performed.[160] The event came in close conjunction with reinstitution of the *salutis augurium,* the solemn augury for the welfare of the state, a ceremony signaling that the nation was at peace; this ceremony, unperformed for three-quarters of a century, was now to be set on a permanent footing.[161] In that very year of 49, a prospective son-in-law of Claudius, L. Iunius Silanus, who had been accused of incest and removed from high office by the emperor, committed suicide. Claudius seized the occasion to exhibit his command of ancient traditions and practices: he ordered expiatory sacrifices that dated back to the time of King Tullus Hostilius six centuries earlier and were now to be carried out by the pontiffs in the sacred grove of Diana.[162] The emperor obviously went out of his way to emphasize his acquaintance with and usage of antique religious formulas. Whenever he struck a treaty with foreign kings, he would sacrifice a sow in the forum, stressing that this was in accord with the ancient ritual of the *fetiales,* the priests who oversaw the sanctity of treaties from the very beginnings of Roman history.[163]

    This was more than sheer antiquarianism. Claudius also endeavored to transfer the Eleusinian Mysteries from Attica to Rome.[164] And he may even have placed on Rome's sacred calendar the festival of Attis that stemmed from Phrygia.[165] The emperor evidently wished to demonstrate his commitment to a thorough and systematic refurbishing of Roman religion in every regard. In this connection, he also fingered certain sects and cults which did not suit the program. The Druids fell under imperial disfavor. Augustus had forbidden Roman citizens to partake of Druidism; Claudius abolished it altogether.[166] Equally notable is the fact that, in the year 52, after yet another Roman aristocrat came under fire for consulting astrologers, the senate, doubtless under the prodding of the emperor, promulgated a decree for banning practitioners of the art from Italy. Tacitus adds, sardonically but quite accurately, that the measure was as cruel as it was unenforceable.[167] The historian, however, may not have caught the true import of the measure. Like previous moves against astrologers, this served more to express public denunciation than to create a host of exiles.

Expulsion of the Jews must be understood in this context. It has, in fact, been suggested that the event comes logically in 52, in conjunction with the measure against astrologers, just as Tiberius had removed Jews and astrologers in tandem. This is a tempting idea, but unnecessary. The year 49 has ancient attestation, not to be lightly dismissed. And that year has its relevant episodes: extension of the *pomerium*, revival of the *salutis augurium*, and the resort to expiatory sacrifices that date back to the regal period of hoary antiquity.[168] Claudius may well have coupled his ostentatious resurrection of national rituals with action against an alien cult, especially if an excuse was found or invented that indicated some disturbance. This reflects no inveterate anti-Judaism on the part of that emperor, let alone a long-standing imperial hostility toward Jews.[169] Nor, on the other hand, should one conclude that Rome acted to put down disturbances and maintain order in the city.[170] Jews had no reason to promote disorder. And there is little likelihood that on this occasion, as on others, large numbers of Jews were, in fact, removed from Rome.[171] Jews were not registered as such, and it would cause far more trouble than it was worth to attempt a round-up. So far as our evidence goes, the Jewish communities in Rome gave the authorities no reason for displeasure through the reign of Nero.[172] Nor did they make a peep during the rebellion in Palestine that followed. Action by the regime in Rome under Claudius, as under Tiberius and in the Republic, came only when it might benefit the government's image—and even then it was largely performance and ceremony.

The realm of the regime provides only part of the picture. Roman officialdom, in general, did not target Jews. The latter minded their own business; and the authorities left well enough alone. But what impressions did Jews leave in the private sphere? Certainly some of the episodes described above, like the pressures exerted by Jews at the trial of Flaccus or at the arrival of envoys after the death of Herod, exhibited to Romans the close ethnic, political, and cultural ties that bound together the Jews resident in Rome with those in the homeland or elsewhere in the diaspora. When the Great Rebellion exploded in Judaea in the 60s CE, engendering harsh and brutal retaliation by Roman forces, one might expect a sharp turn toward hostility against Jews resident in the city. Yet evidence does not always match expectations.

Did the uprising in Palestine bring to the surface latent "anti-semitism" in Rome, or what some now prefer to characterize as "Judeophobia"?[173] Did the Roman populace find its anxieties confirmed by this troublesome and vexatious people, atheists who scorned the proper gods, misanthropes who held aloof from normal society, dangerous proselytizers who contaminated decent Romans, and perpetrators of alarming practices like refusing to perform duties on the Sabbath, refraining from eating pork, and mutilating their genitals?

These are not easy questions to answer. Romans did not deliver themselves of opinions about Jews with any frequency or regularity. But a fair number of remarks exist by various Roman writers from the late Republic through the aftermath of the Great Revolt that offer some entrance into the Roman mentality and permit the construction of at least a tentative picture. That, of course, is not to suggest that their attitudes—or, more precisely, the expressions of their attitudes that have survived for us—are necessarily representative. But they do provide valuable insight into the intellectual atmosphere at Rome insofar as it pertains to Jews. And they afford a glimpse into the understanding—or lack thereof—that the Romans exhibited on questions of Jewish character, principles, and practices. Roman discourse on the Jews from approximately the mid-first century BCE through the early second century CE supplies a window on the conceptual prism through which Jews were perceived.

Inspection of the texts brings one especially surprising result: the Great Revolt itself does not appear to signal a watershed in Roman discourse on the Jews. Official policy toward Judaea changed, to be sure, quite drastically so. The destruction of the Temple, the installation of a major garrison, the decimation of the ruling class, and the imposition of a Roman tax to be delivered annually for support of the cult of Jupiter Capitolinus altered the relationship of the empire to the province of Judaea in the most profound ways.[174] But the Jews of Rome did not take part in that insurrection. And no obvious shift can be discerned in the perception of Jews, or rather the characterization of Jews, in our Roman sources. This is an unexpected conclusion—but a significant one.

Did Roman writers perceive Jewish practices or beliefs as cause for concern? It is not easy to imagine that citizens of the great imperial power felt anxiety about a peculiar, but largely powerless, people in their midst. What would they have to worry about? Jewish monotheism, perhaps? Eminent scholars hold that the single-minded Jewish devotion to Yahweh represented some form of challenge to the religious beliefs of the pagan world, that it defied the pantheon of Roman gods, that it was unpatriotic and blasphemous, an expression of disrespect for the divinities who guaranteed the security of the Roman empire.[175] A reasonable enough surmise, it might be thought. As we have seen, the government, on rare occasions, fastened upon Jews, among other alien groups, for expulsion in order to demonstrate piety and to offer a form of expiation to the gods. But the demonstrations were brief and, so far as the long term was concerned, inconsequential. Composers of extant texts betray no anxieties on this score. The Greeks and Romans did not even have a word for "monotheism." And its opposite, "polytheism," which we cavalierly ascribe to the pagan world, would hardly be comprehensible as a religion—any more than "paganism" was a religion.[176] Of course, the Romans knew that the Jews had but a single deity. Yet none found the idea subversive or menacing. On the contrary. According to St. Augustine, the renowned scholar and greatest student of Roman religion, M. Terentius Varro, writing in the late first century BCE, offered a revealing analysis: he reckoned the god of the Jews as the equivalent of Jupiter, a mere change of names for the same divinity.[177] Even Tacitus, no friend of the Jews (to put it mildly) and writing after Rome had crushed the Great Revolt, did not regard monotheism as such to be an abhorrent practice that needed to be stamped out. In fact, his reference to the Jews as conceiving just a single divinity *(unum numen)* contrasts them not with Romans but with the despised Egyptians, who worship multitudes of animals and multiformed images.[178] *That* was indeed abhorrent. Nothing in the texts implies that adherence to Yahweh constituted a threat to the religious—let alone to the social and political—order of the realm.

To be sure, the Jewish faith did not strike most Romans as especially wise or admirable. Writers in Latin or Greek regularly labeled the creed of the Jews as *superstitio* or *deisidaimonia*. This calumny goes back at least as far as Cicero, who branded Jewish practice as *barbara superstitio*.[179] The phrase surfaces subsequently in writers as different as Seneca, Plutarch, Quintilian, and Tacitus.[180] The Augustan poet Horace points to a Jew in order to epitomize a faith that demands credulity.[181] The comments are snide and contemptuous, an expression of Roman disdain for practices that seemed meaningless or unintelligible. They disclose conventional Roman scorn for alien cults and benighted beliefs.[182] But nothing suggests that Jewish devotion to Yahweh gave the slightest reason for anxiety. If the Jews insisted on their foolishness, leave them to it.

Tacitus, of course, did not much like the ways of the Jews. In his perception, those ways stood at the opposite pole from his own: "they hold all things profane that we regard as sacred, and everything they consider permissible, we consider anathema."[183] Perhaps some of their rites, he observed, have the justification of antiquity; but all the rest are wicked, foul, and abound in depravity.[184] Not exactly a sterling recommendation. But Tacitus reserves his fiercest tirade less for the Jews than for those who have "crossed over" to Judaism; they abandoned their ancestral religions, scorned their native gods, deserted their nation, and even hold cheap their own parents, children, and siblings.[185] Tacitus here excoriates apostates, but suggests no Jewish menace.

Did Romans conceive a more concrete reason for being wary of the Jews? Had the impression emerged (whatever the reality) of a rebellious folk, prone to turbulence, and chafing under Roman rule? Seneca, the first century CE philosopher, in a rare outburst, described the Jews as a most pernicious people *(sceleratissima gens)*.[186] The phrase is often cited as emblematic of Roman hostility, an index that Jews were perceived as a nation prone to criminal activities. Just what Seneca himself meant remains obscure.[187] But it is worth observing that he was not exactly obsessed with fears about Jewish wickedness. In the vast extant corpus of Seneca, one that contains an astonishing array of diverse writings, the Jews nowhere else receive explicit mention—although there are one or two places where he appears to make indirect allusion to them.[188] Furthermore, the notorious passage at issue does not, in fact, come directly from Seneca; it derives secondhand from Augustine's *City of God*. Both the context and the intentions of the writer elude our grasp. If ever a case for caution was justified, this one surely is. The statement hardly qualifies as evidence for any general Roman apprehension about the Jews.

As Romans knew full well, the Jews set up no images to divinity. Was this a challenge to the gods? Varro did not think so—as Augustine reports elsewhere. Quite the reverse: Varro found the practice admirable and worthy of imitation. Indeed, he claimed that the Romans themselves in the earliest days of their history (before things started to go downhill) produced no images of the gods. Had they only stuck to that usage, he maintained, their devotion would be more pious.[189] From Tacitus one might expect a negative slant on this practice. The historian asserts that no statues stand in Jewish cities and none in their temples; they refrain from such adulation toward their own kings and withhold such honor from Roman emperors.[190] How to take this? The assertion might appear to signify a branding of Jews as recalcitrant subjects who reject the authority of the Roman government.[191] In fact, it was nothing of the kind. Roman emperors had long acknowledged Jewish avoidance of ruler worship as legitimate, and accepted readily the substitute gesture of Jews sacrificing to Yahweh on the emperor's behalf, simply another mode of expressing loyalty.[192] The Jews of the diaspora, moreover, made dedications to the emperor in their synagogues.[193] Only Caligula broke the mold—as he did in so many other ways. But his insistence on direct worship was anomalous, aberrant, and abortive. And even he pulled back from the brink, rescinding his order, reluctantly but inevitably.[194] If the emperors themselves did not consider this Jewish custom a slight, other Romans were hardly likely to do so.[195] As for Tacitus, his comment about Jewish unwillingness to worship the emperor need not constitute a reproach. Tacitus was no fan of emperor worship himself.[196] Elsewhere he reports the Jews' resistance to Caligula's order of a statue in the Temple and their readiness to take up arms in a tone that suggests grudging admiration.[197]

The satirist Juvenal, like Tacitus writing after the Revolt, takes, at first glance, a harder line on the subject. He maintains that Jews are wont to despise Roman enactments, preferring instead to learn, obey, and fear Jewish law, which Moses handed down in some secret tome.[198] On the face of it, that looks like a reference to Jewish rejection of the Roman system and embrace of an alternative authority.[199] But it is hazardous to place too serious an interpretation upon Juvenal's sardonic wit. The comments come in the context of Juvenal's broader mockery of Jewish adherence to the Sabbath, dietary laws, circumcision, and rigorous exclusiveness—all, in Juvenal's eyes, more laughable than dangerous. His contrast between Roman *leges* and Jewish *ius* does not present a clash of competing legal and constitutional systems, but a satirist's mode of expressing the absurdity of the Jews' idiosyncratic customs. In short, Roman anxiety is nowhere in evidence. The Romans did not imagine that the empire was in any way menaced or compromised by the laws of Moses.[200]

Jewish peculiarities, of course, did make an impression. From the Roman vantage point, Jews behaved in baffling ways. They held themselves aloof, kept to their own kind, were not great social mixers, indeed preferred to avoid the company of others lest they undermine the constancy of their own customs. This conduct could be construed as antisocial, indeed as misanthropy. The Greeks had commented on this long before the Romans.[201] Tacitus included it in his long list of reasons for displeasure with the Jews: They maintain a rock-steady loyalty among themselves but hate everybody else. They don't eat with other people; they don't sleep with them. There is nothing they won't do with one another—but they won't have intercourse with Gentiles.[202] Such is the Tacitean description, certainly not a generous one. It should, however, be noticed that the historian finds the roots of this exclusivity perfectly explicable in light of Jewish experience in antiquity. As Tacitus has it, when the Hebrews were expelled from Egypt, Moses advised them not to expect help from men or gods, having been abandoned by both. They have to rely on themselves.[203] So Jewish isolationism, if not admirable, is at least intelligible. Juvenal noticed it too—and, characteristically, made a joke of it. The satirist declared that Jews will not even give directions in the street to non-Jews.[204] That might be irritating, but hardly menacing. The Jews, after all, never made a secret of their preference for one another's company. Biblical and post-biblical literature abounds in references to the importance of endogamy and the maintenance of traditions free of alien contamination, themes that recur in Jewish-Hellenistic texts like the *Letter of Aristeas, Tobit,* and *Joseph and Aseneth.*[205] There was nothing here to worry the Romans.

A more serious matter, if indeed it occurred at all, would be Jewish proselytizing. Did it in fact occur? The matter has stirred up high controversy in recent years, unresolved and indecisive; there is no need to reargue the positions here.[206] But one point should be made with emphasis: no unambiguous testimony exists to show that Jews went about accosting Gentiles and endeavoring to turn them into good Jews.[207] Of course, people did convert—male and female, persons who found Judaism or some form of it appealing, those who adopted Jewish practices or beliefs. And Jews doubtless welcomed them into the fold, taking pride in the swelling ranks of their numbers. Why not? That, however, is a very different matter from organized and determined missionary activity. And nothing in the evidence warrants belief in such activity.[208]

A related issue, however, needs to be addressed. Leaving aside the question of whether Jews went about proselytizing, did the Romans have reason for alarm at the prospect of growing numbers of Jews and increasing authority exercised by them?[209] A remark of Seneca might imply it. He observes that the Jewish way of life prevails so widely that it permeates all the lands of the world—so much so that the vanquished impose their laws upon the victors.[210] How significant is that statement? And how representative? First of all, it should be noted that the remarks form part of that same text that reaches us only secondhand through the medium of St. Augustine. We may not have Seneca's *ipsissima verba,* and we certainly do not have the larger context in which they occurred. Further, the statement follows upon other remarks in which Seneca mocks the institution of the Sabbath, berates the Jews for wasting every seventh day in idleness, and notes that they frequently suffer damage at times of crisis because of their *inactivity.*[211] Obviously Seneca is not sounding the alarm to check zealous missionaries.

Tacitus, as we have seen, is angrier at the converts than at the Jews. The former have deserted their native gods, ancestral traditions, homeland, and families.[212] But he makes no claims that Jews are beating the bushes for converts or infiltrating Gentile communities everywhere. Far from it. These remarks are embedded in Tacitus' discussion of the Jews as keeping themselves entirely separate from other peoples and even shunning their company. It would not be easy to proselytize among the Gentiles if one were shunning their company! Tacitus does make mention of increasing numbers of Jews. But he refers to a stepped-up birth rate, not to missionary activity. The Jews, so he affirms, since they believe in the immortality of souls, have a passion for reproduction and a contempt for death.[213] That is not an expression of anxiety.

Juvenal's snide remark about people embracing Mosaic law and scrapping Roman *leges* also applies essentially to converts.[214] But he says nothing about large or menacing numbers. As is notorious, Juvenal complained bitterly about an influx of foreigners into the city: the Orontes river dumping its refuse into the Tiber.[215] But there is no mention of Jews here. Juvenal simply despised easterners generally. Indeed, he saves his most savage vitriol for the Egyptians, that demented folk devoted to monstrous animal deities, who pay reverence to crocodiles, ibises, monkeys, river fish, cats, and dogs—and not a soul to venerate Diana; they won't touch animals, but they dine on human flesh.[216] Nothing that Juvenal has to say about the Jews even approaches that level of vehemence. In sum, conversion, missionary activity, or proselytizing of any kind do not appear as a source of concern.

Was there perhaps apprehension about Jewish economic power? The notion stirs recollection of more recent slurs: the image of the Jew as money-grubber, greedy usurer, unscrupulous capitalist, the financial predator who preys upon innocent Gentiles. That stereotype, however, is sheer anachronism. Tacitus does observe, quite rightly, that converts to Judaism, like other Jews, sent tribute to Jerusalem, thus augmenting the resources of the Jews. The Temple became the repository of great wealth.[217] But the notion that this inspired envy and hostility, that it prompted concern lest Jewish financiers threaten to control the economy of the empire, is quite incredible. Satirists, in fact, far from representing the Jews of Rome as plutocrats, tended to bracket them with beggars. The late first century CE poet Martial presents a typical Jew as one taught by his mother to panhandle.[218] Juvenal, on three separate occasions, refers to mendicant Jews in Rome: to a regular gathering place for them at the Porta Capena, to a beggars' stand associated with a synagogue, and to an impoverished Jewess, stricken with palsy, who plies her begging trade by claiming to tell fortunes and interpret dreams—if you cross her palm with a few pennies.[219] Disdainful remarks of this sort on Jewish indigence and beggary stand at the furthest possible remove from any image of Jews as fat cats.[220]

Any inquiry into the subject of external perceptions of Jews runs a hazard. A natural, even if unconscious, tendency inclines toward the assumption that Romans spent a healthy amount of time thinking about Jews. In fact, Roman writers had many more interesting (to them) subjects to ponder. On the whole, they show indifference to Jews.[221] The preserved remarks are far more often dismissive than probing. The vast majority of Roman references to Judaism fall into a single category: allusions to quaint and curious Jewish traits, practices, and customs that attracted attention precisely because they seemed so outlandish. Romans showed familiarity with religious and cultural activities that stemmed from a wide spectrum of ethnic groups. But Jewish traits seem to have provoked an unusual number of comments.

The institution of the Sabbath, of course, provides an obvious example. In the age of Augustus, the poets Horace and Ovid indicate that knowledge of the Sabbath as a day that placed restrictions on activity and even on the content of conversations was commonplace.[222] Yet confusions permeated and contaminated that knowledge. A widespread notion had it that the Sabbath was observed as a day of fasting. The emperor Augustus himself labored under that misapprehension, evidently already a commonplace in his day. Suetonius reports him saying to Tiberius that he had been fasting all day, more diligently even than a Jew on the Sabbath.[223] Writers in the Augustan era, like Strabo and Pompeius Trogus, simply took for granted the proposition that Jews fasted every Sabbath.[224] Subsequent satirists naturally picked up the idea with pleasure. The Neronian wit Petronius has Jews tremble with trepidation at the prospect of Sabbath fasts imposed by law.[225] And Martial, still more caustically, refers to the fasts of women on the Sabbath which gave them bad breath.[226] Whence this misconception derives escapes detection.[227] But it nicely illustrates the point that most Romans contented themselves with a half-baked idea, frequently repeated but never examined.

Others discerned a logical connection and reached an illogical conclusion. They identified the Sabbath with the day of Saturn, evidently making some association with the planetary system that reckoned Saturn as highest of the seven planets.[228] That interesting tidbit of misinformation can be found in writers as diverse as the Augustan elegiac poet Tibullus, the Flavian military strategist Frontinus, and the ever-fertile Tacitus—although it should be noted that Tacitus does not go on record as endorsing the idea.[229] This delusion provides yet another instance in which Romans preferred to repeat and transmit conjecture rather than investigate its truth. The latter would be too much trouble.

Plutarch, the late first century CE biographer and collector of arcane information, took an altogether different line. In his treatise on banquets, one of the interlocutors offers the intriguing suggestion that the Jewish Sabbath is a form of Dionysiac festival. The grounds for that hypothesis hardly generate confidence: the term "Sabi" served as a designation for Bacchants, the Jews invite one another to enjoy wine on the Sabbath, and (the clincher) the High Priest wears finery once a week that parallels the garb in which Bacchic celebrants clad themselves. Hence, it seemed reasonable to infer that the Jewish Sabbath provided an occasion for drink and revelry.[230] So much for Plutarch's research on the subject. Tacitus knew of this Dionysiac interpretation and rejected it out of hand—not that he had studied the matter with any more care than Plutarch. He gives a comparably fatuous reason for his own conclusion: Bacchic gatherings were joyous and festive, Jewish customs were silly and sordid.[231] Roman impressions of the Sabbath thus ran the gamut from fast day to feast day. As is plain, confusions and distortions were rampant. Romans showed little inclination to conduct serious inquiry into the subject.

When they did bother to pass judgment on Jewish observance of the Sabbath, they reckoned it as monumental folly. It became almost a commonplace among pagan writers to ridicule Jews for refusing to fight on the Sabbath. Various caustic comments derided a senseless observance that caused Jerusalem to fall three times. The parade of critics began as early as the second century BCE, when the Greek historian Agatharchides of Cnidus berated the practice that had delivered Jerusalem into the hands of Ptolemy I. The refrain was picked up by Strabo, for whom the decision not to take up arms on the Sabbath allowed Pompey to capture the city. And a century or so later Frontinus gave the same explanation for Vespasian's seizure of Jerusalem—even though Vespasian was no longer in Judaea at the time![232] Most, or all, of this rests on inaccurate data or misconception.

As the Romans perceived it, even if this silly custom did not precipitate disaster, it represented a colossal waste of time. Seneca supposedly made the crack that, by observing the Sabbath, Jews use up nearly one-seventh of their lives in idleness.[233] That sentiment was echoed by Juvenal: adoption of Jewish ways entails consigning every seventh day to sloth.[234] Tacitus takes the matter a step further. For him, the seductive delights of indolence not only induced Jews to do nothing every seventh day but even prompted them to create the sabbatical year, thus idling away every seventh year.[235]

Pagan writers plainly had a field day in lampooning this institution. The satirist Persius, composing in the reign of Nero, alludes to the habit of lighting lamps on the Sabbath that spew forth smoke on greasy window sills.[236] Seneca too has a laugh at the lighting of lamps, wondering why anyone bothers with it. After all, the gods don't need the light to see, and men just get themselves soiled by soot.[237] And one final twist on the custom of taking one day a week off: the assiduous researcher Pliny the Elder claimed to know of a river in Judaea that dries up every Sabbath.[238] So even the rivers rest one day a week.

Comparable lampooning was directed at another Jewish practice: the abstention from eating pork. This conspicuous characteristic, regularly associated with the Jews, was well known among Romans and drew frequent comments. Cicero knew of it already in the first century BCE.[239] Even the emperors noticed this peculiar habit, as illustrated by a famous joke line attributed to Augustus. In speaking of Herod, ruler of Judaea, who gained wide notoriety for the intrigues and murders that occurred with regularity within his own household, Augustus quipped: "It's better to be Herod's pig than his son."[240] And the emperor Caligula also exhibited familiarity with the dietary restriction. When a delegation of Alexandrian Jews obtained an audience with him in order to argue a case for their rights in Alexandria, the satanic *princeps* led them a merry chase around the gardens and then asked them mockingly "why don't you eat pork?"—a question that made auditors double up with laughter.[241]

Roman satirists had a good deal of fun with the Jewish diet, which inspired some memorable sardonic wit. Petronius, author of the *Satyricon*, concluded that, if Jews don't touch pork, they must worship a pig-god.[242] And Juvenal characterizes Judaea as the place where a long-standing indulgence permits pigs to reach a ripe old age.[243]

Writers of the Roman era puzzled over this weird Jewish revulsion from a culinary delicacy that they held in high esteem. Tacitus postulated a motive for abstention from swine's flesh: the Jews had suffered a disease of epidemic proportions through contact with that animal.[244] His contemporary, the philosopher Epictetus, expressed some irritation over the fact that Jews, Syrians, Egyptians, and Romans quarrel not over whether holiness ought to be preferred to all else but whether eating pork is holy or unholy.[245] Plutarch indeed invented a wholesale dialogue in which the interlocutors debated whether Jews shrank from pork out of reverence for the hog or out of abhorrence of that creature. But it is not easy to take the arguments on either side as altogether serious. The spokesman who maintained that Jews honor the pig offered as reason the fact that pigs first dug up the soil with their protruding snout, thereby giving Jews the idea for invention of the plowshare—the basis for all Jewish agriculture.[246] And the interlocutor on the other side proposed that, among other explanations, Jewish revulsion derived from porcine anatomy: pigs' eyes are so twisted that they point downward and cannot see anything above them unless they are carried upside down![247] Not exactly a compelling reason for refraining from swine's flesh. Plutarch, one might suggest, was having his own little joke in this after-dinner debate. Gentiles evidently could not understand a decision to refrain from the consumption of pork, which they reckoned as one of the pleasures of life. In general, then, the Jews' exclusion of pork from their diet provoked perplexity, much misinformation, and a lot of amused disdain.

Another Jewish custom drew a similar reaction. This one was, to the Roman way of thinking, the most distinctive, even if not the most visible, feature that marked out a Jew: namely, circumcision.[248] For Horace, "circumcised Jews" was a natural expression.[249] Tacitus even supposed that the Jews adopted this peculiar practice precisely in order to make themselves distinct from all other peoples.[250] As Philo noted, circumcision regularly drew ridicule from non-Jews.[251]

The satirists, as one would expect, gibed at it with abandon. In describing a talented Jewish slave who possesses all manner of intellectual and practical skills, Petronius remarked that he has but two faults: he is circumcised and he snores (never mind that he is cross-eyed).[252] Juvenal alleged that Jews are so exclusive in keeping their own company that they won't direct anyone to a water fountain unless he is circumcised. (The satirist does not indicate how they could tell.)[253] Martial has a few obscene poems that make reference to circumcision. One is dedicated to the notorious nymphomaniac Caelia who gives her favors to persons of every imaginable ethnic origin, even to the genitals of circumcised Jews.[254] Another poem refers to a circumcised poet who engages in both plagiarism and pederasty.[255] And still another speaks of a friend who always wore an enormous sheath over his organ, claiming that it allowed him to spare his voice. But when exercising one day, in full view of various spectators (doubtless curious about what lay underneath), the sheath fell off, disclosing that what might have been thought notable for its size was, in fact, notable only for its circumcision.[256] As is clear, the practice of circumcision gave rise to mockery and parody, providing a valuable source of material for jokesters.

What does it all amount to? To analyze Roman attitudes from this assembled testimony as falling into the categories of anti-semitism or philosemitism is far off the mark. The long-standing game of locating Roman writers (and Greek ones too, for that matter) on one side or another of that

divide has run its course and lost its usefulness.[257] Nor will it do to locate them along a spectrum that stretches from admiration to animosity. Romans showed little understanding of Judaism, but they were hardly
inveterate bigots. The texts reveal neither intolerance nor racism. And
nothing in them suggests that Romans were bent on persecution. Jews simply had too little importance to justify harassment or repression. In fact,
they had too little importance even for Roman intellectuals to undertake
any serious research or inquiry about them. The latter seem satisfied with
superficial appearances and impressions; hence they retailed shallow, half-
baked, and misinformed opinions. Why bother to do more? Roman writers either treated Jews with indifference or regarded them with scorn and
disdain. The Revolt itself made hardly a dent in their representations.
Sneers and caricatures occur as readily in Persius and Petronius before the
war as they do in Martial or Juvenal after. And Seneca can mock the Sabbath observance in the same terms as Tacitus. Romans were certainly not
alarmed by Jewish economic power, population growth, proselytism, or
the infiltration of Mosaic law. How could one take seriously a people who
adhered to silly superstitions, who would have no social or sexual intercourse with Gentiles, who begged alms and told fortunes, who wasted every seventh day in idleness, who stained their windows with smoke and
soot from lighting lamps, who would not give you directions in the street,
who did not eat ham or pork chops, and who mangled their genitals?

Where does this leave the Jews themselves? Lacunose testimony does not
lend itself to confident conclusions. Did Jews lead happy and fulfilling lives
in the city of Rome during the Republic and early Principate? The echoes we hear do not include Jewish voices—apart from epitaphs limited in
scope and dating from a subsequent period. But a few findings, by no
means insignificant, do emerge with some clarity.

The Roman government engaged in no systematic persecution of Jews—
nor indeed any persecution at all. The very few and rare instances of "expulsion" resolve themselves into matters of state that had little or nothing
to do with Jews as such. They arose when the government needed to showcase virtues and qualities that reclaimed association with traditional divinities and underscored distinction from alien creeds and groups. Ad hoc circumstances and real or presumed crises called forth the actions. Jews were
usefully conspicuous. They dwelled in readily identifiable communities,
and they made no secret of their peculiar practices and characteristic customs. If public interest required it, they provided convenient targets. But
government action (in the testimony that has come down to us) never fas-

tened on them alone: Chaldeans, magicians, Egyptians, *collegia,* or some other groups simultaneously came under state strictures, thus to accord proper publicity. And the exodus (such as it was) in each instance had few participants and was of brief duration. The gesture alone mattered. The continuity of Jewish communities in Rome seems largely uninterrupted.[258] It would certainly be wrong to imagine that Roman Jews lived in perpetual insecurity, with bags packed and departure vehicles at the ready. Life in the city afforded them a stable existence.

Romans in the private sphere had little reason to trouble themselves over the Jews. Writers scoffed and laughed. The weird ways of the Jews provided a source for amusement, even amazement. But they did not lead to bile, and they did not provoke hostilities. The preserved comments, even in the aftermath of the Revolt, convey mockery rather than malignancy. Jews in Rome roused no fears of insurrection, economic power, or proselytism. They did not require protection or promotion by Gentiles, not even "toleration"—just disregard and detachment. That is what they got. And it was enough.

The Jews in Alexandria

A VIOLENT POGROM rocked the Jews of Alexandria in 38 CE. They were subjected to fearsome indignities, physical attacks, beatings, torture, and murder; their homes were burned, their shops looted, and their synagogues destroyed.[1] The episode is memorable and notorious. It has indeed become emblematic of the vulnerability of diaspora existence, the shaky character of the Jewish place in a Gentile community, and the seething distaste of the Hellenes for that alien *ethnos* in their midst. The devastating set of events raises issues of a broad compass: the degree to which civic rights and privileges were enjoyed by different groups within a *polis,* the access of Jews to full citizenship, the nature of their organization within the larger community, the changes and complexities introduced into a multi-ethnic Hellenistic city by the advent of Roman administration, and, not least, the ambiguities and dangers involved in treading a fine line between assimilation and distinctiveness. Extrapolation from this episode, however, carries its own hazards. How representative was Alexandria, that great city with its peculiar mix of peoples and traditions? And how representative was the explosion of 38 for the experience of Jews in that city? The problems are formidable, and the answers inevitably tentative. A massive literature confronts the researcher. Yet the episode is so central and the reverberations so wide that it demands reassessment.

First, a brief review of the sequence of events, almost all contained in a single source, Philo's treatise *In Flaccum,* composed sometime during the reign of Claudius. The witness was both contemporary and participant—hence can hardly lay claim to detachment or impartiality.

Avillius Flaccus took over as Roman prefect of Egypt in 32 or 33 CE, an appointee of the emperor Tiberius, and a man reckoned among his *amici.* The early years of his tenure in the province went smoothly, as Flaccus showed himself in firm control, instituted needed reform in both military and civil matters, and maintained order and stability. Among other things, he exhibited his authority by dissolving the private clubs and gatherings organized for religious purposes but allegedly given to rowdiness and drunkenness.[2] The situation took a dramatic turn, however, in the sixth year of his administration. Closeness to Tiberius had been an advantage during the emperor's lifetime, but proved a liability after his death in 37. Gaius Caligula ascended the throne in Rome. And Flaccus suddenly found himself in a precarious position. He had been an accuser of Gaius' mother, and a friend of Tiberius' grandson Gemellus and his praetorian prefect Macro, both of whom were murdered early in the new ruler's reign.[3] Flaccus had good reason to worry.

Certain prominent individuals in the Alexandrian community swiftly seized the occasion to their advantage. Philo names Dionysios, Lampon, and Isidoros, all of whom he maligns with epithets such as rabble-rousers, busybodies, troublemakers, and sowers of sedition. In his exposition, these characters took the initiative in prodding Flaccus into action against the Jews. They presented themselves as go-betweens, protectors of Flaccus' interests against his enemies in Rome, advocates of his cause, in return for his services in oppressing the Jews of Alexandria. Flaccus saw the virtue of this proposal and showed his good faith by gradually turning against Jewish litigants at his tribunal.[4] Matters heated up when Agrippa I, recently crowned ruler of a portion of Herod's inheritance, arrived in Alexandria, en route from Rome to his new kingdom. Agrippa's visit triggered turbulence and demonstrations. The Alexandrian leaders fueled Flaccus' fears by portraying Agrippa's advent as signaling the prefect's ruin, and the Alexandrian populace engaged in a demonstration to mock and jeer the king. Flaccus, although responsible for maintaining order, proved either unwilling or unable to curb the outburst.[5] His timidity encouraged the instigators to press Flaccus further into authorizing the installation of statues of the emperor in the synagogues, an act certain to inflame Jewish passions.[6] The governor now took overt steps of his own, with an edict depriving Jews of civic and political privileges and branding them as aliens within the city. For the other inhabitants of Alexandria, this meant that no holds were barred. The Gentiles drove Jews into a single district of the city, looted Jewish homes and shops, stripped many Jews of their professions and livelihood, and left them in dire economic straits.[7]

And that was just the beginning. The pogrom now began in earnest. Mobs used stones and clubs to pummel Jews, swords for execution, and flames to destroy not only homes but trapped families, mocking victims as they tortured them. Philo paints a vivid picture, perhaps suspiciously vivid.[8] Flaccus himself took center stage, flogging leaders of the Jewish

community and members of their senior council in a fashion normally reserved only for the criminal element among lowly Egyptians. And he pre-
sided over executions staged in conjunction with theatrical performances
and popular entertainment.[9] Jewish homes were searched for weapons,
thus to make a show of seeking evidence. But further executions followed
on flimsy testimony, and even women were compelled to swallow swine's
flesh or face the worst that torturers could conceive.[10] The rampages included the burning and destruction of synagogues.[11] No apparent limit was
set upon the atrocities.

The Jews, as Philo makes quite clear, still looked to the imperial government as the source of authority. They prepared a resolution to be sent to
Caligula and even delivered it to Flaccus for transmission to Rome. The
prefect, so we are told, promised to dispatch it but omitted to do so. The
Jews went instead to Agrippa, who had it sent.[12]

The tide now turns in Philo's tale. Caligula commissioned a centurion
to go to Alexandria and place Flaccus under arrest, probably in the fall
of 38. The Jews could at last rejoice in their deliverance.[13] The next episode contains a real surprise. The mercurial and enterprising Isidoros and
Lampon, erstwhile instigators of Flaccus, suddenly appeared in Rome as
accusers of the fallen prefect. Flaccus was convicted, stripped of his property, and exiled to the island of Andros.[14] In the conventional denouement,
the wretched Flaccus acknowledged the power and majesty of the Jewish
god, a clear signal of the story's literary character.[15] This did not alter the
situation, and, of course, would have had no impact on the emperor. Gaius
subsequently ordered Flaccus' execution.[16]

Such is Philo's narrative, a mixture of historical record with embellishment and invention. Even on a conservative and skeptical estimate, however, the Alexandrian Jews suffered a severe blow. And a central issue has
to be addressed. What are the implications of this episode for the relations
of Jews and Gentiles in the diaspora and for the Jewish experience in multi-
ethnic cities in the sphere of the Roman empire?

Who bears responsibility for the attacks on the Jews of Alexandria? In
the *Legatio ad Gaium,* Philo points a finger at the emperor. Gaius, so he
claimed, harbored an unutterable hatred for the Jews.[17] Knowledge of that
passion, according to Philo, inspired the Alexandrian mob to bring its own
fierce detestation to the surface and commence assaults upon the Jews.[18]
Did the persecutions in Alexandria then begin at the top, a feature of imperial anti-semitism, at least for this emperor? That is not very likely. Gaius'
involvement in the Alexandrian situation was remote and detached. In
Philo's systematic and extensive narrative of that situation, set forth in

the *In Flaccum,* the emperor carries no responsibility for the events.[19] On the contrary. Insofar as he appears in the treatise, he is quite blameless. Gaius awarded Agrippa substantial territory in Palestine and advised him to break his journey with a stop in Alexandria.[20] He could hardly have predicted that this stopover would inflame passions. Indeed, Agrippa may have been sent as a friend of the *princeps* and a prominent Jew in order to calm passions.[21] When next the emperor appears in the narrative, he orders Flaccus' removal and arrest, very possibly because the prefect had lost control of affairs in Alexandria.[22] Gaius' behavior in the *In Flaccum* is exemplary. And even the hostile portrayal in the *Legatio* provides no instance of initiative on the emperor's part in the turbulence that wracked Alexandria. Philo alleges Gaius' bitter enmity toward the Jews and infers that the Alexandrians acted on their knowledge of that supposed hatred, both of them unverified assumptions. The author indeed admits as much in an embarrassed aside. He had forgotten himself momentarily and inadvertently (or perhaps with malice aforethought) had charged Gaius with filling the synagogues of Alexandria with images and statues of himself. Philo then adds parenthetically that, by allowing others to dedicate the objects, Gaius was, in effect, doing it himself.[23] A damaging admission. When the emperor did at last meet with a delegation of Alexandrian Jews, he engaged in mockery and derision, but not in any attack. The Jews were reckoned as demented and unfortunate rather than dangerous.[24] Nothing in the emperor's behavior suggests inveterate hatred of the Jews. Even the loony Caligula did not deliberately stir up trouble for the empire in Alexandria. The initiative lay elsewhere.[25]

Can fault be fastened on Flaccus? It is not easy to see why the prefect, already in a precarious position, should make matters worse for himself. The narrative of Philo contains ambiguities, problems, and inconsistencies—by no means a flat indictment of Flaccus.[26] The prefect's early years as governor of Egypt were competent and effective, without any sign of hostility toward Jews.[27] Circumstances shifted when Flaccus lost his supporters in Rome and had greater need to court influential members of the Alexandrian community. Cooperation with those who could give him political cover in the city had become more urgent. How useful Greek leaders would actually be in protecting Flaccus against the wrath of Gaius might well be questioned. But any governor needed to be wary of charges that could be brought by provincials in Rome, and a cultivation of Alexandrian leaders made good sense at this juncture.[28] Flaccus' initial steps were cautious and modest, some judicial rulings against Jewish litigants.[29] Disorder began only with the advent of Agrippa. Philo claims that Flaccus approved of the demonstrations and the insults slung at Agrippa. But he plainly has no evidence and has to resort to rhetoric, in one of the weakest and least plausible paragraphs in the treatise.[30] Flaccus would hardly encourage mockery of Gaius' close friend and appointee. Indeed, he hosted the Jewish prince cordially and treated him with respect. Philo records the fact, and then seeks to wriggle out of it. He insists that beneath the veneer of courtesy, there was secret anger and jealousy. The hypothesis is not very compelling. And how would Philo know? The fact is that the crowd took action, not Flaccus. The most that Philo can say is that he "allowed" it.[31] More likely, Flaccus proved unable to restrain crowd action here.

Pressures on the prefect increased. If Philo is to be believed, Flaccus co-operated with the Gentiles who erected statues in the synagogues. But, once more, our author has nothing concrete to go on. And he resorts again to the same dodge: Flaccus "permitted" them to dedicate the images.[32] He would certainly have been in an awkward position, had he attempted to block the activity. Resistance could readily have been portrayed as a challenge to the worship of the emperor—a portrayal that Flaccus could not afford to risk. The prefect found himself boxed into a corner.

The awkward relations between Flaccus and the Alexandrian leaders may be glimpsed in an intriguing but baffling papyrus fragment. The text belongs to a series of papyri that have been dubbed the *Acta Alexandrinorum*—not historical documents but semi-literary treatments loosely based on actual events and persons, with varying degrees of distance from reality. One of these pieces, in a state too damaged to deliver a clear picture, depicts some form of arrangement between Flaccus and Isidoros and Dionysios. In the preserved portion, the three turned up at the temple of Sarapis for a secret meeting, in the company of a woman and an elderly man. The old man advised Dionysios not to exercise force with Flaccus but to sit down with members of the *gerousia* and to change his mind. Dionysios' response was an affirmative one, despite a previous refusal (either by Flaccus or by himself). The meeting took place; Flaccus assured Isidoros that matters were arranged; and an exchange of five talents in gold took place.[33] The fragment does not permit secure reconstruction of the event. And literary embellishment may account for much of it (especially the meeting in secret, the speech of the old man, the role of the woman, and the very large cash transaction). But the scenario does reflect the tense relationship between Flaccus and the Alexandrian leaders, the friction that had marked their past dealings, and the lengths to which they needed to go to establish cooperation.

A more serious step followed at this juncture. Flaccus, according to

Philo, curtailed Jewish civic and political rights, which amounted to the destruction of their *politeia*. And a few days later he issued a public notice that labeled Jews as aliens and immigrants.[34] The question of what these terms signify with regard to Jewish status in Alexandria both before and after Flaccus' pronouncement must be temporarily postponed. But virulent anti-semitism need not have motivated the prefect. Crowd action escalated the tension and focused on the Jews as targets. The vulnerable Flaccus had to protect his flanks, and also to stay a step ahead of the mob. His pronouncement at least allowed him to assert authority and make the marginalizing of Jews his own decision. A public declaration limiting Jewish prerogatives might also take some steam out of the anti-Jewish movement, and thus head off violence. For, if matters got out of hand, Flaccus' neck would be on the block for failing to keep order.

Matters did indeed get out of hand. And Flaccus could not control the situation. The pogrom proceeded, and the prefect seemed powerless to curb it. Philo still again, this time in the *Legatio,* has Flaccus "allow" the activity.[35] Plainly he did not initiate it, and surely he did not want it. In a little noted episode, Flaccus actually summoned leaders of the Jewish community to a parley in hopes of a reconciliation between them and the rest of the city. Philo, of course, adds that that was only his "ostensible" purpose.[36] But the editorial comment can be ignored. Flaccus had good reason to find a means of cooling down tempers in Alexandria.[37] This effort also came to naught. The prefect had resort to another means. He arrested thirty-eight senior members of the Jewish *gerousia* and had them bound, stripped, and scourged in public. The humiliation was made all the more severe by subjecting them to the sort of beating normally reserved only for Egyptians at the bottom of the social ladder.[38] Although Philo ascribes this to Flaccus' own maliciousness and ferocity, there may be more to it than that. The governor, hard pressed to restore order, perhaps used this means to exhibit his authority and appease the fury of the crowd. Philo lets slip a revealing comment in this connection: Flaccus strove urgently to conciliate the mob that opposed him, thinking that he could thereby have them adopt as their own the ends he had in view.[39] Here the author has it right. The prefect and the Alexandrians had different objectives.[40] Flaccus' hope to keep some control of the situation may also explain the execution of certain Jews, accomplished in grotesque fashion in the theater as part of a lavish public entertainment.[41] The prefect played to the crowd. Those showcase executions could have been designed to head off further private violence.

In short, Flaccus can be crossed off the list of principal villains.[42] He had

no motive for concerted policy against the Jews. Philo's narrative itself undermines his own portrait, one guided more by dramatic needs (a story culminating in Flaccus' fall and repentance) than by history. Flaccus' insecuri-
ties after the loss of his patrons in Rome, his anxieties about alienating
constituencies in Alexandria, and the need to fend off pressures from militant Alexandrians and lobbying by Jewish leaders, while maintaining a
semblance of order in the city lest he be denounced to the authorities at
home, created a bundle of tensions that the prefect never successfully negotiated. No governor who failed to contain disorders in his own seat of government could last for long. Flaccus' removal and demise proved inevitable. His tenure collapsed through ineptitude rather than malice.

Where then to look for the culprits? Did Alexandria harbor a hotbed
of latent anti-semitism that burst to the surface in 38 CE, an exemplar for
the antagonism that held between Greek and Jew in the diaspora? Philo's
presentation puts initiative in the hands of scheming Greeks—Dionysios,
Isidoros, and Lampon—men whom he stigmatizes as panderers to the populace, scribal hacks, sowers of sedition, busybodies, troublemakers, and
inciters of turbulence, a torrent of overlapping epithets.[43] According to
Philo, these men cooked up the plot to victimize Jews, hoodwinked Flaccus
into serving as their front man by promising to protect his interests with
the authorities in Rome, and prodded him into repression of the Jews.[44]
They repeatedly took advantage of the governor's vulnerability, played
upon his need for support among the Alexandrian elite, stoked his jealousy
with regard to Agrippa, and persuaded him of the political profitability of
installing statues of Gaius in Jewish synagogues.[45] Do these men epitomize
Hellenic resentment against Jews, standard-bearers of a broad animosity
that was fanned into flame by the special circumstances of Alexandria?

What little is known about these individuals, in fact, gives some plausibility to Philo's reconstruction. But it suggests that the principal target of
their campaign was not so much the Jews as Flaccus himself. Among the
governor's actions in the early years of his tenure was a crackdown on the
clubs and guilds, the *hetaireiai* and *synodoi,* branded as nests of drunkenness and rowdiness.[46] It is relevant and significant that Isidoros at least was
heavily involved with these organizations, private religious groups that
met for purposes of worship and also as social gatherings for the membership. Whatever truth lay in the disparaging and distorted descriptions by
Philo, Isidoros held a prime place in these religious fraternities and was in a
position to employ them for demonstrations in the streets and the gymnasium.[47] It may well be that Lampon and Dionysios also exercised influence
in the *synodoi.* Flaccus' measures against the associations therefore must

have played a major part in alienating the Alexandrian leaders. Certainly sharp antagonisms ensued. Philo observes with some justice that those who cooperated with Flaccus and were consulted as his principal advisers were the very men who had been his open enemies at the beginning.[48] And his surmise that their reconciliation was a sham and masked a continued bitter enmity rings true.[49] Isidoros, so it is reported, was among the accusers of Macro in Rome.[50] That fits the picture nicely. Macro, the former praetorian prefect, had been a close friend and patron of Flaccus.[51] Another central figure had problems from the past hanging over his head. Lampon had been accused on a charge of impiety toward the emperor in the time of Tiberius, a trial that dragged on for two years; although Lampon escaped conviction, the suspicions had not been dispelled and, according to Philo, the fear of future action still haunted him.[52] He had reason to deflect attention elsewhere. The prodding of Flaccus against the Jews, it can be suggested, involved more than anti-semitism. The prodders endeavored to create disturbances that could demonstrate the incompetence of the prefect.

The plan worked to perfection. Flaccus, nervous about his shaky position and needful of influential support, went along with the attacks on Jews, "allowed" them as Philo concedes. But events spiraled out of his control: chaos followed in the wake of demonstrations, and the hapless governor had to take the blame. Isidoros organized his followers, gathered them in the gymnasium, even bribed a host of demonstrators to hurl public abuse at Flaccus and to give wide exposure to his failings. This time Flaccus lost patience. He set up a tribunal, encouraged accusations against Isidoros and the ringleaders, and prompted confessions on the part of those who had accepted remuneration for raising their voices against Flaccus. Counter-demonstrations materialized to shout down Isidoros and induce his withdrawal from the city.[53] But it was too late. Information reached Gaius about the upheaval in Alexandria, and the emperor soon had Flaccus arrested and brought back to Rome. His erstwhile friends, now his declared enemies, seized the initiative to denounce him in Rome. Isidoros and Lampon emerged as accusers at his trial. Those who had only recently flattered him with epithets like "benefactor" and "savior" now flailed him with harsh censures and calumnies.[54] They may well have been behind the initial denunciations that led to Flaccus' removal to Rome.[55] Just what the exact charges were is nowhere spelled out by Philo, but failure to keep order, leading to sedition, doubtless constituted the principal case against him. Flaccus had been appointed to keep the peace[56]—and on that score he had conspicuously failed. The emperor already had reasons to be suspicious of Flaccus, in view of his connection with Tiberius' grand-son Gemellus and with Macro, both of whom had now been eliminated. Gaius was obviously receptive to the charges. Flaccus' fate thus was sealed. His enemies had had their way.

The scheme to undermine and eventually eliminate Flaccus had worked. But even if this had been the principal motive of the Alexandrian miscre-ants, it does not account for the passions that were unleashed in the popu-lace, the sweeping assaults on the Jews, the desecration of the synagogues, and the horrific pogrom that claimed victims from every level of Jewish so-ciety. Isidoros, Lampon, and Dionysios may have orchestrated events for their own personal or political ends. But the viciousness of the attacks de-mands a different and broader explanation.

Not that explanations are lacking. A whole host of them exist to inspire or intimidate the researcher. Many interpret the hostility as arising out of Hellenic resentment and jealousy: Alexandrian Greeks found offensive the privileges and status enjoyed by the Jews in their midst, thus fueling a fierce anti-semitism.[57] In a variant on this idea, the smoldering animosity di-rected itself not so much against the Jews as against the Romans, who had stripped Alexandria of its autonomy while according protection to the Jews. Since it was futile and dangerous to resist Rome, the Jews could be victimized as protégés of the imperial power.[58] Others, by contrast, see *Ro-man* policy as victimizing the Jews, thus encouraging Greeks to assault the marginalized people.[59] On a different thesis, the Greeks of Alexandria reacted harshly against Jewish efforts to advance or retain their consti-tutional and political station in the city, whether through citizenship or other civic privileges.[60] Another view envisions a class struggle, in which the Alexandrian Greek proletariat struck out against the more success-ful and well-to-do Jewish population.[61] Still another reconstruction sees the hostility of the Alexandrian mob as stemming from a combination of economic envy and religious hatred.[62] The different perspectives overlap and intersect, not in every instance inconsistent with one another. One ele-ment, however, unites them all. The contest is visualized as one that pits Greeks against Jews. A bitter animosity or a heated struggle over privileges marked that stormy relationship. On such an analysis, the diaspora exis-tence of Jews in Alexandria must have been anxiety-ridden, stressful, and fraught with danger.

How involved in fact were the Greeks? Philo makes much of the schem-ing and sinister characters Isidoros, Lampon, and Dionysios. But who ac-tually hit the streets to rally against Jews and then engage in a vicious pogrom? Most assume that members of the *synodoi,* associations of the

Greek common people in the city, run by men like Isidoros, were mobilized to harass and punish the Jews. Yet, as Philo himself records, Flaccus (in the good phase of his governorship) dissolved these clubs.[63] And when Isidoros endeavored to regather supporters through the use of bribery, the demonstrations he organized were against Flaccus, not the Jews. Moreover, they were effectively dispersed with a few arrests, a judicial hearing, and a public humiliation that caused Isidoros to leave the city.[64] The *synodoi* hardly controlled the streets of Alexandria.

One element is missing in almost all interpretations of these events: the Egyptians.[65] Insofar as jealousy and animosity might be justified and intelligible, they are much more readily ascribable to Egyptians than to Greeks. The former stood at the bottom of the social and political structure. Rights guaranteed to the Jews in a Hellenic community where Egyptians lacked any standing whatever would surely generate a bitterness that seethed just below the surface. Philo acknowledges the fact in a broad statement applying to the Roman empire generally. Having summarized the rights and privileges guaranteed to the Jews by Augustus and Tiberius, he remarks that peoples everywhere, even if not by nature inclined to feel kindly toward the Jews, held back from meddling with any of their customs with the intent of destroying them.[66] In the specifically Alexandrian context, a telling episode brings the situation to light in unmistakable fashion. When Flaccus chose to make a show of good faith to his Hellenic collaborators by subjecting members of the Jewish *gerousia* to a public flogging, he employed an especially humiliating mode. Instead of using the flat blade that was standard for Alexandrians, including Alexandrian Jews, he had them beaten with scourges, which were normally applied only to the Egyptians. As Philo puts it, they suffered a punishment suitable to the lowliest Egyptians charged with the most heinous crimes.[67] On this score at least—and it is surely illustrative, not exceptional—Alexandrians and Jews could expect equal treatment, whereas the despised Egyptians faced nothing but degradation. If opportunity presented itself to lash out against those above them, this should cause no surprise. The frightful and vicious assaults inflicted upon the Jews in 38, even if somewhat exaggerated by Philo, indicate a brutal outburst by people long oppressed and debased in their own land.[68] This was no mere rivalry between Jews and Greeks over civic prerogatives. The underclass of Alexandrian society, the ignominious Egyptians, here seized an opportunity to vent their passions.

A close reading of Philo, in fact, confirms the conjecture. The deep-rooted hostility of which he speaks applies primarily to rank and file Egyptians. When Agrippa appeared in the city, says Philo, his arrival set off fierce emotions among those, bursting with envy, who possessed an ancient and, as it were, innate hatred of Jews—for such is the malignant character of the Egyptian race by nature.[69] That he is referring here to Egyptians, and not to the Greeks of Alexandria, is clear and unequivocal. Elsewhere in the *In Flaccum,* he makes comparable remarks about *to Aigyptiakon,* a people given to stirring major upheaval.[70] When Philo, in a striking statement, speaks of "us and them," he means Egyptians, not Greeks.[71] The fact is further underlined in the *Legatio ad Gaium.* Philo records attacks by the mob on Jewish synagogues and the installation of statues of the emperor into the sanctuaries. And he leaves no doubt about the composition of the mob: they were those who deified dogs, wolves, lions, crocodiles, and every manner of animal.[72] That does not apply to Greeks. Indeed, the people who, in Philo's presentation, were most zealous in flattering Gaius' pretensions to divinity were those who reckoned ibises, asps, and other beasts to be gods. It is noteworthy that the author can use the term "Alexandrians" here simply to refer to the Egyptians of Alexandria.[73] Hence, when he identifies the chaotic and turbulent mob of Alexandrians who seized upon the opportunity presented by Gaius' attitude to reveal the hatred that had long been smoldering, he most logically points a finger at the Egyptians.[74]

This conclusion is reinforced by a highly tendentious but, in this context, revealing blast by Josephus. He claims that as long as Greeks and Macedonians held civic privileges in Alexandria, there was no action against the Jews. It was only when a mob of Egyptians swelled their numbers that such action became endemic.[75] Nor is this the only occasion on which Josephus labels the Egyptians as principal antagonists of the Jews, distinguishing them pointedly from Greeks. That motif recurs regularly in his works.[76] The analyses of Philo and Josephus hang together.

The fierce hostility between Jews and Egyptians, however, does not confine itself to the historical narratives of Philo and Josephus. Works of very different genres discharge a venom that indicates deep-rooted animosity between the *ethne.* The Wisdom of Solomon, a philosophical-rhetorical treatise, composed probably in the early Roman Empire, employed the Exodus story as a medium to convey its messages. The author, perhaps a close contemporary of Philo, delivered unrestrained verbal assaults upon the Egyptians, underscoring their ludicrous worship of dumb animals and reveling in the punishments rained down upon them by God.[77] In another category, Jewish and Christian writers ostensibly compiled pagan Sibylline oracles, but, in fact, composed and manipulated them for their own purposes. The earliest layers of composition occur in the *Third Sibylline Oracle* and derive from inventive Jewish writers of the Hellenistic and early Roman periods. They include virulent attacks upon the Egyptians, portrayed as a destructive and immoral race, whose idolatry descends to the level of reverence toward snakes and cats.[78]

Other literary works, of varied forms, echo those attitudes. The romantic novel *Joseph and Aseneth,* an imaginative retelling of the Joseph story for purposes of amusement and edification, contains some harsh denunciation of Egyptian idolatrous practices, setting them at the furthest possible remove from the faith of Joseph's people.[79] The author of III Maccabees, a text produced sometime between the late second century BCE and the early first century CE, gives a fictitious account of Jews nearly martyred by Ptolemy IV, but miraculously saved at the last moment. On the face of it, this should reflect murderous enmity between Jews and a Greek regime. A closer look, however, yields a surprisingly different conclusion. When the king issued his genocidal decree, according to III Maccabees, there was wild rejoicing among the "people of a different race"—but not by the Greeks in the city, who took the part of the Jews and offered them whatever encouragement they could.[80] That is a striking notice. The "people of a different race" whose hatred the author describes as inveterate and deepseated were obviously Egyptians. Finally, in still another genre altogether, the dramatic poet Ezekiel composed a Greek tragedy on the theme of the Exodus. The work notably takes heavy aim not just at the wicked Pharaoh but against the arrogant, oppressive, and fundamentally evil Egyptian people.[81]

The consistency with which Jewish writers, especially Alexandrian Jews, brand Egyptians as villains can hardly be coincidental. That supplies a critical element for understanding the atmosphere that permitted a pogrom. Certain Greek malcontents may have set matters in motion, prodding Flaccus into actions that would discredit him and providing the outlet for pent-up passions among the populace to explode onto the scene. But the pent-up passions belonged primarily to Egyptians rather than to Greeks.

None of this, of course, denies the existence of bigotry or animosity toward Jews in some circles of the Greek community. As is well known, Josephus felt the need to refute calumnies against the Jews conveyed by Alexandrian intellectuals like Apion, Chaeremon, and Lysimachus. And the fragments of the *Acta Alexandrinorum* contain a number of remarks hostile to Jews.[82] Isidoros, Lampon, and Dionysios may well have been part of those circles and shared those sentiments. But the Hellenic component in the riots does not serve to define them. The cynical motives of the leaders tapped into a much more deeply-rooted embitterment that resided in the indigenous people of Egypt.

Upheaval and turbulence claimed Flaccus as a victim. His removal to

Rome in the autumn of 38 must have sobered those who had engaged in
depredations under cover of the prefect's encouragement or indifference.
Flaccus' successor probably arrived shortly thereafter. The imperial government would not leave the province of Egypt ungoverned for long.[83] But
a restoration of stability still left many problems unresolved. Isidoros and
Lampon swiftly pinned all blame on Flaccus, and appeared in Rome as his
accusers. But they and their collaborators could expect some questions to
be raised about their own involvement in the turmoil. At the same time, the
Alexandrian Jews, even if out of immediate danger, had been shattered by
the experience, their vulnerability dramatically exposed and the need for
clarifying their situation now absolutely urgent. In the winter of 38/39 or
39/40, two embassies appeared in Rome to expound their positions before
the emperor.[84]

Gaius Caligula kept them waiting. The Jewish delegation of five persons
included Philo himself, while the Greek embassy was led by Isidoros and
Apion, men with special animus against the Jews.[85] They cooled their heels
for at least half a year, perhaps a year and a half. When first they encountered the emperor, he breezily put them off with the remark that he would
hear them when he had some free time.[86] That time did not come until the
autumn of 40. And even then Caligula consented to receive the missions
only in an informal fashion, while he was touring the gardens and estates
on the Esquiline.[87] The emperor surely was signaling here that he had little
serious interest in the matters brought before him—whether by Jew or by
Greek. Just what petitions the envoys made remains murky. Philo refers to
a Jewish memorandum that outlined what the Jews had suffered and what
they expected to obtain.[88] The essential matter obviously was to secure
some reaffirmation of their rights to carry out customary practices without
fear of disruption or physical danger. Philo's vague references to the "civic
status of Jews" *(politeia)* must have this primarily in view. Gaius' flippant
response, "we would like to know what sort of civic rights you enjoy," presupposes such a presentation.[89] The desecration of the synagogues was certainly on the minds of the Jewish envoys.[90] And this stood for a whole
range of traditions and expectations that had been so violently violated.
The Hellenic embassy must have aimed principally to persuade the emperor that Greek leaders bore no responsibility for the upheaval in Alexandria. To that end, they took the offensive, laying blame directly at the door-
step of the Jews. Isidoros, who had already been instrumental in exposing
the failure of Flaccus to halt the turmoil, now endeavored to win imperial
favor by alleging Jewish disloyalty to the crown: the Jews alone refused to
sacrifice for the emperor's well-being.[91] The motivation here was not raw

anti-semitism, as is often alleged. The Hellenic delegates needed to explain the assaults on Jews as a feature of loyalty to Rome rather than irrational animosity. Philo and his mates, of course, responded vehemently and unanimously that they did indeed sacrifice *for* the emperor—but not *to* him.[92]

Petition and argument, however, seem to have had little effect. Philo, in the *Legatio,* depicts Gaius as implacably hostile to the Jews throughout.[93] He even elaborates wantonly on the character of Helikon, an Egyptian freedman who allegedly had the ear of the emperor and raked up wild charges against the Jews out of sheer malice and depravity.[94] In fact, however, Gaius treated the whole affair with levity rather than animosity. He made a deliberate show of indifference, first by postponing the hearing, then by conducting it while wandering about the mansions and estates on the Esquiline and causing the harried envoys to chase after him in ludicrous fashion.[95] There was no august tribunal here; just frivolity by the mischievous monarch. His response to the Jewish disclaimer about sacrificing for the emperor, "yes, but not *to* me," caused Philo and his fellow delegates to panic.[96] But, as Philo himself has to concede, the whole business resembled a staged comedy.[97] The subject of alien Jewish customs evidently arose in the exchange. When Caligula then asked the obviously mocking question, "so why don't you eat pork?" the remark brought howls of laughter. By the same token, his inquiry about the nature of Jewish civic rights also lacked seriousness.[98] As soon as the Jews sought to marshal a response, he cut them off, preferring to pursue his house inspection, while the envoys tagged along in a vain effort to get a word in edgewise. The emperor's final comment in dismissing the delegates was particularly apt: they are not really wicked but misguided and stupid.[99] And so the interview came to a thudding close. Gaius had treated it all as a piece of theater.[100] And one can well imagine, though we do not get this from Philo's vantage-point, that the Hellenic envoys were treated with the same levity as the Jews.

Anti-semitism is not the issue here. Ethnic or religious animosity between Greek and Jew bears little relevance to what was at stake. The rival legations stemmed from special circumstances in Alexandria that compelled each party to make a case in Rome. And neither got much satisfaction from the roguish *princeps.*

Just what *was* at stake? That question raises the central issue of the place of the Jews in Alexandrian society. It needs to be emphasized, in no uncertain terms, that the calamitous upheaval in 38 CE lacked all precedent. Nothing like it had happened to Jews in Alexandria before—and no seer could have predicted this explosion. Far from being representative, the events are, in fact, altogether exceptional. It would be hazardous to infer that Jews lived under constant threat of danger or awaited impending doom. If anything, the reverse holds. The Jewish experience had been, so far as our evidence goes, remarkably uneventful.

Indeed, one can go further. Testimony, such as it is, on the experience of the Jews in the Ptolemaic era suggests that they fared quite well. The *Letter of Aristeas* reports that Ptolemy I removed up to 100,000 Jews from Palestine to Egypt, and then installed 30,000 of them in garrisons and fortresses throughout his realm.[101] The numbers are inflated and incredible. But the fact of Jewish soldiers serving in the Ptolemaic armies need not be doubted. Ample evidence, literary, epigraphic, and papyrological, attests to it. Jews enrolled in regular units of the army, could obtain officer rank, and received land grants like any others in the lists of the royal forces.[102] Inscriptions in Aramaic and Greek from Alexandrian cemeteries in the early Ptolemaic period disclose Jews, evidently mercenary soldiers, buried alongside Greeks from all parts of the Hellenic world.[103] To be sure, one can hardly credit Josephus when he claims that Ptolemy VI entrusted his entire kingdom to Jews and appointed two Jewish officers as generals over the entire army, particularly when he makes the identical claim for Cleopatra III a generation later.[104] Nevertheless, a substantial Jewish element plainly existed in the armed services of the Ptolemaic domain.[105] Jews, in fact, can be found at various levels of the Hellenistic administration in Egypt, as tax-farmers and tax-collectors, as bankers and granary officials.[106] No barriers, it appears, existed to prevent their engagement in the social and economic world of Ptolemaic Alexandria. By the time of Philo, the Jews in that city were shopowners, farmers, merchants, shippers, traders, and artisans.[107] They even turn up (admittedly outside Alexandria) as policemen.[108]

Jews also had free rein in establishing their own religious institutions. Literary sources report a plethora of synagogues in Alexandria.[109] And documentary evidence confirms the fact. Jews exhibited due respect to the overlordship of the Ptolemies while maintaining an unshaken faith in the traditions of their fathers. The combination is strikingly displayed in inscriptions that record the dedication of Jewish houses of worship *(proseuchai)* in honor of the king or the royal family of Egypt. Several such documents survive, dating from the third through the first centuries BCE, two of them from Alexandria itself and the earliest from Schedia in the near vicinity of Alexandria. As the latter pronounces, the Jewish dedicators constitute their *proseuche* on behalf of King Ptolemy, Queen Berenice, and their children.[110] That standard formula, with variants, characterizes the epigraphic evidence generally, one that closely parallels the terminology in pagan dedications.[111] Jews were fully comfortable in hailing the Gentile rulers of the land while simultaneously dedicating their synagogues to the "Most High God."[112] No tension or inconsistency troubled the two concepts.[113] Royal favor extended to the Jewish places of worship, even to the point of granting them the privilege of *asylia,* the formal status of asylum commonly accorded to pagan temples—a notable mark of official approval.[114]

Jewish success reached even to the upper echelons of the Alexandrian intelligentsia during the reigns of the Ptolemies. Jewish authors adapted the Greek language and Greek literary genres to rewrite biblical stories, to produce historical narratives, and to create fictional fantasies. Names, fragments, and even whole works survive to exhibit the skill and inventiveness of Jewish intellectuals. For many or most of these writers, good reason exists to locate them in Alexandria. They include the translators of the Pentateuch; the historian Demetrius; the authors of historical fiction like the *Letter of Aristeas* and III Maccabees; the tragedian Ezekiel; Aristobulus, the philosophic writer and supposed teacher of Ptolemy VI; and the wildly inventive Artapanus, who recast tales from Genesis and Exodus in his own peculiar mold.[115] The anticipated readership of these authors may have been largely Jewish. But the capacity to compose such works demonstrates that their composers had access to higher education and to the Hellenic cultural traditions available in Ptolemaic Alexandria.

Slender evidence allows only tentative conclusions. But it does appear that Jews enjoyed productive and rewarding lives in the greatest of Hellenistic cities. Integration in the social, economic, and cultural life of Alexandria was open to them, and they took advantage of that opening. Jews served in the armies, obtained administrative posts, took part in commerce, shipping, finance, farming, and every form of occupation, reached posts of prestige and importance, and played a role in the world of the Hellenic intelligentsia. Juridically, the Jews, like other Greek-speaking immigrants to Egypt, were reckoned among the "Hellenes."[116] It might be best to avoid terms like "assimilation" or "accommodation," which have loaded, even pejorative, connotations. Jews did not abandon or compromise their own traditions. We have no hint of internal conflict between the "orthodox" and the "modernists." Nor did the Ptolemaic government require conformity. Jews dwelled where they wished in all parts of the city, but those who preferred the company of their clan concentrated in particular areas.[117] Synagogues sprang up in Alexandria and its environs. As we have seen, the rulers themselves gave synagogues official sanction, awarding the privilege of *asylia* that set them on a par with pagan temples. Thus Jews worshipped their "Most High God" while honoring their Ptolemaic overlords who licensed and legitimated that worship. This was symbiosis, not syncretism.

Only one episode ostensibly marred that symbiosis.[118] The entertaining narrative entitled III Maccabees, composed, in all probability, by an Alexandrian Jew, recounts an attempted massacre of all Jews in the city by Ptolemy IV, an attempt foiled at the last moment by miraculous divine intervention. Josephus reports a very similar tale with a similar conclusion but sets it in the reign of Ptolemy VIII.[119] What historicity, if any, lies behind these narratives remains a matter of dispute. The tale in III Maccabees, on any analysis, is fanciful fiction. And Josephus' version, however different in chronology and detail, contains the same wondrous and magical climax (crazed elephants poised to stampede the Jews were halted at the last moment and swung around to trample the minions of the king). Perhaps some set of circumstances prompted official action against Jews in the reign of Philopator or Physcon, thereby stimulating a later legend. But this hardly emblematized the experience of Jews in the land of the Ptolemies. The story's outcome delivers the main message: Ptolemy did an about-face, punished his counselors, elevated the Jews, and honored their god. Only lunatic lapses disturbed an otherwise harmonious relationship between the Gentile ruler and his Jewish subjects.[120] The text of III Maccabees repeatedly returns to the motif of consistent allegiance by Jews toward the Ptolemies.[121] Whatever the realities of the situation, the Jewish author took pains to stress the long-term tranquillity that prevailed for Jews under Hellenic hegemony in Alexandria. And, although the tale may be fictive fantasy, we need not doubt the fact of a festival instituted to commemorate the outcome, a fact of real significance. That decision receives great emphasis (even duplication) at the conclusion of III Maccabees and is reiterated by Josephus, who indicates that Alexandrian Jews continue to celebrate the occasion in his own day.[122] An effort to recreate reasons for the ceremony may even account for the origin of the legend.[123] Such a ceremony parallels the annual commemoration of the Pentateuch's translation into Greek, celebrated with great festivities and extensive pilgrimages to the island of Pharos at Alexandria, attested by Philo.[124] That constitutes a telling combination. It is suitably symbolic that the two major festivals of Alexandrian Jewry to endure from Ptolemaic into Roman times marked concord between the royal court and the city's Jews.

Few, if any, barriers arose for Jews in the social, economic, cultural, and religious realms. What of the political realm? This is a much tougher question. The issue of where Jews fit in the civic world of Alexandria has stirred tides of scholarly controversy. Brevity would be welcome here. Yet the matter must be squarely faced. The prevailing, nearly universal, view has it that the coming of Rome to Egypt brought about a diminution of Jewish status vis-à-vis other groups in the city, thus highlighting or intensifying a vulnerability that encouraged enemies to seize the advantage.[125] If true, that would go far toward elucidating the backdrop for the pogrom. The evidence for such a scenario, however, is fragile.

The Jews certainly did enjoy an acknowledged status in the Alexandrian community. Just what it was and when it began remain matters of fierce scholarly contention. Josephus traces the Jewish place all the way back to the founding of the city. According to Josephus, Alexander the Great himself settled the Jews, supporters of his cause, in his new foundation and granted them a district for their dwelling.[126] More important, he accorded them civic privileges equal to those possessed by the Macedonians.[127] The accuracy of that claim, however, is more than dubious. Josephus had reason to exaggerate or invent, thereby to lend antiquity and authority to the Jewish situation in Alexandria. It is unlikely in the extreme that Jews accompanied Alexander to Egypt in any numbers (he had not even gone to Judaea). And he would have no reason to confer special distinction upon them. Josephus himself elsewhere attributes to Ptolemy I or to Alexander's successors generally the assignment of a separate district and equal civic rights for the Jews.[128] It need not follow that Josephus fabricated freely and indiscriminately. More probably, he lacked hard data, knew of Jewish privileges in a later period, and gave them an antique pedigree.[129]

The origins can be left in obscurity. What matters is that Jews did have an established place in the city by the end of the first century BCE. The fact is attested by the contemporary Greek geographer Strabo, who had no axe to grind. Josephus naturally seized upon the evidence and eagerly transmitted it. According to Strabo, writing in the age of Augustus, the Jews had a large portion of the city allotted to them, and had their own official, an ethnarch, to govern them, decide disputes, and oversee contracts and decrees, as if he headed an autonomous political entity.[130] The information is fragmentary but fascinating. The Jews plainly had some institutional organization of their own, a political structure and not simply a religious one, with a chief official who held sway—but a structure whose status was something less than full autonomy. This evidently means that Jews governed their internal affairs but were also part of a larger Alexandrian entity to which they owed allegiance. This could account for Josephus' imprecise usage of *isopoliteia* or *isomoiria*.[131]

Egypt fell under Roman authority in 30 BCE. Augustus transformed it into a province of the empire. The Jews of the land, it could be surmised, might feel some anxiety about the new regime. Their compatriots had lent a hand to Julius Caesar, but the benefits of that assistance would not necessarily carry over to the home base of Augustus' bitter and now vanquished foes.[132] Augustus, however, was prepared to be generous. And why not? It would be prudent and practical. Josephus reports that Augustus weakened none of the privileges that Jews had enjoyed since the time of Alexander.[133] Perhaps they did not go back to the latter, but there is good reason to believe that Augustus would refrain from tampering with them. Josephus, in two other places, refers to a tangible document: a bronze stele erected in Alexandria and available for consultation, in which Augustus explicitly guaranteed the Jewish claim to civic rights.[134] Not that Josephus himself ever consulted the document—hence the vague formulation in his text—but a reiteration of previous privileges would be conventional Roman policy.

Augustus did, in fact, intervene in the internal governance of Alexandrian Jewry. The Jewish ethnarch, as it happens, died in the course of the Augustan years. And the *princeps,* probably on the request of contending parties, stepped in to appoint a *gerousia* to oversee the affairs of the Jewish community; the instructions were delivered by the incoming governor of Egypt. Such is the testimony of Philo.[135] It need not follow that Augustus imposed a wholly new structure upon the Jews of Alexandria. He would have little reason for doing so. Josephus, quoting a decree of Claudius in reference to the same event (the death of the ethnarch), in fact states that Augustus did not prevent future ethnarchs.[136] Ethnarch and *gerousia* could well have existed simultaneously.[137] The evidence is simply too slender for confidence. That Augustus took the initiative here is unlikely. Potential instability after the ethnarch's death probably led to a request for imperial intervention. Philo, in any case, regards it as salutary. And a Jewish officialdom continued to govern the Jewish community.[138]

The nature of this governance and its relationship to the broader Alexandrian society elude us. The comment of Strabo, unaffected by pro- or anti-Jewish bias, remains fundamental: the Jewish leader acted as if he headed an autonomous political entity. One may infer that he had a free hand among his own compatriots, but acted within a larger superstructure. Philo's texts refer repeatedly to a Jewish *politeia* or to Jewish *dikaia politika.*[139] The terms notoriously lack precision, and it would be mistaken to endow them with technical significance. But Philo definitely refers to political privileges, as well as to religious rights. *Politeia* can encompass both, but Philo does distinguish them.[140] He can also employ the very interesting phrase *Ioudaioi politai* to denote Jewish inhabitants of Greek cities generally.[141] Evidently he reckons their position to be defined, at least in part, by reference to civic prerogatives. Jewish identity did not confine itself to religious observances.

A key point, however, must be stressed. The political rights of Jews, whatever their particulars, were distinct from the citizenship of Alexandrian Greeks.[142] That distinction appears in III Maccabees, the fanciful treatise composed in the first century BCE or the first century CE. The story has the wicked king Ptolemy IV initiate a wholesale persecution of Jews in Egypt. But he left a loophole. Any Jews who chose to be initiated in the mysteries of Dionysos would enjoy political rights equal to those of the Alexandrians.[143] Their privileges were otherwise evidently distinct. The fact is reinforced by the statement placed in the mouth of the repentant former prefect Flaccus by Philo. Flaccus regretted having castigated the Jews for lack of political rights and the status of foreigners when, in fact, they possessed such rights and had the status of settlers.[144] The last term, *katoikoi,* implies something less than the full enjoyment of a citizen's prerogatives. Jews, in short, did possess civic privileges, but in a form different from that of Alexandrian citizens. The famous letter of the emperor Claudius to the Alexandrians, preserved on papyrus, clinches the matter. The Jews, so Claudius asserts, enjoy what is their own and possess a surplus of benefits in an alien city.[145] From the *princeps'* perspective, at least, Jewish privileges, however bountiful, still fell short of full identification with the city in which they dwelled. Imperial policy had been supportive of Jewish claims to conduct their own affairs. But that support guaranteed the untrammeled practice of religious rites.[146] It did not extend to enforcement of political claims.

A much-debated issue now supervenes. Did Jews labor under a sense of inferiority and thus scramble to secure the citizenship otherwise limited to Alexandrians? Not a single text attests explicitly to such a drive. The absence of any such testimony needs to be underscored. The evidence, such as it is, is indirect, ambiguous, and over-interpreted.

The direct testimony indicates that Jews called themselves "Alexandrians." Greeks in the city had no monopoly on the term.[147] Although, as we have seen, this did not signify duplicate political rights, it surely betokens an assertion of identification with the city—and one that (prior to the events of 38) went unchallenged. The Claudian decree transmitted by Josephus states explicitly that Jews in Alexandria are called "Alexandrians."[148] The Jewish delegation to Gaius in 39 or 40 went there, in part, to point out that they were Alexandrians.[149] When distinguishing Alexandrian Jews from Greeks, Philo refers to the latter as "the other

Alexandrians."[150] Indeed, the Jewish philosopher unhesitatingly calls the city "our Alexandria."[151] Josephus, in grappling with the calumnies of Apion, ridicules the latter's amazement at the fact that Jews are called "Alexandrians" and justifies the appellation.[152] Apion may have balked at the designation, but his cavils confirm that it held sway. Indeed, we have a precious piece of papyrological testimony to add weight. An otherwise unknown Jew, Helenos, in his petition to the Roman governor at the end of the first century BCE (at least in the first draft), refers to himself—and to his father as well—as an "Alexandrian."[153] When Augustus set up a bronze tablet to underline Jewish privileges, it made clear, according to Josephus, that Jews were *politai* of Alexandria.[154] The phrase can hardly denote full citizenship, as already observed, but it fits snugly with the rest of the testimony. Jews claimed a political place in the city of Alexandria.

Did the Jews have a separate political organization of their own, independent of Greeks and Egyptians, a self-sufficient entity conventionally labeled by scholars as a *politeuma*?[155] The controversy over this thesis has been long and long-winded. A full rehearsal is unnecessary.

The term *politeuma* appears only once with regard to the Jews of Alexandria. And the occurrence comes not in any documentary text, but in a fictional narrative, namely the *Letter of Aristeas*.[156] That alone gives some pause. The term surfaces nowhere in Philo or Josephus, nor in the papyrological testimony that bears on Alexandrian Jews. The passage in Pseudo-Aristeas is tortured, convoluted, and possibly non-technical. It relates to the reading out of the completed translation of the Hebrew scrolls into Greek, which prompted various parties to rise and hail the achievement. They are described as "priests and elders of the translators and of those from the *politeuma* and the leaders of the people."[157] Does the *politeuma* constitute a political enclave of Jews in Alexandria? If so, it is not easy to understand why "leaders of the people" should be distinguished from "elders of those from the *politeuma*." In fact, the term *politeuma* has a wide range of meanings. It can signify a private or cultic association, an ethnic organization within a city, or the governing body of a community.[158] None of these readily fits the circumstances described by the *Letter of Aristeas*. Hence some scholars quite properly questioned the existence of a separate Jewish political entity.[159]

The issue, however, stands on a quite different footing as a result of very recent finds. New papyrological texts disclose the existence of a Jewish *politeuma* in Herakleopolis, with a "politarch" and other "archons" in the officialdom, who, among other things, adjudicated disputes between Jews in the city, occasionally even between a Jew and a Gentile.[160] This does not prove the presence of a comparable body in Alexandria, but the proposition has suddenly become much more plausible.

Whether or not *politeuma* is the proper term, the Alexandrian Jews plainly had governing officials of their own: an ethnarch, a *gerousia,* or both. And they possessed political standing in the city, including the exercise of (unspecified) civic privileges, as well as a claim on designations like *politai, dikaia politika,* even *politeia*—and, indeed, the label "Alexandrians." As Strabo discloses, this did not amount to an autonomous entity, although Jewish officials could act almost as if it were. And why should they wish to have an autonomous entity? Jews had little motive to isolate themselves from the great community of Alexandria at large.

Association with that community, however, need not entail full Alexandrian citizenship. What advantage did full citizenship hold for Jews? Or, more fundamentally, does any evidence suggest that they sought it? The view that Jews suffered discrimination in Alexandria after the coming of Rome and thus grasped at Alexandrian citizenship is widely held.[161] But it relies on inference and hypothesis, not tangible data.

A poll-tax was imposed upon Egypt by Augustus after annexation of that land as a province of the Roman empire. It took or acquired the name *laographia,* meaning, strictly, a "register of the people" or a "census." Hence, most interpret it as a mark of degradation, the conqueror's exhibition of supremacy and authority.[162] The issue is not so clear-cut. That the Augustan imposition was a novelty is less than certain. The term *laographia* occurs in Ptolemaic papyri, although the occurrence is local rather than sweeping and the meaning appears to be census rather than poll-tax.[163] The question of Augustus' innovation in this matter, however, can be set aside. The Romans did, in any case, collect a poll-tax in Egypt. And this forms the cornerstone of the prevalent thesis: Alexandrian Greeks had exemption from the tax, but Jews fell under it—hence a reason for seeking full citizenship and erasing the mark of humiliation.

The thesis skates on very thin ice indeed. No text informs us that Jews were subject to the *laographia*—although that has not prevented the proposition from being repeated in work after work. Egyptians certainly paid the price. And the Alexandrians evidently had an exemption.[164] Does it follow that Jews were categorized with Egyptians?

The so-called "Boule-papyrus" has been interpreted to that end. The text evidently preserves (or recreates) an interview between representatives of the Alexandrian government and the Roman emperor, probably Augustus. The Alexandrians, among other things, undertake to guarantee the imperial revenues. They promise the emperor to prevent those liable to the *laographia* from escaping that obligation by gaining enrollment among the ephebes. And they vow to keep the uncultivated and uneducated from tainting the *politeuma* of the Alexandrians and diminishing the income of the empire.[165] Jews go unmentioned here. That they were among the "uncultivated and uneducated," subject to *laographia* and infiltrating the ephebate in order to acquire citizenship and tax-exempt status, is widely assumed.[166] But why? The slur could readily be applied to Egyptians or, indeed more likely, to Greeks without customary access to the ephebate through family or wealth. It is essential to recall that the ephebate normally served as a vehicle for the elite in Greek society; it was hardly available for all Hellenes. Nothing in this papyrus states or suggests that there was a Jewish problem.[167]

The petition of the Alexandrian Jew Helenos, noted earlier in a different context, has also been seized upon to buttress the thesis. Helenos, who describes himself and his father as "Alexandrian," laments that, although he has gone through the appropriate education, he now runs the risk of being deprived of his *patris*.[168] The papyrus then becomes very fragmentary and largely unreadable. But *laographia* is mentioned three times in the preserved portions. That has prompted a common reconstruction: Helenos obtained the education of an ephebe through the gymnasium, which signaled citizenship status and gave exemption from the *laographia;* but he now fears being stripped of his citizenship, being relegated to the liabilities endured by the Jews, and reaching the end of his freedom from the poll-tax.[169] The reconstruction, in fact, is vulnerable at every point. The terms "ephebate" and "gymnasium" result from very shaky readings in the text. The equating of *patris* with "citizenship" is speculation. And the relevance of the *laographia* remains obscure. But even if all these conjectures are conceded, the text fails to sustain the larger thesis. Helenos may well have been anxious about losing his ephebate status and thus being made subject to the *laographia*. But the petition nowhere indicates that his *Jewishness* had rendered him vulnerable—any more than it had rendered his father vulnerable.

The *laographia* receives mention in a literary text that has also been exploited for the master hypothesis.[170] III Maccabees' fictional tale of Ptolemy IV's attack on the Jews includes a notable passage. The king threatens those Jews who fail to perform the proper sacrifices with a servile existence and with *laographia*. If, however, they agree to embrace the cult of Dionysos, they can gain civic privileges equivalent to those of the Alexandrians.[171] That passage has served (by a reference to *laographia*) to date the treatise to the early Empire and to confirm the conjecture that

Jews had been made subject to a poll-tax by the Romans.[172] There is circularity here. And the conclusions are not conclusive. Since *laographia* appears in Ptolemaic texts, the word alone cannot prove composition in the Roman period. In the particular context, moreover, it almost certainly signifies "registration" rather than "tax."[173] And an interpretation of Jewish inferiority to Alexandrians as a consequence of Roman intervention based on a tale set in the Ptolemaic era is a most hazardous one. In any case, the fanciful character of the fable offers only a slippery foothold for historical inference.

Another semi-fictional construct offers testimony commandeered for this purpose. The dossier of fragmentary papyri known as the *Acta Isidori* includes a piece depicting a hostile exchange between the Alexandrian Isidoros and the Jewish king Agrippa at the tribunal of Claudius in Rome. Whether or not such a confrontation ever took place need not be explored here. The item we possess is, at the least, a literary embellishment. One of the fragments contains an intriguing interchange. Isidoros, in responding to Agrippa with regard to the Jews, asserts that they are not of the same temperament as the Alexandrians but follow the mode of the Egyptians. Are they not, he asks, equal to those who pay the tax? Agrippa retorts smartly: the rulers have imposed taxes upon the Egyptians, but no one has done so upon them (the Jews).[174] That little snatch of dialogue has provided ammunition to those who reckon Jews as taxpayers in the category of Egyptians.[175] In fact, it shows just the reverse. Isidoros brackets Jews with Egyptians; Agrippa distinguishes them precisely on the issue of taxes. Even if the debate reflects reality, why believe Isidoros rather than Agrippa? And, more to the point, Isidoros' statement does not maintain that Jews paid the tax—just the opposite. He compares Jews with Egyptians and asks the rhetorical question whether Jews are not equal to those who pay the tax.[176] It follows that Jews are *not* subject to it. Insofar as the text has any historicity, it affirms Jewish privilege rather than disadvantage. The case for Roman reduction of Jews to lower-class taxpayers evaporates into smoke. And with it goes the main motive manufactured by moderns for Jewish hankering after Alexandrian citizenship.[177]

The Jews of Alexandria had their own *politeia* and their own *politika dikaia*. Whatever else those elastic terms might mean, they certainly signify political rights and civic engagement. Those rights were different from—but perhaps preferable to—the juridical citizenship of the Alexandrians. The latter might indeed have some drawbacks for Jews, who could be faced with the prospect of participating in the municipal cults and paying obeisance to the deities of the community.[178] The *locus classicus* is the question that Apion, that Alexandrian baiter of Jews, posed: "if the Jews are citizens, then why don't they worship the same gods that the Alexandrians do?"[179] Josephus, who transmits the comment (whether precisely or not), endeavors to dodge the point. He responds by asserting that, since Egyptians (among whom Apion belonged by birth) fight bitterly with one another about religious differences, they should not be surprised that a people who migrated to Alexandria from elsewhere would hold fast to laws that go back to their origins.[180] The reply may be somewhat extraneous, but the exchange is most interesting. Apion does not, in fact, challenge the *civitas* of the Jews; rather, he complains that, though *cives*, they don't worship the city's gods. The plain implication is that Jews in Alexandria happily escaped the conventional obligations of *cives* without forfeiting their *civitas*.[181] That may have irritated Apion, but it evidently did not diminish Jewish status. More significant, however, is the fact that *cives*, presumably a translation of *politai*, had a meaning distinct from that of "those who held Alexandrian citizenship." Josephus' awkward response makes that clear. His description of the Jews, corresponding to Apion's *cives*, refers simply to immigrants to Alexandria. The Alexandrian Jews, in short, even in the eyes of an avowed opponent, enjoyed civic privileges without compromising religious principle. No pressing need induced them to go after the questionable burdens that accompanied citizenship.[182]

The evidence, ambiguous, complex, and frustratingly fragmentary, nevertheless converges on a central point. The Jews of Alexandria did not suffer oppression under Ptolemaic or Roman governance; they enjoyed freedom to perform traditional rites and to worship the divinity in their own way; and they possessed (unspecified) civic privileges in the larger community. The persecutions in 38 CE during the governorship of Flaccus came as a shocking interruption of their untroubled life, for special and peculiar reasons (as we have seen), not as the culmination of simmering Hellenic anti-semitism nor as resistance to Jewish grasping after Hellenic citizenship.

But the interruption and the shock set off alarm bells. Flaccus' actions entailed, so Philo put it, a destruction of the Jewish *politeia* and a severing of their share in *politika dikaia*.[183] The horrific pogrom that followed mobilized the Jews in energetic fashion. Flaccus' removal gave reason for hope. But the mission to Caligula proved futile. A long wait delayed matters, and then nothing came of it. The monarch's mischievousness left the Jewish emissaries disgruntled and degraded.[184] Caligula's death in January 41, however, opened a whole new set of possibilities. Violent demonstrations resumed in Alexandria, this time with both Jews and Gentiles in arms. The level of ferocity reached the point where it could be termed a "war."[185] The Jewish embassy headed by Philo may still have been in Rome in 41. But the Alexandrian Jews sent another legation to reinforce the case or to justify their own recourse to violence.[186] A rival Greek mission from the city was there as well, arguing vigorously that Jews were responsible for the upheaval.[187] The emperor Claudius, newly installed on the throne, had his hands full right away.

Here, for once, we have the advantage of a first-hand document. A letter of Claudius, preserved on a precious papyrus, gives the imperial pronouncement on the riots in Alexandria. What Caligula had scorned and mocked, Claudius took seriously and addressed directly.[188] The letter itself constitutes a response to the Alexandrian Greeks' embassy that had come in part to deliver formal salutations upon Claudius' accession to the throne. It treats a number of matters not relevant to the Jews.[189] When Claudius gets to the issue of the riots, however, his remarks are pointed and acid. The *princeps* asserts that he will waste no time conducting a precise inquiry to find out who started the trouble. But he adds that he is storing up some remorseless anger against those who had begun hostilities again.[190] And he follows that with a threat: if the contending parties don't put a stop to their obstinate and deadly mutual animosity, he will show them what happens when a generous ruler turns to righteous indignation.[191] Claudius proceeds to admonish both sides. He adjures the Alexandrians to behave kindly and magnanimously toward the Jews, respecting the customs which the latter have practiced freely as in the days of Augustus and which he himself now confirms.[192] At the same time he rebukes the Jews, ordering them not to send again two embassies to which he had to give ear, to refrain from involvement in the games, and to stop bringing in Jews from Syria and Egypt. If they pay no heed, he will lower the boom, treating them like a plague descending upon the universe.[193] The letter concludes on an upbeat note: if both sides leave off their present behavior and agree to live together in a considerate and kindly manner, the emperor will be most solicitous of their city.[194]

Such is the relevant portion of this text. It has been microscopically dissected and repeatedly reinterpreted since the publication of the papyrus three-quarters of a century ago. And most interpretations have Claudius leaning toward the Alexandrian Greeks, taking a hard line on the Jews, and thus perpetuating official displeasure and elite hostility toward that people.[195] Does that give a fair reading of the text? Not very fair at all. The emperor, whatever his proclivities, makes a point of presenting an impartial posture. He reproves both Jew and Greek for the turmoil in the city, unconcerned about who may have started it, and he exhorts them both to behave themselves and to live in harmony with one another.[196] Claudius even refers to the upheaval and *stasis* as "a war against the Jews."[197] This does not absolve Jews of all blame, but it certainly implicates Greeks in the aggression. The emperor dismissed the arguments of Greek envoys who sought to fix responsibility upon the Jews, unwilling to inquire into the matter, but he claimed to harbor remorseless anger against those who would renew the conflict—whether Jew or Greek.[198] To be sure, the emperor expresses irritation at the Jews for having sent two embassies, as if they dwelled in two cities, and orders them not to repeat that action.[199] Perhaps the second mission represented a somewhat more militant posture than the first (which had been sent before Caligula's death and had to proceed more cautiously). Or the two legations may simply have presented different viewpoints, thus exasperating the *princeps,* who already had rival Greek and Jewish positions to adjudicate.[200] But this was hardly a major infraction. Much more significantly, Claudius reaffirmed the policy of Augustus in adjuring Alexandrians to defile none of the customs through which Jews pay homage to their god, but to allow them to continue their own ways as in Augustus' day.[201] This supplies a crucial endorsement of Jewish status. The maintenance of their traditions was not to be infringed, and no repetition of the pogrom would be tolerated.

Claudius' affirmation applied to Jewish religious freedom, not to political standing. Did he then disappoint hopes on the latter score? Such is the prevailing view.[202] But what reason do we have to believe that the Jews sought political aggrandizement? The emperor does indeed direct them "not to grasp after more than they previously had."[203] The phrase has attracted much comment. But nothing suggests that it signifies Jewish efforts to acquire the citizenship of the Alexandrians. Under the circumstances, the Jewish delegates most likely sought guarantees of security, perhaps a pronouncement that would deter future prefects of Egypt from stripping them of civic privileges as Flaccus had done.[204] It would not be surprising if Claudius balked at that. The Roman emperor was the sole supervisor of imperial officials, and he would not have his authority circumscribed by prior promises or guarantees. Claudius, in fact, reminded the Jews that they already enjoyed their own benefits, indeed an abundance of goods, despite living in a city that "belongs to others."[205] The *princeps* got it just right. The Jews had all the advantages of Alexandria, even while others held political authority. Why rock the boat by seeking greater guarantees?

So far, so good. Claudius, however, uttered a most baffling phrase which makes little ostensible sense but has spurred vaulting speculation. He enjoined the Jews not to "pour into" the games organized by the *gymnasiarchoi* or *kosmetai*.[206] Extensive conclusions have been drawn from this, most importantly that Jews had been infiltrating the gymnasia, thus to obtain ephebic education and to acquire credentials that would legitimate citizenship rights.[207] The passage is regularly paired with an earlier pronouncement in the papyrus declaring that Claudius would not sanction Alexandrian citizenship for those of slave parentage who had reached the ephebate.[208] On that view, Jews too used ephebic training to smooth a path toward citizenship. Claudius (it would follow) therefore demanded an end to the practice and blocked the route. Such is the prevailing notion. But the phraseology cannot easily carry so much freight. Nothing connects Claudius' comments on the ephebate with those on the Jews—which come under an altogether separate heading in the papyrus.[209] Neither gymnasiarchical education nor access to citizenship is even hinted at here. The context of the entire section is that of calming passions between the *ethne* and preventing further violence in the city. The sentence must bear relation to that purpose.[210] Claudius directs the Jews not "to pour" into the games. Gymnasia and theaters could serve as staging grounds for demonstrations or turbulence. Not long before, in 38, the display by the crowd in Alexandria, mocking King Agrippa and helping to spark off the riots, took place in the gymnasium.[211] And another mob gathering occurred shortly thereafter in the theater to exert pressure upon Flaccus and prompt the installation of statues in synagogues.[212] In that context, Claudius surely sought to prevent Jews from disrupting the games where large crowds would gather. It can hardly be coincidental that, three lines later, after rebuking the Alexandrian Jews who gained so much benefit from the city, the emperor prohibits them from summoning and bringing in other Jews from Syria and Egypt.[213] The beefing up of Jewish numbers may well have aggravated or intensified the tumult that erupted after Gaius' death, provoked the embassies to Rome, and brought about Claudius' verdict. The *princeps'* pronouncement aimed at restoration of order and maintenance of harmony. With that objective, the phrases hang together and the segment makes sense.

The emperor strove for even-handedness. The idea that his assertions represent special hostility against the Jews does not leap out of the text. Both sides came in for their share of censure.[214] The keystone for the thesis of anti-Judaism coming from the top is Claudius' statement near the end of the letter, which, in most interpretations, characterizes Jews as perpetrating a common plague upon the whole world.[215] In fact, Claudius says nothing of the kind. The offending phrase occurs after the emperor has issued his demands to the Jews to refrain from sending two embassies, from flocking into the games, and from calling in their Syrian and Egyptian compatriots. Then he adds, "*if not,* I shall move against them in every way, *as if* they were stirring up some common plague for the world."[216] The emperor does not here brand the Jews with a slur. Rather, he insists upon implementation of his demands. Disobedience would bring massive imperial retaliation, as if stamping out an epidemic. This is harsh and severe language. But it is not a characterization of the Jews.

Claudius' letter on the whole confirms the picture of a generally prosperous and successful Jewish community in Alexandria. The pogrom in 38 was an exceptional event, and the uprisings after Gaius' death reflected Jewish efforts to restore the status quo ante. That, in effect, is what Claudius did. The *princeps* reprimanded both sides and insisted upon concord. He also reaffirmed the policy of Augustus and assured continuing respect for the practice of Jewish conventions and traditions.

Josephus provides his own sanitized version of Claudius' pronouncement. But he gets the gist of it right. In Josephus' account, the declaration was preceded by suppression of the civic conflict through actions of the Roman prefect and on the orders of the emperor, a perfectly plausible scenario. Josephus then has Claudius issue an edict (rather than a letter) which emphasizes (and exaggerates) imperial favor to the Jews. The emperor refers to Jewish political rights, a status equivalent to that of the Alexandrians, dating back to the time of Alexander, guaranteed by his successors, reaffirmed by Augustus, and undisputed until the riots under Caligula. Claudius then denounces his predecessor as a lunatic, insists that Jewish privileges be reinstated as before, and demands that both parties take care to prevent any further disturbances.[217] That this is a separate pronouncement by the emperor (as most scholars maintain) on the same subject, prompted by the same circumstances, and addressed to the same recipients, seems most unlikely.[218] Claudian edicts may have been prolific, but this would be redundant. And it is altogether implausible that the emperor would label his predecessor as a lunatic in an imperial edict of official character.[219] Josephus, in all probability, did not have access to the original, employed some subsequent report of it, and then framed it to his own agenda. There is no need, therefore, to charge him with forgery or fabrication. It was more a matter of manipulation. The historian underscored Jewish political rights, while Claudius had affirmed only freedom for religious practices—not, perhaps, a contradiction, but a decided shift of emphasis. The harsh rebukes got left out, and only magnanimity remains. But whether one or two declarations issued from the Palatine makes little difference. The bottom line, so to speak, was the same: the emperor confirmed protection of Jewish practices as before and enjoined all to maintain peace in the city.

The situation took a dire and dramatic turn after 66. Repercussions from rebellion in Palestine extended to Egypt. In Alexandria, the citizenry met to vote an embassy to Rome, thus spreading alarm among the Jews. The Alexandrians' purpose, in all likelihood, was to disassociate themselves sharply from the Jewish population and to avoid the taint of disloyalty to Rome. Jews flocked into the assembly, prompting reprisals by the Greeks; there was a rapid escalation of events that resulted in the slaughter of large numbers at the hands of Roman forces.[220] The volatile situation in the wake of the Palestinian upheaval overrode all other considerations. The tumult in 66 need not reflect any long-standing enmity between Greeks and Jews. But it had long-term implications. When rebellion burst out again, a half-century later in the era of Trajan, it emerged from the diaspora, and the bitter legacy helped to inspire Jewish assaults on their enemies in Alexandria.[221]

All that, however, lay in the future. Those events should not obscure a more basic fact. The experience of Jews in Alexandria from the founding of the city to the advent of the Great Revolt—nearly four full centuries—was a predominantly positive one. Jews played a full part in the social, economic, and cultural life of Ptolemaic Alexandria. Their religious institutions and traditions had official sanction and express support from both Ptolemies and Roman emperors. They enjoyed civic privileges together with their own political organs and officialdom. Juridical "citizenship," whatever that might mean, held no special appeal; it was neither an object of desire nor a source of conflict. The Jews were "Alexandrians." In short, the dreadful pogrom of 38 in no way defines or exemplifies the history of Jews in Alexandria. It exploded suddenly and unexpectedly, the product of special circumstances—the peculiar combination of a shaken Roman prefect, the perverse ambitions of certain civic leaders, and the bitterness of an indigenous population. The particular conditions and the motives of the principal actors brought to the surface the repressed emotions of marginalized Egyptians who lashed out against an envied and suddenly vulnerable *ethnos*. The Jews suffered badly, but temporarily, at the hands of violent Egyptians, who reappear with regularity as the chief villains in Hellenistic-Jewish literature. Concentration on that grim episode has distorted the broader history: a lengthy and productive relationship between Jews and Greeks, and the rich and rewarding experience of the Jews in the city of Alexandria.

Jews in the Province of Asia

JEWS WERE conspicuous. One could not miss them. They held stubbornly to practices and beliefs that set them apart from Gentile neighbors—and they made no secret of their peculiarities. Jewish communities in the cities of the Hellenistic world and the Roman empire were readily identifiable. Although diaspora scattered Jews throughout the Mediterranean, they never disappeared into a melting pot.

This tenacity gave them distinctiveness. But it could also render them vulnerable. Testimony is sparse but significant. Some of the most important evidence relates to the Roman province of Asia. On the face of it, Jews found themselves regularly embattled, subject to harassment and oppression in the Greek cities where they dwelled, their privileges often curtailed or under attack, their position precarious, their very distinctiveness a source of animosity and conflict. Hellenic neighbors resented their exclusiveness, their unusual habits, or their odd institutions that did not fit in with civic expectations. Preservation of their ancestral ways required protection. And the Jews found it in the power of Rome. In response to appeal, Roman authority dictated tolerance and privilege, directing Greek communities and leaders to respect Jewish customs and permit them to carry out the commandments. The directives did not always guarantee obedience. Indeed, they occasionally had to be repeated when renewed instances of state interference surfaced. But the general pattern seems consistent: the constriction of Jewish privileges by Greek communities and the summoning of Roman intervention to restore and protect those privileges. Such, in one form or another, is nearly unanimous opinion.[1]

And there is good reason for it. Josephus preserves a number of documents attesting to Jewish complaints about mistreatment in Hellenic cities, almost all of them in Asia Minor, and the responses of Roman officialdom which consistently reaffirm Jewish prerogatives and insist upon their enforcement. The material comprises a collection of official letters, *senatus consulta,* municipal decrees, and imperial edicts. Scholarship has occasionally questioned the authenticity of the documents.[2] But a strong and growing consensus has lined up in support of their genuineness[3]—and rightly so.

The collection itself, to be sure, is a jumble. The documents are quoted usually in part rather than in whole; they are riddled with errors; names are often confused or inaccurate; chronology is askew; duplications and repetitions plague the dossier. No wonder some have sought to dismiss them as forgeries. Josephus assembled the data for avowedly apologetic purposes: he wished to prove that Jews had always been held in high esteem by Rome—a lesson to the Greeks and a means to eliminate groundless hatreds, thus to earn the favor of other nations.[4] With such an objective, one might suspect fabrication and embellishment.

The suspicions, however, do not hold up. Parallels in structure, phraseology, and content can readily be found in authentic Roman documents preserved on stone, bronze, or papyrus. The award of privileges, indeed the repetitive confirmation of them, as a return for loyalty or services, in response to requests or appeals, occurs with frequency in Roman dealings with Greek states from the Hellenistic period through the Principate.[5] *Senatus consulta,* to be sure, could be forged in Rome, and, so it was alleged, occasionally were.[6] But Josephus' dossier includes letters, decrees, and edicts as well as senatorial decisions. And no Roman, in any case, would have a motive for forging *senatus consulta* that awarded privileges to Jews. Josephus, of course, would have such a motive. And the fact that his documents closely resemble in form and substance genuine decrees independently attested does not in itself prove authenticity. An informed forger, whether Josephus or a source, would take pains to replicate standard formulas and conventional structures. Paradoxically enough, it is the very confusion in Josephus' dossier—the errors, disorder, overlap, and redundance—that constitutes the strongest argument *for* authenticity! Any self-respecting forger would have provided a tidier assortment.

Josephus, in all probability, obtained his data with the help of informants from various locations. Jews in diaspora cities would have reason for preserving documents that guaranteed the unhindered practice of traditional rites and authorized adherence to ancestral laws. Josephus need not, indeed probably did not, inspect the original texts, but relied on copies sent by friends or contacts from the archives kept by Jewish communities in Greco-Roman *poleis.* The process was more haphazard than consistent, dependent upon the care and intelligence of different individuals in different places. This would explain why the documents come from only a select number of cities, why duplications exist, why the sequence was confused, why errors occurred in transmission, why names were occasionally garbled, and why the chronology was often imprecise.[7]

The documents therefore can stand—at least in general. On the face of it, they tell the story that buttresses most modern interpretations. The Jews repeatedly drew fire from their Greek neighbors. Jewish institutions stirred private resentments and brought public constraints. Life in the diaspora, on the standard view, was precarious and problematic. Only Roman intervention reasserted privileges and protected ancestral practices. Is that, in fact, the case? The matter could benefit from closer scrutiny. It has significant implications for the experience of diaspora Jews in Greco-Roman antiquity.

One point needs to be set in high profile. The documents in Josephus' collection do not range far and wide in time or space. On the contrary. Most of them belong to a tightly circumscribed period at the end of the Roman Republic and the principate of Augustus, and the vast bulk apply to a narrow geographic region encompassing western Asia Minor.

An instructive example can make the point. Josephus' collection of Jewish privileges authorized by Rome begins (chronologically) with a set of official communications that date to the very first year or so (49–48 BCE) of the Roman civil war that pitted the forces of Pompey against Caesar. The consuls of 49 were bitter opponents of Caesar and advocates of the Pompeian cause. Both of them abandoned Italy when Caesar marched into the peninsula, and one of them, L. Lentulus Crus, conducted vigorous recruitment efforts in the province of Asia. The government, of course, faced a crisis. A buildup of forces in the East was a vital part of the Pompeian strategy to counteract Caesarian successes in the West. Lentulus' sweeping conscription of Roman citizens in Asia netted a full complement of two legions.[8] This supplies the context for the first dossier transmitted by Josephus.

Lentulus issued a decree in 49 exempting the Jews of Ephesus who were Roman citizens from service in the Roman army. The solemn declaration expressed respect for religious feelings and the practice of Jewish rites.[9] That delivered the proper pieties.[10] Did Rome really stand behind the religious prerogatives of faithful Jews here? The request for such an exemption, as stated in another of Josephus' documents, came from a certain Dositheus of Alexandria, presumably a Jew, who petitioned two Romans, evidently officers, and they in turn brought the request to Lentulus, who proceeded to authorize the exemption.[11] The nature of this document is itself obscure; it is more like a narrative to give background to the decision rather than a formal record of it. The text may, in fact, be part of a letter sent by Lentulus to announce his decree.[12] Josephus, in any case, presents it as a formal communication. That in itself is noteworthy and intriguing. Why the need for official explanation? Lentulus had *imperium,* and his recruiting authority was unquestioned. Troops had to be rounded up in substantial numbers—and swiftly. Only Roman citizens could serve in the legions, but all were fair game for recruitment into the auxiliary forces. How much difference would be made by an immunity for Jews who were Roman citizens? It is not easy to believe that large numbers of Jews dwelling in Ephesus—or elsewhere in the province of Asia for that matter—had a legitimate claim on Roman citizenship.[13] The legionaries gathered for the Pompeian cause were more than ample without a Jewish contribution. Jews in theory (though probably not in practice) might still be enrolled in the auxiliaries. But they are rarely found in the ranks of the Roman army.[14] Lentulus could afford to be magnanimous without depleting his manpower.

What then was the value of the gesture? The advantage of harmony in the eastern part of the empire, where Pompeian generals hoped to present a united front against the army of Caesar, was critical. If Jewish representatives asked for immunity from military service on religious grounds, it was a small price to pay. Indeed, the announcement through official communications would underscore Roman generosity. And why the restriction just to Roman citizens? That too may speak to the broader concern for concord. A special exception for Jews could run the risk of resentment by other peoples and ethnic groups subject to call-up in the Roman civil conflict. By releasing only Jews who had the credentials of Roman citizenship, Lentulus could claim a prerogative of the imperial power. And the small numbers involved would hardly provoke bitterness among the inhabitants of Rome's eastern provinces. The additional letter, explaining the grounds for the exemption, might further calm concerns. The policy, it appears, was conspicuously advertised. T. Ampius Balbus, *legatus pro praetore* under Lentulus, also dispatched a letter to the magistrates, council, and *demos* of Ephesus, announcing Lentulus' decision and reporting the concurrence of other Roman officials in the East.[15] Indeed, Romans made sure to spread the word elsewhere. The legate M. Piso proclaimed Lentulus' policy on the island of Delos, thus indicating that it extended beyond the province of Asia, at least into the recruiting grounds of the Aegean. The Delians duly passed a decree in accord with the wishes of Piso.[16]

Nothing in this testimony implies a general Roman thrust to protect the prerogatives of Jews. Nor indeed did Romans intervene here to shield Jews from restrictions imposed by Greeks. The nearest approximation comes in the final phrase of Balbus' letter to the Ephesians, asking them to see to it that no one should trouble the Jews.[17] It does not follow that they had been troubled. Balbus' language is polite, not disciplinary. The whole dossier on military exemptions that gives the context, the decision of Lentulus, and its reportage speaks to a special situation at the outset of the Roman civil war. It reflects an effort by the Pompeian side to develop a united resistance in the East, unmarred by dissension within the ranks.

The next dossier of texts discloses some noteworthy edicts by Julius Caesar the dictator. Caesar, in the year 47 BCE, accorded considerable authority to and reinforced the position of Hyrcanus II, High Priest of Judaea. The documents in the main concern the relationship of Rome to the Jewish homeland. But the enhancement of Hyrcanus' situation had repercussions in the diaspora.

The first and lengthiest decree bestows major honors upon Hyrcanus. The Jewish leader had exhibited loyalty to Rome on more than one occasion in previous years, and was especially instrumental in coming to the aid of Caesar in the immediate past, during the war in Alexandria from which Caesar had only narrowly emerged victorious. In return, the dictator named Hyrcanus high priest and ethnarch of the Jews, those titles to be reserved for him and his children in perpetuity. The beneficiaries were to be numbered among Caesar's friends and allies, and they would hold their privileges in accord with ancestral laws by his command. Any issue that might arise regarding the Jewish way of life would be decided by their own institutions. The Jews were to be free of monetary exactions and the obligation of quartering troops.[18] The privileges assigned here to Hyrcanus and his people are far from unique. A long tradition of Roman formal generosity delivered pronouncements of friendship and alliance, provided rewards for loyalty and military assistance, relieved taxation, and guaranteed the right to operate under ancestral laws.[19] Caesar advertised his magnanimity after the defeat of Pompey at Pharsalus by awarding freedom and autonomy to states that had supported his cause. And after victories in Asia Minor later in the year 47, he presented his ally Mithridates with the title of king and with a tetrarchy in Galatia.[20] He did not single out Hyrcanus and the Jews for special treatment. One item in the decree, however, deserves particular notice. Hyrcanus and his future offspring are to be "ethnarchs of the Jews" and hold the office of "high priest of the Jews."[21] The positions have no territorial definition. Hyrcanus is to hold sway not simply in Judaea but over the Jews in general. That suggests endorsement for the exercise of authority throughout the diaspora.[22]

The endorsement receives reiteration in a *senatus consultum,* issued shortly thereafter to ratify Caesar's edict and reproduced, in part, by Josephus. Hyrcanus and his offspring will possess rule over the nation of the Jews. And, in his capacity as high priest and ethnarch, he will serve as protector of those Jews who suffer injustice.[23] There seems little question that this sanctions Hyrcanus' ascendancy in the diaspora.[24] The decision was to receive full publicity. Bronze tablets recording the provisions would be installed on the Capitol, with copies to be sent to Sidon, Tyre, and Ascalon, and announcements of the edicts to be made everywhere.[25]

Similar inferences may be drawn from another document (or perhaps a version of one of the previous documents). It records Caesar rewarding Hyrcanus for his virtue and benevolence and bestowing upon him and his children the offices of high priests and priests over Jerusalem and "the nation," with the same prerogatives and measures enjoyed by his ancestors.[26] Responsibility for τὸ ἔθνος (the nation) entailed acknowledgment of Hyrcanus' position in the diaspora.

Caesar conferred additional privileges upon the Jews and further distinctions upon Hyrcanus, including significant financial considerations. These all involved Palestine itself, not the diaspora, and thus are not directly pertinent to our purposes.[27] But the repeated elevation of Hyrcanus' prestige is notable, a policy confirmed once again shortly after Caesar's death when his benefactions to the Jews were recorded and inscribed at the behest of the consuls and in the presence of Hyrcanus' envoys.[28] And the Jewish leader is consistently referred to as high priest and ethnarch of the Jews, a position unlimited by geography.[29] Hyrcanus certainly took full account of his status and acted accordingly. After receiving the distinctions and authority accorded by Caesar in 47 BCE, he contacted the Roman governor of Asia, supplying him with documents that guaranteed to the Jews unhindered practice of their religious observances. The governor, C. Rabirius, subsequently sent a letter to the officials in Laodicea and to other cities in his province reaffirming Jewish rights.[30] In late 44 or early 43, when the Roman civil war had erupted again and vigorous recruitment resumed in the East, Hyrcanus wrote to the proconsul of Syria, P. Dolabella, at that time in the province of Asia, and requested exemption of the Jews from military service. The request was swiftly granted.[31] Hyrcanus plainly had no hesitation in stepping into the role of champion of Jews everywhere. No longer simply the chief official in Judaea, he became the representative of the nation scattered through the Mediterranean.

Why this solicitude for Hyrcanus? Caesar doubtless felt appreciation for the loyalty exhibited by the high priest and the assistance he had brought at a time of crisis. Those actions earned favor and honors.[32] But the extension of authority well beyond the borders of Judaea can hardly be due to gratitude alone. International politics took precedence. By beefing up the power of a staunch client ruler whose people were scattered through the eastern Mediterranean, Caesar could hope to substitute his own influence in a region that had hitherto largely owed its allegiance to Pompey and the Pompeians. For the Roman dictator, who had major battles awaiting in the West, a trusted collaborator with connections spread across the East would be an eminently valuable resource. Caesar did not empower Hyrcanus out of affection for the Jews. Neither sentiment nor sympathy motivated this policy. Nor do the decrees that strengthen the Judaean leader's foothold in the diaspora suggest any need for protection of the Jews from the animosity of the Greeks. Julius Caesar had his own agenda. Hyrcanus II was the fortunate beneficiary in a game of power politics, the Roman civil strife that engulfed the Mediterranean.[33]

Turbulent times doubtless stirred tensions within the Hellenic communities of Asia. And Hyrcanus' insistence upon throwing his weight around could not have helped matters. A letter from the magistrates of Laodicea to the Roman proconsul of Asia, C. Rabirius, provides an illuminating instance.[34] Hyrcanus had here taken the initiative, sending envoys to Rabirius with copies of documents affirming the rights of Jews to observe the Sabbath and other practices in accordance with their ancestral laws. Rabirius then directed that no one issue orders to the Jews, friends and allies of Rome, and that no one do them an injustice in his province.[35] The Laodiceans' letter, incorporating Rabirius' request, announces a willingness to comply. Does this mean that Jewish religious rites had been curtailed by the officialdom or inhabitants of Laodicea? Such is the unanimous scholarly verdict.[36] But a note of caution might well be injected here. Hyrcanus plays the principal role in the episode. His envoys bring the documents to the attention of Rabirius, and one of them, a certain Sopatros, actually delivers the proconsul's verdict in writing to Laodicea itself.[37] The high priest's intervention, in all likelihood, came not long after Caesar's establishment of his status as champion of diaspora Jews and watchdog for any injustices suffered by them.[38] Hyrcanus took on that responsibility eagerly and conspicuously. The line paraphrased from Rabirius' letter, that "no one commit an injustice against the Jews," surely came from Hyrcanus' prompting, and so, doubtless, did most or all of the phraseology. The fact that his agents had to deliver the relevant documents to the proconsul indicates that the Jewish issue was not uppermost in Rabirius' mind. His communications to Laodicea and other cities about Jewish privileges may have been no more than pro forma.[39] But they certainly augmented the stature of Hyrcanus among the Jews of Asia Minor. Serious constraints upon Jewish rites need not have motivated the ethnarch's intervention.[40] Hyrcanus was making his presence felt.

A comparable message about respecting the traditional practices of the Jews evidently went to Miletus as well. The next proconsul of Asia, P. Servilius Galba, probably 46 to 44, reported to the magistrates, council, and demos of that city a decision he rendered while conducting assizes at Tralles: after hearing arguments on both sides he determined that Jews in Miletus should not be prohibited from observing the Sabbath, performing other traditional rites, and controlling their produce.[41] Here for the first time we have notice of a direct complaint about mistreatment of Jews brought before the governor. A certain Milesian named Prytanis charged that the Milesians had imposed upon the Jews and prevented them from observing their ancestral practices, a violation of Roman policy.[42] How widespread or serious such restrictions may have been cannot be known. Servilius, in any case, did not automatically uphold the Jewish grievance. He heard arguments on both sides before rendering a verdict.[43] Prytanis perhaps took advantage of the governor's presence at Tralles to register a complaint. It may be significant that a private party raised the issue, not a representative of the high priest in Jerusalem. Prytanis had a hard time, possibly a hard case. The episode did not provoke an official embassy to the Roman authorities. And it would be hazardous to infer from it any systematic policy in Miletus to repress Jewish rights.[44]

Two additional decrees from two other cities in Asia Minor stand on record in these years and express conformity with Roman policy. Neither implies friction or hostility between Greeks and Jews in those cities. One issued from the assembly in Halicarnassus expressing its piety and zeal in following the recommendations of the Roman people, who had written to the city regarding their alliance with the Jews and the pursuance of their sacred rites and customary festivals and gatherings. The Halicarnassian decree guaranteed to the Jews their Sabbath observances, the conduct of their ancestral rites, and the building of synagogues. It even added a sanction: fines would be paid by any public officials or private citizens who interfered with the Jews.[45] The document does not allude to any incident, let alone any policy by the city, that prompted the Roman request. Nor did the Romans necessarily put Halicarnassus on special notice. The written communication mentioned in the decree may refer to one of Caesar's general pronouncements or to a letter dispatched by the proconsul C. Rabirius, who wrote to several cities about the maintenance of Jewish religious practices.[46] Halicarnassus simply broadcast its adherence to Roman pronouncements and respect for Jewish institutions.

A comparable decree, even more generous to the Jews, was promulgated by the council and demos of Sardis. It declared that Jewish citizens dwelling in their city had continually enjoyed great benefits from the Sardians. When representatives of the Jews announced that their freedom and laws had been restored by the Romans and asked that they be permitted to engage in all their customary practices, the Sardian governing bodies readily concurred. The decree specifies the Jews' right to gather on particular days to fulfill their religious requirements, to build and inhabit their own structures, and to obtain food suitable for their dietary demands from city officials.[47] No mention occurs here of Roman urging in the matter. The Jews themselves act as the pressure group. They allude to the fact that their freedom and laws have been reinstated by the Romans, a reference presumably, as in the Halicarnassian decree, to Caesar's affirmation that Jews everywhere should have the final say on all issues concerning the regulation of their own practices. But they present the position directly to the Sardian government and rely on no Roman intermediary. The decree conveys a magnanimous response.[48] The fact that Sardis not only endorses their request but notes that Jews have always received numerous and substantial benefits from the city is significant.[49] The statement accords with the letter of a Roman magistrate sent a few years earlier in 49 during the heavy recruitment in Asia for the opening of civil war. L. Antonius wrote to Sardis on the request of Jewish envoys, who maintained that they had from time immemorial possessed their own association and their own place of gathering in Sardis where they could adjudicate their affairs, and they sought sanction to continue the practice.[50] The need for reaffirmation on both occasions suggests that matters did not always run smoothly. But it is plain that Jews had a long-established presence in Sardis, one that was upheld by the city fathers and reconfirmed in a time of turmoil.

Only one document that falls in this period specifies direct state action to curtail Jewish ritual practices. A Roman magistrate composed a letter reporting appeals from Jews in Delos and some of those sojourning there who complained that they were prohibited by statute from practicing their customary rites. The magistrate declares that he frowns upon such restrictions and recommends that, if any enactment be directed against Jews, friends and allies of Rome, it should be repealed.[51] That is clear testimony for official action by a Greek community against Jewish sacred customs. But how far does it allow for generalization? The text is riddled with problems and peculiarities. The name of the official who sent the letter is much disputed and probably corrupt, leaving the date uncertain and the circumstances obscure. The title of the magistrate is given in an odd form. Even the location to which the missive was directed cannot be determined with confidence. The nearest one comes to some solidity amidst these shifting sands is a reference to "Gaius Caesar," seemingly alive and in charge, which would put the document in the mid-40s.[52] But the context eludes us. Those years constituted a brief period of peace in the East. Caesar's victory at Zela in 47 brought all of Asia Minor firmly into his camp. The dictator's remaining battles were now in the West. His appointed governors could display magnanimity to the eastern communities which, as epigraphic testimony reveals, gained a whole range of benefits from Rome in these years of reconstruction and displays of gratitude.[53] It would be an appropriate time for communities and people to apply to Caesar's appointees for redress of grievances and the support of the imperial power. Why Delos should have statutes on the books that limited Jewish religious activity—or how long they had been on the books—cannot be determined. There had been both a Jewish and a Samaritan presence, indeed very probably a synagogue, on the island for at least a century, but we have no record of their relations with the authorities.[54] The Roman civil war in the East created a new situation and doubtless intensified internal friction. Divided loyalties in Delos and elsewhere may well have provoked measures of state control over dissident or potentially dissident groups. Jews, among others, could serve as convenient scapegoats. The release of pressure after 47 significantly altered the circumstances, and it was a logical time for Delian Jews to seek reversal of the measures. The episode need not signal any long-term campaign of repression.

The death of Caesar in March 44 brought heightened uncertainty and insecurity in the empire. It causes no surprise that Hyrcanus II, one of the dictator's prime beneficiaries, hastened to send delegates to Rome to assure the maintenance of his own interests and those of his people. Hyrcanus' envoys were there in April when the consuls M. Antonius and P. Dolabella promoted measures to ratify all the *acta* of the fallen Caesar. Among them was a *senatus consultum* acknowledging his directives regarding the Jews and declaring that they must be properly inscribed and archived. Hyrcanus' representatives doubtless prompted the move, and they were present, duly recorded as witnesses to the senatorial decree.[55]

Hyrcanus did not stop there. Conflict between the appointees of Caesar and his assassins spilled over quickly to Asia, creating potential hazards for Jewish prerogatives endorsed by the dictator. Dolabella obtained the provincial assignment of Syria, but took the opportunity to gather troops and cash in Asia Minor on the way. He also directed the murder of C. Trebonius, one of the plotters against Caesar and then governor of Asia in early 43.[56] Civil war threatened to erupt again in the region—and heavy recruitment was already in process. Hyrcanus made sure to contact Dolabella as soon as possible to reiterate the privileges previously accorded to the Jews. His agent asked for and obtained exemption from military services and maintenance of traditional practices for his people. Josephus preserves a letter from Dolabella in January, 43, to the city of Ephesus, the principal center of the province, confirming those rights.[57] The missive explicitly names Hyrcanus and his envoy as bringing the matter to Dolabella's notice, thus underscoring the high priest's authority in the diaspora. It also notably cites precedent for the privileges: previous governors had done the same thing.[58] And Dolabella instructs the Ephesians to send copies of his letter to other cities. From the point of view of the Roman general, this emphasized continuity with earlier policy (both Pompeian and Caesarian), gave a sense of stability to the situation, and reiterated a connection with the leader of Jews throughout the East.

Dolabella's letter, it has been observed, speaks simply of military exemption for Jews without specifying that they need be Roman citizens, as had been the case when Lentulus granted that privilege in 49. The action is normally interpreted as a sweeping change in Roman policy, extending immunity to a far larger number of Jews.[59] But that may place too much weight on the wording and not enough on the historical circumstances. If the suggestion offered above concerning Lentulus is correct, he directed his gesture toward those who might be resentful of too broad an exemption for Jews. It surely did not represent a means to enroll non-citizens in substantial numbers. In 43, either the need for such discretion no longer existed, or the language reported by Josephus was broad and inexact. One can hardly imagine that numerous Jews who might otherwise have been conscripted could now breathe a sigh of relief. Hyrcanus had sought confirmation for his *prostasia* over diaspora Jews, and Dolabella gave notice of continued favor to an ethnic group within his domain, thus to strengthen his hand in the coming conflict. The testimony says nothing about Roman sentiment or relief of Jewish oppression. Political considerations were paramount.

But political circumstances changed swiftly in the turbulent months that followed the death of Caesar. Dolabella himself was slain in Syria in the summer of 43, defeated by the forces of the "Liberators" under the anti-Caesarian leader C. Cassius. A reversal of fortunes in Asia Minor seemed imminent. The other principal conspirator against Caesar, the celebrated M. Brutus, gathered troops and cash in Asia to prepare for the onslaught of those carrying Caesar's banner, in late 43 and early 42. Jews, one might well imagine, felt increasing anxiety about the vulnerability of rights guaranteed by Caesar and the Caesarians. Whether Hyrcanus intervened is unrecorded—and unlikely. He had perhaps been too compromised by association with the Caesarian party. But, as another Josephan document discloses, the Jews of Ephesus, probably representing the interests of Jews in the Roman province generally, felt no qualms about appealing to Brutus, the assassin of Caesar. The document conveys a decree by the demos of Ephesus in response to a request by Brutus, who had, in turn, been petitioned by Ephesian Jews to reconfirm their right to observe the Sabbath and other customs without interference.[60] The decree acknowledges Roman support for Jewish entitlements and asserts that no Jew should be prohibited from observing the Sabbath or be fined for doing so.[61] The text has served to reinforce the theory that Jews fell victim to Greek constraint of their practices, suffered monetary penalties when engaged in them, and required Roman protection to feel secure.[62] But the context, once again, is critical. A shift in the power balance had put anti-Caesarian forces in control in the province of Asia. For Jews concerned about the continuity of their prerogatives, application to Brutus was essential. The degree to which the officialdom in Ephesus had actually imposed restraints upon Jewish customs and levied fines for the practice of them cannot be known. The Ephesian edict does not prove rampant repression. The actions of the Jews have more to do with courting Brutus and entrenching their status within the new power structure than with suffering suppression by Ephesus.

Another reversal of fortunes, however, followed soon thereafter. Brutus and Cassius fell at Philippi in late 42, as did the cause of the "Liberators."[63] M. Antonius, avenger of Caesar and triumvir with full authority, soon moved into the East to fill the vacuum. Not surprisingly, Hyrcanus II seized the occasion, as he had in the past, to gain advantage for himself and his people. Envoys from the high priest hastened to meet Antony when he arrived in Ephesus in early 41, seeking the assistance of the Roman dynast in recouping losses suffered under his political enemies. Josephus preserves three documents relevant to the renewal of relations: Antony's reply to Hyrcanus and two letters sent by the Roman to the people of Tyre.[64]

Antony had every reason to resume the connection with Hyrcanus, a valuable asset in entrenching his own influence in the eastern part of the empire. His letter to the high priest stressed the justice of his cause, the delivery of vengeance against the foul assassins of Caesar, and appreciation for the loyalty of the Jewish nation. Antony reported that messages had been sent to various cities demanding that any Jews sold into slav-

ery by Cassius or his officers be restored to their former status, that the
Tyrians return all Jewish possessions and refrain from any violence against
Jews, and, most notably, that the Jews enjoy all the benefits granted them
by Dolabella and himself.[65] The last remark referred to the ratification
of Caesar's edicts on behalf of the Jews promulgated by Antony and
Dolabella upon the death of the dictator and in the presence of Hyrcanus'
envoys in 44.[66] Antony here underscored continuity in a relationship of
mutual benefit that had only temporarily been interrupted by the wickedness of Caesar's foes.

The letters to Tyre rebuked the Tyrians for seizing Jewish territory in the
time of Cassius' proconsulship and insisted upon full restoration of property and persons, with judicial proceedings to be brought against any who
failed to comply with the triumvir's edict.[67] The first missive in particular
stressed the role and authority of Hyrcanus.[68] Like Caesar before him, Antony recognized the value of shoring up the position of this trusted client
ruler to entrench his own party's influence in the East. The documents apply essentially to the recovery of Jewish losses in or near the homeland. But
the reception and warm treatment of Hyrcanus' envoys in Ephesus advertised the ethnarch's position among diaspora Jews in Asia Minor as well.

The declarations of Antony certainly reaffirmed and enhanced
Hyrcanus' prestige. Yet here, as in the case of Caesar, Jewish interests
hardly took top priority. A noteworthy clause concluded Antony's first letter to Tyre. Having endorsed Hyrcanus' claims to lost property, the triumvir added that if the Tyrians have any claims against Hyrcanus in turn, he
will adjudicate them personally when he arrives. The Romans, so Antony
insisted, act in even-handed fashion when judging disputes among their allies.[69] They would have the final say, unfettered by obligations to any nation or people. As usual, Roman leaders kept the objectives of their own
nation and their own faction uppermost in mind. The demands of civil war
and the actions of Roman dynasts created the special circumstances that
provoked the documents recorded by Josephus in the 40s BCE. The documents do not attest to general policies in Greek states toward Jews, let
alone to Roman attitudes toward that people.

A quarter of a century elapsed after the missives of Antony in 41 before
the next recorded measure concerning Jews issued from a Roman magistrate in the East. And it carries alarming implications. Peace and security
had descended upon Asia after the victory of Octavian, the future Augustus, at Actium in 31. A period of reconstruction and reconciliation could
follow. Yet in 14, M. Agrippa, principal lieutenant of Augustus, his son-in-
law, and a man entrusted with oversight of eastern affairs, was approached

by the Jews of Ionia with poignant pleas. They protested mistreatment by the cities of the region: Jews were prohibited from observing their own religious laws, compelled to attend judicial hearings on their holy days, stripped of the monies destined for the Temple in Jerusalem, dragooned into military service, and forced to spend their income on unwanted civic duties, despite all the assurances received from Roman pronouncements in the past.[70] What had happened in the meantime?

Economic deprivations in Asia Minor would seem a logical inference. Financial problems in the cities in the aftermath of war might turn them against a minority group that benefited from exemptions and special privileges.[71] The region's history in the years after M. Antony's arrival offers support for this analysis. In 41 Antony himself insisted that the provincials in Asia supply cash to pay the sums he owed his soldiers, demanding a total equivalent to ten years of taxes to be paid in a two-year period. As this came on the heels of the heavy exactions levied by Brutus and Cassius, Asia could barely shoulder the burden. The triumvir appointed his own agents to make certain that the revenues were gathered. Antony was generous to those who had supported his cause, thus increasing the hardships upon those who had been foolish enough not to do so. Matters only got worse in the following year when the renegade Roman Q. Labienus, now in the service of the Parthians, invaded the province, added his own impositions, and provoked a retaliatory mission by Ventidius Bassus and his army dispatched on the orders of Antony. A series of embassies came to Rome in the early 30s from Greek cities in Asia Minor seeking relief from tribute and other privileges. Antony's determination to mount an expedition against Parthia cannot have helped the situation. In 36, Sex. Pompey, fresh from defeat in Sicily, brought his remaining followers to Asia Minor where he could expect to play upon lingering attachment to the Pompeian name, thus provoking yet another war in the area. And by 32 Antony and Cleopatra engaged in major mobilization to prepare for the great contest against Octavian, still a further drain upon the resources of Asia.[72] The cities must have been exhausted of resources and energy.

But that does not tell the whole tale. The battle of Actium in 31 halted this slide. Octavian may have initially punished some of the towns of Asia that had backed Antony, but, for the most part, he determined to rebuild the region. Numerous benefits were bestowed upon the cities, and the coinage minted at places like Ephesus and Pergamum shows a renewed prosperity. Other communities gained freedom and autonomy. And the *koinon* of Asia enjoyed sufficient affluence to conduct major festivals in honor of the goddess Roma and Augustus. The *princeps* showed special concern for

the region, establishing an extraordinary *imperium* for Agrippa to oversee
its administration in 23 and then visiting it himself from 21 to 19. Additional benefactions stand on record for the major cities of Asia, and new
cults sprang up to honor Augustus in individual communities, quite apart
from the imperial worship by the *koinon* of Asia itself. Taxation was set
upon a firmer and more systematic foundation, thus lending a greater sense
of security to the whole area. The renewed vigor gains confirmation in the
large number of cities that issued their own coins and the roster of places
that could claim the designation of "freedom." Agrippa himself delivered
numerous benefits to the communities of Asia Minor, receiving honors and
distinctions in return.[73]

A surprising conclusion follows. The complaints aired before Agrippa in
14 BCE by the Jews of Ionia did not come, as one might expect, in the period of financial stringency and economic devastation, but at a time when
the region had recovered and prosperity was at hand. Just when the restraints placed upon Jews were imposed by Ionian cities cannot be known.
But there is nothing to show that they were in force for two decades or
more. It may perhaps be significant that when Agrippa and then Augustus
were in Asia in the late 20s, we have no record of any Jewish complaints
brought before the Roman leaders. Expanded opportunities rather than
economic constraints seem to have prompted the episode.

Who, in fact, initiated the hearing in 14? This is a serious and interesting question. Josephus, in *Jewish Antiquities* 16.27, indicates that the Jews
came to the Roman commander to express their grievances against the
Ionians. But elsewhere, in *Jewish Antiquities* 12.125, the historian gives a
very different reason for the opening of the controversy: the Ionians contacted Agrippa first and requested that the *politeia* should be restricted to
them alone and should not include Jews, who declined to worship the gods
of the Ionians. The verdict of Agrippa, in both passages, granted Jews the
right to observe their own customs, thus suggesting that the issue at stake
was constraint on religious rites, not the sharing of civic privileges. And
that is the conclusion of most commentators.[74] But the question deserves
further scrutiny. Would Josephus have gratuitously invented the Ionian request to limit Jewish political rights and then have Agrippa affirm only
their religious privileges? It would have been better to pass over the request
in silence, as he did in Book 16.[75] An initiative on the part of the Ionians in
14, with Agrippa in their territory, makes perfectly good sense. At a time
when the region could anticipate additional benefits from the Roman government, they were not eager to share them too widely. Whatever *politeia*
may mean, it indicates the right to some form of participation in the affairs

of the cities. By limiting that right, the Ionians would also reduce the numbers of those who could enjoy the advantages of Roman *beneficia* to the communities.

The Jews, as it happens, could seize the opportunity as well. Agrippa had arrived with Herod, king of Judaea, who had accompanied him on much of his eastern swing. Herod could be counted on to support their cause, and in his entourage was the gifted and eloquent historian Nicolas of Damascus, who advocated the Jewish position before Agrippa. The Jews neatly turned the tables by pointing to a number of prerogatives to which they were entitled but which had been denied. They specified the offenses as compulsion to appear in court on holy days, deprivation of monies designated for Jerusalem, the requirement to serve in the army, and the obligation to use sacred funds for civic purposes.[76] Did Ionian pressure on the Jews stem from resentment or animosity? It looks rather as if they sought to push the Jewish inhabitants of Ionian cities into a position where they could not claim the advantages bestowed by Roman favor upon the communities of Asia. Greek leaders knew well enough that Jews would not yield up their contributions to the Temple in Jerusalem, or appear in court on the Sabbath and holidays, or accept conscription into the armed forces. By assuring noncompliance, the Ionians could maintain that the Jews themselves had withdrawn, in effect, from the civic body. Hence, the appeal to Agrippa to limit *politeia* to the Greeks of the Ionian cities is perfectly consistent with the other measures. The two passages of Josephus dovetail.[77] Pragmatism may have carried greater weight with the Ionians than hostility toward Jews.

Agrippa had no easy task in the adjudication. Josephus supplies (or rather paraphrases) Nicolas' speech on behalf of the Jews, but provides no arguments on the other side.[78] Agrippa surely did not wish to offend either Greeks or Jews. The verdict, when it came, spoke only to the confirmation of Jewish rights to conduct their customary practices. That occurs in both narratives of Josephus. It simply reasserted standard Roman policy.[79] And it occurs also in the document cited by Josephus, a letter from Agrippa to the magistrates, council, and people of Ephesus. There the Roman commander specifies that Jews should have full control of the monies that go to the Temple, that anyone who confiscates that cash is liable to punishment as a temple-robber, even if he seeks asylum in a shrine, and that the Jews cannot be compelled to appear in court on the Sabbath.[80] On the matter of restricting *politeia* to Greeks, he claimed unwillingness to meddle. Agrippa upheld previous pronouncements, but broke no new ground. Roman leaders regularly confirmed prior decisions, without necessarily expecting to implement them. The Jews were by no means singled out in this regard.[81] Agrippa expressed willingness to consider further Jewish requests—but only if they did not cause difficulty for Roman rule.[82] The interests of the Roman empire remained foremost.

Once again, particular context and circumstances created the issue and determined the outcome. The events do not show repeated friction or long-standing enmity between Greek and Jew in Asia. A period of economic recovery with high expectations for the future encouraged some Greek leaders to limit the numbers of those eligible to share in the benefits. Agrippa's visit triggered an attempt to institutionalize the restriction, but also provoked counterarguments by a spokesman of the Judaean king whose hold on power had been endorsed by Rome. The verdict of Agrippa represented a commitment to continuity—not a Roman campaign on behalf of beleaguered Jews.

The problem, however, would not go away. Despite Agrippa's pronouncement, the Greek cities of Asia persisted in pressuring Jews either to act as full members of the community or to sever ties and be excluded from its services. The annual payments to the Temple in Jerusalem were a particular sore point. They amounted to substantial sums, and they involved pilgrimages to the Holy City that made the practice especially conspicuous. But the practice itself was hardly new. The Jews of Asia had been collecting the cash, city by city, for at least three-quarters of a century—and probably much longer.[83] Why should the city fathers make a special issue of it in the early years of the Augustan principate? That they were strapped for cash is unattested and unlikely. Circumstances had been much worse before. By focusing on the contributions to the Temple, they were pushing the Jews on a most sensitive matter. This would force the issue. If the Jews insisted on maintaining the practice, as of course they would, the municipal governments could regard this as opting out of civic responsibilities and debar Jews from the services and benefits of the community.

The Jews naturally represented the process in a different fashion when appealing to higher authority. Josephus embellishes the account further by having Jewish delegates deplore the inhumanity of the Greeks and complain of insult and injury when applying to Augustus himself.[84] The historian proceeds to convey an Augustan edict to the *koinon* of Asia in 12 BCE or later. Augustus' statement is straightforward and to the point—but hardly suggests that the situation had reached crisis proportions. The *princeps*, like others before him, called upon precedent. He cited the relationship of Caesar and Hyrcanus, and reasserted the policy that Jews should live under their own customs in accordance with ancestral law—

just as they had under Hyrcanus. All of this is conventional language. Then came the specifics. The sacred contributions to Jerusalem should be inviolable, and Jews should not be obliged to give security in legal suits on the Sabbath or the day before. Those who steal sacred books or monies from Jewish meeting houses commit sacrilege and will have their property confiscated and transferred to Rome. And the edict closes with a dire warning: violators of these provisions will suffer no small penalty.[85]

Augustus, so it seems, anticipated the general declaration with instructions to the proconsul of Asia, C. Norbanus Flaccus. Josephus transmits the mandate, or a part thereof, which directed that Jews are not to be interfered with when they gather sacred funds to send to Jerusalem.[86] And we have a record of two letters sent by Norbanus Flaccus to implement Augustus' orders. One went to Sardis, announcing that the *princeps* had written to assure that Jews not be hindered in gathering sums to be sent to Jerusalem.[87] Flaccus sent the second letter to Ephesus with essentially the same message.[88] Presumably others of comparable nature went to various cities in the province. It appears that the imperial pronouncements of Augustus and Agrippa and the reiterations of proconsuls did not always have the desired effect. The Ionians persisted, and the Romans had not resisted. Agrippa had to make much the same demands as Augustus.

The effectiveness of Augustus' general manifesto in 12 BCE or later cannot be assessed with confidence. But it may be relevant that Josephus supplies no further evidence of friction regarding Jews in the province of Asia. He does cite a letter by Iullus Antonius, governor of Asia some time after his consulship of 10 BCE, to the officialdom of Ephesus. The missive, prompted by Jews who had visited the governor perhaps at the outset of his term, confirmed the right of Jews to adhere to their own laws and customs and to bring their offerings to Jerusalem without hindrance. And the proconsul explicitly cites the directives of Augustus and Agrippa (no less than three times) as precedent and authority for his own declaration.[89] The document does not state and need not imply that Jews had suffered in the meantime. It represents pro forma pronouncement by the new governor to restate continuity in policy—or posture. The problem, so far as one can judge, simmered down. And it confined itself to a very short period in the midst of the Augustan principate. One would do well not to draw sweeping conclusions about hostility to Jews by Greeks or about Rome's ride to the rescue. The absence of additional documentation may mean that the Greeks saw no further point in exposing Jewish lack of civic consciousness by laying hands on the funds destined for Jerusalem and demanding court appearances on the Sabbath. Or, equally likely, Augustus, having stated his position (a perfectly conventional one), let matters take their course. Rome had a long record of issuing declarations without seeing to their implementation.[90]

Roman leaders found it useful and convenient to make generous pronouncements to peoples and states who sought their favors. Agrippa made a similar gesture in a letter to the council at Argos, assuring them of Rome's support of their position and restoration of their rights.[91] And ample testimony attests to various occasions on which Augustus himself declared to Greeks his backing for the restoration of their sacred shrines, lands, and properties, the return of confiscated statues of the gods, and the punishment of those who committed sacrilege.[92] In short, the Jews were by no means alone in seeking Roman assistance on matters related to their religious observances—or in receiving assertions of Roman favor.

The documents transmitted by Josephus on the triangular relations among Greeks, Jews, and Romans in Asia Minor tell an ambiguous tale. On the face of it, they present a picture of Hellenic persecution and Roman guardianship. But closer examination demands a more nuanced judgment. Special circumstances and particular exigencies called them forth. And few of them give reason to suppose Greek oppression or Roman deliverance.

Josephus' collection of texts is circumscribed in time and place. Almost all of them apply to Jews in the province of Asia. And the vast majority belong to a few years that fall within the period from Caesar's crossing of the Rubicon to the middle of Augustus' principate. That hardly allows for extensive extrapolation.

The first dossier refers exclusively to the year 49, perhaps spilling into 48, when the consul L. Lentulus and his subordinate officers ardently levied troops in Asia to brace the Pompeian cause for the conflict against Caesar. The edicts and letters exempt Jews from military service in the Roman legions, a harmless and easy concession to make in the interests of a united front in the East. Far from preventing Greek encroachment on Jewish rights, Lentulus anticipated any Greek resentment by limiting his exemption officially to Jews who had Roman citizenship. No friction or conflict lay behind this dossier.

The next group of documents concerns the elevation and support accorded to Hyrcanus II, high priest and ethnarch of the Jews, by Julius Caesar during the years of his dictatorship in the mid-40s BCE. These attest to Caesar's desire for a strong and loyal ruler not only in Judaea but for the diaspora who would help to shore up his position in the eastern empire, where Pompeian sentiment had long been dominant. Pragmatism, not sentiment, dictated Caesarian missives and decrees for Hyrcanus and his people.

The pronouncements of Caesar encouraged Jews to seek confirmation of their rights in various cities, whether through direct initiative or via Roman intermediacy. Proconsuls of Asia, prodded by Jewish representatives, dispatched missives to Laodicea and Miletus reasserting the Jews' privilege of practicing ancestral rites. Decrees from Halicarnassus and Sardis approved Roman policy explicitly or implicitly. In only one of those cases, at Miletus, is there direct testimony to a complaint about Greek mistreatment of Jews. And there is only one instance of reference to official state action against the Jews—at Delos. These count more as exceptions than as illustrations. That some friction surfaced in the aftermath of Caesar's victory in the East, at a time when recriminations must have flown against those suspected of harboring the wrong sympathies, is not surprising. Jews provided convenient targets. But such repression arose from ad hoc circumstances, not considered policy—and appears only rarely in the documents.

The outbreak of renewed civil war after the slaying of Caesar naturally scrambled loyalties again. Jews applied in turn to Caesarian partisans and to those of his enemies in order to assure continuance of their prerogatives. In tumultuous times, reassurances were welcome and desirable—not only for Jews but for those who could use their backing in the conflict. Hostilities among Romans rather than persecution by Greeks provoked Jewish anxieties. And the letters of M. Antony, after defeat of the "Liberators," gave additional reassurance, restored relations, and confirmed allegiance— all in the interests of the Roman triumvir.

Actium brought peace to Asia Minor. And prosperity came on its heels. Paradoxically enough, that may not have been good for Jews. Curtailment of Jewish rights, particularly interference with the transfer of funds to Jerusalem, occurred in an era of rising rather than falling expectations. That suggests something other than anti-semitism. Greek communities hesitated to share too widely the benefits of a more affluent age and manufactured means to segregate those who could be targeted as failing to meet civic obligations. Standard Roman pronouncements followed, this time by Augustus and Agrippa, to reiterate previous policy, duly repeated by governors of Asia. Of actual Roman intervention there is no record. The documents belong only to a short period. And the issue seems to have dissipated quickly.

In sum, the materials assembled by Josephus fall well short of demonstrating persistent persecution by Greeks or the salvation of Jews by Rome. The incidents were episodic and infrequent, engendered by special circumstances, and readily resolved. There was no campaign on the part of Greek

cities in Asia to harass an oppressed minority. As the documents themselves show, the Jews of Sardis had long had their own associations and
settled their own judicial disputes; the Jews of Ionia could be expected to
carry out public liturgies (which required considerable means); and in every city of Asia Jews had no difficulty in gathering substantial funds to
deliver to Jerusalem. Josephus himself acknowledged the fact by having
Nicolas of Damascus speak of Jewish affluence and success in Ionia.[93]
Romans issued periodic pronouncements expressing support for Jewish religious rites and ancestral conventions—a few prompted by actual constraints placed upon Jews, the large majority simply repetitive assertions
citing the precedents of predecessors. This constituted common Roman
practice, far more disinterested than interventionist. Proconsuls might adjudicate disputes between Jews and Greeks brought before their tribunals—and not always in Jewish favor. But Josephus never records a substantive Roman action to safeguard Jews in need of protection. And he
would hardly have omitted any. Rome's decisions derived from the interests of its empire or its leaders, not from any general policy of "toleration,"
let alone from concern for minor ethnic groups within its domain. The
Jews of Asia rarely required defense against Greeks. And the Romans had
bigger fish to fry.

Civic and Sacral Institutions in the Diaspora

Cᴏᴍᴍᴜɴᴀʟ ʟɪꜰᴇ sustained the Jews of the diaspora. The institutions they created and the activities they conducted supplied the means to preserve traditions and advance the interests of the clan. But they did not promote private enclaves or segregated seclusion. Jews strove to engender circumstances that would enable them to maintain their ancient heritage while engaging comfortably and productively in the lands of the classical world wherein they dwelled.

The synagogue was ubiquitous in the diaspora. That fact alone carries wide significance and implications. Jews dwelled almost everywhere around the Mediterranean, and the synagogue, so far as our evidence allows, served as a prime signal of Jewish existence. And, most notably, apart from a minimal handful of exceptions, the synagogue's activities proceeded without disruption or hindrance, a familiar element in the society wherein it functioned. That speaks volumes about the connection of diaspora Jews to the Greco-Roman world in which they found themselves.

Almost any definition of the term "synagogue" runs into difficulty and dispute, or at least raises a large number of questions. An arbitrary rendering is inevitable, but the following may be (relatively) non-controversial: a synagogue was a structure in which or an institution through which Jews could engage in communal activity that helped to define or express a collective identity. This does not imply that synagogues had similar physical features, personnel, or functions across the Mediterranean world.[1] Nor does it preclude changes in structure, activities, or even objectives in the course of decades and centuries. Nor indeed does it require consistency in the application of ancient terminology. The degree of uniformity in time or space simply eludes us. But the definition given above will serve suitably for present purposes.

The extent of synagogal dispersion is itself breathtaking. The volume of data, particularly the material evidence, expands substantially for the period after the destruction of the Temple. Hence the bulk of scholarly study has focused on the later era. But Second Temple testimony, although often fragmentary and frustrating, is strikingly widespread in geographic extent, more than enough to disclose the broad-ranging reach of the synagogue. The survey here will be relatively brief, since fuller studies can readily supply details.[2]

Syria serves as a convenient first stop. A spillover into the neighboring territory would hardly be surprising. Josephus, in fact, proclaims that the Jewish dispersal is heaviest in Syria.[3] He adds the rather dubious proposition that at Antioch, where the Jews were most numerous, they received full civic privileges at the hands of Antiochus IV—and even observes that Antiochus' successors restored to the synagogue all the brass offerings he had confiscated from the Temple![4] But, whatever the embellishments or confusion of Josephus may have been, there is no reason to question the existence of a large Jewish community in Antioch and their membership in a synagogue well before the time of the Great Revolt. They engaged in religious worship, according to Josephus, and their observances even attracted curious Greeks in large numbers.[5] A substantial community settled also in Damascus. As is notorious, Saul (not yet Paul) was struck down on the road to Damascus, where he was heading for the synagogues, armed with a letter from the High Priest. And it was there, after his recovery and conversion, that he preached to the Jews (rather than murdering them).[6] We cannot determine just when they arrived and how long they had been in Damascus. But large numbers of Jews were there when revolt broke out in 66 CE.[7] And they surely did not arrive recently. The principal cities of Syria had housed Jewish synagogues for quite some time.[8]

Jews had found their way to Egypt well before the Greco-Roman period. The notable sanctuary at Elephantine that served a Jewish military colony dates back at least to the sixth century. But the influx speeded up markedly after Ptolemy I's campaigns in Palestine in the late fourth century. The results for Alexandria have already received discussion in Chapter 2. The city enjoyed a plethora of synagogues. And one can go further. A combination of documentary and literary sources attest to Jewish settlements with synagogues (or rather *proseuchai,* as the Egyptian evidence characterizes them) at various sites in the land.[9]

Jews had established themselves in Middle Egypt by the second half of the third century BCE. A stele from Arsinoe-Crocodilopolis that dates to the reign of Ptolemy III (246–221 BCE) records the dedication of a *proseuche* in honor of that ruler, his sister-wife, and their children.[10] And another such structure is attested at Alexandrou-Nesos by a papyrus of

218 BCE, addressed to Ptolemy IV, requesting the recovery of a stolen cloak from a culprit who had sought refuge in a *proseuche*.[11] The institution obviously enjoyed a position of prestige and was acknowledged by the community as a place of sanctuary.

Synagogues show up in Lower Egypt as well (quite apart from Alexandria and its environs, treated earlier). A *proseuche* rose in Xenephyris on a branch of the Nile. An inscription supplies the evidence, composed in now familiar formulas: the Jews dedicated a new gate of their *proseuche* in honor of Ptolemy VIII and two queens. That puts the gate in the later part of the second century BCE. The *proseuche* must have been there before.[12] Comparable language in comparable dedications reveals synagogues in Athribis and Nitriai from the late second and early first centuries BCE.[13] The documents supply a concrete foundation for the otherwise fanciful tale of III Maccabees that has Jews celebrate their liberation and triumph in the time of Ptolemy IV by erecting a stele and dedicating a *proseuche* at Ptolemais. Whether they actually did so or not matters little. Such actions would be fully in step with convention.[14]

As is notorious, a Jewish temple emerged in Leontopolis in the mid-second century BCE, founded by the refugee High Priest Onias IV, with the sanction and patronage of Ptolemy VI. The story, complex and controversial, has been investigated many times and need not be rehashed here.[15] Whatever the character and significance of that institution may have been, the justification for it, as put in the mouth of the High Priest by Josephus, is striking. Onias sought the authority of Ptolemy for his temple on the ground that he (Onias) had visited various sites in Egypt where Jews dwelled and had found that most of them possessed shrines *(hiera)* of an unsuitable nature.[16] The meaning of that strange statement remains impenetrable. The *hiera*, most probably, however, allude to synagogues scattered in the Jewish communities of Egypt. The nature of the alleged improprieties resists inquiry. But the testimony, tainted or confused as it may be, corresponds to the rest of our evidence. Jewish synagogues were a familiar part of the Egyptian landscape.

Jews had made their way also to Cyrenaica on the North African coast—and in significant numbers. Ptolemy I allegedly sent a group of Jewish settlers there to reinforce his control of the area.[17] The numbers clearly grew. By the early first century BCE, according to Strabo (writing two generations later), the city of Cyrene was divided into four groupings: citizens, farmers, metics, and Jews.[18] The Jews were among those whose rights and traditions, such as sending sacred monies to Jerusalem, were reasserted and guaranteed by Agrippa around 14 BCE.[19] That the Jews of Cyrenaica established synagogues in the cities they inhabited can readily be assumed. And explicit testimony comes from an inscription of Berenice, one of the key sites of that region, dated to the second year of Nero's reign, i.e., 55 CE. The stone records a list of donors who contributed to the repairs of a synagogue. Interestingly, the text employs the term *synagoge* in two quite different ways: it signifies both the structure to be repaired and the congregation of Jews in Berenice who authorized the erection of the stele and the honoring of the donors.[20] That a graphic declaration of gratitude to benefactors should be put on public display, in addition to the structure itself which they helped to refurbish, demonstrates that Jews took open pride in the maintenance of their own institutions and in announcing that maintenance to any interested party in the larger community.

A variety of literary references speak of Jews dwelling in Cyprus. Philo includes the island among sites that housed numerous Jewish settlements.[21] Hence it comes as no surprise to learn that the apostles Paul, Barnabas, and Mark proclaimed their message in synagogues of the Jews at Salamis, a chief city of the island.[22] And there is no reason to question it.

Jews, as is well known, scattered themselves all over Asia Minor. And they inhabited the cities in considerable numbers.[23] The fact gains clear confirmation from texts already discussed in other contexts: Cicero's references to the Jews of Asian cities who assiduously collected contributions for the Temple in Jerusalem, and Josephus' assemblage of documents on various communities in the Roman province of Asia which received authorization from the officialdom to carry out their traditional practices.[24] Josephus' transmitted documents do not make explicit mention of synagogues, but the paraphrase by Philo of Augustus' letter to the Roman governors in Asia gives the wanted phraseology: Jews had the right to assemble in their synagogues.[25] That, to be sure, is Philo's language. But he can hardly be far off. The travels of Paul and his colleagues in Asia took them frequently to Jewish synagogues in the cities of Asia Minor. Express testimony exists in the Acts of the Apostles for Pisidian Antioch, Iconium, and Ephesus.[26] And a famous inscription from Acmonia in Phrygia records honors bestowed by the synagogue (evidently the Jewish collective) upon men who had restored and refurbished the building which had originally been erected by a certain Julia Severa. The latter is known to us from independent testimony as a high priestess of the imperial cult in Acmonia in the time of Nero. Whether the initial structure bestowed by Julia Severa was itself a synagogue or was only subsequently transformed into one by the honorands of the document cannot be known. But the inscription indicates a clear continuity, and it is a reasonable inference that the benefactress commissioned the building for the Jewish community of her city.[27]

The testimony for Halicarnassus is nearly as explicit. The city's decree, probably in the 40s BCE, in response to a Roman request and conveyed by Josephus, awarded Jews the privileges of pursuing their own faith and traditions and of constructing synagogues *(proseuchai)* along the sea in accordance with conventional practice.[28] A similar conclusion can be drawn for Sardis, even without direct mention of "synagogues." A Sardian decree of these same years, also following Roman initiative, granted Jews the authority to gather together on the days and in the fashion dictated by their own laws and to construct and inhabit a place set aside for them by the authorities.[29] We can take for granted that the institution, even when not directly attested, served to attach Jews to a common identity in every city of Asia Minor where they gathered in any significant number.

That feature extends even to the shores of the Black Sea. Jews clustered in the cities of the Bosporan kingdom on the north and east coasts of the Black Sea, ancient Hellenic communities in which Jewish immigrants found welcome. The existence of synagogues in those cities is disclosed by a fascinating group of inscriptions that record the freeing of slaves. This remarkable treasure of documents, around ten in number, stems from the cities of Panticapaeum, Phanagoria, and Gorgippia. Three of them are datable to the first century CE, and the others, with similar language but no extant dates, probably fall in or around the same era. Manumission inscriptions, of course, are familiar from other Greek settings, most notably in Delphi where more than a thousand survive. The Temple of Apollo in that sacred city served as the site for these transactions and the repository of their records. It is therefore striking and significant to find comparable actions recorded with reference to the sanctuaries of the Jews in the remote regions of the Black Sea.

Standard formulas, with appropriate variations, mark the documents. And, although interpretation of the particulars generates dispute, a general picture takes form. Typically, the inscription declares the manumission of a slave or slaves in the *proseuche* and sets as the sole price of their freedom a continuing connection with the *proseuche* and the tutelage of the *synagoge* of the Jews. Such, for instance, appears in the best preserved of this collection, an inscription from Panticapaeum, dated explicitly to the year 80/81 CE.[30] The declaration is headed by a reference to the ruling monarch of the Bosporan region, a king identified as "friend of the emperor," "friend of the Romans," and "pious." There follows an indication of the date, then the affirmation by the slave owner that she emancipates her slave in the *proseuche,* and that he is free to move without constraint wherever he wishes, on the condition that he maintain dedication and attachment to the *proseuche,* under the joint supervision of the *synagoge* of the Jews.[31] Similar phraseology can be found in several inscriptions from the Black Sea communities.[32] The precise nature of the ex-slave's obligation to the *proseuche* cannot be determined with certainty and has led to considerable controversy. That heated issue can here be left aside.[33] No solid testimony shows that freedmen discharged religious duties or that they were expected to perform economic services. What the inscriptions do demonstrate quite unmistakably is that the solemn ceremony of manumission took place within the precinct of the *proseuche,* that the emancipated slave retained a close connection with the *proseuche,* and that the community itself (the *synagoge*) took responsibility for his guardianship.[34] This delivers a clear signal of collective solidarity.

The Book of Acts, with its register of Paul's travels, contains tantalizing testimony to synagogues in Macedon and Greece Proper—where the apostle endeavored to preach his message. Specific mentions of such structures occur for Philippi, Thessalonica, and Beroea in Macedon, Athens and Corinth in Greece. And the text employs both *proseuche* and *synagoge* to identify the institution.[35] Whatever suspicion one wants to cast upon the narrative (with its repetitiveness), the references to synagogues can stand. Philo had asserted (through the mouth of Agrippa I) that, among other places, Jews dwelled in Thessaly, Boeotia, Macedonia, Aetolia, Attica, Argos, Corinth, and most of the Peloponnese, including the best parts.[36] Independent testimony exists in abundance for Jews in these and other places of mainland Greece, some of them as early as the second century BCE.[37] We would surely have had to postulate synagogues for them anyway. The Book of Acts supplies welcome confirmation.[38]

The dispersal spread beyond the mainland. Jewish communities sprang up as well in the islands of the Aegean. The First Book of Maccabees conveys a letter from a Roman consul to Egypt in the mid-second century BCE, copies of which were sent to various communities, including the Aegean isles of Delos, Samos, Cos, and Rhodes.[39] The Jews on Delos receive explicit mention in two additional documents preserved by Josephus and dated to the mid-first century BCE, wherein Roman officials guaranteed rights and privileges for the Jewish inhabitants of the island.[40] Their presence in that location is striking and significant. Delos was a holy site, birthplace of Apollo, a point of pilgrimage, and furthermore a major commercial center, a key locus for trade and business, a pivotal place for a whole network of interconnections in the Mediterranean. It may also be the site of the earliest synagogue unearthed through archaeological excavation. The structure, discovered in 1912, went through at least two building phases, placed by excavators in the early second century BCE and the mid-first century BCE. That the building was, at least in its second incarnation, a synagogue has now won widespread scholarly consensus. Complaints by some that it does not contain the symbols and imagery familiar in later Jewish synagogues carry little weight. One cannot predicate expectations for second century BCE synagogues on the basis of artifacts characteristic of such structures three centuries later.[41]

A plausible case can be made for the structure as synagogue. The architectural plan of one portion of the building (Room A) suggests certain similarities with known synagogues. Epigraphic evidence provides a firmer footing. Four inscriptions found in two of the rooms transmit dedications to Theos Hypsistos (God Most High), a common formula employed by Jews—though not by them alone.[42] More tellingly, another dedication uncovered in the vicinity of the building was inscribed "for the *proseuche*."[43] And two remarkable funerary inscriptions from the neighboring island of Rheneia, which served as a burial place for Delians, summon the vengeance of Theos Hypsistos upon the murderers of two young girls, and include a reference to "the day on which every soul humbles itself with supplication"—very possibly an allusion to the Day of Atonement.[44] The cumulative testimony, while inconclusive, carries some weight.

The argument for identification of the structure as a synagogue gained marked support from a recent discovery. Two inscriptions, found very close to the building, attest to the existence of a community of Samaritans on Delos in the third and second centuries BCE. They declare the bestowal of honorific crowns upon benefactors and describe the bestowers as "Israelites on Delos who make offerings to holy Gerizim"—plainly a reference to Samaritans. And one of them honors a donor who backed construction and dedication with his own funds "for the *proseuche*."[45] Does this refer to a Samaritan synagogue independent of but proximate to the Jewish synagogue? Or is the archaeological synagogue itself Samaritan? That synagogues existed on Delos for each of the communities (whether adjoining or not) is perfectly possible. One of the Roman decrees transmitted by Josephus referred to "the Jews in Delos and some of the Jews dwelling in the vicinity." A Roman official could be forgiven for not distinguishing Jews from Samaritans on Delos.[46] Both people had established themselves on that sacred island and bustling depot. Both, in all likelihood, had instituted *proseuchai* to serve as vehicles for communal activities. And one of them employed the structure that constitutes the earliest synagogue unearthed by the spade.

Jews did not confine themselves to the eastern Mediterranean. They resided in Italy long before the destruction of the Temple. The great city of

Rome housed them at least by the mid-second century BCE. The experience of the Jews in Rome has already been examined at length and need not be repeated here. Philo locates them primarily in Trastevere. His comments are notable and pertinent: Augustus knew that the Jews had synagogues and gathered in them, especially on the Sabbath, and he left them intact.[47] There is no reason to question the statement, even though Philo's terminology *(proseuche)* may not have been employed by Roman Jews. Documentary evidence apparently confirms the claims of the philosopher. Funerary epitaphs from the Jewish catacombs in Rome deliver the names of at least eleven synagogues. Three of them are especially intriguing: the synagogues of the Augoustesioi, the Agrippesioi, and the Volumnesioi.[48] It is tempting to postulate that these institutions were named, respectively, after Augustus, Agrippa, and the Roman official Volumnius who supported Herod in his conflicts with the Arabs, thereby dating them all to the late first century BCE or early first century CE.[49] And still another synagogue is termed that "of the Hebrews," perhaps suggesting that it was the earliest of them all, so named to distinguish its members from other ethnic groups in Rome.[50] Caution, to be sure, needs to be exercised. The Jewish catacombs themselves probably date no earlier than the third century CE.[51] Hence the epitaphs cannot supply decisive demonstration of a Second Temple date for any of the synagogues. But the inference is logical and plausible. The large number of Jews settled in Rome during the late Republic and early Empire would surely have gathered in synagogues. Philo did not make it up.

Strong support comes from material evidence elsewhere in Italy. A Jewish synagogue was discovered forty years ago in, of all places, Ostia, the principal harbor for Rome itself, situated near the bank of the Tiber.[52] The visible structure, which includes distinctive Jewish features like an apsidal *aedicula* for Torah scrolls and characteristic imagery like a menorah, lulav, shofar, and ethrog, dates from the fourth century CE. But the excavator identified an earlier structure in *opus reticulatum* which she placed in the first century CE. That the initial building was also a synagogue cannot be established with certainty, especially because one or two major renovations took place before the present edifice. But the indications are potent. The earlier building shows a similar ground plan, possesses features quite different from typical private dwellings in Ostia, and even sported a colonnaded gateway. It seems reasonable to register it as a synagogue from the outset, later refurbished and embellished.[53] Ostia, the port city, took its lead from Rome, the capital of the empire, rather than the reverse. The presence of a synagogue in Ostia almost certainly entails a precedent in Rome.

Thus the Jews had created structures for communal life in two key cities of Italy. There were doubtless more that still await discovery. Even the fragmentary and scattered evidence that survives discloses a remarkable dispersion. Jewish synagogues of the Second Temple period stretched from the Black Sea to North Africa, and from Syria to Italy.

Geographic spread does not tell the whole story. Synagogues also had administrative structures and personnel. These were institutions with established practices, officialdom, and functions—no mere ad hoc arrangements for embattled or fretful diaspora Jews. Unfortunately, the bits and pieces that turn up in our testimony do not permit anything like a secure reconstruction of what these institutions actually did. Instead, we possess numerous titles of functionaries, with little indication of how they functioned. This creates frustration, but not complete paralysis.

Synagogues, it seems, shunned standardization. The idea that some sort of uniform pattern prevailed across the Mediterranean, still held by some, needs to be given up.[54] As is well known, Jewish communities went by more than one name. Even the edifice in which they met, as we have seen, sometimes had the designation *proseuche,* sometimes *synagoge.*[55] Nor do those terms exhaust the possibilities. The texts offer alternatives like *sabbateion, hieron, euxeion,* and *didaskaleion.*[56] There seems little value in seeking precision or technical terminology in the names applied to these institutions.

The same holds for the officialdom. A bewildering variety of officials appears in the evidence, resisting consistent compartmentalization. The post of *archisynagogos* (head of the synagogue) seems promising: that title can be found in both literary and epigraphic attestation, and it occurs with some frequency in an impressively wide range of places.[57] Do we have here the top rung of a Jewish diaspora hierarchy? Not likely. References to *archisynagogoi* show complex roles. In the New Testament, they evidently exercise authority in Jewish congregations.[58] But that authority can carry over into the political realm, as in the case of the *archisynagogos* who appeared at Paul's hearing before the Roman proconsul of Achaea—and got soundly thrashed for his pains.[59] The denomination also regularly applies to donors and benefactors who built or restored synagogues or provided additions to them. Such persons are known from dedicatory inscriptions or honorary decrees. And the titles may, at least in some cases, have been conferred as honorifics, rather than as designation of functionaries. One may be confident of that fact in the case of a seven-year-old *archisynagogos!*[60] The title endures, in various manifestations, to be recorded by Church Fa-

thers, rabbinic texts, the Theodosian Code, the *Historia Augusta,* and epitaphs of late antiquity.[61] But the idea that it fits neatly at the top of a religious or administrative network cannot be sustained. Overlapping and
duplication, rather than clear boundaries, characterize the office—if that
is indeed what it is. Luke refers to the same person as *archisynagogos*
in one passage and *archon tes synagoges* in another.[62] The famous decree
from Acmonia lists as benefactors an *archon,* an *archisynagogos,* and an
archisynagogos for life.[63] The last title is evidently honorific, but the three
individuals do not appear to represent any hierarchical arrangement.[64] In
the post–Second Temple period, at least, several individuals might hold the
title of *archisynagogos* at the same time and in the same community, as attested at Apamea.[65] And the *archisynagogos* could simultaneously hold
other posts or, at least, collect other titles, civilian or even military.[66] This is
no rigidly defined office, with set functions and uniform responsibilities
throughout the diaspora.

A similar conclusion follows for other positions or designations. Fluidity
of nomenclature resists any stable categorization. The leader of the Jewish
community in Alexandria was termed *ethnarch* by Strabo, but *genarch* by
Philo.[67] This suggests not that one or the other was mistaken, but that terminology was unstable. Augustus, in any case, changed the system and installed or authorized the installation of a ruling body, the *gerousia,* whose
members were called *archontes* (chiefs).[68] A comparable arrangement may
have been in place at Berenice in Cyrene. *Archontes* existed there in some
numbers, ten of them named on an inscription as donors for the repair of
the synagogue.[69] More intriguingly, two other inscriptions from Berenice,
honoring persons for their public and private services, were issued in the
name of both the *archontes* and the *politeuma* of the Jews.[70] This implies
that the *archontes* had a corporate existence independent of the communal structure rather than being identified with or representing it. By contrast, at Antioch a single *archon* appears to have held sway.[71] The remarkable new finds from Herakleopolis in Middle Egypt disclose the existence
of annual *archontes,* of unspecified number, operating occasionally in conjunction with a *politarches,* and primarily adjudicating disputes.[72] The
term *archon* occurs with great frequency in the inscriptions of Roman
Jews, all from later antiquity but interesting and revealing for present purposes. They certainly do not present a tidy picture, in which each *archon*
represented an individual synagogue and the whole number gathered in a
collective council.[73] Some were chosen for the office twice or three times;
others held it for life. And here too there are attested instances of child
archontes.[74] This implies a mixture of honorific titles and actual function-

aries. The matter becomes complicated further by modifications of the title, like "*archon* of all dignity" or "*archon* of high order," "*archon* in waiting," and "*ex-archon,*" all in the Roman context. There seems little point in reconstructing some postulated hierarchy. Even for one term in one city, variations dominate.[75] And comparisons across communities simply multiply the complexities. For example, the *gerousia* in Alexandria, as we have seen, consisted of *archontes*. In Rome, the head of the *gerousia* was simply *gerousiarches*.[76] Additional titles are sprinkled about in the diaspora: *prostates* (head man), *archiprostates* (super–head man?), "father (or mother) of the synagogue," *presbyteros* or *geron* (elder), *dynatos* (man of authority), "priest," and various lesser officials or attendants.[77] If homogeneity existed, it escapes detection.

The absence of uniformity should hardly surprise us. A plethora of synagogues in a plethora of communities scattered around the Mediterranean were unlikely to have established (or wish to have established) a fixed pattern. Certainly nothing suggests directives from Jerusalem. And although Jewish settlements in diverse places held communication with one another, they made no point of duplicating arrangements or organizations. The numerous titles, with ostensibly overlapping functions and indistinguishable responsibilities, may not simply be a function of inadequate information. And the effort to find and define *termini technici* may be an illusion. But despite the lack of standardization, an essential fact emerges. Diaspora congregations, each in its own way, did erect an officialdom, however variable and mutable, and did organize their leaders, representatives, and officers in some structured fashion that signified an ongoing community; they were no mere temporary sojourners. This laid the basis for a diaspora existence of stability and endurance.

The synagogue provided a setting for a range of services. Places of assemblage permitted Jews to engage in a variety of civic and sacral activities that marked their distinctiveness and expressed their communal identity.[78] These activities did not mean isolation from surrounding societies. But they announced a continuing commitment to traditions that characterized the clan.

Study and instruction held a prominent place in the functions of the synagogue. Philo, the learned Alexandrian Jew, as one might expect, gives special play to this aspect. The philosopher has Moses inaugurate the practice of weekly gatherings on the Sabbath wherein Jews would have the laws read out to them. And he asserts that the practice persists in his day, with a priest or elder taking responsibility for reading and commenting on the sacred laws, keeping his congregation at it for hours, and providing them with great impetus toward piety.[79] The congregants sit in their synagogues, gather in their customary cluster, read their sacred books, and discuss at length the particulars of their ancestral philosophy.[80] The emperor Augustus himself, according to Philo, acknowledged the Jews' observance of the Sabbath, when they met in synagogues and received instruction in that ancestral philosophy.[81] The Jews hold tenaciously to their traditional learning, devoting every Sabbath to the acquisition of knowledge and the understanding of nature.[82] For Philo, the synagogue qualifies as a Jewish replica of a philosophical academy: the *didaskaleion*. Myriads of schools of learning open up every seventh day to teach prudence, restraint, courage, justice, and all the other virtues—not to forget piety and holiness—while students drink in eagerly the wise words of their teachers.[83] So speaks the philosopher. He might indeed give excessive weight to the intellectual features of the enterprise. But other testimony shows that he cannot be far off the mark. The Book of Acts, which has its own agenda—but a very different one from that of Philo—portrays Paul repeatedly entering Jewish synagogues in various cities of the diaspora and arguing with Jews about the meaning of the scriptures. The exchanges occurred (with perhaps suspicious regularity) in Thessalonica, Athens, Corinth, and Ephesus.[84] That implies at least that the setting was appropriate, presumably customary, for the examination and interpretation of holy writ. Josephus puts into the mouth of Nicolas of Damascus a bold speech addressing Agrippa on behalf of the Jews of Ionia. In the course of it, he proclaims that Jews make no secret of the instructions which guide their lives in matters human and divine and the fact that they spend every Sabbath in the study of their traditions and law.[85] Whatever axes our sources may have to grind, there is no reason to question the consistent notices that Jews gathered in synagogues to study the scriptures.

Did they also come to pray? Some have doubted the proposition. Philo, Acts, and Josephus speak in terms of instruction rather than of prayer. Did diaspora synagogues simply emulate pagan academies, elevating education while subordinating worship? Was the destruction of the Temple a prerequisite for the introduction of liturgical elements into the activities of the synagogue?[86] That is unlikely. The term *proseuche* must count for something. Its basic denotation is simply "prayer," and by metonymy it took on the meaning of "prayer-house" or "synagogue." It appears regularly in Philo with that meaning, as in inscriptions from Egypt, but also outside the Egyptian context in the manumission documents from the Black Sea.[87] Moreover, allusions to religious devotion are by no means absent in Sec-

ond Temple texts. Gentiles certainly assumed that the congregations engaged in some form of worship. Why else would those hostile to the Jews
in Alexandria set up statues of the emperor in the *proseuchai?*[88] And it
is noteworthy that when news arrived of Flaccus' fall, the Alexandrian
Jews flocked to the beaches to send up hymns of thanksgiving to God—
because they had been deprived of their *proseuchai* (where, presumably,
such hymns would otherwise have been offered).[89]

   The situation in Asia supplies confirmation. Josephus explicitly describes the synagogue at Antioch as a *hieron.*[90] Some of the documents
transmitted (or transformed) by the historian contain Roman assurances
of Jewish privileges in Asia that go beyond merely keeping the schools
open. So, for instance, the people of Halicarnassus, following the Roman
lead, declared that Jewish sacred rites, festivals, and gatherings were to be
inviolate, that they be permitted to observe the Sabbath and rituals in accordance with their laws, and that they could go on building *proseuchai*
along the sea in traditional fashion.[91] A comparable Roman letter to
Miletus, at least in Josephus' phraseology, guarantees the Jewish prerogative to keep the Sabbath and to perform ancestral rites.[92] All of this refers
plainly to religious practices associated with congregations and houses of
worship. Even more striking is a Sardian decree reaffirming the rights of
the Jews to have a place where they can assemble with wives and children
and fulfill their traditional vows and sacrifices to God.[93] This need not literally signify sacrifices in synagogues. The Gentile authors of the decree may
have erroneously assumed that holy rites, as in their own temples, included
sacrificial offerings.[94] But it does signal a presumption that the activities
possessed a religious character. Further, the grant of *asylia* to (at least
some) Jewish *proseuchai* in Egypt affords a significant clue to their sacral
character.[95] Finally, the manumission inscriptions from the Bosporan kingdom offer a telling perspective on the matter. The very fact that the ceremony takes place in a *proseuche,* with (occasionally) a dedication to Theos
Hypsistos, through a process closely analogous to the sacral manumissions
in the precinct of Apollo at Delphi, indicates quite clearly that this was
more than a civil proceeding in an academy of higher learning.[96] Were synagogues primarily seats of instruction or places of worship? The dichotomy is a false one. They served perfectly well as both.

   Nor did that exhaust their activities. Synagogues supplied the setting for
communal dining, particularly for the celebration of festivals, the commemoration of key events in Jewish tradition that helped to define the
community. The decrees preserved by Josephus with regard to Jews in Asia
Minor and the Aegean include protection for traditional Jewish festivals.[97]

Philo speaks of the celebration of Sukkoth as being regularly practiced in Alexandria.[98] At Berenice in Cyrene, an honorary decree passed by the Jewish community and its leaders posted as its date the gathering at Sukkoth.[99] In the exuberant formulations of Philo and Josephus, Yom Kippur was observed in every city of the Roman empire, with even Gentiles enticed into the practice.[100] As noted earlier, Roman authors regularly make mention (usually with wit and derision) of Jewish adherence to the Sabbath. Plainly it was observed with regularity in the synagogues of the city.[101] The fanciful tale of III Maccabees concludes with the creation of a new feast day to commemorate the success of the Egyptian Jews over their enemies, punctuated by the installation of a *proseuche* in Ptolemais.[102] Whatever credence one gives to the story, the inauguration of such a festival to be celebrated in a synagogue would itself have been perfectly logical. Diaspora Jews did not shrink from parading their practices in public.

Synagogues might also function for purposes of adjudication. Such at least appears to be the case when the formal process of manumission was ratified in the *proseuchai* of Bosporan Jewish communities.[103] The letter of a Roman magistrate to Sardis, confirmed by a Sardian decree, attests to the existence of a Jewish *topos*, doubtless a synagogue, in that city where Jews rendered decisions on internal controversies.[104] Another letter, this one by Agrippa to Ephesus, discloses Jewish judicial authority there, not only over their own community but over those accused of robbing their sacred treasuries.[105] The New Testament testifies that punishments could be meted out in the synagogues, some at least in the diaspora.[106] All of this provides some confidence in the otherwise invented story of Susanna, which depicts judgment rendered by the Jewish community in Babylon gathered in the synagogue.[107] Adjudication was no small part of Jewish activity in the institutions of the diaspora.

Scattered evidence discloses other purposes to which the synagogue might be put. It provided a place where the community could gather in official assemblage to pass decrees, as in Berenice, or where a burial society could meet to issue a notice, as in Egypt.[108] It might also act as a repository for sacred monies, a means of display for votive offerings and dedicatory inscriptions, and an archive for public records.[109]

The accumulation of testimony, however incomplete and fragmentary, outlines a significant scenario. Diaspora synagogues provided a plethora of activities that declared the distinctiveness of the Jewish community and the adherence to its traditions. Synagogues took root in cities all over the Greco-Roman world, from Italy to the Euphrates, from the Black Sea to Egypt. They possessed official personnel and wholesale administrative structures. They served as schools of instruction to entrench the congregation firmly in the teachings of the Torah and the prophets and to inculcate the traditions of the ancestors. They constituted houses of worship, a locus for prayers, asylum for the refugee, and a place to observe the Sabbath, gather for communal meals, and celebrate the festivals. They housed records, displayed offerings, held sacred funds, and supplied a setting for assemblies to promulgate measures and tribunals to pass judgment. To be sure, one cannot with confidence assume that all these functions were performed in all the synagogues. Local circumstances doubtless dictated numerous divergences, the details of which elude us. But the range of activities is impressive and telling. And they were not carried out in secret enclaves. Synagogues stood in public view; Sabbath observances were well known, even notorious, to Gentiles; inscriptions announced decisions of the congregation; the collection of moneys and their shipment to Jerusalem were conspicuous; and the letters and decrees of the Roman officialdom gave public sanction to Jewish practices, most of which were centered in the synagogue. The impressive testimony underscores the existence of thriving and vigorous Jewish communities, self-assured in the exhibition of their traditions and the fostering of their special character.

Not that all of this was envisioned at the beginning. But then again we do not know when the beginning took place—or indeed what a "beginning" would consist of. Most discussions of the origin of the synagogue (and there have been many) operate on the assumption that it occurred at an identifiable point in time, that it stemmed from specific needs and circumstances, and that a particular explanation (whatever it might be) would account for its multiple manifestations across the Mediterranean. Scholars repeat a litany of lament about inadequate evidence on the motives for creating the synagogue. Yet even if we could pinpoint the invention of the institution in time and place, this would tell us little or nothing about its appearance and objectives in different places at different times. The whole question of "origins" may be the wrong question. But it does raise an issue central to this entire inquiry. Did synagogues represent a diaspora response to loss of or distance from the Temple? Did they serve as substitutes for, rivals to, or reactions against the Temple and its traditions? In short, did they provide a means whereby to reconstitute a Jewish existence that was no longer possible in association with the Temple?

Speculations on the emergence of the synagogue tend to reckon it as a surrogate for the Temple or as an imitation of it.[110] That approach skews the picture from the outset, presupposing a need to fill a gap. So, for instance, many have proposed that synagogues arose in Babylon during the sixth-century exile. Destruction of the First Temple and removal from the homeland prompted the exiles to create new structures for the worship of God and the pursuit of religious traditions. In a variant of this theory, the restoration of the captives in the time of Ezra and Nehemiah instituted the practice of Torah reading in public, thus forming the basis for subsequent synagogues in the land of Israel. Others find a Second Temple diaspora setting as spur for the institution, most notably in Egypt, site of the earliest evidence for *proseuchai*. Jewish communities in that land, remote from Jerusalem, erected "prayer-houses" to meet religious needs, primarily prayer and reading of the Torah, a development prompted or expanded by translation of the Pentateuch into Greek. On yet a different thesis, the synagogue arose in Palestine as a Pharisaic institution responding to new circumstances after the Maccabean rebellion, perhaps a reflection of a growing individualism or even a reaction to Hasmonean control of the Temple, as was certainly the case with the Dead Sea sect. The most recent hypothesis sees the synagogue as a gradual development providing a range of communal activities once carried out at the city gate in biblical society but shifted to new settings after the construction of Hellenistic cities in Palestine revamped the urban structure. On this view, the gap to be filled is not that of the Temple but of a focal point for civic and religious functions.[111]

A contribution to all these conjectures would be pointless here. Theories of origins in Babylonia or in the return of exiles depend on interpretation of rabbinic traditions. Epigraphic evidence exists for synagogues in Egypt as early as the third century, but nothing suggests that this was more than a regional phenomenon or that the Egyptian experience influenced Jews anywhere else. Pharisaic association with the emergence of the synagogue rests on no testimony whatsoever. And the idea that this institution arose to replace functions once performed at the gates of biblical cities in Palestine does not account for the phenomenon of synagogues in the diaspora. The whole concept of a gap to be filled has led inquiry astray. The notable dearth of literary references to synagogues prior to Philo does not, of course, mean that none existed in the Hellenistic period.[112] The material evidence from Egypt and Delos alone demonstrates that they did exist. That is a salutary reminder about the hazards of *argumenta e silentio*. But the absence of notice in the literary sources may carry significance. It suggests that the institution made no dramatic appearance on the landscape and did not constitute a conscious compensation for the loss of religious or communal support elsewhere. When a synagogue does actually receive mention in a Hellenistic diaspora text, the tale of Susanna, the author takes no special notice: the synagogue is simply the site of Susanna's trial in the Jewish community at Babylon.[113] One may reasonably infer that the institution provided a convenient means to conduct the religious and civic functions of Jews dwelling in a diaspora city. The drawing of broader implications is risky and unjustified. Nothing implies the need to find a replacement for or a rival to the Temple.

Synagogues supplied services that were complementary to the Temple, rather than serving as a substitute for it. Indeed, the central characteristic of the Temple cult, namely the performance of sacrifices, was expressly avoided by synagogues. By contrast, the study of Torah and the utterance of prayers, closely associated with synagogue practice, had no official place in the public cult represented by the Temple (at least so far as our evidence goes) before the late Second Temple period. And synagogues developed a wholesale set of officials and hierarchical personnel that were quite separate from but no challenge to the priesthood that ministered to the cult in Jerusalem.[114] Jews dwelling in the diaspora, as we shall see in greater detail, did not view themselves as cut off from the Temple nor in want of a surrogate for it. The shipment of an annual contribution to Jerusalem and the frequent and regular pilgrimages to the city from all over the Mediterranean suffice to establish the continuing connection. The two institutions maintained a symbiotic and mutually reinforcing association.

Did synagogues then take their cue from pagan models? Did the status of aliens in a diaspora setting induce Jews to compensate in a different way, namely to adjust their structures to the surrounding community? That suggestion has appeared in the scholarship, and an ostensibly useful analogy has been seized upon: the *thiasoi, synodoi,* or *collegia,* the voluntary associations in Greco-Roman cities that brought together persons of like-minded interests, occupations, or localities to share common meals and contribute to common purposes.[115] But the resemblances are superficial and the differences fundamental. Membership in synagogues had nothing to do with one's trade or profession; moneys were collected to send contributions to Jerusalem rather than to support the activities of the group; birth and ethnic identity linked synagogue participants; and the bonds that defined them stretched beyond local corporations and civic identities to a larger Jewish world.[116] Nor does it help to propose Egyptian models rather than Greco-Roman ones to account for synagogue structures.[117] That Egyptian Jews may have felt some influence from native buildings or institutions is perfectly possible. But nothing in the Egyptian context goes to the core of synagogue activities.[118] And the peculiar context of that land is hardly transferable elsewhere in the diaspora. Jews did not mold their synagogues in accordance with pagan archetypes—any more than they did in response to the Temple in Jerusalem.

To be sure, diaspora Jews paid attention to the broader community in which they dwelled. Evidence, where we have it, indicates that they eschewed strict segregation or isolation. The documents from Egypt show regular dedication of the *proseuchai* or their appurtenances on behalf of the reigning Ptolemy and his family.[119] Such gestures, of course, were prudent, even perhaps conventional. But not only that: they announced, in effect, that the peculiar Jewish institution belonged also to the larger society wherein it was situated. Homage to the royal house had symbolic significance in a double direction. It brought the Jews into a Ptolemaic context; but it also brought the Ptolemies into a Jewish context. The king could provide benefits—as he did when granting the right of *asylia* to the *proseuche*.[120] But the Jews provided benefits as well by associating the king with the supreme being, the *theos hypsistos,* to whom the synagogue was dedicated. A comparable phenomenon appears in the manumission documents from the Black Sea region. The procedure occurs in the *proseuche;* dedication is made to *theos hypsistos;* due acknowledgment goes to the ruler of the Bosporan kingdom; and an explicit reference notes his close relationship (whatever the reality may have been) with the Roman emperor.[121] Furthermore, and even more striking, dedication to the "highest god" could come side by side with mention of Zeus, Ge, and Helios.[122] This does not amount to "syncretism" or compromise. But it does situate the Jewish experience within the wider framework of the kingdom and the empire.

Adoption of Hellenic conventions in a Hellenic society made perfectly good sense. So, at Berenice in Cyrene, the Jewish officialdom and the community issued honorific decrees to express gratitude to benefactors, whether Jews or non-Jews. They bestowed crowns and fillets in good Greek fashion. And they spoke not only of donations to the *synagoge,* but of repairs to the *amphitheatron.*[123] Embrace of the latter term commands attention. Whether it alludes to the shape of a Greek council hall or a Roman amphitheater, it declares not assimilation but appropriation of the pagan form to a Jewish purpose.[124] Reciprocity might also be expected. At Acmonia in Phrygia, the eminent Julia Severa, high priestess of the imperial cult, erected a building subsequently restored by Jewish benefactors of the synagogue who received their own honorary decree and gilded shield.[125] The conventions were Greco-Roman; the objectives were Jewish.

The synagogue resists reductive categorization. It neither imitated nor compensated for the Temple. It employed pagan conventions but required no pagan models. The institution took diverse forms in diverse times and places. It both promoted association with the surrounding society and maintained unbroken connection with Jerusalem. It negotiated a path between integration and segregation, thereby to serve the sacral and secular needs of Jewish communities in diaspora settings. Through that medium Jews could express their own distinctiveness while fitting within the framework of the Greco-Roman world. The synagogue was sui generis.

Jewish communities in the cities of the diaspora created institutions for the advancement of the flock and the flourishing of the faith. Adequate documentation discloses the mechanisms for internal stability. Much less well documented and much more difficult to discern is the degree to which Jews moved outside their own circles and participated (or were permitted to participate) actively in the wider affairs of the places in which they dwelled. Evidence is scanty but not insignificant. It allows provisional conclusions and the outline of a positive picture.

The gymnasium marked the capstone of higher education in Greek cities all around the Mediterranean and beyond. That institution, with its attendant corps of ephebes, the select youth of upper-echelon families, represented the cultural and intellectual elite of the Hellenistic world. While it may have lost some of its character as a training ground for the military, it retained the central feature of a means to inculcate civic values and to distinguish the next generation of Hellenic leadership in the urban centers of Greek migration.[126] Were Jews excluded or indifferent?

The testimony is slim. But where it exists, it suggests that some Jews could and did partake of this preeminently Greek institution. Two ephebic lists from Cyrene, one from the end of the first century BCE and one from the beginning of the first century CE (each with a number of graffiti from the first half of the first century CE), include unmistakable Jewish names: Jesus, Elazar, and Judas; and several others that may well be Jewish: Jason, Theodotos, and Simon.[127] We possess the end of the first list, with a familiar invocation to pagan gods, in this instance to Hermes and Herakles. It need not follow, as is often assumed, that the Jewish enrollees had forsaken their faith to enter the ranks of the Hellenic elite. Rather, the documents imply that Jews felt a self-assurance in taking part in a Hellenic institution whose token dedication to pagan deities did not compromise their basic beliefs.[128] A similar list of ephebes from the Carian city of Iasos from the early Roman period includes eight names, such as Judas, Theophilos, and Dositheos, that are either definitely or possibly Jewish.[129] In a later era, in the second or third century CE, Jewish ephebes turn up at Korone in

Messenia; and at Hypaipa near Sardis a group of young Jews styled themselves *neoteroi,* following the customary system of arranging themselves in
ephebic categories.[130] In Alexandria, as a crucial but controversial papyrus
informs us, a Jew of that city made reference to his "appropriate *paideia,*"
an apparent reference to ephebic education in the gymnasium.[131] The institution, as is plain, did not systematically ban Jews.[132]

The literary evidence from Alexandria firmly reinforces the conclusion.
The *Letter of Aristeas,* in a celebrated passage, has the High Priest in Jerusalem select as translators of the Pentateuch learned Jewish scholars who
not only mastered the writings of their ancestors but had steeped themselves in the literature of the Greeks.[133] The fictitious treatise may strain
credulity by locating such men in significant numbers in early/mid third
century Jerusalem. But it certainly reflects the circumstances of Hellenistic
Alexandria, where Jews of station could attain the highest levels of the education process—including the author of the *Letter of Aristeas* himself.
Philo, of course, falls most famously into that category. None will question
the breadth and depth of his intellectual training—or his commitment to
Jewish law and tradition. The education available to him in Alexandria
was open to other Jews as well, at least to those of wealth and status (as it
was for Greeks of wealth and status). Philo offers a rare autobiographical
glimpse of his *paideia,* couched in typical allegorical mode. He had set philosophy as his ultimate goal and moved to it through a series of stages—
grammar, geometry, music, and poetry—resisting the charms of each that
had distracted others from the main target, and keeping his eye fixed on
the acquisition of wisdom through philosophy.[134] Elsewhere he speaks of
a whole panoply of instructors: moral guides, household tutors, school
teachers, parents, elders, magistrates, and laws.[135] Parents have a special
responsibility. They set children on the proper path, in order to educate
both body and soul, the former through gymnastic training, the latter
through literature, mathematics, music, and the whole of philosophy.[136]
Most interestingly perhaps, Philo adds, in a different context, that some
pursue such training for unworthy motives, such as exhibiting their cultivated tastes or hoping for high office at the behest of rulers.[137] That is
doubtless true, however much Philo may deplore it. What it implies, however, is that Jews in certain circles (Philo surely refers to Jews here) not only
had access to the schools of higher learning, but could use them as spring-
boards for entrance into the corridors of power.

The cultivated tastes of educated Jews in Alexandria can be further illustrated. They attended the theater, it appears, in appreciable numbers.
Philo, at least, on two separate occasions reports on audience reactions to

Greek drama. In one instance, spectators were swept away by lines of Euripides and burst into spontaneous applause.[138] In another, Philo remarks on diverse responses to musical renditions by actors in dramatic performances or citharodes which drew enthusiasm, revulsion, or indifference.[139] The philosopher notes (without making an issue of it) that he was a frequent attender of the theater.[140] And he was surely not the only Jew to do so. The author of the *Letter of Aristeas* puts into the mouth of a Jewish sage the observation that witnessing dramatic productions was a suitable way to spend one's leisure hours.[141] It may be a stretch to imagine that Jerusalemites did so. But Alexandrian Jews surely did. Indeed, they produced at least one tragic dramatist of their own, the playwright Ezekiel, who composed a tragedy on the theme of the Exodus.[142] Jewish theatergoers found no tension between enjoyment of this genre and adherence to tradition.[143]

High culture was not the only fruit of instruction in the gymnasium. The institution, of course, involved substantial athletic training. The notion that this peculiarly Greek practice was closed to Jews or repellent to them can safely be discarded. Philo places parents' obligations toward their children's physical welfare on a par with that of their intellectual nurturing, the former accomplished through gymnastic exercise.[144] The philosopher was himself well acquainted with athletes' experiences, writing frequently and in some detail about the preparation by athletic contestants and the procedures of contests. Only intimate familiarity would allow him to contrast, for instance, the artificial bulking up by some athletes with the more rigorous training by others.[145] Philo praised the overseers of gymnastic contests for maintaining propriety by banning women spectators, lest they observe men stripping themselves to the nude.[146] His texts speak in specific terms of the announcements by heralds, the actions of referees, the crowning by judges, and the binding of wreaths upon the victors.[147] And he shows a thorough grasp of the sponsorship and organization of the games.[148] Philo was obviously an ardent fan, who attended every form of contest. He could discourse knowledgeably about both the subtle tactics and the brutality of boxers, the fierce and draining battles of the pancratiasts, the tremendous powers of endurance exhibited by wrestlers and pancratiasts, the pitfalls encountered by sprinters and jumpers, and the rabid spectators at chariot races, some of whom rushed out onto the race course and were crushed by the vehicles.[149] In addition, his works frequently made use of the imagery of athletic contests and physical training for purposes of analogy or simile.[150] Philo clearly took for granted that his readers, primarily Jews, had a close acquaintance with them.

The bulk of the evidence on the athletic side is, inescapably, Alexandrian, thanks to the survival of the Philonic corpus. But none will imagine that Jewish experience with sporting events was confined to Alexandria. It is, at the least, intriguing that the Jewish community at Berenice in Cyrene honored a benefactor for refurbishing the "amphitheater."[151] The designation, to be sure, refers to the shape, not the function, of the structure. There is no reason to believe that it housed athletic contests, let alone gladiatorial combats. But appropriation of the name suggests that Jews in the diaspora had no difficulty in associating themselves with Roman institutions that did house such contests—any more than Herod (who built three of them) did in Palestine.[152] Still more intriguing is a notice in Josephus that Jews in Antioch received special dispensation from Seleucus I, who instructed the gymnasiarchs to supply them with money to purchase their own oil since they would not employ that of the Gentiles.[153] Just what this means remains baffling. That Jews required kosher oil to rub themselves down for gymnasial exercises does not seem obvious. Some have conjectured that the reference applies to the distribution of olive oil that Jews would need for eating and ritual purposes. And the notion that such a measure was needed as early as Seleucus I in the early third century BCE appears, in any case, dubious.[154] But even if Josephus' chronology and interpretation are questionable, the role of the gymnasiarch in providing the means for Jewish access to oil implies a connection with the physical exertions of the gymnasium. The indirect testimony concerning Cyrene and Antioch buttresses the explicit comments from Alexandria. Diaspora Jews were no strangers to the athletic activities associated with Greek gymnasia.[155]

The gymnasium emblematized the Hellenic commitment to the training of body and mind that would constitute the fashioning of the *kalos k'agathos,* the elite Greek gentleman. For Jews who had the wherewithal and the social status to share that ideal, the path, so far as we can tell, stood open.

A further question now suggests itself. Jews may have had access to cultural and educational institutions in diaspora cities. But what about access to the organs of government? Once more, the limits on information are quite severe. And even if we had more than fragments and tidbits, they would not (and could not) tell us to what degree Jews desired full incorporation into the body politic. Jews did, as we have seen, enjoy an array of officials and representatives, as well as assemblies to legislate and tribunals to adjudicate within their own ranks. References exist to Jewish *politeumata* in cities of Egypt and Cyrene, which may imply some self-governing responsibilities.[156] But these functions apply to the administration of internal affairs. To what degree did Jews participate in the political life of Gentile communities?

The question is too often put in terms of citizenship. Could Jews aspire to the citizenship of Greek *poleis?* Would they want to? Answers elude us. But the question may be too narrowly and unhelpfully posed. A wider formulation will bring at least some answers in investigating what civic privileges Jews (or some Jews) could expect to possess or acquire in the cities of the diaspora.

The fullest information concerns the Jews of Alexandria—sufficient to cause confusion and stir up controversy, insufficient to reach definitive conclusions. The matter has already been explored above. Only a summary of findings is needed here.[157] Josephus' tracing of Jewish political rights (whatever they may have been) back to Alexander may push the limits of credibility. But Jews did possess a political organization, as is attested by Strabo, who had no Jewish agenda, and their rights were reiterated in a public document by Augustus. Much of the testimony, imprecise and nontechnical, seems to refer to internal governance by the Jews: *politeia* and *politika dikaia.* But the language of Philo in certain key passages alludes intriguingly and significantly to Jewish engagement in the larger civic community. The philosopher makes reference to the Alexandrian Jews' "sharing in political rights."[158] And, on a broader plane, he draws a distinction between the laws specific to the Jews and the common rights they possess in each of the cities where they dwell.[159] Participation of some sort is plainly implied.[160] When Jews termed themselves "Alexandrians," they had more than a geographic designation in mind. Their privileges may not have coincided with Alexandrian "citizenship," but the emperor Augustus could refer to them on a bronze stele as *politai Alexandreon.*[161] That certainly implies an acknowledged role in the political process of the city. Few will have risen as high as the Jewish generals Onias and Dositheus, who held chief military posts under Ptolemy VI, or Chelkias and Ananias, who reached similar heights under Cleopatra in the late second century BCE.[162] But even Apion, the fierce Alexandrian foe of the Jews, makes reference to them as *cives,* if the language of Josephus is to be trusted—and the historian was not here trying to claim them as citizens.[163] Precision is impossible on the basis of this testimony, and it would be pointless to press for it. But it is clear that Jews could play a part in the civic functions of Alexandria.

The newly discovered documents from Herakleopolis in Middle Egypt include a reference to Jewish πολῖται, as contrasted with ἀλλόφυλοι, obviously referring to Gentiles. The term here evidently denotes Jews who belong to the *politeuma* and does not indicate any broader citizenship. But the officials of the *politeuma* could adjudicate cases that involved both Jews and non-Jews.[164]

A tantalizing bit of information comes from Cyrenaica. We know that the Jews had some form of internal organization, as is clear from two documents of the city of Berenice, recording decisions by the *politeuma* and the *archontes*.[165] A separate Jewish identity in Cyrene was noted also by Strabo, who observed that the city was divided into four groups: citizens, farmers, metics, and Jews.[166] This corporate structure, while placing Jews outside the category of citizens, also distinguished them from resident aliens, according them special status as a major element in the community. The semi-independent body gave Jews a convenient vehicle through which to appeal to Augustus and then to Agrippa around 14 BCE regarding funds collected for Jerusalem but confiscated on the pretext that Jews owed taxes to the city.[167] Equally significant, however, is the fact that this organized Jewish enclave did not preclude the participation of Jews in the larger governing structure of Cyrene. An important, though very fragmentary, inscription from Cyrene dating to 60/61 CE records a dedication by the *nomophylakes* of the city and lists several of their names. These officials, as we happen to know, had significant responsibilities in Cyrene, including matters of finance, record keeping, and law enforcement. It is striking, therefore, that among the *nomophylakes* was a certain Eleazar, son of Jason, obviously a Jew—and one who felt no need to mask his identity by assuming a Greek name.[168] How exceptional this instance was we cannot know. Nor can we infer with confidence from this example that Jews generally had eligibility for this office or indeed had had it prior to the Roman period. But this stray and random item nevertheless reveals a notable openness in Cyrenaean political society to the aspirations of (at least some) Jews for involvement in the governing process.

Political privileges for Jews existed also in the great city of Antioch. Here we depend, alas, upon the information supplied by Josephus, who had a case to make and an axe to grind—and whose reports contain their own inconsistencies. The historian claims that Jewish status in Antioch goes all the way back to the progenitor of the Seleucid dynasty, Seleucus I Nicator, who was himself the founder of Antioch. The fullest statement comes in the *Antiquitates*, according to which Seleucus deemed the Jews worthy of *politeia* in Antioch, and affirmed for them privileges equal to those enjoyed by Greeks and Macedonians dwelling there, a *politeia* which Jews still possess in Josephus' own day.[169] A shorter version of the same account appears in *Contra Apionem*.[170] Elsewhere, Josephus gives credit to the successors of

Antiochus Epiphanes who restored to Jews living in Antioch treasures stolen by Epiphanes and gave them the right to a share of privileges in the city equal to that of the Greeks.[171]

These reports have engendered reasonable doubts. The notion of an acknowledged Jewish position dating back practically to the founding of Antioch has little plausibility. Nor can one easily credit the claim of full citizenship equivalent to that of Greeks and Macedonians. And the inconsistency in dating has served to discredit further the statements of Josephus.[172] But none of this justifies jettisoning the account as a whole. *Politeia,* as so often, is taken as signifying "citizenship," a concept incompatible with standard notions of Jews as marginalized and of citizen rights in a *polis* as confined to Greeks. Jewish prerogatives in Antioch may indeed not go back as far as Seleucus Nicator. The date of the origins, however, makes little difference. Antiochene Jews did have civic rights in the time of Josephus; they were inscribed on bronze tablets in the city. And Titus left those privileges intact, even after the Jews' defeat in the Great Revolt.[173] *Politeia,* it must be stressed, need not mean "citizenship" anyway, and Josephus appears to employ it in a non-technical sense. One might note that his phraseology is vague and varied. In addition to *politeia,* he refers to Jews having "equal privileges" *(isotimous)* or "possessing rights" *(dikaia)* of *politeia,* or holding just claims *(dikaiomata),* or "sharing on an equal basis with Greeks."[174] The diverse terminology suggests that Josephus had no clear idea of precise prerogatives. Nor can we recover the particulars. But Jews plainly enjoyed a recognized place in the political scene of Antioch under both the Seleucids and the Roman emperors.[175]

Fragmentary hints only, but intriguing ones, disclose a Jewish role in Greek communities of Asia Minor. In 14 BCE, Greek representatives from Ionian cities confronted M. Agrippa, who was in the vicinity, with some requests about the Jews in their midst. The spokesmen asked that Greeks alone partake of the *politeia* which had been awarded by Antiochus II (more than two centuries earlier); if Jews wished to be their kinsmen, they should worship the same gods.[176] Agrippa delivered some verdicts favorable to the Jews on certain religious issues. But the Roman leader preferred to avoid pronouncements on the distribution of internal political rights. He left the status quo intact.[177] The exact dimensions of this *politeia* are indeterminable. It need not be (and probably was not) coterminous with full citizenship. But the evidence obviously implies a share of civic prerogatives in the Ionian cities. That emerges with clarity from the fact that Jews complained of burdens imposed upon them, including military duties and public liturgies to be funded by their own sacred monies.[178] The Ionians may have stepped up demands upon Jews in order to induce withdrawal from the civic body, anticipating a larger slice of Roman bounty.[179] But the episode discloses the current and past situation: Jews had military and financial responsibilities in Ionian communities. And they could even refer to themselves as kinsmen of their fellow townsmen.[180]

At Sardis the Jews had a flourishing community, with a formal institution *(synodos)* that exercised governance and adjudication within their own ranks.[181] There is, however, also an oblique indication that they played a role in the larger Sardian community. Two different documents in Josephus' collection make reference to Jews of Sardis as *politai*. Each citation is controversial, and the term is not tantamount to "citizen." But the combination gives reason to believe that Jews exercised influence in the Sardian governing process—and not just as lobbyists from a self-contained enclave.[182]

The testimony is tenuous and allows for few details. But the stray items from Alexandria, Antioch, Cyrene, and Asia Minor afford clues that Jews had some access to the political process, occasionally even to high office, and to elite status in cities of the diaspora. Random bits of information add small pieces to the mosaic—like the notice that Paul was a citizen of Tarsus or that a Jerusalemite in Iasos helped to finance the festival of Dionysos in that city.[183] The evidence expands notably after 70 CE, which is outside the bounds of this investigation. But with regard to Jewish involvement in the civic life of Hellenic cities, it is reasonable to surmise that the roots, even where data are lacking, go back to the Second Temple period.[184] And the involvement itself did not oblige Jews to toss their traditions overboard.[185]

Finally, mention must be made of Jewish participation in a still wider spectrum of civic status, namely Roman citizenship. The vast and growing body of citizens certainly included Jews in no small number within its ranks. Those in the city of Rome itself had direct benefit. As we have seen, slaves and war captives brought to Italy could look forward to manumission, and with it came the rights of citizenship. Philo's report collapses the process somewhat, neglecting the fact that within a generation or two of emancipation the stigma of slave descent would have largely worn off. In his own day there must have been a substantial community of Jews in the capital who held that imperial franchise.[186] Sufficient numbers indeed existed in the age of Augustus to warrant special consideration when grain was distributed on the Sabbath—for only citizens were eligible for those distributions.[187] But Philo does make a significant observation: Roman citizenship and Jewish consciousness were entirely compatible.[188] The point is telling.

In ways that escape detection, Jews could acquire Roman citizenship outside Rome itself. Paul is only the most celebrated example.[189] A chance find discloses that one of the Jewish *archontes* at Berenice in Cyrene was M. Laelius Onasion, the *tria nomina* evidently signaling Roman citizenship.[190] There must be many others as yet undiscovered. The documents transmitted by Josephus include one or more declarations by L. Lentulus, consul in 49 BCE, granting exemption from military service to the Jews of Ephesus who were Roman citizens. The declaration was followed by a similar one to the island of Delos and, evidently, to Sardis as well.[191] The exemptions need not imply that large numbers of Asian Jews enjoyed the Roman franchise, and the gesture may have had political ends in view.[192] Nevertheless, even as gesture it would have been empty and ineffective unless the existence of Jews as Roman citizens was familiar in the region. Just how they obtained this status eludes our grasp. Rewards for services, attainment of high office within a community, the patronage of Roman officials or generals, or even manumission of Jewish slaves in Rome who then resettled abroad might be postulated.[193] The precise privileges that accompanied possession of the Roman franchise remain controversial.[194] Status rather than concrete advantage may have been the principal *desideratum* for many. But the fact of Jewish eligibility for and frequent acquisition of that status holds high significance. No barriers excluded Jews from becoming full-fledged beneficiaries of Roman imperial power.

The picture is woefully incomplete. For the vast majority of Jews dwelling in the diaspora, the sources are silent. Hence any conclusions must be hesitant and hazardous. Yet the slender slivers of information leave an impression that is notably more positive than negative. Jews established synagogues in communities all over the Mediterranean. These institutions provided centers for vigorous religious, social, and civic life; they were no mere compensation or consolation for the absence of the Temple. The synagogues borrowed elements from pagan models and fit suitably within pagan society, but they also honored ties with Jerusalem and provided a means to maintain the distinctiveness of Judaism. The structures and/or the gatherings served, among other things, to foster instruction, promote worship, organize communal dining and festivals, maintain records, offices, and funds, enact measures, deliver verdicts, and generally to entrench a sense of collective identity. Jews selected their own officials, created governing bodies, set up tribunals, and enjoyed substantial self-rule. No standardization or uniformity held across the Mediterranean. But the ubiquity of the synagogue is striking. Its leaders, functions, and practices were open to public view and, with rare exceptions, unhindered by external authorities.

Self-governance, however, did not entail withdrawal or isolation. The record, small though it may be, discloses instances of Jewish participation in a whole range of activities connected to the traditions of Greco-Roman society. Individual Jews enrolled in gymnasia, went through the ephebate, attended the theaters, benefited from Hellenic education, and gained familiarity with Hellenic athletics. Some enjoyed civic privileges in certain communities, had access to the larger governing structure, and in a few instances even served as public officials in their cities. And, not least, growing numbers of Jews secured Roman citizenship, a key mark of status on the larger stage of the empire. Of course, this does not translate into untroubled existence everywhere and all the time. But diaspora experience, insofar as we can make it out, managed to combine access to the classical world with affirmation of a traditional identity.

JEWISH CONSTRUCTS
OF DIASPORA LIFE

Diaspora Humor I: Historical Fiction

JEWS OF THE Second Temple period did not perceive themselves as victims of a diaspora. That fact alone arrests attention. Jewish literature of the period refrains from expressions of melancholy on the current condition—indeed avoids explicit rumination on the circumstances of dwelling in scattered communities of the Mediterranean. The absence of express reflections, let alone lamentations, on the subject suggests that diaspora was not a "problem." Nothing compelled the Jews to develop a theory of diaspora, whether as consolation or justification.

The researcher thus runs into roadblocks. Any effort to match what we know of Jewish experience abroad with the comments of writers on their situation faces an uphill battle. Most of the surviving texts constitute inventive retelling of biblical tales or the creation of fanciful narratives, not contemplation of the Jewish plight. But the effort still pays dividends. Analysis of certain works can afford a glimpse, however tentative and indirect, into diaspora mentality and into the manner whereby Jews conceived their own place in diaspora society. An unexpected and striking feature can be discerned in these texts: their witty touches and upbeat quality. That may betray a mood very different from distress or despair—something more akin to the contentment already inferred from other evidence.

The prophet Jeremiah delivered a directive for the diaspora. His letter, addressed to Jews exiled in Babylon, offered sage counsel and consolation. It enjoined Jews in foreign parts to build homes, grow their own food, settle into marriages, become fruitful and multiply. More significantly, they were encouraged to work for the welfare of the city where now they dwell and promote its prosperity, for they prosper when it prospers.[1] Jeremiah, of course, conveying the commands of Yahweh, had the gift of prophecy and forecast a return from exile. But the manifesto itself can serve as a blueprint for diaspora existence, a guide for Jews who were developing strategies for survival and success in lands governed by Gentiles.

A surprising strategy, hardly high on Jeremiah's list but noteworthy and significant, merits consideration: the recourse to humor. Jews employed it to salutary effect. Mirth might brighten the existence or bolster the confidence of those caught in circumstances and places to which they needed to adjust their lives. Jews repeatedly found means both to spoof those set above them and to mock their own foibles, thus to diminish the one and to deflate the other. The jocular mode surfaces in numerous diaspora texts of the Second Temple period, ranging from subtle irony to broad farce. It does not, of course, follow that the comic voice is the only voice in these texts—let alone that interpretation along such lines exhausts the character and meaning of the works. But the exercise of wit and irony exists in abundance. And it may open an avenue into the mentality of Jews adapting to a world of alien culture and Gentile overlords.

Humor, as is notorious, defies definition. No effort to pin it down has much hope of success. Samuel Johnson's celebrated dictum, "comedy has been particularly unpropitious to definers," remains irrefutable. And there is little point in devising a list of criteria to employ as aids for detection. The very diversity of forms and ambiguity of content associated with humor undermine any effort to establish arbitrary boundaries. It can be serious or frivolous; it can have the aspect of savage mockery or gentle irony; it can upset conventions or satirize the unconventional; it can subvert norms or reinforce them; it can deliver cruel parody or generate uplifting laughter; it can be clever sophistication or rollicking slapstick; it can represent sly wit or boisterous exuberance; it employs caricatures and hyperbole but can deride the stereotyper rather than the stereotype. All these varieties and more can be found in Second Temple texts. They cannot be reduced to simple categories or standard formulas.

Nor should one expect a uniformity of response. What is a joke for one reader will fall flat with another. And the equation of one's own reaction with an author's intention is fraught with hazard, at best a suggestive proposal rather than a confident assertion—especially when dealing with a society and culture of so distant an era. The present reader's perspective inescapably shapes, perhaps misshapes, understanding of the texts. Yet the prodding of laughter occurs with remarkable frequency in many diverse and disparate works. Pure projection seems unlikely. Some of these works may have been conceived as comedies from start to finish; others have more sober objectives but include comic features or flashes of humor. The latter are at least equally revealing. They suggest that even authors of somber treatises with moral or religious lessons did not hesitate to inject occasional slices of wit and merriment.

What meaning does this practice carry for diaspora Jews? A convenient and seemingly obvious explanation suggests itself: a people in alien surroundings, suffering or fearing oppression, under the thumb of greater powers, may be "smiling through tears." Freud would appear to have the right answer. Laughter serves to mask a grim reality; humor permits a release of social aggressions by the powerless. By ridiculing the "other," mirth can suppress fear. Comedy serves as compensation.[2] Or, as Lord Byron famously put it, "if I laugh at any mortal thing, 'tis that I may not weep." It all seems logical enough. Yet this emphasis on dark comedy may not strike the right note. In the texts discussed below, humor depends on a sense of detachment and distance. The expression of superiority, a prime ingredient in comedy, commingles with self-criticism. Mockery can direct itself against foreign rulers, but also against Jews themselves—or, more commonly, against both. And much of the humor comes with a light touch, engaging parodies rather than cruel travesties. These texts leave the impression of a folk unburdened by a precarious existence and comfortable with the human comedy.

The comic vein by no means undermines the serious intent. The texts carry meaningful messages, whether reinforcement of religious conviction, collective enlightenment, maintenance of ancient traditions and practices, or reassertion of national identity. For these authors, humor can advance earnest objectives by deriding their foes—or even by mocking their advocates. No inconsistency exists here. Comedy is rarely more effective than when it is serious.

"Historical fiction," as it might be termed, constitutes a favorite medium for delight and edification. The works under scrutiny here provide an apparently plausible historical setting for their narratives, and make reference to known personalities and events. But their authors embellished at will, creating characters, manipulating or inventing facts, and spinning yarns to amuse their readership and advance their own purposes. The historical framework lent an air of familiarity but placed no restraint on creativity and imagination. The question of whether or not this constitutes a literary genre may be left aside. In any case, we know it when we see it. The medium also served as a vehicle for levity, parody, and satire—qualities closely associated with the experience of diaspora.

ESTHER

The Book of Esther appropriately stands at the beginning of this inquiry. Its diaspora setting is central, pivotal to plot and meaning. Its featured players are Jews in Susa under the regime of Persia and in the court of the

Persian king. Its composition came in the Persian era or early in the Hellenistic age, perhaps casting an influence on subsequent works in a comparable vein. And comic elements recur throughout.

A vast scholarly literature on Esther dwarfs the text. This is not the place
to rehash conventional controversies on issues of genre, structure, sources,
diverse versions, and canonicity. The focus here will be on the Masoretic
text, shortest of the extant versions and based on a tale earlier than that of
the two Greek variants with their additions grafted onto the story.[3] It is
also an exemplary comedic text.

The story line is familiar and famous, reproduced annually in every
Purim festival. It needs only a brief summary here. The scene opens at the
court of Ahasuerus, master of the Persian empire, whose domain reached
from India to Ethiopia. The king hosted a lavish banquet for all the officialdom of the realm, thus to put his great wealth on display. The festivities were to culminate in a visit from the ravishing Queen Vashti, summoned by the ruler to exhibit her beauty for his guests. Vashti, however,
refused to parade herself before the assemblage. Ahasuerus swiftly consulted his counselors and retaliated. A royal edict was issued not only banishing Vashti from the king's presence forever and ordering her replacement, but warning all women in the kingdom to be deferential to their
husbands.

That event triggered the plot to follow. Ahasuerus decreed a competition
for Vashti's successor, a contest to find the most comely of the realm's
young virgins to please the king. A large number of girls flocked to the call,
among them the beautiful and shapely Jewess Esther, an orphan raised by
her cousin Mordecai, one of those who had been exiled in the Babylonian
Captivity. After each of the maidens had undergone elaborate cosmetic
treatments and spent a night with Ahasuerus, the king selected Esther as
his favorite (she had concealed her ethnic identity on Mordecai's advice)
and set the regal crown on her head. The event was celebrated by yet another extravagant banquet.

Ahasuerus' principal vizier was the ambitious Haman, promoted and
honored by the king, but ever grasping for more. A royal command had directed that all courtiers and palace officials perform obeisance to Haman
whenever he appeared. There was general compliance, with one exception.
Mordecai, for reasons undisclosed, declined to bend a knee. The minister's
fury knew no bounds, impelling him to seek not only Mordecai's elimination but that of the entire Jewish people of whom he was a part. He persuaded the pliant Ahasuerus to order this genocide on the grounds that
Jews constitute a nation at variance with all others and follow a set of laws

incompatible with those of the empire. The decree was promulgated and published throughout the realm, authorizing the eradication of Jews everywhere—men, women, and children.

Mordecai greeted the news with sackcloth and ashes, as did Jews in every province under Persian rule. But he had a contact on the inside. Mordecai communicated with Esther through an intermediary, asked for her intercession, and suggested that she might have been placed in this position precisely for such a crisis. Esther overcame her initial reluctance and took the grave risk of an unsummoned interview with the king. Fortunately for Esther and for the Jews, Ahasuerus was still smitten with his young consort, promising her anything, up to half his kingdom. Esther played her cards carefully; she invited the king and Haman to dinner on two consecutive evenings, while withholding any explicit request. The vizier, more puffed up than ever by this distinction, pressed ahead with plans to punish the recalcitrant Mordecai—even installing a lofty gallows, on his wife's advice, to string up his enemy.

Fate—or something like it—intervened. Ahasuerus, afflicted with insomnia, had the royal chronicles read out to him. A particular passage hit home: it recorded that Mordecai had once saved the ruler's life by warning him of an assassination plot. And Ahasuerus learned to his dismay that this fine deed had gone unacknowledged. He then inquired of Haman as to how best to reward someone to whom the king wishes to pay signal honor. Haman, of course, surmised that the recipient would be none other than himself. A grave miscalculation. He proposed that the honorand be accorded a royal robe and horse with diadem and be led through the public square by one of the noblest of courtiers, who should proclaim his distinctions to all within earshot. Haman's balloon was swiftly punctured when the king announced that these honors would go to Mordecai and that Haman himself would perform the task of leading his horse and declaring his achievements. The humiliations multiplied. It was not enough that Haman had to humble himself before Mordecai; he had to hear from his own wife that he could not succeed against the Jew. Esther's plan could now come to fruition. At the evening's dinner with Ahasuerus and Haman, she at last unveiled her request: a plea that she and her people be spared destruction at the hands of one determined to annihilate them. The shocked king asked the identity of the villain, and Esther pointed a finger at Haman. The vizier took one last chance and made a desperate appeal to Esther, only to be perceived as attempting a sexual assault. That determined the final humiliation. Ahasuerus directed that Haman be hanged on the same gibbet that he had prepared for Mordecai.

The rescue and reversal for Esther's people ensued. The queen asked Ahasuerus to revoke the orders issued by Haman for extermination of the Jews. The generous Ahasuerus, who had already brought about Haman's demise and transferred his estate to Esther, went further still and gave carte blanche to Esther and Mordecai to compose whatever edict they wished in his own name. Mordecai took full advantage of this offer. The royal edict, whose wording he dictated, was sent to every province of the empire, not only rescinding Haman's letter but authorizing the Jews to take up arms against their enemies, eradicate them all, and confiscate their property. This, of course, led to rejoicing and festival—and also to ruthless implementation. The Jews hanged Haman's ten sons as an exhibit of their triumph, then proceeded to slaughter eight hundred of their foes in Susa and no fewer than seventy-five thousand elsewhere in the Persian dominions. Mordecai, glorying in success, proclaimed that the events should be commemorated annually in a two-day celebration, a practice dutifully followed through Jewish history thereafter. Esther's letters to her people reiterated and reconfirmed those of Mordecai. And Mordecai took his place as the most trusted and powerful of the king's ministers, as well as the chief advocate for the welfare of Jews throughout the realm.

Such is the gist of the Masoretic narrative. Even a bare summary reveals the reversals and ironies that pervade the text. These have long been recognized.[4] And the comic notes that enliven the story have received increasing acknowledgment in recent years.[5] They merit further and fuller scrutiny.

The very opening of the tale alerts the reader to the comedy that is in store. Ahasuerus' banquet is no meager feast. He invited every official in the realm, courtiers of the palace, officers of the imperial army, the Persian aristocracy, and the governors of all the provinces. The banquet lasted for one hundred and eighty days![6] Few readers could be expected to take that seriously. Would Ahasuerus denude his empire of all its officialdom for half a year?[7] And in a continuous revelry that encouraged every guest to drink to his heart's content?[8] The author is perhaps signaling from the outset that hyperbole, not historicity, will characterize this narrative.

Vashti's rebuff of the king's summons has been much discussed. The text offers no reason for the refusal, and rampant speculation has followed, including a rabbinic conjecture that Ahasuerus had asked her to appear in the nude.[9] Whatever the reason, the outcome can only provoke hilarity. The king's ministers panicked over the ramifications of the rebuff. If Vashti can get away with defying the king, will any household in the realm be safe from female dominance? Ahasuerus summoned royal advisers and legal experts. One of his chief ministers drew up a scary scenario: when word gets out to the wives of palace officials, there will be hell to pay—nothing but contempt and scorn for husbands by their spouses. Ahasuerus was persuaded to issue a pronouncement that would go to every imperial province, each in its own language to be sure of intelligibility, and to every household in the land: wives should respect the authority of husbands, and men should be masters in their own homes.[10] The satiric character of this episode could hardly be plainer. The summoning of a panel of judicial experts to advise on Ahasuerus' relations with his queen, the transforming of a domestic squabble into a grave matter of state policy, and the king's promotion of empire-wide publicity for his own embarrassment make the satire unmistakable. Letters demanding wifely submission in every household from one who could not even enforce it in his own underscore the point quite neatly.[11]

The beauty contest to identify Vashti's replacement extends the comedy. Ahasuerus appointed special deputies to scour the satrapies and round up all the lovely young virgins to be brought to the harem. There a eunuch supervised their preparation before each would have a night with the king. And quite a preparation it was. Ahasuerus was evidently not looking for some apple-cheeked, fresh-faced youngster. The contestants would undergo beauty treatments and immersion in cosmetics for a year—six months with myrrh and another six with perfumes and lotions![12] One might expect a bit of sprucing up for the sexual encounter, but a year's worth of makeup seems somewhat excessive. This must be a spoof of the seraglio.

The virtuous Mordecai does not fully escape the author's caustic wit. He evidently pushed his adopted daughter forward as a contestant, yet warned her against revealing her ethnicity and then paced up and down in front of the harem courtyard (for a year?) worrying about her treatment.[13] Mordecai also, though righteously donning sackcloth and ashes upon hearing of Haman's edict, had no hesitation in assuming princely garb to be led on horseback by Haman, and then appearing in royal splendor after promulgation of the pro-Jewish edict.[14]

Impulsiveness and extravagance characterize the actions of the ridiculous ruler. And his vizier Haman possesses comparable characteristics. As Ahasuerus blew up a slight by Vashti into a crisis of societal morals in the empire, so Haman took a snub by Mordecai as justification for a genocidal crusade against the Jews. That is over-reaction on quite a colossal scale. And Haman was prepared to pay top dollar for the privilege. He offered Ahasuerus ten thousand talents of silver, a gigantic sum, to be deposited in the royal treasury and thus to fund the operation. The king, not one to trouble himself unduly even with the gravest matters of state, essentially gave his minister carte blanche: "It's your money; do what you want with those people."[15] So much for the financial arrangements of an empire-wide campaign of the most far-reaching significance. The composer of this work is not concerned with a genuine crisis, but with the gross incongruity represented by the minister's excesses and the king's indifference.

Even in the darkest hour for the Jews, one might detect a sardonic little joke. The promulgation of Haman's decree for mass extermination sent Mordecai into mourning. He employed the traditional mode of behavior: a tearing of his garments and application of sackcloth and ashes. And when Esther learns of this behavior, what is her reaction? She sends Mordecai a new set of clothes![16] An array of sober and serious interpretations marks the scholarship on this episode.[17] But the author may simply have lent a touch of levity by alluding to Esther's naiveté.

A similarly slight note of mirth occurs in recounting Haman's misplaced pleasure at the honor paid him by Esther's dinner invitation. The self-delusion of the vizier is, of course, obvious, a primary feature of the irony enjoyed by the reader. But a gratuitous item is inserted when Haman summoned his friends and his wife to announce his good fortune. He not only boasted about the forthcoming private dinner party with the king and queen, but he recounted the many honors accorded him by the king, the extent of his wealth and resources—and even the large number of his sons. As if his wife needed to be told about the estate and the children![18]

The pivot of the whole piece comes when Ahasuerus is reminded that Mordecai had once saved his life by alerting the palace to an assassination plot. This dramatic discovery, so critical for the narrative, occurs, however, in a setting that exposes once again the whimsicality of the author. Mordecai's good deed had been recorded in the royal chronicles, but had altogether slipped the mind of the witless king. And how did he come upon the information? Ahasuerus had a case of insomnia and instructed his clerks to read aloud selections from the chronicles—evidently the most potent soporific imaginable.[19] The passage mischievously mocks not only the king but the character of the palace records.

Laughter at Haman's egocentrism and at the turnabout that caused his humiliation is, of course, a central ingredient in the effect of the narrative. The minister who had recommended the extravagant honors and expected to be their recipient found himself presenting the royal robe to Mordecai and leading him on horseback in full view of Susa's populace. Mordecai was elevated and Haman was mortified. The author cannot resist injecting a small detail to underline the absurdity. The wearing of a crown would be the most conspicuous mark of royal favor. The crown, however, would be worn not by the honorand but by the horse.[20]

Esther, after keeping the king in suspense for two days and hearing more than once his extravagant promise to gratify any wish up to half his kingdom, finally reveals her request. She pleads for protection for herself and her people from the evil persecutor who seeks wholesale destruction of the Jews. Ahasuerus, shocked and indignant, interrupts Esther and insists upon knowing who would have had the gall to conceive so wicked a scheme.[21] That outburst has been characterized, not unjustly, as "the story's most comic line."[22] Ahasuerus, who just a few days earlier had authorized Haman's plan, sanctioned the massacre, and allowed the edict, ordering it to be sent to every official and province in the empire under his own name, had already forgotten who had thought it all up—even though Haman was sitting right there with him at dinner!

The immediately subsequent scene is a classic instance of tragedy becoming farce. After Esther pointed to Haman as the villain and the furious king repaired to the garden to contemplate his next move, Haman threw himself upon Esther's mercy. Unfortunately for him, Ahasuerus returned at that moment to find Haman sprawled on the couch where Esther reclined. The king immediately concluded that he had interrupted a sexual assault. That sealed the minister's fate. One of Ahasuerus' eunuchs reminded him that Haman had erected a ludicrously lofty gallows on which to hang Mordecai. Ahasuerus directed that Haman himself be impaled upon it.[23] In short, Haman met his end not because he contrived to annihilate all the Jews in the Persian empire, but because the moronic monarch mistook an appeal to clemency for an attempted rape.[24]

The motif of reversal appears most markedly in Esther's request that Ahasuerus repeal the earlier edict on exterminating the Jews and legitimize Jewish retaliation instead. The pliant king yields as swiftly and unthinkingly to Esther as he had done to Haman. And as readers can readily recognize from the language employed to describe delivery of the decrees, the two events are mirror images of each other. Jews are authorized not only to engage in self-defense but to massacre their enemies, as they had themselves been targeted for massacre.[25] Moreover, in addition to the general irony, a more specific twist is injected. The king not only gave Esther and Mordecai full rein to compose the text of the decree, just as he had for Haman; he also observed that use of the royal seal meant that the decree was irrevocable.[26] That remark adds travesty to irony. Ahasuerus proclaims the irreversibility of royal edicts at the same time that he reverses one.[27]

The Jews duly carried out the assaults on their foes which the king's decree legitimized. Frightened Gentiles sought safety in conversion to Judaism—perhaps another sardonic aside by the author.[28] The slaughters themselves certainly did call forth a further bit of derision aimed at the king. Reports of the body count came into the palace: five hundred in the acropolis of Susa had been felled at the hands of the Jews. Ahasuerus announced the result with glee to Esther, and rejoiced at the prospect of what this must mean elsewhere in the kingdom. If five hundred were killed in the citadel, imagine how many had bit the dust in the satrapies![29] Beyond being indifferent to bloodshed, the king positively gloated over the slaying of his own Persians. That must be a dig at the dimwitted sovereign. The comic element may not compromise but it surely complicates any straightforward celebration of Jewish triumph.

None of this suggests that the Scroll of Esther is reducible to a comic sketch—let alone to formulaic carnivalesque.[30] But the humor is persistent and pervasive. Not only does the work mock the buffoonish, irresponsible, and absent-minded king; not only does it puncture the pompous prime minister engulfed in self-delusion; not only is the text filled with hyperbole and gross exaggeration like a 180-day banquet, 127 Persian satrapies, a full year's cosmetic treatment, and a gallows set 50 cubits in the air; but the sly and witty touches recur repeatedly, often unexpectedly. What does it all mean?

For one thing, it should set to rest any debate about the historicity of the tale. To be sure, the author has some facts about the Persian empire: the realm extended from India to Ethiopia in the time of Xerxes, who bears a resemblance to Ahasuerus; it possessed a very effective courier system; its rulers reclined on couches; its court practices included obeisance before high officials and rewards for the king's benefactors; hanging was employed as a punishment; names of persons in the story and a number of nouns in the text do correspond to Persian words.[31] But none of this has any relevance to the question of historicity—only to historical verisimilitude. On the same criteria, the text contains historical howlers: imperial administrative units numbering one hundred twenty-seven, a monarch's marriage to a non-Persian, the appointment of two successive non-Persians as prime minister, the dispatch of official letters in languages other than Aramaic.[32] They are, however, similarly irrelevant. The author was not composing a work of history and made no pretense of it. He signals his playfulness right at the beginning. Knowledgeable readers would know that the Persian empire was not divided into one hundred twenty-seven parts. And it required no knowledge at all to doubt that a royal banquet would keep most of the officialdom of the realm in their cups and away from their jobs for half a year. In the event that anyone missed those signals, the author makes a point of identifying Mordecai as a victim of the Babylonian Captivity, which took place a century before the time of Xerxes. Mordecai would therefore be a centenarian, not the most likely candidate for the demanding job of vizier, and his cousin would hardly be a contender in the Miss Persia contest. The Scroll of Esther can usefully be labeled a "historical novel," if by that is meant that the story is set in a historical context—but not that it conveys history or even that it is based on any historical "core."[33] One might best characterize it as a comic historical novel.

The setting, however, is significant. The story takes place in Susa, Mordecai is a Jew uprooted from Jerusalem and living in exile, Esther is a dependent orphan, and Jews are a minority group scattered through the lands of the Persian empire. The characters themselves are doubtless fictitious. No external evidence corroborates the events of the narrative. But the Scroll of Esther does carry a meaningful authenticity: it evokes the circumstances of Jews dwelling under the aegis of the Persian regime and subject to a mighty imperial power. And that authenticity is not bound by strict chronological limits. Indeed, the date of the text's composition remains beyond our grasp. Its author might have been a Jew living in the Iranian heartland, contemporary with the age of Persian dominance. He was familiar with Persian names and institutions and acknowledged the might of the empire. But he could also have employed the scenario from a distance, looking back on it from the Hellenistic era when the Achaemenids had been replaced by Alexander's successors—and even perhaps from Palestine where an exotic setting might make the novel more appealing.[34]

What matters is the diaspora existence. This holds a central place in the tale and has ramifications well beyond the Persian setting. The Scroll of Esther is often categorized as a *Diasporanovelle,* a reasonable enough designation insofar as it denotes significance for the experience of Jews in the diaspora.[35] The nature of the message delivered, however, is not so easy to characterize. A favored interpretation has it that the book recommends a life-style for diaspora Jews. The success of Mordecai at the conclusion of the tale has him both as second in command to the Shah, ruler of the empire, and as chief advocate for the interests of the Jews.[36] Esther employed her influential position to similar ends—the salvation and elevation of her people. These roles can serve to epitomize the implicit advice of the text: that Jews can be active and engaged participants in Gentile society, while simultaneously maintaining adherence to their own community.[37] On a variant of this analysis, the text teaches Jews that, in circumstances where they have no government or state of their own, no temple or priests, they are thrown back on their own spiritual and intellectual resources. But those who draw on such resources can lead productive and rewarding lives in a diaspora setting that is congenial and encouraging.[38] In other interpretations, however, the diaspora setting is anything but congenial. The book is seen as depicting a dark scenario in which Jews must learn to live with anxieties, to reconcile themselves to their status as a vulnerable minority, and to survive adversity.[39] This concept, framed in a more sophisticated fashion, has recently been portrayed as an identity crisis brought about by exile and dispersion, intensified through being defined externally, and left ambiguous by the text itself.[40] A very different reading of the Scroll of Esther stresses the brutal assaults delivered by Jews upon their foes. It is their power rather than their impotence which leaves the most vivid impression. The harsh revenge appears as gratuitous, even unjustified. Hence, on this reading, the work carries a critique, not a celebration, of Jewish behavior; the irony is directed against naive self-perception of Jewish rectitude.[41]

The diverse answers do not give full satisfaction. An author intent upon urging the compatibility of adherence to Judaism and a comfortable fit in Gentile society would not likely have made the massacre of seventy thousand Gentiles the culminating event of the story—let alone have it lead to the creation of a commemorative celebration. On the other hand, if the object were to remind Jews of the precariousness of diaspora existence and the need to brace themselves for misfortune, why choose the Persian scene for that lesson? In the annals of Jewish history, Persia was the liberator who toppled Babylon and allowed the return from exile. Nothing in the record shows any oppression of Jews in the Persian realm or reason to expect it.[42] Indeed, the Book of Esther itself depicts Persians generally as sympathetic to the would-be victims of Haman. When the vizier's decree of genocide was published, so says the text, the city of Susa was thrown into dismay.[43] And when the reversal of the decree came and Mordecai appeared in princely garb and crown, the city of Susa shouted for joy.[44] Even Haman's wife recognizes the popularity and prestige of the Jews, admonishing her husband that if he chooses to tangle with a Jewish opponent, his demise is certain.[45] Still less plausible is the idea that the work aimed to recall Jews to their ethical principles by censuring the self-perception that attaches to the revenge motive and the perpetration of slaughter. The narrative drops nary a hint of disapprobation for Jewish reprisal—indeed seems to relish the casualty count. This may be irony, but it is not instruction.

The standard explications have a serious drawback: they pay inadequate attention to the comic features that permeate the narrative. Sober didacticism is hardly the dominant mode of the text. Those scholars who have taken special notice of the humorous aspects tend to explain them as a means of alleviating Jewish anxieties in a vulnerable diaspora existence that could, at any moment, end in calamity.[46] Yet this notion of smiling through one's tears does not altogether ring true. Nothing in the text implies that Jews in the Persian domains lived in dread of disaster. The contest was one between Haman and Mordecai, a personal rivalry for influence in the court, not a clash of ethnicities in the empire. As for the "enemies" on whom the Jews avenge themselves, these were persons directed by Haman's edict to conduct genocidal sweeps, not inveterate anti-semites.

The whole idea of the Scroll of Esther as delivering moral admonitions or didactic lessons should be rethought. Even the notorious carnage inflicted by Jews upon their foes contains as much drollery as savagery. The royal edict, dictated by Mordecai, authorized his people to act in self-defense and gave them free rein to slay, destroy, and annihilate their enemies, men, women, and children, all on a specified single day several months in advance—the same day earlier designated for their own massacre.[47] Poetic justice perhaps, but hardly a serious scenario. Would Gentiles target themselves for eradication by behaving wickedly to Jews in the interim? And then present themselves conveniently for the slaughter on the designated day? Evidently so. When the time came, five hundred Persians were available in the citadel of Susa itself (presumably with the gate swung invitingly open) to be cut down by Jews. And no fewer than seventy-five thousand victims made themselves available to be butchered by Jews in the provinces on the same day, all done in "self-defense"—without a single Jewish casualty! That scene contains more slapstick than solemnity.[48]

Laughter need not require justification or rationalization. The humor in the Scroll of Esther carries its own impact. This is not consolation for anxiety-ridden diaspora Jews, nor is it mere vicarious wish-fulfillment against their foes.[49] Moral messages are muted. The mirth itself matters. The book ridicules the witless Ahasuerus and the fatuous Haman, but it can also poke fun at Esther's naiveté and Mordecai's not altogether selfless ambitions. And it turns the Jews' conquest of their opponents into a *reductio ad absurdum*. The jocularity of Purim either inspired the text or was inspired by it.[50] In any case, the topsy-turvy character and frivolity that mark both of them have a close affinity. A festive quality prevails.

This story does indeed have implications for diaspora existence. The whimsicality that portrays rulers as buffoons, Jews as flawed, and high state policy as comic travesty suggests confidence and self-possession in both author and readership. Life in the Persian empire (or its representation in a subsequent diaspora) was comfortable enough to generate witty parody and healthy hilarity. Not a bad recommendation.

TOBIT

The Book of Tobit, unlike Esther, did not make it into the Jewish canon. The reasons, much discussed and debated, remain elusive, and that controversy need not be addressed here.[51] The work has a charm and appeal comparable to the canonical Esther. Its combination of folktale, novelistic, wisdom, pietistic, and pseudo-historical elements give it a special character that may help explain its preservation in Christian circles and, as we now know, made it attractive even in Qumran.[52] And, although the text does not rock with side-splitting comedy, its sardonic humor accords a distinctive flavor that evokes the disposition of diaspora Jews.[53]

The tale, not so familiar as Esther, needs recapitulation. Tobit, like Mordecai, plays his role in exile; victimized by the Assyrian conquest of Israel, he dwells in Nineveh. His good deeds in Israel, his pious adherence to tradition, his devotion to Jerusalem, and his philanthropic activities did not spare him from capture and deportation. The charitable impulse continued in the lands of the Gentiles. But Tobit's career became a roller-coaster. He secured a high position under the Assyrian ruler Shalmaneser, using the opportunity to advance the welfare of his fellow Israelites abroad. And he persisted in such worthy acts even when they became dangerous under the next and less benign monarch, Sennacherib. An informer alerted the king to Tobit's practice of burying slain Israelites, causing our hero and his family to go underground. Happily, however, Sennacherib fell victim to assassins, his own sons, and the next sovereign appointed Tobit's nephew Ahiqar as prime minister of the realm. The good Tobit could now return to his home in Nineveh and resume his gathering of Jewish corpses to provide decent funeral rites. But no good deed goes unpunished. After burying a murdered Jew who had been dumped in the marketplace, Tobit took a nap, evidently exhausted by his labors, only to have sparrows employ his eyes as targets for their droppings and leave him a blind man. The tale turns briefly into a soap opera. With her husband incapacitated, Tobit's wife Anna decided to take a job and shore up the family finances. But that resulted in a domestic quarrel, followed by remorse, verbal self-flagellation, and prayers to God for delivery by death. Tobit was in desperate straits.

A second tale now supervenes. Off in Ecbatana in Media, the virtuous Jewish maiden Sarah suffered parallel agonies of a quite different variety. She had seven marriages, each of which ended abruptly on the wedding night when the hapless husband perished prior to reaching the marriage bed. Poor Sarah was haunted by an evil demon, Asmodeus, who killed off each bridegroom before the marriage could be consummated. On top of all that, she was reproached by one of her father's chambermaids for leading the flower of Ecbatana's Jewish youth to their doom. Sarah contemplated suicide, but thought better of it, resorting to prayer instead. Perhaps God could mercifully hasten her end.

God did indeed step in to set things right. But he chose a roundabout way to undo the damage for both victims. An angel of the Lord, Raphael, would serve as intermediary. When Tobit anticipated that his days were numbered, he delivered some testamentary advice to his son Tobias, a lengthy set of ethical precepts, and he asked him to go to Media where he would find the princely sum of ten silver talents deposited at the home of Tobit's friend and kinsman Gabael. Tobias was ready to comply but did not know how to get there. Raphael now conveniently materialized—the friendly angel disguised as an average Israelite in Assyria, who happened to know the route to Media. Moreover, he claimed to be a close relative, thus earning for himself Tobit's enthusiastic commission to accompany Tobias to Media.

Unbeknownst to the innocent Tobias, Raphael was preparing to solve all of his and his family's problems—and those of Sarah to boot. In the course of the journey, a pause at the river Tigris allowed the travelers to capture a great fish which Tobias, on Raphael's instructions, proceeded to gut and eat, saving the gall, the heart, and the liver for future and better purposes. Upon arrival in Media, Raphael directed his young companion on a detour to Ecbatana where they would lodge with another kinsman, Raguel, who happened to be the father of the luckless multiple widow Sarah. Raphael broached the prospect of an ideal marriage: Tobias and Sarah are nearest kin, hence appropriate, even predetermined, partners according to Mosaic law—a union that Raguel would be bound to bless. Tobias expressed understandable reluctance: he had heard about the fates of Sarah's seven previous bridegrooms. But Raphael offered reassurance, reminding him of the liver and heart of the fish packed away in a sack. Their magical qualities would soon overcome any demon or evil spirit. Tobias took heart. Raguel and his wife Edna rejoiced in meeting the son of their beloved relative Tobit, gave immediate consent to a wedding with their daughter, and drew up a marriage contract. Of course, there was a problem. Raguel was honor-bound to warn Tobias that he had had seven predecessors—none of whom made it through the wedding night alive. But Tobias was fortified. He extracted the fish liver and heart from his bag and deposited them upon the ashes of the incense, just as Raphael had advised him, thus creating an odor that no demon could tolerate. The wicked spirit Asmodeus took one whiff and headed straight for Upper Egypt. Tobias and Sarah could now proceed to deliver thanks to the Lord for the opportunity to grow old together.

Raguel in the meantime was taking no chances. Past experience had given him good cause for concern. He had his servants prepare Tobias' grave, so as to streamline the burial process and put his latest son-in-law away before the neighbors noticed. But when a maidservant announced that the happy couple were still intact, Raguel sent up prayers of joy and gratitude—and hurried to fill in the grave.

One happy ending deserved another. Raphael went off to fulfill Tobias' initial mission. He brought the ten talents of silver from Gabael and brought Gabael himself to help celebrate the wedding festivities. Tobias soon prepared for return to Nineveh with his new bride and new riches. His in-laws were not eager to see him go, making excuses to delay the departure, but had to yield eventually. Tobias' parents were getting anxious, especially his mother who wondered whether he would ever make it back alive, thus prompting yet another quarrel with her husband. But all ended well. Not only did Tobias arrive, with wife and wealth in tow, but Raphael had tutored him on how to put the fish gall to best use. Tobias blew into the unseeing eyes of his father, smeared the fish substance upon them, and then peeled away the bird deposit. Tobit miraculously could see again. There followed embraces all around, ecstatic rejoicing, and heartfelt hymns of thanksgiving. Raphael abandoned his pretense, acknowledged himself an angel of the Lord, and disappeared into heaven, thus prompting a lengthy psalm of praise.

Only the epilogue remains. Tobit's psalm blends joy with foreboding. God deserves gratitude not only for the mercy he shows and the blessings he brings, but also for the pain he has inflicted as penalty for the iniquities of the children of Israel. And there is more to come. On his deathbed, Tobit, having lived to one hundred and twelve, had some sage warning for his son. He advised him to gather his household and head for Media. The Lord's wrath would soon fall upon Nineveh and upon Assyria in general. But the Israelites too would suffer again. The forecasts of the prophets would be fulfilled, the land of Israel ravaged, and its inhabitants scattered. Of course, divine mercy would descend once more, the Temple eventually would be restored, and the exiles would return. But better not to wait. Tobias got the message. He buried his father, then his mother, packed up, and headed straight for Media. There he dwelled securely in the land of his

in-laws, buried them too, and inherited both estates to live comfortably in
Ecbatana. He could now contemplate the destruction of Nineveh at a distance and in safety.

The above summary, while tailored somewhat to present purposes, indicates clearly enough the whimsy and caprice that animate this narrative.
The work itself is a mélange of styles and genres, a blending of sources, a
remolding of models. Its folktale character is obvious, with strong parallels in pagan literature, but the text weaves together at least three tales
or themes.[54] Biblical echoes recur with frequency, including clear reso-
nances from wisdom literature, with its didactic overtones, and even some
allusions to the travails of Job—although Tobit never questions the afflictions he endures. The novelistic quality of the work is plain and unmistakable, but affinities with the Greek romances are overmatched by the differences.[55] As with Esther, the historical setting is relevant and significant, yet
chronological and factual errors undermine any notion of a strong historical consciousness. This is no work of history. Labels are best avoided.
Complexity and variety stand out. The humor, however, repeatedly cap-
tures attention and merits highlighting.

Tobit begins the narrative as narrator.[56] And he wastes no time in asserting his own righteousness: "I walked in the paths of truth and righteousness all the days of my life."[57] That he makes this claim at the outset and in
his own voice is noteworthy. The irony should not be missed. The author
puts the reader on notice right away: perhaps Tobit has reason to insist
upon his virtue. Just how righteous a character is this? Tobit makes a point
of distinguishing himself from his own countrymen and tribesmen. While
they looked to local divinities, he alone maintained tradition, made regular
pilgrimages to Jerusalem, brought his tithes to the Temple, supported orphans, widows, and proselytes.[58] And his stance as sole pillar of the faith
continued into exile. Even members of his family became backsliders and
were assimilated; he alone kept kosher.[59] More than a touch of arrogance
inheres in these statements.[60] Tobit boasts of burying fellow Israelites killed
in Nineveh—acts of courage but perhaps also excessive swagger. He persisted in this practice under a new king even though forced into hiding under his predecessor. Admirable behavior? His neighbors didn't think so.
They derided the reckless Tobit: had he learned nothing from past experience?[61] Shortly thereafter he got his comeuppance: the nap, the sparrow
droppings, and the sightlessness. It is hard to resist the impression that this
portrayal of Tobit's blinding is wickedly satirical. One can imagine a multitude of means to bring about that affliction, but bird excreta would not
spring first to mind. This serves to make Tobit's plight not poignant but ri-

diculous. And another sardonic touch is added: the more the physicians applied their remedies, the worse his eyesight got, until he lost it altogether. So the doctors get their knocks as well.[62]

Tobit did not take his adversity well. When his wife Anna secured employment, this only underscored his incapacity. And when she brought home a young kid from her employer in addition to her regular wages, Tobit immediately suspected that it came through theft rather than as a bonus. His blunt accusation and refusal to believe Anna's denial drew a sharp and appropriate rejoinder from his wife: "And where are your acts of charity? Where are your deeds of righteousness? Look at yourself as others see you!"[63] Tobit's misfortune, it seems, is not altogether undeserved. His pompous sanctimoniousness was punished with bird droppings, and his self-righteousness earned a proper rebuke. And his reaction to Anna's reprimand rendered him still more ridiculous. Tobit resorted to a pitiful prayer, pleading with the Lord to release him from his misery and allow him to die. The misery he specified, however, was not the blindness or any other ailments, just the insults to which he had been subjected![64] A domestic spat, in short, was enough to send Tobit into spasms of self-pity and a death-wish—a rather striking over-reaction. Tobit hardly emerges as an estimable figure.

A comparable analysis can be applied to Tobit's counterpart in Ecbatana, the luckless Sarah, whose boudoir had sent seven suitors to their doom. She too received harsh reproaches, from none other than a domestic employee in her father's household. The servant lashed out at Sarah, blaming her for killing off her bridegrooms, and expressing the wish that she join them rather than keep badgering for more husbands. And the maid had good reason for her outburst: Sarah's frustration had driven her even to beat her servants.[65] The likelihood of a domestic employee chastising her mistress in such language is, of course, small. This only accentuates the topsy-turvy situation projected by the author. Sarah was no innocent waif, and she got her rebuke from an uppity subordinate, just as Tobit got his from an uppity wife. Her over-reaction, moreover, provides a precise parallel: she decides promptly upon suicide. And the driving force again is the humiliation brought by insults—not the aborted marriages.[66] But the text here adds a still more pointed and sardonic aspect. Sarah swiftly changed her mind about hanging herself. It would reflect ill upon her father. And he has no other living relative to be heir to his name and property.[67] A worthy motive, one might suppose, for declining to do away with herself. Yet Sarah went on to pray for death anyway, reemphasizing the insults she had received at a servant's hands—and ignoring the effects this would have upon a bereaved father.[68] Sarah is no more a paragon of virtue than is Tobit. The author cynically subjects the two supposed exemplars of unmerited suffering to a parodic exposure of flawed character.

So much for the central personalities. The exhibition of wry and sometimes bitter humor occurs also in numerous smaller ways at different and often unexpected parts of the text. As an example, note the long and tedious exhortation delivered by Tobit to his son, in the form of testamentary advice, for Tobit expected soon to breathe his last. He urged upon his son a life of exemplary morality, including the honoring of his parents with proper burials, charitable activities, adherence to the Commandments, temperance, industry, and endogamous marriage. Among these pronouncements, Tobit advised his son to avoid arrogance toward his kinsmen, for in arrogance there is ruin.[69] There is a nice irony here: Tobit's own arrogance had brought him low. The close of the speech, however, has the nicest twist. Tobit remarked to Tobias that, although the family had been reduced to poverty, he need have no anxiety, for much good is in store for one who fears God, avoids sin, and performs righteous acts in the eyes of the Lord. That noble sentiment apparently contrasts the absence of material wealth with the spiritual satisfaction of good deeds.[70] Yet the author juxtaposes this with the actual purpose of the mission on which Tobit was sending his son: to collect ten talents of silver that he had deposited with Gabael.[71] Tobit, it seems, did not fully rely on the warm glow that might come from virtuous behavior. He wanted his son to be supplied with cash.

The issue, in fact, sparked another exchange between husband and wife. Anna did not relish the prospect of her son taking off on a distant journey, perhaps never to return. They need him at home. She upbraids Tobit for sending Tobias away. And for what? Money? We can live on what we have.[72] The author does not miss a chance to disclose domestic discord—especially when it suggests that Tobit pays more regard to funds than to family.

That same motif is picked up again later, the occasion for yet another spat between the bickering couple. Anna had been mollified when Tobit reassured her that their son had a reliable traveling companion and would return safe and sound. But as the months went by, with no sign of Tobias, Anna was convinced that he had died abroad and she would never see him again. Tobit too was worried—but not for the same reason. He feared the worst: that Gabael, from whom Tobias was to collect the cash, might be dead and the money gone for good! The mercenary motive once again supersedes parental anxiety. And the parents are at cross-purposes. Anna was inconsolable. When Tobit, confident about his son's safety but concerned for the cash, tried to persuade her that Tobias was merely delayed, she snapped back: "Quiet! And don't lie to me."[73] Tobit, of course, was right about his son's safety. But Anna had the last word. And the narrator, one might infer, makes sport of Tobit's skewed priorities.

The trip to Ecbatana provided another occasion for some tongue-in-cheek. The plot, of course, requires that the travelers acquire some potions or remedies that will solve both Sarah's and Tobit's problems, i.e., exorcise demons and cure blindness. The gall, liver, and heart of a fish would do the trick. Whatever the basis in folklore of such solutions, the means whereby Tobias and Raphael obtained their fish surely points to some whimsy on the author's part. They did not camp on the Tigris for a fishing expedition. Instead a comic scene ensued, in which a huge fish leaped spontaneously out of the water and aimed at Tobias' foot in hopes of gulping it down! The young man gave a shout. And Raphael swiftly issued instructions to grab the fish and hang onto it. Tobias did as he was told and overpowered his prey, dragging it onto dry land. He then proceeded to remove the organs that would serve their purposes and consumed the rest.[74] Just what symbolism, if any, these items conveyed remains elusive. On one theory, the episode constitutes a parody of the Jonah tale; on another, Tobias' "foot" is a euphemism for his genitals, thus giving rise to a host of speculative interpretations.[75] Whatever hypothesis one applies, the spectacle of the great fish hurtling itself out of the river to snatch a part of Tobias' anatomy, with the young man first leaping out of the way and then wrestling the fish into submission, looks irresistibly like a piece of comic entertainment.[76]

The application of the remedies suggests similar facetiousness. Upon entering the bridal chamber Tobias dropped the heart and liver of the fish on incense ashes; the foul odor wafted its way to the demon's nostrils (no one else evidently minded the smell); and he forthwith zoomed off to Upper Egypt—a trek of two thousand miles. Good riddance, one might assume. But Raphael would not leave well enough alone. He raced after the demon to Egypt in order to shackle him hand and foot.[77] That seems unnecessary thoroughness. And nobody appears to have missed Raphael while he was gone. Angels and demons, of course, have their own means of transport. But all of this heightens the comedic spirit of the scene.

The cure for Tobit's blindness seems comparably capricious. The gall of the fish was saved for this purpose. Tobit's eyes were still closed by the white patches resulting from the bird deposits. But, as Raphael had directed him, Tobias had the remedy ready. He first blew into his father's eyes (for reasons unexplained), and then smeared the fish gall upon his eyelids. Lo and behold, the white patches could now just be peeled off—and Tobit's sight was immediately restored.[78] It is not easy to take this as serious medicinal intervention.[79] The Lord works in mysterious ways. But fish substance spread upon bird droppings may have less to do with magic or medicine than with mockery.

The exorcism of the demon Asmodeus allowed Tobias and Sarah to have an untroubled night together. But a hint of the author's wry wit may exist even here. The happy couple begin their evening's activities with a pious prayer. And Tobias vows that he takes his "sister" not out of any lust but in truth. He seeks only mercy for them and an old age together. The prayer concludes with both chanting a double "amen."[80] One can, of course, take this as a pure paean to piety. Or, just perhaps, a sly allusion to incongruity between words and action. They did proceed to sleep together.

One good reason exists for detecting a whimsical tone here. The immediately succeeding scene, which in fact is simultaneous with the couple's nuptial night, is the most hilarious of the piece. Raguel, father of the bride, who had lost seven successive sons-in-law, could not face the embarrassment of an eighth. If his neighbors learned of it, he would be mortified. Raguel therefore instructed his servants to dig a grave in order to have a resting place prepared for the next victim and a swift burial before daybreak, so that no one would be the wiser. Of course, he needed to be sure that Tobias had met the same fate as his predecessors. A maidservant was sent to the bedroom to spy upon the couple, and she dutifully peered in to find them sleeping peacefully together (no sign of lust or loss). When the peeping maid delivered her report, Raguel scrambled to undo the damage. An unfilled grave would be as humiliating as a deceased son-in-law. So the servants hastily covered up the ditch, and when the sun rose Raguel could breathe a sigh of relief—and arrange a great feast.[81] In the midst of this culminating event in the Sarah-Tobias saga, the frazzled Raguel bustles about to avoid becoming a laughingstock to his neighbors. There can be little doubt that this episode was crafted with a delicious sense of humor.

Wherein lies the lesson of this book? It does not, of course, constitute a full-scale satirical novel. And the comedic aspects do not undermine more serious messages delivered in the prayers, the ethical pronouncements, and the overcoming of adversity by the characters. Nevertheless, the sardonic wit has its force; it is no mere sidelight or appendage but an integral part of the text. And this clearly bears relevance to the experience of diaspora Jews.

The diaspora context is critical. All the action of the story occurs in the realm of the Assyrian empire. But no Gentiles take part in the plot. Only the kings of Assyria receive mention, and although the change of rulers does have an effect, they are remote from the field of play. This is a tale of diaspora Jews.

The narrative takes place in a specified historical setting: the aftermath of Assyria's conquest of the Northern Kingdom in the late eighth century and the removal of Israelites to the land of the conqueror. But historicity ends there. No one will confuse this story with a work of history. The author makes little effort to reproduce persons or events with historical accuracy. Even the kings of Assyria are presented out of order and in a confused manner.[82] And the author's knowledge of Mesopotamian geography is decidedly limited.[83] This has led modern scholars to declare that he could not have been a contemporary of the Assyrian conquest.[84] To be sure. The point, however, is not that he makes historical errors, but that historicity is irrelevant. This is creation or recreation of a narrative placed in a historical frame, but making no pretense of an authentic record. Hence it is better seen as exemplifying or illuminating more broadly the experience of Jews compelled to adjust to alien circumstances.

The actual dates and provenance of the author remain indeterminable. For most scholars, the absence of reference to Antiochus IV's persecution or to the ethnic and religious hostilities of the Maccabean age make it definitively pre-Maccabean.[85] For others, by contrast, the prominence of the burial issue would date it precisely to the Maccabean era, when Antiochus prohibited Jewish burials![86] This form of chronological pinpointing, however, is misguided. Arguments from silence carry little weight—especially as we have post-Maccabean treatises that show perfect harmony between Jews and Gentiles, like the *Letter of Aristeas*. And the expectation of a one-to-one or close correspondence between historical events and episodes in the book misconceives its character. The work was certainly composed after the erection of the Second Temple, to which explicit reference is made in the form of prophecy. And it is unlikely to have come after the destruction of the Temple in 70 CE, when this glorious prediction would seem rather empty.[87] It would be prudent not to claim greater precision.[88] The locus of the author is equally irrecoverable. Countless conjectures, ranging from Palestine to Persia, have reached little consensus.[89] A majority of scholars incline to somewhere in the diaspora. But the setting of the piece does not prove this, nor does the fact that it deals with issues endemic to diaspora life. A Palestinian Jew could certainly have composed a work addressing those issues which had become a recurring and enduring part of Jewish existence. One can say no more than that the composition directed itself to the communities of the dispersed.[90]

The Book of Tobit, on the face of it, delivers some empowering mandates for the diaspora. Its tale exhorts those scattered in exile to keep the faith in adversity, to adhere to the teachings of their fathers, to hold their co-religionists to the highest ideals, and to reinforce the solidarity of the clan. In this fashion the career of Tobit, who overcame misfortune, relying on the mercy and beneficence of God, can serve as a model for diaspora Jews—and indeed perhaps inspire even the Gentiles to embrace the true religion. Steadfastness and piety will reap the proper rewards, ultimately achieving the revival of Jerusalem as a beacon to the nations.[91] More explicitly, the work enjoins Jews dwelling in the lands of the Gentiles to maintain their special identity through strict endogamy, a theme that runs throughout the tale, thus assuring survival of the tribe and continuity of its distinctiveness.[92] In one interpretation, this drive for identity by preserving kinship ties is sharpened by male ordering of diaspora existence through the subordination of women.[93] Tobit's reach, however, can extend beyond tribalism. His last prayer and his deathbed speech offer a broader vision in which Jerusalem will eventually encompass Jew and Gentile alike, attracting all the nations of the world to its light.[94]

All this, to be sure, can be found in the text. And its uplifting character need not be denied. But the comic elements must be given their due. The humor that enlivens the narrative also modifies, compromises, and gently subverts the nobler messages. Focus on the family as the bonding link for diaspora Jews is carried to a point bordering on the burlesque. Virtually every character in the story possesses a kinship relationship to the house of Tobit. His wife Anna comes from that stock; so does Gabael, with whom he left his ten talents for safekeeping; and so does Raguel, the father of Sarah, whose whole household is thus linked to that of Tobit. Even Ahiqar, chief minister to the Assyrian crown, is appropriated from another legend to become the nephew of Tobit. And the angel Raphael takes on the role of a close kinsman in order to win the confidence of Tobit.[95] No wonder all the characters, even husbands and wives, greet one another as sister and brother, with ludicrous repetition![96] And no wonder that Tobias and Sarah were meant for each other for eternity.[97] This is endogamy with a vengeance—one big, happy family. The narrator is surely having a bit of fun here. Maintenance of kinship ties might bring some stability to an otherwise fragmented diaspora existence. But clannishness, when carried to excess, prompts ridicule.

The tale does project worthy ideals: endurance in misfortune and the overcoming of adversity through adherence to faith and tradition, which brings divine reward. But the central characters do not always rise to the occasion. The maudlin prayers for death by Tobit and Sarah, when rebuked by uppity subordinates, hardly exemplify courage in adversity. The narrator indeed takes pleasure in exposing the foibles of his creatures: Tobit's pompous piousness, Sarah's self-absorption, Tobias' naiveté and anxieties, Raguel's dread of neighborly disapproval. All achieve happy endings, thanks to the *deus ex machina,* Raphael. And even he has to employ some risible remedies to effect his purposes. The work conveys admirable principles but does not let the reader forget that their practitioners are human, flawed, and, at times, farcical.

If there are lessons here for the diaspora, they are not simplistic or onesided. Tight kinship bonds might preserve continuity within the clan, but, when taken to extreme, they end in narrow interiority. Prayers can evince piety, but not when driven by wounded egos or amour propre. Ethical pronouncements have their place, so long as they do not stem from sanctimoniousness or swagger. The author of Tobit does not indulge in ham-handed travesty but prefers lighthearted lampooning and subtle subversion.

The diaspora existence portrayed in the Book of Tobit is far from an unrelievedly dismal one. Tobit's fortunes have their ups and downs. He is a man of wealth and influence in one reign, a fugitive in the next, and back in favor in the third. Even in his darkest days, he has money stashed away, relatives galore, and friends and family who can move without hindrance through the Assyrian empire. He gets more grief from his wife and from well-aimed bird droppings than from the authorities. Sarah too is plagued by a fiendish spirit, not by menacing Gentiles. Raguel fears his neighbors' scorn rather than official displeasure. And there is more discord within the households than without. It is not altogether incongruous that Tobit's final declarations, which are deadly serious, look beyond constricted clannishness to a broader blending of Jew and Gentile. The comedic features of the tale, while occasionally cutting and parodic, move in step with its upbeat quality. The author can take his Jewish characters down a peg without bemoaning their Assyrian ordeal. If the Book of Tobit is any guide, the Jews negotiated the diaspora rather well.

JUDITH

The Book of Judith delivers an edifying and uplifting message. Although outside the canon, it has held its place through the ages as compelling dramatic fiction—the rescue of the Jews from the brink of disaster by a clever, beautiful, and pious woman who upholds the faith, entraps the enemy general, and provides his head as a prize. The moral lesson of trust in God and adherence to his laws is fundamental, a test of the Jews' faithfulness by pushing them to the point of annihilation. But the didacticism is embedded in a memorable story of greed and arrogance; weakness by the wavering and courage by the devout; shrewdness and ineptitude; salvation for the righteous and destruction for the wicked; the glory and modesty of the heroine; and a blessedly happy ending. As a tale of Jewish success against all odds and over the aggrandizer and oppressor, the narrative had immense appeal and was much retold over the ages.[98] And few major museums in Europe lack a representation of Judith holding the severed head of Holofernes.[99] The work's hold on popular imagination continues unabated. But a principal source of its attractiveness has rarely received attention: its comedic elements.

Diaspora as such does not form part of the tale. The assault comes in Palestine itself. But the narrative is set in the time not long after the Jews' return from exile, a vulnerable period when a new scattering or even destruction still loomed, and when relations with greater and surrounding powers constituted a central feature of that precarious existence.[100] Moreover, the earliest extant texts are the Greek manuscripts of the Septuagint. Although they derive almost certainly from a now lost Hebrew original, the story's appeal to a non-Palestinian readership ensured its preservation. Indeed, the Greek version gained circularity and popularity, while the putative Hebrew model seems to have disappeared already in antiquity. Judith was well known to Clement of Rome in a Greek text by the late first century CE.[101] But no Semitic version has surfaced anywhere, even in the eclectic fragments at Qumran. And Origen explicitly denied the existence of any Hebrew texts of Judith or Tobit in his day.[102] The story, distributed in Greek, obviously carried a meaningful resonance for those who dwelled in the lands of the diaspora.[103]

The highlights of the narrative require rehearsal. The context (wholly imaginary) is a putative military campaign ordered by Nebuchadnezzar, here identified as the mighty monarch of Assyria(!), against various peoples of the Near East, including those dwelling in Judaea and Samaria. The great king had sought the aid of surrounding nations for his war on the Medes. Many refused to heed his call. And once Nebuchadnezzar had brought the Medes to heel, he determined to wreak vengeance upon the recalcitrant nations. The ruler appointed the captain of his hosts, Holofernes, to lead troops against them, to demand obeisance, and to massacre those would not give it. Holofernes swept through the lands, subjugated or slaughtered those in his path, ravaged their fields, and toppled their gods, enforcing worship of Nebuchadnezzar alone.

Only the children of Israel remained on his itinerary. They had them-

selves returned but recently from captivity to reconsecrate their own temple, altar, and sacred vessels. Now they trembled in fear for their well-being. On instruction from the High Priest and his council in Jerusalem, they
blocked the mountain passes, put on sackcloth and ashes, and prayed to
the Lord for rescue. Weeping, wailing, and fasting followed.

Holofernes raged at the Israelites' refusal to capitulate. He inquired as to
what manner of men they were. The Ammonite chieftain Achior, whose
people had already surrendered to the invader, gave Holofernes a thumb-
nail sketch of Israelite history and warned him that the nation was in-
vincible whenever their god favored them, but vulnerable if they have
sinned against him. Holofernes was in no mood for history lessons. His officers and troops, as well as other peoples who had joined his side, reviled
Achior. Holofernes himself delivered a furious blast at Achior's reckless audacity in exalting the god of the Jews and ignoring the might of the true divinity Nebuchadnezzar, whose forces will lay them low. He sent Achior off
packing; his men delivered him at the base of a mountain, trussed and help-
less, to the Jews of Bethulia to suffer with them the siege now prepared by
the army of Assyria.

The inhabitants of Bethulia (an unlocatable town) released Achior from
his bonds, learned of the approaching onslaught, and swiftly became desperate. One hundred seventy thousand Assyrian infantry and twelve thousand cavalry spread across the plain, seemingly threatening to occupy the
whole earth and striking terror into the hearts of the Israelites. Holofernes
seized the springs at the foot of the mountain to cut off the water supply
to Bethulia. As cisterns dried up and men began dropping in the streets,
the citizens of Bethulia pressed their leaders to surrender: better to serve
Assyrians as slaves than to watch the population perish. The city's most
prominent figure, Uzziah, proposed a five-day wait in the hope that God
might intervene, but promised surrender if no sign of such intervention
materialized.

At this point Judith enters the scene. A respected and wealthy widow,
she carried an impressive pedigree with a string of illustrious ancestors, including some biblical figures. Her piety was awesome. Judith had been
fasting for three and a half years since her husband died, eating only on the
Sabbath and the day before, and on the festal days of her people. No one
could say a word to discredit her, a woman who so devoutly feared the
Lord. Judith now summoned the city's elders and flailed them with rebukes. What gives them the arrogance to deliver a deadline to God? Who
are they to threaten surrender if the Lord does not come to their rescue in
five days, as if they were putting him on trial? Are they so obtuse as not to

see that he is putting them to the test, just as he did Abraham, Isaac, and Jacob? Uzziah offered excuses, pleading the lack of water and popular pressure, and asking Judith to pray for rain that might fill the cisterns. Judith brushed off the request but promised to act on behalf of Israel—so long as the city's leaders did not inquire what she was doing. Uzziah and other officials gave her free rein.

Judith first prayed to God for strength and support, then took matters into her own hands. A beautiful as well as a wise woman, she cast off her sackcloth and widow's garb, did up her hair, put on jewelry and perfume, and bedecked herself in her most alluring outfit. With but a single maidservant, Judith marched through the gate of the city, dazzling Uzziah and the elders with her loveliness on the way, and headed straight for the camp of Holofernes—while the city's men could not take their eyes off her. She presented herself to the Assyrians as one who had fled the Israelites in anticipation of their calamity and offered to advise Holofernes on the means whereby to take Bethulia with a minimum of effort. The Assyrians, never questioning her motives and as smitten with her beauty as were the Israelites, ushered her immediately into the tent of Holofernes. Judith duly paid obeisance to the Assyrian general, who had no hesitation in giving her full confidence. She captivated Holofernes not only with her looks but with beguiling and manipulative language, playing up to his ego and persuading him that she would guide him personally to the conquest of all Judaea. The entrancing widow essentially repeated the advice of Achior, affirming that the Israelites will fall only when they have sinned against God. But this time, she said, she will pray to God to tell her just when the sin occurs and she will let Holofernes know, so that he can seize the moment and commence his assault.

Holofernes bought it all. He offered Judith all the food and wine of his elaborate table, but she kept kosher. A few days later came the inevitable invitation to spend the night in Holofernes' tent. She put on her finest apparel but brought her own food. Holofernes, of course, was completely enraptured. Judith roused his desire, then watched as he drank himself into a stupor. And when the intoxicated captain passed out, Judith, armed with prayer and a sword, lopped off his head. She rolled his body off the bed and dropped his head in a sack provided by her maid. The two women slipped from the camp, toting the sack, and returned to the gates of Bethulia. There they had the city's elders display the head of Holofernes on the battlements of the wall. The people stood awestruck at the deed. Achior the Ammonite collapsed in a faint, then praised Judith to the skies, had himself circumcised, and converted to Judaism. The Assyrians, stunned and crestfallen when they discovered Holofernes without a head, thought only of flight. They proved to be an easy prey for the Israelites, who poured out of their gates, routed the enemy, and gathered the vast spoils that had accumulated. Judith received plaudits not only from the citizenry of Bethulia but from the High Priest and his council in Jerusalem (who had come to view the devastation). She in turn led the women of Bethulia in a triumphant dance and delivered a lengthy hymn of thanksgiving to God. But she declined further honors and glory. The devout widow chose to retire to her own estate, emancipated her loyal attendant, and declined all offers of marriage from eager suitors in order to live out her lengthy days in serenity. Judith died at the age of one hundred and five.

The solemn religiosity of Judith underpins the whole tale. Her own successes, even when achieved through guile and audacity, are always accompanied by prayers to Yahweh and humble obeisance to his presumed will, which is ultimately responsible for the outcome. Judith's piety is her most conspicuous characteristic.[104] The narrative reinforces the omnipotence and the clemency of God. He not only smites the wicked Assyrians but spares the faltering Israelites. They can take a lesson from their devout heroine.[105]

But solemnity is not, in fact, the dominant tone of the tale. Wit and humor pervade it, inadequately recognized but vital for understanding. The irony of the author, to be sure, has not escaped notice—the double entendres in Judith's speech and elsewhere, the reversals of form by characters, and the upsetting of expectations.[106] And some have observed the occasional intrusion of humor.[107] But its extensive use holds a more central place and merits closer inspection.

Playfulness begins right at the beginning. The author makes Nebuchadnezzar king of the Assyrians with his capital at Nineveh, has him conduct a triumphant campaign against Arphaxad, ruler of the Medes, and describes him as lord of all the earth.[108] None of this bears the slightest relation to reality. Nebuchadnezzar, of course, ruled in Babylon, not Assyria; he made no war on, let alone conquered, the Medes, whose king Arphaxad is sheer invention; and he never claimed lordship of the earth. To reckon such statements as mistakes, anachronisms, or historical inaccuracies on the author's part is to miss the point altogether.[109] Nor does it help to suppose that real historical events lurk behind this clever disguise—that Nebuchadnezzar's campaign actually stands for the expedition of the Persian monarch Artaxerxes III against Phoenicia and Palestine in the 350s, or that Nebuchadnezzar himself serves as a surrogate for Antiochus IV, with his divine aspirations and determination to bend the Jews to his worship.[110]

Parallels between Artaxerxes' invasion and the narrative in the book of Judith barely exist. And, if the author wished to use a Near Eastern monarch as a screen for Antiochus IV (or on some theories Demetrius I), why choose Nebuchadnezzar, who had suffered no defeat at the hands of Jews, had conquered their land, destroyed their Temple, and sent them into captivity? If the Jewish readers of Judith knew nothing else, they knew that Nebuchadnezzar sat in Babylon, not Nineveh, and that he was responsible for the Babylonian Exile. The author certainly knew it, for he has Achior summarize the highlights of Jewish history, including that exile and the restoration (long after Nebuchadnezzar's death).[111] In short, neither author nor audience was confused. The initial jumble of chronology and personnel had to be deliberate—a signal that the tale was fanciful and that the reader was in for some fun.[112]

Exaggeration and hyperbole reinforce that impression right away. The imaginary ruler of the Medes, Arphaxad, built gigantic fortifications at Ecbatana of impossible heights.[113] And Nebuchadnezzar, after conquering the city, returned home for a banquet with his entire army that lasted one hundred twenty days. This plainly parallels the orgy of feasting that Ahasuerus in the book of Esther enjoyed with his entire officialdom for one hundred eighty days, an equally imaginary event.[114]

The geography is even more cockeyed than the chronology. The text includes numerous sites, altogether unknown or unlocatable. And Holofernes' march, insofar as it can be traced at all, looks like an aimless meandering, backtracking upon itself, taking roundabout routes, and leading the troops on a merry chase—not to mention covering enormous distances in record time. Among other things, if one calculates from the narrative, Holophernes' men must have trekked about three hundred miles from Nineveh to Cilicia in just three days, crossed and recrossed the Euphrates three different times, entered Cilicia twice, and approached the Palestinian coast both by way of Damascus and through Arabia![115] The author evidently indulges in mischief here.

As the Assyrian army marched on Judaea, Joakim the High Priest and his *gerousia* directed the Jews to seize the heights and mountain passes, thus to prevent easy access by the enemy. That would seem a reasonable strategy—especially if, as the text has it, the passes were so narrow that only two men at a time could fit.[116] Having done this, however, the Jews derived little confidence from it. They fell to prayer, fasting, and the spreading of sackcloth and ashes. Indeed, they sprinkled ashes and put sackcloth on everyone and everything available: not only on every Israelite man, woman, and child, but on all hired hands and purchased slaves, on every resident alien who happened to be in the land, and even on the livestock! The altar itself was draped in sackcloth.[117] One wonders how the Israelites managed to locate or produce enough coarse material to wrap the entire population of the land overnight. Or did they have it all stored in warehouses for an emergency? It is hard to take the image of ubiquitous ashes and cattle parading about in sackcloth seriously.[118]

Holofernes goes to the trouble of inquiring into the character of the people whom he is about to assault. But when Achior gives him a précis of Israelite history and good advice, suggesting that he check whether the Jews have sinned recently before he attacks them, Holofernes orders the wise counselor to be arrested and delivered to the enemy.[119] All this, of course, is contrived by the author to heighten Holofernes' arrogance and blindness and to set him up for his own demise, while Achior proves right in the end, a familiar motif in both Greek and Jewish literature. But details of the narrative disclose this author's idiosyncratic touch. The slaves who were ordered to bring Achior to Bethulia took their instructions literally. They attempted to drag their captive up the steep cliffs to the city, only to draw fire from Jewish slingers, who assumed that they were an assault team and pelted them with stones. So much for following instructions. The slaves took a more prudent course. They moved under cover of the ridge, tied up Achior, dumped him at the base of the mountain, and escaped. Better to carry out their orders imperfectly but get back in one piece.[120]

Once Judith enters the picture, the author becomes still more sardonic. The Assyrian hordes who assembled at the base of the heights on which stood the (mythical) city of Bethulia are described as covering the whole face of the earth and possessing a weight that could not be borne by high mountains, hills, or valleys. Yet Holofernes, despite this overwhelming superiority, chose not to engage in battle with the puny Bethulians, preferring instead to stop up their water supply and drive them to surrender without a fight.[121] This is not a sign of great courage or confidence. Nor does the text allot much courage—let alone imagination—to the Jews of Bethulia. As the effects of the siege wore on, the populace of the town railed against their leaders for not yielding sooner to the enemy and insisted that they do so now. Slavery was a better prospect than slaughter. Uzziah and the elders of the community had nothing better to offer than a five-day waiting period to see whether God might come around and rescue his people after all. The distraught Israelites concurred.[122] The boldness and ingenuity of Judith, therefore, serve as contrast not only to the dullness of Holofernes but to the fearful faintheartedness of her fellow-Jews.

Judith is introduced as a woman of the noblest ancestry and the most dedicated piety. The author, however, supplies a fictitious and fantastic genealogy, going straight back (through the male line) to Jacob, a longer lineage than any woman in the Bible enjoyed. Does this underscore the purity of the blood line? Perhaps. It might also be a gibe at the pretentiousness of genealogical claims by the Jewish establishment.[123] And the devoutness of Judith is illustrated through a regimen of fasting that should have brought her to the brink of starvation: three and a half years without a break, apart from two days a week and a few festal days a year.[124] Neither mourning for her deceased husband nor ritual requirements demanded a state of anorexia. And Judith seems not to have lost an ounce of strength over the years. She whacked off Holofernes' head with no difficulty. The author could have denoted his heroine's nobility and religiosity without going to such lengths. There may be mischievousness in this as well.

Judith's denunciations of the Bethulian elders are fierce and vitriolic. In the course of her tirade about the ignorance and blasphemy of putting God to the test and setting a deadline for the Almighty, who could crush or save the Israelites whenever he pleases, she blasts the city's leadership as incapable of ever knowing anything.[125] And the reply of Uzziah confirms every criticism. His pathetic explanation that the people's thirst forced their elders to suggest a five-day hiatus is itself an abdication of leadership. But, even more telling, Uzziah's encouragement of Judith to pray that the Lord send rain to fill the cisterns demonstrates the narrow vision and lack of sensibility that marked the community's elite.[126] Judith not only excoriates them; she manipulates them. She insists on carte blanche to handle matters in her own way, with no questions asked, and the elders, without an inkling of her purpose, meekly agree.[127] The entire exchange dwells more on the fatuity of the Jewish leadership than on the virtues of Judith. And that must be its principal objective.

Judith's virtues, in fact, are not limited by conventional piety. Remarkably, her prayer to Yahweh twice asks for his aid in crushing the enemy through her own deceit. She has no hesitation in implementing divine vengeance by means of deception, the same characteristic she applies to the Lord's foes.[128] The triumph of goodness and light will be secured through craft and duplicity. The author here, in the midst of Judith's lofty prayer, injects his own dose of cynicism.

He also supplies some subtle touches, rarely noticed, in the departure scene. Judith dolls herself up masterfully to facilitate the seduction. She applies perfumes and ointments, does up her hair and fastens it with a headband, puts on the most festive clothes, adds rings, bracelets, earrings, even anklets—every form of jewelry—before setting off.[129] Was the modest and demure Judith only temporarily stepping out of character and painting herself like a tart in order to entice the villain, all in a good cause? Not quite. The author slips in a revealing phrase, usually passed over by commentators. The garb in which she draped herself did not have to be borrowed from the local brothel. It hung in her closet—the clothes in which she used to dress up in the days when her husband was alive.[130] So, she had not always been a self-effacing paragon of humility. The attire, in any case, did its job. The Jews who gathered at the gate to bid Judith farewell were so struck with her beauty that they could not take their eyes off her throughout her lengthy descent down the mountain and passage through the valley, until she disappeared from sight. And all this was supposedly done in the dead of night! Another bit of fun by the author to see whether his readers are alert.[131]

Judith wasted no time in conning her adversaries. She professed to be fleeing the nation of the Jews because they were about to be served up as a meal to the Assyrians.[132] And that was just the beginning of her web of lies. She brazenly asserted to Holofernes that she would utter no falsehoods, then proceeded immediately to cajole him with the most outrageous flatteries: because of Holofernes' qualities the king Nebuchadnezzar has the obeisance not only of men everywhere on earth, but also of animals in the fields and birds in the sky; indeed, the general's wisdom and cleverness were spoken of throughout the world, the one man of virtue in all the kingdom with powerful intelligence and wondrous in the arts of war.[133] This lays it on rather thick. The ironic contrast with Holofernes' dull-witted character is obvious, even heavy-handed. But perhaps a still sharper irony comes in the contrast between Judith's insistence upon her own truthfulness and the fact of her mendacity.[134] She has the guileless Holofernes eating out of her hand when she tells him that she will report to him as soon as the Israelites have committed their latest sin, so it will be safe to attack them. The gullible general swallows it all, even promises to adopt Judith's own god if he accomplishes what she promised.[135] The ravishing widow, with her fancy get-up and seductive wiles, captivates all who come across her. The author cannot resist yet another joke. The Assyrian soldiers who gawked at Judith outside the tent of Holofernes remarked that any people smart enough to have women as beautiful as Judith in their midst have to be taken seriously: we had better kill them all, because they are otherwise liable to take over the world with their cleverness.[136]

Holofernes showed remarkable restraint—or perhaps characteristic thick-headedness. For three days the irresistibly alluring Judith went untouched. She had free rein to play her game of coming and going, ostensibly awaiting a sign to notify the Assyrians and have them commence the assault. Only on the fourth day did Holofernes realize the growing embarrassment, not to mention absurdity, of his own situation. He had to confess to his eunuch that it would be a personal disgrace to him to let such a woman go without having her in bed. If he fails to seduce her, she will laugh him to scorn.[137] In short, it is not so much lust that drives the general, but fear of humiliation! In a paradoxical sense, Judith's calculated plan of seduction worked in ways unanticipated by the calculator. Holofernes finally invited her to spend the night lest he become a laughingstock. And the absurdity is underscored with the author's explanation for Holofernes' delay: he had been looking for the opportunity to deceive Judith from the day he first laid eyes on her.[138] This surprising statement has drawn no surprise from commentators. Yet it flies in the face of everything we know of Holofernes. He is from the start the deceived, not the deceiver, the readily bamboozled general who buys everything Judith says, including the very characterization of the Israelites that he had rejected when it came from the mouth of Achior. The idea of Holofernes shrewdly biding his time in order to catch Judith unawares and then cunningly seducing her would be wholly out of character. And what was he waiting for anyway? Judith had behaved no differently on the day he invited her to his tent than she had in the previous three days. The pseudo-explanation only intensifies the ludicrousness of the situation.

The seduction scene itself and its denouement are riddled with comedy. Holofernes drank too much, of course—the source of his undoing. Just why he did so is unclear. But the author describes it with hyperbolic exaggeration: the general drank more that evening than on any day since the day of his birth, and as he collapsed upon his couch wine had virtually overflowed all about him.[139] Judith now accomplished her deed with remarkable ease. Standing above the prone Holofernes, who was deep in drunken sleep, she took his own sword (as David had taken Goliath's), prayed to God, grabbed Holofernes' hair, and hacked off his head in two swift strokes—not bad for one-handed blows. As the text puts it with mock delicacy, she "took his head from him." Two seemingly gratuitous acts followed. Judith took the trouble to roll Holofernes' body off the bed onto the floor and yanked the canopy off the poles, having her maid stuff it, together with the head, in the food bag, perhaps rubbing in the humiliation of the fallen general.[140] All this was accomplished, to be sure, with the aid of Yahweh, to whom the god-fearing widow repeatedly prayed (although Yahweh himself never makes an appearance). Hence it is striking that Judith refers yet again to her deed as an act of guile and deceit.[141] The authority of the Lord and the piety of the heroine, therefore, issue in duplicity. This is no mere straightforward tale of virtue versus villainy.

Holofernes' head now triggered a chain of reactions, some of them rather startling. When it was hung from the battlements, it recharged the flagging spirits of the Israelites, converting them in an instant from despairing and submissive civilians into buoyant soldiers who rushed to arms.[142] When displayed to the redoubtable Ammonite leader Achior, however, it induced him to drop immediately into a dead faint. As so often, the author declines to offer an explanation. Others had to pick Achior up off the ground, only to have him fall directly (this time consciously) at Judith's feet, to declare his admiration and obeisance, and even to announce his newfound allegiance to the god of Israel. The author describes the conversion in graphic detail: Achior had the flesh of his foreskin cut, and was thus attached to the house of Israel from that day on.[143] Achior's passing out at the sight of a head which Judith had sliced off without blinking an eye must have created quite a spectacle in the Jewish camp. And it can be no coincidence that the author chose an Ammonite chieftain for the role of the zealous convert. This represents a deliberate and direct flouting of the biblical prohibition against the admittance of Ammonites or Moabites into the Israelite flock, a ban imposed for all time.[144] The process only heightens the paradox. At the very moment of triumph for those faithful to the Law, they violate it by welcoming the alien into their midst. This is no inadvertent slip; the author knew exactly what he was doing.[145] Holofernes' head makes one last appearance—or rather non-appearance—in the story. When the Assyrians learned of the Israelite assault, their officers burst into the tent of Holofernes, expecting to rouse him from his erotic night, only to find the headless body lying before them. The author employs consciously coy language to describe the scene: "his head had been taken from him" and "the head is not on him!"[146]

The rest is anti-climax. But comic exaggeration still recurs. The Israelite attack on the enemy engaged every single soldier in the land. The despoiling of the Assyrian camp occupied no fewer than thirty days. And Judith was able to cart off the entire contents of Holofernes' elaborate tent, with furnishings, bed, and all, on the back of a single mule![147]

The triumphant hymn of Judith that concludes the work sings the praises of God, delivers thanks for the salvation of the people and the destruction of their enemies, and details the wiles of the heroine who has lured Holofernes to his doom. It is fitting that the hymn reverts to a theme and a terminology that are so often underscored in the narrative. The Lord may be almighty and Judith a model of piety. But the deed was done by stepping out of character, casting off the clothes of demure widowhood, donning the garb of the seductress, and engaging in deceit.[148] That ironic twist runs throughout the text, reinforced at its very end when Judith returns to the quiet and modest life that she had temporarily abandoned and holds to character for the rest of her many days.[149] Righteousness and faith have much to commend them. But when it comes to the crunch, a bit of duplicity might do the trick.

The sardonic aspects of the narrative do not tell the whole story. But they supply a critical dimension. Diaspora Jews who enjoyed and disseminated the tale evidently found that dimension appealing. The Book of Judith did not labor under the burden of reassuring Jews that God would come to the rescue of the faithful and devout in the face of fearsome foes and crushing odds. The very fanciful nature of the story, set in a pseudo-historical time, laced with transparent chronological and geographic errors, made clear from the outset that amusement would be more important than didacticism. The events and personalities could point out morals but could also subvert them. The Assyrian villains served as useful foils. But the author aimed still sharper shafts at the Israelites. Feeble and incompetent leadership stood exposed at the moment of crisis, as did a populace unsure of its faith and future. Judith's resoluteness set in high relief not only the torpor of Holofernes but the absurdity of the Jewish effort to give God a grace period in which to change his mind. And, lest anyone think that this ostensible morality tale celebrated the traditional virtues, the text repeatedly calls attention to the fact that triumph over the foe came through recourse to chicanery. Holofernes plots deceit, just like Judith—only she is much better at it than he.

The author appears to delight in cultivating incongruities. The very opening lines supply historical particulars in apparently sober detail, while at the same time muddling the sequence of events, creating imaginary characters, and setting kings over the wrong kingdoms. A parade of paradoxes follows. Judith is an adherent of law and ritual but has no hesitation in contriving artifice and trickery. She roundly rebukes Uzziah and the elders, but, far from feeling aggrieved, they give her a green light. She exhibits greater devoutness than the males in her society but also exercises greater ruthlessness. She uses sexual wiles on Holofernes but remains a chaste widow to the end of her days. She plays the most central public role and then retreats to an innocuous private life. She utters repeated prayers to the Lord but, in fact, accomplishes all through her own wits and guile. Holofernes rampages through most of the Near East, and is then content with a long and leisurely siege of a small Judaean town. He swallows wholesale Judith's line about the Israelites and their god, although he had just rejected the same line when uttered by Achior. He waits patiently for four days before trying to seduce Judith—and then falls into a stupor when the opportunity arrives. Other characters behave in comparably peculiar ways. Achior, Gentile though he be, has a clearer vision of Jewish principles than Uzziah, the Judaean magistrate. Achior also, warrior though he be, keels over at the sight of Holofernes' severed head. And Uzziah, chief magistrate though *he* be, gives Judith full authority to proceed with her plan—despite the fact that he had no idea what it was.

These features exhibit the somewhat puckish quality of the author. The appeal of this concoction to diaspora readers does not suggest that they were cowering in terror of imminent repression or eradication and thus in need of an inspirational tale that assured divine favor to the faithful. The offbeat character of the narrative and the playfulness of the author imply an audience prepared to laugh at the fatuousness of the Israelites as well as the ridiculousness of the Gentiles. The subversion goes both ways. Diaspora Jews had sufficient self-assurance to appreciate it.

SUSANNA

The encouragement of laughter directed at the Jews themselves appears in striking fashion in another celebrated saga: the story of Susanna. And here the setting is explicitly a diaspora one. The Jewish community in Babylon supplies the scene, presumably in the period of the Exile—although the alien overlord nowhere makes an appearance. Heroes and villains, the wise and the inept, the innocent and the guilty, are all Jews.

The story surfaces as an addition to the Greek book of Daniel, awkwardly inserted with no ostensible relation to the remainder of the narrative. Hence, in one form or another, it had enjoyed an independent existence. Two Greek versions survive, closely similar but with notable differences, one in the Septuagint, the other a revision by Theodotion in the second century CE. A Semitic original may lie behind one or both, but the matter is unresolvable. The extant form evidently held importance for the diaspora.[150]

The fable is brief and can be swiftly summarized.[151] The introduction of Susanna comes in terms of the men in her life. She was the beautiful and God-fearing daughter of righteous parents who raised her according to the law of Moses, and wife of the wealthy and eminent Joakim, a pillar of the Jewish community in Babylon. Two of the elders of the people, appointed judges in that year, frequented the home of Joakim, and often gazed upon Susanna walking in the garden. Each lusted independently after her, and then, acknowledging their common objective, they conspired together to have her submit to their desires. They hid in the garden, spied upon her in her preparation for the bath, and confronted her with an intimidating proposition: either have intercourse with them or be accused by them of committing adultery with a young man. Susanna, coerced into an unwelcome decision, chose the latter. The lecherous elders then had Susanna brought before a gathering of the people and delivered their indictment, testifying that they had witnessed a sexual encounter between Susanna and her lover; they could not restrain the young man but nabbed Susanna instead. Since they were elders, men of high standing in the community, and judges, their testimony persuaded the congregation, which promptly condemned Susanna to death. The unhappy woman then cried out to God, protesting her innocence but prepared for her doom. The plea took effect. God stirred up the spirit of a youth named Daniel, who roundly rebuked the people and denounced them for exercising peremptory judgment without even interrogating the elders on their testimony. He questioned the validity of their statements and offered to grill them himself. Daniel wisely took the precaution of separating the two men and questioning them independently. He excoriated both of them for a lifetime of wickedness, sinful lust, and injustice. And he put the same question to each: where did the act of intercourse take place? When each responded with a different location, Daniel triumphantly exposed their perjury, and the congregation cheered his success. The elders suffered execution; Susanna was vindicated; her parents, husband, and relatives praised the Lord that she had been found innocent of any shameful deed; and Daniel gained great esteem among the people from that day on.

How best to interpret this text? Folktale elements have long been recognized, and analogous themes have been discovered in the Arabian Nights, Grimm's Fairy Tales, and a variety of eastern and Near Eastern literary creations. In particular, the motifs of the chaste wife falsely accused and the wise youth who outstrips his elders and brings about justice stand out with numerous parallels.[152] Were they adapted and converted to transmit a moral or religious lesson: the virtuous matron vindicated and the evildoers punished through adherence to the Law, faith in the Lord, and the actions of a youth infused with the divine spirit?[153]

That simplistic scenario does not quite work. Susanna fails to qualify fully as a paragon of virtue. Her faith in the Lord falls short of unequivocal. Though confident in the rectitude of her decision, she surprisingly holds out no hope of rescue. Once Susanna elected to stand trial, she was certain that death would follow. Even her prayer to the omniscient God who knows of her innocence expresses the readiness to die.[154] The idea of divine justice, or even mercy, does not occur to her. And the choice of death over adultery reconfirms the conventional morality imposed by a patriarchal society rather than questioning its ethical basis.[155] There may even be a hint in the text's juxtaposition of Susanna's daily walks in the garden with the inflaming of the elders' lust that casts a cloud on the "innocence" of the young woman.[156] That is certainly the tendency of much of the later visual representations of Susanna and the elders.[157] Susanna's dispatch of her maids to seek oils and other preparations for her bath, shutting the garden doors behind them (while the elders remained within) can also raise a question in the reader's mind.[158] When the old lechers made their accusation, Susanna's maids were exceedingly ashamed, never having heard such a reproach to their mistress—but they did not deny it.[159] As an example of impeccable purity, Susanna leaves something to be desired.

Nor does the rectitude of Daniel restrain him from harsh and abusive tactics. His lawyerly techniques hardly embody exemplary justice. Daniel convicts the elders even before questioning them and declares the first to be a lascivious perjurer even though his story had yet to be contradicted.[160] Daniel may have divine inspiration, but any religious messages are muted in this text. Despite some modern interpretations, theology takes a back seat.[161] God's involvement is distant and oblique, alluded to rather than directly felt. He stirred up Daniel's spirit, but the spirit, it seems, was already there.[162] Certainly the Lord plays no role through most of the text. Daniel performed his own task with personal energy and efficiency. Shrewdness, not piety, carried the day. Daniel foiled the libidinous but rather dull-witted scoundrels by interrogating them out of earshot of each other, thereby discovering and exhibiting the inconsistency of their stories. In short, he trounced the villains not as a devout adherent of the faith but as a crafty prosecuting attorney. The scenario itself may derive from a prior folktale. What matters, however, is that the Jewish interpolator had no qualms about casting Daniel in the part of the manipulative and aggressive accuser.[163] This is no simple morality play.[164]

The presence of comedic elements indicates that the tale has more in view than mere didacticism. One may note, for instance, the spectacle of the two dirty old men parting company in Joakim's garden and then ignominiously bumping into each other when each had hoped to sneak back unperceived.[165] That borders on slapstick. And the fun continues a short time later in a scene whose humor seems to have escaped commentators. When Susanna rejects the advances of her would-be lovers, she shouts at the top of her lungs. The action goes unexplained—perhaps a cry to attract attention or a desperate appeal to the Lord. In any case, the startled elders respond by shouting back, evidently to drown her out. One can readily imagine the din.[166] And then one of the elders, suddenly realizing that there will be a trial rather than sex, races to open the garden gate before anyone notices, thus to make their story of a fleeing youth hold up.[167] The yelling and scurrying about accentuate the farcical character of the episode.

The courtroom scene has its own jocular quality. The lustful elders' doltish answers to Daniel's cross-examination display a gross ineptitude that makes a travesty of their august public posts. Daniel also toys with them liberally in his questioning, twice employing puns to increase their discomfiture.[168] The outcome serves less to point a moral than to entertain the readership.

The lecherous judges are the prime targets of ridicule. Their amorous escapades entangle them in their own intrigues and lies, ending in an inglorious fall. Power and authority terminate in disgrace and death. Does the tale of Susanna then represent a social satire, the toppling of the mighty, a challenge to the corrupt system of the elite?[169] Such an analysis misses the mark. There is no class warfare here. Susanna herself belongs to the upper echelons of Jewish society. Her husband enjoys wealth and prestige, even acts as host to the officialdom of the community. Susanna's prime occupation seems to be lolling and bathing in the gardens of her estate; she lives a luxurious life, far from the social margins. Her vindication brings the downfall of the lascivious scoundrels, but only reinforces the social (not to mention the gender) structure. The cheers for her acquittal come from her husband, father, and family—none of whom had stood up for her when it appeared that her adultery had compromised the integrity of the household. They felt relief not because Susanna had escaped the death penalty but because she had not, after all, been a cause for disgrace of the elite family.[170] And the young matron returns meekly to the home of her husband—who, so far as we can tell, had not even been present at her trial. The Susanna tale unambiguously ratifies the status quo.[171]

In fact, the author by no means confines his attacks to the aging Don Juans, as if they were but two rotten apples in an otherwise healthy barrel. The useless Joakim, whose estate and gardens supplied the venue for voyeurism, who welcomed and hosted the lechers, who failed to lift a finger to support his wife in this false accusation, does not exactly emerge as an admirable figure. And Daniel's resort to dubious judicial tactics implies that the "holy spirit" which God had summoned up acts through chicanery. Most important, however, is the fierce critique directed here, as in the book of Judith, at the community as a whole. The two elders held their high offices through appointment by the people, and their word alone sufficed to persuade the entire populace to pass a death sentence on Susanna without hesitation.[172] This is far from a favorable portrait of the Jewish nation. To be sure, public opinion turned around with enthusiasm once Daniel entered the scene.[173] But that only points up the fickle, malleable, and readily manipulated attitudes of leaders and citizenry alike.

Are there signals in this tale that shed light on the attitudes of diaspora Jews? The Jews dwell in Babylon, constituting a self-sustained and sustaining entity within it. They seem unencumbered by exile status or anxiety about external oppression. Indeed, no Gentiles enter the story. The Jews have their own leadership and populace, their own officialdom, their own elite, and their own institutions that engage a broad segment of the community. The house of Joakim enjoys particular esteem and authority. Susanna parades proudly in her gardens, apparently free of Babylonian surveillance, but a prey to her own people.[174] To what degree, if at all, this corresponds to reality cannot be ascertained. But representation of reality is not the point of the fable. The author aims his barbs at the foibles and failings of Jews who run their own affairs in the diaspora: at hypocrisy, false religiosity, inverted values, the ethical indifference of the elite, and the unprincipled vacillation of the rank and file. All this served as a pointed reminder to the nation. Jews who dwell abroad need to clean up their own act. The tale recalled to mind certain basic principles of justice and morality, however flagrantly they were sometimes flouted, that should be observed, especially in Jewish communities that governed their own activities. It provided a subtle reminder that lapses in adherence to those principles could divide Jews internally and erode their own sense of coherence. The freedom with which the author can flay fellow Jews, at all levels of society, remains the most striking feature of this work. Far from displaying nervousness about vulnerability to greater powers, the text exhibits a readiness on the part of Hellenistic Jews to expose their own shortcomings to public scrutiny.[175] And the flashes of levity carry their own message. The comedic mode gave readers a sense of detachment, a welcome distancing from the objects of mockery—hardly indicative of an anxiety-ridden society.

II MACCABEES

A final instance of comedy in historical fiction can round off this discussion. The fictive and fanciful recreation of ostensible historical episodes in distant times or places marks the works considered above. The composer of II Maccabees had somewhat different ends in mind. His treatise dealt with relatively recent times and known events, the background to the Maccabean era and the triumph of Judah Maccabee—and he expected to be taken seriously. The study was based on a lengthy and sober account in five books, now lost, produced by Jason of Cyrene sometime in the second century BCE, within striking distance of the events recorded and setting them forth in great detail. The author of II Maccabees provided a précis of Jason's heavy labors in just one book, seeking a larger audience who would not want to slog through the specifics of the original.[176] He plainly had the right instincts. His epitome survived, while Jason's massive tomes disappeared. The extant text has been commented on interminably by historians and philologists alike. There would be little point in reproducing the gist of this extensive work or analyzing afresh its contribution to our knowledge of the Maccabean era. What matters here is the playfulness and whimsy, altogether overlooked in this author, that surface in select but key episodes and exhibit the sense of humor so frequently found in diaspora writers.

II Maccabees is a peculiar and puzzling work that continues to intrigue researchers.[177] Despite numerous attempts, it refuses to be pigeonholed. It records historical events, but is punctuated by miracles, marvels, and martyrologies. It celebrates the deliverance of Jerusalem, its Temple, and its inhabitants, but it was composed, at least in its fuller form, by a diaspora Jew from Cyrene. It evidently champions Jewish values against the intrusion of Hellenism, yet it was written in Greek by a Jew imbued with Hellenic culture and fully familiar with the terminology and principles associated with the Greeks. No wonder the work has resisted categorization.

Frequent attempts have sought to pin it down to some form of genre. II Maccabees was once reckoned as an example of "tragic history." Thus the author could be bracketed with Greek historians like Duris, Phylarchus, Timaeus, and other writers who suffered the wrath of the "pragmatic" historian Polybius in the second century BCE.[178] But it subsequently dawned upon scholars that Polybius indulged in some of the same rhetorical and dramatic excesses of which he accused others. Hence the genre itself of "tragic history" evaporated.[179]

Others have interpreted II Maccabees as a form of propaganda tract. As one theory has it, the work represents anti-Hasmonean propaganda— an organ of the Hasidim, in opposition to the aggressions of the later Hasmoneans.[180] This is not an easy idea to swallow when the bulk of the work constitutes a celebration of Judah Maccabee's successes. Or, as an alternative, II Maccabees has been characterized as "Temple propaganda."[181] That notion certainly has more to be said for it. But it cannot tell the whole story. The author says little or nothing about the Temple cult itself, and seems to have had hardly any interest in it.[182] And he makes the interesting statement that the Lord did not choose his nation because of the site, but chose the site because of the nation—i.e., he protects the Temple only when the people deserve it.[183]

On still a different theory, II Maccabees is a form of festal legend. It had as its objective to narrate the circumstances and events that gave rise to annual celebrations.[184] One can cite as the most obvious parallel the Book of Esther, thus to account for the rather pagan ceremony of Purim, or III Maccabees, which also attempts to supply background for a celebratory festival whose nature is now beyond our grasp. But this hardly suffices to constitute a whole genre.[185] And those works contain much more than simply the tale of how a festival got started.

II Maccabees has recently received the label of a "historical novel."[186] And one can duly isolate some novelistic features of the work. But the analogy may be somewhat off-base. Historical novels, though set in circumstances that evoke the past and provide verisimilitude, are still fiction—transparently so, as in the case of Esther, Tobit, Judith, and Susanna. All of them constitute pure invention located in a recognizable (or semi-recognizable) historical context—what the film trade calls a "costume drama." II Maccabees stands apart. It certainly contains embellishments and fabrications. But they are attached to a mainline historical narrative that has strong claims on reproducing actual events of the mid-second century BCE, including a host of military and diplomatic episodes. Novelistic touches do not themselves a novel make.

It might, in fact, be prudent to avoid the temptation of labeling or categorizing. II Maccabees does not fit into any neat cubbyhole. And what is to be learned from locating it in some genre? The author himself does not appear concerned with such matters. Moreover, to do so runs the risk of missing some of the striking characteristics of the work that are rarely noted, namely the inventive creativity of the author, and the humor, wit, and irony that one can find in the text. These elements do not, of course, imply that II Maccabees is some form of comedy. Far from it. But they suggest that even in a work of recent history, a mode altogether different from the fictitious histories treated above, jocularity has its place, a characteristic common to so many diaspora compositions.

Only a few instances need be cited to open this much-neglected subject. The Heliodorus story in II Maccabees furnishes a prime exhibit.[187] The events take place in the reign of Seleucus IV, predecessor of the wicked

Antiochus Epiphanes, at a time when the Hellenistic kingdom of the Seleucids held sway over Judaea. Heliodorus, the agent of the king, arrived in Jerusalem to check on reports that the Temple treasury possessed incalculable riches. The High Priest informed him that there were indeed deposits held in trust for widows and orphans, as well as the savings of the wealthy Hyrcanus from the eminent family of the Tobiads. Heliodorus immediately insisted that the monies belonged to the crown and should be handed over to him. He appointed a day and headed for the Temple to conduct an inventory, thus causing alarm among the priests and wholesale weeping and wailing among the people. Sackcloth swiftly turned up, and demonstrations filled the streets. Heliodorus, however, pressed on. He had reached the point of entering the Temple when divine intervention saved the day. An imposing apparition suddenly materialized. A fearsome rider on a mighty horse, splendidly attired, attacked Heliodorus. And then two strapping youths, magnificent in beauty and strength, appeared and pummeled Heliodorus further. The minister had to be carried off in a litter, with acknowledgment of the sovereignty of God. Indeed, it looked as if he would not recover. But the merciful Jewish High Priest Onias III sacrificed to Yahweh for Heliodorus' recovery, and the villain was spared. Heliodorus went back to the Seleucid king and extolled the deeds performed by the Jewish god which he had personally witnessed.

Such is the tale in brief. Scholars eager to give it a label place it in the category of the patron-deity story—if such a genre exists at all. The category encompasses fables that record the epiphany of a god or his surrogates to protect his sacred shrine from those who would violate it. One might compare the legend recorded by Herodotus of superhuman figures arriving to drive the Persians away from the sanctuary at Delphi; or the Babylonian tale of Enlil sending his agent to prevent sacrilege at the temple in Nippur; or Apollo emerging from his shrine at Delphi to draw a bow on the invading Gauls. A biblical parallel also exists: the angel who came from God to drive off the Syrians in answer to the prayers of King Hezekiah and the prophet Isaiah. The Heliodorus episode, as most have recognized, belongs in this company.[188]

But that by no means accounts for everything in the narrative. The author has a wry sense of humor that interpreters have passed by. A case in point exists in the prayer uttered by the priests and the people when Heliodorus was about to violate the Temple treasury. They did not issue a plea to God to protect the sanctity of his house. Rather, they called upon the Lord Almighty to keep the deposits safe and secure for those who had placed their cash there![189] That included the monies of Hyrcanus, perhaps the wealthiest man in Judaea. Thus, the desperate anxieties of the priests and the sackcloth and ashes of the populace summoned the angels of the Lord to protect cash deposits and keep the bank solvent. The author was having a bit of fun here.

The punishment of Heliodorus further subverts seriousness. He got a double dose. It was not enough that a horse charged him, reared up, and kicked him with its hoofs; two powerful young men also arrived out of the blue and beat him to a pulp. That seems like overkill. The two attacks may, of course, have stemmed from two separate tales and two independent sources.[190] The fact remains, however, that this author combined them for his own purposes. They supply, it appears, another example of whimsy on his part.

The humor can hardly be missed in the finale of this episode. Heliodorus, though practically breathing his last, was spared by the High Priest and returned to his king, Seleucus IV, in Antioch. Seleucus then asked him whom he should send next to Jerusalem in order to recover the money. Heliodorus had a ready reply: if you want to send somebody, send your worst enemy; he will get thoroughly thrashed—if he survives at all![191] It is hard to overlook the tongue-in-cheek in that remark. And still another concealed barb can be discerned. Heliodorus said, in a more precise translation, "if you have an enemy or a plotter against the government, send him to Jerusalem." As it happens, it was Heliodorus himself, not long thereafter, who plotted against Seleucus and was responsible for his death.[192] The author of II Maccabees had a good knowledge of contemporary history—and a sardonic cast of mind.

The author's treatment of the dastardly villain Antiochus IV is equally instructive. When the virtuous High Priest Onias III was treacherously murdered, through an agent of the king, Antiochus expressed public sorrow and distress. The composer of II Maccabees spares nothing here. He portrays Antiochus as moved to his very soul and shedding tears when he thought of the moral uprightness and sterling character of Onias.[193] Is that meant to be taken seriously? Few will imagine that the king mourned the death of a Jew in public, let alone shed even crocodile tears. The author was indulging in some malicious mockery.

The description of Antiochus' agonizing death is justly famous.[194] The gory details, including worms swarming about him and flesh rotting off, can readily be paralleled by various Greek texts. They supply a motif for the deaths of cruel tyrants.[195] The author, however, may have added his particular touch by having Antiochus repelled by his own stench.[196] The persecutor repents in the end, so the narrative has it, declaring Jerusalem a free city, granting prerogatives to the Jews, and promising to adorn the Temple with lavish gifts and to finance all its sacrifices.[197] Deathbed penitence, of course, is a common theme. But the characterization of one of Antiochus' promises, a peculiar and interesting one, bears notice: the king vowed that he would give privileges to the Jews equal to those enjoyed by the citizens of Athens.[198] That must be an allusion (if it makes any sense at all) to the golden age of democratic Athens. Such an age, however, had long since passed. Contemporary Athens was hardly a model of autonomy and privilege. This may be yet another little twist of irony. And still more sardonic surely is the concluding description of Antiochus' repentance. He not only intends to treat Jews with respect, but he proclaims his resolve to convert to Judaism itself. And, as if that were not enough, he announces that he would go around the world as a missionary to convert everybody to Judaism![199] The hyperbole here is doubtless deliberate—and derisive.

Finally, the author is not averse to twitting even his own heroes. The counterpart to the evil Antiochus is the High Priest Onias III, the very embodiment of virtue. Onias appears as the shining light in this treatise, the prime model to be emulated. Yet he too comes in for some sly insinuations. When word first arrived of Heliodorus' impending intrusion into the Temple, Onias, far from trusting in rectitude and God, flew into a panic. And his anxiety-ridden countenance set the entire populace off in a state of alarm.[200] This is hardly exemplary behavior. To be sure, this description may be a topos as well. Jewish-Hellenistic literature supplies close parallels. In the apocryphal story of Alexander the Great's march on Jerusalem, the High Priest Jaddus also became nearly paralyzed with fear.[201] And in III Maccabees, when Ptolemy Philopator sought entrance into the "Holy of Holies," the priests were terror-stricken and the people sent up an incredible howl.[202] Jewish-Hellenistic writers did not always depict their religious leaders as secure in their righteousness. More interesting, however, is the comment made by the author of II Maccabees about Onias' motive in asking God to spare the life of the fallen Heliodorus. This was not an act of compassion or moral principle. A very different purpose prevailed. Onias was worried, so says II Maccabees, that if Heliodorus died in Jerusalem, there would be hell to pay from the Syrian king![203] Not exactly the most admirable motivation.

One last item is worth noting. Onias III makes a return appearance near the end of II Maccabees, now an apparition from the other world, in a dream of Judah to encourage him just before the climactic battle with Nicanor.[204] The author introduces Onias, as if for the first time, with fine phrases: he is a man of high character, modest in bearing and of gentle disposition, even an accomplished speaker, and one who practiced virtue all his life. The initial phrase used is *aner kalos kagathos*. Onias, in short, is a good Greek gentleman. There may be more tongue-in-cheek here. And the word used for his speaking prowess is quite intriguing: *lalia*. That often means "chatter" or "prattle," non-serious gossip. The author of II Maccabees, it seems, was poking a bit of fun even at his own hero.

This work as a whole, of course, did not aim for laughs. But that makes the sparks of occasional humor all the more meaningful. The comic ingredient crosses genres and crops up in unexpected places. Its appearance in a text drawn from an extensive scholarly exposition of the Maccabean rebellion, with sober political and/or religious aims, is particularly striking. It suggests a deep-seated inclination to jocularity, a resort to tart witticisms, indeed self-parody, even in tracts of solemn import. Whether that ingredient appeared already in Jason of Cyrene or was added by his Hellenized epitomator, II Maccabees displays the inventive flair and whimsicality of diaspora Jews.

Historical fiction, it seems, appealed widely to Jews of the Hellenistic-Roman period. It gave voice to creativity and imagination. The contexts had vague verisimilitude and included ostensibly familiar personages, but provided an occasion for fanciful events and invented characters. The playful toying with pseudo-history allowed for wit and caprice. And even serious historical narrative could be laced with imaginary episodes and humorous commentary.

The five texts reviewed here all have reverberations for the diaspora. One fable is set in Assyria, one in Babylon, and one in Persia. The other two, placed in Palestine, represent Jews in struggles against larger alien powers, one at least and possibly both composed by diaspora writers. The time of composition cannot be pinpointed for any of them, but all belong approximately within a century of one another. The date when each was composed is, in any event, less important than the fact of their preservation and reproduction over the course of many generations. This signals an enduring resonance and relevance for a long-term readership. The works cross boundaries of time and space and have important implications for diaspora Jews.

The emphasis here has been on humor, a recurrent feature in these compositions, which accords them a distinctive flavor. It brightens dark events and provides happy endings; it cuts foreign princes and generals down to size and holds Jewish follies up to scorn; it exaggerates Israelite accomplishments and mocks Israelite failings. The narratives generally portray

Jews in dire or vulnerable circumstances from which they emerge triumphant or secure—but usually chastened, rebuked, and even ridiculous. The jokes and caricatures are not incidental. Nor do they represent a "smiling through tears" by oppressed people laboring to make the most of a grim situation. If anything, the reverse is true. The authors felt free to expose the blemishes of the Jewish leaders and populace, while lampooning the flaws of their enemies. The texts leave an impression of amused observation and sardonic detachment. Above all, they reveal a self-esteem among diaspora Jews and a sufficiently satisfying life-style that allowed for irony without rancor and burlesque without bitterness.

Diaspora Humor II: Biblical Recreations

HELLENISTIC Jews took great pleasure in retelling biblical tales. They did so with frequency, with variety, and with gusto. The practice took a multitude of forms: history, tragedy, epic, romance, exegesis, or indeed a combination and transformation of genres. Inventiveness was highly prized. Canonical texts were excerpted or augmented, streamlined or enhanced, supplemented or inverted. New and different means of conveying familiar legends or reconceiving biblical heroes appealed widely. None of the reconceptions was designed to substitute for or to subvert the Scriptures. Quite the contrary. They played to a readership fully conversant with the traditional tales, for whom these alternative versions would supply different insights, provocative interpretations, more lively renditions, or merely fanciful fabrications. By revivifying conventional stories and characters, even recasting them in nearly unrecognizable form, they both entrenched the tradition and enlarged it. The authors had wide scope for creativity—and an enthusiasm for entertainment.

Jews, to be sure, had no monopoly on playful rewriting of traditional tales or remolding of mythic figures. Greek and Latin authors regularly took pleasure in the practice. One need think only of Callimachus' whimsical *Hymn to Demeter,* Ovid's *Metamorphoses,* or Lucian's *Dialogues of the Gods.* But their inventions did not amount to tampering with holy books—however much they may have revered Homer. The Jews had little inhibition even on this score. Numerous texts can serve as illustration;[1] but three diverse and fascinating ones will suffice here. They represent a mixture of genres, or rather a free adaptation of them. And they make a liberal use of humor that offers a window on the receptivity and taste of diaspora readers.

THE TESTAMENT OF ABRAHAM

A fascinating, peculiar, and nearly unique text affords an instructive angle on diaspora mentality. The so-called Testament of Abraham has received relatively little exposure. Problems of interpretation are multiple. There is no pseudo-historical setting here offering clues (or traps) for dating and context. Nor is there any pretense of rewriting a biblical tale. Nothing in Genesis provides a basis or even an impetus for the tale told in the Testament of Abraham. Indeed, the testamentary genre itself hardly supplies a model: Abraham refrains from making a testament. The text strikes its own idiosyncratic note.

Or, rather, the texts. Two rescensions of the story exist, a longer (A) and a shorter one (B), each attested by various Greek manuscripts and supported by later editions in other versions and other languages. Both tell the same tale in broad outline, but numerous differences distinguish them, including some major ones of inclusion or omission. This is not the place to explore the diverse suggestions regarding the relationship between the two rescensions—which preceded which, whether A expanded on B or B abbreviated A, or both depended upon a lost original, or each derived from independent earlier versions.[2] Despite the various viewpoints, a broad consensus exists on the origin of the longer edition: it stems from Greek-speaking diaspora Jews in Egypt. The use of Septuagintal vocabulary, the similarity to other texts by Egyptian Jews, and certain themes that echo Egyptian motifs make that conclusion a reasonable and defensible one.[3] The date is well beyond our grasp, most commentators opting for the first century BCE or the first century CE, but with nothing resembling definitive arguments.[4] The longer rescension, in any case, will serve as the text for discussion here. It is the fuller, the more absorbing, the more coherent, and—by far—the funnier.[5]

A résumé of the contents can readily highlight the comic ingredients. Abraham had reached a ripe old age (to put it mildly), nearly a millennium; he was a man of preeminent righteousness, boundless hospitality, and graciousness. But God decided that his time had come. He asked the archangel Michael to break the news to Abraham that he was about to be gathered to his own Master. Michael, however, was not quite up to the task. Abraham's warm and generous welcome, plus healthy doses of flattery, made it most difficult for the archangel to accomplish his mission. A voice from a cypress tree announced that the Lord summons him to those who love him, but Abraham repressed that divine message. Isaac appeared and paid obeisance to the impressive stranger, whom he (unlike his father) recognized instantly as one who does not belong to the race of mortals. Abraham's hospitality extended to washing the feet of his guest, an event that caused Michael, Abraham, and Isaac all to burst into tears—but the archangel's tears turned to precious stones, another mystery that Abraham preferred to keep to himself. When Abraham then laid on a lavish banquet to honor his visitor, Michael simply could not bear to carry out his assignment. He stepped outside, on the pretext of relieving himself, and shot up to heaven. There he had to explain to God that Abraham possessed a greater abundance of every virtue than any man he ever knew, and that there was no way he could bring himself to announce his death.

The merciful Lord relented—not on Abraham but on Michael. He asked the archangel to return to Abraham, but the latter would get the message in an indirect way: Isaac would have a dream, Michael would interpret it, and Abraham would see the light. A nice plan, but it did not quite work. Isaac got the dream all right, and understood its import, racing in to Abraham to hug him while he still could. This generated a new outburst of weeping, with Sarah joining the three men in tears—even without knowing what they were crying about. She did, however, recognize the guest as a celestial figure, one of three whom they had entertained once before, and who had forecast the birth of Isaac. The scales dropped from Abraham's eyes. He now recalled Michael as well. His feet were the tip-off: just like those he had washed in that earlier encounter. And he pulled out the precious stones, the product of Michael's teardrops, a clincher that something supernatural was going on. Isaac proceeded to recount his dream, which involved a man bearing rays of light, coming down from heaven, and removing the sun and moon from around his head. Michael duly interpreted the meaning as the imminent demise of Abraham and Sarah, and reported that he was the agent commissioned to take Abraham's soul on its journey to God. Abraham could no longer conceal the truth from himself. But he had one recourse: "OK, now I know you are the angel of the Lord. But I'm not going."

The mild-mannered Michael raised no objections, just vanished again and raced back to his chief. He explained sheepishly that Abraham would not cooperate. "What do I do now?" God came up with another plan. Michael would return once more, but this time, instead of just announcing the coming death, he would provide a soothing and elaborate justification for it. Abraham would be told not only that he had been singularly blessed by the Lord heretofore but that his descendants would multiply and he would get whatever he asked. Besides, dying isn't so bad. Everybody does it. The

Lord had even refrained from sending his usual agent, the menacing grim reaper, and dispatched instead the amiable Michael, who would give Abraham time to put his affairs in order, say goodbye to Isaac, and make an agreeable departure. So why resist?

The archangel duly brought this comforting news to Abraham. The patriarch humbled himself and expressed compliance. Up to a point. He might not be able to dodge the inevitable, but he could still postpone it. He had a last wish: to see the entire world and every creature in it. Then he would go quietly. Quite a tall order—and it should use up a healthy chunk of time. Michael, having no authorization to act on this request, made yet another journey back to the upper regions to make his latest report. The Lord, ever compassionate, granted that desire too, directing Michael to take Abraham on a flying tour around the globe in a carriage drawn by a heavenly host of cherubim. With this escort Abraham was whisked across the world to witness the whole range of human behavior and experience, both good and evil. The latter made the deepest impression. Abraham kept stopping the chariot to halt criminals and offenders in their tracks by calling upon God to level dire punishments. He had murderers devoured by wild beasts, burglars consumed by fire, and even a couple engaged in unlawful sex swallowed up by the earth! Nothing escaped Abraham's eye. God had to put an end to the trip, lest the righteous Abraham mow down all the sinners on earth. Enough is enough! None would be left but Abraham himself. Mercy, after all, is the Lord's. Since Abraham knows no sin, he has no patience with sinners. God preferred to give them a chance for repentance.

The journey took a detour. On instruction from above, Michael brought Abraham to the seat of judgment where he could witness the fate of those souls whom he had consigned to perdition. There he gained access to an elaborate and complex spectacle. The first vista featured double gates where the pious went to salvation or the wicked to destruction, the latter constituting by far the majority, with Adam presiding over the proceedings on a golden throne and rejoicing or lamenting as the souls filed through one portal or the other. Then a second scene disclosed the exercise of judgment itself, delivered by Abel seated on a crystalline throne, glistening like fire, with a brace of angels recording acts of piety and wickedness respectively, and two more angels, one equipped with a scale to weigh the deeds, the other with fire to put them to the test. The awesome sight sobered Abraham. He swiftly made amends for his previous severity, interceded for one soul whose fate hung in a precarious balance between salvation and perdition, expressed repentance for his own unforgiving character, and then pleaded with God to save those whom he had designated for destruction. Divine compassion heeded the prayer, and the Lord reassured Abraham that not only was he forgiven, but the sinners whom he had condemned suffered only temporary torment and were still salvageable.

One might expect here the cue for a happy ending. And so it appears at first sight. Michael wheeled the chariot around, brought Abraham back home where he could embrace his family once again, and asked him to make his final dispositions before departure for heaven. But, as if nothing had happened in the interim, the patriarch remained unmoved. He asked Michael pointedly whether this request came from God or was just his own idea. The archangel assured him that God himself had issued the order. Not that that made the slightest difference. Abraham repeated his refrain: "I'm not going." Déjà vu. Back went Michael to the Lord, with the same old story: Abraham won't cooperate; what am I supposed to do?

Even God was beginning to lose patience. But not altogether. He turned to Plan B, the summoning of the dread specter, Death, who would carry off Abraham to his end. Yet the Lord would not allow Death to appear before his favorite mortal in his usual hideous aspect and snarling presence. God put him under strict orders to behave himself and speak gently, and he cloaked Death's repulsive visage in a radiant façade, even perfumed his body odor. With so charming an appearance, Death had a hard time convincing Abraham of his identity. The patriarch took him to be the comeliest of angels, and assumed he was pulling his leg. And when Death finally convinced him of his mission, Abraham gave his rote response: "I have no intention of following you."

Unlike Michael, however, Death would not take no for an answer. Rather than chasing back to heaven for new orders, he stayed around to keep the pressure on. But Abraham had yet another dodge to prolong the delay. He demanded that, if Death was really who he claimed to be, he should show his true colors, cast off his disguise, and expose himself in all his ghastly gruesomeness. Death hesitated: no one could tolerate him in the fullness of his horror. But Abraham insisted. Evidently anything seemed more tolerable than shuffling off his mortal coil. Then Death gave him the full treatment: seven fiery dragon heads and fourteen additional faces, ranging from repulsive reptiles to a raging sea. So ferocious was the appearance and so terrifying the noise that all of Abraham's male and female servants, seven thousand of them, dropped dead on the spot. Even the patriarch lost heart. He admitted that this was too much and asked Death to put his handsome camouflage back on—which he was more than pleased to do. Abraham had now undergone a second repentance. Stunned by the loss of his whole household staff in a single instant, he requested that Death join him in prayer to God to restore them to life. The double prayer worked, and the Lord complied.

Despite everything, Abraham still scrambled for ways to defer his own fate. He claimed exhaustion, asking Death to leave him alone. But the specter clung to his side, determined to accomplish his task. Abraham tried another ploy: "I'll go with Michael, not you." And then another: "explain the meaning of all the hideous faces and fearful forms you exhibited earlier." Death put on his professorial mode and duly went through a full explanation. Abraham was running out of stall techniques. He inquired about unexpected deaths—which at this point might have appeared to be a blessing. An exasperated Death now cut off the dialogue. That was the last question he would answer. "There are seventy-two varieties of death, but don't ask me any more questions. The time has come." Abraham begged leave to rest for a while. It was the final reprieve. Family and servants surrounded him to say their farewells. Even in the end, however, Death had to resort to subterfuge to gather the old man to his fathers. He asked Abraham to clasp his right hand so that the patriarch could regain some gaiety, strength, and vitality. The trick worked. Abraham took the bait, and his soul forthwith stuck fast to the hand of Death. The patriarch had at last been entrapped. Michael reappeared, as did a plethora of angels. Abraham got a splendid escort to paradise.

The humor in this text is deliberate and persistent, no mere marginal presence. Of course, the Testament of Abraham has relevance for theology—not to mention eschatology, soteriology, and angelology.[6] But the author evinces a definite fondness for fun. It is going too far to characterize the work as a parody of the pious Abraham.[7] The patriarch's piety is not, in fact, satirized. Rather, it earns him good will, favor, and countless concessions from God and his ministers. Abraham emerges instead as a master manipulator, exploiting his advantages with the divine, and prolonging his mortal existence again and again through a range of delaying tactics. The author does not diminish Abraham's stature but gives him added dimensions—including the very human emotions of spleen, regret, and reluctance to die. And much of it is delivered with tongue in cheek.

The archangel Michael is himself a sympathetic but rather feckless figure. He arrives on earth in splendor, sporting the title of *archistrategos*, "Commander-in-Chief."[8] The designation itself is not surprising. It appears in other Jewish-Hellenistic texts, and is elsewhere applied to Michael.[9] But the title is singularly incongruous when carried by the character in this story. The author seems intent upon employing this denomination with numbing repetitiveness: eight times in the second chapter alone when Michael first encounters Abraham. And the Commander-in-Chief announces it proudly as his title when he identifies himself to Abraham.[10] The military imagery looms large in this context. Michael arrived like a "resplendent soldier," Abraham hailed him as a "most-honored warrior," and then asked what army he had come from.[11] All this contrasts rather sharply with the amiable but wimpish Michael who was swept away by Abraham's benefactions and blandishments and could not bring himself to break the news of impending death, let alone carry out that mission himself. He was unable even to find a suitable means of taking his leave and had to offer the pretext of a need to urinate![12] The befuddled archangel never had a retort to offer when Abraham refused to accompany him, and had to repair repeatedly to the Lord for further instructions. His recurrent trips back and forth between heaven and earth without ever fulfilling his task make him an unmistakably comic character.[13] And that is not all. The confused and inept Michael could not quite handle the role of an angel behaving like a human on earth. Abraham invited him on a horseback ride, but Michael awkwardly put him off: "I don't mount four-footed creatures; let's walk."[14] Even more problematic, what was he to do about eating? Abraham had laid out a sumptuous banquet, but incorporeal angels don't eat or drink. Michael had to consult with the Lord on how to negotiate that embarrassment. "How can I escape notice when I am sitting at the same table with him"—and leaving everything on my plate? God had to make a special arrangement: he would outfit Michael with an internal spirit who devours everything, and the archangel would not have to worry about poor table manners.[15] It is hard to believe that previous commentators missed the joke here.

Abraham, on the other hand, is a master of the evasive action. When clues were dropped, he preferred to ignore them. A tree called to him in human voice, announcing the summons of the Lord. Abraham pretended not to hear anything, hoping that his visitor (Michael) might not have heard it. And later, when Abraham, Isaac, and the mysterious guest all burst into tears for no obvious reason, the stranger's teardrops turned into precious stones. Abraham observed the prodigy, swiftly scooped up the stones, hid them away, and hoped that no one had noticed.[16] The meaning of this is quite uncertain. But it might not be too far off the mark to propose that Abraham, as popular psychological parlance has it, was "in denial." If he did not acknowledge the talking tree or the metamorphosis of tears into jewels, perhaps they would have no effect. The dissimulation here was more like self-deception. But the image of the august patriarch bustling to suppress divine evidence leaves a decidedly comic impression.

Abraham, however, could not deny the facts much longer. Sarah recognized the angel by his face. And she confronted her husband, who still claimed ignorance, with the news that this was one of the heavenly figures who had visited them earlier. The patriarch, with no further room to maneuver, suddenly remembered that the visitor was familiar—not perhaps the face but at least the feet! He had washed them once before. That, surely, is a whimsical note struck by the author.[17]

Evasiveness alternated with stubbornness. When Michael's identity and assignment were disclosed, Abraham simply declined to go with him. The refusal strained even the patience of the Lord. He would not, of course, act precipitately against his favorite, and he supplied Michael with some rhetoric to employ for persuasive purposes. But he had more vigorous and effective means in reserve. God let his restrained demeanor slip for an instant: he directed Michael to ask the patriarch why he balked at coming, and to add that if God were to send Death for him, he'd find out soon enough whether he was coming or not![18] God was not above issuing veiled threats even to the best of mortals. The surprise twist neatly brings the reader up short.

Abraham resorted again to procrastination. This time he asked for a tour of the entire inhabited world before he has to leave it. A tall order and a long journey, but the Lord was agreeable.[19] Abraham, however, overplayed his hand. He kept summoning divine punishment upon every sinner he observed from above, even to the extent of having the earth open up to swallow a couple of lecherous adulterers. God soon realized the mistake he had made. He stepped in to stop the slaughter before Abraham wiped out everyone left standing.[20] The gross imbalance between crime and punishment and the exaggeration of the potential carnage possess more entertainment value than moral suasion.

The judgment scene or scenes, cobbled together, so it seems, from more than one source, are solemn rather than amusing. Yet even here one wonders about the actions of Adam, of awesome aspect and seated on a gilded throne, who observed souls ushered into the narrow gate for the righteous or the broad one that accommodated the far larger number of sinners. He took great delight in the first group, exulting and rejoicing. But he was miserable when witnessing the fate of the second: he threw himself off his throne, wept and wailed, tore at his hair and plucked at his beard.[21] That bit of over-reaction is ill suited to the general solemnity of the scene—perhaps deliberately so.

After Abraham refused yet again to accompany Michael to the next world, the Lord turned to his back-up plan. He called upon Death to finish the job. But that fearsome creature turned to jelly in the presence of God.

He quivered and shivered, moaned and groaned, and panicked at the prospect of orders delivered by the Boss.[22] This is plain parody. And the more so when Death covered his decay and decrepitude with a shining visage, beautiful raiment, and a delectable odor. The disguise was so successful that it nearly backfired. Death had a hard time persuading Abraham of his identity.[23]

The interchange between Abraham and Death operates at the level of comic caricature. The patriarch was at first dazzled by the glorious beauty of this figure from heaven. Then, when convinced (with some difficulty) that he was in fact the grim reaper in the guise of a gorgeous charmer, Abraham wanted only to see the real thing. In an apparent fit of sadomasochism, he pleaded with Death to strip off the façade and display his rot, horror, and savagery in their full loathsomeness. This wild desire for an exhibit of monstrosity was then outdone by the exhibit itself. Death paraded every disgusting face imaginable—and added a few unimaginable ones, including a fiery sword and a lightning flash somehow in the form of faces.[24] The author showed considerable creativity here.[25] Abraham may have satisfied some perverse desire, but it was a good deal more than his servants had bargained for. The fearsome visages and dreadful odors felled seven thousand of them on the spot. This is overkill of a quite literal variety.[26] Abraham now realized that matters were out of hand. He begged Death, with the same earnestness as before, this time to reverse himself and restore the handsome mask to conceal the hideous interior.[27] The topsy-turvy character of this interaction bears a strong affinity to farce. And the final reversal of expectations confirms it. In an instant, Abraham moved across the spectrum from morbid voyeur to pious saviour. On the patriarch's beseeching, Death joined forces with Abraham in prayer to bring back to life the very souls whom he had sent to sudden and premature perdition.[28] If Death can restore life, we are indeed in wonderland.

The dialogue proceeded. Abraham exploited it for his favorite game: foot-dragging to avoid the yielding up of his mortal existence. He tried the tactic of offering to follow Michael if he should return. (He had successfully intimidated the gentle archangel before.) Or, as an alternative, he would yield to Death—but only after prodding him into a lengthy lecture on the symbolism and significance of each of the macabre faces that he had earlier unveiled.[29] Abraham even hoped to prolong the conversation by hearing Death expound on the seventy-two varieties of dying. The patriarch, to the very end, found inventive means of stalling. But the deadly specter cut their discussion short: "I already answered all your questions; stop the stalling and come with me."[30] Abraham, however, never ran out of ruses. Death could capture him only by turning the tables: he used a ruse of his own. The hand-clasping trick finally worked. Abraham was duped into taking Death's hand—and there was no letting go.[31] So, in the end, the master manipulator was himself outmaneuvered. This last twist neatly encapsulates the spirit of the whole. The Testament of Abraham, whatever else it contains, has the characteristics of a light-hearted fantasy.

The work fits into no obvious category or genre. Nor, probably, was it meant to. It surely does not count as a midrash on the biblical tradition. Almost no overlap exists between the Abraham legend in Genesis and our story. The model of the Testaments of the Twelve Patriarchs shows little resemblance to this text. The standard portrait of the aged patriarch who provides sage advice to his sons on his deathbed is missing here altogether. And the absence is hardly accidental. The text refers on several occasions to the issue of Abraham's preparations for departure from this world. God's initial directives to Michael made a point of it: the archangel was to alert Abraham to his coming death so that he could put his affairs in order. When Michael returned to heaven, his task still unaccomplished, the Lord sent him back with the same orders: Abraham needs to arrange for the disposition of his belongings. The same directive was given again when the peripatetic Michael was dispatched for a third time, and on one last occasion when the archangel was ordered to terminate the chariot ride and have Abraham get down to business.[32] The patriarch's studious ignoring of this repeated message is a central element in the comedy itself. Even at the end he seeks to dodge his fate by pretending exhaustion and hoping that Death might just disappear. He gives nary a thought to organizing his affairs or composing counsel to his family. No testament exists in the "Testament of Abraham." Far from fitting into the testament genre, this work is, in a sense, a parody of that genre.[33] Similarly, it ill suits the apocalyptic mold. Abraham did, to be sure, take a trip to the seat of judgment and witnessed souls ushered to their fate. But the description of his experience lacks almost altogether the usual characteristics of celestial tours in apocalyptic texts, including inspection of the layers of heaven and access to the torments of the damned.[34] The Testament of Abraham draws on various genres but belongs to none, a mélange that represents primarily the inventiveness of its creator.[35]

Nor does a single theme predominate. The issue of righteousness and sin, of course, holds an important place. Abraham's rectitude is stressed on numerous occasions. And his detestation of sinful behavior gets him into serious trouble. God had to stay his hand before he massacred most of the inhabitants of the globe. Abraham learned his lesson then. But he

had to relearn it when his request to observe the full grotesqueness of
Death's presence brought about the inadvertent deaths of seven thousand
servants—and for no sins of their own. The Lord's policy was to leave
room for repentance and the exercise of mercy.[36] That theme, however,
does not drive the narrative or determine its denouement.

The confrontation of death, or rather the efforts to avoid its consequences, plays a larger role. The text is liberally sprinkled with Abraham's endeavors to sidestep the inevitable. Scholars detect here a fundamental encounter between divine judgment and the instinctive human
reluctance to accept it. If even Abraham was flawed, we can all feel better
about our own failings. On this view, the Testament of Abraham is largely
a consolatory piece.[37] And perhaps it serves that function for some. But a
didactic interpretation does not readily accord with the tone of the text.
Abraham's evasive tactics and multiple modes of dalliance provide more
entertainment than instruction. The motif of resisting death appears elsewhere in post-biblical Jewish literature, especially in various traditions involving Moses.[38] They may well have exerted an influence. But a critical
difference exists. Moses, in those traditions, staked a claim on immortality
and refused to accept a judgment that would remove him from the world.
Abraham had no such pretensions.[39] His posture was procrastination, not
recalcitrance.[40]

The comic features are more striking than any weighty messages that
may be found in the text. Abraham appears as the artful dodger and inventive manufacturer of pretexts to prolong his earthly existence. Michael is a
genial but inept lieutenant in a commander's costume. And the mercurial
Death adopts a plethora of personae: the quaking subordinate, the fearsome agent, the handsome charmer, the hideous mass murderer, the professorial commentator, and the crafty deceiver. The author has a congenial
sense of humor.

Is there relevance for the diaspora? The Greek text of this long rescension, it can be reasonably inferred, comes from the diaspora, probably
from Egypt.[41] But there is no diaspora setting; the tale is beyond the realm
of history; and the contents have no obvious relation to anything experienced by Jews outside the homeland. Yet the work may yield an indirect insight of real significance. A missing element in the Testament of Abraham
is especially notable: the treatise makes no allusion to differences between
Jew and Gentile. The Children of Israel carry no special distinction; there
is no Chosen People. The sins that Abraham observes and endeavors to
stamp out are common to all: armed robbery, fornication, and burglary.
The means of rehabilitation are also open to all: repentance and forgive-

ness. There is no special access to God through circumcision, keeping the Sabbath, or following the Law. The souls given passage to paradise or condemned to perdition are judged simply on the basis of whether their good deeds outweigh the bad or vice versa, not whether they adhere to a covenant or maintain the faith.[42] All this is quite remarkable for a diaspora author. It suggests an attitude that transcends sectarianism and dismisses barriers between Jews dwelling abroad and their pagan neighbors. The implications of the text indicate circumstances that foster mutual respect and understanding among divergent groups.

In such circumstances, a work of wit and humor finds a comfortable place. The author felt free to play with a patriarchal figure, poke fun at an archangel, remold the grim reaper in a dozen ways, destroy and resurrect thousands in the twinkling of an eye, and invent a lively dialogue that would leave readers smiling. The text may not fit a "testament" genre, but it testifies to the convivial mood of writer and readership in a diaspora context that evidently gave gratification.

THE TESTAMENT OF JOB

The lamentable experience of Job would hardly seem the most obvious invocation to comedy. The God-fearing and prosperous landowner of the biblical tale who suffered grievous losses and unspeakable torments despite his scrupulous piety would not readily inspire recourse to humor.[43] The biblical narrative did take on new forms in the Greco-Roman period. The Septuagint version itself expands on some items and subtracts much else, thus leaving a considerably shortened text. A certain Aristeas produced his own rigorously compressed rendition that transformed Job from an anguished victim protesting against injustice to a steadfast and faithful servant of the Lord, who rewards him in the end.[44] And the Testament of Job picks up that notion, elaborating upon it in fuller fashion, redrawing Job himself, adding or embellishing other characters, and producing an altogether different creation. Nonetheless, the tale of the sorely afflicted Job who endures his sorrows without complaint or wavering and instructs everyone else repeatedly about the glories of God seems an unlikely candidate for jocular treatment. Yet the author did not lack a touch of lightness and frivolity, even when dealing with heavy and somber material.

The Testament of Job, far less familiar and, indeed, far less moving and powerful than the biblical text, warrants a brief summary.[45] The setting, as is suitable for the testament genre, is a deathbed scene in which Job delivers lessons to his children, based on an autobiographical sketch of his life and experiences, in order to underscore the principal virtue he wishes to pass on: that of patience and perseverance.

Job reports the act that provoked the whole sequence of events, his destruction of an idolatrous shrine on the prompting of an angel of the Lord. The angel had also alerted him to the consequences: removing the house of Satan would cause untold evils to rain upon his head but would ultimately bring great rewards and everlasting renown. That was good enough for Job, who leveled Satan's shrine in no time, then went back home and barricaded himself against the coming onslaught. Satan duly arrived, disguised as a beggar, but was rebuffed by Job's maid on her master's orders. Not that that did much good. The devil got authority from God to strip Job of all his wealth and possessions, which he had so generously and philanthropically shared with the community, then to collapse his house and kill his children. The latter task was carried out in a second disguise, this time the robes of a Persian king. Job tore his garments in mourning but never questioned the justice of the Lord. Satan, however, did not stop there. He now inflicted sores on every part of Job's body, which was encased in worms and filth; overturned his throne; and compelled him to make his dwelling a mere pile of dung, on which he sat patiently for nearly half a century.

Job's wife Sitidos sacrificed all to minister to her wretched husband, selling herself out as a maidservant to earn some bread, and then, having too little, resorting to begging, humiliated further by Satan, now in the guise of a bread-seller, who had her cut off all her hair in order to scrounge some loaves. The experience led even the loyal Sitidos to break down, lament her fate, and urge Job to give up the ghost. The unyielding Job, however, would not compromise his faith and condemned his wife's words as manipulated by Satan. The devil then acknowledged his failure, and left off his torments for three years.

Not that matters improved much. Job remained afflicted with sores, still seated on the dunghill. He now received visits from three other kings who had known him in his heyday and could not believe that this was the same man. They had to probe at first to discover whether this was indeed Job, then wept and wailed for him. And when Job waived away their laments, claiming that he awaited a better fate in the next world and scorned all earthly goods, he provoked them to anger or to the conclusion that he had lost his mind. A repartee ensued, brief and pointed (nothing like the lengthy speeches in the biblical legend of Job), leaving the protagonists at loggerheads. The forlorn Sitidos sought at least to extract her children's bones from the house that had collapsed upon them and give them decent burial. But Job, unrelenting as ever, scorned terrestrial matters and insisted that the children's spirits had already been taken up to heaven, even giving his wife and the kings a glimpse of the children's souls crowned with divine splendor. That sufficed for Sitidos, who died shortly thereafter, before she had to resume her servile duties.

One last speaker, Elihu, was prompted by Satan to rail against Job. To no avail. The Lord boomed his disapproval of Elihu through a cloud, but permitted Job to intercede on behalf of the other kings and win them divine favor. Job was now restored to his former splendor, indeed had his estate doubled. He could once again return to his charitable benefactions for the needy.

The tale told, Job then presented his inheritance to the children. The sons got the estate, prompting the daughters to wonder what was left for them. Job gave each of them a sash or cord with magical qualities that provided them with new skills and perceptions and gave them a direct connection with the heavenly powers. Job then died peacefully and happily, his soul lifted to heaven in a divine chariot, a phenomenon witnessed only by the three daughters. His body was set to rest in a tomb, and his name held renown through the ages.

Such is the gist of the narrative. Questions of date, genre, provenance, and purpose, so often discussed in the scholarship, can here be treated with brevity. No definitive answers emerge on any of those counts, and a lengthy inquiry would pay few dividends. The oldest manuscripts are in Greek; no Semitic text survives and no good reason exists to postulate one. The author clearly worked from the Septuagint text, the usages and style thoroughly Greek, and the few Semiticisms readily explained as inevitable among Hellenistic Jews.[46] Use of the Septuagint means that the work can hardly have been composed much before the second century BCE, but no terminus ante quem can be fixed with any degree of certainty.[47] The location of the author is commonly set in Egypt. But the text offers nothing resembling proof on that score. Job is once described as "king of Egypt," a peculiar designation on any reckoning but hardly a sign of provenance for the text.[48] The thorough familiarity with the Septuagint and the presumption of a fully Hellenized readership may well imply a diaspora provenance, but there is no reason to limit the location to Egypt. As for genre, the work generally suits the testament form familiar from the Testaments of the Twelve Patriarchs, with the patriarchs providing directives to their children on their deathbeds through a recounting of their lives, with emphasis on the ethical qualities associated with each particular figure, and concluding with a glimpse of an apocalyptic future and the death of the patriarch. The Testament of Job fits well enough into that category, but with sufficient peculiarities to lift it out of a purely conventional mold. The work keeps exhortation to a minimum and dwells rather on narrative elements, with scenic tableaux akin to drama, and even occasional elements of midrash. It follows no predictable pattern.[49]

Does the treatise have a discernible objective? It has been likened to a martyr tale, with Job voluntarily undergoing torment and suffering, obtaining prophetic vision, and paying witness to the power and truth of God.[50] But that analogy stretches the point. Contrasts are stronger than similarities. Job is no innocent sufferer, but brings on his own plight by overthrowing the idols of the rival god. Moreover, his persecutor acknowledges defeat in the midst of the contest. And Job does not die. He triumphs on earth rather than in the hereafter. This is hardly martyrology. Nor is it a tale of conversion, with implications for missionary activity, whether Jewish or Christian, as some have suggested.[51] Job's initial uncertainties about the divinity to whom sacrifices were made in the idol's shrine may indicate that he was not at first a true believer. But the instruction of the angel won him over immediately. Job shifted from confusion to certainty, but this was no "conversion" from paganism to Judaism.[52] The issue, in any case, arises only at the beginning of the text, and does not recur as a theme of any consequence. Moreover, the theory of a proselytizing intent presumes a non-Jewish readership of some scale, for which there is not the slightest indication or likelihood.[53] Efforts to ascribe this work to a particular sect, like the Essenes or the Therapeutae, are refuted by much that is in the text and carry no conviction.[54] Further speculation would be of little value.

This work came from the pen of a Hellenized Jew, directed toward other Hellenized Jews—a creative retelling of the Job saga in a modified testament guise. Certainly it contains ethical instruction, though not in heavy-handed fashion. And it possesses theological significance, though little that is out of the ordinary, whereas much of central importance to Judaism (like adherence to the Law, or cultic rituals) is omitted. The fundamental questioning of divine justice that underpins the canonical book of Job disappears altogether in this text. The character of Job is flattened out; the hero has unwavering faith and an unchanging disposition. The prime focus rests less on moral or religious didacticism than on the narrative itself, which is more readily graspable than the biblical version and more entertaining. For such a text, the inclusion of comic features is appropriate and an enhancement.

That is not to say that the Testament of Job was conceived as a comedy. Unlike the Testament of Abraham, it does employ the biblical tale (albeit in its Greek version) as a frame, adding or subtracting, embellishing or refashioning, rather than creating an altogether new story. And the sober nature of that original remains dominant. But that did not preclude the occasional insertion of humor, irony, and wit.

The Testament from the outset alters in radical fashion the very nature of Job's relation to God in the biblical version. Pain and suffering came out of the blue in the canonical tale—so far as Job was aware—thus setting the stage for puzzlement and outrage. Not so in the Testament. The angel of the Lord informed Job right at the beginning that overthrow of Satan's shrine would cause him grievous misfortune, predicted the disasters to come, and reassured him that patience would allow him to regain his position, to double his holdings, and to achieve everlasting renown.[55] The happy ending was thus forecast right away—and the nobility of Job's endurance somewhat compromised. He knows that all will turn out well in the end.

Nevertheless, our hero was not exactly eager to confront the consequences. After tearing down the idol's temple, he headed straight home and made sure all the doors were locked. He anticipated Satan's imminent arrival and instructed his doormen to let no one enter. He even left word that anyone who sought him should be told that he was busy and could not be disturbed. And indeed when the inevitable knock on the door came, Job informed his maidservant that he was simply not at leisure to see visitors.[56] That scene, near the opening of the work, sets a comic tone right away. The intrepid Job cowered in the recesses of his home, hoping that doors and servants might somehow postpone his fate or allow him to evade it. Satan played along. Instead of lowering the boom, he appeared in the guise of a beggar, expecting that Job's generosity to the poor would gain him access to the great house. A little cat-and-mouse game followed. The devil asked the housemaid for some bread; Job provided only a burnt loaf as token of his disdain and directed the maid to dismiss the visitor with no expectation of further contact. The hapless girl, unaware of what was going on and not recognizing Satan, substituted a good loaf so as to maintain the proprieties of hospitality. The devil, however, eager to get on with matters, rebuked the servant and insisted on the ashen bread, a token of the conflagration to come. The maid, duly chagrined, went back for the burnt loaf and delivered Job's hostile message. Satan gave her one in return: tell your boss that the burning of this loaf heralds his own burning.[57] This little scene, wholly invented by the author, with Job contriving pointless schemes to keep the devil at bay and the confused servant running back and forth, adds a touch of levity before entering upon the grisly events that had to be adapted from the original.

The Testament includes a long segment on Job's immense generosity

and philanthropy, his bounty for the poor, forgiveness of debts, and readiness to give away food to all in need. But this massive charity operation
had its price. Job's servants grew weary of preparing endless meals for widows and the poor, even resorting to contemptuous slurs against their master. Job, however, had a means of dealing with labor complaints. He picked
up his lyre and strummed while singing the psalms—a nice, soothing response. It supplied the equivalent of wages and put an end to their grous-
ing![58] The reader is thus expected to imagine overworked and protesting
servants happily taking recompense for their services in the form of Job's
warbling.

In the meantime the devil made repeated costume changes. First dressed
as a beggar when he knocked on Job's locked portals, he then put on the
garb of a Persian king and rounded up all the rascals of the realm to complete the job of robbing Job of any remaining belongings. (He had already
laid waste to Job's fields and slaughtered his herds and flocks.)[59] But he
soon doffed that guise as well and dressed himself as a bread-seller, the
better to bargain with Job's wife.[60] One can always posit particular motives
for each camouflage. But the fact is that Satan could have accomplished his
ends without them. The costumes simply add a note of amusing theatrical-
ity to the events.

Job's recourse to a dunghill, of course, derives from the biblical tale. So
does the affliction with worms and sores from head to toe. But the author
added a gratuitous detail. Job, far from resenting his torment, seems to
have reveled in self-mortification. Worms were somehow a source of satisfaction. In fact, if any worm had the temerity to hop off, Job would grab it
and put it back on his body, with the admonishment that it remain there
until further instructions![61] That surely seems contrived to draw a laugh.

The distraught and oppressed Sitidos finally gave way to despair and
urged her husband to denounce God and die. That too stems from the canonical text. But here Job identified her words as really coming from Satan,
who had turned Sitidos into one of those silly women who lead their husbands' innocence astray.[62] The comic metaphor then becomes reality. Satan
was not only the inspiration for the words; he was literally standing behind
Sitidos, concealed by her figure. No costume this time, but a body to serve
as cover. Job had to summon the devil out from behind his wife's skirts and
challenge him to a direct encounter.[63] The climactic confrontation, however, is something of a letdown. Satan, finally now in his own person,
awarded the palm to Job right away, weepily confessing that, like an ath-
lete who pins his opponent but cannot get him to yield, he had failed to
break Job's spirit and so acknowledged defeat.[64] The scene itself resembles

comic drama. But the author seems to have got himself into a bind. Job
gained his triumph too early. The whole interchange with the other kings,
the major portion of the biblical version, had still to be dealt with. It was
too soon for the story to end. Thus, the devil's surrender is turned into a
temporary truce. He withdrew shamefacedly—but just for three years.[65]
This is unlikely to be mere ineptitude on the author's part. He even concludes the section with an exhortation by Job to his children to practice patience (his special virtue) in all that they must endure, a typical terminus in
the testament genre.[66] But half the text remains.[67] The author is evidently
playing with the genre.

The discourses between Job and his friends occupy the vast bulk of the
canonical version. The author of the Testament, by contrast, has little patience with the grave theological issues scrutinized in the original. He cuts
the dialogue to a minimum and expands the narrative. The prologue to the
meeting between Job and his "consolers" in the Bible is told with great
brevity: they heard of his plight, came to sympathize with him, could not
recognize the man they once knew, and loudly lamented his distress.[68] In
the Testament of Job, this introduction grows substantially, with embellishment and exaggeration. The friends who have become kings (as in the
Septuagint) at first could not find him; they had to be led to the dunghill.
And not only did they not recognize him; they insisted that this could not
be Job. When he did identify himself, shock and grief were inadequate
emotions. The three kings all dropped to the ground in a dead faint. When
they came to, they sat for seven days in a state of disbelief.[69] And even then,
they needed convincing. Eliphaz proposed a direct interrogation to see if
this was indeed Job. Unfortunately they could not get too close. The stench
was overpowering. The three kings (who had arrived with their armies!)
were able to approach only by sniffing perfume, while their soldiers scattered incense everywhere—an operation that took three full days.[70] The
spectacle of three monarchs, carrying perfume jars and surrounded by military personnel, timidly approaching a dunghill while the whole area was
fumigated exhibits the author's whimsical imagination.

Eliphaz offered no advice, just lamented Job's misfortunes. And Job responded not with indignation, as in the Bible, but with the serene assur-
ance that his throne rests in the next world, his kingdom to endure forever,
while earthly realms come and go. That did not sit well with Eliphaz, who
took it as an insult and a humiliation—in front of his own troops.[71] Baldad
stepped in to play the reconciler. He was prepared to overlook Job's apparent arrogance in view of the grievous ills he had suffered. His diagnosis,
however, was less than flattering: he surmised that Job had become men-

tally disturbed and that his plight had unhinged his mind.[72] Baldad proceeded to put some questions to Job to see if he was still of sound mind,
questions (such as "why does the sun rise in the east and set in the west?")
that may have required more patience than all the ills that Job had undergone. This time our hero lost his cool, and retorted with a sarcastic question of his own: how is it that we eat and drink through the same throat
but excrete the substances into the latrine through two separate routes?
Baldad was stumped. And Job shut him up by observing that if he didn't
understand the functions of the body, how could he grasp the affairs of
heaven?[73] The author plainly enjoyed himself with this striking put-down.

The humor in the Testament of Job is intermittent and occasional, an
adjunct to the treatise rather than sitting at its core. But the incidental in-
sertions themselves carry weight. The work derives from the diaspora,
whether Egypt or elsewhere, from a Greek-speaking Jewish community
and directed toward other Hellenized Jews. The setting itself is unclear, just
as Job's own background remains elusive. The Hebrew Bible provides him
with no ancestry. But the Septuagint, in a supplement at the conclusion
of the text, makes him a descendant of Esau and ruler of Edom.[74] This
construct is picked up by Aristeas and by the author of the Testament.[75]
But the boundaries of Edom are somewhat stretched. The canonical text
locates Job in Uz, a land identified by Hellenistic Jewish writers as Ausitis
between Idumaea and Arabia.[76] And the stretch goes further in the Testament: Job is designated as "ruling over all Egypt."[77] Just what this confusion amounts to cannot be resolved. But the perception of Job, in any case,
is one of a figure outside the homeland of Judaea.

Should one infer that the emphasis on Job's patience in the face of hor-
rendous trials and tribulations (a feature not prominently present in the
biblical version) delivers a lesson to diaspora communities in adverse circumstances?[78] That seems unlikely. Job suffers and endures as an individual, not as a member of a community. His individual trust in the Lord
stands as the pivot of the piece. The stress on Job's limitless philanthropy
does, to be sure, signal the importance of responsibility to the less fortunate members of the community—perhaps an appeal for solidarity among
diaspora Jews. But the threat exists only from within, not from without.
Satan represents no imperial power. Even the momentary guise of the Persian king identified him with a nation traditionally friendly to the Jews. Rejection of idolatry, adherence to the faith, a belief in the superiority of
heavenly over terrestrial realities, charity to the needy, and perseverance in
misfortune constitute the main themes. The formulas apply essentially to
self-sufficient Jewish communities who need to be reminded of basic prin-

ciples, not to those under the thumb of wicked overlords. With those ideals in view, the Testament of Job avoids heavy-handed exhortation and tempers its message with touches of humor, lightening what had been a ponderous tale and rendering it, at least in part, as a piece of entertainment.

ARTAPANUS

The mysterious and intriguing Artapanus haunts the byways of research on Hellenistic Judaism. Efforts to classify him end in frustration. Artapanus resists labels, eludes characterization, and defies categories. He carries a Persian name, writes in Greek, and has a Jewish perspective. His work jumbles genres and transforms traditions, blending history with fable, propaganda with fantasy, biblical narrative with pagan romance.

Artapanus' output, unlike those treated above, is attached to an author with a name—even if we know nothing about him as a person, and even if the name is a pseudonym. And it pays little heed to doctrine or instruction. Similarities, however, outweigh the differences. The study professes to be a recreation of biblical stories and a retelling of Israelite history. It stems from the diaspora, it is inventive and imaginative, it manipulates rather than reproduces traditions, and it contains a substantial component of levity.

How does one gain a grip on this author? Scholarly treatments proliferate.[79] Most of the work has involved questions of date, provenance, and genre, but they take us only a small distance. The extant fragments of Artapanus derive from Alexander Polyhistor, as preserved by Eusebius— hence a third-hand version at best. But that offers a chronological clue. Artapanus must predate Polyhistor, and thus wrote no later than the early first century BCE. And the Septuagint served as the text with which he worked, thus placing him no earlier than the mid-third century BCE.[80] It would be imprudent to press chronology any further. The question of location seems a bit easier. The surviving texts all concern themselves with Egypt. That may be accidental or perhaps the consequence of Polyhistor's selectivity, but an Egyptian provenance is, at least, a defensible hypothesis. To identify a specific site requires speculation—and the scholarly speculation on that subject is already excessive.[81] Ethnic background is more interesting and more important. On that matter a solid consensus exists: Artapanus is a Hellenized Jew with a zeal for retelling and rewriting biblical stories. No Gentile would have had the motivation do so.[82]

But what is the motivation? The question is tied closely to the issue of genre, a matter that has generated much discussion—to relatively little profit. The work has been classified as either history or romance or some combination thereof, as a vehicle for promoting a syncretistic blend of cultures or a means to refute nasty Gentile depictions of Jews. It can hardly be all of these things at once, and the whole drive for classification may be misguided. Nearly all commentators find an apologetic purpose of some form: Artapanus' aims were patriotic and nationalistic, his work described as "competitive historiography" or "romantic national history," the objective being to elevate Judaism or even to deliver a point-by-point refutation of anti-semitic slanders by the Greco-Egyptian writer Manetho.[83] That sort of interpretation, while it may contain some truth, can hardly be the whole truth. Artapanus is too slippery and elusive a character to pigeonhole. He repeatedly sheds labels and wriggles out of brackets. It may be best to jettison the notion of a single-minded purpose—a sober and serious endeavor to elevate Jewish prestige against the assaults of pagan detractors. That idea rests on a large assumption: that Artapanus' work would be read by Gentile readers. The proposition is not very plausible. How many Gentiles would devour the writings of a Jew (even a pseudonymous Jew) who reproduced or amplified biblical tales that recounted the feats of the Hebrew patriarchs? As propaganda the narrative would win few converts. Artapanus' readers were, in all likelihood, Jews who enjoyed a good yarn. Thus an alternative approach to this writer may be of value. Artapanus was less an embattled apologist engaged in intellectual trench warfare than an imaginative, occasionally jocular, spinner of tales.

Three fragments constitute the corpus of what survives. They derive from a work entitled, so it seems, "On the Jews."[84] Two of the fragments, on Abraham and Joseph, are quite brief and truncated, giving only hints of what the full version might have been like. But the third fragment on Moses is more extensive, more elaborate, and more engaging.

The short paragraph on Abraham parallels a tradition recorded elsewhere that has the patriarch bring the science of astrology to Egypt.[85] Artapanus adds the more vivid detail that Abraham serves as mentor of the Egyptian pharaoh himself. And he supplies further items that he could not have found in the Hebrew Bible, including the statements that Abraham dwelled in Egypt for twenty years and that, when he departed, he left many of his followers behind.[86] This version moves in a discernible direction. Artapanus enhances the association of Abraham with Egypt, thereby to make Egyptian culture, or at least a segment thereof, part of the legacy of the patriarch. But it gives Artapanus less than his due to set his portrait of Abraham in a strictly polemical context, an example of the battle of the books in which various peoples claimed for their own ancestors the prestige of inventing the science of star-interpretation.[87] The work constitutes fanciful recreation for a Jewish-Hellenistic readership, not an endeavor to overtrump Babylonian or Egyptian rivals. By situating Abraham in the context of antique civilizations, Artapanus makes his people part and parcel of the intellectual culture that belongs to the ancient Near East. At the same time, however, he is quite explicit that Abraham has a distinct ethnic identification rather than being a shadowy figure who blends into the larger cultural landscape. It is no accident that he features in a work entitled "On the Jews." Artapanus plays further with appellations. He maintains that the odd term "Hermiouth" was the original designation of Jews. And he adds that the name "Hebrews" actually derives from Abraham himself. What does this terminological jumble amount to? Artapanus moves outside the Near Eastern world to suggest links with the Hellenized Mediterranean of his own experience. The name Hermiouth, nowhere else attested and possibly a concoction by the author, hints at a connection with Hermes, a figure to whom Artapanus alludes elsewhere in his text.[88] This has still broader implications. Abraham appears as ancestor of the Jews, and his people, tied both to the ancient Near East and to the Hellenic world, played a critical part in forming the culture of the Mediterranean. The reverberations from this construct have clear meaning for the Jewish diaspora of Artapanus' day. The descendants of Abraham occupy a secure place in the wider culture that they themselves had helped to shape.

The Joseph fragment, though a bit longer, is still highly condensed by the epitomator. It thereby yields only small insight into the techniques and intent of the author—but enough to reinforce the impression that Artapanus tampered liberally with the biblical tradition. The excerpt is too brief to disclose details of his humor or irony, but it adequately exhibits the caprice of the author.

In Artapanus' version, Joseph, not his brothers, took the initiative in arranging his transfer from Palestine to Egypt. They had conspired against him because he surpassed them in knowledge and intelligence—a very different motive from that ascribed in the Bible, where Jacob's favor and Joseph's perceived or real arrogance had alienated the brothers. Shrewd foresight, however, enabled Joseph to jump the gun on his rivals. Anticipating their plot, he persuaded some neighboring Arabs to convey him to Egypt.[89] Never mind that Arabs were not even around yet.[90] Artapanus' literary license extends well beyond this. On his interpretation, Joseph made his way to Egypt through his own wits, evading the machinations of his brothers, rather than being victimized by them. Joseph is not the naive youth of Genesis, but already exhibits the characteristics that will enable him to rise

to the top in his adopted land. If the preserved fragment of Artapanus accurately represents its author's construct, Joseph swiftly earned the confidence of the pharaoh and gained appointment as chief economic minister of the land. The detour through the household of Potiphar and the
thwarted blandishments of Madame Potiphar are omitted. So is Joseph's
reputation as an acute interpreter of dreams. His installation as the king's
right-hand man comes not from mantic skills or divine assistance but sheer
brain power. The new minister, a quick learner, immediately undertook
sweeping social and economic reforms. He placed Egyptian land tenure,
for the first time, on a fair footing. He intervened to protect the weak from
exploitation by the powerful, allocating possessions in designated lots,
with clearly delineated boundaries, and bringing neglected land back into
cultivation. And he also showed due concern for the religious establishment by setting aside property for the priests.[91] This account veers sharply
away from the biblical narrative. In the Book of Genesis, Joseph's agricultural restructuring resulted in the extension of royal authority and
ownership and made the peasantry of Egypt dependent on the crown.[92]
Artapanus' Joseph, by contrast, acted not to tighten the king's control but
to implement his own broad vision of an equitable society. He became beloved by the people, in large part because he introduced the art of measure-
ments into the land.[93] Joseph, like Abraham, was responsible for enduring
features of Egyptian civilization—and ultimately of all civilizations.

Artapanus obviously felt free to remold the biblical tale to his own
tastes.[94] Joseph emerges as a clever calculator who impressed the pharaoh,
a pragmatic inventor, and an accomplished and humane administrator.
The compressed fragment precludes any extended interpretation. But it
gives some sense of the author's inventiveness.

With Moses, Artapanus really has a field day. The surviving fragment
is far lengthier than the Abraham and Joseph portions combined. And
Artapanus gives full rein to his imagination. Although thoroughly conversant with the Exodus narrative, he employs it only as inspiration for his
own creativity. And the extant text supplies ample evidence for a mischievous sense of humor.

A précis of Artapanus' peculiar rendition can make the point. He begins
in familiar fashion with a wicked pharaoh who oppresses the Israelites
(here called Jews in good Hellenistic fashion), although he applies a name
to him, Chenephres, evidently of his own invention. This king, as in the
Book of Exodus, had a daughter who took up the baby Moses from an
Israelite family and adopted him. She too acquires a name, Merris, at
Artapanus' hands and the added detail that she was otherwise barren—

perhaps a hint that even the Egyptian royal line might need a helping hand from Moses.

The subsequent narrative possesses only the faintest resemblance to what occurs in the Bible.[95] Moses, when he grew up, was given the name Musaeus by the Greeks. So says Artapanus. Just what Greeks might be expected to be around the pharaoh's palace in the Late Bronze Age is anyone's guess. But that was only a small novelty amidst the many inserted into the tale by Artapanus. Musaeus or Moses became the teacher of Orpheus, the legendary singer and father of Hellenic poetry. And his talents displayed themselves in a dazzling diversity of ways. Moses conferred a host of benefits upon mankind, including the invention of ships, mechanisms for stone construction, Egyptian weaponry, hydraulic engines, implements of warfare, and even philosophy. Then, like Joseph—only more so—he showed himself to be adept in revamping Egyptian institutions and fertile in producing new ones. He thought up the nomes as administrative divisions to allow for smoother governance of the nation; he determined the divinities to be assigned to each nome (cats, dogs, and ibises, to be precise); he gave sacred writings to the priests and supplied them with choice land. All this was done with an eye to shoring up the regime, previously wracked with dissent and upheaval. Widespread popularity followed. The masses loved him, and the priests thought him deserving of honors equivalent to those given the gods. The latter accorded him the designation "Hermes," for he had been responsible for their acquisition of sacred scripts.

Everyone seemed pleased with Moses—except the pharaoh Chenephres, who was jealous of his *arete*. Chenephres hit upon the useful idea of sending him off at the head of a makeshift army to wage war on the Ethiopians, fully expecting that he would never make it back alive. But Moses whipped the farmboy conscripts into shape, engaged the Ethiopians for a decade, an epic contest on the scale of the Trojan war, and emerged triumphant. And he had the great prescience to avoid the troubles suffered by the homecomings of the Homeric heroes. He simply did not have his discharged veterans go home. He built a city instead on the site of their triumph where they could all settle, a city to be named after him, Hermopolis (for Hermes), and where the ibis would be consecrated. Even the defeated Ethiopians came to love their conqueror and, on his advice, adopted the practice of circumcision, priests and all. Nothing in the Bible, of course, supplies the smallest warrant for these fantasies.

Nor do the Scriptures prepare readers for what follows in Artapanus' lively narrative. The villain Chenephres, foiled in his plan to rid himself of Moses indirectly, tried a more direct method. He hoped to put his rival off guard by seeking his advice on what else the king might use of benefit to mankind. Moses suggested a strain of oxen which could plow the land. Chenephres took the advice, honored the bull Apis as a divinity, but did all he could to prevent anyone from knowing that the counsel came from Moses. In the meantime he selected assassins and swore his friends to secrecy about the plot. To no avail. The would-be killer planned to commit the foul deed while accompanying Moses to the burial of his mother Merris (whose resting place would be named Meroe after her), but word of the plot leaked out. Moses escaped to Arabia. The assassin followed and sprang at him from ambush. But mighty Moses fought off the knife-wielding assailant and overpowered him.

Artapanus picks up the biblical tale at this point, but only to revise it to his own liking. Moses, seeking refuge from the pharaoh's power, married into the household of an important personage from a neighboring land, although here it is not a Midian priest but an Arabian prince. His new father-in-law, Raguel, had ambitions of his own, urging Moses to wage war on the Egyptians, thus to carve out a realm for himself and his bride as an appendage to Raguel's own kingdom. Moses, however, loyal to his roots, would not lead forces against the land of his birth. Raguel had to content himself with plundering raids. The turning point came with the death of pharaoh Chenephres. And a most suitable end it was. The wicked Chenephres had forbidden Jews to wear woolen garments and required them to dress in linen, so that they could be the more readily identified and victimized. Chenephres succumbed to elephantiasis, the first man ever to die of it. He got what he deserved.

Moses, now hopeful that his people might be relieved of their suffering, encountered the burning bush. The divine voice that issued forth, however, surprisingly commanded him to lead an army against Egypt, just as Raguel had recommended, thereby to free his people of oppression. This would be an invasion in force, no mere request for liberation. Artapanus never hesitated to spin his own variants on the scriptural story. As it happened, the new ruler of Egypt forestalled Moses by summoning him to the palace and then putting him behind bars. A fruitless measure. The prison doors opened spontaneously, the guards either fell into a stupor or perished when their swords splintered, and Moses calmly strolled out to saunter over to the palace. When the astonished pharaoh demanded to know what god had sent him, Moses obliged by whispering the divine name in his ear, thus causing the king to keel over in a faint. Moses had to revive him personally. A scornful priest did not escape so lightly. When he made so bold as to read the Lord's name as inscribed on a sealed tablet, he dropped dead on the spot.

The remainder of the extant text bears at least some resemblance to events recorded in the Book of Exodus. Moses negotiated with the pharaoh for the release of the Israelites, had to prove his authority by turning his rod into a snake and back again (the rod was later taken up into Isis worship), engaged in competition with Egyptian priests and sorcerers, brought about plagues including the flooding of the Nile (the origin of its annual inundation), boils, frogs, locusts, and lice—and, for good measure, Artapanus adds one that the authors of the Bible missed: earthquakes that leveled all the Egyptian homes and most of the temples. That was enough to convince the pharaoh. He did not even need the death of the first-born, which Artapanus provocatively drops from his narrative. There is no Passover here. The Jews were released, grabbing what they could from their neighbors before departure. And the chase scene follows. Artapanus reproduces the familiar tale of the miracle at the Red Sea: Moses caused the waters to divide, he and his people walked across on dry land, and the Egyptian forces, in hot pursuit, found themselves engulfed by the sea and destroyed to a man. That should have sufficed. But Artapanus prefers to complicate matters. He does not even ascribe the story to scriptural authority. Instead, he claims it simply as the version told by the Heliopolitans. And theirs is not the only version. He records another rendition transmitted by the Memphites, the rational rather than the supernatural account: Moses knew the area, waited for the ebb tide, and got his people across before the waters rose. Where does the author stand? No matter. Like Herodotus, Artapanus has deftly led his readers on a merry chase of his own.

This is a remarkable text, replete with twists and turns, offering a surplus of surprises. The Book of Exodus serves as a frame and a skeleton but little more. The rest is imaginative invention. Artapanus does not stitch a seamless narrative. A basic tension exists, for instance, between the Moses figure at the outset who is benefactor of the Egyptians, beloved by them, and devoted to the land, and the later Moses who takes up arms against Egypt and becomes the agent of divine vengeance. But the fragments of Artapanus suggest that he took little interest in consistency or tidiness. His work is learned and ingenious, rich in material drawn from Greek and Egyptian as well as Jewish sources, multiple in theme and content, and, not least, a repository of capricious wit.

Artapanus was determinedly idiosyncratic. Although he credits Moses with a multitude of accomplishments, his extant text leaves out the one achievement with which he was most closely associated by Jew and Gentile alike: the promulgation of laws for the Jews.[96] Why this peculiar omission? That some political or ideological motivation drove him here is most implausible.[97] More likely, the unconventional Artapanus was simply signaling his independence of standard interpretations. His Moses would stand out in arresting fashion. While others might see him as the great lawgiver of the Jews, Artapanus would develop a more colorful and memorable portrait of the man. This toppling of convention characterizes the text again and again.

Artapanus casts Moses in more than one mold. He identifies him in one instance with Hermes, in another with Musaeus. In each case the author dodges responsibility, ascribing the congruence to others: Egyptian priests amalgamated Moses with Hermes, and Greeks gave Moses the name Musaeus.[98] But Artapanus, of course, manipulates the material and blends the traditions. And it is more than simple syncretism. Research and erudition lay behind these constructs. In the case of Hermes, Artapanus welded together various traits of Moses not so much with the Greek divinity as with the Egyptian version of him, namely Thot. Common characteristics included the skills of builders and craftsmen, a connection with the ibis, the exercise of magic, and, most particularly, the ability to interpret sacred writings.[99] Manipulation is clearer still in the matching of Moses and Musaeus. Artapanus not only claims that Greeks made the identification, thus adding an aura of authenticity; he adds that Moses/Musaeus became the teacher of Orpheus, a notion that no informed Greek would have bought. In Hellenic legend, Musaeus was the son or disciple of Orpheus, the celebrated singer of ancient lore.[100] By reversing the sequence, Artapanus made Moses the fount of song and poetry that enriched Hellenic life. For those Jewish readers well versed in Greek literature and myth, this might or might not be edifying—but it was certainly amusing. And that would meet Artapanus' objectives well enough. He presents no activist agenda of persuading Greeks or deluding Jews. He relished the practice of inverting and reshaping traditions. By setting Moses in the guise of both Hermes and Musaeus, Artapanus addresses the perspective and proclivities of diaspora Jews in Hellenistic Egypt: he makes Moses the cultural progenitor of Hellas itself.

In Artapanus' fantasy, Moses was a prime benefactor to humanity in general. But his contributions are not, as one might expect, focused on the realm of high culture. Artapanus' playfulness takes over once again. He offers as samples of Moses' accomplishments the invention of ships and weapons, and of hydraulic and building devices. And one last item is mentioned, almost as an afterthought: philosophy.[101] The sequence is probably not accidental. Artapanus mischievously upsets expectations. He proceeds to assign to Moses the responsibility for various Egyptian institutions: not only the division into nomes, the landed privileges of the priests, and the use of hieroglyphics, but even the apportioning of divinities to each nome and the inauguration of animal worship![102] These last items have given special distress to the scholarly community. What is Artapanus doing? How does one reconcile his laudation of Moses and the Jews with a favorable judgment on pagan rites and animal gods?[103] But efforts at reconciliation may miss the point. The discomfiture of scholars derives from too sober an interpretation of the text. Artapanus cleverly juggled a variety of traditions for those in the know. He appropriated stories about Egyptian and other Near Eastern heroes and divinities, notably Sesostris, Semiramis, Isis, Osiris, and Hermes, most of them subsequently recorded in the first book of Diodorus Siculus. Artapanus gathered together exploits ascribed to one or more of these figures and simply chalked them all up to Moses' credit. Items like the division of Egypt into thirty-six nomes by Sesostris and the consecration of animals by Isis were now transformed into achievements by the Israelite leader.[104] Artapanus was engaging here in some roguish one-upmanship. Moses had outdone all the cultural progenitors of antique civilizations. But it is important to place the matter in proper perspective. Artapanus was not crossing swords with pagan intellectuals in a contest to establish primacy for his hero. Egyptians, if any should by chance happen to read this treatise, would hardly embrace the idea of Moses as originator of animal worship. And few Jews would find it compelling. To label Artapanus as an apologist or polemicist does him less than justice. His expropriation and transformation of pagan legends would amuse a cultivated readership. And he doubtless enjoyed himself thoroughly.

The biblical heroics of Moses were not enough for Artapanus. He added military heroics. Moses turned back an Ethiopian invasion of Egypt and then subdued the mighty Ethiopians with a patchwork army in a war of epic proportions, thereby putting himself in a class with Sesostris, Semiramis, and Osiris. Moreover, he capped his triumph by resettling his loyal farmer-veterans in a brand-new foundation to be named Hermopolis after himself. Moses was thus not only general but colonizer.[105] Hellenic parallels would readily suggest themselves. This was a Moses of many dimensions—to whom the biblical personage bore only the smallest resemblance. Artapanus willfully toyed with traditions.

The author inserted surprises and repeatedly caught readers up short. He has the Ethiopians so charmed by Moses, their conqueror, that they embraced the practice of circumcision which he generously taught them. And, in a typically prankish manner, Artapanus makes a point of noting that not only the Ethiopian rank and file but every one of their priests readily applied the knife.[106] The consecration of Apis, a prime feature of Egyptian worship, became in this story the result of advice from Moses, and the burial of Egypt's sacred animals derived from Chenephres' desire to conceal Moses' initiative in the matter.[107] Moses' potent rod so impressed the Egyptians that they installed rods in each of their temples thereafter and associated them with the worship of Isis.[108] Even the city of Meroe, capital of Ethiopia, owed its name to a Mosaic connection: Moses' adoptive mother Merris was buried there.[109] And Moses' manipulation of the Nile in order to intimidate the king into releasing his people became the origin of the annual inundation of the river.[110] Such comments can only invite mirth.

Whereas the biblical pharaoh served as a stout opponent of Moses, Artapanus transformed Chenephres into a comic figure. His effort to doom Moses by putting him at the head of an inexperienced troop backfired; his appointee as assassin was incompetent; his order to his friends to keep mum about the conspiracy was obeyed by no one; and he went down in history as the first man to die of elephantiasis.[111] The facetious wit can hardly be missed here. And Chenephres' successor was no more formidable. His imprisonment of Moses turned into a joke. The prison doors swung open and the guards' weapons shattered in their hands, while Moses entered the palace unhindered.[112] Moses had merely to whisper God's name in the pharaoh's ear (on the latter's own request) to have him pass out on the spot—which must have created quite a spectacle in the court. He revived only when Moses took hold of him and propped him up.[113]

The lengthy fragment on Moses, as is clear, amplifies the intentions of Artapanus as already adumbrated in his treatments of Abraham and Joseph. He did not enlist in a deadly serious effort to advance Jewish values against the claims of competing nations and cultures. Instead, he exhibits a light touch, a caprice and whimsy that tampered liberally with the Scriptures and inverted or transposed Gentile traditions to place figures of Jewish legend in their midst. The humor is mischievous rather than malicious. Employment of an ostensibly historical narrative allows the author to take on a posture of detachment, disengaged from ideological battle. What stands out is not so much polemics as playfulness.

What inferences might diaspora Jews be expected to draw from so idiosyncratic and beguiling a text? One motif predominates in the fragments: the debt of Egyptian civilization to the genius of Israelite antecedents. Not that Artapanus expected his readers to take the notion literally. They knew their Scriptures. Indeed without that presupposition, much of the whimsicality would be lost. But the motif does at least imply that no irreparable breach existed between the cultures—nor even between the peoples. Abraham was mentor to a pharaoh, Joseph served another loyally, and Moses' reforms were designed to sustain the position of yet another. To be sure, Moses ran into trouble with a couple of pharaohs. But he ingratiated himself with the inhabitants of the land, and with their neighbors as well. The institutions of Egyptians and Ethiopians alike were portrayed as stemming from the inventive insight of the Hebrew leader. None of this should be taken to imply that Hellenized Jews embraced some synthesis with Egyptian culture, let alone that they found animal worship acceptable. But it may well reflect some modus vivendi that characterized diaspora life. Artapanus' text represents no manifesto for assimilation, accommodation, or acculturation. It is a mistake to reckon it as promotional material or propaganda. Artapanus eschews the preaching of a lesson. The facetious and frivolous twists on tradition do, however, betray an unmistakable attitude of self-confidence. Artapanus could poke fun at Egyptian pharaohs while simultaneously garbling the story of the Exodus. His account expands Moses' résumé to comic proportions, has him hailed by Greeks, Egyptians, Ethiopians, and Arabs—a world-historical figure who, like Abraham, represents both a forefather of the Jews and a universal benefactor. Of course, it is all fantasy, as the jocular tone discloses. But the very creation of this fantasy is significant. The audacious revamping of the Exodus legend suggests that Artapanus' readership enjoyed a healthy and successful diaspora existence.

Tinkering with biblical traditions became practically a cottage industry among Jews in the Greco-Roman era. The texts treated here constitute only a sampling. But they illustrate the license accorded to writers who fiddled freely with scriptural stories and took pleasure in injecting them with humor.

The authors transformed tales and reconceived characters in diverting ways. The Testament of Abraham's composer produced a slippery patriarch, a bumbling archangel, and a multifaceted figure of death to keep his readership surprised and off balance. In the altogether different Testament of Job, the hero, who exemplifies patient endurance, nonetheless tries to dodge his tormentor and gives way to an outburst of exasperated sarcasm; Satan emerges as a deft master of disguises that avail him nothing; and the consolers are prone to fainting and are disabled by a whiff of malodors. For Artapanus, Abraham is a counselor of pharaohs, Joseph a clever agricultural reformer, and Moses a combination of inventor, military hero, magician, and founder of both Egyptian and Ethiopian religious and cultural institutions.

These writers did not expect (or want) audiences to take their works as a substitute for the Scriptures. But they could anticipate an amused recognition of feigned resemblance and playful divergence. The texts interestingly and significantly give no hint of conflict between Jew and Gentile, between the "chosen people" and their enemies. Indeed, the reverse seems to hold. Only ethics, not ethnics, matter in the Testament of Abraham. Job's travails are inflicted by divine powers, his consolers are fellow kings, and he bestows his patronage upon all. The Abraham and Moses of Artapanus are culture heroes whose contributions enriched various lands of the Near East and, indirectly, even the Greeks. If these constructs afford a clue to the receptivity of diaspora readers, they suggest self-assurance and comfort in the Greek-speaking lands of the Mediterranean, and a secure confidence in their own traditions that allowed for manipulation, merriment, and mockery.

CHAPTER SEVEN

Jewish Constructs of Greeks and Hellenism

THE ENCOUNTER of diaspora Jews with the language, literature, and learning of the Hellenic world created a cultural revolution. Ancient Judaism was never quite the same again. The adjustments entailed by that encounter played a profound role in the reshaping of Jewish self-conception. The Jews, however, did much more than simply react to the circumstances in which they found themselves. The framing of Jewish identity in lands pervaded by Greek culture presented a significant challenge. And the challenge was met in important part through the conceptions of Greeks and Hellenism conveyed by Jewish intellectuals. They not only engaged with the Hellenized Mediterranean; they constructed that environment for themselves.

A long scholarly tradition has probed the influence of the Hellenic achievement upon the Jewish experience.[1] And researchers have directed much energy toward discerning the attitude of Greeks (or pagans more generally) toward Jews.[2] By contrast, little scrutiny has been applied to an equally revealing and fascinating issue: how was the Hellenic achievement—and those who achieved it—perceived (or, rather, conceived) by the Jews?[3] It is no secret that many Jews became thoroughly familiar with the Greek language, with Hellenic myths, history, traditions, religion, and institutions. They engaged in a protracted effort to redefine themselves within the terms of an ascendant Mediterranean culture that was largely Greek.[4] A significant and neglected part of that endeavor involved Jewish constructs of the Greeks as a people, nation, or society. The formulations of Hellenes and Hellenism yield critical insight into the Jews' reformulations of their own identity.

The issue is a complex and problematic one. Jews do not resolve themselves into a monolithic group with a unitary viewpoint. Attitudes diverge and develop. And there is another complication. It might be tempting to employ Jewish perspectives as an "external" viewpoint on Hellenism. In fact, however, Jews occupy an ambiguous perch as both "external" and "internal" witnesses. They carried their peculiar culture, background, tradition, and history. Yet in the Hellenistic era and in the Greek East of the Roman period, they were part and parcel of a Greek cultural community. Hence Jews needed both to establish their own secure place within a Hellenistic framework and also to avoid being swallowed up by the prevailing culture. Jewish self-conception constituted an ongoing, shifting process, one that was inescapably entangled in the construction of Greek character, values, and beliefs.

One might expect in the first instance an accentuation of distinctiveness. It behooved Jews to underscore the differences that kept them a nation apart and resisted the melting pot. Depiction of the Hellene as the "Other" could serve the purpose of maintaining allegiance to tried-and-true principles. And indeed a number of texts advance that conception.

The author of the Second Book of Maccabees composed a succinct history of the background, circumstances, and consequences of the brutal persecution of Jews by the Hellenistic monarch Antiochus IV Epiphanes. His work offered a condensed and more marketable version of the five volumes devoted to this subject by Jason of Cyrene.[5] As a Hellenized Jew of the late second century BCE who wrote his history in Greek, and an intellectual thoroughly steeped in the traditions of Greek historiography, the author of II Maccabees had a special incentive to stress the contrasts between Greek and Jew. The text, not coincidentally, supplies the first preserved appearances of the terms "Judaism" and "Hellenism." It makes reference to the Seleucid monarchy's efforts to bring Jews to "Hellenic ways."[6] And this, in the author's view, was paralleled by the policy of the High Priest and his faction to lead his countrymen into the "Greek mode of life," thus perpetrating a "peak of Hellenism."[7] Jewish rebels, by contrast, held themselves as champions of "Judaism."[8] To be sure, the text nowhere pairs the two terms, setting them in stark juxtaposition as directly competing concepts.[9] But it certainly delivered the idea that adherents of the two notions went their separate ways in the age of the Maccabees.

That idea was reinforced in an unexpected place. The *Letter of Aristeas* narrates the celebrated fable of the translation of the Pentateuch into Greek, a congenial collaboration between Hellenistic monarch and Jewish High Priest, brought to fruition by Jewish sages at the Ptolemaic capital in Alexandria. No work is more frequently cited as the classic document of harmony and common objectives between Jews and Greeks.[10] But concentration on that aspect, legitimate though it may be, omits a critical message contained in the treatise. Eleazer the High Priest, in responding to queries by Greeks about the peculiar habits of the Jews, delivered some pointed pronouncements. He asserted without equivocation that Jews alone hold to monotheistic beliefs and that those who worship many gods are gripped by foolishness and self-deception. Idolators who revere images of wood and stone, he observed, are more powerful than the very gods to whom they pay homage, since they were themselves responsible for their creation. And he added a touch of sarcasm as well: those who manufactured myths and concocted stories were adjudged the wisest of the Greeks. So much for Greek intelligence.[11] Eleazer proceeded to declare that Moses quite properly fenced the Jews off with unbreakable barriers and iron walls to prevent any mingling with other *ethne,* to keep them pure in body and soul, and to rid them of empty beliefs.[12] Hence even the *Letter of Aristeas,* prime exhibit for intercultural concord, includes a pivotal pronouncement by the chief spokesman for Judaism who sets his creed decisively apart from the ignorant and misguided beliefs of the Greek *ethnos.*

The well-known lines of the apostle Paul bear notice here. He makes direct allusion to the antithesis between the *ethne:* "there is neither Jew nor Greek, slave nor free, male nor female, for you are all one in Jesus Christ."[13] The string of antinomies makes it clear that the two peoples represented conventionally opposite poles. The same phraseology appears in another Pauline text: "we have all been baptized into one body and in one spirit, whether Jews or Greeks, slaves or free."[14] The differentiation held firm in Jewish circles. Paul had an uphill battle to surmount it.

The thoroughly Hellenized philosopher Philo, whose debt to Greek learning is large and unconcealed, nevertheless reminds readers of the distinctions between the peoples. Like Eleazer in the *Letter of Aristeas,* he slips into sarcasm when treating Greek myths. He dismisses the fable of Triptolemos, who sprinkled seeds upon the earth while riding on the backs of winged dragons, as something that can be consigned to Greeks who prefer sophistry to wisdom and sorcery to truth.[15] He mocks the myth of men sown in the earth, springing forth fully formed and even sporting armor. Faith in that tale demonstrates ignorance of the laws of nature.[16] Worse still is the worship of multiple gods, hailed by poetry and song, a different group for each community, and thus a source of laughter and scorn by the others.[17] Further, Greeks place too high a store upon physical beauty, forgetting that the prime of the body lasts only a short time, that its grace is surpassed even by lifeless statues and paintings, not to mention the genuine glory that comes from faith in God.[18] Even the sport of hunting, beloved by Gentiles, comes in for Philo's strictures: it results in the eating of animal flesh already torn apart by dogs, a practice that is anathema to the Jews.[19]

Harsher commentary comes in connection with the Hellenic institution

of the symposium. Philo denounces the extravagant luxury and ostenta-
tion, the gluttony and vulgarity, and the encouragement to pederasty that
mark Greek banquets. These are contrasted in the strongest terms with the
Jewish sect of the Therapeutae, whose symposia are a model of decorum
and piety.[20] Philo further caricatures the rites of Demeter which, in his presentation, lend themselves to licentiousness and transsexuality.[21] Moses, of
course, banned such goings on and repressed mystery cults of every variety.[22] And Philo sets this on a broader scale by caricaturing the festal celebrations of Greeks and barbarians alike—scenes of drunkenness and ca-
rousing, slumbers during the day and wild revelries all night, a suspension
of restraint, piety, and the life of the mind, and an indulgence in the baser
instincts of the belly and the groin.[23] Finally, he holds Jews well apart from
Gentiles on the issue of incest. Whereas Athenian and Spartan lawgivers
permitted certain varieties, Mosaic law prohibited incest in any form. Philo
becomes quite overheated on the subject. He forgets himself sufficiently to
take the Oedipus legend as fact, and even to convey the wild fantasy that
calamitous internecine warfare in Greece and a whole cascade of disasters
followed from the fateful events of that tale.[24]

Insistence upon differences sometimes shaded into sharp criticism of the
habits and morals of the "Other." Philo lashes out against Greek intellectuals whose malice and envy caused them to denigrate Moses because the Torah was so antithetical to the codes of their lawgivers.[25] He castigates both
Greeks and barbarians for the practice of incest authorized by their own
laws.[26] And he condemns them for the loose morals, reckless ambition, and
distrust for one another that produced repeated internal discord and ruin-
ous civil wars.[27] Those conflicts have brought grievous harm to the whole
human race.[28]

This contrast between the cultures found its way into the writings of
Josephus as well. The historian elaborated at length on the distinctions
between Jewish virtues and Greek deficiencies. He delivers an extended
broadside in the *Contra Apionem*. For Josephus, Greek intellectuals directed their precepts only to the elite, whereas Mosaic teachings embraced
all. The Hebrew code eclipsed the imperfections in both the Spartan and
Athenian systems, combining adherence to principle with practical training. While Jews maintained faithful attachment to their laws, Greek history shows nothing but fickleness and inconstancy.[29] Josephus even exploited Hellenic writings themselves to drive home his point. He cited
Plato and others who censured their own poets and statesmen for concoct-
ing preposterous myths about their gods, celebrating their immoralities,
and broadcasting their follies. The contrast with Jewish piety and fidelity
could hardly be greater.[30]

Still more hostile comments can be found in a diverse collection of texts. Greeks regularly viewed other *ethne* as *barbaroi,* a familiar cliché. The author of II Maccabees, however, neatly turned the tables. In his presentation, the Jews who fought for Judaism against the policies of Antiochus IV drove out the "barbarian hordes."[31] The standard Hellenic designation for the alien was thus reversed and applied to the Hellenes themselves. That portrayal became yet more intensified in the martyrologies recorded by II Maccabees. The elderly sage Eleazer resisted to the death any compromise of Jewish practice by spurning the cruel edicts of Antiochus, calmly accepting his agonizing torture. The same courage manifested itself in the devout mother who witnessed proudly the savage slaying of her seven steadfast sons and joined them herself in death, a memorable testimony to Jewish faith and Hellenic barbarity.[32] Those tales reappeared many generations later at a time when the fierce emotions of the Maccabean era were a distant memory. The text known as IV Maccabees elaborated in exquisite detail the torments inflicted upon Eleazer and the mother with her seven sons. Its author, a Jew, probably of the first century CE and trained in Greek philosophy, employed the martyrologies to illustrate Stoic doctrines of the command of reason over the passions. The Hellenic medium thus served to convey Jewish commitment to the Torah in contrast with the irrationality and atrocities of the Greeks themselves—an irony not lost on the author.[33]

The abhorrence of philosophically minded Jews for the excesses of the Greeks surfaces indirectly in another treatise roughly contemporary with IV Maccabees. The so-called Wisdom of Solomon falls within the tradition of Jewish wisdom literature but comes from the hand of a Hellenized Jew thoroughly familiar with Greek philosophy.[34] The setting itself of the treatise is strictly biblical, but resonance for a later era is unmistakable. The author drops an interesting remark, perhaps inadvertent—but all the more revealing for that. He ascribes to the unspeakable Canaanites every form of loathsome practice, including orgiastic mystery rites, human sacrifice, and cannibalism. And he describes them in terms of participants in a Dionysiac *thiasos.*[35] The notorious Hellenic ritual thereby serves to epitomize barbaric behavior.

A comparably intriguing term, mentioned just once but with reverberating overtones, occurs in the Greek additions to the Book of Esther. There the villainous vizier Haman, prime foe of the Jews in the Persian court at Susa, is labeled not a Persian at all but a Macedonian.[36] The Hellenistic Jewish composer of the additions made a deliberate choice to insert that substitute ethnicity. The chief advocate of genocide was thus identified with the imperial conquerors from the Hellenic world.

Jewish imagination went further still on this score. A full-scale story, almost entirely fictitious, depicted the lunatic crusade of a Hellenistic king against the nation of the Jews. The text appears in some of the manuscripts of the Septuagint, misleadingly entitled III Maccabees (for it has nothing whatever to do with the history or legend of the Maccabees).[37] It depicts the mad monarch Ptolemy IV, determined to eradicate the Jews of Egypt because their compatriots had denied him access to the Holy of Holies in Jerusalem. A frenzy of hatred drove Ptolemy to his scheme of ethnic cleansing. He ordered subordinates to round up all the Jews in the land, confine them in the hippodrome outside Alexandria, and have them trampled en masse by a herd of crazed elephants. A happy ending concluded the tale when God's messengers turned the great beasts around to crush the minions of the king. But the Jews had suffered a fearsome travail. The narrow escape only highlighted the hostility of those committed to the elimination of the Jews. Ptolemy's enmity did not stand alone. A group of friends, advisers, and soldiers urged the destruction of that *genos* which refused to conform to the ways of other nations.[38] And a far wider populace rejoiced at the prospect of Jewish demise, their festering hatred now given free rein in open exultation.[39] And the salvation of the Jews in the end elevates them to a position of authority, esteem, and respect among their "enemies."[40] This evidently reinforces the convention that pits Jews against Greeks, and brands the latter as a nation standing outside the bounds of morality and humane behavior.

The diverse indictments of Greeks reappear in every form and with full intensity in the prophecies of the *Third Sibylline Oracle*. The Sibyl had venerable roots in pagan antiquity, but the surviving collection of pronouncements stems from Jewish and Christian compilers who recast them for their own ends. The contents of the Third Sibyl represent the earliest portion, almost entirely the product of Jewish invention, with some parts at least dating to the era of the Maccabees.[41] One group of verses echoes the dire forecasts of Daniel, even the imagery, with reference to the kingdoms of the Macedonians who impose an evil yoke and deliver much affliction upon Asia but whose race *(genos)* will be destroyed by the very race it seeks to destroy.[42] The text also repeats in different form Daniel's sequence of empires, including the Greeks as arrogant and impious and the Macedonians as bearing a fearful cloud of war upon mortals. Internal rot will follow, extending from impiety to homosexuality and afflicting many lands— but none so much as Macedon itself, evidently the prime offender.[43] Elsewhere the Sibyl condemns Greeks for overbearing behavior, the fostering of tyrannies, and moral failings. She predicts that their cities in Asia Minor

and the Near East will be crushed by a terrible divine wrath: Greece itself
will be ravaged and its inhabitants consumed in strife for gain.[44] This bitter
and wrathful composition brands the people of Hellas as insolent, sacrile-
gious, and brutal, doomed to suffer the vengeance of the Lord.

The collective testimony seems straightforward enough—and not very
heartening. Jewish compositions constructed the Hellenes as foils, as
aliens, as the "Other," thereby the better to set off the virtues and qualities
of their own nation. The characterizations cross genre boundaries, appearing in apocalyptic texts, histories, philosophical treatises, and imaginative
fiction. The diverse formulations range from the relatively mild strictures
in the *Letter of Aristeas,* castigating Greeks for foolish and delusive idolatry, to the fierce portrayals of Hellenic character as barbaric, irrational,
and murderous in the martyrologies of II and IV Maccabees, the fictive tale
of III Maccabees, and the apocalyptic visions of the Third Sibyl.

To halt there, however, would be to leave a distinctly distorted impression.
Jewish constructs of the Greeks were more complex and varied. Indeed,
much of the evidence points in directions very different from single-minded
antithesis or hostility. Moreover, the very authors and works that deliver
negative perceptions can modify, soften, or even invert them.

The *Letter of Aristeas* is a prime case in point. Eleazer, the High Priest,
as we have seen, insisted on fundamental differences between Jewish and
Hellenic ways of seeing the world—a vital ingredient in that treatise. But
that does not preclude sympathetic engagement and amicable cooperation.
Quite the contrary. The tale itself has as its principal story line the collaboration of Jewish sages and a Hellenistic court in rendering the Hebrew Bible into Greek. Ptolemy II, according to the narrative, authorized and subsidized the project, paid the expenses of the translators, plied them with
expensive gifts, and hosted them generously with kosher banquets in Alexandria. The Jewish elders, men of cultivation and erudition, were the appointees of the High Priest, chosen for their expertise in the Torah as well
as their command of Greek language and learning. Ptolemy showed deep
respect for the hallowed scrolls of the Law, and the Jews of Alexandria
welcomed with great enthusiasm the Hellenic version of the Pentateuch.
The theme of harmony between Jewish principles and the Hellenistic society pervades the treatise.[45]

The harrowing narrative of III Maccabees, in most interpretations,
stands at the opposite end of the spectrum. The portrayal of the vindictive
and sadistic Ptolemy IV, bent on extermination of the Jews and thwarted

only by divine intervention, would appear to deliver a dark and disturbing image of Jewish life in the realm of Hellenic royalty.[46] Not necessarily so. A closer reading shows that even the king is hardly an unmitigated monster. The text presents him more as irrational or deranged than as fundamentally wicked, his rantings as no more than a temporary interruption of an otherwise cordial relationship. Ptolemy in fact more than once emerges from his temporary bouts with lunacy to express praise and gratitude to the Jews for their fidelity to the crown, and concord reigns at the end.[47] The real enemies of the Jews are wicked and envious courtiers, a familiar cliché in biblical and post-biblical fables. And they receive their due comeuppance. The Jews themselves, as the treatise affirms repeatedly, are indeed loyal subjects of the realm, not rebels or aliens, but the most trustworthy of peoples.[48] This is no subversive tract.[49] More specifically and more tellingly, the tract pronounces a positive verdict upon relations between Jew and Greek generally. Although the Jews had their foes at court and some malevolent people who rejoiced at their plight, the Alexandrian Greeks themselves offered sympathy, encouragement, and even clandestine assistance.[50] So even this ostensibly most polemical concoction leaves the broader lesson of concord rather than conflict. The mutual respect of the *ethne* counts for more than the ephemeral aberrations of the king and the malignant jealousies of his flatterers.

Philo unsurprisingly gives high marks to Greeks for intelligence and sagacity. He transmits (with exaggeration and perhaps some mischievousness) the conventional thesis of geographic determination that makes the rocky soil of Greece responsible for the most important products—namely, the best and wisest of men.[51] But he admires the Greeks for more than just brain power. In a long section of his treatise on the Stoic doctrine of liberty, Philo lauds the Greeks for espousing personal and individual freedom, even in the face of fearful compulsion. Whereas II and IV Maccabees held up as models those Jews who preferred torture and death to the abandonment of principle, Philo finds comparable models among Stoic heroes and in Greek literary texts. The Jewish philosopher cites Euripides and Aeschylus for the steadfast support of free speech, Anaxarchus, Zeno, and other thinkers for defiance of tyranny with supreme confidence in their own virtue, and the caustic Diogenes for unbridled puncturing of the proud and the powerful.[52] Still more notable is Philo's retelling of the legend that has the Septuagint produced by Jewish scholars at the court of Ptolemy II. The king receives handsome plaudits as the very model of monarchic munificence and an authentic admirer of Jewish law.[53] And Philo places special stress upon the close correspondence of the Hebrew and Greek texts. The two versions stand equal in their ability to inspire wonder and reverence—two sisters, indeed one and the same entity.[54] This constitutes a powerful statement for the affinity of the cultures.

Other illustrations can readily be produced. But a collection of comments, some exuding bitterness and estrangement, others expressing admiration and collaboration, misses the mark. No comparisons and contrasts, weighing and adding up of the negative and the positive, will get to the heart of the matter. The fact that both can be found in the same authors and the same texts suffices to show the futility of tabulation. How then can we interpret this ostensible dissonance and incongruity?

Any neat resolution would be suspect. Discrepancies exist, not to be explained away. Yet a cardinal coherence transcends them. Jewish intellectuals, grappling with the issue of how to conceive their relationship with Hellenism, a repeated and extended exertion, developed a discriminate strategy. The insistence on differentiation, even an unbridgeable gap, between the cultures on the one hand, and high esteem for the Greek achievement and those responsible for it on the other, could reinforce rather than cancel out each other—to the advantage of the Jews. Jewish writers opted less for antagonism or admiration than for appropriation.

The thrust of thinking on this score is exemplified by the work of Aristobulus. A man of wide philosophical and literary interests (though the depths of his mastery can be questioned), he produced an extensive composition, evidently a form of commentary on the Torah, at an uncertain date in the Hellenistic period.[55] Strong temptation exists to identify him with the Aristobulus named by II Maccabees as belonging to a family of anointed Jewish priests and also serving as teacher to King Ptolemy of Egypt. The identification would neatly epitomize the conjunction of Jewish traditional piety with engagement in the cultural and political world of the Greeks.[56] Whatever the identity of Aristobulus, his work itself aptly characterizes a central ingredient of Jewish-Hellenistic thought.

Only a meager portion of Aristobulus' lengthy tome now survives. The fragments, however, disclose the direction and objectives: Aristobulus presented the Bible as the foundation stone for much of the Greek intellectual and artistic heritage. Moses, in his presentation, emerges as a culture hero, precursor and inspiration for Hellenic philosophical and poetic traditions. In Aristobulus' vision, the Torah, the principal legacy of the Israelite lawgiver, provided the impetus for a host of Hellenic attainments. Aristobulus imagines that the venerable Greek sage Pythagoras, in the sixth century BCE, borrowed extensively from the books of Moses and inserted their lessons into his own teachings.[57] More impressive still, Plato, foremost among Greek philosophers, was a devoted reader of the Scriptures, poring over every detail, and faithfully followed their precepts.[58] Never mind that the Pentateuch had not yet been translated into Greek by the time of Plato—let alone that of Pythagoras. Aristobulus had a canny way around that problem. He simply proposed that prior translations of the Bible, or parts thereof, had circulated long before the commissioned enterprise of Ptolemy II, before the coming of Alexander, even before Persian rule in Palestine![59] Of course, Aristobulus was engaging here in creative fiction, compounding the concoction to save the thesis. But it was all in a good cause. He had made Moses responsible for the best in Greek philosophy.

In the imaginative construct of Aristobulus, other philosophers too came under the sway of the Torah. The "divine voice" to which Socrates paid homage owed its origin to the words of Moses.[60] And Aristobulus made a still broader generalization. He found concurrence among all philosophers in the need to maintain reverent attitudes toward God, a doctrine best expressed, naturally, in the Hebrew Scriptures which preceded (and presumably determined) the Greek precepts. Indeed, all of Jewish law was constructed so as to underscore piety, justice, self-control, and the other qualities that represent true virtues—i.e., the very qualities subsequently embraced and propagated by the Greeks.[61] Aristobulus thereby brought the whole tradition of Greek philosophizing under the Jewish umbrella.

The inventive Aristobulus did not stop there. In addition to philosophy, he discovered echoes of the Torah in Greek poetry from the earliest times to his own day. The Sabbath, a vital part of Jewish tradition stemming from Genesis, proved serviceable for this purpose. Aristobulus reckoned it as a preeminent principle that was widely adopted and signaled by the mystical quality ascribed to the number seven.[62] He managed to find ostensible proof in the verses of Homer and Hesiod. This required some fancy footwork. Aristobulus cavalierly interpreted a Hesiodic reference to the seventh day of the month as the seventh day of the week. And he (or his source) emended a line of Homer from the "fourth day" to the "seventh day." He quoted additional lines of those poets to similar effect—lines that do not correspond to anything in our extant texts of Homer and Hesiod. One might properly suspect manipulation or fabrication.[63]

Aristobulus was endlessly creative. He also enlisted in his cause poets who worked in the distant mists of antiquity, namely the mythical singers Linus and Orpheus. Linus, an elusive figure variously identified as the son of Apollo or the music master of Herakles, conveniently left verses that celebrated the number seven as representing perfection itself, associating it with the heavenly bodies, with an auspicious day of birth, and as the day when all is made complete.[64] The connection with the biblical origin of the Sabbath is strikingly close—and too good to be true. Aristobulus summoned up still greater inventiveness in adapting or improvising a poem devoted to monotheism and assigned to Orpheus himself. The composition delivers sage advice from the mythical singer to his son or pupil Musaeus, counseling him to adhere to the divine word and describing God as complete in himself while completing all things—the sole divinity with no rivals, hidden to the human eye but accessible to the mind, a source of good and not evil, seated on a golden throne in heaven, commanding the earth, its oceans, and mountains, and in control of all.[65] The poem, whether or not it derives from Aristobulus' pen, belongs to the realm of Hellenistic Judaism. It represents a Jewish commandeering of Orpheus, emblematic of Greek poetic art, into the ranks of those proclaiming the message of biblical monotheism.

Aristobulus did not confine himself to legendary or distant poets; he made bold to interpret contemporary verses in ways suitable to his ends. One sample survives. Aristobulus quoted from an astronomical poem entitled the *Phaenomena*, by the Hellenistic writer Aratus of Soli. Its opening lines proved serviceable. By substituting "God" for "Zeus," Aristobulus turned Aratus' invocation into a hymn for the Jewish deity.[66] Brazenness and ingenuity mark the enterprise of Aristobulus. One can only imagine what novel fancies existed in those portions of his work that no longer survive. He evidently conducted a concerted campaign to convert Hellenic writings into footnotes on the Torah.

In that endeavor Aristobulus had much company. Resourceful Jewish writers searched through the scripts of Attic dramatists, both tragic and comic, for passages whose content suggested acquaintance with Hebrew texts or ideas. And where they did not exist, alterations or fabrications could easily be inserted. Verses with a strikingly Jewish flavor were ascribed to Aeschylus, Sophocles, and Euripides, and others to the comic playwrights Menander, Diphilus, and Philemon, again a combination of classical and Hellenistic authors. The fragments are preserved only in the Church Fathers, and the names of the transmitters are lost to us. But the milieu of Jewish-Hellenistic intellectuals is unmistakable.[67] Verses from Aeschylus emphasized the majesty of God, his omnipotence and omnipresence, the terror he can inspire, and his resistance to representation or understanding in human terms.[68] Sophocles insisted upon the oneness of the Lord who fashioned heaven and earth, the waters and the winds; he railed against idolatry; he supplied an eschatological vision to encourage the just and frighten the wicked; and he spoke of Zeus' disguises and philandering—doubtless to contrast delusive myths with authentic divinity.[69] Euripides too came in handy. Researchers found lines affirming that God's presence cannot be contained within structures fashioned by mortals and that he sees all but is himself invisible.[70] Attribution of comparable verses to comic poets is more confused in the tradition, as Christian sources provide conflicting notices on which dramatist said what. But the recorded writers Menander, Philemon, and Diphilus supplied usefully manipulable material. One or another spoke of an all-seeing divinity who will deliver vengeance upon the unjust and wicked, who lives forever as Lord of all, who apportions justice according to deserts, who scorns offerings and votives but exalts the righteous at heart.[71]

All of this attests to feverish activity on the part of Hellenistic Jews. Which of these texts are authentic but taken out of context and which were manufactured for the occasion can no longer be determined with confidence. No matter. The energy directed itself to discernible goals. Jewish writers appropriated, massaged, reinterpreted, or fabricated the words of classical and contemporary Greek authors to demonstrate dependence on the doctrines of the Torah. The purpose of this contrivance is plain enough. It implied that the Hellenic achievement, far from being alien to the Hebraic, simply restated its principles. The finest of Greek philosophers from Pythagoras to Plato, poets from Homer to Aratus, and even the legendary singers Orpheus and Linus were swept into the wake of the Jews.

This game of fanciful appropriation attracted numerous players. It appealed, among others, to the fertile imagination of Artapanus, a Hellenized Jew from Egypt in the second or first century BCE.[72] As we have seen, his idiosyncratic recreation of biblical stories includes an elaborate account of Moses' exploits that goes well beyond any scriptural basis. Apart from ascribing to Moses the inception of a host of Egyptian institutions and technologies, he also excogitated a Greek connection. The name Moses, Artapanus claimed, induced Greeks to identify him with Musaeus, the legendary poet and prophet from Attica, son or pupil of Orpheus, who stands at the dawn of Hellenic song and wisdom. Artapanus, however, gave a slight but significant twist to the legend. He made Musaeus the mentor of Orpheus, rather than the other way around.[73] Moses therefore becomes the father of Greek poetic and prophetic traditions. In Artapanus' fantasy, those traditions count as part of a Hebrew heritage.

A more obscure allusion in Artapanus has Moses receive the designation of Hermes by the Egyptian priests who honored him as the interpreter of hieroglyphics.[74] The Hellenic aspect is not in the forefront here. Artapanus makes reference to the Egyptian version of Hermes, an equivalent to Thot, the mythical progenitor of much of Egyptian culture.[75] But his creative reconstruction clearly amalgamates the cultural strands. Artapanus writes ostensibly about Pharaonic Egypt but looks, in fact, to contemporary Ptolemaic Egypt. His Moses absorbs both Musaeus and Hermes and becomes the fount of Greek culture in the Hellenistic era.

A familiar story, but not one normally cited in this connection, fits the pattern. Paul's celebrated visit to Athens further exemplifies the genre of appropriation. The tale is told in the Acts of the Apostles.[76] Paul proselytized among the Jews and "God-fearers" in the synagogue—and with any person who happened to pass by in the *agora,* This upset certain Stoics and Epicureans, who hauled him before the tribunal of the Areopagus and questioned him about the new doctrine he was peddling. The author of Acts adds the snide remark that Athenians have nothing better to do with their time than to talk or hear about the latest fad.[77] Paul was quick to turn the situation to his own advantage—and in a most interesting way. He remarked to the Athenians that they were an uncommonly religious people. He had wandered through many of their shrines and had found one altar inscribed to an "unknown god."[78] This was a perfect opportunity for him to tell them precisely who that "unknown god" happened to be. Paul proceeded to speak of the sole divinity, creator of the world and all that is in it, a god who dwells in no temples and can be captured in no images.[79] The description plainly applies to the god of the Hebrew Bible, with no Christian admixture. Paul, like other inventive Jews, quoted Greek poetry to underpin his claims. So, he remarked to the Athenians, "as some of your own poets have said, 'We too are his [God's] children.'"[80] The poet in question happened to be Aratus of Soli, no Athenian at all. But that detail can be happily overlooked. The parallels with other texts cited above are glaring. Paul, as conceived by the author of Acts, deployed Greek poetic utterances as certification for Jewish precepts. And he cited a Greek dedicatory inscription as evidence for Hellenic worship of the right deity—even if the Athenians themselves were unaware of his identity.

This calculating construct of Hellenic dependence on Jewish precedents took hold early and developed over the generations. It did not await the Church Fathers for resurrection. Philo conveys the message in full-blown form. He quotes Heraclitus on the death of the soul and declares that he followed the teachings of Moses.[81] On a rather less lofty note, he allows that Socrates might have learned from Moses the motives of the Creator in forming the parts of the human body that provide the excretory functions![82] Stoic philosophy too derived central precepts from the Pentateuch. According to Philo, Zeno's insistence that the wise must dominate the foolish is taken directly from Isaac's command that Esau serve his brother Jacob.[83] Greek lawgivers, in his presentation, had the Mosaic code before them when they drew up statutes for their own states. He supplies a specific example: the ban on hearsay evidence, a prohibition lifted directly from the holy tablets of Moses.[84] The Stoic doctrine that the wise man alone is ruler and king actually stems, in Philo's view, from a reference in Genesis to Abraham.[85] And he goes well beyond this. Whereas individual Hellenic communities regularly discard institutions adopted by other Hellenic communities and Gentiles generally reject one another's enactments, Jewish law alone has earned the respect of all peoples, no matter where they dwell or what their ethnic traditions may be.[86] The Sabbath itself, so Philo claims, has gained universal acceptance, and the Day of Atonement inspires admiration and reverence even among Greeks, whose own sacred periods run more to feasts than fasts.[87] These extravagant statements supply the backdrop for Philo's account of the translation of the Hebrew Bible into Greek: it was motivated by Greek desire to emulate the ways of the Jews.[88] And its accomplishment remains dear to all, king and commoner alike, regardless of the fortunes of the Jewish nation itself.[89]

The pattern of appropriation persisted. Its echoes find resonance in Josephus. He too reiterates the line that many Greeks have embraced Jewish laws—though some have been more consistent in maintaining them than others. He goes so far as to claim that Jews are more divided from Greeks by geography than by institutions.[90] Like Aristobulus, Philo, and others, Josephus finds Greek philosophers hewing closely to the concept of God which they obtained from acquaintance with the Books of Moses—noting in particular Pythagoras, Anaxagoras, Plato, and the Stoics.[91] The prescriptions in Plato's *Republic* obliging citizens to study closely all the laws of their state and prohibiting social intercourse with foreigners in order to keep the polity pure for those who abide by its regulations exhibit, according to Josephus, direct imitation of Moses.[92] Toward the end of his treatise *Contra Apionem*, Josephus makes still more exaggerated claims. Greek philosophers were only the first of those drawn to the laws of the Torah, adopting similar views about God, teaching abstinence from extravagance and harmony with one another. The masses followed suit. Their zeal for Jewish religious piety has now spread around the world so that there is a hardly a single *polis* or *ethnos*, whether Greek or barbarian, unaffected by observance of the Sabbath, various Jewish practices, and even dietary restrictions. Indeed, they labor to emulate the concord, philanthropy, industry, and undeviating steadfastness characteristic of the Jews.[93] The hyperbole can safely be set aside. But Josephus' insistence on the Greek quest to duplicate Jewish ethics, religion, institutions, and customs follows upon a long and strong tradition.

A habit of Philo pointedly discloses the Jewish adaptation of a Hellenic convention. The Greeks, as is notorious, divided the world between two *ethne*: Hellenes and barbarians. Philo picks up the construct without hesitation. He employs the dualism on numerous occasions—and unselfconsciously. The Jewish philosopher embraced the notion like any good Greek. Where is the Jewish place in this division of the races? In several instances, Jews are subsumed, unmentioned, or irrelevant. The world simply consists of Greeks and barbarians. Philo employs the Hellenic convention as a natural mode of expression—without giving it a second thought.[94] Indeed, when applying this dichotomy to the world's languages, namely Greek and "barbarian," Philo includes his own people's ancestral tongue under the latter rubric![95] Nor does he shrink even from bracketing the Jews with that half of mankind who count as "barbarians" rather than Greeks.[96] Philo plainly did not deprecate his compatriots here.[97] Far from it. Jews, for the most part, stand altogether outside this bifurcation. Philo refers frequently to Greeks and barbarians by contrast with Jews who fall under neither heading—and whose practices are decidedly preferable to both. Jews shun the love of luxury, the concern with physical beauty, the revelries, the imperialist ambitions and rivalries, the mutual distrusts, and the internecine warfare that mark the experience of Greeks and barbarians alike.[98] The Jewish philosopher unhesitatingly employed Hellenic categories and endorsed the traditional differentiation dear to the Greeks. The advantage, however, went to his own nation.

Diaspora intellectuals found it convenient and edifying to fit into the broader world of Hellenistic culture. But the mode of adaptation had a decided bias. Jews deliberately eschewed blending, syncretism, or assimilation. They molded Hellenism to their own design, underscoring rather than covering up distinctiveness, and placing a premium on moral, intellectual, and even cultural superiority.

The *Letter of Aristeas* offers a lively illustration. Common goals and mutual benefits at the court of Ptolemy Philadelphus constitute the main line of the narrative. But, as we have seen, the Jewish High Priest had already pronounced on the preference of Jewish practices. And, more subtly but significantly, that message seeps through in the rest of the tale. The author conjured up the names of some Greek intellectuals, the historian Hecataeus of Abdera, the philosopher Theopompus, the tragic poet Theodectus, and the librarian of Alexandria, Demetrius of Phaleron, to have them testify to the august and awe-inspiring quality of the Hebrew Scriptures, a spiritual power that laid low those who sought to exploit them in frivolous fashion.[99] Ptolemy himself, while orchestrating the whole project of translation, paid due homage to the majesty of the Torah, the god of the Jews, and the admirable principles that distinguished their creed.[100] The king even performed *proskynesis,* to demonstrate his reverence to the Scrolls.[101] The Jewish sages exhibited their wisdom and piety most authoritatively in a sequence of symposia wherein their answers to the king's questions left him nearly breathless with admiration—and induced the Greek philosophers who witnessed their virtuosity to concede the supremacy of Jewish intellect.[102] The *Letter* celebrates cooperation and shared aims. But the implication that Jewish values served to enhance Hellenism holds a central place. This was not an equal bargain.[103]

Philo makes that point repeatedly, in diverse contexts, and with conviction. Scattered comments set the wisdom and sagacity of Moses ahead of Greek philosophers. The latter boasted that Heraclitus first developed the idea that only the contemplation of opposites leads to understanding of the whole. Not so, according to Philo: Moses had it right long before Heraclitus.[104] Elsewhere, Philo invents the fantasy that the young Moses received instruction from both Egyptian and Greek teachers, with the latter responsible for higher learning. But, Philo notes, Moses swiftly surpassed his masters, who had nothing more to teach him, and found themselves befuddled by his expounding of matters beyond their grasp. His schooling had the character more of recollection than of education.[105] Philo echoes the Platonic assertion that states can move toward desirable goals only when kings become philosophers or philosophers kings. But he adds the claim that Moses not only blended those capacities but possessed the combined characteristics of lawgiver, high priest, and prophet—far exceeding anything Plato might hold out for Greek aspirations.[106] The Jewish thinker does credit Plato with an accurate understanding of the cosmos: it came into being through creation, and it is indestructible. The idea, he notes, appears already in Hesiod. But, of course, it arose long before either of them. Moses had it in the sacred books.[107] Philo indulges elsewhere in a quite gratuitous bit of one-upmanship. He observes that Greek philosophers reckon as wise men those who first applied names to things. Moses, however, had gone them one better. He gave that distinction not to a group of ancient thinkers, but to Adam himself.[108] Just how this enhances Moses' luster is not obvious. But Philo somehow found it useful.

In addition to outstripping Greek philosophers, Moses also outdid Greek legislators. Philo compares him favorably to the lawgiver of the Spartans, who made a fetish of austerity, and to those of the Ionians and Sybarites, who catered to effeminacy and luxury. The Hebrew legislator cut the proper path between the two.[109] Whereas the laws that govern Greeks and other peoples failed to prevent wars, violence, despotism, and every form of excess, the code of Moses, Philo insists, remains unshaken and authoritative from the time of its enactment to the present day.[110] On a far smaller scale, Philo still finds ways to give Moses the advantage. He acknowledges that other legislators sponsored the humane measure that pregnant women condemned to death should be allowed to live until their children were born. But Moses was more compassionate still: he had advocated the same treatment for animals![111] Philo did not miss a bet.

Greek philosophers, though admired, regularly fall short of the noblest ideals espoused in Jewish tradition. Philo contrasts Anaxagoras and Democritus, whose commitment to higher thought allowed their lands to be overrun, with the Therapeutae, equally abstemious, who gave their possessions away to benefit others.[112] Socrates rightly stressed self-scrutiny; his motto "know thyself" was a salutary reminder of down-to-earth thinking. But the precept, in Philo's view, was better expressed by Terah, father of Abraham, whose move from Chaldea to Haran symbolized the shift from airy speculation to serious grappling with the world.[113] Elsewhere he takes a snide swipe at the sophists: they are mere phrase-mongers and hair-splitters, in no way helpful in guidance to a life of virtue.[114] They sell their so-called wisdom for whatever price it fetches, like peddlers hawking their wares in the market.[115] Indeed, Philo can even rebuke the whole tribe of Greek philosophers for failure to reach agreement on the most basic of issues, such as the nature and origin of the universe, and the principles of morality.[116] The theme appears persistently in Philo's tracts. Hellenic accomplishments, even when laudable and admirable, don't measure up to those of the Jews.[117]

The ultimate expression of Jewish appropriation and superiority comes in the *Third Sibylline Oracle*. Jews here usurped a far-famed feature of the Hellenic tradition. The alleged prognostications of the Sibyl date back to the mists of antiquity, forecasting the fates of inquirers. Collections of the Sibyl's prophecies, appropriately edited, fashioned, or fabricated, circulated among the creative and the gullible in the classical world. Jews subsequently recast the genre, articulating their own apocalyptic visions by setting them in the mouth of the pagan prophetess—delivered in proper Homeric hexameters.[118] They include, as we have seen, some grave stric-

tures upon and dire predictions for the Greeks. But a more momentous
message also lurks in the lines of the oracle. Jews utilized the fictitious forecast not only to demonstrate ascendancy but to display magnanimity. The
Greeks need not doom themselves to perdition. The Sibyl extends a hand
to the Hellenic world, exhorting Greeks to dispose of deceitful rulers, to
abandon idolatry, and to acknowledge the authority of God. Time remains for remorse and repentance. Sacrifice and prayers to the Lord and
walking in the paths of righteousness would still bring Greeks within the
fold. Disasters inflicted upon Hellas are not irrevocable and can be reversed by divine order.[119] The Sibyl, in essence, urges Greeks to adopt the
commandments and morality of the Jews, thus to gain salvation on the day
of judgment.[120]

None of this amounts to a call for conversion. Readers of these verses
were largely, almost exclusively, Jews, not Gentiles. But the Sibyl manifests
a significant diaspora mentality: Jewish precepts are seen as informing and
improving the wider world, bringing within their embrace Greeks who acknowledge their majesty and earn indulgence. A divine deliverance can
thus bring both cultures to a common destiny—in which the values of the
Jews prevail. Jews adroitly adapted the Greek medium to present Greeks as
adapting to Jewish ways.

The perceptions and conceptions by Jews of Greeks do not compose a neat
pattern. Inquiry turns up hostile, even antagonistic, representations of the
Hellenic "Other." Or it encounters laudatory evaluations and admiring appreciation. Or both. The same texts and authors can move in either direction, or in variations thereof. This may reflect discordant voices, diverse
judgments, perhaps inadequate reasoning. Yet a fundamental consistency
prevails, underlying and informing the complex conceptualizations. Jewish
intellectuals of the diaspora had access to the literary and philosophical
world of Hellenism, indeed held a place within it—while forever reexamin-
ing and rearticulating their own traditions. They stood simultaneously inside and outside the Greco-Roman cultural community, a fact that explains
much in their construction of that community.

An attempt to balance "positive" and "negative" assessments misses
the mark. They overlap and interweave in ways that render the terminology meaningless. Jewish texts could both assert common values and insist upon differentiation between the peoples. They both eschewed and
embraced Greek characteristics, conveniently censuring those whose deficiencies could set Jewish practices in the best light and hailing others
whose inspiration could be credited to the Torah. In the Jewish construct,

Greeks are prone to credulity, naive believers in their own myths, adherents to false deities, lured by luxury, inured to internecine quarrels, and lacking the commitment to morality that holds prime place among Jews. On the other hand, Hellenic thinkers and artists advanced noble ideals, offered uplifting precepts, and even comprehended the unity of God. But they were not in the class of Jewish sages. And their best ideas depended on perusal of the Pentateuch. Either way, the Greeks fall short. The strategy was complex and calculated. Jews managed to buy into Hellenic conventions and twist them to Jewish ends. Insofar as this signals a diaspora mentality, it suggests neither rejection nor adoption of Hellenism. No such stark choice confronted the Jews. They preferred to appropriate the best in Hellenic culture and make it their own.

CHAPTER EIGHT

Diaspora and Homeland

DIASPORA LIES deeply rooted in Jewish consciousness. It existed in one form or another almost from the start, and it persists as an integral part of the Jews' experience of history. The status of absence from the center has demanded time and again that Jews confront and, in some fashion, come to terms with a seemingly inescapable concomitant of their being.[1] The images of uprootedness, dispersal, and wandering haunt Jewish identity. Jews have written about diaspora incessantly, lamented it or justified it, dismissed it or grappled with it, embraced it or deplored it.

At a theoretical level, that experience has been deconstructed from two quite divergent angles. The gloomy approach holds primacy. On this view, diaspora dissolves into *galut*, exile, a bitter and doleful image, offering a bleak vision that leads either to despair or to a remote reverie of restoration. The negative image dominates modern interpretations of the Jewish psyche. Realization of the people's destiny rests in achieving the "Return," the acquisition of a real or mythical homeland.[2] The alternative approach takes a very different route. It seeks refuge in a comforting concept: that Jews require no territorial sanctuary or legitimation. They are "the people of the Book." Their homeland resides in the text—not just the canonical Scriptures but an array of Jewish writings that help to define the nation and give voice to its sense of identity. Their "portable Temple" serves the purpose. A geographic restoration is therefore superfluous, even subversive. To aspire to it deflects the focus from what really counts: the embrace of the text, its ongoing commentary, and its continuous reinterpretation.[3] Diaspora, in short, is no burden, indeed a virtue in the spread of the word. This justifies a primary attachment to the land of one's residence, rather than the home of the fathers.

The destruction of the Temple in 70 CE, of course, constitutes a principal watershed for the Jews of antiquity. Both of the analyses mentioned above apply primarily as constructs to comprehend Jewish mentality in the generations, even centuries, after that cataclysmic event. The elimination of the center, source of spiritual nourishment and preeminent symbol of the nation's identity, compelled Jews to reinvent themselves, to find other means of religious sustenance, and to adjust their lives to an indefinite period of displacement. That story has been told many times and in many ways.[4]

But another story demands closer attention. Jews faced a more puzzling and problematic situation prior to the loss of the Temple. Diaspora did not await the fall of Jerusalem to Roman power and destructiveness. The scattering of Jews had begun long before—occasionally through forced expulsion, much more frequently through voluntary migration. The major push came with the arrival of the Greeks—the Hellenistic period. Alexander the Great's conquests stimulated wholesale settlements of Greek veterans, merchants, travelers, and adventurers in the lands of the eastern Mediterranean and the former subject areas of the Persian empire. That development proved to be an irresistible magnet. Jews migrated to the new settlements and expanded their communities in substantial numbers. A Greek diaspora, in short, brought the Jewish one in its wake. Vast numbers of Jews dwelled outside Palestine in the roughly four centuries that stretched from Alexander to Titus.[5] The era of the Second Temple brought the issue into sharp focus, inescapably so. The Temple still stood, a reminder of the hallowed past, and, through most of the era, a Jewish regime existed in Palestine. Yet the Jews of the diaspora, from Italy to Iran, far outnumbered those in the homeland.[6] Although Jerusalem loomed large in their self-perception as a nation, few of them had seen it, and few were likely to. How then did diaspora Jews of the Second Temple period conceive their association with Jerusalem, the emblem of ancient tradition?

In modern interpretations, a dark picture prevails. Diaspora is something to be *overcome*.[7] Thunderous biblical pronouncements had presented it as the terrible penalty exacted by God for the sins of the Israelites. They will be scattered among the nations and pursued by divine wrath.[8] Spread among the lands, they will worship false gods and idols and enjoy no repose from the anger of the Lord.[9] Abandonment of ancestral precepts means that the children of Israel will have to enter the servitude of foreign lords in foreign parts.[10] They will be dispersed among peoples unknown to them or to their fathers and will suffer God's vengeance until their destruction.[11] Failure to heed the divine commandments or the warnings of prophets produces the scattering of Israel at the hands of the Lord.[12] The dismal character of exile seems reinforced by the words of Philo in the first century CE. For him, banishment far exceeds death as the most feared penalty. Death at least puts an end to one's misery; exile perpetuates it, the equiva-

lent of a thousand deaths.[13] No solace lies in adjustment. There seems
nothing worth adjusting to. Only a single goal can keep flickering hopes
alive: the expectation, however distant, of returning from exile and regain-
ing a place in the Promised Land. The Bible offers that possibility. Obedience to the Lord and eradication of past errors will induce him to regather
the lost souls spread across the world and restore them to the land of their
fathers.[14] He will raise a banner among the nations and assemble the people of Judah from the four corners of the earth.[15] Given such a tradition,
it causes no surprise that the grim sense of diaspora and a correspond-
ingly gloomy attitude are conventionally ascribed to Jews of the Second
Temple.[16]

Yet that convention ignores a grave implausibility. It is not easy to imagine that millions of ancient Jews dwelled in foreign parts for generations
mired in misery and obsessed with a longing for Jerusalem that had little
chance of fulfillment. Many of them lived hundreds, even thousands, of
miles away from Jerusalem, in Memphis, or Babylon, or Susa, or Athens,
or Rome. To assume that they repeatedly lamented their fate and pinned
their hopes on recovery of the homeland is quite preposterous. Moreover,
the desirability of such a return, let alone its likelihood, can be seriously
questioned. However much milk and honey flowed in Palestine, it could
hardly support an influx of refugees that would swamp the indigenous
population. Would most peasant farmers or urban dwellers who had put
down roots abroad relish the prospect of starting afresh and competing for
scarce resources in an unfamiliar site? The proposition is implausible.

Signs of a shift in scholarly attitudes are now discernible. Some recent
works tip the balance away from the center to the periphery. It seems only
logical that Jews sought out means whereby to legitimize a diaspora existence that most of them inherited from their parents and would bequeath
to their descendants.[17] As we have seen, large and thriving Jewish communities existed in numerous areas of the Mediterranean, with opportunities
for economic advancement, social status, and even political responsibilities.[18] The essential facts are not in dispute.[19] Does it follow then that the
displaced and dispersed had recourse to the thesis that mobility takes preference over territoriality, that the nation is defined by its texts rather than
its location?

The dichotomy is deceptive. Hellenistic Jews did not have to face the
eradication of the Temple. It was there—but they were not. Yet they nowhere developed a theory or philosophy of diaspora. The whole idea of
privileging homeland over diaspora, or diaspora over homeland, derives
from a modern rather than an ancient obsession. The issue is too readily

conceived in terms of mutually exclusive alternatives: either the Jews regarded their identity as unrealizable in exile and the achievement of their
destiny as dependent upon reentry into Judaea; or they clung to their heritage abroad, shifting attention to local and regional loyalties, and cultivating a permanent attachment to the diaspora. Those alternatives, of course,
have continuing contemporary resonance.[20] But Second Temple Jews did
not confront so stark a choice.

Hellenistic texts, upon initial examination, would appear to support a solemn conclusion: life in foreign parts came as a consequence of divine disfa-
vor, a banishment from the homeland. The characterization of diaspora as
exile occurs with some frequency in the works of Hellenistic Jewish writers.[21] And this has prompted what seems to be a natural assumption: that
the gloom represents Jewish attitudes in the contemplation of their current
fate. But the assumption is shaky and vulnerable. A caveat has to be issued
from the start. The majority of these grim pronouncements refer to the biblical misfortunes of the Israelites—expulsion by the Assyrians, the destruction of the Temple, and the Babylonian Captivity. Were they all metaphors
for the Hellenistic diaspora? The inference would be hasty.[22] And it begs
the question.

Ben Sira laments the sins of his forefathers and records the fierce retaliation of the Lord that brought uprooting from their land and dispersal into
every other land.[23] The reference, however, is to the era of Elijah and
Elisha, to the ills of the Northern Kingdom, and to the Assyrian conquest
that scattered the Israelites. It may indeed have contained a warning to Ben
Sira's contemporaries, whose shortcomings paralleled those of his ancestors—but it did not condemn the current diaspora. The Book of Tobit tells
a tale that ostensibly takes place in the Assyrian Captivity as well. Tobit be-
wails his own fate, prompted by the sins of his forefathers, and the fate of
his countrymen, now an object of scorn and a vulnerable prey to those in
the nations whence they have been dispersed.[24] A later prayer by Tobit
once again labels the diaspora as a penalty for Israel's abandonment of tradition, but looks ahead to divine mercy and redemption.[25] And a final prediction anticipates another calamity, the loss of the Temple, the desolation
of the land, and yet another dispersal abroad.[26] To suppose that the author
of Tobit sees in all this a reflection of his present circumstances is a simplistic leap. Tobit also forecasts the recovery of the Temple and portrays the
outcome as the culmination of Israelite dreams, a happy ending to endure
indefinitely.[27] That hardly suggests that the Hellenistic diaspora is a vale of
tears.

One can reach the same conclusion regarding the Book of Judith. Achior, the Ammonite leader, briefly sketches the highlights of Israelite history to Holofernes and includes the deportation to Babylon and the scattering of Jews as a devastating penalty for waywardness. But the penalty was canceled with the return from exile and the rebuilding of the Temple.[28] Nothing in Judith suggests that subsequent dispersion, when the Temple remained intact, derived from sin and punishment.

The dire predictions that occur in the Testaments of the Twelve Patriarchs include the calamity of dispersal to the four corners of the earth, wrought by the wrath of God, the equivalent of captivity among the nations. Here too the sons of Jacob foresaw the capture of the Temple and the grief of their people in Babylon—but also the renewal of divine compassion and eventual restoration.[29] These texts make no direct, and probably no indirect, allusion to diaspora Jews of the Greco-Roman era.[30] Similar conclusions apply to various other statements in Second Temple texts. Jubilees reports the afflictions suffered by Israelites who succumbed to idolatry and were scattered by God into captivity amidst the nations.[31] The Psalms of Solomon include a hymn praising the righteousness of the Lord in expelling Israel's neglectful inhabitants from their land and sending them into exile around the world.[32] The Greek additions to Jeremiah, incorporated as I Baruch in the Septuagint, echo the self-reproach for misdeeds that produced the Lord's dispersal of the Israelites and landed them in an accursed exile.[33] And the thunderous forecasts of the Third Sibylline Oracle contain a segment on abandonment of the Temple, enslavement by Assyrians, desolation of the land, and distribution of the despised throughout earth and sea.[34] A repeated theme runs through these texts, extending over a lengthy stretch of time. The biblical allusions are stern and severe, reminders of past punishments and warnings against future apostasy.[35] Diaspora dwellers in the Greco-Roman world are put on notice, lest they lapse again. But a notable fact needs emphasis. The texts do not make the current scattering itself a target of reproach or a source of discontent.[36]

Our sources do, it can be conceded, make reference to Jews in Ptolemaic Egypt who did not arrive there of their own free will. Convoluted and controversial evidence applies to the transfer of Jews to Egypt in the wake of Ptolemy I's campaigns in Palestine. The *Letter of Aristeas* reports that some Jews migrated south after being removed from Jerusalem by the Persians and a far greater number, more than one hundred thousand, came as prisoners of war after Ptolemy I's invasion.[37] Josephus, however, preserves a different version, ostensibly drawn from Hecataeus of Abdera, but almost certainly composed by a Jewish writer cloaking himself in the persona of Hecataeus. In this happy account, the Jews accompanied Ptolemy voluntarily and enthusiastically, impressed by his gentleness and magnanimity, making a contented home for themselves in his country.[38] The truth of the matter may not be determinable. It is, in any case, irrelevant for our purposes. Even the harsh version in the *Letter of Aristeas* is immediately softened. Ptolemy I employed the newly arrived Jews in his army, paid them handsomely, and set them up in garrisons.[39] His son went much further. Ptolemy II excused his father's severe actions as necessary to appease his troops and then proceeded not only to liberate all Jewish captives in Egypt, but to enroll many in the forces, and even to promote the more trustworthy leaders to official positions in the realm.[40] The reality or unreality of this rosy picture makes no difference. This was the image conveyed by Egyptian Jews. They did not portray themselves as laboring under the yoke. Josephus, extrapolating from the narrative of "Pseudo-Hecataeus," pointedly contrasts the forcible expulsion of the Jews to Babylon by the "Persians" with their migration to Egypt and Phoenicia after the death of Alexander the Great.[41]

The inventive tale of III Maccabees places the Jews of Egypt in the gravest peril. Thrice they were almost annihilated by the wicked schemes of the mad monarch Ptolemy IV. The text alludes to the Jews' precarious existence at the mercy of their enemies. They were to perish unjustly, a foreign people in a foreign land.[42] But the dire forecast did not come to pass. The Jews triumphed in the tale, their enemies thwarted and their apostates punished. More significantly, the vindication of the victors would be celebrated by an annual festival—in Egypt.[43] The diaspora existence, in III Maccabees as in the *Letter of Aristeas,* could go on indefinitely and contentedly.

What of restoration to the homeland, the presumed sole remedy for the anguish of exiles? Such a promise derives from the Pentateuch: the Lord who issued the banishment will eventually return the children of Israel from the most remote regions to the land of their fathers.[44] That happy ending recurs in the same Hellenistic writers who bemoan the transgressions that brought about dispersal in the first place. Tobit affirms that God's fury will be followed by his mercy, thus to produce an ingathering of the exiles and even conversion of the Gentiles.[45] Achior in the Book of Judith informs the Assyrian general that the Israelites have regained their city and their temple. To be sure, they might lose them again if they go astray— but that anticipates perilous times in Palestine, not the drawbacks of diaspora existence.[46] The prophecy in Asher's testament foresees the same reinstatement of the scattered faithful through the benevolence of God.[47] Similar sentiments are expressed in the Psalms of Solomon.[48] And God himself

makes the identical promise to Moses in the text of Jubilees: after consigning his people to captivity among their foreign enemies, he will reassemble
them once more in the place of their origins to revere their newly rebuilt
sanctuary.[49] But in each instance the termination of exile and return to the
homeland are connected to the reconstruction of the Temple. As symbol of
the faith, its demolition had rendered foreign enslavement—or its representation—especially wrenching. A comparable condition, however, did
not hold in the Hellenistic diaspora.[50] The Temple stood again in Jerusalem. And few Jews abroad were held there by constraint.[51]

Just one text takes up this theme and applies it to the ingathering of exiles in the Hellenistic age. The preamble of II Maccabees contains a letter
purportedly sent by Judah Maccabee, the council of elders, and the people
of Jerusalem and Judaea to the Jews of Egypt. The vexed questions of
whether or not the letter is authentic, whether Judah ever sent it, whether it
was composed by the author of II Maccabees or attached later, what parts
are original and what parts interpolated can all be set aside here.[52] It is, on
any reckoning, a Hellenistic composition. The missive concludes with the
hope that God, who has now delivered Jews from great evils (the persecutions by Antiochus IV) and has purified the sanctuary, will show compassion and reassemble Jews from all regions of the world to the holy place.[53]
Do we have here then a reflection of a continued wish for dissolving the diaspora and repopulating Judaea with those languishing abroad?

The inference is far from inevitable. This concocted letter, whatever its
genuineness or lack thereof, represents a Maccabean line. Judah deliberately and pointedly echoes the biblical theme.[54] The final lines of the epistle
follow closely the wording in Deuteronomy 30.3–5. And they are not the
only allusion to this motif of regathering the dispersed. Earlier in the letter
Judah cites Nehemiah, recently returned to Jerusalem, who issues a prayer
after erection of the Second Temple that God will liberate the enslaved
among the nations and reassemble those in the diaspora.[55] Later he makes
reference to Jeremiah at the time of the exile and the prophet's promise that
God will show pity and bring his people together again.[56] The latter two
passages are inventions by the composer, without authority in the Scriptures. The purpose plainly is to link Judah's achievement in the purification
of the Temple to grand moments of the Israelite past. The letter alludes
not only to the rebuilding of the Temple in the time of Nehemiah but to its
initial construction by King Solomon himself and even to divine signs
vouchsafed to Moses.[57] Judah is set in the line of the great figures of biblical antiquity. That context accounts for the phraseology of regathering the

exiles; it is a dramatic plea with scriptural resonance, not a mirror of contemporary longings by diaspora Jews.

The point can be strengthened. Judah's epistle was directed to the Jews of Egypt. Its principal objective was to declare the celebration of Hanukkah (or its original version as a Feast of Tabernacles) and to encourage the Judaeans' Egyptian compatriots to celebrate it as well.[58] The message contemplates no dissolution of that diaspora community—but rather presupposes its continued existence.

A consistency holds amidst these texts. Dismal memories of misery and exile recall the biblical era, sufferings under Assyrians and Babylonians. But redemption came; the promise of a new Temple was kept. The lamentations do not apply to current conditions. Hellenistic constructs have Jews thrive in Egypt, overcome their enemies, and enjoy festivities that celebrate triumphs won in Palestine and the diaspora alike.

How compelling was the notion of a "homeland" to Jews dwelling in distant and dispersed communities of the Mediterranean?[59] In principle, the concept held firm. The sanctity of Jerusalem retained a central place in the consciousness of Hellenistic Jews, wherever they happened to reside. They had not wrapped themselves in the texts as the real meaning of their identity, embracing their location in the diaspora and indifferent to their territorial roots. Judah Maccabee labels Jerusalem as the "holy city" in his epistle to the Egyptian Jews, as one might expect.[60] The phrase also appears several times in the work of Philo, who never doubts the primacy of Jerusalem.[61] And the Jews' devotion to their sacred "acropolis" is observed even by the pagan geographer Strabo.[62] Numerous other texts characterize Palestine as the "holy land." That designation occurs in II Maccabees, the Wisdom of Solomon, the Testament of Job, the Sibylline Oracles, and Philo.[63] Most, if not all, of these works stem from the diaspora. They underscore the reverence with which Jews around the Mediterranean continued to regard Jerusalem and the land of their fathers.[64]

Loyalty to one's native land was a deep commitment in the rhetoric of the Hellenistic world.[65] A striking passage in the *Letter of Aristeas* pronounces that precept in unequivocal fashion. Amidst the myriad questions put to his Jewish guests by Ptolemy II at his week-long symposium was one that asked "how should one be a lover of one's country?" The respondent made as strong a contrast as can be imagined between a native land and residence abroad, between *patris* and *xenia*. It is a noble thing, he said, to live and die in one's own country; by contrast, *xenia* brings contempt to the

poor and shame to the rich—as if they had been expelled for criminal behavior.[66] The statement, surprisingly enough, has received almost no comment from scholars.[67] Prima facie, it looks like a *locus classicus* for Jewish
belief that life in Palestine alone is worth living, and that diaspora existence
is mere despair and disgrace.

Philo more than once endorses the idea that adherence to one's *patris*
has compelling power. He speaks of the charms of kinsmen and homeland;
trips abroad are good for widening one's horizons, but nothing is better
than coming home.[68] Failure to worship God is put on a level with neglecting to honor parents, benefactors, and *patris*.[69] Defending one's country is
a prime virtue.[70] And, as Philo has Agrippa say to Caligula, love of one's
native land and compliance with its precepts are deeply ingrained in all
men.[71]

Palestine as the *patris* appears as a recurrent theme. The diaspora author
of II Maccabees brands the Jewish villains of his piece, Simon, Jason, and
Menelaus, as betrayers of their homeland.[72] And Judah Maccabee is a preeminent champion of his *patris* and its laws.[73] The Hebrews, according to
Philo, had migrated to Egypt as if it were a second fatherland. But they
eventually conceived a longing for the real thing, their ancient and native
land.[74] A comparable formulation can be found in Artapanus' recreation
of the Exodus.[75] The same is true of the Greek drama on that theme composed by Ezekiel.[76] That the term *patris* is no mere shorthand expression
for traditions, practices, the site of their faith, or even Jerusalem is clear
from an unambiguous assertion in II Maccabees. Judah Maccabee called
upon his troops to fight nobly and to the death for their laws, their temple,
their city, their *patris,* and their way of life.[77] *Patris* is not synonymous with
any of the rest. The native land is Palestine.

Thus, Jerusalem as concept and reality remained a powerful emblem of
Jewish identity—not supplanted by the Book or disavowed by those who
dwelled afar. How then should we interpret this tenacious devotion? Do
these pronouncements entail a widespread desire to pull up stakes and return to the fatherland? It might seem logical, even inevitable, to conclude
that diaspora Jews set their hearts upon such a return. Fulfillment could
come only with a reconnection to the *patris*.[78]

Logical perhaps, but not inevitable. Broad pronouncements about love
of one's country accord with general Hellenistic attitudes and expressions.[79] They do not require that residence abroad be abandoned and native environs reinhabited lest life remain incomplete. References to the Hebrews' migration to Egypt from the fatherland and subsequent recovery of
that fatherland are perfectly reasonable and acceptable—without imposing

upon them the burden of standing for aspirations by Hellenistic Jews. It is noteworthy that the texts that speak of reverence for the *patris* do not speak of the "Return."

The bald and forceful statement in the *Letter of Aristeas,* noted above, offers an ostensibly formidable obstacle. The Jewish spokesman, in a Hellenistic composition and a Hellenistic setting, draws a stark contrast between the nobility of living and dying in one's *patris* and the ignominy of dwelling abroad.[80] Is the reference here to Palestine? That is not an obvious conclusion. In the context of the whole work, a disparagement of Egypt as residence for Jews would be absurd. The main message of the *Letter* directs itself to Egyptian Jews for whom the Hebrew Scriptures are rendered into Greek—an accomplishment they greet with fervid gratitude. Indeed, they insist that not a word be changed in the translation, so that it will remain forever inviolable.[81] The entire tale rests on the premise that diaspora Jews will now have direct access to the tenets of their faith and a solid foundation for enduring communities abroad. Why then this statement in the symposium? It is well to remember that each question posed by Ptolemy II seeks advice from a Jewish sage on some aspect of how to govern his kingdom or how to lead a good life. In this instance, the king asks how he might be a genuine lover of his country.[82] The first part of the answer, that which contrasts native land and foreign residence, seems curiously irrelevant. And the last part, which advises Ptolemy to bestow benefits on all, just as he regularly does, thus to be reckoned a real patriot, presupposes (if it carries any substantive meaning) the continued and contented community of resident aliens. Like so many of the swift and brief retorts by Jewish sages at the banquet, this one is bland and unsatisfying, containing statements that barely pertain to the king's query. The passage, whatever its significance, can hardly serve as a touchstone for the thesis that diaspora Jews were consumed with a desire to forsake their surroundings.

Did Jewish settlements abroad carry a stigma? A term sometimes employed to characterize them might, at first sight, seem to suggest it. They were viewed as *apoikiai,* "colonies." That designation presented them as offshoots from the metropolis, secondary and inferior to the original. But the term, in customary Greek usage, lacked pejorative overtones. And, as employed by Jewish writers, its implications were, in fact, decidedly positive.

In the fantasy depicted in III Maccabees, the Jews hounded and herded in Alexandria faced nearly certain death. A final prayer reached God from the elderly and respected priest Eleazer. Among his pleas, Eleazer included a reference to possible impieties committed by Jews in their *apoikia.*[83] But the sins, not the location, provide the grounds for potential destruction. And the happy ending vindicates and perpetuates the colony. The new festival instituted by the Egyptian Jews to celebrate their rescue and triumph would hold for generations to come and throughout the time of their settlement abroad—here designated as *paroikia*.[84]

Philo uses the word *apoikia* with reference to Moses leading the Hebrews out of their abode in Egypt. No negative overtones characterize that statement. The same phraseology in the same context was employed three and a half centuries earlier by the Greek writer Hecataeus of Abdera.[85] Indeed, Philo elsewhere makes clear his very positive assessment of Jewish "colonies" abroad. God reassured Moses that Jews dwelling abroad in future generations would be on the same footing as Jews in Palestine with regard to fulfilling sacred rites. The diaspora Jews, Philo affirms explicitly, live at a distance through no transgression but through the need of an overpopulated nation to send out *apoikiai*.[86] The philosopher reiterates that statement in fuller form in Agrippa's letter to Caligula, proudly detailing the colonies that had been sent out from Judaea over the years to places all over the Mediterranean and the Near East.[87] Josephus echoes Philo in asserting that Jewish participation in colonies established abroad by other nations gave them an honored presence in those settlements from the start.[88] In a most revealing passage, Philo, in fact, asserts that in the case of those sent to a colony, by contrast to those simply away from home, the *apoikia*, rather than the *metropolis*, becomes the *patris*.[89] Jerusalem was indeed the mother city.[90] But, as is clear, the expression "colony" had a ring of pride and accomplishment, signaling the spread of the faith and its adherents, not a fall from grace.[91]

Jews formed stable communities in the diaspora, entering into the social, economic, and political life of the nations they joined, aspiring to and often obtaining civic privileges in the cities of the Hellenistic world. Adequate evidence attests a Jewish assertion of full and acknowledged membership and a genuine sense of belonging. Philo expresses the principle of the matter clearly enough. He declares that *xenoi* (foreigners) should be reckoned as residents and friends eager to enjoy privileges equal to those of citizens, and indeed hardly any different from the indigenous people themselves.[92] Josephus maintains that Jews have every right to designate themselves as Alexandrians, Antiochenes, Ephesians, or whatever name belongs to the city in which they have settled.[93] Further, in discussing elsewhere the Jews of Ionia who sought redress from Rome against their opponents in the time of Augustus, he claims that they established their status as "natives."[94] Philo indeed referred to his city as "our Alexandria."[95] That form of identification emerges more poignantly in the petition of an Alexandrian Jew threatened with loss of his privileges. He labels himself an "Alexandrian" at the head of the document—alluding to his father, also an Alexandrian, and the proper education he had received—and expresses his fear of being deprived of his *patris*. The petitioner or the scribe who composed the letter in its final form then altered the term "Alexandrian" to "a Jew from Alexandria."[96] Whatever legal meaning this terminology might have carried, it signals the petitioner's clear affirmation of his roots in the community.[97] A comparable sentiment might be inferred from an inscription of the Phrygian city Acmonia, alluding to fulfillment of a vow made to the "whole *patris*." A Jew or a group of Jews must have commissioned it, for a menorah appears beneath the text. Here again the "native city" is honored, presumably through a gift for civic purposes. The donor pronounces his local loyalty in a conspicuous public manner.[98]

The most telling statement comes in Philo's *In Flaccum*. The passage is frequently cited for its reference to the impressive span of the Jewish diaspora, the spread of Jews to the most numerous and most prosperous places of Europe and Asia, whether on islands or on the mainland. But Philo proceeds to offer a striking depiction of Jewish attitudes both toward Jerusalem and toward the lands where Jews now (and for generations) have made their home. As Philo puts it, they considered the holy city as their "metropolis," but the states in which they were born and raised and which they acquired from their fathers, grandfathers, and distant forefathers they adjudged their *patrides*.[99] That fervent expression eradicates any idea of the "doctrine of return." Diaspora Jews, in Philo's formulation at least, held an intense attachment to the adopted lands of their ancestors.

Jews living around the Mediterranean were unapologetic and unembarrassed by their situation. They did not describe themselves as part of a diaspora. They did not suggest that they were cut off from the center, leading a separate, fragmented, and unfulfilled existence. Peoples from communities and nations everywhere settled outside their places of origin in the fluid and mobile Hellenistic world without abandoning their identities as Athenians, Macedonians, Phoenicians, Antiochenes, or Egyptians. The Jews could eschew justification, rationalization, or tortured explanation for their choice of residence. They felt no need to construct a theory of diaspora.

Commitment to the community and devotion to Jerusalem were entirely compatible. That devotion had a public and conspicuous demonstration every year: the payment of a tithe to the Temple from Jews all over the

Mediterranean.[100] The ritualistic offering carried deep significance as a bonding device. Its origins are obscure and require no investigation here. That it rests on a biblical prescription, the half-shekel imposed by the Lord upon Israelites counted in a census in the wilderness, may be questioned.[101] A more direct link perhaps comes with Nehemiah's establishment of a one-third shekel tax to help finance maintenance of the new Temple's operations.[102] When such a contribution was first expected of Jews in the diaspora can only be guessed at. The Seleucid overlords of Palestine had subsidized the financial needs of the Temple in the early second century BCE, as the Ptolemies may have done before them, and the Persian kings before them.[103] At some time after the installation of Hasmonean rule, support for the Temple came in from abroad; this soon became a matter of established practice and an accepted obligation of the faithful.[104]

The fact impressed itself notably among the Romans. Events of the mid-60s BCE brought it to their attention in a forceful fashion. Economic circumstances in Rome and abroad had prompted a series of decrees forbidding the export of gold. The Roman governor of Asia, L. Valerius Flaccus, enforced the policy in various ways, including a ban on the sending of gold by the Jews of Asia Minor to Jerusalem.[105] The action not only prompted resentment among the Jews in Flaccus' province but also stirred up a hornet's nest of opposition by the Jews in Rome itself. Cicero, who conducted Flaccus' defense at his trial for extortion in 59, comments bitterly about the horde of Jews crowding around the tribunal, exercising undue pressure upon the proceedings, and passionately exhibiting their "barbaric superstition."[106] The account, of course, is partisan, rhetorical, and exaggerated. But Cicero conveys some precious information. First, he indicates the earnest commitment of Jews everywhere to provide funds annually to the Temple from Italy and from all the provinces of the Roman empire.[107] Next, his record of Flaccus' activities indicates that tribute for the Temple was collected by Jewish communities, city by city, wherever they possessed sufficient numbers in Asia Minor.[108] And, what is most revealing, Cicero's speech, however embellished and overblown, shows that the plight of Asian Jews who were prevented from making their accustomed contributions to the Temple stirred the passions of their compatriots far off in Rome and provoked impressively noisy demonstrations on their behalf. Cicero remarks both on the pressure and size of the Jewish assemblage and on its community of interests—features, he claims, well known in Rome.[109] The whole episode exhibits the solidarity of sentiments among diaspora Jews from Italy to the Near East in the matter of expressing their allegiance to Jerusalem.[110]

The centrality of Jewish commitment to the tithe is demonstrated again and again. Philo reinforces the testimony of Cicero. His comment on the large Jewish community in Rome at the time of Augustus once again associates it with zeal for gathering the sacred tithes to be delivered by envoys to Jerusalem—a fact with which the *princeps* was well acquainted.[111] The size of contributions over the years had brought substantial wealth to the Temple. Josephus proudly observes that the donations had come from Jews all over Asia and Europe, indeed from everywhere in the world, for a huge number of years.[112] When that activity was interfered with by local authorities, Jews would send up a howl to Rome. So, for instance, when M. Agrippa, overseeing the eastern provinces for Augustus, appeared in Ionia, Jews from various Ionian communities complained loudly of Greek interference with their prerogatives, naming first and foremost the seizure of cash destined as contributions to Jerusalem.[113] If Josephus' collection of Roman decrees is to be trusted, the emperor Augustus himself intervened to assure the untroubled exercise of Jewish practices in the province of Asia. In promulgating an edict to put Roman muscle behind the guarantee of Jewish privileges, Augustus placed at the head of the list the inviolability of sacred monies sent to Jerusalem and designated for the treasury officials of the Temple.[114] That prerogative and that alone is noted in the emperor's letter to the proconsul of Asia.[115] Agrippa followed it up with directives to officials in Ephesus and Cyrene, as did the Roman governor in a message to Sardis.[116] The active support by Augustus and Agrippa for Jewish interests on this matter is attested also by Philo, a close contemporary.[117] Monies collected for Jerusalem form the centerpiece in each of the Roman pronouncements. That emphasis must come from Jews pressing their claims upon the imperial government. Indeed, areas beyond the reach of Roman power also contained Jews who pursued the same practice with rigor and consistency. Communities in Babylon and other satrapies under Parthian dominion sent representatives every year over difficult terrain and dangerous highways to deposit their contributions in the Temple.[118] Even if the documents are not genuine, they reflect the order of priorities expressed by the Jewish sources of Philo and Josephus. The issue of paying homage to Jerusalem was paramount.[119]

Proof, if proof be needed, is provided by a hostile witness with no axe to grind on this score. Tacitus, in supplying a list of depraved and deplorable Jewish habits, sets in first place the institution of collecting tribute and donations to increase the resources of the Jews.[120] And there is ironic significance to the fact that when the Romans destroyed the Temple they refrained from destroying this institution; rather, they altered its recipient.

The annual tithe would no longer go to the nonexistent sacred shrine; it would metamorphize into a Roman tax. The cash would now serve to subsidize the cult of Jupiter Capitolinus.[121]

The stark symbolism of the tithe had a potent hold upon Jewish sentiment. That annual act of obeisance was a repeated reminder, or rather display, of affection and allegiance. Jerusalem cast the most compelling image, and gripped the imaginations of Jews everywhere in the Mediterranean and the Near East. The repeated, ritualistic contributions emblematized the unbroken attachment of the diaspora to the center. Even the Romans recognized the symbolic power of the payment. Its transformation into a subsidy for the preeminent deity of the empire would serve as dramatic signifier of a new loyalty.

What implications does the tithe possess for the questions addressed here? Did the outpouring of cash for the Temple by Jews from Italy to Iran imply that the diaspora was reckoned as fleeting and temporary, an interim exile or refuge, an affliction to be endured until restoration to the Holy City? In fact, the reverse conclusion holds. The continuing pledge of allegiance proclaimed that the diaspora could endure indefinitely and quite satisfactorily. The communities abroad were entrenched and successful, even mainstays of the center. Diaspora Jews did not and would not turn their backs on Jerusalem, the principal emblem of their faith. Their fierce commitment to the tithe delivered that message unequivocally. But the gesture did not signify a desire for the Return. On the contrary: it signaled that the Return was unnecessary.

A comparable phenomenon demands attention: the pilgrimage of diaspora Jews to Jerusalem. How often this occurred and in what numbers is unclear.[122] Major festivals could attract Jews with some frequency and in quantity. If Philo is to be believed, myriads came from countless cities for every feast, over land and sea, from all points of the compass, to enjoy the Temple as a serene refuge from the hurly-burly of everyday life abroad.[123] The most celebrated occasion occurred after the death of Jesus. The feast of Pentecost had brought numerous persons into the city from far-flung and diverse locations: peoples from Parthia, Media, and Elam, from Mesopotamia and Cappadocia, from Pontus and Asia, from Phrygia and Pamphylia, from Egypt and Cyrene, from Crete and Arabia, and, indeed, even from Rome—all witness to the miracle of the disciples speaking in the whole array of diverse tongues.[124] When the Roman governor of Syria visited Jerusalem at the time of Passover in the mid-60s CE, he encountered crowds of incalculable numbers.[125] Even the Great Revolt did not discourage pilgrims from coming at Passover. A large number found themselves trapped in the city and perished in the Roman siege.[126] Huge crowds from abroad, including Gentiles, at Passover were evidently common.[127] The women's court at the Temple was large enough to accommodate those who resided in the land and those who came from abroad—a clear sign that female pilgrims in some numbers were expected visitors.[128]

The delivery of the annual tithe itself brought diaspora Jews to Jerusalem on a regular basis, a ritual performance analogous to, even identical with, a pilgrimage. Philo attests to the sacred messengers who not only deposit the monies but perform the sacrifices.[129] And they might be accompanied by many others, especially when arduous and perilous journeys required numbers for protection.[130] The adherents of Paul who went with him to Jerusalem from Greece, Macedon, and Asia may also have been performing a pilgrimage.[131] The Holy City exercised tremendous force as a magnet. Josephus' romantic tale about the conversion to Judaism by the royal family in far-off Adiabene, whatever its authenticity, illustrates the point nicely. The queen mother Helena, an ardent proselyte, naturally felt that confirmation of her new status required a visit to the sacred site and worship in the Temple. Helena proceeded to shower Jerusalem with gifts, a gesture duplicated by her son Izates, the king of Adiabene. Izates himself sent his five young sons to Palestine to receive training in Hebrew language and culture. And both mother and son were buried not in Adiabene but outside Jerusalem in monuments whose construction Helena herself had directed.[132] The experience of the royal house, at least as represented in the tale, recapitulates the behavior of diaspora Jews, which they had, in effect, become.[133] The visits to Jerusalem and gifts to the Temple followed the appropriate mode of expressing homage. But the demonstration of devotion did not entail a desire for migration. Pilgrimage, in fact, by its very nature, signified a temporary payment of respect. The Holy City had an irresistible and undiminished claim on the emotions of diaspora Jews. It was indeed a critical piece of their identity. But home was elsewhere.

The self-perception of Second Temple Jews projected a tight solidarity between center and diaspora. The images of exile and separation did not haunt them. They were not compelled to choose between restoration to Eretz Israel and recourse to the Word as their "portable homeland." What affected the dwellers in Jerusalem affected Jews everywhere. The theme of intertwined experience and interdependent identity is reiterated with impressive frequency and variety.

Many of the texts already noted, and a good number of others besides, fortify this conclusion. The author of II Maccabees—or at least of the let-

ters attached to the beginning of that work—gives pointed expression to
the idea. The Jews of Jerusalem take for granted the intimate relationship
that exists with their brethren in Egypt. The preamble of the first letter
greets them as "brothers" to "brothers" and alludes to their common heritage: God's covenant with Abraham, Isaac, and Jacob.[134] And the central
message of both missives is that the Egyptian Jews should celebrate the
new festival honoring the recovery and purification of the Temple after
the desecration by Antiochus IV.[135] The concluding lines of the second letter make reference to the desired reunion of all Jews in the holy site. As argued earlier, this is not a call for an end to the diaspora. It represents the
party line of the Maccabeans.[136] But even on a closer analysis, it signifies no
more than a summons to a festival—and thus a reaffirmation of solidarity
among Jews everywhere. It reflects the practice of pilgrimage rather than a
program to dissolve the dispersal.

The *Letter of Aristeas* makes the connection between Jerusalemites and
other Jews still more forceful and unequivocal. King Ptolemy's letter to the
High Priest in Judaea asserts that his motive in having the Hebrew Bible
rendered into Greek was to benefit not only the Jews of Egypt but all Jews
throughout the world—even those not yet born.[137] And it is fitting that,
when the scholars from Jerusalem completed their translation and it was
read out to the Jews of Egypt, the large assemblage burst into applause—a
dramatic expression of the unity of purpose.[138]

The narrative of III Maccabees depends on that same unity of purpose.
It presupposes and never questions the proposition that the actions of
Jerusalemites represent the sentiments of Jews anywhere in the diaspora.
When Ptolemy IV was thwarted in his design to enter the Holy of Holies in
Jerusalem, he reacted immediately upon return to Egypt to inflict punishment upon the Jerusalemites' compatriots in that land. The king had determined to bring public shame upon the *ethnos* of the Jews generally.[139] A
few were prepared to yield to his blandishments and accept civic privileges
in Alexandria in return for apostasy. But most of them held firm, regarding
the apostates as enemies of the nation and refusing them any part in communal life and mutual services.[140] Whatever Ptolemy IV may in fact have
thought, the author of III Maccabees certainly presumed a commonality of
interests within the Jewish *ethnos* as a whole. Egyptian Jews were "fellow-
tribesmen" of those who dwelled in Judaea.[141]

The Book of Tobit offers a parallel episode. A principal theme of that
work concerns proper burial rites. Tobit, dwelling in exile at Nineveh, felt
it incumbent upon himself, despite the dangers and difficulties involved, to
bury the bodies of all Jews executed on the orders of the Assyrian king

Sennacherib. Like the wicked Ptolemy of III Maccabees, Sennacherib wreaked vengeance upon Israelites in Assyria because of a rout he had suffered at the hands of their compatriots in Palestine.[142] Once again, the assumption of solidarity between Jews in the center and those abroad underpins the narrative.

Apart from putative pagans, real ones attested to Jewish solidarity as well. The notorious passage of Cicero, discussed earlier, offers a vivid example. When a Roman governor sought to prevent the export of gold from Asia for the Temple in Jerusalem, a large crowd of Jews in Rome protested vociferously and exerted heavy pressure on public proceedings.[143]

In the perceptions of Philo and Josephus, no breach existed, no discernible difference even, between the practices of Palestinian Jews and of those abroad. The priestly classes in the diaspora maintain the same rigid adherence to genealogical purity as do those in the homeland. Moreover, the scrupulous records of the former are regularly sent to Jerusalem as a token of esteem and a sign of solidarity. Josephus in this connection employs the term *diesparmenoi* ("scattered")—and plainly without any derogatory undertone.[144] Philo asserts the equivalence of diaspora Jews, with regard to the ritual of honoring the dead, in still more forceful terms: those who settle abroad have committed no wrongs and cannot be denied equal privileges. The nation has simply spilled over its borders and can no longer be confined to a single land.[145]

The community of interests could have a direct effect on the events of Jewish history. In the late second century BCE, Cleopatra III, queen of Egypt, gained the upper hand in a war against her son Ptolemy Lathyrus and heard tempting advice from some of her advisers that she should seize the opportunity for an invasion of Judaea. The plan never materialized because better advice came from another quarter. The Jewish military man Ananias, a loyal and effective general in Cleopatra's army, dissuaded her with a compelling argument. He counted the High Priest in Judaea, Alexander Jannaeus, as his own kinsman. And any attack on the High Priest, so he claimed, would make enemies of all the Jews in Egypt. Cleopatra reconsidered the matter, dropped plans for an invasion, and instead concluded an alliance with Jannaeus.[146]

A half-century later, the close ties of Judaean and Egyptian Jews and the prestige of the High Priest once more had a telling effect on the course of historical events. At the height of the Roman civil war, Julius Caesar found himself besieged in Alexandria in 48/47 BCE. A troop of three thousand Jewish soldiers marched to his rescue under their general Antipater, who had rounded up additional support from Arabia, Syria, and Lebanon. But their path was blocked by Egyptian Jews who dwelled in the Oniad district, i.e., in the enclave of Leontopolis, site of a long-standing Jewish community. Antipater, however, overcame any resistance by appealing to their common nationality and, indeed, their loyalty to the High Priest Hyrcanus. Antipater brandished a letter from Hyrcanus requesting that Egyptian Jews support the cause of Caesar. No further persuasion was necessary. The Jews of both Leontopolis and Memphis declared themselves for Caesar and helped to turn the tide of the war.[147] The sense of Jewish solidarity and the respect for the High Priest's authority in Jerusalem had an impressive impact. No sign of an "exilic" mentality here. Leontopolis itself endured as an autonomous center of Judaism with its own temple for well over two hundred years, until its destruction by the Romans in the wake of the Great Revolt. But, as this episode indicates, there was no schismatic separatism here. The Jews of Leontopolis continued to acknowledge the ascendancy of Jerusalem.[148]

One might note also the active involvement of Roman Jews in pressing Augustus to put an end to Herodian rule in Judaea after the death of Herod the Great. Fifty envoys came from Judaea for this purpose, and eight thousand Jews resident in Rome joined in their lobbying efforts.[149] When a pretender to the throne emerged, claiming to be a reincarnation of one of Herod's sons, he found widespread support from Jews in Crete, in Melos, and in Rome itself.[150] These events provide a revealing window upon the lively interest and occasionally energetic engagement of diaspora Jews in the affairs of Palestine.

The affiliations and interconnections emerge perhaps most dramatically in the grave crises that marked the reign of the emperor Caligula. Harsh conflict erupted in Alexandria, bringing dislocation, persecution, and death upon large numbers in the Jewish community of that city. And a still worse menace loomed over Jerusalem when the erratic emperor proposed to have a statue of himself installed in the Temple. Philo's accounts of these events contain their own bias and agenda, but they do convey the reflections of an eyewitness and participant. And they afford an insight into the attitudes of articulate Jews in the diaspora. The attacks upon the Alexandrian Jewish community came under the authority of the Roman prefect of Egypt, A. Flaccus. And when they came, so Philo maintains, the word spread like wildfire. Once synagogues were destroyed in Alexandria, reports would swiftly sweep not only through all the districts of Egypt but from there to the nations of the east and from the borders of Libya to the lands of the west. Jews had settled all over Europe and Asia, and the news of a pogrom anywhere would race through the entire network.[151] So

Philo says. And, although his claim of such speedy communications might stretch a point, the concept of tight interrelationships among Jews of the diaspora can hardly be denied. Flaccus, of course, eventually perished for his misdeeds, an appropriate ending to the morality tale. And Philo makes sure to emphasize that this was no peculiar Alexandrian affair: Flaccus is described as the "common enemy of the Jewish nation."[152]

Philo himself headed the delegation to the emperor that would plead the cause of the Jewish community in Alexandria. The timing of their arrival in Rome only heightened the drama. Word soon arrived of the larger crisis: Gaius' decision to install his statue in the Temple at Jerusalem. The initial motive for the embassy now seemed paltry by comparison. Philo's words are arresting: this most grievous calamity fell unexpectedly and brought peril not to one part of the Jewish people but to the entire nation at once.[153] Indeed, Philo berates himself for even thinking about parochial Alexandrian matters when a much greater catastrophe threatened the very existence of the Jewish polity and the name common to the nation as a whole.[154] The magnitude of this step had already occurred to P. Petronius, the legate of Syria whose task it was to oversee the erection of the statue. Petronius dragged his feet and reached for excuses to postpone the job. For he knew (or so Philo reconstructs his thoughts) that such an act would outrage Jews everywhere and would provoke resistance not only in Judaea where their ranks are especially strong but from the large number of Jews dwelling across the Euphrates in Babylon and all the provinces of the Parthian empire—indeed almost throughout the world.[155] The letter of Agrippa I, a friend of the emperor and recently accorded a kingdom among the Jews, urgently alerted Gaius to the severe gravity of the situation. Agrippa's plea to the Roman ruler maintained, among other things, that an affront to Jerusalem would have vast repercussions: the Holy City was not merely metropolis of Judaea but of most nations in the world, since Jewish colonies thrived all over the Near East, Asia Minor, Greece, Macedon, Africa, and the lands beyond the Euphrates.[156] No matter how self-serving Agrippa's statement may have been—or indeed the account of Philo in which it is embedded—the image of Jerusalem as binding together Jews everywhere in the *oikoumene* surely held a prominent place in the self-perception of the diaspora. And, in Philo's account at least, that perception is not confined to Jews. If Gentiles in any city received authorization to attack Jews, their counterparts in all cities would take it as a green light to conduct their own terrorist activities.[157]

The consistency of this portrait leaves a potent impression. Philo articulated an unbroken bond among diaspora Jews and between them and Jerusalem. No trauma in one community would go unfelt in the rest. And the ripples from any threat to Jerusalem would quickly extend throughout the Jewish world.

A moving passage elsewhere in Philo's corpus neatly encapsulates the theme stressed here. It stands outside the context of crisis and turmoil, outside the fears of pogrom in Alexandria or the megalomania of a Roman monarch. Philo, who thrived in the diaspora, enjoyed its advantages, and broadcast its virtues, nevertheless found even deeper meaning in the land of Israel. In his discussion of Jewish festivals, he interprets the Shavuot Festival as a celebration of the Jews' possession of their own land, a heritage now of long standing, and a means whereby they could cease their wandering over continents and islands and their existence as foreigners and vagabonds dwelling in the countries of others.[158] Philo saw no inconsistency or contradiction in this. Diaspora Jews might find fulfillment and reward in their communities abroad. But they honored Judaea as a refuge for the formerly displaced and unsettled, and the prime legacy of all.

Josephus makes the point in a quite different context but with equal force. In his rewriting of Numbers, he places a sweeping prognostication in the mouth of the Midianite priest Balaam. To the consternation of the king of Moab, who had expected a dark oracle for the Israelites, Balaam projected a glorious future. They will not only occupy and hold forever the land of Canaan, a chief signal of God's favor, but their multitudes will fill all the world, islands and continents, outnumbering even the stars in the heavens.[159] That is a notable declaration. Palestine, as ever, merits a special place. But the diaspora, far from being a source of shame to be overcome, represents a resplendent achievement.

The respect and awe paid to the Holy Land by Jews living elsewhere stood in full harmony with commitment to local community and allegiance to Gentile governance. Diaspora Jews did not bewail their fate or pine away for the homeland. Nor, by contrast, did they ignore the homeland and regard the Book as surrogate for the Temple. The postulated alternatives are severe and simplistic. Palestine mattered, and it mattered in a territorial sense—but not as a required residence. Gifts to the Temple and pilgrimages to Jerusalem announced simultaneously a devotion to the symbolic heart of Judaism and a singular pride in the accomplishments of the diaspora. Jewish Hellenistic writers took the concurrence for granted. They were not driven to apologia. Nor did they feel obliged to reconcile the contradiction. As they saw it, there was none.

Abbreviations · Notes · Bibliography · Index

Abbreviations

AJAH	*American Journal of Ancient History*
AJP	*American Journal of Philology*
Ann. Scuol. arch. di Atene	*Annali della Scuola archeologica di Atene*
ANRW	*Aufstieg und Niedergang der römischen Welt.* Berlin, 1972–
BA	*Biblical Archaeologist*
BCH	*Bulletin de Correspondance Hellénique*
BGU	*Berliner Griechische Urkunden* (Ägyptische Urkunden aus den Königlichen Museen zu Berlin). Berlin, 1895–1912
CA	*Classical Antiquity*
CBQ	*Catholic Biblical Quarterly*
Charles, *APOT*	R. H. Charles, ed., *The Apocrypha and Pseudepigrapha of the Old Testament in English,* 2 vols. Oxford, 1913
Charlesworth, *OTP*	J. H. Charlesworth, ed., *The Old Testament Pseudepigrapha,* 2 vols. New York, 1983–1985
CHI	*The Cambridge History of Iran,* 8 vols. Cambridge, 1968–1991
CHJ	*The Cambridge History of Judaism,* 3 vols. Cambridge, 1984–1999
CIJ	J.-B. Frey, ed., *Corpus Inscriptionum Judaicarum,* 2 vols. Rome, 1936–1952
CIRB	*Corpus inscriptionum regni Bosporani.* Leningrad, 1965
CJZC	G. Lüderitz. *Corpus jüdischer Zeugnisse aus der Cyrenaika.* Wiesbaden, 1983
CP	*Classical Philology*
CPJ	V. A. Tcherikover, A. Fuks, and M. Stern, eds., *Corpus Papyrorum Judaicarum,* 3 vols. Jerusalem, 1957–1964
CQ	*Classical Quarterly*
GRBS	*Greek, Roman, and Byzantine Studies*
Holladay, *Fragments*	C. R. Holladay, *Fragments from Hellenistic Jewish Authors,* 4 vols. Chico/Atlanta, 1983–1996

HSCP	*Harvard Studies in Classical Philology*
HTR	*Harvard Theological Review*
HUCA	*Hebrew Union College Annual*
IC	M. Guarducci, ed., *Inscriptiones Creticae*, 4 vols. Rome, 1935–1950
ID	*Inscriptions de Délos*, 6 vols. Paris, 1923–1937
IG	*Inscriptiones Graecae*
IGRR	*Inscriptiones Graecae ad Res Romanas Pertinentes*, 4 vols. Paris, 1911–1927
ILS	H. Dessau, ed., *Inscriptiones Latinae Selectae*. Berlin, 1892–1916
Inscr. Ital.	*Inscriptiones Italiae*
JBL	*Journal of Biblical Literature*
JIGRE	W. Horbury and D. Noy, *Jewish Inscriptions of Graeco-Roman Egypt*. Cambridge, 1992
JIWE	D. Noy, *Jewish Inscriptions of Western Europe*, 2 vols. Cambridge, 1993–1995
JJP	*Journal of Juristic Papyrology*
JJS	*Journal of Jewish Studies*
JQR	*Jewish Quarterly Review*
JR	*Journal of Religion*
JRA	*Journal of Roman Archaeology*
JRS	*Journal of Roman Studies*
JSHRZ	*Jüdische Schriften aus hellenistisch-römischer Zeit.* Gütersloh, 1973–
JSJ	*Journal for the Study of Judaism in the Persian, Hellenistic, and Roman Period*
JSP	*Journal for the Study of the Pseudepigrapha and Related Literature*
JSQ	*Jewish Studies Quarterly*
MMR	T. R. S. Broughton, *The Magistrates of the Roman Republic*, 3 vols. New York/Atlanta, 1951–1986
NT	*Novum Testamentum*
NTS	*New Testament Studies*
PIR	*Prosopographia Imperii Romani Saeculi I. II. III*
PP	*La parola del passato*
Proc. of XXth Int. Congr. of Papyrologists	*Proceedings of the XXth International Congress of Papyrologists.* Copenhagen, 1994
PsVTGr	A.-M. Denis and M. de Jonge, eds., *Pseudepigrapha Veteris Testamenti Graece.* Leiden, 1967–
RDGE	R. K. Sherk, *Roman Documents from the Greek East: Senatus Consulta and Epistulae to the Age of Augustus.* Baltimore, 1969
RE	A. Pauly, G. Wissowa, and W. Kroll, eds., *Real-Encyclopädie der classischen Altertumswissenschaft.* Munich, 1893–
REJ	*Revue des études juives*

RevBib	*Revue Biblique*
RevHistPhilRel	*Revue d'histoire et de philosophie religieuses*
RHR	*Revue de l'histoire des religions*
RIDA	*Revue internationale des droits de l'Antiquité*
Safrai and Stern, *Jewish People*	S. Safrai and M. Stern, eds., *The Jewish People in the First Century*, 2 vols. Philadelphia, 1974–1976
Schürer, *History*	Emil Schürer, *The History of the Jewish People in the Age of Jesus Christ*, 3 vols. Edinburgh, 1973–1987 (revised and edited by Geza Vermes, Fergus Millar, Matthew Black, and Martin Goodman)
SCI	*Scripta Classica Israelica*
SEG	*Supplementum Epigraphicum Graecum*
Stone, *Jewish Writings*	M. E. Stone, ed., *Jewish Writings of the Second Temple Period*. Philadelphia, 1984
StudClassOrient	*Studi Classici e Orientali*
Syll	W. Dittenberger, ed., *Sylloge Inscriptionum Graecarum*, 4 vols. 3rd ed., Leipzig, 1915–1924
VDI	*Vestnik Drevnej Istorii*
VigChr	*Vigiliae Christianae*
ZAW	*Zeitschrift für die alttestamentliche Wissenschaft*
ZNW	*Zeitschrift für die neutestamentliche Wissenschaft*
ZPE	*Zeitschrift für Papyrologie und Epigraphik*

Notes

INTRODUCTION

1. I Macc. 15.22–23.
2. Strabo, *apud* Jos. *Ant.* 14.114–115.
3. Philo, *Leg.* 281–283.
4. Josephus puts 120,000 Jews in Egypt in the early third century BCE; *Ant.* 12.11. According to Philo, they numbered more than a million by 38 CE; *Flacc.* 43. In Alexandria alone, 50,000 Jews perished in a massacre in 66 CE; Jos. *BJ,* 2.497. In Damascus, 10,500 fell in that same year; Jos. *BJ,* 2.561; cf. 7.368. After the death of Herod in 4 BCE, 8,000 Jews in Rome turned up to demonstrate against his successor; Jos. *BJ,* 2.80; *Ant.* 17.300. And 4,000 able-bodied young Jewish males were deported from Rome to Sardinia in 19 CE; Jos. *Ant.* 18.83–84; Tac. *Ann.* 2.85; Suet. *Tib.* 36. In Cyrene in 70 CE, wealthy Jewish males alone numbered 3,000; Jos. *BJ,* 7.445. The figures are by no means all reliable.
5. *LetArist.* 12—although the numbers given, 100,000, are highly inflated. Cf. Jos. *Ant.* 12.7.
6. Cf. Jos. *Ant.* 12.138–139, 12.144.
7. I Macc. 9.70–72; 10.33; Jos. *Ant.* 13.337, 13.344. The fact of Jewish slaves in Delphi, as attested by manumission decrees of the second century BCE, indicates that some war captives were sold on the slave marts; *CIJ,* I, nos. 709–711.
8. Cf., e.g., Jos. *Ant.* 13.125, 13.133, 13.383, 14.21; *BJ,* 1.98; I Macc. 11.21, 11.25, 15.16–24.
9. See, especially, Philo, *Leg.* 155; cf. also Jos. *BJ,* 1.154, 1.180; *Ant.* 14.71, 14.79, 14.97, 14.120, 14.275, 14.304, 14.313, 14.321, 20.244.
10. Pseudo-Hecataeus, *apud* Jos. *CAp.* 1.194.
11. *LetArist.* 13–14, 23–27; Jos. *CAp.* 2.44.
12. The departure of the High Priest Onias IV and his supporters for Egypt in the Maccabean period is an exception; Jos. *Ant.* 12.387, 13.62; *BJ,* 1.31–33, 7.423. They stayed on in Egypt for generations, but not under duress.
13. Jos. *Ant.* 12.149–153.
14. Val. Max. 1.3.3; Cic. *Pro Flacco,* 66.
15. Philo, *Leg.* 155.

16. Overpopulation: Philo, *Flacc.* 45–46; indebtedness: Ben Sira, 29.18.
17. Extensive data exist on Jews in this profession. See the useful survey by A. Kasher, in A. Shinan, ed., *Emigration and Settlement in Diaspora in the Hellenistic-Roman Period* (Jerusalem, 1982), 84–91 (Hebrew).
18. Kasher, op. cit., 80–84 (Hebrew).
19. Cf. Jos. *Ant.* 4.115–116.
20. Psalm 137.1–6. The translation is that of *The New Jerusalem Bible* (New York, 1990), 711–712.
21. Jeremiah 29.4–7 (*New Jerusalem Bible,* 971). The strategy, to be sure, is presented as a temporary one, for two generations, until Yahweh will restore his people to Israel.
22. *CIJ,* I, no. 711b.
23. Jos. *Ant.* 20.100; *BJ,* 2.309.
24. *LetArist.* 139.
25. III Sibyl. 218–247.
26. Philo, *Flacc.* 55; cf. Jos. *BJ,* 2.495.
27. E.g., Hecataeus, *apud* Diod. 40.3.4; Manetho, *apud* Jos. *CAp.* 1.239; Pompeius Trogus, *apud* Justin, 36.2.15; Tac. *Hist.* 5.5.1–2; Juv. 14.102–104.
28. Many of these comments are discussed in Chapter 1. For full references, see M. Stern, *Greek and Latin Authors on Jews and Judaism,* 2 vols. (Jerusalem, 1976, 1980).
29. Jos. *BJ,* 2.457–480.
30. Alexandria: Jos. *BJ,* 2.487–498; Antioch: Jos. *BJ,* 7.47–62.
31. See, especially, the actions of the Antiochenes and Alexandrians in the wake of Rome's victory; Jos. *BJ,* 7.100–111; *Ant.* 12.121–124.
32. For the events and sources, see E. M. Smallwood, *The Jews under Roman Rule* (Leiden, 1981), 389–427.

1. THE JEWS IN ROME

1. See the sensible calculations of H. Solin, *ANRW,* II.29.2 (1983), 698–701, with reference to earlier discussions. Cf. D. Noy, *Foreigners at Rome: Citizens and Strangers* (London, 2000), 257–258.
2. Val. Max. 1.3.3.
3. Philo, *Leg.* 155.
4. Cf. Jos. *BJ,* 1.154; *Ant.* 14.71, 79.
5. Cic. *Pro Flacco,* 66.
6. Val. Max. 1.3.3 (Paris epitome): *Iudaeaos, qui Sabazi Iovis cultu Romanos inficere mores conati erant, repetere domos suas coegit.*
7. Val. Max. 1.3.3 (Nepotianus epitome): *Iudaeos quoque, qui Romanis tradere sacra sua conati erant, idem Hispalus urbe exterminavit arasque privatas e publicis locis abiecit.*
8. See E. N. Lane, *JRS,* 69 (1979), 35–38; as against, e.g., M. Hengel, *Judaism and Hellenism* (London, 1974), I, 263.
9. See the discussion of P. R. Trebilco, *Jewish Communities in Asia Minor* (Cambridge, 1991), 140–142.
10. Cf. H. J. Leon, *The Jews of Ancient Rome* (Philadelphia, 1960), 3–4; Hengel,

Judaism and Hellenism, I, 263; M. Stern, *Greek and Latin Authors on Jews and Judaism* (Jerusalem, 1976), I, 359, with earlier bibliography; idem, *Zion,* 44 (1979), 7–8 (Hebrew); P. Schäfer, *Judeophobia* (Cambridge, Mass., 1997), 51; H. D. Slingerland, *Claudian Policymaking and the Early Imperial Repression of Judaism at Rome* (Atlanta, 1997), 41–42.

11. Lane, *JRS,* 69 (1979), 37; rejected, without argument, by D. Wardle, *Valerius Maximus: Memorable Deeds and Sayings, Book 1* (Oxford, 1998), 150–151.

12. The idea is accepted without difficulty by E. M. Smallwood, *The Jews under Roman Rule* (Leiden, 1981), 129–130; L. H. Feldman, *Jew and Gentile in the Ancient World* (Princeton, 1993), 93, 301–302. Denied by M. Goodman, *Mission and Conversion* (Oxford, 1994), 82–83.

13. As does S. Alessandri, *StudClassOrient,* 17 (1968), 187–198, who argues that the absence of other testimony and the unlikelihood of anti-Jewish actions at a time when Rome and Judaea had good diplomatic relations undermine the reliability of Valerius' evidence. See also A. J. Marshall, *Phoenix,* 29 (1975), 140–141; J. M. G. Barclay, *Jews in the Mediterranean Diaspora* (Edinburgh, 1996), 286. But arguments from silence are shaky in so ill-documented a subject. And formal relations between the states have no real bearing on actions toward immigrants in Rome.

14. Cf. Alessandri, *StudClassOrient,* 17 (1968), 198; Barclay, *Jews in the Mediterranean Diaspora,* 286. Alessandri's conclusion that Valerius conceived the episode to ingratiate himself with Tiberius has little to recommend it, despite the recent endorsement by Slingerland, *Claudian Policymaking,* 43–45.

15. Cf. Leon, *Jews of Ancient Rome,* 3–4; Schürer, *History,* I, 197; Smallwood, *Jews under Roman Rule,* 129–130, with earlier bibliography; eadem in *CHJ,* III, 172.

16. On the embassy, see I Macc. 14.17–18, 14.24, 14.40. The chronology is discussed by Stern, *Greek and Latin Authors,* I, 359–360; idem, *Zion,* 44 (1979), 5 (Hebrew); J. Sievers, *The Hasmoneans and Their Supporters* (Atlanta, 1990), 117.

17. The idea appears in Leon, *Jews of Ancient Rome,* 4, with bibliography; M. Stern, in Safrai and Stern, *Jewish People,* I, 160–161; idem, *Zion,* 44 (1979), 8 (Hebrew); Feldman, *Jew and Gentile,* 301; Schäfer, *Judeophobia,* 255, n. 8.

18. So E. Bickerman, *RIDA,* 5 (1958), 150; Goodman, *Mission and Conversion,* 82–83.

19. For Antiochus' benefactions, see Jos. *Ant.* 12.136–146; for the transfer of Jews to Asia Minor, Jos. *Ant.* 12.147–153.

20. Cf. C. Guignebert, *Le monde juif vers le temps de Jésus* (Paris, 1950), 235; cited by Leon, *Jews of Ancient Rome,* 4.

21. Val. Max. (Paris epitome): *levibus et ineptis ingeniis fallaci siderum interpretatione quaestuosam mendaciis suis caliginem inicientes.* The expulsion of Chaldeans is confirmed by Livy, *Oxyr. Per.* 54. Cf. also Servius, *Ad Aen.* 8.187. Rightly noted by Alessandri, *StudClassOrient,* 17 (1968), 188. On the Chaldeans as astrologers and possible reasons for expulsion, see Wardle, *Valerius Maximus,* 149.

22. So, rightly, Stern, *Zion*, 44 (1979), 9–10 (Hebrew).

23. Suet. *Rhet.* 1.2; Gellius, 15.11.1. See the discussion by E. S. Gruen, *Studies in Greek Culture and Roman Policy* (Leiden, 1990), 170–174.

24. See sources and discussion in Gruen, *Studies*, 174–177.

25. Athenaeus, 12.547a; Aelian, *VH*, 9.12; Suda, s.v. Epikouros.

26. One might note, for instance, the severe crackdown on the Bacchanalian cult in the 180s, followed closely by the burning of "Pythagorean" books ascribed to the legendary king Numa Pompilius, and the passage of the *lex Orchia*, the first sumptuary law to impose restrictions on the lavishness of the dinner table. The next sumptuary measure, the *lex Fannia,* came in 161, also the year of the expulsion of Greek professors. The subject is treated in some detail, with full references, in Gruen, *Studies*, 34–78, 158–179.

27. Macrobius, *Sat.* 3.17.6.

28. Macrobius, *Sat.* 3.17.7ff. Lucilius, fr. 1200, 1307, M; Gellius, 2.24.11–12; *Vir. Ill.* 72; Pliny, *NH*, 8.223.

29. Cic. *Pro Flacco*, 67: *exportari aurum non oportere cum saepe antea senatus tum me consule gravissime iudicavit.* That the ban encompassed silver, as well as gold, is clear from Cic. *In Vat.* 12.

30. Cic. *Pro Flacco*, 67–68.

31. Cic. *Pro Flacco*, 67: *multitudinem Iudaeorum flagrantem non numquam in contionibus.* B. Wardy, *ANRW,* II.19.1 (1979), 603, 609, wrongly asserts that these were Jewish witnesses from Asia. They were, in fact, a crowd of demonstrators on the fringe of the tribunal; Cic. *Pro Flacco,* 69: *vox in coronam turbamque effunditur.* On the Aurelian Steps as a site for *contiones,* cf. Cic. *Pro Cluent.* 93.

32. Cic. *Pro Flacco*, 67: *cum aurum Iudaeorum nomine quotannis ex Italia et ex omnibus nostris provinciis Hierosolymam exportari soleret.*

33. See discussion with sources in Schürer, *History,* I, 236–242.

34. Cic. *Pro Flacco*, 67: *barbarae superstitioni;* 69: *istorum religio sacrorum a splendore huius imperii, gravitate nominis nostri, maiorum institutis abhorrebat . . . quam cara dis immortalibus esset docuit, quod est victa.*

35. Cic. *Pro Flacco*, 3, 6–26, 60–66.

36. This was observed long ago by Y. Levi, *Zion,* 7 (1942), 109–124 (Hebrew). See also Stern, *Greek and Latin Authors,* I, 194; Wardy, *ANRW,* II.19.1 (1979), 601–609; Marshall, *Phoenix,* 29 (1975), 141–142; Barclay, *Jews in the Mediterranean Diaspora,* 287–288. Cicero's statements as a reflection of Roman perceptions of Jews are taken more seriously by Feldman, *Jew and Gentile,* 173–174, and Schäfer, *Judeophobia,* 181–182. J.-E. Berard, *SCI,* 19 (2000), 113–131, sees them as a feature of Cicero's political, religious, and moral conservatism.

37. Cic. *Pro Flacco*, 67.

38. It does not follow that Jews received a special exemption from the general ban on export of gold, an exemption violated by Flaccus, as was argued by J. Juster, *Les Juifs dans l'empire romaine* (Paris, 1914), I, 379–381. See the cogent arguments of Marshall, *Phoenix,* 29 (1975), 144–146.

39. E. S. Gruen, *The Last Generation of the Roman Republic* (Berkeley, 1974), 426–427.

40. Marshall, *Phoenix*, 29 (1975), 150–151.

41. A. Drummond, *Athenaeum*, 87 (1999), 138–144.

42. Cic. *Pro Flacco*, 67: *multitudinem Iudaeorum flagrantem non numquam in contionibus.*

43. Cic. *Pro Flacco*, 66: *illa turba . . . scis quanta sit manus, quanta concordia, quantum valeat in contionibus.*

44. For this notion, see Levi, *Zion*, 7 (1942), 129–132 (Hebrew); Leon, *Jews of Ancient Rome*, 8; Stern, in Safrai and Stern, *Jewish People*, I, 161; Wardy, *ANRW*, II.19.1 (1979), 610–611; M. Pucci Ben Zeev, *Athenaeum*, 65 (1987), 338–339; Schäfer, *Judeophobia*, 181.

45. Notice that Cicero also claims that Phrygians and Mysians frequently disrupt Roman *contiones; Pro Flacco*, 17. That evidently refers to immigrant communities, not liberated slaves. At *Pro Flacco*, 70, Cicero, having gone through the charges leveled by Greeks and complaints of the Jews, turns to the allegations of *cives Romani*. This, in fact, leads into his assault on the notorious *negotiator* Appuleius Decianus, another witness against Flaccus. It does not follow that the Jews, who were there as protestors, not as witnesses, had no Roman citizens among them.

46. Philo, *Leg.* 155.

47. For the campaign of Pompey, see Jos. *BJ*, 1.138–154; *Ant.* 14.48–79; for Gabinius' victory, Jos. *BJ*, 1.162–174; *Ant.* 14.82–97; for Cassius' takeover and conquest, Jos. *BJ*, 1.180–181; *Ant.* 14.119–122.

48. Josephus specifies only the family of Aristobulus as brought to Rome for Pompey's triumph; *BJ*, 1.154, 157–158; *Ant.* 14.71, 79. Gabinius took three thousand captives; Jos. *BJ*, 1.163; *Ant.* 14.85; Cassius also corralled three thousand; Jos. *BJ*, 1.180; *Ant.* 14.120. There is no indication as to how many of these captives were transported to Rome.

49. On the synagogue inscriptions, see, most recently, P. Richardson, in K. P. Donfried and P. Richardson, eds., *Judaism and Christianity in First-Century Rome* (Grand Rapids, 1998), 17–29. The evidence of the catacombs is too late to shed much light on Jewish dwellings in the period of the Republic and early Empire. See L. V. Rutgers, *The Hidden Heritage of Diaspora Judaism* (Leuven, 1998), 45–71.

50. G. Fuks, *JJS*, 36 (1985), 29–30, rightly warns against assuming that emancipation came very swiftly.

51. There is, to be sure, a distinction between formal and informal manumission, the latter, at least from the Augustan age, according fewer privileges and defining a separate status (the Junian Latins), something less than full citizenship, thus postponing transition to the latter—although the goal would be reached in a subsequent generation. On the forms of manumission, see, e.g., A. M. Duff, *Freedmen in the Early Roman Empire* (Oxford, 1928), 21–28; A. Watson, *The Law of Persons in the Later Roman Republic* (Oxford, 1967), 185–200; S. Treggiari, *Roman Freedmen during the Late Republic* (Oxford, 1969), 20–31; A. Watson, *Roman Slave Law* (Baltimore, 1987), 23–26; J. F. Gardner, *Being a Roman Citizen* (London, 1993), 8–11. On limitations, the Augustan reforms, and the category of Junian Latins, see Duff, op. cit., 36–49, 75–85; Watson, *Roman Slave Law*, 28–32; Gardner, op. cit., 20–48.

P. R. C. Weaver, *Chiron*, 20 (1990), 275–304, provides a salutary reminder that movement from Junian Latin status to that of full citizenship was slower than has often been thought. For sons of freedmen, see Treggiari, op. cit., 52–67.

52. See the letter of Philip V, king of Macedon, in 217, commenting with surprise and admiration on the Roman practice of granting citizenship to ex-slaves; *Syll.*[3] 543. The reasons for the practice are traced by Gardner, *Being a Roman Citizen*, 19–20, very interestingly, to the idea that the slave who had been an integral part of his master's *familia* would now be embraced by the larger *familia* that constituted Roman society.

53. The main sources are Dio, 37.9.5; Cic. *De Off.* 3.47; *De Leg. Agrar.* 1.13.

54. Cf. the analysis of Gruen, *Last Generation*, 409–411.

55. Tertullian, *Ad Nat.* 1.10, drawing on Varro, a contemporary of the events. Cf. Tertullian, *Apol.* 6; Arnob. 2.73; S. A. Takács, *Isis and Sarapis in the Roman World* (Leiden, 1995), 60–63.

56. Actions against the Isis cult were taken again in 53, Dio, 40.47.3; in 48, Dio, 42.26; and perhaps in 50, Val. Max. 1.3.4, with Wardle, *Valerius Maximus*, 151–152; *contra*: Takács, *Isis and Sarapis*, 57–59.

57. On the *collegia*, see the classic works of J. P. Waltzing, *Étude historique sur les corporations professionelles chez les romains*, 4 vols. (Louvain, 1895–1900), and F. M. De Robertis, *Il diritto associativo romano* (Bari, 1938).

58. Asconius, 7, Clark: *senatus consulto collegia sublata sunt quae adversus rem publicam videbantur esse constituta.*

59. See, e.g., J. Linderski, *Roman Questions: Selected Papers* (Stuttgart, 1995), 165–203 (first published 1968); Treggiari, *Roman Freedmen*, 168–177; J.-M. Flambard, *Ktema*, 6 (1981), 143–166.

60. Sources in *MRR*, II, 196. Most recent discussion in W. J. Tatum, *The Patrician Tribune: Publius Clodius Pulcher* (Chapel Hill, 1999), 117–119.

61. Asconius, 75, Clark: *postea collegia et s.c. et pluribus legibus sunt sublata prater pauca atque certa quae utilitas civitatis desiderasset.*

62. These points and others were made long ago by Juster, *Les Juifs*, I, 413–424, against Mommsen. Some of his arguments are stronger than others, and his position has generally been rejected. But the counter-arguments of S. L. Guterman, *Religious Toleration and Persecution in Ancient Rome* (London, 1951), 130–156, do not shake Juster's case. The similarities he finds between synagogues and *collegia* are superficial, and the basic differences, as noted above, remain fundamental. Guterman's position, that synagogues were equivalent to *collegia,* at least in Roman eyes, still holds the field. See, e.g., G. La Piana, *Foreign Groups in Rome During the First Centuries of the Empire* (Cambridge, Mass., 1927), 348–351; Smallwood, *Jews under Roman Rule*, 133–135; eadem, *CHJ*, III, 170–171; Marshall, *Phoenix*, 29 (1975), 149–150; Barclay, *Jews in the Mediterranean World*, 291–292; W. Cotter, in J. S. Kloppenborg and S. G. Wilson, eds., *Voluntary Associations in the Graeco-Roman World* (London, 1996), 77; P. Richardson, in Kloppenborg and Wilson, op. cit., 90–93. A notable exception is M. H. Williams, in M. Goodman, ed., *Jews in a Graeco-Roman World* (Oxford, 1998), 216–217.

63. Suet. *Iul.* 42: *Cuncta collegia praeter antiquitus constituta distraxit.*

64. Suet. *Aug.* 32: *collegia praeter antiqua et legitima dissolvit.* The term *legitima,* distinct from *antiqua,* may be a *terminus technicus,* thus indicating prior legislation, which must be that of Caesar. See the analysis of De Robertis, *Il diritto associativo,* 177–178; followed and expanded upon by Linderski, *Roman Questions,* 217–223.

65. See on this the discussion of Z. Yavetz, *Julius Caesar and His Public Image* (Ithaca, 1983), 88–90.

66. Jos. *Ant.* 14.215. On the document generally, see above, pp. 92–93.

67. Josephus' phrase is ἐν τῷ διατάγματι. The term διάταγμα should mean an edict rather than a law; see H. J. Mason, *Greek Terms for Roman Institutions* (Toronto, 1974), 127.

68. The proposition, peculiar though it may be, has been embraced by almost all scholars. Cf. Stern, in Safrai and Stern, *Jewish People,* I, 163; idem, *Zion,* 44 (1979), 10–11 (Hebrew); Smallwood, *Jews under Roman Rule,* 134; U. Baumann, *Rom und die Juden* (Frankfurt, 1983), 252; H. Castritius, in T. Klein, ed., *Judentum und Antisemitismus von der Antike bis zur Gegenwart* (Düsseldorf, 1984), 22–23; Yavetz, *Julius Caesar,* 95; Barclay, *Jews in the Mediterranean Diaspora,* 291–292; Cotter, in Kloppenborg and Wilson, *Voluntary Associations,* 76–78; Richardson, in Kloppenborg and Wilson, op. cit., 93; M. Pucci Ben Zeev, *Jewish Rights in the Roman World* (Tübingen, 1998), 111–112, 459–460; Smallwood, *CHJ,* III, 170–171. But see the doubts of Williams, in Goodman, *Jews in a Graeco-Roman World,* 217–221, on grounds somewhat different from those proposed here.

69. As Williams, in Goodman, *Jews in a Graeco-Roman World,* 218–221, is inclined to do.

70. This renders otiose the question of whether the term *thiasos,* used in Josephus' text here, implies classification of the Jewish synagogues as *collegia.* The paraphrase of Caesar's law, which may have gone through more than one version before the document was transmitted by Josephus, could well have rendered *collegium* with θίασος—a perfectly reasonable rendering. But it does not follow that Jewish associations were formally classified as *collegia.*

71. The phrase *religio licita,* frequently used by, e.g., Guterman, *Religious Toleration,* 103–129, and Smallwood, *Jews under Roman Rule,* 135–136, 344–345, eadem, *CHJ,* III, 169, has no technical authority. It appears only in Tertullian, *Apol.* 21.1. So, rightly, Castritius, in Klein, *Judentum und Antisemitismus,* 22.

72. The events themselves are outlined in Schürer, *History,* I, 330–335.

73. Jos. *BJ,* 2.14–25; *Ant.* 17.219–229.

74. Jos. *BJ,* 2.37–38; *Ant.* 17.248–249.

75. Jos. *BJ,* 2.80; *Ant.* 17.299–300.

76. See Jos. *BJ,* 2.90–91; *Ant.* 17.314.

77. Jos. *BJ,* 2.80; *Ant.* 17.300.

78. Jos. *BJ,* 2.81; *Ant.* 17.301.

79. Suet. *Iul.* 84: *exterarum gentium multitudo circulatim suo quaeque more lamentata est praecipueque Iudaei, qui etiam noctibus continuis bustum frequentarunt.*

80. Jos. *BJ*, 2.101–110; *Ant.* 17.324–338.
81. Jos. *Ant.* 17.330; *BJ*, 2.105.
82. Philo, *Leg.* 155–157.
83. So, for instance, the Augustan measure on *collegia*, reprising or expanding that of Caesar, which dissolved all except the "ancient and legitimate ones" (Suet. *Aug.* 32), surely gave no special concession to Jews—any more than Caesar's had. Philo rightly makes no mention of it. Smallwood's assertion, *Jews under Roman Rule,* 136, that Augustus exempted Jews from this ban is without foundation. A similar view is found in Barclay, *Jews in the Mediterranean Diaspora,* 292.
84. Philo, *Leg.* 158. Philo's assertion that recipients got either money or food is questionable, perhaps a confusion with later imperial largesse in the form of *congiaria.* Cf. E. M. Smallwood, *Legatio ad Gaium* (Leiden, 1961), 158. That Augustus took steps to regulate the grain distribution is well known; cf. G. Rickman, *The Corn Supply of Ancient Rome* (Oxford, 1980), 61–66, 179–185; D. Kienast, *Augustus,* 2nd ed. (Darmstadt, 1999), 198–200. The issue may have arisen in connection with Augustus' reduction of numbers on the grain lists; Suet. *Aug.* 40, 42; Dio, 55.10.1.
85. Philo does record Augustus' gifts to the Temple in Jerusalem and his subsidies for sacrifices made there; *Leg.* 157, 317; cf. 319; Jos. *Ant.* 5.562–563. But this need be no more than an instance of the *princeps'* general policy of supporting cults and shrines in the empire. For Augustus' private views on the Temple, see Suet. *Aug.* 93: he praised his grandson Gaius for passing through Judaea *without* making supplication in Jerusalem. As is well known, one of the synagogues in Rome, as much later inscriptions inform us, was called "synagogue of the Augustesioi" in Trastevere; *CIJ,* I, no. 284 = *JIWE,* II, no. 547; *CIJ,* I, no. 301 = *JIWE,* II, no. 301; *CIJ,* I, no. 338 = *JIWE,* II, no. 169; *CIJ,* I, no. 368 = *JIWE,* II, no. 189; *CIJ,* I, no. 416 = *JIWE,* II, no. 194; *CIJ,* I, no. 496 = *JIWE,* II, no. 542. It is possible, though by no means provable, that the synagogue received that designation in the lifetime of Augustus and as tribute to his benefaction to the Jews. See, e.g., Leon, *Jews of Ancient Rome,* 142; Richardson, in Donfried and Richardson, *Judaism and Christianity,* 20–21. But if the title expressed gratitude to Augustus, it may well refer to his benefactions to diaspora Jews in the East, on which see above, pp. 101–102. Another Roman synagogue enjoyed the name of "synagogue of the Agrippesioi" (*CIJ,* I, no. 365 = *JIWE,* II, no. 170; *CIJ,* I, no. 425 = *JIWE,* II, no. 130; *CIJ,* I, no. 503 = *JIWE,* II, no. 549). If this pays honor to Agrippa, it too probably recalls his letters and edicts on Asian Jews. See above, Chapter 3. There is nothing on record of any acts by Agrippa on behalf of Jews in Rome. The same can be said of the "synagogue of the Volumnesioi" (*CIJ,* I, no. 343 = *JIWE,* II, no. 167; *CIJ,* I, no. 402 = *JIWE,* II, no. 100; *CIJ,* I, no. 417 = *JIWE,* II, no. 163; *CIJ,* I, no. 523 = *JIWE,* II, no. 577). This may owe its designation to a certain Volumnius, a Roman official, possibly governor of Syria, who supported Herod in conflicts with Arabs, and perhaps in other matters as well; Jos. *BJ,* 1.535–542; *Ant.* 16.277–283, 16.344–369; see the discussions of Leon, op. cit., 157–159, and Richardson, op. cit., 22. If so, this supplies another instance of Roman syna-

gogues paying honor to Romans who advanced Jewish causes abroad. It says nothing about benefits supplied to Jews in Rome.

86. On eligibility for grain, see D. van Berchem, *Les distributions de blé et d'argent à la plèbe romain sous l'empire* (Geneva, 1939), 27–31; Kienast, *Augustus,* 198–200.

87. The notion that Jews required a series of specified exemptions and explicit privileges sets the whole issue on its head. For this approach, see, e.g., La Piana, *Foreign Groups,* 343–345.

88. Jos. *Ant.* 18.65–80.

89. Ibid., 18.81–84.

90. Tac. *Ann.* 2.85. There is no reason to question Tacitus' date. Josephus appears to put the events in the procuratorship of Pontius Pilate (26–36 CE), but that is not his only chronological blunder; see Stern, *Zion,* 44 (1979), 13–15 (Hebrew).

91. Suet. *Tib.* 36.

92. Dio, 57.18.5a.

93. Seneca, *Epist. Moral.* 108.22.

94. So, e.g., E. M. Smallwood, *Latomus,* 15 (1956), 315–322; eadem, *Jews under Roman Rule,* 203–210; eadem, *CHJ,* III, 173–174; Stern, *Greek and Latin Authors,* II, 70–71; idem, *Zion,* 44 (1979), 26–27 (Hebrew); Feldman, *Jew and Gentile,* 302–303; D. R. Schwartz, in R. S. Wistrich, ed., *Demonizing the Other: Antisemitism, Racism, and Xenophobia* (Amsterdam, 1999), 78. Schäfer, *Judeophobia,* 109–111, maintains that Tiberius was concerned not about Jewish proselytizing activities but about the growing number of proselytes. Barclay, *Jews in the Mediterranean Diaspora,* 298–301, similarly sees the explanation as "Roman fear of cultural invasion." In the view of E. L. Abel, *REJ,* 127 (1968), 383–386, only the proselytes were actually banished, which flies in the face of most of the evidence.

95. Dio, 57.18.5a: τῶν τε Ἰουδαίων πολλῶν ἐς τὴν Ῥώμην συνελθόντων καὶ συχνοὺς τῶν ἐπιχωρίων ἐς τὰ σφέτερα ἔθη μεθιστάντων, τοὺς πλείονας ἐξήλασεν.

96. As M. H. Williams, *Latomus,* 48 (1989), 767–768, is inclined to do. To be sure, the fragment could refer to any year between 17 and 20 CE, not necessarily 19. But the likelihood of two expulsions of Jews within a four-year period is infinitesimal; so, rightly, Feldman, *Jew and Gentile,* 302. And it would not weaken Dio's authority anyway.

97. So Goodman, *Mission and Conversion,* 83, 144. See, on Jews generally, Dio, 37.16.5–17.1: τὸ γένος τοῦτο κολουσθὲν μὲν πολλάκις, αὐξηθὲν δὲ ἐπὶ πλεῖστον.

98. Tacitus, *Ann.* 2.85, speaks of *quattuor milia libertini generis ea superstitione infecta,* but the idea that "infected with this superstition" refers to converts is unacceptable. The four thousand *libertini* of military age were hardly all converts—and conversion to Judaism was certainly not confined to freedmen. To be sure, Tacitus' comment about renunciation of the wicked rituals as allowing for exemption, *nisi certam ante diem profanos ritus exuissent,* might apply more easily to converts, but framers of the escape clause may never have expected to have many takers. Suetonius, *Tib.* 36, speaks of the removal of

the "rest of that nation or those holding similar beliefs" *(reliquos gentis eiusdem vel similia sectantes),* but, even if the latter do signify proselytes (by no means an obvious conclusion), they are not the main targets, and Suetonius does not even hint that proselytizing activity provoked the expulsion. The fact that Fulvia, in Josephus' tale, is a convert *(Ant.* 18.82) in no way implies that conversion was the issue at stake. The villains of the piece had nothing to do with her conversion.

99. That, of course, is especially true of the Isis story. Josephus is at pains to show that the punishment of Paulina's deceivers fits the crime far more suitably than does the victimization of Jews. See the analysis of H. R. Moehring, *NT,* 3 (1959), 293–304; cf. Williams, *Latomus,* 48 (1989), 775–778; Slingerland, *Claudian Policy,* 67–69. The Josephan tall tales were taken seriously by W. A. Heidel, *AJP,* 41 (1920), 38–47, who saw Roman punishment as the result of indignation at Jews seeking to make Fulvia into a temple prostitute! The imaginative thesis is adequately refuted by Smallwood, *Latomus,* 15 (1956), 317–319. Leon, *Jews of Ancient Rome,* 17, also accepts Josephus' explanation for Tiberius' motive.

100. H. Solin, *ANRW,* II.29.2 (1983), 686; and, especially, Williams, *Latomus,* 48 (1989), 765–784. L. V. Rutgers, *CA,* 13 (1994), 64–65, is critical of Williams' arguments but leaves open the possibility that unrest in 19 CE prompted Roman action against Jews and Isis worshippers, and regards the issue of law and order as paramount; op. cit., 67–70.

101. Cic. *Pro Flacco,* 66–67; Suet. *Iul.* 84; Horace, *Sat.* 1.4.143; all cited by Williams, *Latomus,* 48 (1989), 780.

102. A more serious comment is that of Suetonius with regard to the reign of Claudius, referring to the Jews as *assidue tumultuantes;* Suet. *Claud.* 25.4. But that needs fuller treatment; see above, pp. 38–39.

103. See R. F. Newbold, *Athenaeum,* 52 (1974), 110–121. Note, especially, Tac. *Ann.* 4.6.

104. See the powerful argument of Slingerland, *Claudian Policymaking,* 50–63, who also gives copious reference to modern scholarship—although devoting too much space to quarreling with it.

105. Tac. *Ann.* 2.85.4: *actum et de sacris Aegyptiis Iudaicisque pellendis . . . ceteri cederent Italia, nisi . . . profanos ritus exuissent.*

106. Suet. *Tib.* 36: *externas caerimonias, Aegyptios Iudaicosque ritus compescuit . . . reliquos gentis eiusdem vel similia sectantes.*

107. Dio, 57.18.5a.

108. Seneca, *Epist. Moral.* 108.22: *alienigena tum sacra movebantur et inter argumenta superstitionis ponebatur quorundam animalium abstinentia.*

109. Philo, *Leg.* 160–161.

110. Slingerland, *Claudian Policymaking,* 69–77, does his best to undermine Philo's testimony and to claim Sejanus as a mere instrument of the emperor's will. But he cannot get around Philo's express statements about Tiberian measures and actions. On all this, see above, pp. 35–36.

111. Philo, *Leg.* 160.

112. Dio, 60.6.6. See above, pp. 36–38.

113. Tac. *Ann.* 2.87; cf. M. H. Williams, *Latomus,* 14 (1989), 782.

114. A summary of the events, with sources, may be conveniently found in B. Levick, *Tiberius the Politician* (London, 1976), 154–157.

115. Tac. *Ann.* 2.69: *reperiebantur solo ac parietibus erutae humanorum corporum reliquiae, carmina et devotiones et nomen Germanici plumbeis tabulis insculptum, semusti cineres ac tabo obliti aliaque malefica, quis creditur animas numinibus infernis sacrari.* Cf. 3.13.

116. Tac. *Ann.* 2.82.

117. The discussion of popular reactions and official commemorations of Germanicus comes in *Ann.* 2.82–84, the expulsion in 2.85.

118. It is noted in the *Fasti Antiates; Inscr. Ital.* XIII, 2.209.

119. See Tac. *Ann.* 2.71–72; cf. 3.16.

120. Tac. *Ann.* 2.27–32; Suet. *Tib.* 36; Dio, 57.15.8.

121. Tac. *Ann.* 2.85; Suet. *Tib.* 36; Jos. *Ant.* 18.84.

122. Among the useful discussions, see E. T. Merrill, *CP,* 14 (1919), 366–371; Stern, *Greek and Latin Authors,* II, 72; idem, *Zion,* 44 (1979), 12 (Hebrew); Smallwood, *Jews under Roman Rule,* 207–208; Williams, *Latomus,* 48 (1989), 770; Slingerland, *Claudian Policymaking,* 52–53.

123. Tac. *Ann.* 2.85: *si ob gravitatem caeli interissent, vile damnum.*

124. The references in Eusebius are plainly drawn from Philo and do not represent independent testimony; see Smallwood, *Latomus,* 15 (1956), 323–324; D. Hennig, *L. Aelius Seianus* (Munich, 1975), 164–169; Stern, *Zion,* 44 (1979), 16 (Hebrew).

125. Philo, *Flacc.* 1.

126. Philo, *Leg.* 159–160.

127. Philo, *Flacc.* 161.

128. So, rightly, Merrill, *CP,* 14 (1919), 372; Smallwood, *Latomus,* 15 (1956), 324–329. The mistaken conflation of Philo's evidence with the testimony on 19 may be found, e.g., in Leon, *Jews of Ancient Rome,* 16–17; Stern, in Safrai and Stern, *Jewish People,* I, 164. Hennig, *Seianus,* 170–173, argues unconvincingly that Philo deliberately obscured the events of 19 in order to blame them on Sejanus. Similarly, see Stern, *Zion,* 44 (1979), 15–17 (Hebrew). For Slingerland, *Claudian Policymaking,* 69–77, Sejanus' actions simply carried out the consistent and unwavering policy of the emperor designed to repress Judaism. But this thesis requires that Philo's praises of Tiberius be sheer invention and deception, a hard case to make.

129. See Tac. *Ann.* 4.59.

130. Philo, *Leg.* 160.

131. Any connection between the slanders in Rome and the accusations in the provinces is altogether obscure. Philo associates the machinations of Sejanus only with the former. The latter may, in fact, have arisen in individual provincial cities, perhaps of a variety similar to those dealt with by Augustus or Agrippa earlier; see above, Chapter 3. Tiberius, in any case, reasserted prior policy of endorsing the protection of Jewish practices.

132. For Agrippa and the accession of Claudius, see Jos. *Ant.* 19.236–245; *BJ,* 207–209; cf. Dio, 60.82–3. Agrippa's role is doubtless exaggerated by

Josephus. See V. Scramuzza, *The Emperor Claudius* (Cambridge, Mass., 1940), 51–63. For the award of territory, see Jos. *Ant.* 19.274–275; *BJ*, 2.215–216.

133. On all this, see above, pp. 79–83.

134. Dio, 60.6.6: τούς τε Ἰουδαίους πλεονάσαντας αὖθις, ὥστε χαλεπῶς ἂν ἄνευ ταραχῆς ὑπὸ τοῦ ὄχλου σφῶν τῆς πόλεως εἰρχθῆναι, οὐκ ἐξήλασε μὲν, τῷ δὲ δὴ πατρίῳ βίῳ χρωμένους ἐκέλευσε μὴ συνεθροίζεσθαι.

135. See the cogent arguments of H. D. Slingerland, *JQR*, 79 (1989), 307–308; idem, *Claudian Policymaking*, 98–99; H. Botermann, *Das Judenedikt des Kaisers Claudius* (Stuttgart, 1996), 104–107, with extensive bibliography.

136. Dio, 60.6.6.

137. Cf. Slingerland, *Claudian Policymaking*, 107–108.

138. So Slingerland, *Claudian Policymaking*, 131–134.

139. As the Loeb translation has it: "ordered them, while continuing their traditional mode of life, not to hold meetings." Botermann, *Das Judenedikt*, 103, 124–132, goes too far in this direction, and has Claudius order the Jews both to hold to traditional ways and not to gather; *er befahl ihnen, bei ihrer überkommenen Lebensweise zu bleiben und sich nicht zu versammeln*. This not only does violence to the text, but it requires belief that the emperor had to compel Jews to practice Judaism! The argument is needed to bolster Botermann's thesis that Jewish communities were being disrupted by Christian proselytizing.

140. See above, Chapter 3.

141. *CPJ*, II, no. 153, lines 86–87.

142. Dio, 60.6.7.

143. Posturing plainly prevails here. The text does not indicate even that the gatherings had generated any disturbances, only that the *princeps* sought to reform the life-style of his subjects; Dio, 60.6.7. There had certainly been no Jewish uprisings. Dio speaks simply of what *might happen* if Claudius resorted to expulsion.

144. Suet. *Claud.* 25.4: *Iudaeos impulsore Chresto assidue tumultuantis Roma expulit.*

145. See, e.g., Scramuzza, *Claudius*, 150–151; Leon, *Jews of Ancient Rome*, 23–27; S. Benko, *Theologische Zeitschrift*, 25 (1969), 406–408; Stern, *Greek and Latin Authors*, II, 114–116; idem, *Zion*, 44 (1979), 20–22 (Hebrew); G. Luedemann, *Paul, Apostle to the Gentiles: Studies in Chronology* (Philadelphia, 1984), 6–7, 164–171; Schürer, *History*, III.1, 77; Feldman, *Jew and Gentile*, 303–304. Further bibliography can be found in Slingerland, *JQR*, 79 (1989), 306. D. R. Schwartz, *Agrippa I* (Tübingen, 1990), 94–95, combines the sources by interpreting Dio as referring to a partial expulsion—which distorts the text.

146. So, rightly, Slingerland, *Claudian Policymaking*, 105–109. Most scholars now recognize that Dio and Suetonius refer to separate episodes, the first a ban on assemblies, the second an expulsion; see, e.g., A. Momigliano, *Claudius: The Emperor and His Achievement* (Oxford, 1934), 31–33; Smallwood, *Jews under Roman Rule*, 210–216; Barclay, *Jews in the Mediterranean Diaspora*, 303–306; Botermann, *Das Judenedikt*, 48–49, 54–57,

104–107; Slingerland, *Claudian Policymaking*, 97–110. There is little help to be had from the Scholiast on Juvenal, 4.11, who refers to Jews moving to Aricia after being expelled from Rome. We have no way of knowing whether this applies to the expulsion under Tiberius or to that under Claudius—or to yet another event; cf. Stern, *Greek and Latin Authors*, II, 655.

147. Orosius, 7.6.15. The text, unfortunately, presents puzzles of its own. Orosius claims Josephus as his source for the date of the expulsion, and goes on to quote Suetonius, on whose information he places greater weight. But the extant text of Josephus has nothing to this effect.

148. According to H. D. Slingerland, *JQR*, 83 (1992), 140–142, and idem, *Claudian Policymaking*, 123–129, Orosius simply made it up, using the fact of a famine in the next year as a means to demonstrate divine retaliation for Claudius' persecution of Christians; cf. also Feldman, *Jew and Gentile*, 304. That is excessive speculation. Botermann, *Das Judenedikt*, 55–56, with valuable bibliography, questions Orosius' testimony but gives no grounds for dismissing it. Similarly, Schürer, *History*, III.1, 77, n. 92. But the silence of Tacitus is not decisive. And the idea of sheer fabrication on Orosius' part is hard to credit.

149. Acts, 18.2.

150. For Paul's hearing, see Acts, 18.12–17. On the date of Gallio's proconsulship, see *Syll.*³ 801, an inscription from Delphi giving a letter of Claudius and making reference to Gallio. For discussion, see *PIR*, IV, J, no. 757. The chronology is challenged by Slingerland, *JBL*, 110 (1991), 439–449. But see the proper criticism by J. Murphy-O'Connor, *JBL*, 112 (1993), 315–317. Even on Slingerland's strained chronology, however, Gallio's tenure would fall between 49 and 54, allowing readily for the possibility that Claudius' expulsion edict came in 49. The idea of two separate expulsion decrees within a three- or four-year period would be most implausible indeed. The suggestion of Leon, *Jews of Ancient Rome*, 25, adopted by Stern, *Zion*, 44 (1979), 21 (Hebrew), that Aquila and Priscilla may have been wandering around Italy for some years after expulsion from Rome and before reaching Corinth is a tortured and desperate effort to retroject the date. The arguments of Luedemann, *Paul*, 164–171, that Acts, 18 gives no support for an expulsion in 49, are extreme and unpersuasive.

151. Cf. Slingerland, *Claudian Policymaking*, 152–159, 226–227.

152. Benko, *Theologische Festschrift*, 25 (1969), 406–418, who regards Chrestus as a Jewish zealot stirring up insurrection, gives a list of Jewish-Gentile tensions over the decade and a half prior to the Claudian edict—but none of them occurred in Rome.

153. See the illuminating survey of scholarship on this matter, going back to the fifteenth century, by Botermann, *Das Judenedikt*, 72–95. Botermann follows a long line of scholars who find a reference to Christ or Christianity in the testimony of Suetonius; op. cit., 95–102. Add also Stern, *Zion*, 44 (1979), 19–23 (Hebrew). Momigliano, *Claudius*, 33, even stated that the onus of proof rests upon those who wish to deny it; similarly, Smallwood, *Jews under Roman Rule*, 211; eadem, *CHJ*, III, 176. More properly, Slingerland, *Claudian Policymaking*, 203–217, shifts the burden to the other side.

154. Botermann's recent suggestion, *Das Judenedikt*, 98–101, that Jewish converts to Christianity in Rome would have asserted "Christ lives," thus leading gullible Roman officials to conclude that he was in Rome and directing subversion in the synagogues, is ingenious but most implausible—especially as she concedes that Suetonius knew very well the difference between Christ and his followers.

155. This is well known. See now the recent survey of testimony by Slingerland, *Claudian Policymaking*, 179–201. But Slingerland's bold and original hypothesis, op. cit., 151–168, 227–241, that Chrestus was an imperial freedman who instigated Claudius to take action against the Jews, founders on philological grounds. The ablative absolute in Suet. *Claud.* 25.4 occurs within the participial phrase, bracketed by *Iudaeos* and *tumultuantis*. Suetonius cannot be taken to mean that *impulsore Chresto* modifies the verb.

156. It does not help to enlist Aquila and Priscilla in this cause. They may have become Christian converts after coming under Paul's influence; Acts, 18.18, 18.26. But they are identified only as Jews when they left Italy; Acts, 18.2.

157. Dio, 60.23.1.

158. Tac. *Ann.* 11.15: *ne vetustissima Italiae disciplina per desidiam exolesceret.*

159. Tac. *Ann.* 11.11; Suet. *Claud.* 21.2; Pliny, *NH,* 6.159, 8.160.

160. Tac. *Ann.* 12.23–24; Gellius, 13.14.

161. Tac. *Ann.* 12.23; cf. Dio, 37.24.1–2.

162. Tac. *Ann.* 12.3, 12.8; cf. Seneca, *Apoc.* 8.2.

163. Suet. *Claud.* 25.5. These instances of Claudian piety are usefully collected and commented on by Momigliano, *Claudius,* 27–28, and Scramuzza, *Claudius,* 145–156.

164. Suet. *Claud.* 25.5.

165. The evidence for this is late: the sixth-century writer John Lydus, *de Mensibus,* 4.59. Scramuzza, *Claudius,* 152–155, is at pains to dispute this information, perhaps unnecessarily so.

166. Suet. *Claud.* 25.5; cf. Pliny, *NH,* 29.53–54.

167. Tac. *Ann.* 12.52: *de mathematicis Italia pellendis factum senatus consultum atrox et irritum.*

168. See above, p. 40.

169. That is the basic thesis of Slingerland's *Claudian Policymaking.* Cf. Noy, *Foreigners at Rome,* 42.

170. So, e.g., Scramuzza, *Claudius,* 151; Smallwood, *Jews under Roman Rule,* 215–216; B. Levick, *Claudius* (London, 1990), 87, 121; Rutgers, *CA,* 13 (1994), 56–74.

171. The phrase in Suet. *Claud.* 25.4: *Judaeos tumultuantis . . . expulit,* most likely means "he expelled those Jews engaged in the (putative) rioting," not all Jews. And even those who left may have soon returned. Aquila and Priscilla seem to have done so; Rom. 16.3–4.

172. Cf. Acts, 28.17–31.

173. There is no need here to rehash the innumerable arguments on the propriety of labeling pagans as "anti-semitic," a phrase unknown before the late nineteenth century. Among many other works, see I. Heinemann, *RE,* Suppl. V (1931), 3–43; N. W. Goldstein, *JR,* 19 (1939), 346–364; R. Marcus, in K. S.

Pinson, ed., *Essays on Antisemitism* (New York, 1946), 61–78; M. Simon, *Verus Israel* (Oxford, 1986; first published 1964), 202–233; R. R. Ruether, *Faith and Fratricide: The Theological Roots of Anti-Semitism* (New York, 1974), 23–63; J. N. Sevenster, *The Roots of Pagan Anti-Semitism in the Ancient World* (Leiden, 1975); J. L. Daniel, *JBL,* 98 (1979), 45–65; J. G. Gager, *The Origins of Anti-Semitism* (Oxford, 1985), 13–88; Pucci Ben Zeev, *Athenaeum,* 65 (1987), 335–359; N. de Lange, in S. L. Gilman and S. T. Katz, eds., *Anti-Semitism in Times of Crisis* (New York, 1991), 21–37; Z. Yavetz, *JJS,* 44 (1993), 1–22; Feldman, *Jew and Gentile,* 123–187; D. Rokeah, *REJ,* 154 (1995), 281–294; Yavetz, *Judenfeindschaft in der Antike* (Munich, 1997), 17–43, 46–53, 95–114; Schäfer, *Judeophobia,* 34–118, 163–211.

174. Cf. M. Goodman, *The Ruling Class of Judaea* (Cambridge, 1987), 31–251.

175. Cf. Feldman, *Jew and Gentile,* 149–153; idem, *JSP,* 16 (1997), 44, 51–52; Schäfer, *Judeophobia,* 183–192.

176. Neither "monotheism" nor "polytheism" constitutes a single phenomenon, definable and identifiable. And "paganism," of course, only came into existence as a Christian concept. Cf. M. Beard, J. North, and S. Price, *Religions of Rome* (Cambridge, 1998), I, 212, 286–287, 312. Jewish monotheism is itself problematical; cf. P. Hayman, *JJS,* 42 (1991), 1–15.

177. Varro, *apud* Augustine, *De Consensu Evangelistarum,* I.30: *Varro autem ipsorum, quo doctiorem aput se neminem inveniunt, deum Iudaeorum Iovem putavit nihil interesse censens;* so also I.31, I.42.

178. Tac. *Hist.* 5.5.4: *Aegyptii pleraque animalia effigiesque compositas venerantur, Iudaei mente sola unumque numen intellegunt.* Schäfer, *Judeophobia,* 39–41, rightly stresses that Tacitus' comment on the Jewish god is a favorable one. The passage seriously undermines the view of H. Heinen, *Trierer Theologische Zeitschrift,* 101 (1992), 124–149, that Tacitus' excursus on the Jews was drawn largely from anti-Jewish Egyptian sources.

179. Cic. *Pro Flacco,* 67.

180. Seneca, *apud* Augustine, *CD,* 6.11; Plutarch, *De Stoic. Rep.* 38; *De Superst.* 69C; Quintilian, 3.7.21; Tac. *Hist.* 2.4, 5.8.2–3, 5.13.1; *Ann.* 2.85. Cf. also Pliny, *NH,* 13.46. It appears once again in the inscription of the Epicurean Diogenes of Oinoanda probably in the first half of the second century, in a recently published fragment; M. F. Smith, *Anatolian Studies,* 48 (1998), 132, III, lines 12–14.

181. Horace, *Sat.* 1.5.97–101.

182. On *superstitio,* see Beard, North, and Price, *Religions of Rome,* I, 214–227.

183. Tac. *Hist.* 5.4.1: *profana illic omnia quae apud nos sacra, rursum concessa apud illos quae nobis incesta.*

184. Tac. *Hist.* 5.5.1: *cetera instituta, sinistra foeda, pravitate valuere.*

185. Tac. *Hist.* 5.5.2.

186. Seneca, *apud* Augustine, *CD,* 6.11.

187. Some speculation can be found in Z. Yavetz, *Historia,* 47 (1998), 87.

188. Seneca, *Epist. Moral.* 95.47, 108.22. The same holds true for Quintilian, who once refers to Jews as a *perniciosa gens* (3.7.21), but makes no mention of that people anywhere else in his work. The Oinoanda inscription of the early second century CE sets Jews with Egyptians as among the most superstitious

and most abominable of peoples; Smith, *Anatolian Studies,* 48 (1998), 132, III, lines 12–16. But this need not reflect *Roman* attitudes.

189. Varro, *apud* Augustine, *CD,* 4.31: *quod si adhuc, inquit, mansisset, castius dii observarentur.*

190. Tac. *Hist.* 5.5.4.

191. So, e.g., Wardy, *ANRW,* II.19.1 (1979), 629–631; K. Rosen, *Gymnasium,* 103 (1996), 115–117.

192. Cf. Philo, *Leg.* 157, 232, 280, 356; Jos. *BJ,* 2.197, 2.409; *CAp.* 2.77.

193. Philo, *Leg.* 133; *Flacc.* 49.

194. Philo, *Leg.* 330–333; Jos. *Ant.* 18.299–301. Philo's story that Caligula changed his mind once again and ordered the construction of a new statue in Jerusalem, *Leg.* 337–338, is a dubious concoction. Nothing, in any case, came of the matter.

195. This, of course, would not prevent some enemies of the Jews elsewhere from attempting to use the issue against them, as Apion did in Alexandria—but evidently to no effect; Jos. *CAp.* 2.73.

196. Cf. Tac. *Ann.* 15.74.

197. Tac. *Hist.* 5.9.2: *iussi a C. Caesare effigiem eius in templo locare arma potius sumpsere.*

198. Juv. 14.100–102: *Romanas autem soliti contemnere leges/ Iudaicum ediscunt et servant ac metuunt ius,/ tradidit arcano quodcumque volumine Moyses.*

199. So Schäfer, *Judeophobia,* 185.

200. Rosen's argument, *Gymnasium,* 103 (1996), 107–126, that Tacitus feared a resumption of Jewish hostilities on the basis of anti-Roman prophecies is highly improbable.

201. See, e.g., Hecataeus of Abdera, *apud* Diod. 40.3.4; Manetho, *apud* Jos. *CAp.* 1.239; Posidonius, *apud* Diod. 34/5.1–3; Apollonius Molon, *apud* Jos. *CAp.* 2.148.

202. Tac. *Hist.* 5.5.1–2.

203. Ibid., 5.3.1.

204. Juv. 14.103–104.

205. On Jewish isolationism, see Sevenster, *Roots of Pagan Anti-Semitism,* 89–119. On its perception as misanthropy and Jewish responses, see Feldman, *Jew and Gentile,* 125–153.

206. The strongest advocate for Jewish missionary activity is L. H. Feldman, who has made the case repeatedly and with powerful argumentation. See, e.g., Feldman, in M. Mor, ed., *Jewish Assimilation, Acculturation, and Accommodation* (Lanham, Md., 1992), 24–37; idem, in H. W. Attridge and G. Hata, eds., *Eusebius, Christianity, and Judaism* (Detroit, 1992), 372–408; idem, *Jew and Gentile,* 288–341, with valuable earlier bibliography at 553–554. But an increasing number of scholars have taken up the cudgels on the other side: e.g., S. McKnight, *A Light among the Gentiles: Jewish Missionary Activity in the Second Temple Period* (Minneapolis, 1991), 11–77; E. Will and C. Orrieux, *Proselytisme juif? histoire d'une erreur* (Paris, 1992), passim; S. J. D. Cohen, in Mor, op. cit., 14–23; M. Goodman, in J. Lieu, J. North, and T. Rajak, eds., *Jews among Pagans and Christians in the Roman Empire*

(London, 1992), 53–78; idem, *Mission and Conversion*, 60–90; L. V. Rutgers, *JQR*, 85 (1995), 363–370. The position of Schäfer seems curiously inconsistent; *Judeophobia*, 106–118, 183–192.

207. See the cogent arguments of Goodman, *Mission and Conversion*, 60–90.

208. The lines of the poet Horace, *Sat.* 1.4.139–143, writing in the age of Augustus, are often taken to imply vigorous missionary activity; so, e.g., Stern, *Greek and Latin Authors*, I, 323; Sevenster, *Roots of Pagan Anti-Semitism*, 203; Feldman, *Jew and Gentile*, 299. But Horace says only that "we [the band of poets], like the Jews, will compel you to defer to this throng" *(ac veluti te Iudaei cogemus in hanc concedere turbam)*. There is no good reason to think that Horace is here speaking of conversion. The Jews never, on any reckoning, "compelled" persons to convert! And it is taking the lines too seriously to interpret them as showing that the Jews constituted a known pressure group in Rome. For this interpretation, see J. Nolland, *VigChr*, 33 (1979), 347–355; Barclay, *Jews in the Mediterranean Diaspora*, 295–296; Schäfer, *Judeophobia*, 107–108.

209. So, e.g., Daniel, *JBL*, 98 (1979), 62–64; Gager, *Origins of Anti-Semitism*, 59–61; Pucci Ben Zeev, *Athenaeum*, 65 (1987), 344–348; Rosen, *Gymnasium*, 103 (1996), 116, 121; Schäfer, *Judeophobia*, 183–192; Yavetz, *Historia*, 47 (1998), 96–98.

210. Seneca, *apud* Augustine, *CD*, 6.11: *cum interim usque eo sceleratissimae gentis consuetudo convaluit, ut per omnes iam terras recepta sit; victi victoribus leges dederunt.*

211. Ibid.: *multa in tempore urgentia non agendo laedantur.*

212. Tac. *Hist.* 5.5.1–2.

213. Tac. *Hist.* 5.5.3: *hinc generandi amor et moriendi contemptus.*

214. Juv. 14.100–102.

215. Juv. 3.60–66.

216. Juv. 15.1–13.

217. Tac. *Hist.* 5.5.1, 5.8.1.

218. Martial, 12.57.13.

219. Juv. 3.10–16, 3.296, 6.542–547.

220. On the economic situation of Jews in the Hellenistic and Roman periods, see the useful collection of material and discussion by Sevenster, *Roots of Pagan Anti-Semitism*, 57–88; S. Applebaum, in Safrai and Stern, *Jewish People*, II, 631–727. The argument of Feldman, *Jew and Gentile*, 107–113, that references to Jewish beggary are ironic, signifying that Jews were actually envied for their wealth, is hard to credit.

221. So, rightly, Feldman, *JSP*, 16 (1997), 39–42.

222. Horace, *Sat.* 1.9.60–78; Ovid, *Ars Amat.* 1.75–76, 1.415–416; cf. *Remed. Amor.* 217–220. Just what Horace means by equating the Sabbath with the "thirtieth" remains a mystery. See the discussions of Stern, *Greek and Latin Authors*, I, 326; R. Goldenberg, *ANRW*, II.19.1 (1979), 436–438; Feldman, *SCI*, 10 (1989–1990), 87–112; Schäfer, *Judeophobia*, 85.

223. Suet. *Aug.* 76.2.

224. Strabo, 16.2.40; Trogus, *apud* Justin, 36.2.14.

225. Petronius, fr. 37 (Ernout).

226. Martial, 4.4.7.
227. For some conjectures, see Goldenberg, *ANRW*, II.19.1 (1979), 439–441; Feldman, *Jew and Gentile*, 161–163.
228. Cf. Tac. *Hist.* 5.4.4.
229. Tibullus, 1.13.8; Frontinus, *Strat.* 2.1.17; Tac. *Hist.* 5.4.4.
230. Plut. *Quaest. Conviv.* 4.6.2.
231. Tac. *Hist.* 5.5.5: *quippe Liber festos laetosque ritus posuit, Iudaeorum mos absurdus sordidusque.*
232. Agatharchides, *apud* Jos. *CAp.* 1.209–210 and Jos. *Ant.* 12.5–6; Dio, 37.16.1–4; Strabo, 16.2.40; Frontinus, *Strat.* 2.1.17; cf. Plut. *De Superst.* 8.169C. On the vexed question of whether Jews would fight on the Sabbath, see Goldenberg, *ANRW*, II.19.1 (1979), 430–433; A. J. Holladay and M. D. Goodman, *CQ*, 36 (1986), 165–171; B. Bar-Kochva, *Judas Maccabaeus* (Cambridge, 1989), 474–493.
233. Seneca, *apud* Augustine, *CD*, 6.11: *septimam fere partem aetatis suae perdant vacando.*
234. Juv. 14.105–106.
235. Tac. *Hist.* 5.4.3.
236. Persius, 5.179–182.
237. Seneca, *Epist. Moral.* 95.47: *nec lumine dii egent et ne homines quidem delectantur fuligine.*
238. Pliny, *NH*, 31.24: *In Judaea rivus sabbatis omnibus siccatur.*
239. Plut. *Cic.* 7.
240. Macrobius, *Sat.* 2.4.11: *melius est Herodis porcum esse quam filium.* In all likelihood, Augustus made the gag in Greek, where he could pun on the words υἱός and ὗς.
241. Philo, *Leg.* 361.
242. Petronius, fr. 37 (Ernout): *numen porcinum.*
243. Juv. 6.159–160: *et vetus indulget senibus clementia porcis.* Cf. 14.98–99. Schäfer, *Judeophobia*, 77–81, correctly observes the absence of polemic in the satirists' comments.
244. Tac. *Hist.* 5.4.2.
245. Epictetus, *apud* Arrian, *Dissertationes*, 1.22.4 (Souilé).
246. Plut. *Quaest. Conviv.* 4.5.2.
247. Ibid., 4.5.3. The arguments are taken perhaps too seriously by Schäfer, *Judeophobia*, 72–74, 77.
248. Cf. Feldman, *Jew and Gentile*, 153–158; S. D. J. Cohen, *The Beginnings of Jewishness: Boundaries, Varieties, Uncertainties* (Berkeley, 1999), 39–49.
249. Horace, *Sat.* 1.9.70: *curtis Iudaeis.*
250. Tac. *Hist.* 5.5.2: *circumcidere genitalia instituerunt, ut diversitate noscantur.*
251. Philo, *Spec. Leg.* 1.1–2.
252. Petronius, *Sat.* 68.4–8; cf. 102.14; fr. 37 (Ernout).
253. Juv. 14.103–104.
254. Martial, 7.30.5.
255. Martial, 11.94.
256. Martial, 7.82.
257. For efforts along these lines, see, e.g., Daniel, *JBL*, 98 (1979), 45–65; Gager,

Origins of Anti-Semitism, 35–88; L. H. Feldman, in D. Berger, ed., *History and Hate: The Dimensions of Anti-Semitism* (Philadelphia, 1986), 29–36; idem, *Jew and Gentile,* 123–287, passim; idem, *JSP,* 16 (1997), 39–52.

258. See the sensible comments of Barclay, *Jews in the Mediterranean Diaspora,* 310, 318–319.

2. THE JEWS IN ALEXANDRIA

1. Philo, *Flacc.* 65–96; *Leg.* 127–134.
2. Philo, *Flacc.* 2–5, 8.
3. Ibid., 9–11, 14–16.
4. Ibid., 20–24.
5. Ibid., 25–40.
6. Philo, *Flacc.* 41–44, 51; *Leg.* 132, 134, 346.
7. Philo, *Flacc.* 53–57, 62–64; *Leg.* 121–123, 132.
8. Philo, *Flacc.* 65–72; *Leg.* 127–131.
9. Philo, *Flacc.* 73–85.
10. Ibid., 86–91, 95–96.
11. Philo, *Leg.* 132–134.
12. Philo, *Flacc.* 97–103; *Leg.* 178–179. The resolution probably hailed Gaius upon his accession to the throne or, less likely, gave thanks for his recovery from illness in late 37. Cf. E. M. Smallwood, *The Jews under Roman Rule* (Leiden, 1981), 236–237; D. R. Schwartz, *Agrippa I* (Tübingen, 1990), 76.
13. Philo, *Flacc.* 109–115, 121–124.
14. Ibid., 125–126, 147–151, 181.
15. Ibid., 169–170.
16. Ibid., 185–191.
17. Philo, *Leg.* 133.
18. Ibid., 120–121, 133, 162–165.
19. R. Barraclough, *ANRW,* II.21.1 (1984), 459–461, claims to detect hostility toward Gaius in Philo's *In Flaccum,* but can find no instances of action against the Jews.
20. Philo, *Flacc.* 26, 31.
21. A. Kushnir-Stein, *JJS,* 51 (2000), 227–242, interestingly proposes that Agrippa came to Alexandria on invitation of the Jews, who sought his aid in forwarding a petition to the emperor. This, of course, requires jettisoning Philo's evidence as tendentious and apologetic. But not only that. Would it not have been far more effective for the Jews to contact Agrippa in Rome, where he could deliver the petition in person, than to summon him to Alexandria in order to present him with a document that he would later dispatch from Palestine?
22. Philo, *Flacc.* 109–115; cf. *Flacc.* 5.
23. Philo, *Leg.* 346.
24. Ibid., 361–368; see, especially, 367.
25. By contrast, H. D. Slingerland, *Claudian Policymaking and the Early Imperial Repression of Judaism at Rome* (Atlanta, 1997), 77–81, prefers the portrait of Gaius in the *Legatio ad Gaium* as determinedly hostile to the Jews to

that of the *In Flaccum,* but he can produce no concrete instance of a relevant imperial action with regard to Alexandria. Gaius' policy on the Temple in Jerusalem, of course, is a different matter altogether and would require separate treatment.

26. Barraclough, *ANRW,* II.21.1 (1984), 461–468, sees the portrait of Flaccus as a strictly negative one.

27. Philo, *Flacc.* 2–5, 8.

28. See the cogent arguments of A. N. Sherwin-White, *Latomus,* 31 (1972), 820–828.

29. Philo, *Flacc.* 24.

30. Ibid., 35, 40.

31. Ibid., 32–33.

32. Ibid., 43–44. Cf. also *Flacc.* 51; *Leg.* 132.

33. The text can be conveniently consulted in *CPJ,* II, no. 154. For discussion, see H. A. Musurillo, *The Acts of the Pagan Martyrs* (Oxford, 1954), 93–104; Tcherikover, *CPJ,* II, 60–64; J. Mélèze-Modrzejewski, *The Jews of Egypt* (Philadelphia, 1995), 167–169.

34. Philo, *Flacc.* 53–54.

35. Philo, *Leg.* 132.

36. Philo, *Flacc.* 76.

37. One might observe also that when Jewish leaders prepared a resolution for Caligula, they presented it first to Flaccus, asking him to pass it on to the emperor; Philo, *Flacc.* 97–101; *Leg.* 178–179. The document was probably no more than the conventional praise bestowed by provincials upon the accession of a new *princeps* to the throne. Flaccus dragged his feet on the matter, perhaps to avoid friction with those who were pressing for action against the Jews. But the very fact that Jewish leaders brought the resolution to Flaccus is noteworthy. They obviously did not regard him as an implacable foe.

38. Philo, *Flacc.* 73–81.

39. Ibid., 82: ἀλλ' ἔσπευδε καὶ κατήπειγεν ἕνεκα τῆς πρὸς τὸν ἐναντίον ὄχλον ἀρεσκείας, ταύτῃ νομίζων ἐξοικειώσασθαι μᾶλλον αὐτὸν εἰς ἅπερ διενοεῖτο.

40. Certainly Flaccus would not have encouraged the burning of synagogues—which would entail the destruction of dedications to the emperor contained therein; Philo, *Flacc.* 49; *Leg.* 133. Nor is there any indication that Flaccus ordered the herding of Jews into a single district of the city; Philo, *Flacc.* 55; *Leg.* 124.

41. Philo, *Flacc.* 84–85.

42. Philo elsewhere makes a mysterious reference to a recent official known to him, "in charge of Egypt," who made a vain attempt to force Jews to abandon observance of the Sabbath, engaging in some fiercely arrogant, even megalomaniacal, language; *Somn.* 2.123–132. It is most unlikely that the official in question is Flaccus, for whom no such acts are recorded in the *In Flaccum.* The postulate would require that Philo compose the *De Somnis* and the bulk of his treatises late in life. See E. R. Goodenough, *The Politics of Philo Judaeus: Practice and Theory* (New Haven, 1938), 29–30; Barraclough, *ANRW,* II.21.1 (1984), 532. Some have assigned the reference to Ti. Julius

Alexander, either as prefect of Egypt or in a lesser capacity; D. R. Schwartz, *Studia Philonica Annual*, 1 (1989), 63–69; R. A. Kraft, in B. A. Pearson, ed., *The Future of Early Christianity* (Minneapolis, 1991), 131–141. But his prefecture too raises chronological problems. The official may, in fact, be a tax collector in an unspecified region of Egypt. See Philo, *Spec. Leg.* 3.159–162, a passage largely ignored and nowhere analyzed in connection with *Somn.* 2.123–132. Both passages are introduced by πρώην and refer to a ruthless official. In any case, neither one implicates Flaccus or even refers explicitly to Alexandria.

43. Philo, *Flacc.* 20. Cf. *Flacc.* 137.
44. Ibid., 18–23.
45. Ibid., 22–23, 29–31, 41.
46. Ibid., 4. It is quite unjustifiable to label these associations as "anti-semitic clubs," as, e.g., J. G. Gager, *The Origins of Anti-Semitism* (Oxford, 1985), 48–50; W. Bergmann and C. Hoffmann, in R. Erb and M. Schmidt, *Antisemitismus und jüdische Geschichte* (Berlin, 1987), 28–35.
47. Philo, *Flacc.* 135–138.
48. Ibid., 18: τοῖς δ' ἐξ ἀρχῆς ἀνομολογηθεῖσιν ἐχθροῖς ἐσπένδετο καὶ συμβούλοις περὶ πάντων ἐχρῆτο. This analysis is buttressed by the papyrus fragment noted above that indicates strained relations between Flaccus, Dionysios, and Isidoros, later patched up by an arrangement and a monetary transaction; *CPJ*, II, no. 154. See above, p. 58.
49. Philo, *Flacc.* 19: οἱ δ' ἐγκότως γὰρ εἶχον τὸ κατηλλάχθαι δοκεῖν λόγῳ μόνον ἐπιμορφάσαντες, ἔργοις δὲ κατὰ διάνοιαν ἀσύμβατα μνησικακοῦντες.
50. *CPJ*, II, no. 156a, lines 17–19.
51. Philo, *Flacc.* 10–16.
52. Ibid., 128–129.
53. The narrative appears in Philo, *Flacc.* 137–145. Just when this episode, offered as an excursus by Philo, occurred in the course of events cannot be determined. But Philo's statement that Isidoros had once earned favor with Flaccus and subsequently had a falling out suggests that this confrontation came late in Flaccus' tenure; *Flacc.* 138.
54. Philo, *Flacc.* 125–127; cf. *Flacc.* 135.
55. A papyrus fragment mentions a comment of Isidoros in connection with a trial in Rome at the time of Caligula; *CPJ*, II, no. 155, lines 24–35. This probably has no direct link to the charges against Flaccus. (Caligula ordered the accuser in this case to be burned.) But it places Isidoros in Rome and indicates his influence at court.
56. Philo, *Flacc.* 5.
57. So, e.g., H. I. Bell, *JRS*, 31 (1941), 3–8; V. Tcherikover, *Hellenistic Civilization and the Jews* (Philadelphia, 1959), 309–332; idem, *JJS*, 14 (1963), 7–20; Barraclough, *ANRW*, II.21.2 (1984), 422–424; A. A. Barrett, *Caligula: The Corruption of Power* (London, 1989), 184–185; Z. Yavetz, *Judenfeindschaft in der Antike* (Munich, 1997), 102–103.
58. Smallwood, *Jews under Roman Rule*, 233–235; Gager, *Origins of Anti-Semitism*, 43–50; J. M. G. Barclay, *Jews in the Mediterranean Diaspora* (Edin-

burgh, 1996), 48–49; Yavetz, *Judenfeindschaft,* 103–104; D. R. Schwartz, in R. S. Wistrich, ed., *Demonizing the Other: Antisemitism, Racism, and Xenophobia* (Amsterdam, 1999), 75–77; A. Jakab, *Henoch,* 21 (1999), 151.

59. Modrzejewski, *Jews of Egypt,* 161–173; R. Alston, *Greece and Rome,* 44 (1997), 165–175.

60. Tcherikover, *CPJ,* I, 55–56; idem, *JJS,* 14 (1963), 17–20; Barraclough, *ANRW,* II.21.2 (1984), 426–428; Barclay, *Jews in the Mediterranean Diaspora,* 60–71. In the formulation of Bergmann and Hoffmann, in Erb and Schmidt, *Antisemitismus und jüdische Geschichte,* 15–46, the clash grew out of shifts or feared shifts in the political balance, with the Greeks and Flaccus collaborating in a calculated effort to resist or reduce Jewish claims on civic privileges. See the criticisms (too harshly expressed) by P. Schäfer, *Judeophobia* (Cambridge, Mass., 1997), 156–160.

61. L. Cracco-Ruggini, in J. H. D'Arms and C. C. Kopff, *The Seabourne Commerce of Ancient Rome* (Memoirs of the American Academy in Rome, 26) (1980), 55–76. Legitimate criticisms are leveled by M. Pucci Ben Zeev, *JSJ,* 21 (1990), 227–235.

62. L. H. Feldman, *Jew and Gentile in the Ancient World* (Princeton, 1993), 113–117.

63. Philo, *Flacc.* 4.

64. Ibid., 136–145.

65. A notable exception is Schäfer, *Judeophobia,* 143–145.

66. Philo, *Leg.* 159.

67. Philo, *Flacc.* 78–80.

68. Philo, *Flacc.* 55–72, 95–96; *Leg.* 120–131.

69. Philo, *Flacc.* 29: οἱ δ᾽ ὑπὸ φθόνου ῥηγνύμενοι—βάσκανον γὰρ φύσει τὸ Αἰγυπτιακόν—καὶ . . . ἅμα διὰ τὴν παλαιὰν καὶ τρόπον τινὰ φύσει γεγενημένην πρὸς Ἰουδαίους ἀπέχθειαν.

70. Philo, *Flacc.* 17. The distinction between "Egyptians" and "Alexandrians" is explicit in *Flacc.* 78: τοὺς μὲν γὰρ Αἰγυπτίους . . . τοὺς δὲ Ἀλεξανδρέας. Cf. *Flacc.* 92.

71. That is plain from his reference to those dwelling in the city and "all Egypt"; Philo, *Flacc.* 43: ὅτι καὶ ἡ πόλις οἰκήτορας ἔχει διττούς, ἡμᾶς τε καὶ τούτους, καὶ πᾶσα Αἴγυπτος.

72. Philo, *Leg.* 132–139. E. M. Smallwood, *Philonis Alexandrini Legatio ad Gaium* (Leiden, 1961), 86, 88, repeatedly inserts the word "Greeks" in her translation of this segment, whereas the term does not appear in the original. Cf. eadem in *CHJ,* III, 182. And the reference to animal worship in *Leg.* 139 rules it out. Cf. *Leg.* 166.

73. Philo, *Leg.* 162–164.

74. Ibid., 120: "The promiscuous and unruly mob of Alexandrians, perceiving this and thinking that a most suitable opportunity had arrived, attacked us and displayed the hatred which had long been smoldering, throwing everything into chaos and confusion." The fact that Philo does censure the Egyptians as culprits has long been recognized but repeatedly explained away as a deliberate insult to the Alexandrian Greeks by lumping them with Egyp-

tians, or as a rhetorical device to disguise Greek opposition as Egyptian. See, e.g., H. Willrich, *Judaica* (Göttingen, 1900), 128–130; H. Box, *Philonis Alexandrini In Flaccum* (London, 1939), 79; Smallwood, *Legatio*, 225, 246; Barclay, *Jews in the Mediterranean Diaspora*, 74. This begs the question. And it fails to account for Philo's sharp differentiation between Alexandrians and Egyptians in *Flacc.* 78. K. Goudriaan, in P. Bilde et al., eds., *Ethnicity in Hellenistic Egypt* (Aarhus, 1992), 86–93, appears to believe that the adversaries of the Jews were "Graeco-Egyptians," recent immigrants from the countryside to Alexandria who wished to be regarded as Hellenes. This is purely speculative. For P. Borgen, in Bilde, op. cit., 128, Philo includes Alexandrian Greeks within a larger category of "Egyptians" by contrast with Jews as part of a theological dualism.

75. Jos. *CAp.* 2.69.

76. Cf. Jos. *CAp.* 2.28–32, 2.65–67, 2.121–124; *BJ*, 2.487.

77. See, especially, *Wisdom*, 10.15–21, 11.5–16, 12.23–27, 15.14–19, 17.2–21, 19.13–17. On the date and character of the work, see D. Winston, *The Wisdom of Solomon* (Garden City, 1979), 3–69.

78. See III Sibyl. 29–45, 314–318, 348–349, 596–600. The nature and objectives of this compilation more generally are disputed. Cf. the contrasting interpretations of Barclay, *Jews in the Mediterranean Diaspora*, 216–228, E. S. Gruen, *Heritage and Hellenism: The Reinvention of Jewish Tradition* (Berkeley, 1998), 268–290, and J. J. Collins, *Between Athens and Jerusalem: Jewish Identity in the Hellenistic Diaspora* (2nd ed., Grand Rapids, 2000), 83–97, 160–165.

79. See, e.g., *Jos. As.* 2.3–5, 3.10, 7.1, 8.4–5, 9, 10.13–14, 11.7–9, 12.5. The scholarship on this work is vast and growing. See the bibliography in Schürer, *History*, III.1, 550–552. For recent literature, see the items cited by Collins, *Between Athens and Jerusalem*, 230–239.

80. III Macc. 3.2–10: οἱ ἀλλόφυλοι, by contrast with οἱ δὲ κατὰ τὴν πόλιν Ἕλληνες; 4.1: τοῖς ἔθνησιν. The effort of Barclay, *Jews in the Mediterranean Diaspora*, 196–197, to dismiss this as a "rhetorical ploy" is unpersuasive. III Maccabees repeatedly pits Jews against τὰ ἔθνη or ἀλλοεθνεῖς, not against Greeks; cf., e.g., 4.6, 5.6, 5.13, 6.9, 6.13, 6.15, 7.4. Cf. Collins, *Between Athens and Jerusalem*, 126–127.

81. Ezekiel, in Euseb. *PE*, 9.28.2: κακούμενον κακῶν ὑπ' ἀνδρῶν καὶ δυναστείας χερός; 9.28.12: ὕβριν ἀνθρώπων κακῶν; 9.29.14. The fragments of Ezekiel are assembled, with valuable commentaries, by H. Jacobson, *The Exagoge of Ezekiel* (Cambridge, 1983), 50–67, and Holladay, *Fragments*, II, 344–405.

82. On the Alexandrian writers challenged by Josephus, see Jos. *CAp.* 1.288–2.78. On the *Acta Alexandrinorum*, see the texts assembled by Musurillo, *Acts of the Pagan Martyrs*—although only a few contain snide remarks about the Jews.

83. The successor was C. Vitrasius Pollio, who was certainly there by April, 39; *ILS*, no. 8899.

84. Philo, *Leg.* 190, reports that the Jewish embassy at least left in the winter. The Greek one would hardly have allowed much time to elapse. The year itself re-

mains disputed. The full-scale hearing before Gaius apparently did not take place before the autumn of 40. Gaius himself was away on campaign between mid-39 and mid-40. This means that the envoys might have been sitting in Rome for well over a year before they were heard, not an impossible scenario. It is somewhat less likely that they waited for at least a year before sending embassies. The evidence is presented fairly and in full by Smallwood, *Legatio,* 47–50, who opts for winter, 39/40, but acknowledges that the issue remains open. A case for 38/39 is made by Schwartz, *Agrippa I,* 196–199.

85. Philo, *Leg,* 172, 174, 355, 370; Jos. *Ant.* 18.257.
86. Philo, *Leg.* 181.
87. Ibid., 349–351.
88. Ibid., 178. Philo describes this memorandum as a summary of the petition earlier transmitted by Agrippa. But since much had happened in Alexandria since Agrippa's presence there, the envoys must have added a good deal—or expected to do so in oral testimony. Cf. Smallwood, *Legatio,* 252–253.
89. Philo, *Leg.* 193–194, 349, 363.
90. Ibid., 191.
91. Ibid., 355. Cf. Jos. *Ant.* 18.257–258, who ascribes these accusations to Apion.
92. Philo, *Leg.* 356.
93. Ibid., 177, 180, 349–360, 373. Cf. Jos. *Ant.* 18.260.
94. Philo, *Leg.* 166–178. It is hazardous to pin much faith on this fanciful portrait of Helikon, the sinister anti-Jewish influence on Gaius, as Barclay, *Jews in the Mediterranean Diaspora,* 55, appears to do.
95. Philo, *Leg.* 358–359.
96. Ibid., 357.
97. Ibid., 359. Cf. ibid., 368. Smallwood's effort to find a serious exchange here (*Jews under Roman Rule,* 244–245) is unpersuasive.
98. Philo, *Leg.* 361–363.
99. Ibid., 367.
100. Cf. ibid., 368: ἀντὶ δικαστηρίου θέατρον.
101. *LetArist.* 12–13, 35–36; cf. Jos. *CAp.* 1.186, 2.44; *Ant.* 12.8, 12.45–47. On Jewish immigration into Egypt, see the comments of Tcherikover, *CPJ,* I, 3–5; Modrzejewski, *Jews of Egypt,* 73–74; Barclay, *Jews in the Mediterranean Diaspora,* 20–22, 27–29.
102. For the relevant papyri see *CPJ,* I, nos. 18–32, with the comments of Tcherikover, *CPJ,* I, 11–16, 146–147. Cf. *CIJ,* II, no. 1531 = *JIGRE,* no. 115; P. Köln, III, 144. It does not follow that they organized themselves in separate Jewish units, as is argued by A. Kasher, *The Jews in Hellenistic and Roman Egypt* (Tübingen, 1985), 38–48. See also Modrzejewski, *Jews of Egypt,* 83–87.
103. *CIJ,* II, nos. 1424–1431 = *JIGRE,* nos. 1–8. See the comments of Horbury and Noy, *JIGRE,* xiii–xvi and *ad loc.* Cf. Modrzejewski, *Jews of Egypt,* 77–80.
104. Jos. *CAp.* 2.49 (Ptolemy VI); *Ant.* 13.285–287, 13.349 (Cleopatra III). Josephus drew on Strabo for the latter notice, but his direct quotation from Strabo does not assert that Cleopatra's whole force was placed in their hands.

105. Other references to Jewish soldiers in the Ptolemaic period can be found in Jos. *CAp.* 1.200–204, 2.64; *Ant.* 14.99, 14.131–132; *BJ,* 1.175, 1.190–192.

106. See the discussion of Tcherikover, *CPJ,* I, 194–203, with nos. 48–124, 127, 132, 137. Cf. Kasher, *Jews in Egypt,* 58–63. See also Jos. *Ant.* 20.147.

107. Philo, *Flacc.* 56–57; *Leg.* 129; cf. III Macc. 3.10; Jos. *Ant.* 18.159. See Tcherikover, *CPJ,* I, 48–50.

108. Tcherikover, *CPJ,* I, 17; Kasher, *Jews in Egypt,* 55–58.

109. Philo, *Flacc.* 41, 45, 48, 53; *Leg.* 132, 134, 137–138, 152, 191, 346; *Mos.* 2.216. Cf. III Macc. 2.28, 3.29, 4.18, 7.20; Philo, *Somn.* 2.127; Jos. *Ant.* 13.65–66. This includes the "largest and most celebrated" synagogue, mentioned by Philo (*Leg.* 134) and elaborately described in rabbinic sources; see Smallwood, *Legatio,* 222–223; Kasher, *Jews in Egypt,* 349–351; L. I. Levine, *The Ancient Synagogue: The First Thousand Years* (New Haven, 2000), 84–89.

110. *CIJ,* II, no. 1440 = *JIGRE,* no. 22: ὑπὲρ βασιλέως Πτολεμαίου καὶ βασιλίσσης Βερενίκης ἀδελφῆς καὶ τῶν τέκνων τὴν προσευχὴν οἱ Ἰουδαῖοι.

111. The Alexandrian inscriptions are *CIJ,* II, no. 1432 = *JIGRE,* no. 13 and *CIJ,* II, no. 1433 = *JIGRE,* no. 9. Others from elsewhere in Egypt, with comparable formulas, include *CIJ,* II, no. 1443 = *JIGRE,* no. 27; *CIJ,* II, no. 1444 = *JIGRE,* no. 28; *CIJ,* II, no. 1441 = *JIGRE,* no. 24; *CIJ,* II, no. 1442 = *JIGRE,* no. 25; *CIJ,* II, no. 1449 = *JIGRE,* no. 125; *CPJ,* II, no. 1532a = *JIGRE,* no. 117; *JIGRE,* no. 126. See the invaluable bibliographical notes supplied by Horbury and Noy for each of these entries. Among other useful discussions, see P. M. Fraser, *Ptolemaic Alexandria* (Oxford, 1972), I, 282–285; II, 440–444; Kasher, *Jews in Egypt,* 106–119; idem, in D. Urman and P. V. D. Flesher, *Ancient Synagogues* (Leiden, 1995), 205–220; J. M. Griffiths, in Urman and Flesher, op. cit., 3–16; Modrzejewski, *Jews of Egypt,* 87–98; D. D. Binder, *Into the Temple Courts: The Place of the Synagogues in the Second Temple Period* (Atlanta, 1999), 233–252.

112. Although the term "synagogue" is regularly applied to the house of worship in the New Testament, Egyptian Jews generally employed the word *proseuche* to denote the structure, while *synagoge* signified "congregation" or "assemblage." The two terms are explicitly distinguished in *CPJ,* I, no. 138, line 1: ἐπὶ τῆς γ[ε]νηθείσης συναγωγῆς ἐν τῆι προσευχῆι. See also the same distinction in the Bosporan manumission decrees; *CIJ,* I, nos. 1, 683, 683a, 684. Donation to a *synagoge* in an inscription possibly from Alexandria surely refers to the assemblage—and may not even be Jewish; *CIJ,* II, no. 1447 = *JIGRE,* no. 20.

113. Fraser, *Ptolemaic Alexandria,* I, 283, misleadingly states that "the Judaism, whatever its nature, was largely concealed beneath the pagan exterior." There was no concealment.

114. The grant comes on a bilingual (Greek and Latin) decree issued by Ptolemy Euergetes, probably Ptolemy VIII, and his queen, with the Latin version added later; *CIJ,* II, no. 1449 = *JIGRE,* no. 125: βασιλίσσης καὶ βασιλέως προσταξάντων ἀντὶ τῆς προανακειμένης περὶ τῆς ἀναθέσεως τῆς προσευχῆς πλακὸς ἡ ὑπογεγραμμένη ἐπιγραφήτω. [vacat] βασιλεὺς

Πτολεμαῖος Εὐεργέτης τὴν προσευχὴν ἄσυλον. *Regina et rex iusserunt.* On the exercise of *asylia* in a Jewish *proseuche,* see *CPJ,* I, no. 129, lines 3–6; cf. Binder, *Into the Temple Courts,* 238–240, 436–439.

115. This is not the place to examine their work and that of other Jewish intellectuals. See, especially, the surveys of Y. Gutman, *The Beginnings of Jewish-Hellenistic Literature,* 2 vols. (Jerusalem, 1958, 1963) (Hebrew); M. Goodman in Schürer, *History,* III.1, 470–704; Holladay, *Fragments.* Cf. also Fraser, *Ptolemaic Alexandria,* I, 687–716; Gruen, *Heritage and Hellenism,* passim; Collins, *Between Athens and Jerusalem,* passim.

116. Cf. J. M. Modrzejewski, in S. J. D. Cohen and E. S. Frerichs, eds., *Diasporas in Antiquity* (Atlanta, 1993), 79–80; idem, *Jews of Egypt,* 81–83; W. Clarysse, *Proc. of XXth Int. Congr. of Papyrologists* (Copenhagen, 1994), 193–203. On Jewish adaptation to Greek law in Egypt—too complex a topic to enter into here—see the summary comments by Modrzejewski, *Jews of Egypt,* 112–119.

117. Philo, *Flacc.* 55; Jos. *BJ,* 2.488, 2.495; *CAp.* 2.33–36.

118. It is foolhardy to draw any inference about a persecution from Jordanes, *Rom.* 81, a very late text which does not, in any case, report Ptolemaic oppression. See the persuasive arguments of I. Levy, *HUCA,* 23 (1950/51), 127–136.

119. Jos. *CAp.* 2.51–55.

120. This interpretation of III Maccabees is argued much more fully by S. R. Johnson, *History as it Should Have Been* (Berkeley, forthcoming), and by Gruen, *Heritage and Hellenism,* 222–236. A darker analysis appears in Barclay, *Jews in the Mediterranean Diaspora,* 192–203. The more benign version has most recently been reiterated by Collins, *Between Athens and Jerusalem,* 122–131. Cf. also the remarks of Modrzejewski, *Jews of Egypt,* 152–153.

121. See III Macc. 1.22–23, 3.3, 5.31, 6.26, 7.7, 7.11.

122. III Macc. 6.36, 7.19–20; Jos. *CAp.* 2.55.

123. Cf. E. J. Bickermann, *RE,* 19 (1928), 800; J. Tromp, *Henoch,* 17 (1995), 315–318.

124. Philo, *Mos.* 2.41–42.

125. Tcherikover, *Hellenistic Civilization and the Jews,* 311–328; idem, *CPJ,* I, 60–66; *JJS,* 14 (1963), 2–7; S. Applebaum, in Safrai and Stern, *Jewish People,* I, 444–445; Smallwood, *Jews under Roman Rule,* 230–232; eadem, *CHJ,* III, 181; Modrzejewski, *Jews of Egypt,* 163–164; Jakab, *Henoch* 21 (1999), 151–153.

126. Jos. *CAp.* 2.35; cf. *BJ,* 2.487; *Ant.* 19.281.

127. Jos. *CAp.* 2.35: ἴσης παρὰ τοῖς Μακεδόσι τιμῆς ἐπέτυχον. The term employed in *BJ,* 2.487, is ἰσοτιμίας or, as two manuscripts have it, ἰσουμοίρας, i.e., presumably, ἰσομοιρίας.

128. Jos. *Ant.* 12.8: τοῖς Μακεδόσιν ἐν Ἀλεξανδρείᾳ ποιήσας ἰσοπολίτας. Cf. Jos. *BJ,* 2.487; *Ant.* 19.281.

129. Cf. Tcherikover, *Hellenistic Civilization and the Jews,* 120–124, with a different analysis of Josephus' motives. See also Barclay, *Jews in the Mediterranean Diaspora,* 70.

130. Strabo, *apud* Jos. *Ant.* 14.117. Cf. Jos. *Ant.* 19.283. The term used for

this official by Philo is "genarch," which must be another expression for ethnarch; *Flacc.* 74; cf. Box, *In Flaccum,* 102–103; Kasher, *Jews in Egypt,* 253. An ἀρχεῖον τῶν Ἰουδαίων, some form of a notary office, is mentioned in a papyrus of the Augustan era; *CPJ,* II, no. 143, line 7.

131. Cf. the discussion of A. Kasher in P. Bilde et al., eds., *Ethnicity in Hellenistic Egypt* (Aarhus, 1992), 109–117, who, however, sees the Jews as possessing a political body quite separate and independent of the Alexandrian Greeks. Philo, *Mos.* 1.34–36, in speaking of the Hebrews in Egypt prior to the Exodus, makes the very interesting statement that foreign settlers ought to be treated as people "bordering on citizens": γειτνιῶντες ἤδη πολίταις. If this is an indirect or even unconscious allusion to Egyptian Jews of his own day, it suggests an acknowledged civic status but one short of full citizenship.

132. For Jewish support to the Caesarian cause, see Jos. *Ant.* 14.127–136, 14.193; *BJ,* 1.187–192; *CAp.* 2.60–61.

133. Jos. *BJ,* 2.488.

134. Jos. *CAp.* 2.37; *Ant.* 14.188. Josephus ascribes the act to "Julius Caesar." But the reference is almost certainly to Augustus. Caesar was in no position to declare Jewish rights in Alexandria, since Egypt had not yet been annexed as a Roman province. And Augustus' name, in any case, was also "Julius Caesar"; hence, an easy error to commit. Cf. Tcherikover, *CPJ,* I, 56.

135. Philo, *Flacc.* 74.

136. Jos. *Ant.* 19.283.

137. For various opinions on this subject, see Box, *In Flaccum,* 102–103; Tcherikover, *Hellenistic Civilization and the Jews,* 412; idem, *CPJ,* I, 57; M. Stern, *Greek and Latin Authors on Jews and Judaism* (Jerusalem, 1974), I, 280–281; Schürer, *History,* III.1, 93; Kasher, *Jews in Egypt,* 254; Schwartz, *Agrippa I,* 104; M. Pucci Ben Zeev, *Jewish Rights in the Roman World* (Tübingen, 1998), 302.

138. Philo, *Flacc.* 74, 76, 80. Philo also makes reference to Jewish ἄρχοντες; *Flacc.* 76, 80, 117. But they are evidently identical with members of the γερουσία.

139. Philo, *Flacc.* 53; *Leg.* 193–194, 349, 363, 371.

140. See Philo, *Flacc.* 53: ἀποκοπέντων . . . ἐθῶν τε πατρίων καὶ μετουσίας πολιτικῶν δικαίων. Cf. Philo, *Leg.* 371. L. Troiani, in F. Parente and J. Sievers, eds., *Josephus and the History of the Greco-Roman Period* (Leiden, 1994), 12–20, rightly disassociates πολιτεία and πολίτης from the strict sense of "citizenship" and "citizen." But he overemphasizes its connotation with reference to the laws of Moses. Many of the citations in Philo and Josephus noted above clearly point to the exercise of civic rights. S. Honigman, *JJS,* 48 (1997), 62–90, by contrast, notes with acuity the institutional character of these phrases and recognizes the influence both of Stoic theory and of the Roman conception of *civitas.* See, especially, Philo, *Leg.* 155–157, 193–194; Jos. *CAp.* 2.38–40. Yet, although she acknowledges the cultural as well as juridical nature of the *politeia,* she holds to the traditional line that Jews sought Alexandrian citizenship in a strict sense in order to escape a situation of inferiority.

141. Philo, *Flacc.* 47. See also Jos. *Ant.* 14.235: *Ioudaioi politai.*

142. The distinction is rightly insisted upon by Kasher, *Jews in Egypt,* 233–261,

and passim. But his further conclusions that Jews possessed an autonomous *politeuma* need not follow.

143. III Macc. 2.30. On the face of it, this seems in direct contradiction to Josephus' statements that the Jews already had *isopoliteia* with the Greeks and Macedonians in Alexandria; *Ant.* 12.8, 19.281; *BJ*, 2.487. In fact, it shows only the diverse and non-technical manner in which the term can be employed.

144. Philo, *Flacc.* 172: ὠνείδισά ποτε ἀτιμίαν καὶ ξενιτείαν αὐτοῖς ἐπιτίμοις οὖσι κατοίκοις. Similarly, Jos. *CAp.* 2.7, 2.33, 2.44; *Ant.* 14.113, 14.117. See also Jos. *Ant.* 14.259, a decree of the Sardians, referring to Jews in their city: οἱ κατοικοῦντες ἡμῶν ἐν τῇ πόλει Ἰουδαῖοι πολῖται. The somewhat cumbersome description implies that Jews enjoyed political rights but not full citizenship in Sardis. Comparable wording, regarding Jews in Antioch, can be found in Jos. *CAp.* 2.39. Cf. the discussions of Kasher, *Jews in Egypt*, 242–243; Pucci Ben Zeev, *Jewish Rights*, 219–220, with additional bibliography.

145. *CPJ*, II, no. 153, lines 94–95 καρπουμένους μὲν τὰ οἰκῖα ἀπολά[υ]οντας δὲ ἐν ἀλλοτρίᾳ πόλει περιουσίας ἀπθόνων ἀγαθῶν.

146. Cf. Philo, *Flacc.* 49–50; *Leg.* 114, 161, 240, 311–313.

147. The term could be used with a juridical meaning, but could also have an informal designation. See D. Delia, *Alexandrian Citizenship during the Roman Principate* (Atlanta, 1991), 23–28. As an analogy, one might note the widespread use of the term *Romaioi* by and for Italians settled in communities of the Greek East, only some of whom were actually Roman citizens; see J. Hatzfeld, *Les Trafiquants italiens dans l'Orient hellénique* (Paris, 1919), 17–51; A. J. N. Wilson, *Emigration from Italy in the Republican Age of Rome* (Manchester, 1966), 88–93, 105–111, 152–155.

148. Jos. *Ant.* 19.281.

149. Philo, *Leg.* 194. Smallwood's translation of δεικνύντας as "to prove" is too strong.

150. Philo, *Leg.* 183.

151. Ibid., 150. On Philo and the attitudes and position of Alexandrian Jews, see Kasher, *Jews in Egypt*, 233–261.

152. Jos. *CAp.* 2.38–39. Apion's famous question, "if they are citizens, why do they not worship the same gods as the Alexandrians?" employs the term *Alexandrini* to signify non-Jews in Alexandria; Jos. *CAp.* 2.65: *quomodo... si sunt cives, eosdem deos quos Alexandrini non colunt?* But that is his usage, not the Jewish one. And, if accurately reported, the statement indicates that Jews claimed political privileges that Apion did not directly challenge.

153. *CPJ*, II, no. 151, lines 2–3: παρὰ Ἑλένου το(ῦ)Τρύφωνο(ς) Ἀλεξαδρέω(ς)... ὢν ἐκ πατρὸς Ἀλεξανδρέ(ως). It is true that the petitioner (or his scribe) revised this version, deleted the first "Alexandrian" and replaced it with Ἰουδαίου τῶν ἀπὸ Ἀλεξαδρε(ίας). This correction may, however, have the purpose of providing a more precise or more informative designation in the formal petition. It need not signify acknowledgment of a diminished status. The widespread notion that the term Ἀλεξανδρεύς would signify Alexandrian citizenship and that Helenos was, therefore, obliged to change it is not directly buttressed by the text. There are, in fact, several corrections in this

document, clearly indicating that it is a rough draft. That citizenship is not at issue here is rightly argued by Kasher, *Jews in Egypt,* 200–207; see also Delia, *Alexandrian Citizenship,* 26. The standard view is most prominently formulated by Tcherikover, in his edition of the document at *CPJ,* II, 29–33, and in *Hellenistic Civilization and the Jews,* 312. So also Modrzejewski, *Jews of Egypt,* 164–165; I. M. Gafni, *Land, Center, and Diaspora: Jewish Constructs in Late Antiquity* (Sheffield, 1997), 45; Schäfer, *Judeophobia,* 155. Barclay, *Jews in the Mediterraenan Diaspora,* 50, wavers between both alternatives.

154. Jos. *Ant.* 14.188.

155. The idea of a separate political entity is advanced by, e.g., V. M. Scramuzza, *The Emperor Claudius* (Cambridge, Mass., 1940), 72–76; Tcherikover, *CPJ,* I, 6–10; Smallwood, *Legatio,* 6–12; eadem, *Jews under Roman Rule,* 227–230; eadem, *CHJ,* III, 177–178; Kasher, *Jews in Egypt,* 208–211, and passim; cf. J. J. Collins, *Jewish Wisdom in the Hellenistic Age* (Louisville, 1997), 140–142; idem, *Between Athens and Jerusalem,* 114–115, 120–122.

156. *LetArist.* 310. To be sure, the term appears also in Jos. *Ant.* 12.108. But that is mere paraphrase of the *Letter of Aristeas.*

157. *LetArist.* 310: στάντες οἱ ἱερεῖς καὶ τῶν ἑρμηνέων οἱ πρεσβύτεροι καὶ τῶν ἀπὸ τοῦ πολιτεύματος οἵ τε ἡγούμενοι τοῦ πλήθους.

158. See the illuminating discussions of C. Zuckerman, *SCI,* 8–9 (1985–1988), 171–185, and G. Lüderitz, in J. W. van Henten and P. W. van der Horst, eds., *Studies in Early Jewish Epigraphy* (Leiden, 1994), 183–225.

159. Zuckerman, *SCI,* 8–9 (1985–1988), 181–184, proposed that *politeuma* here refers to the Jewish state in Palestine, which would suit the Greek well enough, but lacks any parallels. The suggestion of Lüderitz, in van Henten and van der Horst, *Studies,* 206–208, that the reference is to the community of Alexandrian Greeks does at least have a documentary parallel; *CPJ,* II, no. 150, line 5. But who then are the "leaders of the people"? If they are the principal figures of the Greek community, the passage is redundant. If they head the Jewish community in Alexandria, the passage has to refer, in sequence, to elders of the (Jewish) translators, elders of the (Greek) *politeuma,* and leaders of the (Jewish) people in Alexandria. This is awkward and highly implausible. Lüderitz himself has to concede that his reconstruction requires "a somewhat free translation."

160. The new papyri have now been published in exemplary fashion by J. M. S. Cowey and K. Maresch, *Urkunden des Politeuma der Juden von Herakleopolis (144/3–133/2 v. Chr.) (P. Polit. Jud.) Papyrologica Coloniensia,* XXIX (Wiesbaden, 2001). The *politeuma* of Jews is explicitly recorded in documents no. 1, 2, 4, 7, 8. See the discussion by Cowey and Maresch, op. cit., 4–9. One other Jewish *politeuma* is directly attested by documentary evidence: a *politeuma* in the city of Berenice in Cyrenaica, mentioned in two epigraphic decrees; *CJZC,* nos. 70 and 71. But this could be either a political body or a private association.

161. E.g., Box, *In Flaccum,* xxvii–xxx, xxxviii; Tcherikover, *Hellenistic Civilization and the Jews,* 311–328; idem, *CPJ,* I, 61–62; *JJS,* 14 (1963), 4–9; Smallwood, *Legatio,* 12–14, 25; eadem, *Jews under Roman Rule,* 231–235; Schäfer, *Judeophobia,* 156. Barclay, *Jews in the Mediterranean Diaspora,* 65–

71, takes a similar line but believes that the striving after citizenship was confined to only a minority of Alexandrian Jews.

162. The case is made most forcefully by V. A. Tcherikover, *JJP*, 4 (1950), 179–207; idem, *Hellenistic Civilization and the Jews*, 311–318; *CPJ*, I, 60–66; cf. Smallwood, *Jews under Roman Rule*, 231–232; Modrzejewski, *Jews of Egypt*, 163; Collins, *Jewish Wisdom*, 143–144; idem, *Between Athens and Jerusalem*, 116–118; Schäfer, *Judeophobia*, 155 (in modified form); Jakab, *Henoch*, 21 (1999), 151–152. On the poll-tax generally as a symbol of subjection to Rome, see A. K. Bowman and D. Rathbone, *JRS*, 82 (1992), 112–114; Rathbone, *Cahiers du Centre G. Glotz* 4 (1993), 86–99.

163. P Tebt. 103, 121, 189; P Ryl. 667. S. L. Wallace, *AJP*, 59 (1938), 418–422, endeavored to make a case for a Ptolemaic poll-tax that was simply adapted by the Romans, without implication of a new conqueror flexing muscles. But the case is almost entirely speculative.

164. Even that presumption, universally held, depends upon indirect testimony. See S. L. Wallace, *Taxation in Egypt from Augustus to Diocletian* (Princeton, 1938), 119. It rests largely on Josephus' statement in *BJ*, 2.385, regarding population figures for Egypt, exclusive of Alexandria, which he drew from tax records. It is noteworthy, however, that he does not use the term *laographia* here. Other evidence is conveniently summarized by Delia, *Alexandrian Citizenship*, 30–31.

165. *CPJ*, II, no. 150, lines 2–6: φημὶ γὰρ ταύτην φρ[ο]ντιεῖν ἵνα μή τι τῶν μελλόντων τινὲς λαογραφεῖσθαι, τοῖς κατ᾽ ἔτος ἐφήβοις σενεγγραφόμενοι ἐπὶ τὴν δημοσίαν γρα[φήν, τὴν] πρόσοδον ἐλασσῶσι καὶ τὸ π[ο]λίτευμα τῶν Ἀλεξανδρείων ἀ[κ]έραιον ὑπάρχον ἄθρεπτοι καὶ ἀνάγωγοι γεγονότες ἄνθρωποι μολύνωσι. The date cannot be established definitively, and some put it in the time of Claudius. For a summary of the debates and bibliography, see Musurillo, *Acts of the Pagan Martyrs*, 83–92; Tcherikover, *CPJ*, II, 25–29; Delia, *Alexandrian Citizenship*, 117–119.

166. E.g., Tcherikover, *JJP*, 4 (1950), 199; idem, *Hellenistic Civilization and the Jews*, 313; Collins, *Jewish Wisdom*, 144–145; idem, *Between Athens and Jerusalem*, 117.

167. A useful parallel exists in Claudius' letter to the Alexandrians, also preserved on papyrus. Claudius responds to an Alexandrian request by affirming that he will guarantee the Alexandrian πολιτεία for all those enrolled as ephebes up to the time of his accession, with the exception of those who reached the ephebate despite having been born of slave parents; *CPJ*, II, no. 153, lines 53–55. This plainly reflects the same problem aired in the "Boule-papyrus." Persons unqualified by birth were slipping into the ephebate and gaining unjustified access to the Alexandrian *politeia*. But there is no word of Jews.

168. *CPJ*, II, no. 151, lines 5–8: μεταλαβὼν . . . [τῆ]ς ἀρεσκούσης παιδείας, κινδυνεύω . . . τῆς ἰδίας πατρίδος στερηθῆναι.

169. So Tcherikover, *JJP*, 4 (1950), 201; idem, *CPJ*, II, 29–33; Modrzejewski, *Jews of Egypt*, 164–165.

170. Tcherikover, *JJP*, 4 (1950), 201–202; idem, *Hellenistic Civilization and the Jews*, 317–318. Kasher, *Jews in Egypt*, 211–228, takes issue with Tcherikover on almost every point but becomes so enmeshed in polemics that his own view is left obscure.

171. III Macc. 2.28–30.
172. So, most recently, Collins, *Between Athens and Jerusalem,* 124–126, with useful bibliography.
173. III Macc. 2.28–29: πάντας δὲ τοὺς Ἰουδαίους εἰς λαογραφίαν καὶ οἰκετικὴν διάθεσιν ἀχθῆναι . . . τούς τε ἀπογραφομένους χαράσσεσθαι. Cf. 2.32: ἐπειρῶντο ἑαυτοὺς ῥύσασθαι ἐκ τῶν ἀπογραφῶν.
174. *CPJ,* II, no. 156c, lines 25–30: οὔκ εἰσιν Ἀλ[εξανδρεῦσιν] ὁμοιοπαθεῖς, τρόπῳ δὲ Αἰγυπτ[ίων ὁμοῖοι.] οὔκ εἰσι ἴσοι τοῖς φόρον τελ[οῦσι]; Ἀγρίππας: [Αἰ]γ[υπτ]ίοις ἔστησαν φόρους [ο]ἱ ἄρχ[οντες]. . . . . . . ν. τούτοις δὲ οὐδείς. It is here assumed that φόρος stands for λαογραφία, as most scholars take it.
175. E.g., Tcherikover, *JJP,* 4 (1950), 200–201; idem, *CPJ,* II, 79; Collins, *Between Athens and Jerusalem,* 117–118.
176. *CPJ,* II, no. 156c, line 27: οὔκ εἰσι ἴσοι τοῖς φόρον τελ[οῦσι].
177. Some have inferred that Alexandrian citizenship was desirable as a prerequisite for Roman citizenship from the evidence of Pliny, *Ep.* 10.6. So, Scramuzza, *The Emperor Claudius,* 77; Applebaum, in Safrai and Stern, *Jewish People,* I, 444–445; B. Levick, *Claudius* (London, 1990), 183; Bowman and Rathbone, *JRS,* 82 (1992), 116. But it is hard to believe that Alexandrian citizens alone were eligible for the Roman franchise—and hence for service in the Roman legions. See the discussion by Delia, *Alexandrian Citizenship,* 39–45. In any case, Pliny's point applies to Egyptians, not to other *peregrini;* see 10.6.2: *quia inter Aegyptios ceterosque peregrinos nihil interesse credebam.* There is no reason to conclude that Jews required that route to Roman franchise. D. R. Schwartz suggests, *per litt.,* that Pliny is distinguishing here not between Egyptians and other *peregrini* in the land but between all dwellers in Egypt and other *peregrini* elsewhere in the empire. This is a possible, but less likely, reading. Why should Rome require Alexandrian citizenship as a stepping-stone for all who resided in Egypt but demand nothing comparable in the rest of the Roman world? Josephus, in fact, claims that Rome singled out (ethnic) Egyptians as the only people barred from Roman citizenship; *CAp.* 2.41. And the *Gnomon of the Idios Logos* (*BGU,* no. 1210), 55, includes a regulation excluding Egyptians from the Roman army. Cf. A. N. Sherwin-White, *The Letters of Pliny: A Historical and Social Commentary* (Oxford, 1966), 568–569. Roman policy evidently did put ethnic Egyptians into an exceptional (and undesirable) category.
178. The problem is noted, e.g., by Tcherikover, *Hellenistic Civilization and the Jews,* 310–311, and Smallwood, *Legatio,* 13–14. But the answer, that a "modernist party" among the Jews sought citizenship and was prepared to compromise, while the "orthodox" Jews shunned it on religious grounds, is pure construct. The whole distinction between the "orthodox" and the assimilationists, as formulated, e.g., by L. H. Feldman, *Jewish Social Studies,* 22 (1960), 215–237, has no basis in the texts.
179. Jos. *CAp.* 2.65: *quomodo ergo, inquit, si sunt cives, eosdem deos quos Alexandrini non colunt?*
180. Ibid., 2.67: *si autem in vobis Aegyptiis tantae differentiae opinionum sunt, quid miraris super his, qui aliunde in Alexandriam advenerunt, si in legibus a principio constitutis circa talia permanserunt.*

181. The assertion by Honigman, *JJS*, 48 (1997), 68–69, that Apion's remark must have been stimulated by a Jewish attempt to seek expansion of the citizenship, has no foundation.
182. That these burdens could be a problem is indicated by the issue that arose for Jews in Ionia in the Augustan era; see Jos. *Ant.* 12.125–126; cf. 16.27–28.
183. Philo, *Flacc.* 53.
184. See above, pp. 66–67.
185. The word is used by Claudius in his response to the Alexandrians; *CPJ*, II, no. 153, lines 73–74. That the Jews themselves took up arms is stated by Josephus, *Ant.* 19.278.
186. That two Jewish delegations were in Rome seems clear from Claudius' statement; *CPJ*, II, no. 153, lines 88–92. One of them was presumably that headed by Philo, still in Rome in 41; the other was sent after the renewed fighting. See Tcherikover, *CPJ*, I, 71–73; idem, *CPJ*, II, 50–52, although his view that Claudius held three separate hearings is implausible. Cf. Barclay, *Jews in the Mediterranean Diaspora*, 57. On the chronology of the embassies which cannot be pinned down, see the discussions of Tcherikover, *CPJ*, II, 50–51; Smallwood, *Jews under Roman Rule*, 245–248; Kasher, *Jews in Egypt*, 323–325. Nothing supports the conjecture of A. Momigliano, *Claudius, the Emperor and His Achievement* (Oxford, 1934), 97–98, that one embassy represented Jews with citizenship, the other Jews without.
187. *CPJ*, II, no. 153, lines 75–76.
188. The older bibliography is registered with thoroughness by Tcherikover, *CPJ*, II, 36–37.
189. For the formal purpose of the mission, see *CPJ*, II, no. 153, lines 14–22.
190. *CPJ*, II, no. 153, lines 74–78.
191. Ibid., lines 79–82.
192. Ibid., lines 82–88.
193. Ibid., lines 88–100.
194. Ibid., lines 100–104.
195. So, e.g., Tcherikover, *CPJ*, I, 73–74; idem, *CPJ*, II, 48; idem, *Hellenistic Civilization and the Jews*, 313–314; Modrzejewski, *Jews of Egypt*, 183; H. Botermann, *Das Judenedikt des Kaisers Claudius* (Stuttgart, 1996), 112; Schäfer, *Judeophobia*, 151–152; and, especially, Slingerland, *Claudian Policymaking*, 143–150.
196. *CPJ*, II, no. 153, lines 77–83, 100–102.
197. Ibid., lines 73–74: τῆς δὲ πρὸς Ἰουδαίους ταραχῆς καὶ στάσεως, μᾶλλον δ' εἰ χρὴ τὸ ἀληθὲς εἰπεῖν τοῦ πολέμου.
198. Ibid., lines 74–78: πότεροι μὲν αἴτιοι κατέστησαν καίπερ ἐξ ἀντικαταστάσεως πολλὰ τῶν ἡμετέρων πρέσβεων φιλοτειμηθέντων ... οὐκ ἐβουλήθην ἀκριβῶς ἐξελέγξαι, ταμιευόμενος ἐμαυτῶι κατὰ τῶν πάλειν ἀρξαμένων ὀργὴν ἀμεταμέλητον.
199. Ibid., lines 88–91.
200. Cf. the speculations of Tcherikover, *CPJ*, II, 50–53.
201. *CPJ*, II, no. 153, lines 85–88: καὶ μηδὲν τῶν πρὸς θρησκείαν αὐτοῖς νενομισμένων τοῦ θεοῦ λοιμένωνται, ἀλλὰ ἐῶσιν αὐτοὺς τοῖς ἔθεσιν χρῆσθαι ὗς καὶ ἐπὶ τοῦ θεοῦ Σεβαστοῦ, ἅπερ καὶ ἐγὼι διακούσας ἀμφοτέρων ἐβεβαίωσα.

202. So, e.g., Scramuzza, *The Emperor Claudius*, 77–78; Tcherikover, *CPJ*, I, 73–74; idem, *CPJ*, II, 53; idem, *JJS*, 14 (1963), 19–20; Applebaum, in Safrai and Stern, *Jewish People*, I, 444; Smallwood, *Jews under Roman Rule*, 249–250; eadem, *CHJ*, III, 185; Schwartz, *Agrippa I*, 105–106; Yavetz, *Judenfeindschaft*, 110–112; Barclay, *Jews in the Mediterranean Diaspora*, 58–60; Schäfer, *Judeophobia*, 151–152; Collins, *Jewish Wisdom*, 145–147; idem, *Between Athens and Jerusalem*, 120–122.

203. *CPJ*, II, no. 153, lines 88–90: καὶ Ἰουδέοις δὲ ἄντικρυς κελεύωι μηδὲν πλήωι ὧν πρότερον ἔσχον περιεργάζεσθαι.

204. See Philo, *Flacc.* 53–57. Kasher, *Jews in Egypt*, 322–323, rightly denies that citizenship was an issue here, but needlessly suggests that the Jews wanted an expansion of political rights.

205. *CPJ*, 153, lines 94–95: καρπουμένους μὲν τὰ οἰκῖα ἀπολά[υ]οντας δὲ ἐν ἀλλοτρίᾳ πόλει περιουσίας ἀπθόνων ἀγαθῶν.

206. Ibid., lines 92–93: μηδὲ ἐπισπαίειν γυμνασιαρχικοῖς ἢ κοσμητικοῖς ἀγῶσει. The verb remains disputed. The papyrus appears to read ἐπισπαίρειν, meaning to "be in alarm." But this meaning bears no relation to the context and the verb is, in any case, very rare. Hence, most have rightly adopted the emendation ἐπισπαίειν, which carries the sense of "pouring in." See Aristophanes, *Plutus*, 805. A. Kasher, *AJAH*, 1 (1976), 152–156; idem, *Jews in Egypt*, 314–321, seeks to retain the original reading, but translates it, quite illegitimately, as "harassing."

207. E.g., Scramuzza, *The Emperor Claudius*, 77; Tcherikover, *CPJ*, II, 53; Smallwood, *Jews under Roman Rule*, 249; Barclay, *Jews in the Mediterranean Diaspora*, 58–60, 65–71; Schäfer, *Judeophobia*, 150–152; Collins, *Jewish Wisdom*, 145–149.

208. *CPJ*, II, no. 153, lines 53–57.

209. See ibid., line 73. Kasher, *Jews in Egypt*, 310–314, rightly disconnects them.

210. Schäfer's assertion, *Judeophobia*, 151, that the immediate context does not concern itself with disturbances is indecisive. The whole section is framed by parallel statements insisting that Jews and Alexandrians cease hostility toward one another; *CPJ*, II, no. 153, lines 79–82, 100–104.

211. Philo, *Flacc.* 33–39.

212. Ibid., 41. Cf. also the Alexandrian upheaval in 66 CE, during which both Jews and Greeks spilled into the amphitheater; Jos. *BJ*, 2.490–491. These episodes are rightly pointed to by Kasher, *AJAH*, 1 (1976), 154–155; idem, *Jews in Egypt*, 317–319.

213. *CPJ*, II, no. 153, lines 96–97: μηδὲ ἐπάγεσθαι ἢ προσείεσθαι ἀπὸ Συρίας ἢ Αἰγύπ[τ]ου καταπλέοντας Ἰουδαίους.

214. The claim that Claudius is angrier with the Jews because he uses the verb διαμαρτύρομε (line 82) in adjuring the Greeks, but κελεύωι (line 89) in ordering the Jews, is unacceptable nit-picking.

215. See, most recently, Slingerland, *Claudian Policymaking*, 146–147.

216. *CPJ*, II, no. 153, lines 98–100: εἰ δὲ μή, πάντα τρόπον αὐτοὺς ἐπεξελεύσομαι καθάπερ κοινήν τεινα τῆς οἰκουμένης νόσον ἐξεγείροντας.

217. Jos. *Ant.* 19.278–285.

218. Its separateness is argued for (or asserted) by, e.g., Momigliano, *Claudius*, 30–31; Scramuzza, *The Emperor Claudius*, 74; Tcherikover, *CPJ*, I, 69–71;

idem, *CPJ*, II, 49–50; Smallwood, *Jews under Roman Rule*, 245–246; Kasher, *Jews in Egypt*, 263–274. But see the persuasive arguments for Josephus' manipulation of the letter by D. Hennig, *Chiron*, 5 (1975), 328–330, and Schwartz, *Agrippa I*, 99–105. So also Botermann, *Das Judenedikt*, 107–109.

219. In her recent discussion, Pucci Ben Zeev, *Jewish Rights*, 294–327, makes the most extensive and effective case for a separate edict promulgated prior to the letter recorded on the papyrus. Yet the reconstruction depends on seeing Josephus' introduction to his own document as belonging, in fact, after that event and representing circumstances that pertain to the (subsequent) papyrological letter. This is somewhat awkward and tortured. As for Claudius' reference to the madness of Caligula, Pucci Ben Zeev assembles an impressive array of testimony to emperors' criticisms of their predecessors (op. cit., 324–326). But none is a close parallel to this direct slur on an ostensibly official document.

220. The events are chronicled in Jos. *BJ*, 2.487–498. Josephus, to be sure, interprets the tumult as yet another episode of "unceasing encounters" with the Greeks; *BJ*, 2.489. But this is rhetorical extrapolation and exaggeration. Although simmering hostility and intermittent outbursts may have occurred between Jew and Egyptian, neither Josephus nor any other source specifies other incidents between Jew and Greek in Alexandria. In fact, the "unending strife" (ἀεὶ μὲν ἦν στάσις) to which Josephus alludes a few lines earlier (*BJ*, 2.487) is that between Jews and Egyptians, not Jews and Greeks.

221. See the evidence and discussion in Smallwood, *Jews under Roman Rule*, 389–396, 406–409. For some specifics, cf. the cogent article of M. Pucci Ben Zeev, *JSJ*, 20 (1989), 31–48.

3. JEWS IN THE PROVINCE OF ASIA

1. See, e.g., M. S. Ginsburg, *Rome et la Judée* (Paris, 1928), 94–97; A. M. Rabello, *ANRW*, II.21.2 (1984), 1290, 1292; T. Rajak, *JRS*, 74 (1984), 122–123; eadem, in W. Green, ed., *Approaches to Ancient Judaism*, V (Atlanta, 1985), 28–30; P. R. Trebilco, *Jewish Communities in Asia Minor* (Cambridge, 1991), 8–12; J. M. G. Barclay, *Jews in the Mediterranean Diaspora* (Edinburgh, 1996), 271–278; M. Pucci Ben Zeev, *Jewish Rights in the Roman World* (Tübingen, 1998), 229–230; E. M. Smallwood, *CHJ*, III, 169.

2. See, especially, H. R. Moehring, in J. Neusner, ed., *Christianity, Judaism, and Other Greco-Roman Cults* (Leiden, 1975), III, 124–158. Cf. also the skepticism of U. Baumann, *Rom und die Juden* (Frankfurt, 1983), 69–87.

3. See the lengthy bibliography collected by Pucci Ben Zeev, *Jewish Rights*, 9. She also provides the most recent and thorough argument for authenticity, op. cit., 357–368.

4. Jos. *Ant.* 14.186–187, 14.266–267, 16.174–178.

5. The most valuable collection can readily be consulted in R. K. Sherk, *RDGE*. Pucci Ben Zeev, *Jewish Rights*, 16–21, 382–387, very usefully points to the numerous parallels with documents found in Josephus.

6. Cf. Cic. *Agrar.* 2.37; *Phil.* 5.12, 12.12; *Ad Att.* 15.26.1, *De Domo*, 50.

7. See E. Schürer, *History*, I, 52–53; Rajak, in Green, *Approaches to Ancient Judaism*, V, 33, n. 11; most fully and convincingly argued by Pucci Ben Zeev, *SCI*, 13 (1994), 46–59. Her subsequent thought, credited to Rajak, that Josephus' information came from an anonymous compiler who copied the documents in diaspora archives, *Jewish Rights*, 405–408, is less persuasive.

8. Caes. *BC*, 3.41.

9. Jos. *Ant.* 14.240: "Lentulus set forth the following decree. In view of their religious piety I have released before the tribunal those Jews who are Roman citizens and are accustomed to practice Jewish rites in Ephesus." Very much the same formulation occurs in Jos. *Ant.* 14.228 and again in 14.234. Although Josephus presents these as three separate enactments, they plainly represent three versions of a single original, a good example of Josephus' dependence on different informants whose information he did not always sort out properly. That all versions reflect the same document is generally acknowledged; see, e.g., J. Juster, *Les Juifs dans l'empire romain* (Paris, 1914), I, 143–144; C. Saulnier, *RevBib*, 88 (1981), 164–165; G. Forni, in G. Wirth, K. H. Schwarte, and J. Heinrichs, eds., *Romanitas-Christianitas: Untersuchungen zur Geschichte und Literatur der römischen Kaiserzeit* (Berlin, 1982), 154–163; Pucci Ben Zeev, *Jewish Rights*, 158–159, 174–175. Full bibliographies can be found in Pucci Ben Zeev, op. cit., 150, 173, 186. The question of Lentulus' legal authority to issue edicts, which has exercised some scholars, hardly requires comment. Civil war engendered a revolutionary situation. But Lentulus as consul had wide authority anyway. There is no constitutional problem here.

10. The reference to *deisidaimonia* almost certainly refers to Jewish, not Roman piety, but either would be appropriate. Cf. Pucci Ben Zeev, *Jewish Rights*, 153.

11. Jos. *Ant.* 14.236–237.

12. So Juster, *Les Juifs*, I, 143; Pucci Ben Zeev, *Jewish Rights*, 185.

13. Schürer, *History*, III.1, 120–121, 133–135, took the exemption to imply that large numbers of Jews in the region were Roman citizens. If so, it is difficult to know why Lentulus tied his own hands. The evidence, cited by Schürer, for Jewish *libertini* in Rome is irrelevant. So is the fact of many Roman citizens in Asia; that says nothing about Jews who were Roman citizens. The assumption that Asia contained many Jews who possessed Roman citizenship is widely embraced; see, e.g., V. Tcherikover, *Hellenistic Civilization and the Jews* (Philadelphia, 1959), 330; M. Stern, in Safrai and Stern, *Jewish People*, I, 152; Barclay, *Jews in the Mediterranean Diaspora*, 271. E. M. Smallwood, *The Jews under Roman Rule from Pompey to Diocletian* (Leiden, 1981), 127–128, is rightly skeptical. Pucci Ben Zeev, *Jewish Rights*, 151–153, proposes that most of these *politai* were Junian Latins rather than full Roman citizens. But this rests on inferences from the manumission process in Rome. And it is hard to imagine that large numbers of Jews were emancipated in Rome in the decade or so after being enslaved by Pompey—and then mi-

grated to Asia Minor. On the whole issue of Roman citizenship and its availability (or desirability) to Jews, see above, Chapter 4.

14. See S. Applebaum, in S. Applebaum, ed., *Roman Frontier Studies, 1967* (Tel Aviv, 1971), 181–182.

15. Jos. *Ant.* 14.230. Balbus' statement that Lentulus exempted the Jews in Asia from military service (without mentioning the requirement of Roman citizenship) may reflect his own misunderstanding or perhaps an error in the transmission. So, rightly, Pucci Ben Zeev, *Jewish Rights,* 164.

16. Jos. *Ant.* 14.231–232. A similar decree was passed by the Sardians, according to Josephus, *Ant.* 14.232, although he provides no text. A letter to the Sardians did go out in this year from L. Antonius, proquaestor and propraetor in 49, referring, so it seems, to Jews who held Roman citizenship (if the reading ἡμέτεροι be preferred to ὑμέτεροι); Jos. *Ant.* 14.235. Hence this may indicate that Sardis too had been alerted to Lentulus' decree and responded suitably; cf. Juster, *Les Juifs,* I, 145; Saulnier, *RevBib,* 88 (1981), 165. The content of the letter, however, as given by Josephus, does not remark on military exemptions, but on the Jews' own jurisdiction within Sardis. Hence a connection with Lentulus' decree remains uncertain. See the discussion of Pucci Ben Zeev, *Jewish Rights,* 180–181.

17. Jos. *Ant.* 14.230.

18. Ibid., 14.190–195. The huge bibliography on this edict is conveniently collected by Pucci Ben Zeev, *Jewish Rights,* 31–32. See, especially, the still valuable discussion of F. Rosenthal, *Montatsschrift für Geschichte und Wissenschaft des Judentums,* 28 (1879), 176–183, 216–228, 302–306.

19. The excellent commentary of Pucci Ben Zeev, *Jewish Rights,* 34–53, provides numerous illuminating parallels in other Roman decrees for the various clauses of this document. See, in particular, the close comparison with the decree for Seleukos of Rhosos; *RDGE,* no. 58; M. Pucci Ben Zeev, *JSJ,* 26 (1995), 113–121. But it is not clear why Pucci Ben Zeev draws the conclusion that Caesar's guarantee of Jews' rights to live under their own laws had "a precise legal value"; *Jewish Rights,* 415, 422, following Juster, *Les Juifs,* I, 213–217.

20. Strabo, 13.1.27; Plut. *Caes.* 48.1; Appian, *BC,* 2.88. On Mithridates, see Dio, 42.48.4. This is the same Mithridates actually mentioned in the decree for Hyrcanus; Jos. *Ant.* 14.193.

21. Jos. *Ant.* 14.194.

22. The inference was drawn long ago by Rosenthal, *Monatsschrift für Geschichte und Wissenschaft des Judentums,* 28 (1879), 216–222; cf. Ginsburg, *Rome et la Judée,* 90–91. See also Pucci Ben Zeev, *Jewish Rights,* 49–50, with further bibliography.

23. Jos. *Ant.* 14.196: ὅπως τὰ τέκνα αὐτοῦ τοῦ Ἰουδαίων ἔθνους ἄρχῃ ... καὶ ὁ ἀρχιερεὺς αὐτὸς καὶ ἐθνάρχης τῶν Ἰουδαίων προιστῆται τῶν ἀδικουμένων.

24. The fact is widely recognized. See the bibliographical citations in Pucci Ben Zeev, *Jewish Rights,* 65–66.

25. Jos. *Ant.* 14.197–198.

26. Ibid., 14.199. On the date of the document, perhaps a *senatus consultum* of

47, recording a Caesarian decree of 48, see Pucci Ben Zeev, *Jewish Rights,* 71–73, with bibliography.

27. Jos. *Ant.* 14.200–210. See the analysis by Rosenthal, *Monatsschrift für Geschichte und Wissenschaft des Judentums,* 28 (1879), 306–313. For Ginsburg, *Rome et la Judée,* 86–87, this was part of a grandiose scheme by Caesar to unify all the nations and bring about a harmonious consolidation of the Roman empire—a dubious and unsupported hypothesis.

28. Jos. *Ant.* 14.211–212, 219–222. Cf. A. Momigliano, *Ricerche sull'orginazzazione della Giudea sotto il dominio romano* (63 a.C.–70 d.C.) (Amsterdam, 1967), 16–18.

29. Jos. *Ant.* 14.200, 211; cf. 222.

30. Ibid., 14.241–243.

31. Ibid., 14.223–224.

32. Cf. Rajak, in Green, *Approaches to Judaism,* V, 24–25.

33. D. Piatelli, *Israel Law Review,* 14 (1979), 14–26, acknowledges the political aspects but fails to note internecine Roman struggles and sees everything as part of a general Roman design to administer Judaea through Jewish surrogates. That analysis misses all the nuances.

34. Jos. *Ant.* 14.241–243. The date is probably 47 or 46; see *MRR,* III, 181, with bibliography. T. Reinach, *REJ,* 38 (1899), 161–171, argued that the Hyrcanus mentioned here is Hyrcanus I, not Hyrcanus II, and that Rabirius' intervention belongs to the late second century BCE, a case reiterated more forcefully now by C. Eilers in a forthcoming study. That alternative certainly merits consideration, especially in view of a document recorded shortly thereafter by Josephus which certainly does refer to Hyrcanus I; *Ant.* 14.247–255. But the circumstances of the mid-40s, when Hyrcanus II had recently received Caesar's endorsement and was conspicuously exercising his authority, seem marginally preferable.

35. Jos. *Ant.* 14.242.

36. See, e.g., Barclay, *Jews in the Mediterranean Diaspora,* 270; Pucci Ben Zeev, *Jewish Rights,* 196–197.

37. Jos. *Ant.* 14.241.

38. Ibid., 14.196.

39. It is worth noticing that Rabirius' letter to the Laodiceans also delivered instructions on matters apart from the Jews; Jos. *Ant.* 14.243. That he wrote to other cities as well is indicated at Jos. *Ant.* 14.242.

40. A reference in the document to complaints by the people of Tralles is regularly taken to indicate that Jews were persecuted in that city as well; Jos. *Ant.* 14.242; cf., e.g., Juster, *Les Juifs,* I, 146–147; Rajak, *JRS,* 74 (1984), 119; Barclay, *Jews in the Mediterranean Diaspora,* 270; Pucci Ben Zeev, *Jewish Rights,* 196–197. But one might observe that the text does not actually specify the issues raised by the Roman decrees to which the people of Tralles objected.

41. Jos. *Ant.* 14.244–246. On the date, see *MRR,* II, 298; III, 196. C. Eilers' suggestion *(per litt.)* that the individual involved is P. Servilius Globulus, governor of Asia in 63, is intriguing but implausible.

42. Jos. *Ant.* 14.245.
43. Ibid., 14.246.
44. Pucci Ben Zeev, *Jewish Rights,* 204, assumes the existence of unrecorded decrees issued against the Jews. The phrase αὐτόν τε κατὰ τοὺς νόμους τεθεικέναι τὸ ψήφισμα (Jos. *Ant.* 14.245) is baffling. But it can hardly refer to a decree passed by the Milesian assembly; cf. Juster, *Les Juifs,* I, 147–148.
45. Jos. *Ant.* 14.256–258.
46. Cf. ibid., 14.195, 241–242. Pucci Ben Zeev, *Jewish Rights,* 197–198, 214–215, proposes that Caesar may have granted explicit permission to observe the Sabbath and other practices in parts of his edicts not recorded by Josephus.
47. Jos. *Ant.* 14.259–261.
48. Pucci Ben Zeev, *Jewish Rights,* 223–224, questions the magnanimity by pointing out that the privileges explicitly granted do not correspond fully to the requests of the Jews. But that may be excessive parsing of the text. The fact that the decree details the specific items sought by the Jews surely implies that the Sardians did not hold back.
49. Jos. *Ant.* 14.259: πολλὰ καὶ μεγάλα φιλάνθρωπα ἐσχηκότες διὰ παντὸς παρὰ τοῦ δήμου.
50. Ibid., 14.235: ἐπέδειξαν αὐτοὺς σύνοδον ἔχειν ἰδίαν κατὰ τοὺς πατρίους νόμους ἀπ᾽ ἀρχῆς καὶ τόπον ἴδιον.
51. Ibid., 14.213–216.
52. Ibid., 14.215: Γάιος Καῖσαρ ὁ ἡμέτερος σταρτηγὸς καὶ ὕπατος. M. Pucci Ben Zeev, *RevBib,* 103 (1996), 237–243, argued that the author of the letter, given in the manuscripts as Ἰούλιος Γάιος, is actually young Octavian and dated the letter to his consulship of 43, a view she subsequently modified to put the date in late 42 or 41; *Jewish Rights,* 115–116. But the reference to Caesar clearly implies that he is alive and in office; so, rightly, Juster, *Les Juifs,* I, 142. The actual title, στρατηγὸς ὕπατος, assigned in the document both to the letter's composer and to Caesar, is an archaic one, indicating confusion or ignorance on the part of the copyist. On the title, see M. Holleaux, Στρατηγὸς ὕπατος (Paris, 1918), 1–9. Similarly problematic is the place to which the letter was directed. The manuscripts give Παριανῶν, evidently the city of Parium in the Troad. But a correction to Παρίων, the island of Paros in the vicinity of Delos, seems reasonable. For discussions, see Juster, *Les Juifs,* I, 142; Saulnier, *RevBib,* 88 (1981), 189–190; Pucci Ben Zeev, *Jewish Rights,* 109–110, 114–118. C. Eilers *(per litt.)* cuts the knot by proposing that the *governor* is in Delos and that the Jews of Parium went to him there. But the word order of the Greek stands against that construct. A skeptical view of the whole document has recently been expressed by M. H. Williams, in M. Goodman, *Jews in a Graeco-Roman World* (Oxford, 1998), 217–221. But she focuses, as do most commentators on the text, upon the issue of Caesar's supposed exemption of Jews from a general ban on *collegia,* an issue not directly relevant here.
53. See the treatment by D. Magie, *Roman Rule in Asia Minor* (Princeton, 1950), I, 416–418.
54. The letter of a Roman consul in the mid-second century BCE, expressing sup-

port for Jews all over the Mediterranean, went to numerous states and communities, including Delos; I Macc. 14.23. The Samaritans appear on two recently discovered Delian inscriptions; P. Bruneau, *BCH*, 106 (1982), 465–504. On the synagogue, see above, Chapter 4. It is possible that the "sojourning Jews," distinguished from "the Jews in Delos" in Jos. *Ant.* 14.213, were Samaritans.

55. Jos. *Ant.* 14.219–222.
56. On Dolabella's activities, see the sources collected by Broughton, *MRR*, II, 317, 344, and the discussion by Magie, *Roman Rule*, I, 418–420.
57. Jos. *Ant.* 14.223–227.
58. Ibid., 14.227.
59. See, e.g., Smallwood, *Jews under Roman Rule*, 125; Baumann, *Rom und die Juden*, 248; Trebilco, *Jewish Communities*, 17; Pucci Ben Zeev, *Jewish Rights*, 148.
60. Jos. *Ant.* 14.262–264. The name of the Roman proconsul unfortunately appears in corrupt form in the manuscripts. But identification with M. Brutus, who exercised *imperium* in western Asia Minor in early 42, remains the most logical and plausible one. See Juster, *Les Juifs*, I, 148–149; Schürer, *History*, III.1, 117; Pucci Ben Zeev, *Jewish Rights*, 228. On Brutus' movements in these months, see the sources in *MRR*, II, 346–347, 361, and the reconstruction by Magie, *Roman Rule*, I, 421–426.
61. Jos. *Ant.* 14.263.
62. See, e.g., Rajak, *JRS*, 74 (1984), 119; Barclay, *Jews in the Mediterranean World*, 270; Pucci Ben Zeev, *Jewish Rights*, 229–230.
63. For the sources on Cassius' actions, see *MRR*, II, 343–344.
64. Jos. *Ant.* 14.304–322. Cf. Juster, *Les Juifs*, I, 149.
65. Jos. *Ant.* 14.306–313.
66. Ibid., 14.217–222.
67. Ibid., 14.314–322. Letters to similar effect were also sent to Sidon, Antioch, and Aradus; ibid., 14.323.
68. Ibid., 14.314, 317.
69. Ibid., 14.318.
70. Ibid., 16.27–29. A different version of this appears in Jos. *Ant.* 12.125–127, where the issue at stake seems to be Jewish claims on citizenship in the Ionian communities. There can be little doubt that Josephus is referring to the same event in both passages: Ionian Jews appeal to Agrippa and their cause is taken up by Nicolas of Damascus in each instance. The doubts of Juster, *Les Juifs*, I, 150, are unwarranted. There is general agreement on the identity of the two episodes. See Tcherikover, *Hellenistic Civilization and the Jews*, 330; Smallwood, *Jews under Roman Rule*, 140–141; Baumann, *Rom und die Juden*, 258–259; Schürer, *History*, III.1, 129–130; Trebilco, *Jewish Communities*, 168–169; Barclay, *Jews in the Mediterranean Diaspora*, 271–272; Pucci Ben Zeev, *Jewish Rights*, 268–270. For the complex and tortured issue of Jewish citizenship in Greek cities, see above, Chapter 4.
71. That is the explanation presented most recently and forcefully by Barclay, *Jews in the Mediterranean Diaspora*, 268–274; endorsed in full by Pucci Ben Zeev, *Jewish Rights*, 271–272.

72. See the sources collected by Broughton, *MRR*, II, 371, 383, 388, 400, 406–409, 417–418, and the discussion by Magie, *Roman Rule*, I, 427–440.
73. Evidence and discussion are given in Magie, *Roman Rule*, I, 468–479.
74. See, e.g., Tcherikover, *Hellenistic Civilization and the Jews*, 329–330; Schürer, *History*, III.1, 129–130; Trebilco, *Jewish Communities*, 168–169; P. Richardson, *Herod: King of the Jews and Friend of the Romans* (Columbia, S.C., 1996), 270–271; cf. Pucci Ben Zeev, *Jewish Rights*, 269–270.
75. Some have suggested that Agrippa actually upheld the Ionian request and Josephus chose to pass over *that* fact in silence; Smallwood, *Jews under Roman Rule*, 140–141; Baumann, *Rom und die Juden*, 258–259; Barclay, *Jews in the Mediterranean Diaspora*, 271–272. It would surely have been easier, in that event, to leave out this embarrassing feature altogether, rather than call attention to it.
76. Jos. *Ant.* 16.27–28.
77. Note the reference in Jos. *Ant.* 12.125–126 to the Ionian assertion that if Jews were their kinsmen they would worship Ionian gods: εἰ συγγενεῖς εἰσιν αὐτοῖς 'Ιουδαῖοι, σέβεσθαι τοὺς αὐτῶν θεούς. This too indicates an effort to demonstrate that Jews had opted out of the civic community. Comparable measures may well have been taken against other minority groups—who had no Josephus to record them for us.
78. Jos. *Ant.* 16.31–57. Barclay, *Jews in the Mediterranean Diaspora*, 268–269, takes the words put into Nicolas' mouth by Josephus perhaps too seriously as a genuine reflection of the situation. So also Pucci Ben Zeev, *Jewish Rights*, 271–272. For B. Z. Wacholder, *Nicolaus of Damascus* (Berkeley, 1962), 28–29, and J.-M. Roddaz, *Marcus Agrippa* (Rome, 1984), 458, Josephus employed an actual speech of Nicolas preserved in his historical work. But see the cautionary comments of M. Stern, *Greek and Latin Authors on Jews and Judaism* (Jerusalem, 1976), I, 231–232.
79. Jos. *Ant.* 12.126; 16.60.
80. Ibid., 16.167–168. The decision is alluded to also in Philo, *Leg.* 240. C. Eilers, *Tyche*, 14 (1999), 77–86, places this letter at the time of Agrippa's earlier visit to the East in the 20s. But "Silanus the *strategos*," to whom Agrippa also sent a letter, may well be the consul of 17 BCE rather than the consul of 25 BCE.
81. This is rightly noticed by Pucci Ben Zeev, *Jewish Rights*, 419–427, although she places greater emphasis on the legal status conferred by these confirmations.
82. Jos. *Ant.* 16.60. Roddaz, *Marcus Agrippa*, 461–462, correctly questions the sympathy of Agrippa for the Jews and recognizes the political dimension.
83. Cic. *Pro Flacco*, 67–68. Cf. Jos. *Ant.* 14.112–113.
84. Jos. *Ant.* 16.160–161. Josephus indicates that similar complaints came from the Jews of Cyrene, but he does not here supply a document to illustrate it.
85. Jos. *Ant.* 16.162–165. Pucci Ben Zeev, *Jewish Rights*, 238–251, provides numerous illuminating parallels in other Roman edicts to Greek states. On the date, see G. W. Bowersock, *HSCP*, 68 (1964), 207–210; Pucci Ben Zeev, *Jewish Rights*, 252. The document gives Augustus as pontifex maximus, and hence cannot be earlier than 12 BCE. And a marginal note in a Latin manuscript has the tribunician year as XI (12 BCE). But references in Augus-

tus' edict to C. Marcius Censorinus, the consul of 8 BCE, may place it somewhat later. This Augustan edict is probably referred to by Philo, *Leg.* 311–
313.

86. Jos. *Ant.* 16.166. The document, unfortunately, is undated. Norbanus
Flaccus is either the consul of 38 or the consul of 24. The latter, who would
have been governor of Asia some time after 24 BCE, is more likely. The
document probably preceded the Augustan edict of 12 BCE or later. Many
date it to the very year of 12 BCE; see, e.g., E. M. Smallwood, *Philonis
Alexandrini Legatio Ad Gaium* (Leiden, 1961), 309–310; followed by
Schürer, *History*, III.1, 119; Pucci Ben Zeev, *Jewish Rights*, 259–261. See also
R. J. Evans, *Historia*, 36 (1987), 128. But this requires a lengthy gap between
consulship and proconsulship for Norbanus Flaccus.

87. Jos. *Ant.* 16.171.

88. Philo, *Leg.* 314–315.

89. Jos. *Ant.* 16.172–173. The date is much discussed. See the bibliography in
Pucci Ben Zeev, *Jewish Rights*, 289–290. But there is no compelling reason to
place it in 4 BCE, as do Juster, *Les Juifs*, I, 150, and Pucci Ben Zeev, loc. cit.

90. As a close parallel in these same years, the Jews of Cyrene came to Augustus
complaining about theft of sacred monies and other injuries; Jos. *Ant.*
16.160–161. The *princeps* then dispatched communications to the governor
of Libya and other officials, directing them to protect the transfer of contributions to Jerusalem; Jos. *Ant.* 16.169. But that plainly did not suffice. At some
time thereafter, Agrippa received the same complaints and had to write directly to the magistrates, council, and people of Cyrene instructing them to
return the funds to the Jews and see to the matter of compensation; Jos. *Ant.*
16.169–170; see S. Applebaum, *PP*, 97 (1964), 297–303; Pucci Ben Zeev,
Jewish Rights, 233–235, 273–280. On Rome's past history of failing to carry
through on pronouncements, see E. S. Gruen, *The Hellenistic World and the
Coming of Rome* (Berkeley, 1984), passim.

91. See J. H. Oliver, *Greek Constitutions of Early Emperors from Inscriptions
and Papyri* (Philadelphia, 1989), no. 3. Rightly noted by Pucci Ben Zeev, *Jewish Rights*, 267.

92. See, e.g., Oliver, *Greek Constitutions*, no. 2; *RDGE*, no. 61. Other texts and
bibliography are helpfully collected by Pucci Ben Zeev, *Jewish Rights*, 255–
256.

93. Jos. *Ant.* 16.41. Barclay, *Jews in the Mediterranean Diaspora*, 268–269,
276–277, rightly points to the well-being of Jews in these Greek communities. But his inference that growing Jewish prosperity and influence engendered Gentile hostility may owe too much to modern experience.

4. CIVIC AND SACRAL INSTITUTIONS IN THE DIASPORA

1. The variety of diaspora experiences is now generally recognized and need not
be argued; cf. A. T. Kraabel, *JJS*, 33 (1982), 445–464 = Kraabel, in J. A.
Overman and R. S. MacLennan, eds., *Diaspora Jews and Judaism* (Atlanta,
1992), 21–33; J. J. Price, *SCI*, 13 (1994), 169–186. This is assumed in what
follows, even where the generic expression "diaspora" is employed.

2. See the very valuable collection of testimony, the bibliography, and the ser-

viceable comments in Schürer, *History*, III.1, 1–86. With special reference to Second Temple synagogues, see the excellent new compilation of data and important analysis by D. D. Binder, *Into the Temple Courts: The Place of the Synagogues in the Second Temple Period* (Atlanta, 1999), 227–341. L. I. Levine's sweeping new study includes significant discussions of pre-70 diaspora synagogues; *The Ancient Synagogue: The First Thousand Years* (New Haven, 2000), 74–159. A useful checklist of diaspora synagogues appears in L. V. Rutgers, *The Hidden Heritage of Diaspora Judaism* (Leuven, 1998), 127–130. Epigraphic testimony is discussed by L. H. Kant, *ANRW*, II.20.2 (1987), 692–698. On the visual and archaeological aspects, see R. Hachlili, *Ancient Jewish Art and Archaeology in the Diaspora* (Leiden, 1998), passim. Cf. the overviews by A. T. Kraabel, *ANRW*, II.19.1 (1979), 475–510, and L. M. White, *Building God's House in the Roman World* (Baltimore, 1990), 60–101. And one may consult now the summary by H. Bloedhorn and G. Hüttenmeister, *CHJ*, III, 267–297.

3. Jos. *BJ*, 7.43. Cf. also Philo, *Leg.* 245.

4. Jos. *BJ*, 7.43–45. Elsewhere, he ascribes the grant of civic privileges to Seleucus I—an even more questionable proposition; *CAp.* 2.39; *Ant.* 12.119. Still more dubious material is found in Malalas, *Chron.* 8.206–207, 10.261.

5. Jos. *BJ*, 7.45. They suffered grievously during the Revolt; Jos. *BJ*, 7.46–62. On the Jews in Antioch, see C. H. Kraeling, *JBL*, 51 (1932), 130–160; I. Levinskaya, *The Book of Acts in its Diaspora Setting* (Grand Rapids, 1996), 127–135; Levine, *Ancient Synagogue*, 116–118.

6. Acts, 9.2, 9.20.

7. Jos. *BJ*, 2.559–561, 7.368.

8. Josephus remarks that Jews dwelled in every city of Syria; *BJ*, 2.462–463; cf. 2.479. But he does not speak explicitly of synagogues at that point.

9. See the recent valuable survey of the evidence by Levine, *Ancient Synagogue*, 75–82.

10. *JIGRE*, no. 117: ὑπὲρ βασιλέως . . . οἱ ἐν Κροκ[ο]δίλων πόλει Ἰου[δαῖ]οι τὴν προ[σευχήν]. That *proseuche* or another in Crocodilopolis is mentioned also in a papyrological document recording a land survey in the region; *CPJ*, I, no. 134; cf. A. Kasher, *The Jews in Hellenistic and Roman Egypt* (Tübingen, 1985), 138–140; Binder, *Into the Temple Courts*, 236–238.

11. *CPJ*, I, no. 129; Kasher, *Jews of Egypt*, 146–148.

12. *CIJ*, II, no. 1441 = *JIGRE*, no. 24, lines 5–6: τὸν πυλῶνα τῆς προσευχῆς. Cf. Kasher, *Jews in Egypt*, 111–112; Binder, *Into the Temple Courts*, 242–243.

13. Athribis: *CIJ*, II, no. 1443 = *JIGRE*, no. 27; *CIJ*, II, no. 1444 = *JIGRE*, no. 28. Nitriai: *CIJ*, II, no. 1442 = *JIGRE*, no. 25. Of uncertain provenance is another private donation of a *proseuche*; *JIGRE*, no. 126. See Kasher, *Jews in Egypt*, 114–119.

14. III Macc. 7.18–20. So, rightly, Binder, *Into the Temple Courts*, 245–246.

15. For a recent analysis, with extensive bibliography, see E. S. Gruen, *SCI*, 16 (1997), 47–70. See also D. R. Schwartz, *Zion*, 62 (1997), 5–22 (Hebrew).

16. Jos. *Ant.* 13.65–66.

17. Ibid., 2.44. For Jews in Cyrene in the mid-second century BCE, see I Macc. 15.23.

18. Strabo, *apud* Jos. *Ant.* 14.115.
19. Jos. *Ant.* 16.160, 16.169–170. See the discussion, with extensive bibliography, by M. Pucci Ben Zeev, *Jewish Rights in the Roman World* (Tübingen, 1998), 273–280.
20. *SEG,* 17, no. 823 = *CJZC,* no. 72, lines 3–6: ἐφάνη τῇ συναγωγῇ τῶν ἐν Βερνεικίδι Ἰουδαίων τοὺς ἐπιδιδόντες εἰς ἐπισκευὴν τῆς συναγωγῆς ἀναγράψαι αὐτοὺς εἰστήλην λίθου Παρίου. On the inscription, see the comments of S. Applebaum, *Jews and Greeks in Ancient Cyrene* (Leiden, 1979), 161–164, 192–193; Binder, *Into the Temple Courts,* 109–111, 260–262. Whether this structure is identical with the ἀμφιθεάτρον mentioned in two earlier inscriptions from Berenice need not be resolved here; *CJZC,* nos. 70, 71; cf. the discussions of Applebaum, op. cit., 160–167; Binder, op. cit., 140–145; Levine, *Ancient Synagogue,* 89–96. The term *synagoge* appears also on a very fragmentary text from the city of Cyrene; *Ann. Scuol. arch. di Atene,* 39–40 (1961–1962), no. 116. But there is nothing to show that this is a Jewish document. See Applebaum, op. cit., 193–194; Binder, op. cit., 256–257.
21. Philo, *Leg.* 282. See also I Macc. 15.23; Jos. *Ant.* 13.284–287; Acts, 4.36, 11.20.
22. Acts, 13.5. Binder, *Into the Temple Courts,* 270, unnecessarily questions the plural here.
23. See Philo, *Leg.* 245.
24. Cic. *Pro Flacco,* 67–69; Jos. *Ant.* 14.223–230, 14.234–267, 16.160–168, 16.171–173.
25. Philo, *Leg.* 311: ἵνα ἐπιτρέπωσι τοῖς Ἰουδαίοις μόνοις εἰς τὰ συναγώγια συνέρχεσθαι. See also Jos. *Ant.* 16.164, referring to a σαββατεῖον.
26. Acts, 13.14, 13.43, 14.1, 18.19, 18.26, 19.8.
27. *CIJ,* I, no. 766 = B. Lifshitz, *Donateurs et fondateurs dans les synagogues juives* (Paris, 1967), no. 33. For Julia Severa's position in Acmonia, see Schürer, *History,* III.1, 31. As a high priestess of the imperial cult, she was almost certainly not a Jewess. For recent discussions of the document see P. R. Trebilco, *Jewish Communities in Asia Minor* (Cambridge, 1991), 58–60; Binder, *Into the Temple Courts,* 145–147, 287–288; T. Rajak, in S. Fine, ed., *Jews, Christians, and Polytheists in the Ancient Synagogue* (London, 1999), 161–173; Levine, *Ancient Synagogue,* 111–112.
28. Jos. *Ant.* 14.258. See the discussion by Pucci Ben Zeev, *Jewish Rights,* 206–216.
29. Jos. *Ant.* 14.260–261; cf. 14.235. See Pucci Ben Zeev, *Jewish Rights,* 217–225; Binder, *Into the Temple Courts,* 283–284.
30. The stone is published in *CIJ,* I, no. 683 = *IGRR,* I, no. 881 = *CIRB,* no. 70.
31. *CIRB,* no. 70, lines 6–7: ἀφείημι ἐπὶ τῆς πρ[ο]σευχῆς θρεπτόν; lines 13–15: χωρὶς εἰς τ[ὴ]ν προσευχὴν θωπείας τε καὶ προσκαρτερήσεως; lines 18–19: συνεπ[ιτ]ροπευούσης δὲ καὶ τῆς συναγωγῆς τῶν Ἰουδαίων.
32. *CIRB,* nos. 71, 73, 985, 1123, 1127; *SEG,* 43, no. 510. A recent find from Phanagoria, dated to 51 CE, shows similar phraseology; D. A. Danshin, *VDI,* 204 (1993), 60 (Russian). See these and others collected by Levinskaya, *Book of Acts,* 231–242; E. L. Gibson, *The Jewish Manumission Inscriptions of the Bosporan Kingdom* (Tübingen, 1999), 159–172.
33. That the freedman had some religious obligation to the synagogue seems un-

likely. The term θωπεία, normally rendered as "flattery," is not readily conso-
nant with piety. The point is made most recently and cogently by Gibson,
Jewish Manumission Inscriptions, 134–144. This renders otiose the even
more extreme claims that the phraseology points to conversion on the part of
the ex-slaves; as, e.g., J. Juster, *Les Juifs dans l'empire romain* (Paris, 1914), I,
268–269; H. Bellen, *Jahrbuch für Antike und Christentum*, 8–9 (1965/66),
171–176. Gibson's understanding of θωπεία as subservience or a subservient
attitude, however (op. cit., 144–149), does not suit the positive context of the
inscription and would seem to make the oversight of the *synagoge* somewhat
superfluous. The term προσκαρτέρησις is commonly interpreted as some
form of work obligation due to the *proseuche*; e.g., B. Nadel, *VDI*, 1 (1948),
203–206 (Russian); Levinskaya, *Book of Acts*, 231–242; Gibson, op. cit.,
144–149. But the parallel passages adduced (Dem. *Neaira*, 120; Acts 8.13,
10.7; *IG*, 2.2, no. 1028; *IC*, 2.11.3) by no means prove the proposition. The
term indicates only perseverance, not labor, let alone servile labor. The analogy with Delphic manumission documents which include a *paramone* clause
binding the freedman for services to his former master does not work. The
clause appears in two of the Bosporan inscriptions, obligating the emancipated slave to perform duties for the ex-master until the latter's death; *CIRB*,
no. 73, lines 10–11 (mostly restored), and *CIRB*, no. 74, lines 8–10. But such
duties are not connected with the synagogue. On *paramone* clauses generally,
see A. Samuel, *JJP*, 15 (1965), 256–284. With regard to προσκαρτέρησις in
the Bosporan inscriptions, see the sensible discussion of J. A. Overman in
H. C. Kee and L. H. Cohick, eds., *Evolution of the Synagogue: Problems and
Progress* (Harrisburg, 1999), 150–151, who rightly sees it as signifying adherence to the Jewish community in some sense—although it stretches a point
to interpret the term in conjunction with *proseuche* in Rom. 12.12 as meaning adherence to the synagogue. Levine, *Ancient Synagogue*, 113–115, passes
over these controversies.

34. It does not, of course, follow that the freedman in any sense "converted"
to Judaism. On the clause, συνεπιτροπευούσης τῆς συναγωγῆς τῶν
Ἰουδαίων, see Overman, in Kee and Cohick, *Evolution of the Synagogue*,
151–155. For other reecent discussions of the Bosporan documents, see
Schürer, *History*, III.1, 36–38; Levinskaya, *Book of Acts*, 105–116; Binder,
Into the Temple Courts, 272–276, 439–445; Gibson, *Jewish Manumission
Inscriptions*, 124–152.

35. Acts, 16.13, 16.16, 17.1, 17.10, 17.17, 18.4, 18.7; cf. 18.8, 18.17.

36. Philo, *Leg.* 281.

37. Most, but by no means all, of this evidence is later. See the summary in
Schürer, *History*, III.1, 64–68; Levinskaya, *Book of Acts*, 154–166.

38. Cf. the treatment in Binder, *Into the Temple Courts*, 289–297.

39. I Macc. 15.23. Note the presence of a military commander in Rhodes at the
end of the fourth century BCE named Ananias—quite possibly a Jew. Diod.
20.97.7. This stray bit of information reminds us of how much our sources
omit.

40. Jos. *Ant.* 14.213–216, 14.231–232.

41. A history of the scholarship on this subject need not be rehearsed here. The

initial identification of the structure as a synagogue was made by the excavator A. Plassart, *Mélanges Holleaux* (Paris, 1913), 201–215 = *RevBib*, 11 (1914), 523–534. A full review of the scholarly debates was made by P. Bruneau, *Recherches sur les cultes de Délos à l'époque hellénistique et à l'époque impériale* (Paris, 1970), 480–493. Briefer summaries since that time may be found in Kraabel, *ANRW*, II.19.1 (1979), 491–494; L. M. White, *HTR*, 80 (1987), 136–140; B. H. McLean, in J. S. Kloppenborg and S. G. Wilson, eds., *Voluntary Associations in the Graeco-Roman World* (London, 1996), 192–195; Binder, *Into the Temple Courts*, 297–317; Levine, *Ancient Synagogue*, 100–105. Whether the initial phase of the building was a synagogue or served some other function cannot be determined with confidence. White, op. cit., 147–152, takes the first structure as a private dwelling. But see the arguments of Binder, op. cit., 307–315.

42. The documents are *CIJ*, I, 727–730 = *ID*, nos. 2328, 2330–2332. The phraseology may be found in the Septuagint (e.g., Genesis, 14.20); Philo, *Flacc.* 46; *Leg.* 278; Jos. *Ant.* 16.163; *CIJ*, II, no. 1537. See A. T. Kraabel, *GRBS*, 10 (1969), 81–86.

43. *CIJ*, I, no. 726 = *ID*, no. 2329: Ἀγαθοκλῆς καὶ Λυσίμαχος ἐπὶ προσευχῆι. The dedicator Lysimachos appears also in one of the inscriptions from the building itself; *CIJ*, I, no. 729 = *ID*, no. 2328.

44. *CIJ*, I, no. 725 a-b, lines 10–12: ᾧ πάσα ψυχὴ ἐν σήμερον ἡμέραι ταπεινοῦται μεθ᾽ ἱκετείας.

45. The documents are published by P. Bruneau, *BCH*, 106 (1982), 465–504. See especially no. 2, lines 4–5: κατασκευάσαντα καὶ ἀναθέντα ἐκ τῶν ἰδίων ἐπὶ προσευχά.

46. Jos. *Ant.* 14.213–214. See the cogent discussion by White, *HTR*, 80 (1987), 141–147. McLean, in Kloppenborg and Wilson, *Voluntary Associations*, 193, prefers a single synagogue that is Samaritan. Among other treatments, see A. T. Kraabel, *BA*, 47 (1984), 44–46; Schürer, *History*, III.1, 71; Binder, *Into the Temple Courts*, 305, 472–474; Levine, *Ancient Synagogue*, 102–103.

47. Philo, *Leg.* 156–157: ἠπίστατο οὖν καὶ προσευχὰς ἔχοντας καὶ συνιόντας εἰς αὐτάς, καὶ μάλιστα ταῖς ἱεραῖς ἑβδόμαις . . . οὔτε ἐνεωτέρισεν εἰς τὰς προσευχὰς.

48. Augoustesioi: *CIJ*, I, no. 284 = *JIWE*, II, no. 547; *CIJ*, I, no. 301 = *JIWE*, II, no. 301; *CIJ*, I, no. 338 = *JIWE*, II, no. 169; *CIJ*, I, no. 368 = *JIWE*, II, no. 189; *CIJ*, I, no. 416 = *JIWE*, II, no. 194; *CIJ*, I, no. 496 = *JIWE*, II, no. 542; Agrippesioi: *CIJ*, I, no. 365 = *JIWE*, II, no. 170; *CIJ*, I, no. 425 = *JIWE*, II, no. 130; *CIJ*, I, no. 503 = *JIWE*, II, no. 549; Volumnesioi: *CIJ*, I, no. 343 = *JIWE*, II, no. 167; *CIJ*, I, no. 402 = *JIWE*, II, no. 100; *CIJ*, I, no. 417 = *JIWE*, II, no. 163; *CIJ*, I, no. 523 = *JIWE*, II, no. 577.

49. So, e.g., H. J. Leon, *The Jews of Ancient Rome* (Philadelphia, 1960), 140–142, 157–159; Schürer, *History*, III.1, 95–98; Levinskaya, *Book of Acts*, 182–185; P. Richardson, in K. P. Donfried and P. Richardson, *Judaism and Christianity in First-Century Rome* (Grand Rapids, 1998), 19–22. D. Noy, *Foreigners at Rome: Citizens and Strangers* (London, 2000), 284, questions the connection with Volumnius.

50. *CIJ*, 291, 317, 510, 535. Cf. Leon, *Jews of Ancient Rome*, 147–149. On the use of the term "Hebrews" generally by Jews, see G. Harvey, in S. Jones and S. Pearce, eds., *Jewish Local Patriotism and Self-Identification in the Graeco-Roman Period* (Sheffield, 1998), 132–147, who suggests that it designates an association with religious conservatism. See also Noy, *Foreigners at Rome*, 265. This does not, however, seem especially likely in the diaspora context at Rome. Were other synagogues content to take names that suggested less adherence to ancestral traditions?

51. See Rutgers, *Hidden Heritage*, 45–71.

52. The most complete publication is by the principal excavator, M. F. Squarciapino, *La sinagoga di Ostia* (Rome, 1964). A useful summary in English can be found in *Archaeology*, 16 (1963), 194–203.

53. Such was the opinion of the excavator (see the previous note), followed by most scholars; e.g., A. T. Kraabel, *ANRW*, II.19.1 (1979), 497–500; Rutgers, *Hidden Heritage*, 111–112; Hachlili, *Ancient Jewish Art*, 53–55. L. M. White, in Donfried and Richardson, *Judaism and Christianity in First Century Rome*, 30–68, made a case for regarding the original building as a home or a collegial hall; noted without comment by Levine, *Ancient Synagogue*, 255–256. But the case was rickety and largely demolished by Binder, *Into the Temple Courts*, 322–336. The fact of a synagogue, at least in its later stages, was demonstrated by an inscription found in the site recording a donor's dedication of the "ark for the holy law"; *JIWE*, I, no. 13: καὶ τὴν κειβωτὸν ἀνέθηκεν νόμῳ ἁγίῳ. See also *CIJ*, I, 533, probably from the early second century CE, which registers a community of Jews in the vicinity of Ostia, and *JIWE*, I, no. 14, from Ostia recording an *archisynagogos*. Cf. Schürer, *History*, III.1, 81–82. On the date of the original synagogue, see the recent debate between A. Runesson and L. M. White in *HTR*, 92 (1999), 409–464.

54. This is typical in the older literature; e.g., Juster, *Les Juifs*, I, 438–456; Schürer, *History*, II, 427–439; III.1, 87–107; S. Krauss, *Synagogale Alterthümer* (Hildesheim, 1966), 103–112 (originally published 1922). The approach is soundly criticized by T. Rajak and D. Noy, *JRS*, 83 (1993), 81–83. But it is revived again, most recently, by Binder, *Into the Temple Courts*, 371.

55. It is sometimes said that *proseuche* was the earlier term, subsequently superseded by *synagoge,* or that the distinction was a geographic one: *synagoge* in Palestine, *proseuche* in the diaspora; see, e.g., M. Hengel, *Judaica et Hellenistica: Kleine Schriften,* I (Tübingen, 1996), 171–195 (first published 1971); Bloedhorn and Hüttenmeister, in *CHJ*, III, 268—269. Yet Josephus can still use *proseuche* (albeit rarely) to mean a building; Jos. *Vita*, 277; *Ant.* 14.256–258. Juvenal employs it in the early second century CE; *Sat.* 3.292–296. It occurs also in the Bosporan inscriptions of the mid-first century or later; *CIRB*, nos. 70, 71, 73, 1123; *SEG*, 43, no. 510. Philo, by contrast, though addicted to the term *proseuche*, can also apply *synagogoi* to the sacred places of the Essenes; *Prob.* 81. And he employs the term elsewhere as well; *Somn.* 2.127; *Leg.* 311–312. The famous Theodotus inscription, probably no later than the mid-first century, speaks of two earlier generations of

archisynagogoi; CIJ, II, no. 1404. Further, *proseuche* and *synagoge* can be employed side by side (with different meanings) in the Bosporan inscriptions (see citations above, nn. 30–32), while in Cyrene the same document uses *synagoge* twice for two different purposes; *CJCZ*, no. 72. It seems fruitless to draw clear-cut geographic or chronological distinctions.

56. For *sabbateion*, see Jos. *Ant.* 16.164; for *hieron*, III Macc. 2.28; Jos. *BJ*, 7.44–45; for *euxeion*, *CPJ*, II, no. 223; for *didaskaleion*, Philo, *Spec. Leg.* 2.62. Cf. Levine, *Ancient Synagogue*, 119–120.

57. See the collection of epigraphic testimonia in Rajak and Noy, *JRS*, 83 (1993), 89–92. The geographic spread is summarized by L. I. Levine, in M. Goodman, ed., *Jews in a Graeco-Roman World* (Oxford, 1998), 201.

58. Mark, 5.22, 5.35–36, 5.38; Luke, 8.49, 13.14; Acts, 13.15, 18.8, 18.17.

59. Acts, 18.12–17.

60. *CIJ*, I, no. 587 = *JIWE*, I, no. 53—a very late testimonium, to be sure. The possibility of *archisynagogos* as an honorary title may be considered also for women who held that designation. In general, on *archisynagogoi* as donors and benefactors, see Rajak and Noy, *JRS*, 83 (1993), 84–89, with references.

61. See the comprehensive and judicious study of Levine, in Goodman, *Jews in a Graeco-Roman World*, 195–213.

62. Luke, 8.41, 8.49.

63. *CIJ*, II, no. 766.

64. Binder, *Into the Temple Courts*, 350–351, implausibly suggests that the *archisynagogos* for life was an emeritus *archisynagogos*.

65. *CIJ*, II, no. 803.

66. See Levine, in Goodman, *Jews in a Graeco-Roman World*, 211.

67. Strabo, *apud* Jos. *Ant.* 14.117; Philo, *Flacc.* 74.

68. Philo, *Flacc.* 80, 117.

69. *CJCZ*, no. 72.

70. Ibid., no. 70, line 12: ἔ[δοξε τοῖς ἄ]ρχουσι καὶ τῶι πολιτεύματι; ibid., no. 71, lines 21–22: ὧν χάριν ἔδοχε τοῖς ἄρχουσι καὶ τῶι πολιτεύματι.

71. Jos. *BJ*, 7.47.

72. See J. M. S. Cowey and K. Maresch, *Urkunden des Politeuma der Juden von Herakleopolis (144/3–133/2 b. Chr.) (P. Polit. Iud) Papyrologica Coloniensia*, XXIX (Wiesbaden, 2001), 10–18. *Archontes* are addressed by petitioners in almost all the documents. See especially no. 17 that gives both *archontes* and the *politarches* rendering a decision.

73. So Leon, *Jews of Ancient Rome*, 173–176.

74. For those named *dis archon* or *tris archon*, see, e.g., *CIJ*, I, nos. 289, 316, 391, 494. For *archontes dia biou*, see *CIJ*, I, nos. 266, 398, 416, 417, 480, 503. Child *archontes* are registered in *CIJ*, I, nos. 88, 120.

75. See especially M. H. Williams, *ZPE*, 104 (1994), 129–141. Other discussions, with references, can be found in Leon, *Jews of Ancient Rome*, 173–180; Schürer, *History*, III.1, 98–100; Levinskaya, *Book of Acts*, 187–190; Binder, *Into the Temple Courts*, 344–348. Note also the *politarchon*, perhaps at Leontopolis; *CPJ*, III, no. 1530a = *JIGRE*, no. 39. On this office, see G. H. R. Horsley, in D. W. J. Gill and C. Gempf, eds., *The Book of Acts in its Greco-Roman Setting* (Grand Rapids, 1994), 419–431. The recent effort by

M. Williams, *JJS*, 51 (2000), 77–87, to interpret *exarchon* as a leader of liturgical singing is unpersuasive. The parallel literary term is *exarchos*, not *exarchon*.

76. E.g., *CIJ*, I, nos. 95, 106, 119, 147, 368. See also *CIJ*, I, no. 561 = *JIWE*, I, no. 23, from the vicinity of Puteoli.

77. Many of these functionaries appear in the Roman funerary inscriptions. See Leon, *Jews of Ancient Rome*, 180–194; Williams, *ZPE*, 104 (1994), 134–141; Levinskaya, *Book of Acts*, 190–192. *Prostates* also occurs as early as the second century BCE in Egypt; *CIJ*, II, no. 1441 = *JIGRE*, no. 24. Other testimonia can be found in Schürer, *History*, II, 427–439; III.1, 101–104. And see the valuable discussion by Binder, *Into the Temple Courts*, 352–370.

78. Two recent works provide excellent surveys of these activities at greater length than is possible here: Binder, *Into the Temple Courts*, 389–450; Levine, *Ancient Synagogue*, 124–159.

79. Philo, *Hyp.* 7.11–13.

80. Philo, *Somn.* 2.127; cf. *Leg.* 311–312. Philo here interestingly uses the term *synagoge*, rather than his more customary *proseuche*.

81. Philo, *Leg.* 156. Here the term is *proseuche*.

82. Philo, *Mos.* 2.215–216.

83. Ibid., 2.216. A very similar formulation occurs in *Spec. Leg.* 2.62. Cf. *Leg.* 115, 210; *Spec. Leg.* 2.233; *Praem.* 66.

84. Acts, 17.2–3, 17.17, 18.4, 18.19, 19.8–9; cf. 18.26. At Pisidian Antioch, Paul and Barnabas arrived in the synagogue on the Sabbath and listened to the reading of the law and prophets; Acts, 13.14–15. Cf. Acts, 15.21.

85. Jos. *Ant.* 16.43. Cf. Jos. *CAp.* 2.204. Josephus, like Philo, attributes the origin of this prescription to Moses; *CAp.* 2.175. See also Philo, *Opif.* 128; Acts, 15.21. On the question of when reading of the prophets was added to that of the Torah, see Levine, *Ancient Synagogue*, 135–143.

86. So, e.g., E. Fleischer, *Tarbiz*, 59 (1990), 397–441 (Hebrew); H. C. Kee, *NTS*, 36 (1990), 1–24; H. A. McKay, *Sabbath and Synagogue: The Question of Sabbath Worship in Ancient Judaism* (Leiden, 1994), passim. For some persuasive counter-arguments, see P. W. van der Horst, in Fine, ed., *Jews, Christians, and Polytheists*, 18–43; E. P. Sanders, in Fine, op. cit., 6–12; Binder, *Into the Temple Courts*, 404–415; and Levine, *Ancient Synagogue*, 151–158.

87. The view of L. I. Levine, in L. I. Levine, ed., *The Synagogue in Late Antiquity* (Philadelphia, 1987), 22, and *Ancient Synagogue*, 155, that the term *proseuche* was applied by diaspora Jews, anxious about their minority status and distance from Jerusalem, in order to give their institutions an aura of sanctity, is speculative and implausible. This presupposes a nervousness and need for security that begs the principal question. A similar idea is expressed by M. Goodman, in B. Isaac and A. Oppenheimer, eds., *Studies on the Jewish Diaspora in the Hellenistic and Roman Periods* (Tel Aviv, 1996), 15, who proposes that diaspora Jews ascribed the concept of sacrality to synagogues only in adaptation of Gentile perceptions and in order to protect synagogue sites and personnel. By contrast, A. Kasher, in D. Urman and P. V. M. Flesher, eds., *Ancient Synagogues: Historical Analysis and Archaeological Discovery* (Leiden, 1995), 205–220, finds the sacral character of Egyptian synagogues as primary, with other communal functions as secondary.

88. Philo, *Flacc.* 41–43; *Leg.* 134–137.

89. Philo, *Flacc.* 122–124. See the cogent comments of Binder, *Into the Temple Courts,* 408–409.

90. Jos. *BJ,* 7.44–45. Cf. Jos. *Ant.* 13.66–67.

91. Jos. *Ant.* 14.257–258.

92. Ibid., 14.244–246.

93. Ibid., 14.260.

94. Philo can occasionally use *thyein* (to sacrifice) in a vaguer and broader sense; *Spec. Leg.* 3.171; *Deus,* 8; cf. Binder, *Into the Temple Courts,* 406–407. But it is not likely that this accounts for the language of the Sardian decree.

95. *CIJ,* II, no. 1449; cf. *CPJ,* I, no. 129; see above, p. 69.

96. See above, pp. 109–110.

97. Jos. *Ant.* 14.257. See also ibid., 14.214–216, 14.261; cf. 16.164. A fragmentary ostracon from Apollinopolis Magna of the first century BCE records contributions to a common feast, very possibly to take place in a synagogue; *CPJ,* I, no. 139.

98. Philo, *Flacc.* 116.

99. *CJCZ,* no. 71, lines 1–2: ἐπὶ συλλόγου τῆς σκηνοπηγίας.

100. Jos. *CAp.* 2.282; Philo, *Mos.* 23.

101. E.g., Horace, *Serm.* 1.9.69; Ovid, *Ars Amat.* 1.416; Seneca, *apud* Aug. *CD,* 6.11; Petronius, fr. 37; Suet. *Aug.* 76.2. See above, Chapter 1.

102. III Macc. 7.15–20.

103. E.g., *CIRB,* nos. 70, 71, 73, 1123; *SEG,* 43, no. 510. See above, pp. 109–110.

104. Jos. *Ant.* 14.235, 14.260.

105. Ibid., 16.168. Cf. also Strabo's reference to adjudication by the Jewish ethnarch in Alexandria, which may well have employed a synagogue as venue; Strabo, *apud* Jos. *Ant.* 14.117.

106. Cf. Matt. 10.17–18, 23.34; Mark, 13.9; Luke, 12.11, 21.12; Acts, 22.19; II Cor. 11.23–24. Further references and discussion can be found in Trebilco, *Jewish Communities,* 20–21.

107. Daniel, 13.28 (the version of Theodotus): καὶ ἐλθόντες ἐπὶ τὴν συναγωγὴν τῆς πόλεως.

108. Berenice: *CJZC,* no. 71; Egypt: *CPJ,* I, no. 138.

109. Repository for monies: Philo, *Spec. Leg.* 1.78; *Leg.* 311–312; Jos. *Ant.* 16.164; 16.168; cf. Cic. *Pro Flacco,* 68. Votive offerings: Philo, *Leg.* 133; *CIJ,* I, nos. 727–730. Dedicatory inscriptions: *CJZC,* nos. 70–72. Archival records: *CIJ,* I, nos. 683a, 690, 690a, 691; II, no. 1449 = *JIGRE,* no. 125; *CPJ,* II, no. 143; cf. Jos. *Ant.* 16.165. See the useful remarks of Binder, *Into the Temple Courts,* 426–433.

110. Some see it as a rival of the Temple: e.g., V. A. Tcherikover, *Hellenistic Civilization and the Jews* (Philadelphia, 1959), 124–125; P. V. M. Flesher, in Urman and Flesher, *Ancient Synagogues,* 28–31; others as an imitation of the Temple: e.g., Kasher, in Urman and Flesher, op. cit., 205–220; Binder, *Into the Temple Courts,* 31–39.

111. This last is the thesis argued by L. I. Levine, *JBL,* 115 (1996), 425–448; idem, *Ancient Synagogue,* 26–41, who also supplies a useful summary of prior views and bibliography; op. cit., 20–26. See, particularly, J. Gutmann, in J.

Gutmann, ed., *The Synagogue: Studies in Origins, Archaeology, and Architecture* (New York, 1975), 72–76; Hengel, *Judaica et Hellenistica*, I, 171–195; Levine, in Levine, *Synagogue in Late Antiquity,* 7–31; L. L. Grabbe, in Urman and Flesher, *Ancient Synagogues,* 17–26; Kasher, in Urman and Flesher, op. cit., 205–220; R. Hachlili, *JSJ,* 28 (1997), 34–47.

112. The allusion in Agatharchides of Cnidus (second century BCE) to Sabbath prayers ἐν τοῖς ἱεροῖς (*apud* Jos. *CAp.* 1.209) may simply be a reference to the Temple, with an erroneous use of the plural. In any case, Agatharchides is here speaking about Jerusalem, not the diaspora. *Contra:* Hengel, op. cit., 176.

113. Daniel, 13.28 (the Septuagint version): ἐπὶ τὴν συναγωγήν.

114. See the remarks of S. J. D. Cohen, in *CHJ,* III, 299–313. Cf. also E. P. Sanders, in Fine, *Jews, Christians, and Polytheists,* 4–12.

115. The case was made by S. L. Guterman, *Religious Toleration and Persecution in Ancient Rome* (London, 1951), 130–156, particularly with regard to the Roman context, recently revived and expanded by P. Richardson, in Kloppenborg and Wilson, *Voluntary Associations,* 90–109; cf. also, with a different angle, Binder, *Into the Temple Courts,* 35–37.

116. The distinctions were rightly brought to the fore by Juster, *Les Juifs,* I, 413–424. Guterman's objections, *Religious Toleration,* 135–148, are inadequate. The matter is usually discussed only in the Roman context, on which see above, pp. 24–26.

117. As is proposed by J. G. Griffiths, in Urman and Flesher, *Ancient Synagogues,* 3–16.

118. Griffiths, op. cit., 11–15, can point to little more than possible architectural similarities, themselves conjectural; the feature of asylum, which is hardly peculiar to the Egyptians; and the combination of worship and instruction, which existed only for the priestly elite in Egypt.

119. *JIGRE,* nos. 13, 22, 24, 25, 28.

120. Ibid., no. 125.

121. *CIRB,* nos. 69, 70, 73, 1123, 1124, 1125, 1126; *SEG,* 43, no. 510.

122. *CIRB,* nos. 1123, 1126; cf. 74, 1021.

123. *CJZC,* nos. 70–72. See the discussions of Applebaum, *Jews and Greeks in Ancient Cyrene,* 160–167, and Binder, *Into the Temple Courts,* 109–110, 140–145, 257–263.

124. Cf. the stelai at Delos recording dedications for the *proseuche* and gratitude to *theos hypsistos.* See Binder, *Into the Temple Courts,* 303–306, and above, p. 111.

125. Lifshitz, *Donateurs,* no. 33.

126. Cf. H. I. Marrou, *A History of Education in Antiquity* (London, 1956), 102–115.

127. *SEG,* 20, no. 740 = *CJZC,* no. 6; *SEG,* 20, no. 741 = *CJZC,* no. 7. Other possible Jewish names, as postulated by Applebaum, *PP,* 97 (1964), 291–292; idem, *Jews and Greeks,* 177–178, are less plausible.

128. So, rightly, M. Hengel, *Judaism and Hellenism* (London, 1974), I, 68. L. H. Feldman, *Jewish Social Studies,* 22 (1960), 224–228, maintained that such participation required deviation from "orthodoxy," a view modified in *Jew and Gentile in the Ancient World* (Princeton, 1993), 57–59.

129. L. Robert, *REJ*, 101 (1937), 85–86.
130. Korone: *IG*, V (1), 1398, lines 91–92; Robert, *Hellenica*, III (1946), 100; Hypaipa: *CIJ*, I, no. 755. Cf. Trebilco, *Jewish Communities*, 177.
131. *CPJ*, II, no. 151, line 6: [τῆ]ς ἀρεσκούσης παιδείας. The papyrus may also have included explicit reference to the gymnasium and the ephebate, but the reading of both terms is much too uncertain to supply any confidence.
132. That Jews engaged in separate and comparable gymnasia, but not in Greek ones, as maintained by H. A. Wolfson, *Philo: Foundations of Religious Philosophy in Judaism, Christianity, and Islam* (Cambridge, Mass., 1947), I, 80–81, is implausible and refuted by the ephebic lists from Cyrene and Iasos.
133. *LetArist.* 121; cf. 3.
134. Philo, *Congr.* 74–79. The thesis of Wolfson, *Philo*, I, 81, that this is a theoretical formulation, unconnected to any real educational experience, is strained and unconvincing; see A. Mendelson, *Secular Education in Philo of Alexandria* (Cincinnati, 1982), 25–26.
135. Philo, *Migr.* 116.
136. Philo, *Spec. Leg.* 229–230.
137. Philo, *Leg. All.* 167.
138. Philo, *Prob.* 141.
139. Philo, *Ebr.* 177.
140. Ibid.
141. *LetArist.* 284.
142. The fragments of Ezekiel are conveniently collected by Holladay, *Fragments*, II, 344–405.
143. Wolfson, *Philo*, I, 81, needlessly postulates separate performances staged and attended by Jews. This view is rightly criticized by Feldman, *Jew and Gentile*, 61–63, who presents the evidence fairly but nevertheless presumes tension and "deviation from orthodoxy," for which there is no evidence.
144. Philo, *Spec. Leg.* 2.229–230.
145. Ibid., 2.91.
146. Ibid., 3.176.
147. Philo, *Agr.* 112–113; *Vita Cont.* 43.
148. Philo, *Prov.* 44, 46; *Opif.* 78; *Flacc.* 130.
149. Boxers: Philo, *Cher.* 81; *Agr.* 114; wrestlers and pancratiasts: *Prob.* 26, 110; *Somn.* 2.134, 1.145–146; sprinters and jumpers: *Deus*, 75; *Agr.* 115, 177, 180; *Migr.* 133; chariot races: *Prov.* 58.
150. E.g., Philo, *Deus*, 38, 75; *Migr.* 166; *Fuga*, 97–98; *Agr.* 119–121; *Mos.* 2.171, 2.291; *Somn.* 1.69, 1.129–130; *Spec. Leg.* 1.38; *Plant.* 76; *Opif.* 47; *Praem.* 4–6. Several other examples have been collected by H. A. Harris, *Greek Athletics and the Jews* (Cardiff, 1976), 55–70.
151. *CJZC*, no. 70; cf. Applebaum, *Jews and Greeks*, 164–167; Binder, *Into the Temple Courts*, 140–145; Levine, *Ancient Synagogue*, 89–93.
152. Jos. *Ant.* 15.268–271, 15.341, 17.194. Amphitheaters were already well established in Republican Italy; see K. Welch, *JRA*, 7 (1994), 59–80.
153. Jos. *Ant.* 12.120: τοὺς Ἰουδαίους μὴ βουλομένους ἀλλοφύλῳ ἐλαίῳ χρῆσθαι λαμβάνειν ὡρισμένον τι παρὰ τῶν γυμνασιάρχων εἰς ἐλαίου τιμὴν ἀργύριον ἐκέλευσεν. Cf. Jos. *Vita*, 74; *BJ*, 2.591.
154. See discussions by Harris, *Greek Athletics*, 74–75; Kasher, *Jews in Egypt*,

303–304; M. Goodman, in P. R. Davies and R. T. White, eds., *A Tribute to Geza Vermes* (Sheffield, 1990), 227–245; J. M. G. Barclay, *Jews in the Mediterranean Diaspora* (Edinburgh, 1996), 256–257, n. 63.

155. One might observe also, whatever one makes of the notorious set of events, that it was a diaspora Jew, Jason of Cyrene, who recorded the installation of a gymnasium, with athletic activities, and an ephebate in Jerusalem itself; II Macc. 4.9–14.

156. See above, pp. 74–75.

157. See above, Chapter 2.

158. Philo, *Flacc.* 53: μετουσίας πολιτικῶν δικαίων.

159. Philo, *Leg.* 371: καὶ τὰ ἐξαίρετα νόμιμα καὶ τὰ κοινὰ πρὸς ἑκάστας τῶν πόλεων αὐτοῖς δίκαια.

160. Cf. Philo, *Mos.* 1.34–36—with reference to the Hebrews in pre-Exodus Egypt, but perhaps an indirect allusion to Philo's contemporaries.

161. Jos. *Ant.* 14.188.

162. Jos. *CAp.* 2.49–52; *Ant.* 13.285–287; cf. *CIJ,* II, no. 1450.

163. Jos. *CAp.* 2.65–67.

164. Cowey and Maresch, *Urkunden,* 22–23. Jewish *politai* are recorded in document no. 1, lines 16–18. For disputes between Jews and non-Jews heard by the *archontes* of the *politeuma,* see documents no. 10 and 11, with the discussion of Cowey and Maresch, op. cit., 11–13.

165. *CJZC,* nos. 70, 71. See above, n. 70. The *politeuma* may well have been a representative body, rather than encompassing all the Jews of the city. Such is suggested by the voting procedure; *CJZC,* no. 70, line 21. See G. Lüderitz, in J. W. van Henten and P. W. van der Horst, *Studies in Early Jewish Epigraphy* (Leiden, 1994), 210–221.

166. Strabo, *apud* Jos. *Ant.* 14.114–115.

167. Jos. *Ant.* 16.161, 16.169–170. The circumstances are obscure and the outcome of the appeal to Agrippa unknown. Evidently the earlier one to Augustus, who then wrote to the Roman governor, did not have much effect. See the rather speculative reconstruction by Applebaum, *PP,* 97 (1964), 296–302, whose claim that the Jews' citizenship status was at stake has no foundation in the texts. See also idem, *Jews and Greeks,* 183–185; Pucci Ben Zeev, *Jewish Rights,* 276–280. The argument of M. W. B. Bowsky, *AJP,* 108 (1987), 495–510, that *CJZC,* no. 71, honoring M. Tittius, a Roman official who showed favor to the Jews of Berenice, belongs to 14/13 BCE and thus indicates implementation of Agrippa's letter is less than compelling. Nothing in the inscription suggests that Tittius preserved Jewish control over their funds, and Bowsky's dating depends on a putative Cyrenean era that begins in 67 BCE, for which there is no evidence whatsoever.

168. *CJZC,* no. 8, lines 4–5: οἱ συνάρξαντες νομοφύλακες. Eleazar appears in line 7: Ἐλαζα[ρ Ἰ]άσονος. On this office, see the discussion by Applebaum, *PP,* 97 (1964), 292–295; idem, *Jews and Greeks,* 186–189.

169. Jos. *Ant.* 12.119: πολιτείας αὐτοὺς ἠξίωσε καὶ τοῖς ἐνοικισθεῖσιν ἰσοτίμους ἀπέφηνε Μακεδόσιν καὶ Ἕλλησιν, ὡς τὴν πολιτείαν ταύτην ἔτι καὶ νῦν διαμένειν.

170. Jos. *CAp.* 2.39.

171. Jos. *BJ*, 7.44.

172. It does not help much that Josephus used as evidence the fact that Antiochene Jews got money from Seleucid officials for their own oil rather than having to use that of the Gentiles, a decidedly weak, even irrelevant argument; *Ant.* 12.120. Serious doubts are expressed by Tcherikover, *Hellenistic Civilization and the Jews*, 328–329. By contrast, Kasher, *Jews in Egypt*, 297–309, seeks, implausibly, to reconcile all of Josephus' testimony and finds it all acceptable—so long as it refers to a Jewish *politeuma* in Antioch. According to C. H. Kraeling, *JBL*, 51 (1932), 138–139, Seleucus Nicator rewarded some Jewish veterans in his forces with Antiochene citizenship, thus accounting for Josephus' conclusion—a strained hypothesis. More guarded interpretations may be found in Schürer, *History*, III.1, 126–127; Barclay, *Jews in the Mediterranean Diaspora*, 244–245.

173. Jos. *BJ*, 7.106–111.

174. Jos. *Ant.* 12.119, 12.121; *BJ*, 7.44, 7.110. The notion that *isopoliteia* gave Jews the right to full citizenship upon rejection of their own religious practices has no basis in the evidence. See A. D. Nock, *Essays on Religion and the Ancient World* (ed. Z. Stewart, Oxford, 1972), II, 960–962.

175. No direct evidence exists for Jewish participation in the political scene of other Syrian cities. The claim of G. Downey, *A History of Antioch in Syria from Seleucus to the Arab Conquest* (Princeton, 1961), 115, and Applebaum, in Safrai and Stern, *Jewish People*, I, 453, that Jews possessed a *politeuma* in Seleucia on the Tigris, is not warranted by Jos. *Ant.* 18.372 and 18.378. But the existence of Jewish communities with established governing bodies elsewhere in Syria would not be surprising.

176. Jos. *Ant.* 12.125: ἵνα τῆς πολιτείας ἣν αὐτοῖς ἔδωκεν Ἀντίοχος . . . μόνοι μετέχωσιν, ἀξιούντων δ᾽, εἰ συγγενεῖς εἰσιν αὐτοῖς Ἰουδαῖοι, σέβεσθαι τοὺς αὐτῶν θεούς. The same encounter is recorded in Jos. *Ant.* 16.27–29, with Jews, rather than Asian Greeks, taking the initiative, and no mention of *politeia*. The former version is the more likely. See above, pp. 98–99.

177. Jos. *Ant.* 12.126.

178. Ibid., 16.28.

179. See the interpretation argued above, Chapter 3. Earlier studies have focused too exclusively on the issue of whether Jews possessed citizenship. See, e.g., Applebaum, in Safrai and Stern, *Jewish People*, I, 441–442; Smallwood, *Jews under Roman Rule*, 140–141; Schürer, *History*, III.1, 129–130; Trebilco, *Jewish Communities*, 168–169; Barclay, *Jews in the Mediterranean Diaspora*, 271–272.

180. Josephus elsewhere adds that the Jews in Ephesus and all over Ionia took the same ethnic designation as indigenous citizens of the towns; *CAp.* 2.39.

181. Jos. *Ant.* 14.235, 14.260–261.

182. A letter from L. Antonius in 49 BCE to the Sardians refers to Jews as Ἰουδαῖοι πολῖται ἡμέτεροι; Jos. *Ant.* 14.235. So at least most of the manuscripts have it. That would signify that Jewish envoys from Sardis who came to Antonius were Roman citizens. But a variant has ὑμέτεροι instead of ἡμέτεροι. The latter receives support from the other document, a decree by the Sardians confirming Jewish privileges in the city and designating them as οἱ κατοικοῦντες

ἡμῶν ἐν τῇ πόλει Ἰουδαῖοι πολῖται; Jos. *Ant.* 14.259. The last term has sometimes been seen as an interpolation: W. W. Tarn and G. T. Griffith, *Hellenistic Civilization* (3rd ed., London, 1952), 221; Schürer, *History*, III.1, 130; Trebilco, *Jewish Communities*, 171. The two passages, however, buttress one another. And it is not implausible that both refer to the political status of Jews in Sardis—without any inferences about citizenship. Reference to the Jews as κατοικοῦντες should signify something other than full citizens. As usual, too much of the scholarship concerns itself with the irresolvable—and probably irrelevant—citizenship issue. See, e.g., Applebaum, in Safrai and Stern, *Jewish People*, I, 442; Trebilco, op. cit., 169–171; Barclay, *Jews in the Mediterranean Diaspora*, 271; Pucci Ben Zeev, *Jewish Rights*, 177–178, 219–220.

183. Paul and Tarsus: Acts, 21.39; Nicetas the Jerusalemite and Iasus: *CIJ*, I, no. 749.
184. See testimony and discussions in Juster, *Les Juifs*, II, 1–27; Applebaum, in Safrai and Stern, *Jewish People*, I, 420–463; Schürer, *History*, III.1, 126–137; Trebilco, *Jewish Communities*, 167–185 and passim.
185. See Nock, *Essays*, II, 960–962.
186. Philo, *Leg.* 155. See the fuller discussion, with references and bibliography, above, Chapter 1.
187. Philo, *Leg.* 158.
188. Ibid., 157: οὔτε τὴν Ῥωμαϊκὴν αὐτῶν ἀφείλετο [Augustus] πολιτείαν, ὅτι καὶ τῆς Ἰουδαϊκῆς ἐφρόντιζον.
189. Acts, 16.37–39, 22.25–29, 23.27. Cf. B. Rapske, *The Book of Acts and Paul in Roman Custody* (Grand Rapids, 1994), 83–90, with bibliography.
190. *CJZC*, no. 71, lines 5–6.
191. Ephesus: Jos. *Ant.* 14.228, 14.234, 14.240; cf. 14.237. Delos and Sardis: ibid., 14.231–232; cf. 14.235.
192. See above, Chapter 3, for fuller discussion and bibliography.
193. Cf. A. N. Sherwin-White, *The Roman Citizenship* (2nd ed., Oxford, 1973), 245–248; Pucci Ben Zeev, *Jewish Rights*, 152, with bibliography. Note, for instance, Octavian's award of citizenship to Seleucus of Rhosus for his military services; *RDGE*, no. 58, II, lines 12–23. The bestowal of Roman citizenship upon Antipater, father of Herod (Jos. *BJ*, 1.194), is, of course, hardly representative.
194. Cf. Schürer, *History*, III.1, 134–135.

5. DIASPORA HUMOR I: HISTORICAL FICTION

1. Jeremiah, 29.4–7.
2. See, e.g., the recent statement of this Freudian analysis, with regard to biblical criticism generally, by A. Brenner, in *JSOT*, 63 (1994), 40–41. On a more general level, see the thoughtful and penetrating comments of W. Sypher, in W. Sypher, ed., *Comedy* (New York, 1956), 193–258.
3. For discussions of the three versions, see C. A. Moore, *Daniel, Esther, and Jeremiah: The Additions* (Garden City, 1977), 161–165; D. J. A. Clines, *The Esther Scroll: The Story of the Story* (Sheffield, 1984), 9–92; K. Jobes, *The Alpha-Text of Esther: Its Character and Relationship to the Masoretic*

Text (Atlanta, 1996); C. V. Dorothy, *The Books of Esther: Structure, Genre, and Textual Integrity* (Sheffield, 1997), 13–19; J. D. Levenson, *Esther* (Louisville, 1997), 27–34; A. Lacocque, *Biblical Interpretation*, 7 (1999), 308–322. And see now the extensive study, with hypothetical reconstructions, by R. Kossmann, *Die Esthernovelle vom Erzählten zur Erzählung* (Leiden, 2000), who finds the "Alpha-Text" in Greek as the best witness to the original version.

4. E.g., S. B. Berg, *The Book of Esther: Motifs, Themes and Structure* (Missoula, 1979), 103–113; E. L. Greenstein, in J. Neusner, B. A. Levine, and E. S. Frerichs, eds., *Judaic Perspectives on Ancient Israel* (Philadelphia, 1987), 235–237; S. Goldman, *JSOT*, 47 (1990), 15–31; M. V. Fox, *Character and Ideology in the Book of Esther* (Columbia, S.C., 1991), 158–163.

5. See, especially, B. W. Jones, *CBQ*, 39 (1977), 171–181, 225–243; J. Sasson, in R. Alter and F. Kermode, eds., *The Literary Guide to the Bible* (Cambridge, Mass., 1987), 335–342; S. Niditch, *Underdogs and Tricksters: A Prelude to Biblical Folklore* (New York, 1987), 128–131, 133–134, 144–145; Greenstein, in Neusner et al., *Judaic Perspectives*, 225–241; Fox, *Character and Ideology*, 25, 168, 171, 173–177, 182–184, 198, 253; Levenson, *Esther*, 12–14; J. W. Whedbee, *The Bible and the Comic Vision* (Cambridge, 1998), 171–190; A. Berlin, *Esther* (Philadelphia, 2001), xv–xxii; eadem, *JBL*, 120 (2001), 6–7, 13–14. K. M. Craig, *Reading Esther: A Case for the Literary Carnivalesque* (Louisville, 1995), passim, recognizes some of this but is too intent upon forcing Esther into the Bakhtinian conception of literary carnivalization; cf. Berlin, *Esther*, xxi–xxii. The fascinating and insightful work of T. K. Beal, *The Book of Hiding* (London, 1997), occasionally acknowledges farcical features in the text (e.g., pp. 22, 118), but Beal confines his analysis to its serious intent. By contrast, Y. T. Radday, in Y. T. Radday and A. Brenner, eds., *On Humour and the Comic in the Hebrew Bible* (Sheffield, 1990), 295–313, in a hilarious reconstruction, finds comedy almost everywhere in the work, even in its structure and its style (e.g., frequent use of the passive voice!), an overkill that even the most determined humorist would find excessive.

6. Esther, 1.3–4.

7. Cf. Radday, in Radday and Brenner, *Humour and the Comic*, 296; Levenson, *Esther*, 45.

8. Esther, 1.8. See Fox, *Character and Ideology*, 17.

9. For some suggestions, see L. M. Paton, *The Book of Esther* (New York, 1908), 149–150; E. J. Bickerman, *Four Strange Books of the Bible* (New York, 1967), 185–186; C. A. Moore, *Esther* (New York, 1971), 13; Berlin, *Esther*, 11–15.

10. Esther, 1.12–22.

11. Cf. Clines, *Esther Scroll*, 31–33; Fox, *Character and Ideology*, 168.

12. Esther, 2.3, 2.12. Cf. the treatment of K. De Troyer, in A. Brenner, ed., *A Feminist Companion to Esther, Judith, and Susanna* (Sheffield, 1995), 47–70.

13. Esther, 2.10–11.

14. Ibid., 4.1, 6.7–11, 8.15.

15. Ibid., 3.11. The text literally reads "the silver is given to you." It is rendered

as "keep the money" by the Septuagint: τὸ μὲν ἀργύριον ἔχε. But that misses the meaning. Haman did, in fact, deposit the cash; cf. Esther, 4.7, 7.4. The translation given above follows Moore, *Esther*, 40; see also Fox, *Character and Ideology*, 52; Levenson, *Esther*, 72.

16. Esther, 4.1–4.
17. See, e.g., Moore, *Esther*, 48; Fox, *Character and Ideology*, 57–58; L. R. Klein, in A. Brenner, *A Feminist Companion*, 162; Beal, *Book of Hiding*, 70; Berlin, *Esther*, 46. For B. Wyler, in Brenner, op. cit., 123, Esther was unaware of Jewish practices because she was too assimilated.
18. Esther, 5.10–11. Cf. Levenson, *Esther*, 92.
19. Esther, 6.1.
20. Ibid., 6.8. It is not impossible that the Persian king's horse might occasionally have paraded with something like a crown. Cf. Paton, *Book of Esther*, 248–249; Moore, *Esther*, 65; Fox, *Character and Ideology*, 77. But that would not compromise the comedy of the text—indeed might enhance it. For Craig, *Reading Esther*, 108, the crowned horse adds a carnivalesque flavor.
21. Esther, 7.5.
22. Sasson, in Alter and Kermode, *Literary Guide*, 337. Efforts to rationalize this response miss the point; cf. Levenson, *Esther*, 103.
23. Esther, 7.6–10.
24. Moore, *Esther*, 72, overlooks the humor and implausibly takes this as understandable error on Ahasuerus' part. For Paton, *Book of Esther*, 263, and Fox, *Character and Ideology*, 87, the king feigned misunderstanding in order to find a pretext to eliminate Haman; cf. further Kossmann, *Die Esthernovelle*, 203–204. That analysis also ignores the comedy. A better appreciation is given by Levenson, *Esther*, 104, who reckons it the funniest scene in the whole book. So also Greenstein, in Neusner et al., *Judaic Perspectives*, 228; Radday, in Radday and Brenner, *Humour and the Comic*, 308. Berlin, *Esther*, 70–71, sees the farce but considers the king's misapprehensions as deliberate. Cf. L. M. Wills, *The Jew in the Court of the Foreign King* (Minneapolis, 1990), 171, 177; Whedbee, *The Bible and the Comic Vision*, 181–182. Goldman, *JSOT*, 47 (1990), 18–19, suggests that Esther manipulated the entire scenario.
25. Esther, 8.4–14; cf. 3.12–15.
26. Ibid., 8.8. On this, see Jones, *CBQ*, 39 (1977), 179–180.
27. The remark almost certainly is Ahasuerus', not that of the narrator; see Fox, *Character and Ideology*, 95, as against Moore, *Esther*, 79. But it hardly follows, as Fox thinks, that the king is here explaining his favor to Esther on the grounds that he cannot personally repeal his own edict; so also Levenson, *Esther*, 109; Whedbee, *The Bible and the Comic Vision*, 182. Are we to suppose that both edicts, authorizing mutual massacre, were on the books simultaneously? So, e.g., Clines, *Esther Scroll*, 18–19, 67, 176. That would be black comedy indeed.
28. Esther, 8.17. Commentators usually treat this with solemn seriousness: Fox, *Character and Ideology*, 104–106; Levenson, *Esther*, 117; Beal, *Book of Hiding*, 103; Kossmann, *Die Esthernovelle*, 309–310; Berlin, *Esther*, 80–81. But see Moore, *Esther*, 82, citing D. N. Freedman.

29. Esther, 9.6–12. Cf. Jones, *CBQ*, 39 (1977), 180; Berlin, *Esther,* 86.

30. So, e.g., Greenstein, in Neusner et al., *Judaic Perspectives,* 231: "the story of Esther is a skit, not a drama . . . a cartoon, and thus precisely the sort of show one would expect to see on Purim." For the carnivalism, see Craig, *Reading Esther,* passim; Berlin, *Esther,* xxi–xxii.

31. See the parallels collected by Paton, *The Book of Esther,* 64–71; Moore, *Esther,* xli; Fox, *Character and Ideology,* 134–136.

32. These and other implausibilities are canvassed by Paton, *Book of Esther,* 71–77; Moore, *Esther,* xlv–xlvi; Fox, *Character and Ideology,* 131–134; Levenson, *Esther,* 23–25. The effort by R. Gordis, *JBL,* 100 (1981), 382–388, to find a factual basis for much of this is strained and unpersuasive.

33. Fox, *Character and Ideology,* 138, 148–150, who properly discounts any historical basis for the story, nevertheless believes that its author expected it to be read as fact rather than fiction. In view of the grotesque exaggerations and transparent implausibilities, that is hard to swallow. Cf. Berlin, *JBL,* 120 (2001), 6–7. Various suggestions on the genre of the work are canvassed by Kossmann, *Die Esthernovelle,* 24–26.

34. Scholarly discussions of the date only exhibit the tenuousness and speculative character of any suggestion. A recent study of the language confirms merely that it is "late Biblical Hebrew," but conclusions on anything more specific are qualified and provisional; R. L. Bergey, "The Book of Esther: Its Place in the Linguistic Milieu of Post-Exilic Biblical Hebrew Prose" (Ph.D. diss., Dropsie College, 1983). Moore, *Esther,* lix–lx, puts the composition prior to the Maccabean period, claiming that a Gentile ruler would not likely have been portrayed in sympathetic fashion after that time; similarly, Levenson, *Esther,* 26; Berlin, *Esther,* xlii. By contrast, Paton, *Book of Esther,* 60–63, L. M. Wills, *The Jewish Novel in the Ancient World* (Ithaca, 1995), 98–100, and I. Frölich, *Time and Times and Half a Time* (Sheffield, 1996), 144–146, incline toward a post-Maccabean date precisely because the hostility against Gentiles, as reflected in Jewish retaliation at the end of the Esther story, fits better at that time. Neither suggestion is especially compelling. To begin, one might well question the proposition that Ahasuerus receives a sympathetic portrayal. Moreover, Gentile monarchs certainly do receive favorable treatment in Hellenistic Jewish texts. One need think only of Alexander the Great or Ptolemy Philadelphus in the *Letter of Aristeas,* among others. On tales involving Greek rulers and Jews, see E. S. Gruen, *Heritage and Hellenism: The Reinvention of Jewish Tradition* (Berkeley, 1998), 189–245. And Jewish ferocity against the nation's enemies hardly awaited the coming of the Maccabees. Biblical tradition is full of it. Fox, *Character and Ideology,* 139–140, prefers a Hellenistic to a Persian date on the grounds that no contemporary of the Persian era could have ascribed 127 satrapies to the empire and have expected to be taken seriously. But that presumes a serious intent. The number is hyperbolic, in the same class as the 180 days of banqueting, the 50-cubit-high gallows, and the 75,000 Gentiles slain by the Jews. The only chronological indicator of any import is the "fourth year of Ptolemy and Cleopatra" when, so the colophon to the Septuagint version reports, the Greek translation of Esther was brought to Egypt; Esther, Add. F, 11. Depending on

which Ptolemy and Cleopatra, the date would be 114/113, 78/77, or 49/48, most likely one of the first two; cf. E. J. Bickerman, *JBL,* 63 (1944), 339–362. But this gives only a terminus for the Greek translation. The Hebrew Esther could be much earlier. Berlin, *JBL,* 120 (2001), 9–11, and eadem, *Esther,* xxviii–xxxii, xli–xliii, regards the most comparable texts to be those written by Greeks in the Persian period. But this, as she acknowledges, falls well short of proof of a Persian date. For T. Ilan, *Integrating Women into Second Temple History* (Tübingen, 1999), 133–135, the work itself was composed shortly before the translation and aimed to buttress the reign of the Hasmonean queen Shlomzion who took the throne in 76, a novel but wholly unsupported and implausible idea. The opening of the book sets Ahasuerus' reign in the past, evidently a somewhat distant past; Esther, 1.1–2; cf. 10.2. If he is indeed Xerxes (485–465 BCE), that would put the composition no earlier than the late fifth century. That is as far as one may prudently go. The current consensus for a late Persian or early Hellenistic date may well be right. But there can be no great confidence about it. The sensible discussion by Berg, *Book of Esther,* 169–173, with further bibliography, arrives at no firm conclusions.

35. On this category, see A. Meinhold, *ZAW,* 87 (1975), 306–324; *ZAW,* 88 (1976), 72–93; cf. A. Lacocque, *The Feminine Unconventional* (Minneapolis, 1990), 56–59; Fox, *Character and Ideology,* 145–148; Berlin, *Esther,* xxxiv–xxxvi. Other possible genres and models are discussed by Dorothy, *Books of Esther,* 302–327.

36. Esther, 10.3.

37. See the interpretations of D. Daube, *JQR,* 37 (1946–47), 139–147; W. L. Humphreys, *JBL,* 92 (1973), 214–217, 222–223; S. A. White, in P. L. Day, *Gender and Difference in Ancient Israel* (Minneapolis, 1989), 164–165, 170–173; Klein, in Brenner, *Feminist Companion,* 172–175; Levenson, *Esther,* 14–17; Berlin, *Esther,* 95; S. R. Johnson, *History as it Should Have Been* (Berkeley, forthcoming).

38. Fox, *Character and Ideology,* 147–148; cf. Kossmann, *Die Esthernovelle,* 310–313, 359–361.

39. So, e.g., Jones, *CBQ,* 39 (1977), 171, 181; Greenstein, in Neusner et al., *Judaic Perspectives,* 235; Lacocque, *Feminine Unconventional,* 70–71. T. S. Laniak, *Shame and Honor in the Book of Esther* (Atlanta, 1998), 6, 62, 66, 86, 172–174, essentially adopts this perspective, but finds the happy ending as something "the Jews occasionally enjoyed and always hoped for."

40. Beal, *Book of Hiding,* 119–122.

41. Goldman, *JSOT,* 47 (1990), 22–26.

42. There is some testimony indicating a forcible expulsion of Jews from Palestine in the Persian period; *Letter of Aristeas,* 35; Jos. *CAp.* 1.191, 1.194. The accuracy of those statements is most questionable. But even if they are accepted, they refer to Palestinian Jews, not to any oppression of diaspora Jews. On their accuracy, see B. Bar-Kochva, *Pseudo-Hecataeus, "On the Jews"* (Berkeley, 1996), 91–97, 143–145. Any oppression of religious minorities would be at variance with the general policy of the Persian empire; see M. Boyce, in *CHJ,* I, 279–307; M. Schwartz, in *CHI,* II, 664–697.

43. Esther, 3.15; cf. Levenson, *Esther,* 76–77. Berlin, *Esther,* 43, sees this simply as a reaction to the extremism of the decree.
44. Esther, 8.15.
45. Ibid., 6.13. See the discussions by Clines, *Esther Scroll,* 43–44, and Goldman, *JSOT,* 47 (1990), 23–24.
46. See Jones, *CBQ,* 39 (1977), 171, 181. A slightly different formulation is given in Niditch, *Underdogs and Tricksters,* 144–145; Greenstein, in Neusner et al., *Judaic Perspectives,* 239. A. Brenner, in Brenner, *Feminist Companion,* 79–80, notices the humor but stresses the didacticism.
47. Esther, 3.12–13, 8.12–13.
48. The farce is recognized by Jones, *CBQ,* 39 (1977), 180; cf. Wills, *Jewish Novel,* 95–98; Berlin, *Esther,* 87.
49. For the idea of wish-fulfillment, see Lacocque, *Feminine Unconventional,* 77–78.
50. On the origins of Purim, a much disputed topic, see Paton, *The Book of Esther,* 77–94; Berlin, *Esther,* xlv–xlix. Scholarship on the subject is summarized by Kossmann, *Die Esthernovelle,* 9–15.
51. A summary and sensible discussion can be found in C. A. Moore, *Tobit* (New York, 1996), 48–53, with important bibliography. Moore's commentary, in general, is an outstanding contribution.
52. On the manuscripts and the various versions, see D. C. Simpson, in Charles, *APOT,* I, 174–182; F. Zimmerman, *The Book of Tobit* (New York, 1958), 127–138; Schürer, *History,* III.1, 227–230; Moore, *Tobit,* 53–64.
53. The comedic elements have gained increasing appreciation in recent years. See Wills, *Jewish Novel,* 68–92; D. McCracken, *JBL,* 114 (1995), 401–418; Moore, *Tobit,* 24–26. J. Schwartz, *RevHistPhilRel,* 67 (1987), 295–297, even claims to find affinities with Menander and Greek New Comedy, but the parallels he cites are thin and strained.
54. Folklorists long ago isolated the motifs of "The Grateful Dead Man" and "The Monster in the Bridal Chamber" as principal components in this narrative. But numerous other strands also entered into this mix, including a borrowing from the story of Ahiqar, minister of the Assyrian king, who turns up here as a nephew of Tobit. See Simpson, in Charles, *APOT,* I, 187–194; R. H. Pfeiffer, *History of New Testament Times with an Introduction to the Apocrypha* (New York, 1949), 264–271; Zimmerman, *Book of Tobit,* 5–12; Schürer, *History,* III.1, 226–227; Wills, *Jewish Novel,* 73–76; Moore, *Tobit,* 11–14. The work does not, however, follow any prescribed pattern. See the remarks of W. Soll, *SBL Seminar Papers,* 27 (1988), 39–53. Whether Tobit qualifies as a "folktale" or a "fairy tale" is not a particularly helpful question; cf. J. Blenkinsopp, *JSOT,* 20 (1981), 27–46; P. J. Milne, *JSOT,* 34 (1986), 35–60. On the connections with wisdom literature, see M. Rabenau, *Studien zum Buch Tobit* (Berlin, 1994), 27–66.
55. Wills, *Jewish Novel,* 68–73, 91–92, judges the bulk of the text to be a popular novel, designed primarily for entertainment.
56. The shift from Tobit's own voice to that of an omniscient narrator later in the work has engendered extensive discussion. See, especially, I. Nowell, *SBL Seminar Papers,* 27 (1988), 27–38; B. Bow and G. W. E. Nickelsburg, in A.-J.

Levine, ed., *"Women Like This": New Perspectives on Jewish Women in the Greco-Roman World* (Atlanta, 1991), 127–128; J. E. Miller, *JSP,* 8 (1991), 53–61; McCracken, *JBL,* 114 (1995), 403–409; Moore, *Tobit,* 143–144.

57. Tobit, 1.3.

58. Ibid., 1.5–8.

59. Ibid., 1.10.

60. See the apt remarks of McCracken, *JBL,* 114 (1995), 407–409; cf. G. W. E. Nickelsburg, *Jewish Literature between the Bible and the Mishnah* (Philadelphia, 1981), 32–33; idem, in Stone, *Jewish Writings,* 41–42.

61. Tobit, 2.8: καὶ οἱ πλησίον μου κατεγέλων λέγοντες οὐ φοβεῖται οὐκέτι. The effort of Zimmermann, *Book of Tobit,* 57, to translate κατεγέλων in a positive sense as "marveled," rather than "derided," is implausible and unpersuasive. See Moore, *Tobit,* 129.

62. Tobit, 2.9–10. The satirical character is detected by T. Craven, *Artistry and Faith in the Book of Judith* (Chico, 1983), 116, n. 7; Wills, *Jewish Novel,* 82; and McCracken, *JBL,* 114 (1995), 402. Cf. Moore, *Tobit,* 131. Bird dung, to be sure, was regarded in antiquity as a cure for a bewildering variety of ailments; see, e.g., Pliny, *NH,* 30.26, 30.32, 30.58, 30.67–68, 30.70, 30.75, 30.107, 30.117, 30.137. If the author of Tobit makes allusion to this folkwisdom, he is plainly inverting it.

63. Tobit, 2.14: καὶ ποῦ εἰσιν αἱ ἐλεημοσύναι σου; ποῦ εἰσιν αἱ δικαιοσύναι σου; ἰδὲ ταῦτα μετὰ σοῦ γνωστά ἐστιν. The last phrase is obviously tortuous to translate. Moore, *Tobit,* 126, offers "Look where they've got you!" which is somewhat far from the text but gets the gist. The sarcasm is clear on any rendering; cf. Moore, op. cit., 134–135. A.-J. Levine, in J. A. Overman and R. S. MacLennan, eds., *Diaspora Jews and Judaism* (Atlanta, 1992), 110–111, rightly observes Tobit's discomfiture at Anna's entering the work force but fails to notice that this undermines his rather than her stature.

64. Tobit, 3.6: διότι λυσιτελεῖ μοι ἀποθανεῖν μᾶλλον ἢ ζῆν, ὅτι ὀνειδισμοὺς ψευδεῖς . . . καὶ μὴ ἀκούειν ὀνειδισμούς. Cf. McCracken, *JBL,* 114 (1995), 406–407. The effort of D. A. Bertrand, *RevHistPhilRel,* 68 (1988), 270–271, to see in this episode a reflection of Tobit's piety in seeking a pure offering for Passover is implausible.

65. Tobit, 3.7–9; see, especially, 3.9: τί ἡμᾶς μαστιγοῖς περὶ τῶν ἀνδρῶν σου. Zimmermann's translation, "Why do you vex us for husbands of yours?" loses the force of μαστιγοῖς.

66. Tobit, 3.10: ὅπως ἀποθάνω καὶ μηκέτι ὀνειδισμοὺς ἀκούσω ἐν τῇ ζωῇ μου; cf. 3.13; 3.15.

67. Tobit, 3.10, 3.15.

68. Ibid., 3.11—15.

69. Ibid., 4.13.

70. Ibid., 4.21.

71. Ibid., 4.20; cf. 4.1–2.

72. Ibid., 5.18–20.

73. Ibid., 10.1–7.

74. Ibid., 6.1–5.

75. See Moore, *Tobit,* 198–200, for a variety of alternatives and useful bibliographical references.

76. Cf. McCracken, *JBL,* 114 (1995), 402.

77. Tobit, 8.1–3; cf. 6.17. A number of ingenious explanations have been offered for this scene, which require no rehearsal here. See references and summary in Moore, *Tobit,* 236–237.

78. Tobit, 11.7–12; cf. 6.9.

79. B. Kollmann, *ZAW,* 106 (1994), 289–299, sees a combination of magic and medicine here. So also Moore, *Tobit,* 201–202. It is, of course, true that numerous prescriptions for ancient remedies included the use of fish products. Pliny indeed cites the value of fish gall for improving vision; *NH,* 29.125, 32.69–70. And still closer parallels appear in the late antique compilation of pseudo-medicinal works preserved under the title of *Cyranides.* One remedy has fish gall as healing white spots in the eye, and another has fish liver as curing blindness; 4.13. See the edition of D. Kaimakis, *Die Kyraniden* (Meisenheim am Glan, 1976), 252. It does not follow that the author of Tobit held a brief for such medications. In fact, audience familiarity with them would give special point to the mockery. The same may well hold for the *Cyranides'* references, 4.13, 4.55, to fish parts driving out demons; Kaimakis, op. cit., 252, 283. Further evidence can be found in Kallmann, *ZAW,* 106 (1994), 292–297.

80. Tobit, 8.5–9. On the overuse, perhaps in a whimsical way, of the terms "brother" and "sister" in this work, see Wills, *Jewish Novel,* 78–79.

81. Tobit, 8.10–19. Earlier scholars, disappointingly, found nothing funny in this scene; e.g., Zimmermann, *Book of Tobit,* 95–97. But see Craven, *Artistry and Faith,* 116, n. 7; Wills, *Jewish Novel,* 80; McCracken, *JBL,* 114 (1995), 412–413; Moore, *Tobit,* 239–240.

82. The author has Shalmaneser as conqueror of Israel and presents a sequence of Shalmaneser, Sennacherib, and Esarhaddon on the Assyrian throne; Tobit, 1.2, 1.10–15, 1.21. In fact, Sargon II was the son of Shalmaneser; he completed the conquest; and he was the father of Sennacherib. The actual deportation of Israelites from Naphtali, Tobit's tribe, occurred earlier, in the reign of Tiglath-Pileser, the predecessor of Shalmaneser. See the discussions of Zimmermann, *Book of Tobit,* 15, 50–51, and Moore, *Tobit,* 101–102, 119. There is even more hopeless confusion in the text's reference to the fall of Nineveh and its supposed conqueror at 14.15. See Moore, *Tobit,* 296–297.

83. Cf. C. C. Torrey, *JBL,* 41 (1922), 237–245; Zimmermann, *Book of Tobit,* 16.

84. Zimmermann, *Book of Tobit,* 15, 22.

85. So, e.g., Simpson, in Charles, *APOT,* I, 183; Nickelsburg, *Jewish Literature,* 35; idem, in Stone, *Jewish Writings,* 45; Schürer, *History,* III.1, 224; Rabenau, *Studien zum Buch Tobit,* 182; Moore, *Tobit,* 41.

86. Zimmermann, *Book of Tobit,* 23–24; Wills, *Jewish Novel,* 72. Zimmermann even sees Nineveh as a disguise for Antioch, the purported location of the book's composer; op. cit., 19–20.

87. Tobit, 13.16–17, 14.4–5. The argument of Zimmermann, *Book of Tobit,* 24–26, followed by Wills, *Jewish Novel,* 86–87, that these two final chapters were composed independently of the main corpus and subsequent to the destruction of the Second Temple, are strained and inconclusive. And the argument is severely damaged by the fact that at least parts of these chapters appear in the Qumran texts; 4QTob. a, c–e. The texts may be consulted, with

valuable commentary by J. A. Fitzmyer, in J. VanderKam et al., eds., *Discoveries in the Judaean Desert*, XIX (Oxford, 1995), 1–76.

88. The Aramaic fragments from Qumran have prompted a host of suggestions, but they cannot themselves determine a date of composition. See J. A. Fitzmyer, *CBQ*, 57 (1995), 655–675. The proposal of J. Lebram, *ZAW*, 76 (1964), 328–331, that the text can be fixed to ca. 300 BCE, on the grounds that the author alludes to the sequence of world kingdoms but does not register the Macedonians (14.4–7), is altogether speculative. Earlier discussions of the date are usefully summarized by Simpson, in Charles, *APOT*, I, 183–185.

89. A summary of earlier opinions can be found in Simpson, in Charles, *APOT*, I, 185–187. He himself opts for Egypt, on flimsy grounds. See the criticisms of Zimmermann, *Book of Tobit*, 15–21, whose choice of Antioch has little to recommend it. The thesis of J. Milik, *RB*, 73 (1966), 522–530, that the author was a Samarian with links to the house of the Tobiads (endorsed by Rabenau, *Studien zum Buch Tobit*, 175–182, and Wills, *Jewish Novel*, 72), lacks any substance. The majority view of an eastern diaspora provenance is well expressed by Nickelsburg, in Stone, *Jewish Writings*, 45. See also Moore, *Tobit*, 42–43, with a valuable summary of previous scholarship. But a case has also been made for Palestinian authorship; see, e.g., Pfeiffer, *History of New Testament Times*, 275; J. C. Dancy et al., eds., *The Shorter Books of the Apocrypha* (Cambridge, 1972), 10.

90. Cf. the cautious formulation of Schürer, *History*, III.1, 223.

91. The glowing anticipation occurs most vividly at the end of the work, in Tobit's final prayer and in the testamentary advice to his son; Tobit, 13.1–17, 14.11. On the centrality of these lessons, see, e.g., Simpson, in Charles, *APOT*, I, 186–187; Nickelsburg, *Jewish Literature*, 32–35; idem, in Stone, *Jewish Writings*, 43–45; M. Delcor, in *CHJ*, II, 474–475; McCracken, *JBL*, 114 (1995), 417–418; Moore, *Tobit*, 22–24, with an instructive sampling of various opinions. And see now Johnson, *History as it Should Have Been* (Berkeley, forthcoming).

92. E.g., Tobit, 1.9, 3.15, 4.12–13, 6.11–13, 7.10. Cf. Dancy et al., *Shorter Books*, 8; Rabenau, *Studien zum Buch Tobit*, 121–126; W. Soll, in C. A. Evans and J. A. Sanders, eds., *The Function of Scripture in Early Jewish and Christian Tradition* (Sheffield, 1998), 166–175. Levine, in Overman and MacLennan, *Diaspora Jews*, 105, puts it nicely: "it delineates Israel by means of genealogy rather than geography."

93. Levine, in Overman and MacLennan, *Diaspora Jews*, 105–117.

94. Tobit, 13.13, 14.6. See McCracken, *JBL*, 114 (1995), 415–417.

95. Tobit, 1.9, 1.14, 1.21, 5.11–14, 6.11.

96. The terms "brother" and "sister" occur sixty-six times in the text. This was overlooked by almost all commentators but is acutely noted by Wills, *Jewish Novel*, 78, who recognizes the satirical character here.

97. Tobit, 6.18.

98. A number of useful commentaries can be consulted. See, especially, A. E. Cowley, in Charles, *APOT*, I, 242–267; M. S. Enslin, *The Book of Judith* (Leiden, 1972); Dancy et al., *Shorter Books*, 67–131; E. Zenger, *JSHRZ*, I.6; C. A. Moore, *Judith* (Garden City, 1985), with substantial bibliography at 109–117. On the texts, see R. Hanhart, *Text und Textgeschichte des Buches*

Judith (Göttingen, 1979). The fullest treatment of the later Judith traditions may be found in A. M. Dubarle, *Judith: Formes et sens des diverses traditions* (Rome, 1966), 2 vols.

99. See N. Stone, in J. C. VanderKam, ed., *"No One Spoke Ill of Her": Essays on Judith* (Atlanta, 1992), 73–93; M. Bal, in A. Brenner, ed., *A Feminist Companion to Esther, Judith, and Susanna* (Sheffield, 1995), 253–285.

100. Judith, 4.1–3.

101. I Clement, 55.4.

102. Origen, *Ep. Ad Afr.* 13. Craven, *Artistry and Faith, 5,* even ventures to suggest that there was no Hebrew original and that the tale was initially composed in Greek. The numerous Hebraisms in the Greek make this unlikely. See Cowley, in Charles, *APOT,* I, 244–245; Zenger, *JSHRZ,* I.6, 430–431; Moore, *Judith,* 66–67. But the matter remains unsettled; cf. Schürer, *History,* III.1, 219–220.

103. It is not impossible that the text was composed in the diaspora. The phraseology, οἱ υἱοὶ Ισραηλ οἱ κατοικοῦντες ἐν τῇ Ιουδαίᾳ (Judith, 4.1), would be quite unusual coming from one who dwelled in Judaea; so S. Zeitlin, in Enslin, *Book of Judith,* 31–32. Moore, *Judith,* 70, 147, considers the use of the term "children of Israel" as a deliberate archaism. But that does not account for the phrase "children of Israel dwelling in Judaea"—which implies a diaspora perspective.

104. Judith, 8.6–8, 8.25, 9.1–14, 10.9, 12.8, 13.4–7, 13.14–16, 16.1–5, 16.13–17, 16.19. The notion that this work represents orthodox Pharisaism, however, or the doctrines of any particular sect is questionable. See the remarks of D. Winston, in L. Alonzo-Schökel, *Narrative Structures in the Book of Judith* (Berkeley, 1974), 64; Craven, *Artistry and Faith,* 118–122; and Lacocque, *Feminine Unconventional,* 44–45.

105. Cf. Johnson, *History as it Should Have Been* (Berkeley, forthcoming).

106. Alonso-Schökel, *Narrative Structures,* 8–11; Moore, *Judith,* 78–85. Dancy et al., *Shorter Books,* 67, 129, sees this only in the second part of the work. On the subversion of gender roles, see A.-J. Levine, in VanderKam, ed., *"No One Spoke Ill of Her,"* 17–28; Wills, *Jewish Novel,* 142–152; M. Stocker, *Judith: Sexual Warrior: Women and Power in Western Culture* (New Haven, 1998), 3–10.

107. Craven, *Artistry and Faith,* 115–116; Wills, *Jewish Novel,* 134–139.

108. Judith, 1.1, 1.5, 1.13–16, 2.5.

109. So, e.g., Pfeiffer, *History of New Testament Times,* 297; O. Eissfeldt, *The Old Testament* (Oxford, 1965), 586; Nickelsburg, *Jewish Literature,* 106; cf. Enslin, *Book of Judith,* 58: "historical slips."

110. The campaign of Artaxerxes III included generals named Orophernes (Holofernes?) and Bagoas (Diod. 16.47.4, 31.19.2–3), both of whom play a role in the Judith tale, thereby inducing some to see it as inspired by that expedition. For a list of scholars who have held that view, see Schürer, *History,* III.1, 217–218. Add also Cowley, in Charles, *APOT,* I, 246. The notion that "Nebuchadnezzar" actually substitutes for Antiochus IV or another Seleucid king and thus helps to establish a Maccabean or post-Maccabean date for the book's composition is widespread; see, e.g., Pfeiffer, *History of*

New Testament Times, 294–295; M. Delcor, *Klio,* 49 (1967), 151–179; Zeitlin, in Enslin, *Book of Judith,* 28–30; Dancy et al., *Shorter Books,* 70; Nickelsburg, *Jewish Literature,* 108–109; Zenger, *JSHRZ,* I.6, 442–443; Schürer, *History,* III.1, 218–219; Frölich, *Time and Times and Half a Time,* 121–122, 127. A summary of opinions can be found in Moore, *Judith,* 49–56; cf. 67–70. And see now S. Burstein, in F. B. Titchener and R. F. Moorton, Jr., eds., *The Eye Expanded: Life and the Arts in Greco-Roman Antiquity* (Berkeley, 1999), 105–112. D. Mendels, *The Land of Israel as a Political Concept in Hasmonean Literature* (Tübingen, 1987), 51–56, believes that territorial indications in the text allow him to pinpoint a date between 140 and 134 BCE. Ilan, *Integrating Women,* 136–137, 150–151, prefers a time around 77 BCE, as propaganda for Shlomzion's acquisition of the Hasmonean throne. But Judith's withdrawal into private life would hardly serve to advance the interests of a Jewish queen.

111. Judith, 5.18–19.
112. This was recognized long ago by C. C. Torrey, *The Apocryphal Literature: A Brief Introduction* (New Haven, 1945), 89–90. See also Craven, *Artistry and Faith,* 71–74; Moore, *Judith,* 79; Lacocque, *Feminine Unconventional,* 31–32.
113. Judith, 1.1–4. The point was to contrast Nebuchadnezzar's ability to capture massive fortifications wth his inability to take the small town of Bethulia. So, rightly, Moore, *Judith,* 124–125.
114. Judith, 1.16; cf. Esther, 1.4.
115. Judith, 2.21–28. Moore, *Judith,* 137–139, attempts tortuously to make some rational sense out of this muddle. Cf. also Zenger, *JSHRZ,* I.6, 461–463. The attempt is best abandoned; cf. Enslin, *Book of Judith,* 71–74. Dancy et al., *Shorter Books,* 80, may miss the point by suggesting that the author neither knew nor cared about geography.
116. Judith, 4.5–7.
117. Ibid., 4.9–12.
118. Craven, *Artistry and Faith,* 115, rightly sees the humor. Commentators generally pass over the matter as an exhibit of the gravity of the situation and of the Jews' earnestness. Cf. Enslin, *Book of Judith,* 82–83; Zenger, *JSHRZ,* I.6, 469; Moore, *Judith,* 152. It is true that the placing of sackcloth on livestock also occurs in the book of Jonah, 3.7–8. But it may very well serve as caricature in that text as well. On Jonah as comedy, see J. Miles, *JQR,* 65 (1975), 168–181; J. W. Whedbee, *Semeia,* 7 (1977), 1–39; idem, *Bible and Comic Vision,* 191–220. The placing of sackcloth over the altar is nowhere else attested, evidently a creation of the author.
119. Judith, 5–6.
120. Ibid., 6.10–13.
121. Ibid., 7.4, 7.17–18.
122. Ibid., 7.19–32.
123. Ibid., 8.1. See the acute analysis of M. Steinmann, *Lecture de Judith* (Paris, 1953), 72–74, who suggests that this made-up ancestry may be a dig at the author's contemporary aristocrats. The argument of E. J. Bruns, *CBQ,* 18

(1956), 19–22, that an authentic tradition underlies the genealogy is unpersuasive.

124. Judith, 8.6.
125. Ibid., 8.13.
126. Ibid., 8.30–31. There may here be an echo of Aaron's response to Moses in Exodus 32.21–24; cf. Zenger, *JSHRZ*, I.6, 491.
127. Judith, 8.32–35.
128. Ibid., 9.10: πάταξον δοῦλον ἐκ χειλέων ἀπάτης μου ἐπ' ἄρχοντι; 9.13: δὸς λόγον μου καὶ ἀπάτην εἰς τραῦμα καὶ μώλωπα αὐτῶν; cf. 10.4: ἐκαλλωπίσατο σφόδρα εἰς ἀπάτησιν ὀφθαλμῶν ἀνδρῶν. And note the use of ἀπάτη to refer to the Lord's enemies in 9.3.
129. Judith, 10.3–4.
130. Ibid., 10.3: ἐν οἷς ἐστολίζετο ἐν ταῖς ἡμέραις τῆς ζωῆς τοῦ ἀνδρὸς αὐτῆς Μανασση.
131. Ibid., 10.7–10. That this took place at night is clear from 8.33, 9.1, 11.3. Dancy et al., *Shorter Books*, 106–107, noticed the anomaly and ascribed it to the author's forgetfulness! Moore, *Judith*, 202, remarks that "the author was not concerned with the question of how the women could be seen at night." Most commentators pay no heed to the matter.
132. Judith, 10.12.
133. Ibid., 11.5–8.
134. The insistence on her truthfulness comes also at Judith, 11.10.
135. Judith, 11.17–18, 11.23.
136. Ibid., 10.19.
137. Ibid., 12.12.
138. Ibid., 12.16: ἐτήρει καιρὸν τοῦ ἀπατῆσαι αὐτὴν ἀφ' ἧς ἡμέρας εἶδεν αὐτήν.
139. Ibid., 12.20, 13.2. See the deliberate contrast between 12.18 and 12.20.
140. Ibid., 13.6–10. See 13.8.
141. Ibid., 13.16: ἠπάτησεν αὐτὸν τὸ πρόσοπόν μου εἰς ἀπώλειαν αὐτοῦ. The repeated use of ἀπάτη is not accidental.
142. Ibid., 14.1–2, 14.11.
143. Ibid., 14.6–10.
144. Deut. 23.3–4.
145. It is quite impossible to believe that this was an oversight on the part of the author. So, e.g., Cowley, in Charles, *APOT*, I, 264: "The author overlooks the law of Deut. xxiii.3"; Enslin, *Book of Judith*, 160: "the author is seemingly unconcerned with the prohibition of Ammonites." It helps little to postulate a broad-minded attitude toward non-Jews on the part of the author, an attitude nowhere else exhibited; so Zenger, *JSHRZ*, I.6, 512; or to explain Achior's conversion as an exception to the rule; as does Dancy et al., *Shorter Books*, 120; Moore, *Judith*, 235–236. The very concrete description of the circumcision shows a purposeful effort to call attention to it, as does the insistence upon the lasting nature of the conversion; Judith, 14.10: περιετέμετο τὴν σάρκα τῆς ἀκροβυστίας αὐτοῦ καὶ προσετέθη εἰς τὸν οἶκον Ισραηλ ἕως τῆς ἡμέρας ταύτης. Some have taken this episode as a reason for failure of the text to make it into the canon; e.g., Steinmann, *Lecture de Judith*, 61–62;

Lacocque, *Feminine Unconventional*, 40–41. That puts too great a burden on this event. Many other possible elements bear on the issue of non-canonicity; see Craven, *Artistry and Faith*, 117–118; Moore, in VanderKam, *"No One Spoke Ill of Her,"* 61–71.

146. Judith, 14.15.

147. Ibid., 15.3, 15.11.

148. Ibid., 16.6–9; 16.8. Note the use, once more, of ἀπάτη.

149. Ibid., 16.22–23.

150. On the original language, see the discussions of F. Zimmerman, *JQR*, 48 (1957/58), 236–241; C. A. Moore, *Daniel, Esther, and Jeremiah: The Additions* (Garden City, 1977), 81–84, with bibliography. For comparison of the two versions in the Septuagint and Theodotion, see J. Schüpphaus, *ZAW*, 83 (1971), 49–72; Moore, op. cit., 78–80; H. Engel, *Die Susanna-Erzählung* (Göttingen, 1985), 10–17, 55–77. A useful review of the principal scholarship may be found in M. J. Steussy, *Gardens in Babylon: Narrative and Faith in the Greek Legends of Daniel* (Atlanta, 1993), 49–54.

151. The summary is based on the slightly longer and fuller edition of Theodotion. Some of the comments that follow are adapted from the discussion in Gruen, *Heritage and Hellenism*, 173–177.

152. The patterns were discerned by G. Huet, *RHR*, 65 (1912), 277–284; W. Baumgartner, *Archiv für Religionswissenschaft*, 24 (1926), 268–280; B. Heller, *ZAW*, 54 (1936), 281–287; and now widely adopted: e.g., Pfeiffer, *History of New Testament Times*, 453–454; Moore, *Additions*, 88–89; Wills, *Jew in the Court*, 76–79.

153. Cf. Nickelsburg, *Jewish Literature*, 25–26; Steussy, *Gardens in Babylon*, 141–142, 191.

154. Susanna, 43.

155. See the trenchant comments of J. A. Glancy, in Brenner, *Feminist Companion*, 288–302; cf. also A.-J. Levine, in Brenner, op. cit., 306–313, 319–323. The demure and passive character of Susanna decisively undermines the thesis of Ilan, *Integrating Women*, 149–150, that this text has any connection with the reign of queen Shlomzion in the early first century BCE.

156. Susanna, 7–8: ἐθεώρουν αὐτὴν οἱ δύο πρεσβύτεροι καθ᾽ ἡμέραν εἰσπορευομένην καὶ περιπατοῦσαν καὶ ἐγένοντο ἐν ἐπιθυμίᾳ αὐτῆς. See M. Bal, *Biblical Interpretation*, 1 (1993), 4; Levine, in Brenner, *Feminist Companion*, 313. Note that Daniel accuses one of the elders of having been led astray by beauty and perverted by lust; Susanna, 56: τὸ κάλλος ἐξηπάτησέν σε, καὶ ἡ ἐπιθυμία διέστρεψεν τὴν καρδίαν σου.

157. See M. Miles, *Carnal Knowing: Female Nakedness and Religious Meaning in the Christian West* (Boston, 1989), 121–124; Bal, *Biblical Interpretation*, 1 (1993), 1–18; Glancy, in Brenner, *Feminist Companion*, 292–294; E. Spolsky, in E. Spolsky, *The Judgment of Susanna* (Atlanta, 1996), 101–117.

158. It is noteworthy that, according to the text, the maids left the garden and shut the door without seeing the elders, but no explicit statement denies that Susanna was aware of their presence. She did not express surprise when they accosted her. See Susanna, 15–22.

159. Susanna, 27.

160. Ibid., 49, 54–55.
161. Among the theological interpretations, see Baumgartner, *Archiv für Religionswissenschaft*, 24 (1926), 279–280; Pfeiffer, *History of New Testament Times*, 454; R. A. F. MacKenzie, *Canadian Journal of Theology*, 211–218; Moore, *Additions*, 89–90.
162. Susanna, 45: ἐξήγειρεν ὁ θεὸς τὸ πνεῦμα τὸ ἅγιον παιδαρίου νεωτέρου. In the Septuagint version, an angel bestows the πνεῦμα upon Daniel. But it does not follow, as suggested by R. Dunn, *Christianity and Literature*, 31 (1982), 22–24, that Daniel's actions are subsequently dictated by the angel, whereas his free agency exists only in Theodotion's edition.
163. On the trickery of Daniel as a means to reinforce the passivity of Susanna and confirm the patriarchal order, see S. Sered and S. Cooper in Spolsky, *Judgment of Susanna*, 43–55.
164. The expression is used by Wills, *Jewish Novel*, 57.
165. Susanna, 13–14. The humor here is actually more vivid in the Septuagint version than in Theodotion's.
166. Susanna, 24: καὶ ἀνεβόησεν φωνῇ μεγάλῃ Σουσαννα, ἐβόησαν δὲ καὶ οἱ δύο πρεσβῦται κατέναντι αὐτῆς.
167. Ibid., 25: καὶ δραμὼν ὁ εἷς ἤνοιξεν τὰς θύρας τοῦ παραδείσου.
168. Ibid., 54–55: σχῖνον . . . σχίσει; 58–59: πρῖνον . . . πρῖσαι.
169. So, e.g., Dunn, *Christianity and Literature*, 31 (1982), 24–26; Lacocque, *Feminine Unconventional*, 27–30. The idea goes back to D. M. Kay, in Charles, *APOT*, I, 642, who reckoned that the story would be unpopular with the elders of Jewish society, thus explaining its absence in the canon. This is itself a reflection of the debate among the Church Fathers. Cf. B. Halpern-Amaru, in Spolsky, *Judgment of Susanna*, 24–31.
170. See Susanna, 63. The family had raised no objection, for instance, when Susanna, according to the Septuagint text, had been stripped at her trial, on the demand of the accusers; Susanna, 32. Theodotion softens this by having her stripped simply of her veil.
171. See, especially, Glancy, in Brenner, *Feminist Companion*, 292, 301; Levine, in Brenner, op. cit., 310–313; Sered and Cooper, in Spolsky, *Judgment of Susanna*, 54–55; A. Bach, *Women, Seduction, and Betrayal in Biblical Narrative* (Cambridge, 1997), 69–72.
172. Susanna, 5, 41.
173. Ibid., 50.
174. As Levine wittily puts it, in Brenner, *Feminist Companion*, 312, "Rather than lamenting by the waters of Babylon, she bathes in them."
175. The efforts of Steussy, *Gardens in Babylon*, 183–195, to make a direct connection between the Additions to Daniel and the experiences of Jews in various diaspora communities seem strained and forced. Nor is it obvious that the diaspora community is vulnerable and can survive only with divine help, with Daniel as the hope of the future to rescue Israel from its distress; so Levine, in Brenner, *Feminist Companion*, 319–320; cf. also Sered and Cooper, in Spolsky, *Judgment of Susanna*, 55: "Daniel emerges as the model of a Diaspora leader."
176. II Macc. 2.19–31.

177. The edition with text, translation, and notes by F.-M. Abel, *Les Livres des Maccabées* (Paris, 1949) remains fundamental. See also J. R. Bartlett, *The First and Second Books of the Maccabees* (Cambridge, 1973). The very learned and valuable, though often quirky, commentary of J. A. Goldstein, *II Maccabees* (Garden City, 1983) is indispensable. For a useful summary of the main issues and bibliography, see Schürer, *History*, III.1, 531–537.

178. Cf., e.g., E. J. Bickermann, *Der Gott der Makkabäer* (Berlin, 1937), 147; C. Habicht, *JSHRZ*, I.3, 189.

179. See F. W. Walbank, *Historia*, 9 (1960), 216–234; R. Doran, *Temple Propaganda* (Washington, 1981), 84–89.

180. Goldstein, *II Maccabees*, 14–19.

181. Doran, *Temple Propaganda*, 47–76.

182. Cf. D. Arenhoevel, *Die Theokratie nach dem 1. und 2. Makkabäerbuch* (Mainz, 1967), 102–106, 112–113, 118–120.

183. II Macc. 5.19.

184. J. G. Bunge, *Untersuchungen zum zweiten Makkabäerbuch* (Bonn, 1971), 184–190; A. Momigliano, *CP*, 70 (1975), 81–88.

185. Cf. Doran, *Temple Propaganda*, 105–107.

186. Wills, *Jewish Novel*, 193–201.

187. II Macc. 3.1–40.

188. For the Hezekiah episode, see II Chron. 32.1–22; II Kings, 18.17–19, 18.36. Other parallels are cited in Doran, *Temple Propaganda*, 47–48; Goldstein, *II Maccabees*, 198.

189. II Macc. 3.15: ἐπεκαλοῦντο εἰς οὐρανὸν τὸν περὶ παρακαταθήκης νομοθετήσαντα τοῖς παρακαταθεμένοις ταῦτα σῶα διαφυλάξαι; 3.22: οἱ μὲν οὖν ἐπεκαλοῦντο τὸν παγκρατῆ κύριον τὰ πεπιστευμένα τοῖς πεπιστευκόσιν σῶα διαφυλάσσειν μετὰ πάσης ἀσφαλείας.

190. See J. Moffatt, in Charles, *APOT*, I, 135; E. J. Bickermann, *Studies in Jewish and Christian History* (Leiden, 1980), 172–190; Goldstein, *II Maccabees*, 210–212.

191. II Macc. 3.37–38: εἴ τινα ἔχεις πολέμιον ἢ πραγμάτων ἐπίβουλον, πέμψον αὐτὸν ἐκεῖ, καὶ μεμαστιγωμένον αὐτὸν προσδέξῃ, ἐάνπερ καὶ διασωθῇ.

192. Appian, *Syr.* 45.

193. II Macc. 4.37.

194. Ibid., 9.4–10.

195. Cf. T. W. Africa, *CA*, 1 (1982), 1–17; O. W. Allen, Jr., *The Death of Herod: The Narrative and Theological Function of Retribution in Luke-Acts* (Atlanta, 1997), 29–74.

196. II Macc. 9.12.

197. Ibid., 9.13–16.

198. Ibid., 9.15.

199. Ibid., 9.17: πρὸς δὲ τούτοις καὶ Ἰουδαῖον ἔσεσθαι, καὶ πάντα τόπον οἰκητὸν ἐπελεύσεσθαι καταγγέλλοντα τὸ τοῦ θεοῦ κράτος.

200. Ibid., 3.16–18.

201. Jos. *Ant.* 11.326.

202. III Macc. 1.16–29.

203. II Macc. 3.32.
204. Ibid., 15.12.

6. DIASPORA HUMOR II: BIBLICAL RECREATIONS

1. Many other texts along these lines are discussed, with somewhat different purposes, in E. S. Gruen, *Heritage and Hellenism: The Reinvention of Jewish Tradition* (Berkeley, 1998), 110–188. The texts treated here and in that work stand somewhat apart from what is often referred to as "the rewritten Bible," efforts to recreate biblical narrative with some variation and supplementation, while remaining close to the original, as in Jubilees, Josephus, Pseudo-Philo, or the Genesis Apocryphon. Cf. D. J. Harrington, in R. A. Kraft and G. W. E. Nickelsburg, eds., *Early Judaism and Its Modern Interpreters* (Atlanta, 1986), 239–247; P. Alexander, in D. A. Carson and H. G. N. Williamson, eds., *It Is Written: Scripture Citing Scripture* (Cambridge, 1988), 99–121; B. Halpern-Amaru, *Rewriting the Bible* (Valley Forge, 1994), 4.

2. For the view that both rescensions derived from a single original, see M. R. James, *The Testament of Abraham* (Cambridge, 1892), 34–49; G. H. Box, *The Testament of Abraham* (London, 1927), xii–xv; M. Delcor, *Le Testament d'Abraham* (Leiden, 1973), 5–14. By contrast, E. P. Sanders, in J. H. Charlesworth, *OTP*, I, 871–872, holds that each had a separate Vorlage. For G. W. E. Nickelsburg, in G. W. E. Nickelsburg, ed., *Studies on the Testament of Abraham* (Missoula, 1976), 47–60, 85–93, the longer version precedes the shorter, whereas F. Schmidt, in Nickelsburg, op. cit., 65–83, reaches the reverse conclusion, arguing that Rescension A constitutes a reworking and expansion of Rescension B. A strong case for Rescension A as the earlier has now been made in a forthcoming study by J. Ludlow, *Abraham Meets Death: Narrative Humor in the Testament of Abraham*. The evidence will not readily allow for confident results; see the sober remarks of R. A. Kraft, in Nickelsburg, op. cit., 121–137. On the texts and versions of the two rescensions, see the full study by Schmidt, *Le Testament grec d'Abraham* (Tübingen, 1986). The most thoroughgoing commentary available is that of Delcor, op. cit.

3. See the arguments of James, *Testament of Abraham*, 76; N. Turner, "The Testament of Abraham" (diss., London, 1953), 177–185; and Delcor, *Le Testament d'Abraham*, 28–34, 67–73. Cf. Nickelsburg, *Jewish Literature Between the Bible and the Mishnah* (Philadelphia, 1981), 253; Sanders, in Charlesworth, *OTP*, I, 875. Schmidt, in Nickelsburg, *Studies*, 78–80, although he sees Rescension B as the original version and reckons it as the product of Palestinian Jews, finds the longer version to be a composition of the Jewish diaspora in Egypt. Palestinian provenance is claimed by E. Janssen, *JSHRZ*, III.2, 198–199, on flimsy grounds. Kraft, in Nickelsburg, *Studies*, 129–130, considers the evidence inadequate for a conclusion.

4. See the discussions, quite indecisive, of James, *Testament of Abraham*, 7–29; Delcor, *Le Testament*, 73–77; Janssen, *JSHRZ*, III.2, 198; Sanders, in Charlesworth, *OTP*, I, 874–875.

5. Very little attention has been paid to the amusing aspects of this work.

Nickelsburg, *Jewish Literature,* 250–251, alludes to "humorous touches" but does not explore them. By contrast, L. M. Wills, *The Jewish Novel in the Ancient World* (Ithaca, 1995), 249–256, regards the whole work as a "satirical novel," rather an extreme position, but even he overlooks many of the more amusing features of it. Ludlow, *Abraham Meets Death,* provides a valuable treatment of the subject.

6. On the eschatology, see, especially, Delcor, *Le Testament,* 52–63; Nickelsburg, in Nickelsburg, *Studies,* 23–64; P. B. Munoa, III, *Four Powers in Heaven: The Interpretation of Daniel 7 in the Testament of Abraham* (Sheffield, 1998), 43–81. The angelic figures are studied by A. B. Kolenkow, in Nickelsburg, op. cit., 153–162.

7. So Wills, *Jewish Novel,* 250.

8. T Abr. 1.4, 2.1–4, etc.

9. See examples collected by Delcor, *Le Testament,* 91. And, in general, see J. P. Rohland, *Der Erzengel Michael: Arzt und Feldherr* (Leiden, 1977).

10. T Abr. 7.11: καὶ λέγει ὁ ἀρχιστράτηγος ἐγώ εἰμι Μιχαὴλ ὁ ἀρχιστράτηγος.

11. Ibid., 2.2–5.

12. Ibid., 4.5–6. Cf. Wills, *Jewish Novel,* 253, who sees the absurdity in this.

13. T Abr. 4.5–6, 5.1, 8.1, 9.1, 9.7, 10.1, 15.11.

14. Ibid., 2.9–12.

15. Ibid., 4.9–10: καὶ νῦν, κύριε, τί ποιήσω; πῶς διαλάθω μετὰ τούτων καθήμενος ἐν μιᾷ τραπέζῃ μετ᾽ αὐτοῦ; ὁ δὲ κύριος εἶπε . . . ἐγὼ ἀποστελῶ ἐπὶ σὲ πνεῦμα παμφάγον . . . καὶ συνευφράνθητι καὶ σὺ μετ᾽ αὐτοῦ. A noteworthy parallel appears in Tobit, 12.19. On angels and food, see the note by Delcor, *Le Testament,* 108.

16. T Abr. 3.1–4, 3.9–12. On parallels for the legend of the speaking tree, see James, *Testament of Abraham,* 59–64.

17. T Abr. 6.1–6. The whimsicality is rightly recognized by Wills, *Jewish Novel,* 253. One might note also that recognition by his feet sits ill with the notion of Michael as "incorporeal"—perhaps another little twist by the author. Thanks are due to George Nickelsburg for this observation.

18. T Abr. 8.12: ἐὰν ἐάσω τὸν θάνατον ἀπελθεῖν σοι τότε ἂν εἶχον ἰδεῖν κἂν ἔρχῃ κἂν οὐκ ἔρχῃ.

19. Ibid., 9.5–8.

20. Ibid., 10.4–13.

21. Ibid., 11.4–7.

22. Ibid., 16.3.

23. Ibid., 16.6–13.

24. Ibid., 17.4–17.

25. On possible Egyptian influences on some of these imaginings, see James, *Testament of Abraham,* 56–58; Delcor, *Le Testament,* 162–164.

26. T Abr. 17.18.

27. Ibid., 17.19–18.1.

28. Ibid., 18.9–11.

29. Ibid., 19.4–16.

30. Ibid., 20.1–3.

31. Ibid., 20.8–9: πεπλάνηκεν γὰρ τὸν Ἀβραὰμ ὁ θάνατος; καὶ ἠσπάσατο τὴν χεῖρα αὐτοῦ, καὶ εὐθέως ἐκολλᾶτο ἡ ψυχὴ αὐτοῦ ἐν τῇ χειρὶ τοῦ θανάτου.

32. Ibid., 1.4, 4.11, 8.11, 15.1, 15.7.

33. So, rightly, Nickelsburg, in Nickelsburg, *Studies,* 87–88. Kolenkow, in Nickelsburg, op. cit., 139–162, correctly notes the significant differences between the Testament of Abraham and works in the standard testament genre. So also Delcor, *Le Testament,* 42–45. Kolenkow further argues, less plausibly, that its main point is Abraham's repentance of his sinful desire to destroy all sinners—in this way paralleling a feature (the confession of sinners) that does appear in other testament works. That feature exists, to be sure, but hardly as the pivot of the piece. And it has nothing to do with the actual references to Abraham's final dispositions—which he consciously and deliberately avoided.

34. Cf. Janssen, *JSHRZ,* III.2, 196; Sanders, in Charlesworth, *OTP,* I, 880. On heavenly tours in general, see M. Himmelfarb, *Ascent to Heaven in Jewish and Christian Apocalypses* ((New York, 1993), who properly excludes the Testament of Abraham from this category; op. cit., 8. K. Kohler, *JQR,* 7 (1895), 581–606, misleadingly regards the text as "the Apocalypse of Abraham." Some have insisted that the whole story turns on the judgment scene; e.g., James, *Testament of Abraham,* 52; J. J. Collins, *The Apocalyptic Imagination* (New York, 1984), 201–204; Munoa, *Four Powers,* 28–42. That narrows the text's focus in unacceptable fashion.

35. Cf. Wills, *Jewish Novel,* 254.

36. This aspect is stressed by Nickelsburg, *Jewish Literature,* 251–252. So also Kolenkow, in Nickelsburg, *Studies,* 147–148.

37. See, especially, Collins, *Apocalyptic Imagination,* 202–204. Similiarly, Janssen, *JSHRZ,* III.2, 197–198; Nickelsburg, *Jewish Literature,* 251.

38. See references and discussion by James, *Testament of Abraham,* 64–70. Cf. also Sanders, in Charlesworth, *OTP,* I, 879.

39. See the important articles by S. E. Loewenstaam, in Nickelsburg, *Studies,* 185–217, 219–225. Abraham had no doubts about his mortality; T Abr. 9.5.

40. This departs from the idea of Nickelsburg, *Jewish Literature,* 251, that the work constitutes a parody of Abraham's most prominent biblical virtue, his unflagging faith; cf. also Wills, *Jewish Novel,* 254. In fact, Abraham nowhere directly defies God. Instead, he questions God's agents as to whether their declarations come from him or represent themselves; T Abr. 15.8, 19.4. And he explicitly affirms willingness to abide by God's will. He merely sought means to postpone its implementation; T Abr. 9.5. Abraham's obedience is not at issue.

41. See above, n. 3.

42. These features are rightly observed by Sanders, in Charlesworth, *OTP,* I, 877–878; so also, in a different fashion, much earlier by Kohler, *JQR,* 7 (1895), 594–606.

43. But see the provocative discussion by J. W. Whedbee, *The Bible and the Comic Vision* (Cambridge, 1998), 221–262, who does find the book of Job to have the structure of comedy and identifies a number of comic elements within it.

44. For Aristeas, see the text as printed by Holladay, *Fragments,* I, 268–270. Cf. the analysis of Gruen, *Heritage and Hellenism,* 118–120.

45. The most useful editions of the Greek text are those of S. P. Brock, *Testamentum Iobi,* in *PsVTGr,* II, 1–59, and R. A. Kraft, *The Testament of Job According to the SV Text* (Missoula, 1974), with translation. A valuable summary of scholarship on the work may be found in R. P. Spittler, in M. A. Knibb and P. W. van der Horst, eds., *Studies on the Testament of Job* (Cambridge, 1989), 7–32.

46. The notion of a Hebrew original was argued by M. R. James, *Apocrypha Anecdota, Second Series* (Cambridge, 1897), 5.1, xciv–cii. C. C. Torrey, *The Apocryphal Literature* (New Haven, 1945), 142–143, preferred an Aramaic original; so also R. H. Pfeiffer, *History of New Testament Times with an Introduction to the Apocrypha* (New York, 1949), 70. Neither view has any support in recent investigations. That the text was composed in Greek now has near-unanimous support. Cf. M. Philonenko, *Semitica,* 18 (1968), 12; D. Rahnenfuhrer, *ZNW,* 62 (1971), 68–69; H. C. Kee, *SBL Seminar Papers,* 1 (1974), 54–55; B. Schaller, *JSHRZ,* II.3, 307–308; R. P. Spittler, in Charlesworth, *OTP,* I, 830; Schürer, *History,* III.1, 553. The one portion that may derive, directly or indirectly, from a previous Semitic version is the hymn of Eliphaz in T Job, 43. On the composition of the text, see B. Schaller in Knibb and van der Horst, *Studies,* 46–92.

47. Some set 70 CE as a terminal date on the grounds that references to sacrifices in the text imply that the Temple still stood; cf. Philonenko, *Semitica,* 18 (1968), 24. But such references already existed in canonical Job, 1.5, 42.8, and have no bearing on the date of T Job.

48. T Job, 28.7. See M. Philonenko, *Semitica,* 8 (1958), 41–53; Spittler, in Charlesworth, *OTP,* I, 833–834. Rightly questioned by Schaller, *JSHRZ,* III.3, 309.

49. See J. J. Collins, *SBL Seminar Papers,* 1 (1974), 37–39, 51; Schaller, *JSHRZ,* III.3, 312–313; Spittler, in Charlesworth, *OTP,* I, 831–832.

50. So I. Jacobs, *JJS,* 21 (1970), 1–3; endorsed by Collins, *SBL Seminar Papers,* 1 (1974), 51. See the fuller exposition by C. Haas in Knibb and van der Horst, *Studies,* 136–138.

51. James, *Apocrypha Anecdota,* 5.1, xciii–xciv; Jacobs, *JJS,* 21 (1970), 4–10; Rahnenfuhrer, *ZNW,* 62 (1971), 88–93; Haas, in Knibb and van der Horst, *Studies,* 136–138.

52. T Job, 2–5.

53. So, rightly, Schaller, *JSHRZ,* III.3, 314. Note especially T Job, 45.3, where Job exhorts his sons to take no foreign wives—hardly compatible with proselytism. That this is a work of Jewish, not Christian, provenance is now generally accepted and need not be reargued. Cf. Philonenko, *Semitica,* 18 (1968), 21–22; Schaller, *JSHRZ,* III.3, 308–309, 314–316; Schürer, *History,* III.1, 553.

54. K. Kohler, in G. A. Kohut, ed., *Semitic Studies in Memory of Rev. Dr. Alexander Kohut* (Berlin, 1897), 265–275, offered the Essene/Therapeutae hypothesis, refined and expanded by Philonenko, *Semitica,* 8 (1958), 41–53; idem, *Semitica,* 18 (1968), 14–16, 21–23; cf. Spittler, in Charlesworth, *OTP,* I, 834.

The idea was effectively demolished by Schaller, *JSHRZ*, III.3, 309–310. For Kee, *SBL Seminar Papers*, 1 (1974), 53–76, the milieu of the tract is that of Merkebah mysticism. Cf. Philonenko, *Semitica*, 18 (1968), 17–18. But the mystical elements play only a small role in the text as a whole. And allusions to magic do not appear until the concluding portion in the amulets supplied by Job as a legacy for his daughters. Cf. P. W. van der Horst, *Essays on the Jewish World of Early Christianity* (Göttingen, 1990), 107–108.

55. T Job, 4.3–11.
56. Ibid., 5.3–6.7.
57. Ibid., 7.2–12.
58. Ibid., 13.4–14.5.
59. Ibid., 17.1–2.
60. Ibid., 23.1. He was also not averse to appearing as a whirlwind; ibid., 20.5.
61. Ibid., 20.9: εἴποτε ἀφήλατο σκώληξ, ἦρον αὐτὸν καὶ κατήγγιζον εἰς τὸ αὐτὸ λέγων παράμεινον ἐν τῷ αὐτῷ τόπῳ ἐν ᾧ ἐτέθης ἄχρις οὗ ἐπισταλθῇ σοι ὑπὸ τοῦ κελεύσαντός σοι.
62. Ibid., 26.7–8. On the author's treatment of Sitidos in general, see van der Horst, *Essays*, 96–100.
63. T Job, 27.1.
64. Ibid., 27.2–5.
65. Ibid., 27.6.
66. Ibid., 27.7.
67. On the structure of the work as a whole and the possibility that the author put various pieces together, see the remarks of Collins, *SBL Seminar Papers*, 1 (1974), 46–48; Schaller, *JSHRZ*, III.3, 304–306, with bibliography; idem, in Knibb and van der Horst, *Studies*, 48–88.
68. Job, 2.11–12.
69. T Job, 28.7–30.5. The seven-day period does occur in the canonical version. The rest is accretion.
70. T Job, 31.1–4.
71. Ibid., 34.1–5.
72. Ibid., 35.1–5. Cf. the parallel in Wisdom, 5.4, pointed to by Nickelsburg, *Jewish Literature*, 269, n. 35.
73. T Job, 37–38.
74. Job (Septuagint version), 42.17. This, of course, is based on an identification of Job with Jobab in Genesis, 36.33, an identification adopted by both Aristeas and the Testament of Job.
75. Aristeas, in Euseb. *PE*, 9.25.1; T Job, 1.6.
76. Job, 1.1; Job (Septuagint version), 1.1, 42.17; Aristeas, in Euseb. *PE*, 9.25.1; cf. T Job, 28.7.
77. T Job, 28.7.
78. Cf. Collins, *SBL Seminar Papers*, 1 (1974), 50: "The emphasis on Job's endurance suggests a time of persecution."
79. The older bibliography was collected by C. Holladay, *Theios Aner in Hellenistic-Judaism* (Missoula, 1977), 199–232. His subsequent edition of the fragments, with characteristically fair appraisal and sound judgment, brought the subject up to date a few years later; *Fragments*, I, 189–243. Addi-

tional work was summarized by G. E. Sterling, *Historiography and Self-Definition: Josephos, Luke-Acts, and Apologetic Historiography* (Leiden, 1992), 167–186. No startling revelations have burst on the scene since that time. One ought, however, to mention the interesting contribution of D. Flusser and S. Amorai-Stark, *JSQ*, 1 (1993/94), 217–233, on Artapanus and Egyptian traditions, and the brief but balanced remarks of J. M. G. Barclay, *Jews in the Mediterranean Diaspora* (Edinburgh, 1996), 127–132. The segment on Artapanus here is an expansion of comments made by Gruen, *Heritage and Hellenism*, 87–89, 150–151, 155–160. A different view appears in Johnson, *History as it Should Have Been*.

80. See the comments and bibliography in Sterling, *Historiography and Self-Definition*, 173–175.

81. See, e.g., P. M. Fraser, *Ptolemaic Alexandria* (Oxford, 1972), I, 706, II, 985; Holladay, *Theios Aner*, 212–214; N. Walter, *JSHRZ*, I.2 (1980), 124–125; J. J. Collins, in Charlesworth, *OTP*, II, 891.

82. The classic study by J. Freudenthal, *Alexander Polyhistor* (Breslau, 1875), 143–174, decisively demolished earlier conjectures about Artapanus as pagan. But his own reconstruction that sees Artapanus as a Jew masquerading as a pagan adds unnecessary complication. See the sensible remarks of Sterling, *Historiography and Self-Definition*, 167–168.

83. See, e.g., Freudenthal, *Alexander Polyhistor*, 160–162; M. Braun, *History and Romance in Graeco-Oriental Literature* (Oxford, 1938), 26–31; D. L. Tiede, *The Charismatic Figure as Miracle Worker* (Missoula, 1972), 148–150; Fraser, *Ptolemaic Alexandria*, I, 705–706; Walter, *JSHRZ*, I.2, 125; Holladay, *Theios Aner*, 212–218, 231–232; idem, *Fragments*, I, 190–191; J. J. Collins, *Between Athens and Jerusalem*, 2nd ed. (Grand Rapids, 2000), 39–44; idem, in Charlesworth, *OTP*, II, 891–892; M. Goodman, in Schürer, *History*, III.1, 522–523; D. Georgi, *The Opponents of Paul in Second Corinthians* (Edinburgh, 1987), 124–126; van der Horst, *Essays*, 202–203; A. J. Droge, *Homer or Moses?* (Tübingen, 1989), 30–32; Sterling, *Historiography and Self-Definition*, 182–184. A more cautious treatment can be found in R. Doran, *ANRW*, II.20.1 (1987), 258–263, but he too embraces the notion that Artapanus' work constituted a response to Manetho's anti-Jewish tirade; so also Barclay, *Jews in the Mediterranean Diaspora*, 129–130; Johnson, *History as it Should Have Been*. The one clear dissent was issued long ago by Y. Gutman, *The Beginnings of Jewish-Hellenistic Literature* (Jerusalem, 1963), II, 128, 133–134 (Hebrew), but was not pursued at any length.

84. Euseb. *PE*, 9.23.1: περὶ Ἰουδαίων; Clement, *Strom.* 1.23.154.2: περὶ Ἰουδαίων. A variant is found in Euseb. *PE*, 9.18.1: ἐν τοῖς Ἰουδαϊκοῖς—which need not be a formal title.

85. This occurs in a long fragment ascribed to Eupolemus by Alexander Polyhistor and preserved also by Eusebius, *PE*, 9.17. See the discussion in Gruen, *Heritage and Hellenism*, 146–150, with bibliography.

86. Euseb. *PE*, 9.18.1. The latter assertion is in direct conflict with Genesis, 12.20–13.1.

87. So Sterling, *Historiography and Self-Definition*, 177–178.

88. On the term "Hermiouth," still obscure, see Freudenthal, *Alexander Polyhistor*, 153; Walter, *JSHRZ*, I.2, 127. A different interpretation is given by G. Mussies, in M. H. van Voss et al., *Studies in Egyptian Religion* (Leiden, 1982), 112.

89. Euseb. *PE, 9.23.1*.

90. The designation itself is common among Hellenistic writers; see Holladay, *Fragments*, I, 228.

91. Euseb. *PE, 9.23.2*.

92. Genesis, 47.13–26.

93. Euseb. *PE, 9.24.3*.

94. One might observe also that Artapanus omitted the whole rationale for Joseph's policy as given in Genesis—the need to shore up resources in the years of plenty in order to preserve them for the coming famine. For Artapanus, Joseph received his post simply to reorganize the country's economic system. The last sentence of the fragment as reported by Eusebius, to be sure, does make allusion to the storage of grain surplus during seven years of plenty; *PE, 9.23.4*. But the passage is out of place, unconnected, and inconsistent with what went before, an afterthought at best and perhaps wrongly inserted and attributed to Artapanus; cf. Walter, *JSHRZ*, III.2, 287; ibid., I.2, 128. In another obvious change, the subsequent arrival of Jacob and his brothers appears unmotivated by any crisis, merely a reunion with Joseph and a resettlement; Euseb. *PE, 9.23.3*.

95. The narrative is preserved by Euseb. *PE, 9.27.1–37*, conveniently reproduced, with translation and notes, by Holladay, *Fragments*, I, 208–225, 230–243.

96. On Hellenistic conceptions of Moses as lawgiver, see, e.g., Hecataeus of Abdera *apud* Diod. 40.3.3; Eupolemus *apud* Euseb. *PE, 9.26.1*; Aristobulus *apud* Euseb. *PE, 13.12.1–3*; Pseudo-Longinus, *On the Sublime*, 9.9; Philo, *Mos.* 1.1, 1.162, 2.3, 2.12; Jos. *CAp.* 2.145, 2.154–156, 2.279–280.

97. Droge, *Homer or Moses?*, 29, suggests that Artapanus associated himself with those who disparaged Mosaic laws. But Moses receives only the most positive evaluations throughout the text.

98. Euseb. *PE, 9.27.3, 9.27.6*.

99. For the utilization of Hermes/Thot traits by Artapanus, see Gutman, *Beginnings*, II, 120–122 (Hebrew), and Mussies, in Voss et al., *Studies in Egyptian Religion*, 97–108.

100. See the references collected by Holladay, *Theios Aner*, 224.

101. Euseb. *PE, 9.27.4*.

102. Ibid., 9.27.4: καὶ ἑκάστῳ τῶν νομῶν ἀποτάξαι τὸν θεὸν σεφθήσεσθαι . . . εἶναι δὲ καὶ αἰλούρους καὶ κύνας καὶ ἴβεις.

103. So, for instance, Freudenthal, *Alexander Polyhistor*, 143–153, was driven to conceive of Artapanus as a Jew writing in pagan guise in order to reach his audience. And Goodman, in Schürer, *History*, III.1, 523, tries to soften the blow by claiming that the "sacred animals were not so much worshipped as 'consecrated' to God." That distinction, if it exists, would surely be lost on Artapanus' readers. Various other efforts at explanation are usefully documented by Holladay, *Theios Aner*, 201–204. More recently, Flusser and

Amorai-Stark, *JSQ*, 1 (1993/94), 225–231, argue that, for Artapanus, Moses' religious innovations only sought to provide stability to Egypt and animals were consecrated for their benefit to mankind, whereas Egyptian paganism was regarded as foolishness. This last idea finds no support in the fragments. See the brief but sensible comments of Barclay, *Jews in the Mediterranean World,* 131–132, who, however, puts too much emphasis on Artapanus' "syncretism."

104. On all this, see the treatments by Braun, *History and Romance,* 26–31, and, especially, Tiede, *Charismatic Figure,* 151–177; cf. Holladay, *Theios Aner,* 209–212.

105. Euseb. *PE,* 9.27.7–9. A longer and very different version of Moses' campaign against the Ethiopians appears in Jos. *Ant.* 2.238–253. See T. Rajak, *JJS,* 29 (1978), 111–122; D. Runnalls, *JSJ,* 14 (1983), 135–156, with further bibliography.

106. Euseb. *PE,* 9.27.10: οὐ μόνον δὲ τούτους, ἀλλὰ καὶ τοὺς ἱερεῖς ἅπαντας. Cf. the discussion of Holladay, *Fragments,* 236, with bibliography.

107. Euseb. *PE,* 9.27.12.

108. Ibid., 9.27.32.

109. Ibid., 9.27.16.

110. Ibid., 9.27.28.

111. Ibid., 9.27.7–8, 9.27.13–14, 9.27.20.

112. Ibid., 9.27.23–24.

113. Ibid., 9.27.24–25:διακρατηθέντα δὲ ὑπὸ τοῦ Μωύσου πάλιν ἀναβιῶσαι.

7. JEWISH CONSTRUCTS OF GREEKS AND HELLENISM

1. The most detailed and influential study of the past generation remains that of M. Hengel, *Judaism and Hellenism,* 2 vols. (London, 1974). His arguments on the early and extensive spread of Hellenism among the Jews were, however, challenged by L. H. Feldman, *Jew and Gentile in the Ancient World* (Princeton, 1993), passim, especially 42–44, 416–422, with bibliography. The classic work on this subject for Palestine and for a slightly later period is S. Lieberman, *Hellenism in Jewish Palestine* (New York, 1950).

2. A vast literature can be cited on this subject. The relevant texts are conveniently collected by M. Stern, *Greek and Latin Authors on Jews and Judaism,* 2 vols. (Jerusalem, 1976, 1980). Among more recent works, with reference to earlier scholarship, see particularly J. G. Gager, *The Origins of Anti-Semitism* (Oxford, 1985); Z. Yavetz, *JJS,* 44 (1993), 1–22; P. Schäfer, *Judeophobia: Attitudes toward the Jews in the Ancient World* (Princeton, 1997).

3. The treatment by C. Sirat, in K. J. Dover, ed., *Perceptions of the Ancient Greeks* (Oxford, 1992), 54–78, makes very little use of Second Temple texts. M. Goodman, in G. Abramson and T. Parfitt, eds., *Jewish Education and Learning* (Chur, 1994), 167–174, gives just a brief sketch and concentrates almost entirely on Josephus.

4. A valuable and sensible treatment appeared recently by J. M. G. Barclay, *Jews in the Mediterranean Diaspora* (Edinburgh, 1996).

5. For a register of scholarship on II Maccabees, see E. Schürer, *History,* II.1, 536–537.

6. II Macc. 6.9, 11.24. Cf. Tac. *Hist.* 5.8.

7. II Macc. 4.10, 4.13, 4.15. Cf. Jos. *Ant.* 12.240–241.

8. II Macc. 2.21, 8.1, 14.38.

9. See E. S. Gruen, *Heritage and Hellenism: The Reinvention of Jewish Tradition* (Berkeley, 1998), 3–4.

10. For scholarship on the treatise, see Schürer, *History,* III.1, 685–687. Recent discussions appear in Gruen, *Heritage and Hellenism,* 206–222; J. J. Collins, *Between Athens and Jerusalem: Jewish Identity in the Hellenistic Diaspora* (2nd ed., Grand Rapids, 2000), 97–103.

11. *LetArist.* 134–137: καὶ νομίζουσιν οἱ ταῦτα διαπλάσαντες καὶ μυθοποιήσαντες τῶν Ἑλλήνων οἱ σοφώτατοι καθεστάναι.

12. Ibid., 139: ὁ νομοθέτης . . . περιέφραξεν ἡμᾶς ἀδιακόποις χάραξι καὶ σιδηροῖς τείχεσιν, ὅπως μηθένι τῶν ἄλλων ἐθνῶν ἐπιμισγώμεθα κατὰ μηδέν, ἁγνοὶ καθεστῶτες κατὰ σῶμα καὶ κατὰ ψυχήν, ἀπολελυμένοι ματαίων δοξῶν. Cf. the discussion by R. Feldmeier, in M. Hengel and A. M. Schwemer, eds., *Die Septuaginta zwischen Judentum und Christentum* (Tübingen, 1994), 20–36. It is noteworthy that Philo's rendition of this story omits the assertions of Eleazer; *Mos.* II.26–44.

13. Gal. 3.28. See the expanded and more complex version in Col. 3.11.

14. I Cor. 12.13. Cf. also I Cor. 10.32; Rom. 1.16, 2.9–10, 3.9, 10.12; Acts, 19.10, 19.17, 20.21. See C. D. Stanley, *JSNT,* 64 (1996), 123. The Greeks are themselves made equivalent to *ta ethne;* I Cor. 1.22–24.

15. Philo, *Praem.* 8.

16. Philo, *Aet.* 57–58. Other examples can be found in H. A. Wolfson, *Philo* (Cambridge, Mass., 1947), I, 33–43. On Philo's shrewd use of Plato to sharpen the distinction between Hellenic myth-making and Holy Scripture, see M. Niehoff, in G. N. Stanton and G. G. Strousma, eds., *Tolerance and Intolerance in Early Judaism and Christianity* (Cambridge, 1998), 135–158.

17. Philo, *Spec. Leg.* 2.164; cf. 1.28.

18. Philo, *Abr.* 267–268; *Prov.* 2.15–16.

19. Philo, *Spec. Leg.* 4.119–121.

20. Philo, *Vita Cont.* 40–90. This contrast dominates most of the treatise.

21. Philo, *Spec. Leg.* 3.37–42.

22. Ibid., 1.319–323. On Philo and mystery cults, see Wolfson, *Philo,* I, 43–55; D. I. Sly, *Philo's Alexandria* (London, 1996), 99–111.

23. Philo, *Cher.* 91–96; *Mos.* 2.23.

24. Philo, *Spec. Leg.* 3.15–16, 3.22–24.

25. Philo, *Mos.* 1.2–4.

26. Philo, *Spec. Leg.* 3.12–15, 22–24.

27. Philo, *Jos.* 30, 56–57; *Mos.* 2.12–13; *Spec. Leg.* 3.15–16.

28. Philo, *Dec.* 153.

29. Jos. *CAp.* 2.168–174, 2.220–224. See the discussion of C. Schäublin, *Hermes,* 110 (1982), 324–335.

30. Jos. *CAp.* 2.239–254, 2.271. On the objectives of the *Contra Apionem,* cf. the recent remarks of M. Goodman, in M. Edwards, M. Goodman, and

S. Price, eds., *Apologetics in the Roman Empire* (Oxford, 1999), 45–58. On Josephus' contrast of Jews and Greeks in other texts, see T. Rajak, in J. J. Collins and G. E. Sterling, eds., *Hellenism in the Land of Israel* (Notre Dame, 2001), 244–262.

31. II Macc. 2.21: τοῖς ὑπὲρ τοῦ Ἰουδαϊσμοῦ φιλοτίμως ἀνδραγαθήσασιν, ὥστε . . . τὰ βάρβαρα πλήθη διώκειν. Cf. 5.22, 10.4.

32. II Macc. 6.18–7.41.

33. IV Macc. 4–18. For recent discussions of the text, with bibliography, see Schürer, *History*, III.1, 588–593; J. W. van Henten, *The Maccabean Martyrs as Saviours of the Jewish People: A Study of 2 and 4 Maccabees* (Leiden, 1997), 58–82.

34. See the excellent treatment by D. Winston, *The Wisdom of Solomon* (Garden City, 1979), 3–69.

35. Wisdom, 12.3–5: σπλαγχνοφάγον ἀνθρωπίνων σαρκῶν θοῖναν καὶ αἵματος ἐκ μέσου μύστας θιάσου. Cf. Winston, *Wisdom*, 238–240, with references.

36. Esther, Add. E.10: ὡς γὰρ Αμαν Αμαδαθου Μακεδῶν, ταῖς ἀληθείαις ἀλλότριος τοῦ τῶν Περσῶν αἵματος; cf. E.14.

37. A valuable summary of scholarship on this text may be found in F. Parente, *Henoch*, 10 (1988), 150–168. See, more recently, J. M. Modrzejewski, *The Jews of Egypt* (Philadelphia, 1995), 141–153; Barclay, *Jews in the Mediterranean Diaspora*, 192–203; Gruen, *Heritage and Hellenism*, 222–236; Collins, *Between Athens and Jerusalem*, 122–131.

38. III Macc. 3.2, 3.6–7, 5.3, 6.23–24, 7.3.

39. Ibid., 4.1: δημοτελὴς συνίστατο τοῖς ἔθνεσιν εὐωχία μετὰ ἀλαλαγμῶν καὶ χαρᾶς ὡς ἂν τῆς προκατεσκιρωμένης αὐτοῖς πάλαι κατὰ διάνοιαν μετὰ παρρησίας νῦν ἐκφαινομένης ἀπεχθείας.

40. Ibid., 3.21.

41. The chronology is complex and contested. For recent and contrasting views, see E. S. Gruen, in M. Goodman, ed., *Jews in a Graeco-Roman World* (Oxford, 1998), 15–29; Collins, *Between Athens and Jerusalem*, 84–86.

42. III Sibyl. 381–400.

43. Ibid., 166–190.

44. Ibid., 202–204, 341–349, 545–555, 638–645.

45. There is no need to elaborate on the specifics here. Among the serviceable editions and commentaries on the *Letter*, see R. Tramontano, *La lettera di Aristea a Filocrate* (Naples, 1931); M. Hadas, *Aristeas to Philocrates* (New York, 1951); A. Pelletier, *Lettre d'Aristée à Philocrate* (Paris, 1962); N. Meisner, *JSHRZ*, II.1, 35–87.

46. So, most recently, Barclay, *Jews in the Mediterranean Diaspora*, 192–203.

47. See III Macc. 3.21, 5.31, 6.26, 7.7.

48. III Macc. 1.22–23, 3.3, 7.11.

49. This argument is made more fully in Gruen, *Heritage and Hellenism*, 231–233, and most extensively by S. R. Johnson, *History as it Should Have Been* (Berkeley, forthcoming). Cf. also Collins, *Between Athens and Jerusalem*, 129–131.

50. III Macc. 3.8–10: οἱ δὲ κατὰ τὴν πόλιν ἕλληνες . . . παρεκάλουν δὲ καὶ δυσφόρως εἶχον . . . καί τινες . . . πίστεις ἐδίδουν συνασπιεῖν καὶ πᾶν ἐκτενὲς προσοίσεσθαι πρὸς ἀντίλημψιν.

51. Philo, *Prov.* 66–68.

52. Philo, *Prob.* 98–160. See also the story of unknown provenance, but plainly drawn from some Hellenic author, that has female prisoners of the Macedonians drown their own children rather than subject them to slavery, thus setting them on the path to genuine freedom; *Prob.* 115. This shows a close parallel to the martyrologies in II and IV Maccabees.

53. Philo, *Mos.* 2.29–33.

54. Ibid., 2.40: τῇ τε Χαλδαικῇ καὶ τῇ ἑρμηνευθείσῃ, καθάπερ ἀδελφὰς μᾶλλον δ' ὡς μίαν καὶ τὴν αὐτὴν ἔν τε τοῖς πράγμασι καὶ τοῖς ὀνόμασι τεθήπασι καὶ προσκυνοῦσιν.

55. The fullest treatment of Aristobulus may be found in N. Walter, *Der Thoraausleger Aristobulos* (Berlin, 1964). Among other important contributions, see Y. Gutman, *The Beginnings of Jewish-Hellenistic Literature*, 2 vols. (Jerusalem, 1958), I, 186–200 (Hebrew); Hengel, *Judaism and Hellenism*, I, 163–169, II, 105–112; Walter, *JHSRZ*, III.2, 261–279; P. Pilhofer, *Presbyteron Kreitton* (Tübingen, 1990), 164–172; D. Dawson, *Allegorical Readers and Cultural Revision in Ancient Alexandria* (Berkeley, 1992), 78–82; Barclay, *Jews in the Mediterranean Diaspora*, 150–158. The whole subject was recently placed on a firmer footing by the excellent edition of the fragments, with translation, notes, and bibliography, by Holladay, *Fragments*, III. See the useful analysis of scholarship by D. Winston, *Studia Philonica Annual*, 8 (1996), 155–166. More recent comments may be found in Gruen, *Heritage and Hellenism*, 246–251; Collins, *From Athens to Jerusalem*, 186–190.

56. II Macc. 1.10; Clement, *Strom.* 1.22.150.1, 5.14.97.7; Euseb. *PE*, 8.9.38. For discussions of the identification, see works in n. 55 above.

57. Aristobulus, *apud* Euseb. *PE*, 13.12.1.

58. Ibid.: φανερὸν ὅτι κατηκολούθησεν ὁ Πλάτων τῇ καθ' ἡμᾶς νομοθεσίᾳ καὶ φανερός ἐστι περιειργασμένος ἕκαστα τῶν ἐν αὐτῇ.

59. Ibid.

60. Ibid., 13.12.3–4; Clement, *Strom.* 5.14.99.3.

61. Aristobulus, *apud* Euseb. *PE*, 13.12.8. See Gutman, *Beginnings*, I, 192–199 (Hebrew).

62. Aristobulus, *apud* Euseb. *PE*, 13.12.12. See, on this, Gutman, *Beginnings*, I, 203–210 (Hebrew); Walter, *Der Thoraausleger Aristobulus*, 68–81; Holladay, *Fragments*, III, 230–232.

63. Aristobulus, *apud* Euseb. *PE*, 13.12.13–15; Clement, *Strom.* 5.14.107.1–3. See the careful discussion of Walter, *Der Thoraausleger*, 150–158, with reference to the relevant Homeric and Hesiodic lines; cf. Gutman, *Beginnings*, I, 210–212 (Hebrew); Holladay, *Fragments*, III, 234–237.

64. Aristobulus, *apud* Euseb. *PE*, 13.12.16: ἑβδομάτῃ δ' ἠοῖ τετελεσμένα πάντα τέτυκται. See Walter, *Der Thoraausleger*, 158–166; Hengel, *Judaism and Hellenism*, I, 166–167; Holladay, *Fragments*, III, 237–240.

65. Aristobulus, *apud* Euseb. *PE*, 13.12.4–5. Various versions of the poem are preserved by Christian authors in addition to Eusebius, and scholarly disputes over its transmission and over what counts as authentic Aristobulus remain unsettled. The subject now claims a whole volume to itself; Holladay, *Fragments*, IV.

66. Aristobulus, *apud* Euseb. *PE*, 13.6–7; cf. Clement, *Strom.* 5.14.101.4b.
67. The fragments are collected by A.-M. Denis, *Fragmenta Pseudepigraphorum Graeca*, in *PsVTGr*, III, 161–174. See the valuable discussion by M. Goodman in Schürer, *History*, III.1, 667–671, with bibliographies.
68. Pseudo-Justin, *De Monarchia*, 2; Clement, *Strom.* 5.14.131.2–3; Euseb. *PE*, 13.13.60.
69. Pseudo-Justin, *De Monarchia*, 2–3; Clement, *Strom.* 5.14.111.4–6, 5.14.113.2, 5.14.121.4–122.2; Euseb. *PE*, 13.13.38, 13.13.40, 13.13.48. Cf. Philo, *Prob.* 19.
70. Clement, *Strom.* 5.11.75.1; *Protr.* 6.68.3. The second passage is attributed by Pseudo-Justin, *De Monarchia*, 2, to the comic poet Philemon.
71. Clement, *Strom.* 5.14.119.2, 5.14.121.1–3, 5.14.133.3; Euseb. *PE*, 13.13.45–47, 13.13.62; Pseudo-Justin, *De Monarchia*, 2–5.
72. The fragments of Artapanus are collected and commented upon by Holladay, *Fragments*, I, 189–243. See the discussions of J. Freudenthal, *Alexander Polyhistor* (Breslau, 1875), 143–174; Gutman, *Beginnings*, II, 109–135 (Hebrew); C. R. Holladay, *Theios Aner in Hellenistic Judaism* (Missoula, Mont., 1977), 199–232; G. E. Sterling, *Historiography and Self-Definition: Josephos, Luke-Acts, and Apologetic Historiography* (Leiden, 1992), 167–186; Barclay, *Jews in the Mediterranean Diaspora*, 127–132. For sharply contrasting interpretations, see Gruen, *Heritage and Hellenism*, 87–89, 150–151, 155–160, and Collins, *Between Athens and Jerusalem*, 37–46. And see Chapter 6 above.
73. Artapanus, *apud* Euseb. *PE*, 9.27.3–4. Cf. Holladay, *Theios Aner*, 224.
74. Artapanus, *apud* Euseb. *PE*, 9.27.6: ὑπὸ τῶν ἱερέων . . . προσαγορευθῆναι Ἑρμῆν, διὰ τὴν τῶν ἱερῶν γραμμάτων ἑρμηνείαν.
75. On Artapanus' manipulation of the Hermes/Thot characteristics, see Gutman, *Beginnings*, II, 120–122 (Hebrew); G. Mussies, in M. H. van Voss, *Studies in Egyptian Religion* (Leiden, 1982), 97–108.
76. Acts, 17.16–33.
77. Ibid., 17.21.
78. Ibid., 17.23.
79. Ibid., 17.24–26.
80. Ibid., 17.28.
81. Philo, *Leg. All.* 1.108. Cf. Pilhofer, *Presbyteron Kreitton*, 179–182.
82. Philo, *Q Genesis*, 2.6.
83. Philo, *Prob.* 53–57.
84. Philo, *Spec. Leg.* 4.59–61.
85. Philo, *Mut.* 152; *Somn.* 2.244; cf. *Abr.* 261; *Sobr.* 57; *Migr.* 197. See Genesis, 23.6.
86. Philo, *Mos.* 2.17–20.
87. Ibid., 2.21–24.
88. Ibid., 2.25–27.
89. Ibid., 2.43.
90. Jos. *CAp.* 2.121–123: τῶν Ἑλλήνων δὲ πλέον τοῖς τόποις ἢ τοῖς ἐπιτηδεύμασιν ἀφεστήκαμεν.
91. Ibid., 2.168; cf. 1.162. Cf. Pilhofer, *Presbyteron Kreitton*, 200–205.

92. Jos. *CAp.* 2.257: μάλιστα δὲ Πλάτων μεμίμηται τὸν ἡμέτερον νομοθέτην. On Josephus and Plato's *Laws,* see Schäublin, *Hermes,* 110 (1982), 335–341.
93. Jos. *CAp.* 2.280–284.
94. Philo, *Ebr.* 193; *Conf. Ling.* 6; *Mut.* 35; *Abr.* 136; *Jos.* 134; *Spec. Leg.* 1.211, 2.44, 2.165; *Praem.* 165; *Prob.* 73–75, 94, 98, 138; *Vita Cont.* 21; *Leg.* 8, 83, 102, 141, 145, 147, 162. Cf. the treatment by K. Goudriaan, in P. Bilde et al., eds., *Ethnicity in Hellenistic Egypt* (Aarhus, 1992), 82–86. Paul followed the same line, in similar fashion. He proclaimed his message to "Greeks and barbarians, the wise and the ignorant." No pagan could have said it better; Rom. 1.14. Josephus follows suit; see, e.g., *BJ,* 5.17; *Ant.* 4.12; *CAp.* 2.282.
95. Philo, *Conf. Ling.* 190; cf. Jos. *BJ,* 1.3, 1.6.
96. Philo, *Mos.* 2.27; *Prob.* 73–75.
97. See Philo, *Mos.* 2.27.
98. Philo, *Opif.* 128; *Cher.* 91; *Plant.* 67; *Abr.* 180–181, 267; *Jos.* 30, 56; *Mos.* 2.12, 2.18–20; *Spec. Leg.* 4.120; *Vita Cont.* 48; *Dec.* 153; cf. *Abr.* 178–181; *Leg.* 292–293.
99. *LetArist.* 31, 312–316.
100. Ibid., 38–40, 42, 175–181, 312, 317, 321.
101. Ibid., 177, 317.
102. Ibid., 187–296. See, especially, 200–201, 235, 296. The whole banquet scene may be a clever spoof, rather than a serious presentation, by the author of the *Letter;* Gruen, *Heritage and Hellenism,* 218–220. But the point of Jewish intellectuals surpassing the best of Greek philosophers holds on any interpretation.
103. So, rightly, Feldmeier, in Hengel and Schwemer, *Septuaginta,* 20–37.
104. Philo, *Her.* 207–214.
105. Philo, *Mos.* 1.21–24: ὧν ἐν οὐ μακρῷ χρόνῳ τὰς δυνάμεις ὑπερέβαλεν εὐμοιρίᾳ φύσεως φθάνων τὰς ὑφηγήσεις, ὡς ἀνάμνησιν εἶναι δοκεῖν, οὐ μάθησιν, ἔτι καὶ προσεπινοῶν αὐτὸς τὰ δισθεώρητα. See the discussion of Pilhofer, *Presbyteron Kreitton,* 187–190.
106. Philo, *Mos.* 2.2.
107. Philo, *Aet.* 13–19.
108. Philo, *Leg. All.* 2.15. On Philo's theory of divine language and the connection with the origin of names, see M. Niehoff, *JSQ,* 2 (1995), 220–227, who does not, however, include this passage.
109. Philo, *Spec. Leg.* 4.102: μέσην ἀτραπὸν ἀμφοῖν ἀνατεμών.
110. Philo, *Mos.* 2.12–14.
111. Philo, *Virt.* 139–140. Not that Jewish law was always characterized as being milder than its Gentile counterparts. Philo can also maintain that in other systems offenders received lax and indulgent treatment, whereas the Mosaic code was rigorous and undeviating in its enforcement; *Hyp.* 7.1–3.
112. Philo, *Vita Cont.* 14–16.
113. Philo, *Somn.* 1.52–58.
114. Philo, *Agr.* 136–145.
115. Philo, *Gig.* 39.
116. Philo, *Ebr.* 198–202.
117. Cf. Dawson, *Allegorical Readers,* 116–124.

118. For some of the more important bibliography, see Gruen, in Goodman, *Jews in a Graeco-Roman World*, 16, n. 1; see further Barclay, *Jews in the Mediterranean Diaspora*, 216–228; Collins, *Between Athens and Jerusalem*, 83–97.

119. III Sibyl. 545–572, 624–656.

120. Ibid., 732–766. See Gruen, in Goodman, *Jews in a Graeco-Roman World*, 31–33.

8. DIASPORA AND HOMELAND

1. See the stimulating discussion by A. M. Eisen, *Galut* (Bloomington, 1986). Eisen recapitulates his thesis in C. Taylor, *Sources of the Self* (Cambridge, Mass., 1987), 219–225.

2. See, in general, the important works of Y. F. Baer, *Galut* (New York, 1947); Y. Kaufmann, *Exile and Estrangement* (Hebrew), 2 vols. (Tel Aviv, 1962); Eisen, *Galut*. See also D. Vital, *The Origins of Zionism* (Oxford, 1975), 1–10; E. Levine, in E. Levine, ed., *Diaspora: Exile and the Jewish Condition* (New York, 1983), 1–11. For the notion of exile and return as an invented construct by composers of the Pentateuch, dominating Jewish self-definition ever thereafter, see J. Neusner, in J. M. Scott, *Exile: Old Testament, Jewish, and Christian Conceptions* (Leiden, 1997), 221–237, summarizing his lengthier presentation in Neusner, *Self-Fulfilling Prophecy: Exile and Return in the History of Judaism* (Boston, 1987). So also J. Assmann, *Das kulturelle Gedächtnis* (Munich, 1999), 197–228. In a similar vein, with specific reference to the Assyrian and Babylonian "exiles," see R. P. Carroll, in L. L. Grabbe, ed., *Leading Captivity Captive: "The Exile" as History and Ideology* (Sheffield, 1998), 62–79; T. L. Thompson, in Grabbe, op. cit., 101–118; P. R. Davies, in Grabbe, op. cit., 128–138. This concept of the Jewish experience has become a paradigm for the diaspora mentality everywhere. Cf. W. Safran, *Diaspora*, 1 (1991), 83–99. The use of such an ideal type is rightly criticized in the acute discussion of J. Clifford, *Routes: Travel and Translation in the Late Twentieth Century* (Cambridge, Mass., 1997), 244–277.

3. See especially G. Steiner, *Salmagundi*, 66 (1985), 4–25. On the ambivalence of exile and homecoming in recent Jewish conceptions, see the comments of S. D. Ezrahi, *Michigan Quarterly Review*, 31 (1992), 463–497; idem, *Booking Passage: Exile and Homecoming in the Modern Jewish Imagination* (Berkeley, 2000), 3–23.

4. The recent article by C. Milikowsky, in Scott, *Exile*, 265–281, argues, most interestingly, that early midrashic texts do not single out the Roman conquest as a pivotal turning point, but conceive a more continuous period of exile and subjugation, stretching through the Second Temple era and beyond. The notion of the Temple's fall as a caesura emerges only in later rabbinic writings.

5. For population estimates, see J. Juster, *Les Juifs dans l'empire romain* (Paris, 1914), I, 209–212; S. Baron, *Encyclopedia Judaica*, 13 (Jerusalem, 1971), 866–903; L. H. Feldman, *Jew and Gentile in the Ancient World* (Princeton, 1993), 23, 468–469, 555–556. No reliable testimony exists on specific numbers. See the salutary skepticism of L. V. Rutgers, *JQR*, 85 (1995), 363–367.

6. Cf. the remark of Strabo, *apud* Jos. *Ant.* 14.115, that Jews have settled ev-

erywhere and that hardly a place exists in the world without their presence—
a positive, not a negative statement, in which Josephus takes pride.

7. A doleful portrait of diaspora for Hellenistic Jews is drawn most forcefully
by W. C. van Unnik, *Das Selbstverständnis der jüdischen Diaspora in der
hellenistich-römischen Zeit* (Leiden, 1993), a posthumous publication of papers actually delivered in 1967. Van Unnik shows that the term "diaspora"—
or more usually its verbal form—is almost always employed with a negative connotation in the Septuagint (which uses it to render various Hebrew
words); op. cit., 89–107. It has a negative meaning also in the large majority
of its appearances in Hellenistic Jewish writers; op. cit., 108–147.

8. Lev. 26.33.

9. Deut. 4.26–28, 28.63–65.

10. Jeremiah, 5.19.

11. Ibid., 9.15.

12. Daniel, 9.4–7.

13. Philo, *Abr.* 64.; cf. *Conf. Ling.* 120–121, 196.

14. Deut. 30.2–5; cf. I Kings, 8.33–34, 8.46–51; II Chron. 6.24–25, 6.36–39; Jeremiah, 29.10–14.

15. Isaiah, 11.12.

16. Baer, *Galut,* 9–13; Eisen, *Galut,* 3–34. As noted in n. 7 above, the most
sweeping argument on melancholy Jewish attitudes toward the diaspora in
the Second Temple era is made by van Unnik, *Das Selbstverständnis,* passim.
See also the useful survey by W. D. Davies, *The Territorial Dimension of Judaism* (Berkeley, 1982), 28–34, 61–100.

17. Davies, *Territorial Dimension,* 116–126, endeavors to resolve the "contradiction" between commitment to the Land at the center and the realities of
life on the periphery, concluding that, although the pull of the Land is personal and powerful, it is not territorial. In the view of A. T. Kraabel, in L. I.
Levine, ed., *The Synagogue in Late Antiquity* (Philadelphia, 1987), 56–58,
Jews shifted from an "Exile theology" to a "Diaspora theology," although he
appears to believe that this really took hold only after the destruction of the
Temple. The trenchant review article of J. J. Price rightly stresses the diversity
of diaspora communities and the successes enjoyed by Jews therein; *SCI,* 13
(1994), 170–179. But he plays down too much the power still wielded by the
concept of the Holy Land. J. M. G. Barclay, *Jews in the Mediterranean Diaspora* (Edinburgh, 1996), 418–424, offers a sensible and balanced statement,
arguing that attachment to the "motherland" could coexist with rootedness
in regions abroad, although he regards the degree of attachment as dependent
on circumstances. The fine study of I. M. Gafni, *Law, Center, and Diaspora*
(Sheffield, 1997), 19–40, explores various strategies whereby diaspora Jews
sought to account for or legitimize their situation. He places perhaps too
much emphasis, however, upon the apologetic character in Hellenistic Jewish
representations of local patriotism; op. cit., 42–52. A recent general survey by
M. H. Williams, in J. Huskinson, *Experiencing Rome: Culture, Identity, and
Power in the Roman Empire* (London, 2000), 305–333, finds a balance between diaspora assimilation and self-identity but omits the idea of the homeland in the latter.

18. The classic study is Juster's 2-volume work, *Les Juifs dans l'empire romain,* passim. Among recent treatments, see M. Stern, in Safrai and Stern, *Jewish People,* I, 117–183; Schürer, *History,* III.1, 1–176; Barclay, *Jews in the Mediterranean Diaspora,* 19–81, 231–319; I. Levinskaya, *The Book of Acts in its Diaspora Setting* (Grand Rapids, 1996), 127–193. And see above, Chapter 4.

19. On the variety of motives and circumstances that induced Jews to settle in various parts of the Mediterranean, see the evidence assembled and the discussion by A. Kasher, in A. Shinan, ed., *Emigration and Settlement in Jewish and General History* (Jerusalem, 1982), 65–91 (Hebrew).

20. See the contrasting views expressed by E. E. Urbach, in M. Davis, ed., *World Jewry and the State of Israel* (New York, 1977), 217–235, and J. J. Petuchowski, *Judaism,* 9 (1960), 17–28. Davies, *Territorial Dimension,* 91–100, usefully summarizes the positions.

21. Not that the two terms were reckoned as equivalent in antiquity. Indeed, *galut* or *golah* is never translated as *diaspora* in Greek. The Septuagint employs a variety of Greek words, including ἀποικία (colony), μετοικεσία (change of abode), παροικία (residence abroad), and αἰχμαλοσία (captivity). See van Unnik, *Das Selbstverständnis,* 80–85. Van Unnik, op. cit., 150–152, even argues, paradoxically and implausibly, that diaspora was a grimmer concept for Jews than exile. See the just criticisms by J. M. Scott, in Scott, *Exile,* 180–184.

22. Scott, in Scott, *Exile,* 185–187, notes certain passages in the Septuagint on the expulsion of the Jews to which the translators added phrases such as "until this day"; Deut. 29.28; II Kings, 17.23; II Chron. 29.9. It hardly follows that these were intended to apply to the Hellenistic era.

23. Ben Sira, 48.15: ἕως ἐπρονομεύθησαν ἀπὸ γῆς αὐτῶν/ καὶ διεσκορπίσθησαν ἐν πάσῃ τῇ γῇ. Elsewhere he offers up a prayer for divine deliverance in an ostensibly contemporary context, including a plea for gathering all the tribes of Jacob and restoring their inheritance as from the beginning; 36.10. But Ben Sira here echoes biblical language and by no means implies a longing for return felt in the diaspora.

24. Tobit, 3.3–4.

25. Ibid., 13.3–6, 13.10–11.

26. Ibid., 14.4.

27. Ibid., 13.10–11, 14.5–7.

28. Judith, 5.18–19.

29. T Levi, 10.3–4, 15.1–2, 16.5; T Judah, 23.3–5; T Iss. 6.1–4; T Zeb. 9.6–8; T Dan, 5.8–13; T Asher, 7.2–6.

30. The Testament of Naphtali, 4.1–5, speaks of two separate calamities inflicted by God, an exile and a scattering, after each of which he restores his favor to the children of Israel. For van Unnik, *Das Selbstverständnis,* 119–120, the second one actually refers to the Hellenistic diaspora. But it may well allude to the aftermath of the destruction in 70 CE; so M. de Jonge, *The Testaments of the Twelve Patriarchs* (Leiden, 1978), 85.

31. Jubilees, 1.9–13.

32. Ps. Solomon, 9.1–2.

33. I Baruch, 3.8.

34. III Sibyl. 266–279.
35. Even Josephus, who rarely indulges in this form of outburst, expands on Deuteronomy and has Moses warn his people of dispersal and servitude everywhere in the inhabited world as a consequence of their rebellion; *Ant.* 4.189–191. In the view of B. Halpern-Amaru, *JQR,* 71 (1980/81), 219–221, Josephus here obliquely alludes to the Jewish revolt of 66–70 CE. So also van Unnik, *Das Selbstverständnis,* 141–142.
36. As is assumed, e.g., by Price, *SCI,* 13 (1994), 172.
37. *LetArist.* 12, 35. Similarly, Jos. *Ant.* 12.7.
38. Jos. *CAp.* 1.186; cf. *Ant.* 12.9. That this is the work of a Jewish "Pseudo-Hecataeus" is cogently argued by B. Bar-Kochva, *Pseudo-Hecataeus, "On the Jews": Legitimizing the Jewish Diaspora* (Berkeley, 1996), 71–82.
39. *LetArist.* 13–14, 36. Josephus even adds that he bestowed citizen privileges equivalent to those of the Macedonians; *Ant.* 12.8.
40. *LetArist.* 19–27, 36–37.
41. Jos. *CAp.* 1.194. On the truth of these matters, see the discussion by Bar-Kochva, *Pseudo-Hecataeus,* 101–105, 143–144.
42. III Macc. 6.3: λαὸν ἐν ξένῃ γῇ ξένον ἀδίκως ἀπολλύμενον. Cf. 6.10: κατὰ τὴν ἀποικίαν; 6.15: ἐν τῇ γῇ τῶν ἐχθρῶν αὐτῶν.
43. Ibid., 6.36, 7.15, 7.19.
44. Deut. 30.1–5; cf. Jeremiah, 23.8; Ezek. 11.16–17. Philo's reference, *Praem.* 115, to the change from a "spiritual diaspora" to wisdom and virtue allegorizes the prophecy in Deuteronomy but does not refer to Hellenistic expectations or desire for return to Judaea; cf. U. Fischer, *Eschatologie und Jenseitserwartung im hellenistischen Diasporajudentum* (Berlin, 1978), 208–209. Nor does his gloss on Deut. 30.4 at *Conf. Ling.* 197.
45. Tobit, 13.5, 13.10–11, 13.13, 14.5–7.
46. Judith, 5.19.
47. T Asher, 7.7.
48. Ps. Solomon, 8.28.
49. Jubilees, 1.15–17. Cf. the analysis of B. Halpern-Amaru, in Scott, *Exile,* 139–141. See also I Baruch, 2.29–35.
50. The arguments of Scott, in Scott, *Exile,* 209–213, for a continuing hope of return through the Greco-Roman period lack foundation in the evidence. The texts cited do not derive from the diaspora.
51. Philo, in a puzzling passage, does make reference to Jews in Greek and barbarian islands and continents, enslaved to those who had taken them captive, and ultimately to strive for the one appointed land; *Praem.* 164–165. He draws here on the texts of Lev. 26.40–45 and Deut. 30.1–10. But the language must be metaphorical, and the sense is allegorical, with messianic overtones, as the Jews will be conducted by a divine and superhuman vision; *Praem.* 165: ξεναγούμενοι πρός τινος θειοτέρας ἢ κατὰ φύσιν ἀνθρωπίνην ὄψεως. Cf. van Unnik, *Das Selbstverständis,* 132–136. It is unjustified to see here a concrete concept of the Return, as does J. M. Scott, *SBL Seminar Papers,* 34 (1995), 567, or a belief in the eventual disappearance of the diaspora, as proposed by H. A. Wolfson, *Philo: Foundations of Religious Philosophy in Judaism, Christianity, and Islam* (Cambridge, Mass., 1947), II, 407;

cf. also J. J. Collins, *Between Athens and Jerusalem* (2nd ed., Grand Rapids, 2000), 134–136. The passage is best understood as a symbolic voyage to God or true wisdom. Philo expresses a closely comparable idea in *Conf. Ling.* 81. In any case, Philo's references to the ingathering of the exiles, even in an obscure fashion, occur almost exclusively in the *De Praemiis et Poenis*. Cf. the treatment by B. Halpern-Amaru, in L. A. Hoffmann, ed., *The Land of Israel: Jewish Perspectives* (Notre Dame, 1986), 83–85. On Philo's messianic ideas, see the valuable discussions with surveys of earlier opinions by R. D. Hecht, in J. Neusner, W. S. Green, and E. S. Frerichs, eds., *Judaisms and their Messiahs at the Time of the Christian Era* (Cambridge, 1987), 139–168, and P. Borgen, in J. H. Charlesworth, ed., *The Messiah* (Minneapolis, 1992), 341–361. Fischer, *Eschatologie,* 202–210, questions the messianic implications, but sees the passage as an allegorical representation of misguided souls brought to wisdom by the *Logos.*

52. II Macc. 1.10–2.18. See, e.g., E. J. Bickermann, *ZNW,* 32 (1933), 234–235; J. Bunge, *Untersuchungen zum zweiten Makkabäerbuch* (Bonn, 1971), 32–94; C. Habicht, *JSHRZ,* I.3, 201–202; B. Z. Wacholder, *HUCA,* 49 (1978), 89–133; J. A. Goldstein, *II Maccabees* (Garden City, 1983), 154–188.

53. II Macc. 2.18.

54. See, most recently, T. A. Bergren, *JSJ,* 28 (1997), 249–270.

55. II Mac. 1.27: ἐπισυνάγαγε τὴν διασπορὰν ἡμῶν, ἐλευθέρωσον τοὺς δουλεύοντας ἐν τοῖς ἔθνεσιν.

56. Ibid., 2.7: ἕως ἂν συναγάγῃ ὁ θεὸς ἐπισυναγωγὴν τοῦ λαοῦ καὶ ἵλεως γένηται.

57. Ibid., 8–12.

58. Ibid., 1.9, 1.18, 2.16.

59. This, of course, is not the place to examine the concept of the "Land of Israel" in Jewish thought generally, a vast topic. See the succinct and valuable study by Davies, *Territorial Dimension,* passim.

60. II Macc. 1.12.

61. Philo, *Leg.* 225, 281, 288, 299, 346; *Somn.* 2.246. See also his emphasis upon the centrality of the Temple in Jewish practice and allegiance; *Spec. Leg.* 1.66–68. Cf. A. Kasher, *Cathedra,* 11 (1979), 48–49 (Hebrew).

62. Strabo, 16.2.37.

63. II Macc. 1.7; Wisdom, 12.3; T Job, 33.5: ἐν τῇ ἁγίᾳ γῇ; III Sibyl 267: πέδον ἀγνὸν; 732–735; V Sibyl 281; Philo, *Her.* 293; *Somn.* 2.75; *Spec. Leg.* 4.215; *Flacc.* 46; *Leg.* 202: τῆς ἱερᾶς χώρας; 205, 330. Cf. Zech. 2.16. On Philo and the "Holy Land," see B. Schaller, in G. Strecker, ed., *Das Land Israel in biblischer Zeit* (Göttingen, 1983), 175–182, who finds the philosopher's appeal to this concept largely determined by the particular circumstances in which he was writing—most of the references coming when Judaea was under threat. Cf. R. L. Wilken, *The Land Called Holy* (New Haven, 1992), 34–37; G. Delling, *Die Bewältigung der Diasporasituation durch das hellenistische Judentum* (Göttingen, 1987), 37–39.

64. Philo, in fact, indicates that even the migration of Abraham to Canaan was more like a return to his native land than a movement to foreign parts, thus

associating the Jews with Palestine from the dawn of history; *Abr.* 62. Cf. Artapanus, *apud* Euseb. *PE*, 9.18.1; Wisdom, 12.2–7; Jos. *Ant.* 1.159–160.

65. Cf. Polybius, 1.14.4.

66. *LetArist.* 249: ὅτι καλὸν ἐν ἰδίᾳ καὶ ζῆν καὶ τελευτᾶν. ἡ δὲ ξενία τοῖς μὲν πένησι καταφρόνησιν ἐργάζεται, τοῖς δὲ πλουσίοις ὄνειδος, ὡς διὰ κακίαν ἐκπεπτωκόσιν.

67. Cf., e.g., the standard commentaries: R. Tramontano, *La lettera di Aristea a Filocrate* (Naples, 1931), 211–212; H. G. Meecham, *The Letter of Aristeas* (Manchester, 1935), 290–291; M. Hadas, *Aristeas to Philocrates* (New York, 1951), 197; A. Pelletier, *Lettre d'Aristée à Philocrate* (Paris, 1962), 212, 250.

68. Philo, *Abr.* 63, 65.

69. Philo, *Mos.* 2.198; *Mut.* 40; cf. *Spec. Leg.* 1.68; *Plant.* 146; *Ebr.* 17; *Fug.* 29; *Deus,* 17.

70. Philo, *Cher.* 15; *Abr.* 197; *Leg.* 328.

71. Philo, *Leg.* 277. Cf. *Migr.* 217; *Spec. Leg.* 1.68, 4.16–17. Philo's references to *patris* in the metaphorical sense, as abandonment of the territorial homeland for the true *patris,* are not, of course, relevant to this point. See, e.g., *Spec. Leg.* 1.51–53; *Conf. Ling.* 78, 81. Other references can be found in S. Pearce, in S. Jones and S. Pearce, eds., *Jewish Local Patriotism and Self Identification in the Graeco-Roman Period* (Sheffield, 1998), 100.

72. II Macc. 4.1, 5.8–9, 5.15, 13.3.

73. Ibid., 8.21, 13.10.

74. Philo, *Mos.* 1.36; *Hyp.* 6.1.

75. Artapanus, *apud* Euseb. *PE*, 9.27.21.

76. Ezekiel, *Exagoge, apud* Euseb. *PE*, 9.28.12.

77. II Macc. 13.14: παρακαλέσας τοὺς σὺν αὐτῷ γενναίως ἀγωνίσασθαι μέχρι θανάτου περὶ νόμων, ἱεροῦ, πόλεως, πατρίδος, πολιτείας.

78. So, e.g., Kasher, *Cathedra,* 11 (1979), 52–56 (Hebrew).

79. Cf. I. Heinemann, *Zion,* 13-14 (1948), 3–6 (Hebrew); Kasher, *Cathedra,* 11 (1979), 45–50 (Hebrew).

80. *LetArist.* 249. See n. 66 above.

81. *LetArist.* 308–311.

82. Ibid., 249.

83. III Macc. 6.10: εἰ δὲ ἀσεβείαις κατὰ τὴν ἀποικίαν ὁ βίος ἡμῶν ἐνέσχηται.

84. Ibid., 6.36: ἐπὶ πᾶσαν τὴν παροικίαν αὐτῶν εἰς γενεάς; 7.19: ταύτας ἄγειν τὰς ἡμέρας ἐπὶ τὸν τῆς παροικίας αὐτῶν χρόνον εὐφροσύνους. The latter may be a doublet of the former. These passages do not imply that the author emphasized the temporary character of the sojourn in Egypt and looked ahead with enthusiasm to the "ingathering of the exiles," *pace* Heinemann, *Zion,* 13-14 (1948), 7 (Hebrew); Scott, in Scott, *Exile,* 192.

85. Philo, *Mos.* 1.71; Hecataeus, *apud* Diod. 40.3.3.

86. Philo, *Mos.* 2.232. On this passage, see Gafni, *Land,* 58–59. Cf. Josephus' reference to the same principles that apply to priestly practices both in Judaea and wherever there is a community of Jews; *CAp.* 1.32, employing the term *systema.* Josephus, citing (Pseudo) Hecataeus, also draws a connection between large population and migration; *CAp.* 1.194.

87. Philo, *Leg.* 281–282. Y. Amir, in A. Oppenheimer, U. Rappaport, and M. Stern, eds., *Jerusalem in the Second Temple Period* (Jerusalem, 1980), 154–157 (Hebrew), presses the analogy with Greek colonization a little too far.

88. Philo, *Flacc.* 46; Jos. *CAp.* 2.38. The view of Kasher, *Cathedra*, 11 (1979), 49–53 (Hebrew), that this sets "colonies" in a lower or dependent status with regard to the metropolis, misplaces the emphasis.

89. Philo, *Conf. Ling.* 78: τοῖς μὲν γὰρ ἀποικίαν στειλαμένοις ἀντὶ τῆς μητροπόλεως ἡ ὑποδεξαμένη δήπου πατρίς, ἡ δ' ἐκπέμψασα μένει τοῖς ἀποδεδημηκόσιν, εἰς ἣν καὶ ποθοῦσιν ἐπανέρχεσθαι. Scott, *SBL Seminar Papers*, 34 (1995), 562–563, misses the contrast between the μὲν and the δὲ clauses and wrongly sees the passage as a negative comment on the contemporary diaspora.

90. Cf. Jos. *BJ,* 7.375; *Ant.* 3.245.

91. Cf. Philo's use of the term in a very different context; *Spec. Leg.* 4.178. J. Mélèze-Modrzejewski, in S. J. D. Cohen and E. S. Frerichs, eds., *Diasporas in Antiquity* (Atlanta, 1993), 66–70, rightly points out that the Septuagint often translates *galut* (exile) or *golah* (the collective exiled) as *apoikia*, thus, in effect, offering an *interpretatio Graeca*. His further assertion, however, that Jews, unlike Greeks, invariably expected a return to the land of their fathers, is questionable. Scott, in Scott, *Exile,* 189–193, unconvincingly takes the connotation of *apoikia* in a negative sense.

92. Philo, *Mos.* 1.35.

93. Jos. *CAp.* 2.38–39.

94. Jos. *Ant.* 16.59: οἱ δὲ ἐγγενεῖς τε αὐτοὺς ἐδείκνυσαν.

95. Philo, *Leg.* 150: τὴν ἡμετέραν Ἀλεχάνδρειαν. Cf. *Leg. All.* 2.85. On Philo's attitude toward Alexandria, see, most recently, Pearce, in Jones and Pearce, *Jewish Local Patriotism,* 97–104. Philo was, of course, fiercely hostile to Egyptians, their practices, institutions, and beliefs. This served him well in distinguishing the superior qualities of the Jews and their association with Greco-Roman culture. Cf. K. Goudriaan, in P. Bilde et al., eds., *Ethnicity in Hellenistic Egypt* (Aarhus, 1992), 81–85; Pearce, op. cit., 83–97. But that would not compromise his affection for Alexandria, might indeed reinforce it.

96. *CPJ,* II, no. 151. Just what this change signified has been much debated and need not be explored here. See above, Chapter 2. The discussion of Kasher, *Cathedra,* 11 (1979), 53 (Hebrew), concentrates only on the political aspect.

97. Cf. also the epitaph of a young woman from Leontopolis, thus evidently a Jewess, which refers to her "homeland and father"; *CPJ,* III, no. 1530 = *JIGRE,* no. 38, line 2: πάτραν καὶ γενέτην. To be sure, the *patris* here is the land of Onias, a Jewish enclave in Egypt, but the inscription discloses an unequivocal local allegiance. Cf. Gafni, *Land,* 48.

98. *CIJ,* II, no. 771: ὑπὲρ εὐχῆ[ς] πάσῃ τῇ πατρίδι. The *patris* here almost certainly refers to the city of Acmonia, not to the Jewish community; see P. R. Trebilco, *Jewish Communities in Asia Minor* (Cambridge, 1991), 81–82. Gafni, *Land,* 49–50, questions the degree to which conventional formulations of this sort disclose any genuine feelings of local patriotism.

99. Philo, *Flacc.* 46: μητρόπολιν μὲν τὴν ἱερόπολιν ἡγούμενοι . . . ἃς δ' ἔλαχον ἐκ πατέρων καὶ πάππων καὶ προπάππων καὶ τῶν ἔτι ἄνω προγόνων οἰκεῖν ἕκαστοι πατρίδας νομίζοντες, ἐν αἷς ἐγεννήθησαν καὶ ἐτράφησαν. Cf. Schaller, in Strecker, *Das Land Israel,* 174–175.

100. See the useful summary of testimony and the discussion by S. Safrai, in Safrai and Stern, *Jewish People,* I, 186–191.

101. Exodus, 30.11–16; cf. Philo, *Her.* 186; *Spec. Leg.* 1.77–78.

102. Nehemiah, 10.32–34.

103. For the Seleucids, see II Macc. 3.3; Jos. *Ant.* 12.138–144; cf. II Macc. 9.16; Jos. *Ant.* 11.16. For the Ptolemies, see Jos. *Ant.* 12.40–41. For the Persian kings, see Ezra, 6.8–10, 7.18–21.

104. It was certainly well entrenched by the early first century BCE; Jos. *Ant.* 14.110–113; Cic. *Pro Flacco,* 67.

105. On possible reasons for Roman policy here, see A. J. Marshall, *Phoenix,* 29 (1975), 139–154, and, more fully, above, Chapter 1.

106. Cic. *Pro Flacco,* 66–68.

107. Ibid., 67: *cum aurum Iudaeorum nomine quotannis ex Italia et ex omnibus nostris provinciis Hierosolymam exportari soleret.*

108. The Ciceronian speech singles out Apamea, Laodicea, Adramyttium, and Pergamum; *Pro Flacco,* 68. Cf. Philo, *Spec. Leg.* 1.78.

109. Cic. *Pro Flacco,* 66: *scis quanta sit manus, quanta concordia, quantum valeat in contionibus.*

110. Modern discussions of Cicero's attitude toward the Jews pay little attention to the implications of his statements on this score. So, e.g., Y. Levi, *Zion,* 7 (1942), 109–134; B. Wardy, *ANRW,* II.19.1 (1979), 596–613.

111. Philo, *Leg.* 155–156.

112. Jos. *Ant.* 14.110; cf. 18.312–313; *BJ,* 7.45.

113. Jos. *Ant.* 16.28, 16.45.

114. Ibid., 16.163. Cf. further a ruling by Julius Caesar which also appears to guarantee the Temple tithe; ibid., 14.202.

115. Ibid., 16.166.

116. Ibid., 16.167–171. Another similar letter by the governor of Asia to Ephesus is preserved by Philo, *Leg.* 315.

117. Philo, *Leg.* 291, 312.

118. Ibid., 216.

119. Cf. Philo, *Spec. Leg.* 1.76–77. In addition to the annual contributions felt as an obligation by all Jews, there were more substantial gifts by wealthy diaspora donors to express their reverence; Jos. *BJ,* 4.567, 5.5, 5.201–205; *Ant.* 18.82, 20.51–53.

120. Tac. *Hist.* 5.5.1: *cetera instituta, sinistra foeda, pravitate valuere; nam pessimus quisque spretis religionibus patriis tributa et stipes illuc congerebant, unde auctae Iudaeorum res.*

121. Jos. *BJ,* 7.218; Dio, 66.7.2.

122. The biblical prescription indicates three times a year: Exodus, 23.17; cf. Jos. *Ant.* 4.203. But actual practice varied widely; cf. Safrai, in Safrai and Stern, *Jewish People,* I, 191–194; A. Kerkeslager, in D. Frankfurter, ed., *Pilgrimage and Holy Space in Late Antique Egypt* (Leiden, 1998), 106–107.

123. Philo, *Spec. Leg.* 1.69: μυρίοι γὰρ ἀπὸ μυρίων ὅσων πόλεων . . . καθ᾽ ἑκάστην ἑορτὴν εἰς τὸ ἱερόν.
124. Acts, 2.1–11; cf. 6.9.
125. Jos. *BJ*, 2.280. Josephus' figure of "no less than three million" is, of course, preposterous. Cf. also ibid., 6.422–425.
126. Ibid., 6.420–421.
127. Ibid., 6.426–427. Cf. Jos. *Ant.* 17.214. On the numbers, see J. Jeremias, *Jerusalem in the Time of Jesus* (Philadelphia, 1969), 77–84.
128. Jos. *BJ*, 5.199.
129. Philo, *Leg.* 156: χρήματα συνάγοντας ἀπὸ τῶν ἀπαρχῶν ἱερὰ καὶ πέμποντας εἰς Ἱεροσόλυμα διὰ τῶν τὰς θυσίας ἀναξόντων. So also 216, 312; *Spec. Leg.* 1.78. Philo could also, of course, employ the concept of pilgrimage in an allegorical sense; cf. Amir, in Oppenheimer et al., *Jerusalem in the Second Temple Period,* 158–165 (Hebrew).
130. See Jos. *Ant.* 18.312–313; cf. 17.26.
131. Acts, 20.4, 21.29.
132. The tale of the royal house of Adiabene and its conversion is told in a long excursus by Josephus, *Ant.* 20.17–96. For the attachment to Jerusalem, see 20.49–53, 20.71, 20.95; cf. *BJ*, 5.55, 5.119, 5.147. The desire to be buried in Jerusalem is attested also by epitaphs recording the transferral of bones to the holy city. See, e.g., J. A. Fitzmyer and D. J. Harrington, *A Manual of Palestinian Aramaic Texts* (Rome, 1978), no. 68 (first century BCE or first century CE). Cf. I. M. Gafni, *The Jerusalem Cathedra,* 1 (1981), 96–104.
133. For additional evidence, including rabbinic texts and discussion of diaspora pilgrimages to Jerusalem, see S. Safrai, *Die Wallfahrt im Zeitalter des Zweiten Tempels* (Neukirchen, 1981), 65–97. A condensed version can be found in Safrai and Stern, *Jewish People,* I, 191–204. Cf. Delling, *Die Bewältigung,* 36–37. On visitors to Jerusalem generally, see the testimony and discussion by Jeremias, *Jerusalem,* 58–77. The speculation of M. Goodman, in L. I. Levine, ed., *Jerusalem: Its Sanctity and Centrality to Judaism, Christianity, and Islam* (New York, 1999), 69–76, that large-scale pilgrimage began only in the reign of Herod, encouraged by the king for economic reasons, rests on little more than an argument from silence.
134. II Macc. 1.1–2: τοῖς ἀδελφοῖς τοῖς κατ᾽ Αἴγυπτον Ἰουδαίοις χαίρειν οἱ ἀδελφοὶ οἱ ἐν Ἱεροσολύμοις Ἰουδαῖοι . . . εἰρήνην ἀγαθήν.
135. Ibid., 1.9, 1.18, 2.16–17. A similar promotion of a festival advocated by Jerusalemites for diaspora Jews occurs with regard to Purim. See the Greek supplements to Esther, Addition, F, 11.
136. Ibid., 2.18. See above, pp. 238–239. It does not follow that the letter represents Hasmonean policy to claim ascendancy over diaspora Jews, as is argued by U. Rappaport, in B. Isaac and A. Oppenheimer, eds., *Studies on the Jewish Diaspora in the Hellenistic and Roman Periods* (Tel Aviv, 1996), 3–4 (Hebrew).
137. *LetArist.* 38: βουλομένων δ᾽ ἡμῶν καὶ τούτοις χαρίζεσθαι καὶ πᾶσι τοῖς κατὰ τὴν οἰκουμένην Ἰουδαίοις καὶ τοῖς μετέπειτα.
138. Ibid., 307–311.
139. III Macc. 2.21–27: προέθετο δημοσίᾳ κατὰ τοῦ ἔθνους διαδοῦναι ψόγον.

140. Ibid., 2.28–33: ὡς πολεμίους τοῦ ἔθνους ἔκρινον καὶ τῆς κοινῆς συναναστροφῆς καὶ εὐχρηστίας ἐστέρουν.
141. Ibid., 3.21: τοὺς ὁμοφύλους.
142. Tobit, 1.18: καὶ εἴ τινα ἀπέκτεινεν Σενναχηριμ, ὅτε ἀπῆλθεν φεύγων ἐκ τῆς Ἰουδαίας, . . . ἔθαψα. The subject of ἀπῆλθεν is certainly Sennacherib, as observed by C. A. Moore, *Tobit* (New York, 1996), 120. Cf. II Kings, 19.35.
143. Cic. *Pro Flacco*, 66–67, 69.
144. Jos. *CAp.* 1.32–33.
145. Philo, *Mos.* 2.232: μὴ χωρούσης διὰ πολυανθρωπίαν τὸ ἔθνος μιᾶς χώρας.
146. Jos. *Ant.* 13.352–355: ὅτι τὸ πρὸς τοῦτον ἄδικον ἐχθροὺς ἅπαντας ἡμᾶς σοι τοὺς Ἰουδαίους καταστήσει. Cf. M. Stern, *Zion*, 50 (1985), 101–102 (Hebrew).
147. Jos. *Ant.* 14.127–137. See, especially, 14.131: πείθει δὲ καὶ τούτους τὰ αὐτῶν φρονῆσαι κατὰ τὸ ὁμόφυλον Ἀντίπατρος, καὶ μάλιστα ἐπιδείξας αὐτοῖς τὰς Ὑρκανοῦ τοῦ ἀρχιερέως ἐπιστολάς. Cf. also Jos. *BJ*, 1.190.
148. For this interpretation of Leontopolis, see E. S. Gruen, *SCI*, 16 (1997), 47–70, with bibliography. A different view is found in D. R. Schwartz, *Zion*, 62 (1997), 5–22 (Hebrew). The authority of the High Priest in diaspora communities is attested also by the request of Saul (Paul) for letters from the High Priest to the synagogues in Damascus, authorizing him to arrest Christians in their midst and bring them back to Jerusalem; Acts, 9.1–2.
149. Jos. *Ant.* 17.300–301.
150. Ibid., 17.321–338.
151. Philo, *Flacc.* 45–46.
152. Ibid., 124: κοινὸν ἐχθρὸν τοῦ ἔθνους. Cf. 1, 117.
153. Philo, *Leg.* 184: ἕτερον κατασκήπτει βαρύτατον ἐξαπιναίως ἀπροσδόκητον κακόν, οὐχ ἑνὶ μέρει τοῦ Ἰουδαϊκοῦ τὸν κίνδυνον ἐπάγον, ἀλλὰ συλλήβδην ἅπαντι τῷ ἔθνει. Cf. 178, 351, 373.
154. Ibid., 193–194.
155. Ibid., 213–217: ὀλίγου δέω φάναι πᾶσα ἡ οἰκουμένη.
156. Ibid., 277–283. Cf. 330: οὐ μόνον τοῖς τὴν ἱερὰν χώραν κατοικοῦσιν ἀλλὰ καὶ τοῖς πανταχοῦ τῆς οἰκουμένης Ἰουδαίοις.
157. Ibid., 371; cf. 159–161.
158. Philo, *Spec. Leg.* 2.168. Cf. Schaller, in Strecker, *Das Land Israel*, 176–178. Van Unnik, *Das Selbstverständis*, 127–137, who finds no optimistic assessment of the diaspora in Philo, notably omits this passage.
159. Jos. *Ant.* 4.115–116: τὴν δ᾿ οἰκουμένην οἰκητήριον δι᾿ αἰῶνος ἴστε προκειμένην ὑμῖν, καὶ τὸ πλῆθος ὑμῶν ἔν τε νήσοις καὶ κατ᾿ ἤπειρον βιοτεύσετε ὅσον ἐστὶν οὐδ᾿ ἀστέρων ἀριθμὸς ἐν οὐρανῷ. Josephus departs quite substantially here from the corresponding text in Numbers, 23.6–10. See the good discussion by Halpern-Amaru, *JQR*, 71 (1980/81), 225–229; eadem, in Hoffman, *Land of Israel*, 81–82; cf. also Price, *SCI*, 13 (1994), 171. For comparable statements in Josephus, see *Ant.* 1.282: οἷς ἐγὼ τὸ ταύτης κράτος τῆς γῆς δίδωμι καὶ παισὶ τοῖς αὐτῶν, ὃ πληρώσουσιν ὅσην ἥλιος ὁρᾷ καὶ γῆν καὶ θάλασσαν; 2.213, 14.115 (citing Strabo); *BJ*, 7.43. On Josephus᾿ generally positive attitude toward diaspora, see L. H. Feldman, in Scott, *Exile*, 145–172.

Bibliography

Abel, E. L. "Were the Jews Banished from Rome in 19 AD?" *REJ,* 127 (1968): 383–386.

Abel, F.-M. *Les Livres des Maccabées.* Paris, 1949.

Abramson, G., and T. Parfitt, eds. *Jewish Education and Learning.* Chur, 1994.

Africa, T. W. "Worms and the Death of Kings: A Cautionary Note on Disease and History." *CA,* 1 (1982): 1–17.

Alessandri, S. "La presunta cacciata dei Giudei da Roma nel 139 a. Chr." *StudClassOrient,* 17 (1968): 187–198.

Alexander, P. S. "Retelling the Old Testament." In D. A. Carson and H. G. M. Williamson, eds., *It Is Written: Scripture Citing Scripture, Essays in Honour of Barnabas Lindars,* 99–121. Cambridge, 1988.

Allen, O. W., Jr. *The Death of Herod: The Narrative and Theological Function of Retribution in Luke-Acts.* Atlanta, 1997.

Alonso-Schökel, L. *Narrative Structures in the Book of Judith* (Protocol of the Center for Hermeneutical Studies in Hellenistic and Modern Culture, Coll. 11). Berkeley, 1974.

Alston, R. "Philo's *In Flaccum:* Ethnicity and Sacred Space in Roman Alexandria." *Greece and Rome,* 44 (1997): 165–175.

Alter, R., and F. Kermode, eds. *The Literary Guide to the Bible.* Cambridge, Mass., 1987.

Amir, Y. "Philo's Version of the Pilgrimage to Jerusalem." In A. Oppenheimer, U. Rappaport, and M. Stern, eds., *Jerusalem in the Second Temple Period,* 154–165. Jerusalem, 1980. (Hebrew)

Appelbaum, S. "Jewish Status at Cyrene in the Roman Period." *PP,* 97 (1964): 291–303.

——— "Jews and Service in the Roman Army." In S. Appelbaum, ed., *Roman Frontier Studies, 1967,* 181–184. Tel-Aviv, 1971.

——— "The Legal Status of the Jewish Communities in the Diaspora." In Safrai and Stern, *Jewish People,* I (1974), 420–463.

——— "The Organization of the Jewish Communities in the Diaspora." In Safrai and Stern, *Jewish People,* I (1974), 464–503.

——— "Economic Life in Palestine." In Safrai and Stern, *Jewish People,* II (1976), 631–700.

——— "The Social and Economic Status of the Jews in the Diaspora." In Safrai and Stern, *Jewish People,* II (1976), 701–727.

——— *Jews and Greeks in Ancient Cyrene.* Leiden, 1979.

Arenhoevel, D. *Die Theokratie nach dem 1. und 2. Makkabäerbuch.* Mainz, 1967.

Assmann, J. *Das kulturelle Gedächtnis.* Munich, 1999.
Attridge, H. W., and G. Hata, eds. *Eusebius, Christianity, and Judaism.* Detroit, 1992.
Bach, A. *Women, Seduction, and Betrayal in Biblical Narrative.* Cambridge, 1997.
Baer, Y. *Galut.* New York, 1947.
Bal, M. "The Elders and Susanna." *Biblical Interpretation,* 1 (1993): 1–19.
——— "Head Hunting: 'Judith' on the Cutting Edge of Knowledge." In A. Brenner, ed., *A Feminist Companion to Esther, Judith, and Susanna,* 253–285. Sheffield, 1995.
Bar-Kochva, B. *Judas Maccabaeus: The Jewish Struggle against the Seleucids.* Cambridge, 1989.
——— *Pseudo-Hecataeus, "On the Jews:" Legitimizing the Jewish Diaspora.* Berkeley, 1996.
Barclay, J. M. G. *Jews in the Mediterranean Diaspora from Alexander to Trajan (323 BCE–117 CE).* Edinburgh, 1996.
Baron, S. W. "Population." *Encyclopedia Judaica,* vol. 13, 866–903. Jerusalem, 1971.
Barraclough, R. "Philo's Politics, Roman Rule, and Hellenistic Judaism." *ANRW,* II.21.1 (1984): 417–553.
Barrett, A. A. *Caligula: The Corruption of Power.* London, 1989.
Bartlett, J. R. *The First and Second Books of the Maccabees.* Cambridge, 1973.
Baumann, U. *Rom und die Juden: Die römisch-jüdischen Beziehungen von Pompeius bis zum Tode des Herodes (63 v.Chr.–4 v.Chr.).* Frankfurt am Main, 1983.
Baumgartner, W. "Susanna: Die Geschichte einer Legende." *Archiv für Religionswissenschaft,* 24 (1926): 259–280.
Beal, T. K. *The Book of Hiding: Gender, Ethnicity, Annihilation, and Esther.* London, 1997.
Beard, M., J. North, and S. Price. *Religions of Rome,* 2 vols. Cambridge, 1998.
Bell, H. I. "Anti-Semitism in Alexandria." *JRS,* 31 (1941): 1–18.
Bellen, H. "Συναγωγὴ τῶν Ἰουδαίων καὶ θεοσεβῶν. Die Aussage einer bosporanischen Freilassungsinschrift (CIRB 71) zum Problem der Gottesfürchtigen (mit 1 Tafel)." *Jahrbuch für Antike und Christentum,* 8–9 (1965/1966): 171–176.
Benko, S. "The Edict of Claudius of A.D. 40 and the Instigator Chrestus." *Theologische Zeitschrift,* 25 (1969): 406–418.
Berard, J.-E. "Philosophie politique et antijudaïsme chez Cicéron." *SCI,* 19 (2000): 113–132.
Berg, S. B. *The Book of Esther: Motifs, Themes, and Structure.* Missoula, 1979.
Bergey, R. L. "The Book of Esther: Its Place in the Linguistic Milieu of Post-Exilic Biblical Hebrew Prose." Ph.D. diss., Dropsie College, 1983.
Berger, D., ed. *History and Hate: The Dimensions of Anti-Semitism.* Philadelphia, 1986.
Bergmann, W., and C. Hoffmann. "Kalkül oder Massenwahn? Eine soziologische Interpretation der antijüdischen Unruhen in Alexandria 38 n. Chr." In R. Erb and M. Schmidt, eds., *Antisemitismus und jüdische Geschichte: Studien zu Ehren von Herbert A. Strauss,* 15–46. Berlin, 1987.
Bergren, T. A. "Nehemiah in 2 Maccabees 1:10–2:18." *JSJ,* 28 (1997): 249–270.
Berlin, A. *Esther.* Philadelphia, 2001.

———— "The Book of Esther and Ancient Storytelling." *JBL*, 120 (2001): 3–14.

Bertrand, D. A. "Le chevreau d'Anna: la signification de l'anecdotique dans le livre de *Tobit*." *RevHistPhilRel*, 68 (1988): 267–274.

Bickermann, E. J. "Makkabäerbücher (III)." *RE*, 19 (1928): 797–800.

———— "Ein jüdischer Festbrief vom Jahre 124 v. Chr. (II Macc I 1–9)." *ZNW*, 32 (1933): 233–254.

———— *Der Gott der Makkabäer: Untersuchungen über Sinn und Ursprung der makkabäischen Erhebung.* Berlin, 1937.

———— "The Colophon of the Greek Book of Esther." *JBL*, 63 (1944): 339–362.

———— "The Altars of Gentiles: A Note on the Jewish Ius Sacrum." *RIDA* (3rd ser.), 5 (1958): 137–164. (= *Studies in Jewish and Christian History, Part Two*, 324–346. Leiden, 1980.)

———— *Four Strange Books of the Bible.* New York, 1967.

———— *Studies in Jewish and Christian History, Part Two.* Leiden, 1980.

Bilde, P., et al., eds. *Ethnicity in Hellenistic Egypt.* Aarhus, 1992.

Binder, D. D. *Into the Temple Courts: The Place of the Synagogues in the Second Temple Period.* Atlanta, 1999.

Blenkinsopp, J. "Biographical Patterns in Biblical Narrative." *JSOT*, 20 (1981): 27–46.

Bloedhorn, H., and G. Hüttenmeister. "The Synagogue." In *CHJ*, III (1999): 267–297.

Borgen, P. "'There Shall Come Forth a Man': Reflections on Messianic Ideas in Philo." In J. H. Charlesworth, ed., *The Messiah: Developments in Earliest Judaism and Christianity*, 341–361. Minneapolis, 1992.

Botermann, H. *Das Judenedikt des Kaisers Claudius: römischer Staat und Christiani im 1. Jahrhundert.* Stuttgart, 1996.

Bow, B., and G. W. E. Nickelsburg. "Patriarchy with a Twist: Men and Women in Tobit." In A.-J. Levine, ed., *"Women Like This": New Perspectives on Jewish Women in the Greco-Roman World*, 127–143. Atlanta, 1991.

Bowersock, G. W. "C. Marcius Censorinus, Legatus Caesaris." *HSCP*, 68 (1964): 207–210.

Bowman, A. K., and D. Rathbone. "Cities and Administration in Roman Egypt." *JRS*, 82 (1992): 107–127.

Bowsky, M. W. B. "M. Tittius Sex.f. Aem. and the Jews of Berenice (Cyrenaica)." *AJP*, 108 (1987): 495–510.

Box, G. H. *The Testament of Abraham.* London, 1927.

Box, H. *Philonis Alexandrini In Flaccum.* London, 1939.

Boyce, M. "Persian Religion in the Achemenid Age." *CHJ*, I (1984): 279–307.

Braun, M. *History and Romance in Graeco-Oriental Literature.* Oxford, 1938.

Brenner, A. "Who's Afraid of Feminist Criticism? Who's Afraid of Biblical Humour? The Case of the Obtuse Foreign Ruler in the Hebrew Bible." *JSOT*, 63 (1994): 38–55.

———— ed. *A Feminist Companion to Esther, Judith, and Susanna.* Sheffield, 1995.

Brock, S. P. "*Testamentum Iobi.*" In *PsVTGr*, II (1967): 1–59.

Bruneau, P. *Recherches sur les cultes de Délos à l'époque hellénistique et à l'époque impériale.* Paris, 1970.

———— "Les Israélites de Délos et la juiverie délienne." *BCH*, 106 (1982): 465–504.

Bruns, E. J. "The Genealogy of Judith." *CBQ*, 18 (1956): 19–22.

Bunge, J. G. *Untersuchungen zum zweiten Makkabäerbuch.* Bonn, 1971.

Burstein, S. "Cleitarchus in Jerusalem: A Note on the *Book of Judith.*" In F. B. Titchener and R. F. Moorton, Jr., eds., *The Eye Expanded: Life and the Arts in Greco-Roman Antiquity,* 105–112. Berkeley, 1999.

Carroll, R. P. "Exile! What Exile? Deportation and the Discourses of Diaspora." In L. L. Grabbe, ed., *Leading Captivity Captive: "The Exile" as History and Ideology,* 62–79. Sheffield, 1998.

Carson, D. A., and H. G. N. Williamson, eds. *It Is Written: Scripture Citing Scripture, Essays in Honour of Barnabas Lindars.* Cambridge, 1988.

Castritius, H. "Die Haltung Roms gegenüber den Juden in der ausgehenden Republik und der Prinzipatzeit." In T. Klein, ed., *Judentum und Antisemitismus von der Antike bis zur Gegenwart,* 15–40. Düsseldorf, 1984.

Charles, R. H., ed. *The Apocrypha and Pseudepigrapha of the Old Testament in English,* 2 vols. Oxford, 1913.

Charlesworth, J. H., ed. *The Old Testament Pseudepigrapha,* 2 vols. New York, 1983–1985.

——— ed. *The Messiah: Developments in Earliest Judaism and Christianity.* Minneapolis, 1992.

Clarysse, W. "Jews in Trikomia." *Proceedings of the XXth International Congress of Papyrologists,* 193–203. Copenhagen, 1994.

Clifford, J. *Routes: Travel and Translation in the Late Twentieth Century.* Cambridge, Mass., 1997.

Clines, D. J. A. *The Esther Scroll: The Story of the Story.* Sheffield, 1984.

Cohen, S. J. D. "Was Judaism in Antiquity a Missionary Religion?" In M. Mor, ed., *Jewish Assimilation, Acculturation, and Accommodation: Past Traditions, Current Issues, and Future Prospects,* 14–23. Lanham, 1992.

——— *The Beginnings of Jewishness: Boundaries, Varieties, Uncertainties.* Berkeley, 1999.

——— and E. S. Frerichs, eds. *Diasporas in Antiquity.* Atlanta, 1993.

Collins, J. J. "Structure and Meaning in the Testament of Job." *SBL Seminar Papers,* 1 (1974): 35–51.

——— *The Apocalyptic Imagination: An Introduction to the Jewish Matrix of Christianity.* New York, 1984.

——— "Artapanus." In Charlesworth, *OTP,* II (1985): 889–904.

——— *Jewish Wisdom in the Hellenistic Age.* Louisville, 1997.

——— *Between Jerusalem and Athens: Jewish Identity in the Hellenistic Diaspora,* 2nd ed. Grand Rapids, 2000.

——— and G. E. Sterling, eds. *Hellenism in the Land of Israel.* Notre Dame, 2001.

Cotter, W. "The Collegia and Roman Law: State Restrictions on Voluntary Associations, 64 BCE–200 CE." In J. S. Kloppenborg and S. G. Wilson, eds., *Voluntary Associations in the Graeco-Roman World,* 74–89. London, 1996.

Cowey, J. M. S., and K. Maresch. *Urkunden des Politeuma der Juden von Herakleopolis (144/3–133/2 b. Chr.) (P. Polit. Iud) Papyrologica Coloniensia,* XXIX. Wiesbaden, 2001.

Cowley, A. E. "Judith." In Charles, *APOT,* I (1913): 242–267.

Cracco-Ruggini, L. "Nuclei immigrati e forze indigene in tre grandi centri commerciali dell' Impero." In J. H. D'Arms and C. C. Kopff, eds., *The Seabourne Commerce of Ancient Rome* (Memoirs of the American Academy at Rome, 36), 55–76. Rome, 1980.

Craig, K. M., Jr. *Reading Esther: A Case for the Literary Carnivalesque*. Lousiville, 1995.

Craven, T. *Artistry and Faith in the Book of Judith*. Chico, 1983.

Dancy, J. C., et al., eds. *The Shorter Books of the Apocrypha: Tobit, Judith, Rest of Esther, Baruch, Letter of Jeremiah, Additions to Daniel and Prayer of Manasseh*. Cambridge, 1972.

Daniel, J. L. "Anti-Semitism in the Hellenistic-Roman Period." *JBL*, 98 (1979): 45–65.

Danshin, D. A. "Phanagorian Community of Jews." *VDI*, 204 (1993): 59–72. (Russian)

Daube, D. "The Last Chapter of Esther." *JQR*, 37 (1946/1947): 139–147.

Davies, P. R. "Exile? What Exile? Whose Exile?" In L. L. Grabbe, ed., *Leading Captivity Captive: "The Exile" as History and Ideology*, 128–138. Sheffield, 1998.

—— and R. T. White, eds. *A Tribute to Geza Vermes: Essays on Jewish and Christian Literature and History*. Sheffield, 1990.

Davies, W. D. *The Territorial Dimension of Judaism*. Berkeley, 1982.

Davis, M., ed. *World Jewry and the State of Israel*. New York, 1977.

Dawson, D. *Allegorical Readers and Cultural Revision in Ancient Alexandria*. Berkeley, 1992.

Day, P. L., ed. *Gender and Difference in Ancient Israel*. Minneapolis, 1989.

de Jonge, M. *The Testaments of the Twelve Patriarchs*. Leiden, 1978.

de Lange, N. "The Origins of Anti-Semitism: Ancient Evidence and Modern Interpretations." In S. L. Gilman and S. T. Katz, eds., *Anti-Semitism in Times of Crisis*, 21–37. New York, 1991.

De Robertis, F. M. *Il diritto associativo romano*. Bari, 1938.

De Troyer, K. "An Oriental Beauty Parlour: An Analysis of Esther 2.8–18 in the Hebrew, the Septuagint and the Second Greek Text." In A. Brenner, ed., *A Feminist Companion to Esther, Judith, and Susanna*, 47–70. Sheffield, 1995.

Delcor, M. "Le livre de Judith et l'époque grecque." *Klio*, 49 (1967): 151–179.

—— *Le Testament d'Abraham*. Leiden, 1973.

—— "The Apocrypha and Pseudepigrapha of the Hellenistic Period." *CHJ*, II (1989): 409–503.

Delia, D. *Alexandrian Citizenship during the Roman Principate*. Atlanta, 1991.

Delling, G. *Die Bewältigung der Diasporasituation durch das hellenistische Judentum*. Göttingen, 1987.

Denis, A.-M. "*Fragmenta Pseudepigraphorum Graeca*." In *PsVTGr*, III (1970): 45–238.

Donfried, K. P., and P. Richardson, eds. *Judaism and Christianity in First-Century Rome*. Grand Rapids, 1998.

Doran, R. *Temple Propaganda: The Purpose and Character of 2 Maccabees*. Washington, 1981.

—— "The Jewish Hellenistic Historians Before Josephus." *ANRW*, II.20.1 (1987): 246–297.

Dorothy, C. V. *The Books of Esther: Structure, Genre, and Textual Integrity*. Sheffield, 1997.

Dover, K. J., ed. *Perceptions of the Ancient Greeks*. Oxford, 1992.

Downey, G. *A History of Antioch in Syria from Seleucus to the Arab Conquest*. Princeton, 1961.

Droge, A. J. *Homer or Moses? Early Christian Interpretations of the History of Culture.* Tübingen, 1989.

Drummond, A. "Tribunes and Tribunician Programmes in 63 B.C." *Athenaeum,* 87 (1999): 121–168.

Dubarle, A. M. *Judith: Formes et sens des diverses traditions,* 2 vols. Rome, 1966.

Duff, A. M. *Freedmen in the Early Roman Empire.* Oxford, 1928.

Dunn, R. "Discriminations in the Comic Spirit in the Story of Susanna." *Christianity and Literature,* 31 (1982): 19–31.

Edwards, M., M. Goodman, and S. Price, eds. *Apologetics in the Roman Empire.* Oxford, 1999.

Eilers, C. "M. Silanus, Stratoniceia, and the Governors of Asia under Augustus." *Tyche,* 14 (1999): 77–86.

Eisen, A. M. *Galut: Modern Jewish Reflection on Homelessness and Homecoming.* Bloomington, 1986.

——— "Exile." In C. Taylor, ed., *Sources of the Self: The Making of the Modern Identity,* 219–225. Cambridge, Mass., 1989.

Eissfeldt, O. *The Old Testament: An Introduction, Including the Apocrypha and Pseudepigrapha, and Also the Works of Similar Type from Qumran.* Oxford, 1965.

Engel, H. *Die Susanna-Erzählung.* Göttingen, 1985.

Enslin, M. S. *The Book of Judith.* Leiden, 1972.

Erb, R., and M. Schmidt, eds. *Antisemitismus und jüdische Geschichte: Studien zu Ehren von Herbert A. Strauss.* Berlin, 1987.

Evans, C. A., and J. A. Sanders, eds. *The Function of Scripture in Early Jewish and Christian Tradition.* Sheffield, 1998.

Evans, R. J. "Norbani Flacci: The Consuls of 38 and 24 B.C." *Historia,* 36 (1987): 121–128.

Ezrahi, S. D. "Our Homeland, the Text . . . Our Text, the Homeland." *Michigan Quarterly Review,* 31 (1992): 463–497.

——— *Booking Passage: Exile and Homecoming in the Modern Jewish Imagination.* Berkeley, 2000.

Feldman, L. H. "The Orthodoxy of the Jews in Hellenistic Egypt." *Jewish Social Studies,* 22 (1960): 215–237.

——— "Anti-Semitism in the Ancient World." In D. Berger, ed., *History and Hate: The Dimensions of Anti-Semitism,* 15–41. Philadelphia, 1986.

——— "Was Judaism a Missionary Religion in Ancient Times?" In M. Mor, ed., *Jewish Assimilation, Acculturation, and Accommodation: Past Traditions, Current Issues, and Future Prospects,* 24–37. Lanham, 1992.

——— "Jewish Proselytism." In H. W. Attridge and G. Hata, eds., *Eusebius, Christianity, and Judaism,* 372–408. Detroit, 1992.

——— *Jew and Gentile in the Ancient World: Attitudes and Interactions from Alexander to Justinian.* Princeton, 1993.

——— "Reflections on Jews in Graeco-Roman Literature." *JSP,* 16 (1997): 39–52.

——— "The Concept of Exile in Josephus." In J. M. Scott, ed., *Exile: Old Testament, Jewish, and Christian Conceptions,* 145–172. Leiden, 1997.

Feldmeier, R. "Weise hinter 'eisernen Mauern.'" In M. Hengel and A. M. Schwemer, eds., *Die Septuaginta zwischen Judentum und Christentum,* 20–37. Tübingen, 1994.

Fine, S. *Jews, Christians, and Polytheists in the Ancient Synagogue: Cultural Interaction during the Greco-Roman Period.* London, 1999.

Fischer, U. *Eschatologie und Jenseitserwartung im hellenistischen Diaspora-judentum.* Berlin, 1978.

Fitzmyer, J. A. "Tobit." In J. VanderKam et al., eds., *Discoveries in the Judaean Desert,* XIX, 1–76. Oxford, 1995.

—— "The Aramaic and Hebrew Fragments of Tobit from Qumran Cave 4." *CBQ,* 57 (1995): 655–675.

—— and D. J. Harrington. *A Manual of Palestinian Aramaic Texts.* Rome, 1978.

Flambard, J.-M. "*Collegia Compitalica:* phénomène associatif, cadres territoriaux et cadres civiques dans le monde romain à l'époque republicaine." *Ktema,* 6 (1981): 143–166.

Fleischer, E. "On the Beginnings of Obligatory Jewish Prayer." *Tarbiz,* 59 (1990): 397–441. (Hebrew)

Flesher, P. V. M. "Palestinian Synagogues before 70 c.e.: A Review of the Evidence." In D. Urman and P. V. M. Flesher, eds., *Ancient Synagogues: Historical Analysis and Archaeological Discovery,* I, 27–39. Leiden, 1995.

Flusser, D., and S. Amorai-Stark. "The Goddess Thermuthis, Moses, and Artapanus." *JSQ,* 1 (1993/1994): 217–233.

Forni, G. "Intorno al Consilium di L. Cornelio Lentulo console nel 49 a.C." In G. Wirth, K. H. Schwarte, and J. Heinrichs, eds., *Romanitas-Christianitas: Untersuchungen zur Geschichte und Literatur der römischen Kaiserzeit,* 154–163. Berlin, 1982.

Fox, M. V. *Character and Ideology in the Book of Esther.* Columbia, S.C., 1991.

Frankfurter, D., ed. *Pilgrimage and Holy Space in Late Antique Egypt.* Leiden, 1998.

Fraser, P. M. *Ptolemaic Alexandria,* 3 vols. Oxford, 1972.

Freudenthal, J. *Alexander Polyhistor.* Breslau, 1875–1879.

Fröhlich, I. *"Time and Times and Half a Time": Historical Consciousness in the Jewish Literature of the Persian and Hellenistic Eras.* Sheffield, 1996.

Fuks, G. "Where Have All the Freedmen Gone? On an Anomaly in the Jewish Grave-Inscriptions from Rome." *JJS,* 36 (1985): 25–32.

Gafni, I. M. "Reinterment in the Land of Israel: Notes on the Origin and Development of the Custom." *The Jerusalem Cathedra,* 1 (1981): 96–104.

—— *Land, Center, and Diaspora: Jewish Constructs in Late Antiquity.* Sheffield, 1997.

Gager, J. G. *The Origins of Anti-Semitism: Attitudes Toward Judaism in Pagan and Christian Antiquity.* Oxford, 1985.

Gardner, J. F. *Being a Roman Citizen.* London, 1993.

Georgi, D. *The Opponents of Paul in Second Corinthians.* Edinburgh, 1987.

Gibson, E. L. *The Jewish Manumission Inscriptions of the Bosporan Kingdom: Release in the Prayerhouse.* Tübingen, 1999.

Gill, D. W. J., and C. Gempf, eds. *The Book of Acts in its Graeco-Roman Setting.* Grand Rapids, 1994.

Gilman, S. L., and S. T. Katz, eds. *Anti-Semitism in Times of Crisis.* New York, 1991.

Ginsburg, M. S. *Rome et la Judée: contribution à l'histoire de leurs relations politiques.* Paris, 1928.

Glancy, J. A. "The Accused: Susanna and Her Readers." In A. Brenner, ed., *A Feminist Companion to Esther, Judith, and Susanna,* 288–302. Sheffield, 1995.

Goldenberg, R. "The Jewish Sabbath in the Roman World." In *ANRW,* II.19.1 (1979): 414–447.

Goldman, S. "Narrative and Ethical Ironies in Esther." *JSOT,* 47 (1990): 15–31.

Goldstein, J. A. *II Maccabees.* Garden City, 1983.

Goldstein, N. W. "Cultivated Pagans and Ancient Anti-Semitism." *JR,* 19 (1939): 346–364.

Goodenough, E. R. *The Politics of Philo Judaeus: Practice and Theory.* New Haven, 1938.

Goodman, M. *The Ruling Class of Judaea: The Origins of the Jewish Revolt against Rome A.D. 66–70.* Cambridge, 1987.

———— "Kosher Olive Oil in Antiquity." In P. R. Davies and R. T. White, eds., *A Tribute to Geza Vermes: Essays on Jewish and Christian Literature and History,* 227–246. Sheffield, 1990.

———— "Jewish Proselytizing in the First Century." In J. Lieu, J. North, and T. Rajak, eds., *Jews among Pagans and Christians in the Roman Empire,* 53–78. London, 1992.

———— *Mission and Conversion: Proselytizing in the Religious History of the Roman Empire.* Oxford, 1994.

———— "Jewish Attitudes to Greek Culture in the Period of the Second Temple." In G. Abramson and T. Parfitt, eds., *Jewish Education and Learning,* 167–174. Chur, 1994.

———— "Sacred Space in Diaspora Judaism." In B. Isaac and A. Oppenheimer, eds., *Studies on the Jewish Diaspora in the Hellenistic and Roman Periods,* 1–16. Tel-Aviv, 1996.

———— "Josephus' Treatise *Against Apion.*" In M. Edwards, M. Goodman, and S. Price, eds., *Apologetics in the Roman Empire,* 45–58. Oxford, 1999.

———— "The Pilgrimage Economy of Jerusalem in the Second Temple Period." In L. I. Levine, ed., *Jerusalem: Its Sanctity and Centrality to Judaism, Christianity, and Islam,* 69–76. New York, 1999.

———— ed. *Jews in a Graeco-Roman World.* Oxford, 1998.

Gordis, R. "Religion, Wisdom and History in the Book of Esther—A New Solution to an Ancient Crux." *JBL,* 100 (1981): 359–388.

Goudriaan, K. "Ethnical Strategies in Graeco-Roman Egypt." In P. Bilde et al., eds., *Ethnicity in Hellenistic Egypt,* 74–99. Aarhus, 1992.

Grabbe, L. L. "Synagogues in Pre-70 Palestine: A Re-assessment." In D. Urman and P. V. M. Flesher, eds., *Ancient Synagogues: Historical Analysis and Archaeological Discovery,* I, 17–26. Leiden, 1995.

———— ed. *Leading Captivity Captive: "The Exile" as History and Ideology.* Sheffield, 1998.

Green, W. S., ed. *Approaches to Ancient Judaism,* V, *Studies in Judaism in Its Greco-Roman Context.* Atlanta, 1985.

Greenstein, E. L. "A Jewish Reading of Esther." In J. Neusner, B. A. Levine, and E. S. Frerichs, eds., *Judaic Perspectives on Ancient Israel,* 225–243. Philadelphia, 1987.

Griffiths, J. G. "Egypt and the Rise of the Synagogue." In D. Urman and P. V. M. Flesher, eds., *Ancient Synagogues: Historical Analysis and Archaeological Discovery,* I, 3–16. Leiden, 1995.

Gruen, E. S. *The Last Generation of the Roman Republic.* Berkeley, 1974.

———— *The Hellenistic World and the Coming of Rome.* Berkeley, 1984.

———— *Studies in Greek Culture and Roman Policy.* Leiden, 1990.

—— "The Origins and Objectives of Onias' Temple." *SCI*, 16 (1997): 47–70.

—— *Heritage and Hellenism: The Reinvention of Jewish Tradition.* Berkeley, 1998.

—— "Jews, Greeks, and Romans in the Third Sibylline Oracle." In M. Goodman, ed., *Jews in a Graeco-Roman World*, 15–36. Oxford, 1998.

Guignebert, C. *Le monde juif vers le temps de Jésus.* Paris, 1950.

Guterman, S. L. *Religious Toleration and Persecution in Ancient Rome.* London, 1951.

Gutman, Y. *The Beginnings of Jewish-Hellenistic Literature*, 2 vols. Jerusalem, 1958–1963. (Hebrew)

Gutmann, J. "The Origin of the Synagogue: The Current State of Research." In J. Gutmann, ed., *The Synagogue: Studies in Origins, Archaeology, and Architecture*, 36–40. New York, 1975.

—— ed. *The Synagogue: Studies in Origins, Archaeology, and Architecture.* New York, 1975.

Haas, C. "Job's Perseverance in the Testament of Job." In M. A. Knibb and P. W. van der Horst, eds., *Studies on the Testament of Job*, 117–154. Cambridge, 1989.

Habicht, C. *2. Makkabäerbuch* (JSHRZ, I.3). Gütersloh, 1976.

Hachlili, R. "The Origin of the Synagogue: A Reassessment." *JSJ*, 28 (1997): 34–47.

—— *Ancient Jewish Art and Archaeology in the Diaspora.* Leiden, 1998.

Hadas, M. *Aristeas to Philocrates (Letter of Aristeas).* New York, 1951.

Halpern-Amaru, B. "Land Theology in Josephus' *Jewish Antiquities*." *JQR*, 71 (1980/1981): 201–229.

—— "Land Theology in Philo and Josephus." In L. A. Hoffmann, ed., *The Land of Israel: Jewish Perspectives*, 65–73. Notre Dame, 1986.

—— *Rewriting the Bible: Land and Covenant in Postbiblical Jewish Literature.* Valley Forge, 1994.

—— "The Journey of Susanna Among the Church Fathers." In E. Spolsky, ed., *The Judgment of Susanna: Authority and Witness*, 21–34. Atlanta, 1996.

—— "Exile and Return in Jubilees." In J. M. Scott, ed., *Exile: Old Testament, Jewish, and Christian Conceptions*, 127–144. Leiden, 1997.

Hanhart, R. *Text und Textgeschichte des Buches Judith.* Göttingen, 1979.

Harrington, D. J. "The Bible Rewritten (Narratives)." In R. A. Kraft and G. W. E. Nickelsburg, eds., *Early Judaism and Its Modern Interpreters*, 239–246. Atlanta, 1986.

Harris, H. A. *Greek Athletics and the Jews.* Cardiff, 1976.

Harvey, G. "Synagogues of the Hebrews: 'Good Jews' in the Diaspora." In S. Jones and S. Pearce, eds., *Jewish Local Patriotism and Self-Identification in the Graeco-Roman Period*, 132–147. Sheffield, 1998.

Hatzfeld, J. *Les Trafiquants italiens dans l'Orient hellénique.* Paris, 1919.

Hayman, P. "Monotheism—A Misused Word in Jewish Studies?" *JJS*, 42 (1991): 1–15.

Hecht, R. D. "Philo and Messiah." In J. Neusner, W. S. Green, and E. S. Frerichs, eds., *Judaisms and Their Messiahs at the Time of the Christian Era*, 139–168. Cambridge, 1987.

Heidel, W. A. "Why Were the Jews Banished from Italy in 19 AD?" *AJP*, 41 (1920): 38–47.

Heinemann, I. "Antisemitismus." *RE*, Suppl. V (1931): 3–43.

———— "The Relationships between the Jewish People and Its Land in Jewish-Hellenistic Literature." *Zion*, 13–14 (1948): 1–9. (Hebrew)

Heinen, H. "Ägyptische Grundlagen des antiken Antijudaismus." *Trierer Theologische Zeitschrift*, 101 (1992): 124–149.

Heller, B. "Die Susannaerzählung: ein Märchen." *ZAW*, 54 (1936): 281–287.

Hengel, M. *Judaism and Hellenism: Studies in Their Encounter in Palestine during the Early Hellenistic Period*, 2 vols. London, 1974.

———— *Judaica et Hellenistica: Kleine Schriften*, 2 vols. Tübingen, 1996.

———— and A. M. Schwemer, eds. *Die Septuaginta zwischen Judentum und Christentum*. Tübingen, 1994.

Hennig, D. *L. Aelius Seianus*. Munich, 1975.

———— "Zu neuveröffentlichen Bruchstücken der 'Acta Alexandrinorum.'" *Chiron*, 5 (1975): 317–335.

Himmelfarb, M. *Ascent to Heaven in Jewish and Christian Apocalypses*. New York, 1993.

Hoffmann, L. A., ed. *The Land of Israel: Jewish Perspectives*. Notre Dame, 1986.

Holladay, A. J., and M. D. Goodman. "Religious Scruples in Ancient Warfare." *CQ*, 36 (1986): 151–171.

Holladay, C. R. *Theios Aner in Hellenistic-Judaism: A Critique of the Use of This Category in New Testament Christology*. Missoula, 1977.

———— *Fragments from Hellenistic Jewish Authors*, 4 vols. Chico/Atlanta, 1983–1996.

Holleaux, M. Στρατηγὸς ὑπατός. Paris, 1918.

Honigman, S. "Philon, Flavius Josèphe, et la citoyenneté alexandrine: vers une utopie politique." *JJS*, 48 (1997): 62–90.

Horsley, G. H. R. "The Politarchs." In D. W. J. Gill and C. Gempf, eds., *The Book of Acts in Its Graeco-Roman Setting*, 419–431. Grand Rapids, 1994.

Huet, G. "Daniel et Susanne." *RHR*, 65 (1912): 277–284.

Humphreys, W. L. "A Life Style for the Diaspora: A Study of the Tales of Esther and Daniel." *JBL*, 92 (1973): 211–223.

Huskinson, J., ed. *Experiencing Rome: Culture, Identity, and Power in the Roman Empire*. London, 2000.

Ilan, T. *Integrating Women into Second Temple History*. Tübingen, 1999.

Isaac, B., and A. Oppenheimer, eds. *Studies on the Jewish Diaspora in the Hellenistic and Roman Periods*. Tel-Aviv, 1996.

Jacobs, I. "Literary Motifs in the Testament of Job." *JJS*, 21 (1970): 1–10.

Jacobson, H. *The Exagoge of Ezekiel*. Cambridge, 1983.

Jakab, A. "Le Judaisme hellénisé d'Alexandrie depuis la fondation de la ville jusqu'à la révolte sous Trajan." *Henoch*, 21 (1999): 147–164.

James, M. R. *The Testament of Abraham*. Cambridge, 1892.

———— *Apocrypha Anecdota, Second Series*, 5.1. Cambridge, 1897.

Jannsen, E. *Testament Abrahams (JSHRZ, III.2)*. Gütersloh, 1975.

Jeremias, J. *Jerusalem in the Time of Jesus: An Investigation into Social and Economic Conditions during the New Testament Period*. Philadelphia, 1969.

Jobes, K. *The Alpha-Text of Esther: Its Character and Relationship to the Masoretic Text*. Atlanta, 1996.

Johnson, S. R. *History as it Should Have Been*. Berkeley, forthcoming.

Jones, B. W. "Two Misconceptions about the Book of Esther." *CBQ*, 39 (1977): 171–181.

Jones, S., and S. Pearce, eds. *Jewish Local Patriotism and Self-Identification in the Graeco-Roman Period*. Sheffield, 1998.

Juster, J. *Les Juifs dans l'empire romaine*, 2 vols. Paris, 1914.

Kaimakis, D. *Die Kyraniden*. Meisenheim am Glan, 1976.

Kant, L. H. "Jewish Inscriptions in Greek and Latin." *ANRW*, II.20.2 (1987): 671–713.

Kasher, A. "The Jewish Attitude to the Alexandrian Gymnasium in the First Century A.D." *AJAH*, 1 (1976): 148–161.

———— "Jerusalem as 'Metropolis' in Philo's National Consciousness." *Cathedra*, 11 (1979): 45–56. (Hebrew)

———— "Jewish Emigration and Settlement in Diaspora in the Hellenistic-Roman Period." In A. Shinan, ed., *Emigration and Settlement in Diaspora in the Hellenistic-Roman Period*, 65–91. Jerusalem, 1982. (Hebrew)

———— *The Jews in Hellenistic and Roman Egypt: The Struggle for Equal Rights*. Tübingen, 1985.

———— "The Civic Status of the Jews in Ptolemaic Egypt." In P. Bilde et al., eds., *Ethnicity in Hellenistic Egypt*, 100–121. Aarhus, 1992.

———— "Synagogues as 'Houses of Prayer' and 'Holy Places' in the Jewish Communities of Hellenistic and Roman Egypt." In D. Urman and P. V. M. Flesher, eds., *Ancient Synagogues: Historical Analysis and Archaeological Discovery*, I, 205–220. Leiden, 1995.

Kaufmann, Y. *Exile and Estrangement*, 2 vols. Tel-Aviv, 1962. (Hebrew)

Kay, D. M. "Susanna." In Charles, *APOT*, I (1913): 638–651.

Kee, H. C. "Satan, Magic, and Salvation in the Testament of Job." *SBL Seminar Papers*, 1 (1974): 53–76.

———— "The Transformation of the Synagogue after 70 C.E.: Its Import for Early Christianity." *NTS*, 36 (1990): 1–24.

———— and L. H. Cohick, eds. *Evolution of the Synagogue: Problems and Progress*. Harrisburg, 1999.

Kerkeslager, A. "Jewish Pilgrimage and Jewish Identity in Hellenistic and Early Roman Egypt." In D. Frankfurter, ed., *Pilgrimage and Holy Space in Late Antique Egypt*, 99–225. Leiden, 1998.

Kienast, D. *Augustus*, 2nd ed. Darmstadt, 1999.

Klein, L. R. "Honor and Shame in Esther." In A. Brenner, ed., *A Feminist Companion to Esther, Judith, and Susanna*, 149–175. Sheffield, 1995.

Klein, T., ed. *Judentum und Antisemitismus von der Antike bis zur Gegenwart*. Düsseldorf, 1984.

Kloppenborg, J. S., and S. G. Wilson, eds. *Voluntary Associations in the Graeco-Roman World*. London, 1996.

Knibb, M. A., and P. W. van der Horst, eds. *Studies on the Testament of Job*. Cambridge, 1989.

Kohler, K. "The Pre-Talmudic Haggada II: The Apocalypse of Abraham and its Kindred." *JQR*, 7 (1895): 581–606.

———— "The Testament of Job. An Essene Midrash on the Book of Job." In G. A. Kohut, ed., *Semitic Studies in Memory of Rev. Dr. Alexander Kohut*, 264–338. Berlin, 1897.

Kohut, G. A., ed. *Semitic Studies in Memory of Rev. Dr. Alexander Kohut*. Berlin, 1897.

Kolenkow, A. B. "The Genre Testament and the Testament of Abraham." In

G. W. E. Nickelsburg, Jr., ed., *Studies on the Testament of Abraham*, 139–152. Missoula, 1976.

—— "The Angelology of the Testament of Abraham." In G. W. E. Nickelsburg, Jr., ed., *Studies on the Testament of Abraham*, 153–162. Missoula, 1976.

Kollmann, B. "Göttliche Offenbarung magisch-pharmakologischer Heilkunst im Buch Tobit." *ZAW*, 106 (1994): 289–299.

Kossmann, R. *Die Esthernovelle vom Erzälten zur Erzählung*. Leiden, 2000.

Kraabel, A. T. "ὕψιστος and the Synagogue at Sardis." *GRBS*, 10 (1969): 81–93.

—— "The Diaspora Synagogue: Archaeological and Epigraphic Evidence Since Sukenik." *ANRW*, II.19.1 (1979): 477–510.

—— "The Roman Diaspora: Six Questionable Assumptions." *JJS*, 33 (1982): 445–464.

—— "New Evidence of the Samaritan Diaspora Has Been Found on Delos." *BA*, 47 (1984): 44–46.

—— "Unity and Diversity among Diaspora Synagogues." In L. I. Levine, ed., *The Synagogue in Late Antiquity*, 49–60. Philadelphia, 1987.

Kraeling, C. H. "The Jewish Community at Antioch." *JBL*, 51 (1932): 130–160.

Kraft, R. A. *The Testament of Job According to the SV Text*. Missoula, 1974.

—— "Reassessing the 'Recensional Problem' in Testament of Abraham." In G. W. E. Nickelsburg, Jr., ed., *Studies on the Testament of Abraham*, 121–137. Missoula, 1976.

—— "Philo and the Sabbath Crisis: Alexandrian Jewish Politics and the Dating of Philo's Works." In B. A. Pearson, ed., *The Future of Early Christianity: Essays in Honor of Helmut Koester*, 131–141. Minneapolis, 1991.

—— and G. W. E. Nickelsburg, eds. *Early Judaism and Its Modern Interpreters*. Atlanta, 1986.

Krauss, S. *Synagogale Altertümer*. Hildesheim, 1966 (originally published 1922).

Kushnir-Stein, A. "On the Visit of Agrippa I to Alexandria in AD 38." *JJS*, 51 (2000): 227–242.

La Piana, G. *Foreign Groups in Rome During the First Centuries of the Empire*. Cambridge, Mass., 1927.

Lacocque, A. *The Feminine Unconventional: Four Subversive Figures in Israel's Tradition*. Minneapolis, 1990.

—— "The Different Versions of Esther." *Biblical Interpretation*, 7 (1999): 301–322.

Lane, E. N. "Sabazius and the Jews in Valerius Maximus: A Re-examination." *JRS*, 69 (1979): 35–38.

Laniak, T. S. *Shame and Honor in the Book of Esther*. Atlanta, 1998.

Lebram, J. "Die Weltreiche in der jüdischen Apokalyptik: Bemerkungen zu Tobit." *ZAW*, 76 (1964): 328–331.

Leon, H. J. *The Jews of Ancient Rome*. Philadelphia, 1960.

Levenson, J. D. *Esther: A Commentary*. Louisville, 1997.

Levi, Y. "Cicero on the Jews." *Zion*, 7 (1942): 109–134. (Hebrew)

Levick, B. *Tiberius the Politician*. London, 1976.

—— *Claudius*. London, 1990.

Levine, A.-J. "Diaspora as Metaphor: Bodies and Boundaries in the Book of Tobit." In J. A. Overman and R. S. MacLennan, eds., *Diaspora Jews and Judaism: Essays in Honor of, and in Dialogue with, A. Thomas Kraabel*, 105–117. Atlanta, 1992.

—— "Sacrifice and Salvation: Otherness and Domestication in the Book of Judith." In J. C. VanderKam, ed., *"No One Spoke Ill of Her": Essays on Judith,* 17–30. Atlanta, 1992.

—— "'Hemmed in on Every Side': Jews and Women in the Book of Susanna." In A. Brenner, ed., *A Feminist Companion to Esther, Judith, and Susanna,* 303–323. Sheffield, 1995.

—— ed. *"Women Like This": New Perspectives on Jewish Women in the Greco-Roman World.* Atlanta, 1991.

Levine, E. "The Jews in Time and Space." In E. Levine, ed., *Diaspora: Exile and the Jewish Condition,* 1–11. New York, 1983.

Levine, E., ed. *Diaspora: Exile and the Jewish Condition.* New York, 1983.

Levine, L. I. "The Second Temple Synagogue: The Formative Years." In L. I. Levine, ed., *The Synagogue in Late Antiquity,* 7–32. Philadelphia, 1987.

—— ed. *The Synagogue in Late Antiquity.* Philadelphia, 1987.

—— "The Nature and Origin of the Palestinian Synagogue Reconsidered." *JBL,* 115 (1996): 425–448.

—— "Synagogue Leadership: the Case of the Archisynagogue." In M. Goodman, ed., *Jews in a Graeco-Roman World,* 195–214. Oxford, 1998.

—— *The Ancient Synagogue: The First Thousand Years.* New Haven, 2000.

—— ed. *Jerusalem: Its Sanctity and Centrality to Judaism, Christianity, and Islam.* New York, 1999.

Levinskaya, I. *The Book of Acts in Its Diaspora Setting.* Grand Rapids, 1996.

Levy, I. "Ptolémée Lathyre et les Juifs." *HUCA,* 23.2 (1950/1951): 127–136.

Lewy, H. "Tacitus on the Origin of the Jews." *Zion,* 8 (1942/1943): 1–34, 61–84. (Hebrew)

Lieberman, S. *Hellenism in Jewish Palestine: Studies in the Literary Transmission, Beliefs and Manners of Palestine in the I Century B.C.E.–IV Century C.E.* New York, 1950.

Lieu, J., J. North, and T. Rajak, eds. *Jews among Pagans and Christians in the Roman Empire.* London, 1992.

Lifshitz, B. *Donateurs et fondateurs dans les synagogues juives.* Paris, 1967.

Linderski, J. *Roman Questions: Selected Papers.* Stuttgart, 1995.

Loewenstaam, S. E. "The Death of Moses." In G. W. E. Nickelsburg, Jr., ed., *Studies on the Testament of Abraham,* 185–218. Missoula, 1976.

—— "The Testament of Abraham and the Texts Concerning the Death of Moses." In G. W. E. Nickelsburg, Jr., ed., *Studies on the Testament of Abraham,* 219–226. Missoula, 1976.

Lüderitz, G. "What Is the Politeuma?" In J. W. van Henten and P. W. van der Horst, eds., *Studies in Early Jewish Epigraphy,* 183–225. Leiden, 1994.

Ludlow, J. *Abraham Meets Death: Narrative Humor in the Testament of Abraham.* Sheffield, forthcoming.

Luedemann, G. *Paul, Apostle to the Gentiles: Studies in Chronology.* Philadelphia, 1984.

MacKenzie, R. A. F., S. J. "The Meaning of the Susanna Story." *Canadian Journal of Theology,* 3 (1957): 211–218.

Magie, D. *Roman Rule in Asia Minor to the End of the Third Century after Christ,* 2 vols. Princeton, 1950.

Marcus, R. "Antisemitism in the Hellenistic-Roman World." In K. S. Pinson, ed., *Essays on Antisemitism,* 61–78. New York, 1942.

Marrou, H. I. *A History of Education in Antiquity.* London, 1956.

Marshall, A. J. "Flaccus and the Jews of Asia (Cicero, *Pro Flacco* 28.67–69)." *Phoenix,* 29 (1975): 139–154.

Mason, H. J. *Greek Terms for Roman Institutions.* Toronto, 1974.

McCracken, D. "Narration and Comedy in the Book of Tobit." *JBL,* 114 (1995): 401–418.

McKay, H. A. *Sabbath and Synagogue: The Question of Sabbath Worship in Ancient Judaism.* Leiden, 1994.

McKnight, S. *A Light among the Gentiles: Jewish Missionary Activity in the Second Temple Period.* Minneapolis, 1991.

McLean, B. H. "The Place of Cult in Voluntary Associations and Christian Churches on Delos." In J. S. Kloppenborg and S. G. Wilson, eds., *Voluntary Associations in the Graeco-Roman World,* 186–225. London, 1996.

Meecham, H. G. *The Letter of Aristeas: A Linguistic Study with Special Reference to the Greek Bible.* Manchester, 1935.

Meinhold, A. "Die Gattung der Josephusgeschichte und des Estherbuches: Diasporanovelle I." *ZAW,* 87 (1975): 306–324.

——— "Die Gattung der Josephsgeschichte und des Estherbuches: Diasporanovelle II." *ZAW,* 88 (1976): 72–93.

Meisner, N. *Aristeasbrief (JSHRZ,* II.1). Gütersloh, 1973.

Mélèze-Modrzejewski, J. "How To Be a Greek and Yet a Jew in Hellenistic Alexandria." In S. J. D. Cohen and E. S. Frerichs, eds., *Diasporas in Antiquity,* 65–92. Atlanta, 1993.

——— *The Jews of Egypt from Ramses II to Emperor Hadrian.* Philadelphia, 1995.

Mendels, D. *The Land of Israel as a Political Concept in Hasmonean Literature: Recourse to History in Second Century B.C. Claims to the Holy Land.* Tübingen, 1987.

Mendelson, A. *Secular Education in Philo of Alexandria.* Cincinnati, 1982.

Merrill, E. T. "The Expulsion of the Jews from Rome under Tiberius." *CP,* 14 (1919): 365–372.

Miles, J. A. "Laughing at the Bible: Jonah as Parody." *JQR,* 65 (1975): 168–181.

Miles, M. R. *Carnal Knowing: Female Nakedness and Religious Meaning in the Christian West.* Boston, 1989.

Milik, J. T. "Fragment d'une Source du Psautier (4Q Ps 89): et fragments des Jubilés, du document de Damas, d'un Phylactère dans la Grotte 4 de Qumran." *RevBib,* 73 (1966): 94–106.

Milikowsky, C. "Notions of Exile, Subjugation and Return in Rabbinic Literature." In J. M. Scott, ed., *Exile: Old Testament, Jewish, and Christian Conceptions,* 265–296. Leiden, 1997.

Miller, J. E. "The Redaction of Tobit and the Genesis Apocryphon." *JSP,* 8 (1991): 53–61.

Milne, P. J. "Folktales and Fairy Tales: An Evaluation of Two Proppian Analyses of Biblical Narratives." *JSOT,* 34 (1986): 35–60.

Moehring, H. R. "The Persecution of the Jews and the Adherents of the Isis Cult at Rome A.D. 19." *NT,* 3 (1959): 293–304.

——— "The *Acta pro Judaeis* in the *Antiquities* of Flavius Josephus: A Study in Hellenistic and Modern Apologetic Historiography." In J. Neusner, ed., *Christianity, Judaism, and Other Greco-Roman Cults: Studies for Morton Smith at Sixty,* III, 124–158. Leiden, 1975.

Moffat, J. "2 Maccabees." In Charles, *APOT,* I (1913): 125–154.

Momigliano, A. *Claudius: The Emperor and His Achievement.* Oxford, 1934.

────── *Ricerche sull'organizzazione della Giudea sotto il dominio romano (63 a. C.–70 d. C.).* Amsterdam, 1967.

────── "The Second Book of Maccabees." *CP,* 70 (1975): 81–88.

Moore, C. A. *Daniel, Esther, and Jeremiah: The Additions.* Garden City, 1977.

────── *Judith.* Garden City, 1985.

────── "Why Wasn't the Book of Judith Included in the Hebrew Bible?" In J. C. VanderKam, ed., *"No One Spoke Ill of Her": Essays on Judith,* 61–71. Atlanta, 1992.

────── *Tobit.* New York, 1996.

Mor, M., ed. *Jewish Assimilation, Acculturation, and Accommodation: Past Traditions, Current Issues, and Future Prospects.* Lanham, 1992.

Munoa, P. B., III. *Four Powers in Heaven: The Interpretation of Daniel 7 in the Testament of Abraham.* Sheffield, 1998.

Murphy-O'Connor, J. "Paul and Gallio." *JBL,* 112 (1993): 315–317.

Mussies, G. "The Interpretatio Judaica of Thot-Hermes." In M. H. van Voss et al., eds., *Studies in Egyptian Religion: Dedicated to Professor Jan Zandee,* 89–120. Leiden, 1982.

Musurillo, H. A., S. J. *The Acts of the Pagan Martyrs: Acta Alexandrinorum.* Oxford, 1954.

Nadel, B. "On the Economic Meaning of the Proviso of the Bosporan Manumissions." *VDI,* 1 (1948): 203–206. (Russian)

Neusner, J. *Self-Fulfilling Prophecy: Exile and Return in the History of Judaism.* Boston, 1987.

────── "Exile and Return as the History of Judaism." In J. M. Scott, ed., *Exile: Old Testament, Jewish, and Christian Conceptions,* 221–238. Leiden, 1997.

────── ed. *Christianity, Judaism, and Other Greco-Roman Cults: Studies for Morton Smith at Sixty,* 4 vols. Leiden, 1975.

──────, W. S. Green, and E. S. Frerichs, eds. *Judaisms and Their Messiahs at the Time of the Christian Era.* Cambridge, 1987.

──────, B. A. Levine, and E. S. Frerichs, eds. *Judaic Perspectives on Ancient Israel.* Philadelphia, 1987.

Newbold, R. F. "Social Tension at Rome in the Early Years of Tiberius' Reign." *Athenaeum,* 52 (1974): 110–143.

Nickelsburg, G. W. E., Jr. "Review of the Literature." In G. W. E. Nickelsburg, Jr., ed., *Studies on the Testament of Abraham,* 9–22. Missoula, 1976.

────── "Eschatology in the Testament of Abraham: A Study of the Judgment Scene in the Two Recensions." In G. W. E. Nickelsburg, Jr., ed., *Studies on the Testament of Abraham,* 23–64. Missoula, 1976.

────── *Jewish Literature between the Bible and the Mishnah: A Historical and Literary Introduction.* Philadelphia, 1981.

────── ed. *Studies on the Testament of Abraham.* Missoula, 1976.

Niditch, S. *Underdogs and Tricksters: A Prelude to Biblical Folklore.* New York, 1987.

Niehoff, M. "What's in a Name? Philo's Mystical Philosophy of Language." *JSQ,* 2 (1995): 220–252.

────── "Philo's Views on Paganism." In G. N. Stanton and G. G. Strousma, eds., *Tolerance and Intolerance in Early Judaism and Christianity,* 135–158. Cambridge, 1998.

────── *Philo on Jewish Identity and Culture.* Tübingen, 2001.

Nock, A. D. *Essays on Religion and the Ancient World*, ed. Z. Stewart, 2 vols. Oxford, 1972.

Nolland, J. "Proselytism or Politics in Horace Satires I, 4, 138–143?" *VigChr,* 33 (1979): 347–355.

Nowell, I. "The Narrator in the Book of Tobit." *SBL Seminar Papers,* 27 (1988): 27–38.

Noy, D. *Foreigners at Rome: Citizens and Strangers.* London, 2000.

Oliver, J. H. *Greek Constitutions of Early Emperors from Inscriptions and Papyri.* Philadelphia, 1989.

Oppenheimer, A., U. Rappaport, and M. Stern, eds. *Jerusalem in the Second Temple Period: Abraham Schalit Memorial Volume.* Jerusalem, 1980. (Hebrew)

Overman, J. A. "Jews, Slaves, and the Synagogue on the Black Sea: The Bosporan Manumission Inscriptions and Their Significance for Diaspora Judaism." In H. C. Kee and L. H. Cohick, eds., *Evolution of the Synagogue: Problems and Progress,* 141–157. Harrisburg, 1999.

——— and R. S. MacLennan, eds. *Diaspora Jews and Judaism: Essays in Honor of, and in Dialogue with, A. Thomas Kraabel.* Atlanta, 1992.

Parente, F. "The Third Book of Maccabees as Ideological Document and Historical Source." *Henoch,* 10 (1988): 143–182.

——— and J. Sievers, eds. *Josephus and the History of the Greco-Roman Period: Essays in Memory of Morton Smith.* Leiden, 1994.

Paton, L. M. *The Book of Esther.* New York, 1908.

Pearce, S. "Belonging and Not Belonging: Local Perspectives in Philo of Alexandria." In S. Jones and S. Pearce, eds., *Jewish Local Patriotism and Self-Identification in the Graeco-Roman Period,* 79–105. Sheffield, 1998.

Pearson, B. A., ed. *The Future of Early Christianity: Essays in Honor of Helmut Koester.* Minneapolis, 1991.

Pelletier, A. *Lettre d'Aristée à Philocrate.* Paris, 1962.

Petuchowski, J. J. "Diaspora Judaism—an Abnormality?" *Judaism,* 9 (1960): 17–28.

Pfeiffer, R. H. *History of New Testament Times with an Introduction to the Apocrypha.* New York, 1949.

Philonenko, M. "Le Testament de Job et les Thérapeutes." *Semitica,* 8 (1958): 41–53.

——— "Le Testament de Job." *Semitica,* 18 (1968): 1–75.

Piatelli, D. "An Enquiry into the Political Relations between Rome and Judaea from 161 to 4 BCE." *Israel Law Review,* 14 (1979): 195–236.

Picard, A., ed. *Mélanges Holleaux: Recueil de Mémoires concernant L'Antiquité Grecque offert à Maurice Holleaux en souvenir de ses années de direction à l'École Française d'Athènes (1904–1912).* Paris, 1913.

Pilhofer, P. *Presbyteron Kreitton: Der Altersbeweis der jüdischen und christlichen Apologeten und seine Vorgeschichte.* Tübingen, 1990.

Pinson, K. S., ed. *Essays on Antisemitism.* New York, 1946.

Plassart, A. "La synagogue juive de Délos." In A. Picard, ed., *Mélanges Holleaux: Recueil de Mémoires concernant L'Antiquité Grecque offert à Maurice Holleaux en souvenir de ses années de direction à l'École française d'Athènes (1904–1912),* 201–216. Paris, 1913. (= *RevBib,* 11 (1914): 523–534.)

Price, J. J. "The Jewish Diaspora of the Graeco-Roman Period." *SCI,* 13 (1994): 169–186.

Pucci Ben Zeev, M. "Cosa pensavano: Romani degli Ebrei?" *Athenaeum*, 65 (1987): 335–359.

—— "Greek Attacks Against Alexandrian Jews During Emperor Trajan's Reign." *JSJ*, 20 (1989): 31–48.

—— "New Perspectives on the Jewish-Greek Hostilities in Alexandria during the Reign of Emperor Caligula." *JSJ*, 21 (1990): 227–235.

—— "Roman Documents in Josephus' Antiquities: What Was Josephus' Source?" *SCI*, 13 (1994): 46–59.

—— "Seleukos of Rhosos and the Jews." *JSJ*, 26 (1995): 113–121.

—— "Who Wrote a Letter Concerning Delian Jews?" *RevBib*, 103 (1996): 237–243.

—— *Jewish Rights in the Roman World: The Greek and Roman Documents Quoted by Josephus Flavius*. Tübingen, 1998.

Rabello, A. M. "L'observance des fêtes juives dans l'Empire romain." *ANRW*, II.21.2 (1984): 1288–1312.

Rabenau, M. *Studien zum Buch Tobit*. Berlin, 1994.

Radday, Y. T. "Esther with Humour." In Y. T. Radday and A. Brenner, eds., *On Humour and the Comic in the Hebrew Bible*, 295–313. Sheffield, 1990.

—— and A. Brenner, eds. *On Humour and the Comic in the Hebrew Bible*. Sheffield, 1990.

Rahnenführer, D. "Das Testament des Hiob und das neue Testament." *ZNW*, 62 (1971): 68–93.

Rajak, T. "Moses and Ethiopia: Legend and Literature." *JJS*, 29 (1978): 111–122.

—— "Was There a Roman Charter for the Jews?" *JRS*, 74 (1984): 107–123.

—— "Jewish Rights in the Greek Cities under Roman Rule: a New Approach." In W. S. Green, ed., *Approaches to Ancient Judaism*, V, *Studies in Judaism in Its Greco-Roman Context*, 19–35. Atlanta, 1985.

—— "The synagogue within the Greco-Roman city." In S. Fine, ed., *Jews, Christians, and Polytheists in the Ancient Synagogue: Cultural Interaction during the Greco-Roman Period*, 161–173. London, 1999.

—— "Greeks and Barbarians in Josephus." In J. J. Collins and G. E. Sterling, eds., *Hellenism in the Land of Israel*, 246–264. Notre Dame, 2001.

—— and D. Noy. "*Archisynagogoi*: Office, Title, and Social Status in the Greco-Jewish Synagogue." *JRS*, 83 (1993): 75–93.

Rappaport, U. "The Jews of Eretz-Israel and the Jews of the Diaspora During the Hellenistic and Hasmonaean Periods." In B. Isaac and A. Oppenheimer, eds., *Studies on the Jewish Diaspora in the Hellenistic and Roman Periods*, 1–9. Tel-Aviv, 1996. (Hebrew)

Rapske, B. *The Book of Acts and Paul in Roman Custody*. Grand Rapids, 1994.

Rathbone, D. "Egypt, Augustus, and Roman Taxation." *Cahiers du Centre G. Glotz*, 4 (1993): 81–112.

Reinach, T. "Antiochus Cyzicène et les Juifs." *REJ*, 38 (1899): 161–171.

Richardson, P. *Herod: King of the Jews and Friend of the Romans*. Columbia, S.C., 1996.

—— "Early Synagogues as Collegia in the Diaspora and Palestine."In J. S. Kloppenborg and S. G. Wilson, eds., *Voluntary Associations in the Graeco-Roman World*, 90–109. London, 1996.

—— "Augustan-Era Synagogues in Rome." In K. P. Donfried and P. Richardson, eds., *Judaism and Christianity in First-Century Rome*, 17–29. Grand Rapids, 1998.

Rickman, G. *The Corn Supply of Ancient Rome*. Oxford, 1980.

Robert, L. "Un corpus des inscriptions juives." *REJ*, 101 (1937): 73–86. (= *Hellenica*, III (1946): 90–108.)

Roddaz, J.-M. *Marcus Agrippa*. Rome, 1984.

Rohland, J. P. *Der Erzengel Michael, Arzt und Feldherr: Zwei Aspekte des vor- und frühbyzantinischen Michaelskultes*. Leiden, 1977.

Rokeah, D. "Tacitus and Ancient Anti-Semitism." *REJ*, 154 (1995): 281–294.

Rosen, K. "Der Historiker als Prophet: Tacitus und die Juden." *Gymnasium*, 103 (1996): 107–126.

Rosenthal, F. "Die Erlässe Cäsars und die Senatsconsulte in Josephus Alterth. XIV, 10 nach ihrem historischen Inhalte untersucht." *Montatsschrift für Geschichte und Wissenschaft des Judentums*, 28 (1879): 176–183.

Ruether, R. R. *Faith and Fratricide: The Theological Roots of Anti-Semitism*. New York, 1974.

Runesson, A. "The Oldest Original Synagogue Building in the Diaspora: A Response to L. Michael White." *HTR*, 92 (1999): 409–433.

Runnalls, D. "Moses' Ethiopian Campaign." *JSJ*, 14 (1983): 135–156.

Rutgers, L. V. "Roman Policy towards the Jews: Expulsions from the City of Rome during the First Century c.e." *CA*, 13 (1994): 56–74.

——— "Attitudes to Judaism in the Greco-Roman Period: Reflections on Feldman's *Jew and Gentile in the Ancient World*." *JQR*, 85 (1995): 361–395.

——— *The Hidden Heritage of Diaspora Judaism*. Leuven, 1998.

Safrai, S. "Relations between the Diaspora and the Land of Israel." In Safrai and Stern, *Jewish People*, I (1974), 184–215.

——— *Die Wallfahrt im Zeitalter des Zweiten Tempels*. Neukirchen-Vluyn, 1981.

——— and M. Stern. *The Jewish People in the First Century*, 2 vols. Philadelphia, 1974–1976.

Safran, W. "Diasporas in Modern Societies: Myths of Homeland and Return." *Diaspora*, 1 (1991): 83–99.

Samuel, A. "The Role of *Paramone* Clauses in Ancient Documents." *JJP*, 15 (1965): 221–311.

Sanders, E. P. "Testament of Abraham." In Charlesworth, *OTP*, I (1983): 871–902.

——— "Common Judaism and the Synagogue in the First Century." In S. Fine, ed., *Jews, Christians, and Polytheists in the Ancient Synagogue: Cultural Interaction during the Greco-Roman Period*, 1–17. London, 1999.

Sasson, J. "Esther." In R. Alter and F. Kermode, eds., *The Literary Guide to the Bible*, 335–342. Cambridge, Mass., 1987.

Saulnier, C. "Lois Romaines sur les Juifs selon Flavius Josèphe." *RevBib*, 88 (1981): 161–198.

Schäfer, P. *Judeophobia: Attitudes toward the Jews in the Ancient World*. Cambridge, Mass., 1997.

Schaller, B. *Das Testament Hiobs (JSHRZ, III.3)*. Gütersloh, 1976.

——— "Philon von Alexandria und das 'Heilige Land.'" In G. Strecker, ed., *Das Land Israel in biblischer Zeit*, 172–187. Göttingen, 1983.

Schäublin, C. "Josephus und die Griechen." *Hermes*, 110 (1982): 316–341.

Schmidt, F. "The Two Recensions of the Testament of Abraham: In Which Way Did the Transformation Take Place?" In G. W. E. Nickelsburg, Jr., ed., *Studies on the Testament of Abraham*, 65–84. Missoula, 1976.

——— *Le Testament grec d'Abraham.* Tübingen, 1986.

Schüpphaus, J. "Das Verhältnis von LXX- und Theodotion-Text in den apokryphen Zusätzen zum Daniel buch." *ZAW,* 83 (1971): 49–72.

Schürer, E. *The History of the Jewish People in the Age of Jesus Christ,* 3 vols. Edinburgh, 1973–1987 (revised and edited by G. Vermes, F. Millar, M. Black, and M. Goodman).

Schwartz, D. R. "Philonic Anonyms of the Roman and Nazi Periods: Two Suggestions." *Studia Philonica Annual,* 1 (1989): 63–73.

——— *Agrippa I: The Last King of Judaea.* Tübingen, 1990.

——— "The Jews of Egypt between the Temple of Onias, the Temple of Jerusalem, and Heaven." *Zion,* 62 (1997): 5–22. (Hebrew)

——— "Antisemitism and Other -ism's in the Greco-Roman World." In R. S. Wistrich, ed., *Demonizing the Other: Antisemitism, Racism, and Xenophobia,* 73–87. Amsterdam, 1999.

Schwartz, J. "Remarques littéraires sur le roman de Tobit." *RevHistPhilRel,* 67 (1987): 293–297.

Schwartz, M. "The Religion of Achaemenian Iran." In *CHI,* II (1985): 664–697.

Scott, J. M. "Philo and the Restoration of Israel." *SBL Seminar Papers,* 34 (1995): 553–575.

——— "Exile and the Self-Understanding of Diaspora Jews in the Greco-Roman Period." In J. M. Scott, ed., *Exile: Old Testament, Jewish, and Christian Conceptions,* 173–218. Leiden, 1997.

——— ed. *Exile: Old Testament, Jewish, and Christian Conceptions.* Leiden, 1997.

Scramuzza, V. M. *The Emperor Claudius.* Cambridge, Mass., 1940.

Sered, S., and S. Cooper. "Sexuality and Social Control: Anthropological Reflections on the Book of Susanna." In E. Spolsky, ed., *The Judgment of Susanna: Authority and Witness,* 43–56. Atlanta, 1996.

Sevenster, J. N. *The Roots of Pagan Anti-Semitism in the Ancient World.* Leiden, 1975.

Sherwin-White, A. N. *The Letters of Pliny: A Historical and Social Commentary.* Oxford, 1966.

——— "Philo and Avillius Flaccus: a Conundrum." *Latomus,* 31 (1972): 820–828.

——— *The Roman Citizenship,* 2nd ed. Oxford, 1973.

Shinan, A., ed. *Emigration and Settlement in Diaspora in the Hellenistic-Roman Period.* Jerusalem, 1982. (Hebrew)

Sievers, J. *The Hasmoneans and Their Supporters from Mattathias to the Death of John Hyrcanus I.* Atlanta, 1990.

Simon, M. *Verus Israel: A Study of the Relations Between Christians and Jews in the Roman Empire, 135–425.* Oxford, 1986. (first published 1964)

Simpson, D. C. "Tobit." In Charles, *APOT,* I (1913): 174–241.

Sirat, C. "The Jews." In K. J. Dover, ed., *Perceptions of the Ancient Greeks,* 54–78. Oxford, 1992.

Slingerland, H. D. "Suetonius, *Claudius,* 25.4 and the Account in Cassius Dio." *JQR,* 79 (1989): 305–322.

——— "Acts 18:1–18: The Gallio Inscription and Absolute Pauline Chronology." *JBL,* 110 (1991): 439–449.

——— "Suetonius, *Claudius* 25.4, Acts 18 and Paulus Orosius' *Historiarum Adversum Paganos Libri VII:* Dating the Claudian Expulsion(s) of Roman Jews." *JQR,* 83 (1992): 127–144.

——— *Claudian Policymaking and the Early Imperial Repression of Judaism at Rome.* Atlanta, 1997.

Sly, D. I. *Philo's Alexandria.* London, 1996.

Smallwood, E. M. "Some Notes on the Jews under Tiberius." *Latomus,* 15 (1956): 314–329.

——— *Philonis Alexandrini Legatio ad Gaium.* Leiden, 1961.

——— *The Jews under Roman Rule from Pompey to Diocletian.* Leiden, 1981.

——— "The Diaspora in the Roman period before CE 70." In *CHJ,* III (1999): 168–191.

Smith, M. F. "Excavations at Oinoanda 1997: The New Epicurean Texts." *Anatolian Studies,* 48 (1998): 125–170.

Solin, H. "Juden und Syrer im westlichen Teil der römischen Welt. Eine ethnisch-demographische Studie mit besonderer Berücksichtigung der sprachlichen Zustände." In *ANRW,* II.29.2 (1983): 587–789.

Soll, W. "Tobit and Folklore Studies, with Emphasis on Propp's Morphology." *SBL Seminar Papers,* 27 (1998): 39–53.

——— "The Family as Scriptural and Social Construct in Tobit." In C. A. Evans and J. A. Sanders, eds., *The Function of Scripture in Early Jewish and Christian Tradition,* 166–175. Sheffield, 1998.

Spittler, R. P. "The Testament of Job: A History of Research and Interpretation." In M. A. Knibb and P. W. van der Horst, eds., *Studies on the Testament of Job,* 7–32. Cambridge, 1989.

Spolsky, E. "Law or the Garden: The Betrayal of Susanna in Pastoral Painting." In E. Spolsky, ed., *The Judgment of Susanna: Authority and Witness,* 101–118. Atlanta, 1996.

——— ed. *The Judgment of Susanna: Authority and Witness.* Atlanta, 1996.

Squarciapino, M. F. *La sinagoga di Ostia.* Rome, 1964.

Stanley, C. D. "Neither Jew nor Greek: Ethnic Conflict in Graeco-Roman Society." *JSNT,* 64 (1996): 101–124.

Stanton, G. N., and G. G. Strousma, eds. *Tolerance and Intolerance in Early Judaism and Christianity.* Cambridge, 1998.

Steiner, G. "Our Homeland, the Text." *Salmagundi,* 66 (1985): 4–25.

Steinmann, M. *Lecture de Judith.* Paris, 1953.

Sterling, G. E. *Historiography and Self-Definition: Josephos, Luke-Acts, and Apologetic Historiography.* Leiden, 1992.

Stern, M. "The Jewish Diaspora." In Safrai and Stern, *Jewish People,* I (1974): 117–183.

——— "Expulsions of the Jews from Rome in Antiquity." *Zion,* 44 (1979): 1–27. (Hebrew)

——— *Greek and Latin Authors on Jews and Judaism,* 2 vols. Jerusalem, 1976–1980.

——— "The Relations between the Hasmonean Kingdom and Ptolemaic Egypt, in View of the International Situation during the 2nd and 1st Centuries B.C.E." *Zion,* 50 (1985): 81–106. (Hebrew)

Steussy, M. J. *Gardens in Babylon: Narrative and Faith in the Greek Legends of Daniel.* Atlanta, 1993.

Stocker, M. *Judith: Sexual Warrior. Women and Power in Western Culture.* New Haven, 1998.

Stone, M. E., ed. *Jewish Writings of the Second Temple Period.* Philadelphia, 1984.

Stone, N. "Judith and Holofernes: Some Observations on the Development of the Scene in Art." In J. C. VanderKam, ed., *"No One Spoke Ill of Her": Essays on Judith,* 73–93. Atlanta, 1992.

Strecker, G., ed. *Das Land Israel in biblischer Zeit.* Göttingen, 1983.

Sypher, W. "The Meanings of Comedy." In W. Sypher, ed., *Comedy,* 193–260. New York, 1956.

——— ed. *Comedy.* New York, 1956.

Takács, S. A. *Isis and Sarapis in the Roman World.* Leiden, 1995.

Tarn, W. W., and G. T. Griffith. *Hellenistic Civilization,* 3rd ed. London, 1952.

Tatum, W. J. *The Patrician Tribune: Publius Clodius Pulcher.* Chapel Hill, 1999.

Taylor, C., ed. *Sources of the Self: The Making of the Modern Identity.* Cambridge, Mass., 1989.

Tcherikover, V. A. "*Syntaxis* and *Laographia.*" *JJP,* 4 (1950): 179–207.

——— *Hellenistic Civilization and the Jews.* Philadelphia, 1959.

——— "The Decline of the Jewish Diaspora in Egypt in the Roman Period." *JJS,* 14 (1963): 1–32.

Thompson, T. L. "The Exile in History and Myth: A Response to Hans Barstad." In L. L. Grabbe, ed., *Leading Captivity Captive: "The Exile" as History and Ideology,* 101–118. Sheffield, 1998.

Tiede, D. L. *The Charismatic Figure as Miracle Worker.* Missoula, 1972.

Titchener, F. B., and R. F. Moorton, Jr., eds. *The Eye Expanded: Life and the Arts in Greco-Roman Antiquity.* Berkeley, 1999.

Torrey, C. C. "'Nineveh'" in the Book of Tobit." *JBL,* 41 (1922): 237–245.

——— *The Apocryphal Literature: A Brief Introduction.* New Haven, 1945.

Tramontano, R. *La lettera di Aristea a Filocrate.* Naples, 1931.

Trebilco, P. R. *Jewish Communities in Asia Minor.* Cambridge, 1991.

Treggiari, S. *Roman Freedmen during the Late Republic.* Oxford, 1969.

Troiani, L. "The πολιτεία of Israel in the Graeco-Roman Age." In F. Parente and J. Sievers, eds., *Josephus and the History of the Greco-Roman Period: Essays in Memory of Morton Smith,* 11–22. Leiden, 1994.

Tromp, J. "The Formation of the Third Book of Maccabees." *Henoch,* 17 (1995), 311–328.

Turner, N. "The Testament of Abraham." Ph.D. diss., London, 1953.

Urbach, E. E. "Center and Periphery in Jewish Historic Consciousness: Contemporary Implications." In M. Davis, ed., *World Jewry and the State of Israel,* 217–235. New York, 1977.

Urman, D., and P. V. M. Flesher, eds. *Ancient Synagogues: Historical Analysis and Archaeological Discovery,* 2 vols. Leiden, 1995.

van Berchem, D. *Les distributions de blé et d'argent à la plebe romain sous l'empire.* Geneva, 1939.

van der Horst, P. W. *Essays on the Jewish World of Early Christianity.* Göttingen, 1990.

——— "Was the Synagogue a Place of Sabbath Worship Before 70 CE?" In S. Fine, ed., *Jews, Christians, and Polytheists in the Ancient Synagogue: Cultural Interaction during the Greco-Roman Period,* 18–43. London, 1999.

van Henten, J. W. *The Maccabean Martyrs as Saviours of the Jewish People: A Study of 2 and 4 Maccabees.* Leiden, 1997.

——— and P. W. van der Horst, eds. *Studies in Early Jewish Epigraphy.* Leiden, 1994.

van Unnik, W. C. *Das Selbstverständnis der jüdischen Diaspora in der hellenistisch-römischen Zeit.* Leiden, 1993.

van Voss, M. H., et al., eds. *Studies in Egyptian Religion: Dedicated to Professor Jan Zandee.* Leiden, 1982.

VanderKam, J. C., ed. *"No One Spoke Ill of Her": Essays on Judith.* Atlanta, 1992.

―――― et al., eds. *Discoveries in the Judaean Desert,* XIX. Oxford, 1995.

Vital, D. *The Origins of Zionism.* Oxford, 1975.

Wacholder, B. Z. *Nicolaus of Damascus.* Berkeley, 1962.

―――― "The Letter from Judah Maccabee to Aristobulus: Is 2 Maccabees 1:10b–2:18 Authentic?" *HUCA,* 49 (1978): 89–134.

Walbank, F. W. "History and Tragedy." *Historia,* 9 (1960): 216–234.

Wallace, S. L. "Census and Poll-Tax in Ptolemaic Egypt." *AJP,* 59 (1938): 418–442.

―――― *Taxation in Egypt from Augustus to Diocletian.* Princeton, 1938.

Walter, N. *Der Thoraausleger Aristobulos: Untersuchungen zu seinen Fragmenten und zu pseudepigraphischen Resten der jüdisch hellenistischen Literatur.* Berlin, 1964.

―――― *Fragmente jüdisch-hellenistischer Exegeten (JSHRZ,* III.2). Gütersloh, 1975.

―――― *Fragmente jüdisch-hellenistischer Historiker (JSHRZ,* I.2). Gütersloh, 1976.

Waltzing, J. P. *Étude historique sur les corporations professionelles chez les romains,* 4 vols. Louvain, 1895–1900.

Wardle, D. *Valerius Maximus: Memorable Deeds and Sayings, Book 1.* Oxford, 1998.

Wardy, B. "Jewish Religion in Pagan Literature during the Late Republic and Early Empire." In *ANRW,* II.19.1 (1979): 592–644.

Watson, A. *The Law of Persons in the Later Roman Republic.* Oxford, 1967.

―――― *Roman Slave Law.* Baltimore, 1987.

Weaver, P. R. C. "Where Have All the Junian Latins Gone? Nomenclature and Status in the Early Empire." *Chiron,* 20 (1990): 275–305.

Welch, K. "The Roman Arena in Late-Republican Italy: A New Interpretation." *JRA,* 7 (1994): 59–80.

Whedbee, J. W. "The Comedy of Job." *Semeia,* 7 (1977): 1–39.

―――― *The Bible and the Comic Vision.* Cambridge, 1998.

White, L. M. "The Delos Synagogue Revisited: Recent Fieldwork in the Graeco-Roman Diaspora." *HTR,* 80 (1987): 133–160.

―――― *Building God's House in the Roman World: Architectural Adaptation among Pagans, Jews, and Christians.* Baltimore, 1990.

―――― "Synagogue and Society in Imperial Ostia: Archaeological and Epigraphic Evidence." In K. P. Donfried and P. Richardson, eds., *Judaism and Christianity in First-Century Rome,* 30–68. Grand Rapids, 1998.

―――― "Reading the Ostia Synagogue: A Reply to A. Runesson." *HTR,* 92 (1999): 435–464.

White, S. A. "Esther: A Feminine Model for Jewish Diaspora." In P. L. Day, ed., *Gender and Difference in Ancient Israel,* 161–177. Minneapolis, 1989.

Wilken, R. L. *The Land Called Holy: Palestine in Christian History and Thought.* New Haven, 1992.

Will, E., and C. Orrieux. *"Proselytisme juif"? histoire d'une erreur.* Paris, 1992.

Williams, M. H. "The Expulsion of the Jews in A.D. 19." *Latomus*, 48 (1989): 765–784.

—— "The Structure of Roman Jewry Re-Considered: Were the Synagogues of Ancient Rome Entirely Homogeneous?" *ZPE*, 104 (1994): 129–141.

—— "The Structure of the Jewish Community in Rome." In M. Goodman, ed., *Jews in a Graeco-Roman World*, 215–228. Oxford, 1998.

—— "Exarchon: An Unsuspected Jewish Liturgical Title from Ancient Rome." *JJS*, 51 (2000): 77–87.

—— "Jews and Jewish Communities in the Roman Empire." In J. Huskinson, ed., *Experiencing Rome: Culture, Identity, and Power in the Roman Empire*, 305–334. London, 2000.

Willrich, H. *Judaica: Forschungen zur hellenistisch-jüdischen Geschichte und Litteratur*. Göttingen, 1900.

Wills, L. M. *The Jew in the Court of the Foreign King: Ancient Jewish Court Legends*. Minneapolis, 1990.

—— *The Jewish Novel in the Ancient World*. Ithaca, 1995.

Wilson, A. J. N. *Emigration from Italy in the Republican Age of Rome*. Manchester, 1966.

Winston, D. *The Wisdom of Solomon*. Garden City, 1979.

—— "Aristobulus: From Walter to Holladay." *Studia Philonica Annual*, 8 (1996): 155–166.

Wirth, G., K. H. Schwarte, and J. Heinrichs, eds. *Romanitas-Christianitas: Untersuchungen zur Geschichte und Literatur der römischen Kaiserzeit*. Berlin, 1982.

Wistrich, R. S., ed. *Demonizing the Other: Antisemitism, Racism, and Xenophobia*. Amsterdam, 1999.

Wolfson, H. A. *Philo: Foundations of Religious Philosophy in Judaism, Christianity, and Islam*, 2 vols. Cambridge, Mass., 1947.

Wyler, B. "Esther: The Incomplete Emancipation of a Queen." In A. Brenner, ed., *A Feminist Companion to Esther, Judith, and Susanna*, 111–135. Sheffield, 1995.

Yavetz, Z. *Julius Caesar and His Public Image*. Ithaca, 1983.

—— "Judeophobia in Classical Antiquity: A Different Approach." *JJS*, 44 (1993): 1–22.

—— *Judenfeindschaft in der Antike*. Munich, 1997.

—— "Latin Authors on Jews and Dacians." *Historia*, 47 (1998): 77–107.

Zeitlin, S. "The Books of Esther and Judith: A Parallel." In M. S. Enslin, ed., *The Book of Judith*, 1–37. Leiden, 1972.

Zenger, E. *Das Buch Judit (JSHRZ I.6)*. Gütersloh, 1981.

Zimmerman, F. "The Story of Susanna and Its Original Language." *JQR*, 48 (1957/1958): 236–241.

—— *The Book of Tobit*. New York, 1958.

Zuckerman, C. "Hellenistic Politeumata and the Jews: A Reconsideration." *SCI*, 8–9 (1985/1986): 171–185.

Index